Respectfully yet relentlessly pressing Horton's many conversation partners in New Testament, this thorough, systematic, and far-ranging work advances a reading both distinctive and yet more traditional than many of today's dominant paradigms. Horton also exposes some of our blind spots, properly challenging mischaracterizations of the Reformers. In contrast to some New Testament scholars driven too much by modern philosophic premises, Horton is often more faithful to ancient interpretations relevant to the biblical cultures. As a New Testament scholar, I profited repeatedly from his historical context for various theological approaches in modern New Testament scholarship.

Craig Keener, F. M. and Ada Thompson Professor of
Biblical Studies, Asbury Theological Seminary

This is a superb theological study that creatively retrieves the doctrine of justification from the patristic era to the Reformation. Horton seeks to revitalize the contemporary ecumenical discussion regarding justification by showing not only the enduring merits of the Reformation's exegetical, theological, and pastoral legacy, but also its hermeneutical and theological superiority to alternative views, namely, Roman Catholic, Radical Orthodoxy, the new perspective on Paul, and new Finnish interpretations. Some of his interpretations are questionable, for example, "the triumph of Nominalism occurred with the Counter-Reformation (Council of Trent) rather than with the Reformation." Still, I came away from reading this engaging book marked by a careful and generous listening to others, both reenergized with a passion for understanding the long-running doctrinal conversation about God, grace, and justification and challenged to engage critically the author's vision.

Eduardo J. Echeverria, professor of philosophy and systematic
theology, Sacred Heart Major, Archdiocesan Seminary of Detroit

This is a serious and important work coming from a leading Reformed theologian. It concerns a pivotal doctrine that was at the heart of the Reformation and that continues to provoke differences between Protestants and Catholics. Both Protestant and Catholic readers—not only scholars but also theologically interested laity—will profit by wrestling with this learned historical study.

Gerald R. McDermott, Anglican Chair of
Divinity, Beeson Divinity School

It is not often one finds a book ranging across the three "CDs"—the Damascus Document, Augustine's *City of God*, and Barth's *Church Dogmatics*! This is a volume bristling with theological insight and intellectual energy. Add to that Horton's learning and clarity, and you have that rare thing—a gripping and intelligent treatment of justification.

Simon Gathercole, reader in New Testament, University of Cambridge, fellow and director of studies in theology, Fitzwilliam College

Doctrine, as the Reformers never tired of saying, flows from and leads back to Scripture. Michael Horton has demonstrated this thesis with *Justification,* a project that is at once a rich and rigorous exegetical investigation of the doctrine of justification and at the same time a model of theologically engaged scriptural interpretation. As all theology must, this book drinks from the well of Scripture as it walks the path of reading and doctrine towards the horizon of praise and proclamation. The result, both exegetically informed and theologically significant, is good news "for your bones and mine" (Luther): God justifies the ungodly in Christ, an unconditioned gift given in the word of promise that creates faith.

J. A. Linebaugh, lecturer in New Testament, Cambridge University, fellow, Jesus College

This work is very impressive and a major contribution to the clarification of the significant issues. Horton anchors his presentation of the Protestant Reformers' teaching on the justification of the sinner in an extensive, carefully wrought exploration of the biblical roots, and he anchors conceptualizations of the relationship between sinners and their Creator within a covenantal framework that takes seriously both the sacramental nature of how God operates and the re-creative power of the gospel delivered by Christ. He challenges false interpretation of the Reformers' understanding of justification with thorough, perceptive assessments of patristic and medieval doctrines of justification, providing an alternative that capitalizes on the sixteenth-century insights to address the twenty-first-century person in the midst of the turmoil of our times.

Robert Kolb, professor emeritus of systematic theology, Concordia Seminary, Saint Louis

NEW STUDIES IN DOGMATICS

JUSTIFICATION
VOLUME 2

NEW STUDIES IN DOGMATICS

JUSTIFICATION
VOLUME 2

MICHAEL HORTON

MICHAEL ALLEN AND SCOTT R. SWAIN,
GENERAL EDITORS

ZONDERVAN

Justification, Volume 2
Copyright © 2018 by Michael Horton

This title is also available as a Zondervan ebook.

Requests for information should be addressed to:
Zondervan, *3900 Sparks Dr. SE, Grand Rapids, Michigan 49546*

ISBN 978-0-310-57838-3

CONTENTS

SERIES PREFACE

New Studies in Dogmatics follows in the tradition of G. C. Berkouwer's classic series, Studies in Dogmatics, in seeking to offer concise, focused treatments of major topics in dogmatic theology that fill the gap between introductory theology textbooks and advanced theological monographs. Dogmatic theology, as understood by editors and contributors to the series, is a conceptual representation of scriptural teaching about God and all things in relation to God. The source of dogmatics is Holy Scripture; its scope is the summing up of all things in Jesus Christ; its setting is the communion of the saints; and its end is the conversion, consolation, and instruction of creaturely wayfarers in the knowledge and love of the triune God until that knowledge and love is consummated in the beatific vision.

The series wagers that the way forward in constructive theology lies in a program of renewal through retrieval. This wager follows upon the judgment that much modern theology exhibits "a stubborn tendency to grow not higher but to the side," to borrow Alexander Solzhenitsyn's words from another context. Though modern theology continues to grow in a number of areas of technical expertise and interdisciplinary facility (especially in both the exegetical and historical domains), this growth too often displays a sideways drift rather than an upward progression in relation to theology's subject matter, scope, and source, and in fulfilling theology's end. We believe the path toward theological renewal in such a situation lies in drawing more deeply upon the resources of Holy Scripture in conversation with the church's most trusted teachers (ancient, medieval, and modern) who have sought to fathom Christ's unsearchable riches. In keeping with this belief, authors from a broad evangelical constituency will seek in this series to retrieve the riches of Scripture and tradition for constructive dogmatics. The purpose of retrieval is neither simple repetition of past theologians nor repristination of an earlier phase in church history; Christianity, at any rate, has no golden age east of Eden and short of the kingdom of God. Properly understood, retrieval is an inclusive and enlarging venture, a matter of tapping into a vital root and, in some cases, of relearning a lost grammar of theological discourse, all for the sake of equipping the church in its contemporary vocation to think and speak faithfully and fruitfully about God and God's works.

While the specific emphases of individual volumes will vary, each volume will display (1) awareness of the "state of the question" pertaining to the doctrine under discussion; (2) attention to the patterns of biblical reasoning (exegetical, biblical-theological, etc.) from which the doctrine emerges; (3) engagement with relevant ecclesiastical statements of the doctrine (creedal, conciliar, confessional), as well as with leading theologians of the church; and (4) appreciation of the doctrine's location within the larger system of theology, as well as of its contribution to Christian piety and practice.

Our prayer is that by drawing upon the best resources of the past and with an awareness of both perennial and proximate challenges to Christian thought and practice in the present, New Studies in Dogmatics will contribute to a flourishing theological culture in the church today. Soli Deo Gloria.

MICHAEL ALLEN AND SCOTT R. SWAIN

ACKNOWLEDGMENTS

There are too many friends and colleagues to thank for their input on these two volumes, especially the second. I mention only the following: my Westminster Seminary California colleagues David VanDrunen, Zach Keele, and Joshua Van Ee. There are many other scholars whose ears I have bent to rehearse the arguments that appear in both volumes, especially Mike Allen and Jono Linebaugh. In addition, Tom Wright has been a generous conversation partner, critic, and friend over the years and in various opportunities that we have had to wrestle together over these issues that we both take so seriously. Despite substantial disagreements on this subject, he has helpfully challenged my exegesis at certain points. Another colleague Silverio Gonzalez gave great feedback on some chapters, and for that I'm grateful. These scholars have offered sources that enhanced my arguments and critiques that at least reduced the number of obvious errors, for which I alone am responsible.

I am also indebted to my White Horse Inn colleagues: three decades of collaboration and (more importantly) friendship with fellow Reformed minister Dr. Kim Riddlebarger, Dr. Rod Rosenbladt and his Lutheran cohorts, and Baptist pastor Ken Jones. Our producer, Shane Rosenthal, gave invaluable input and resources. I am also thankful to Mark Green and my assistant, Leslie Wilson, who carved out writing hours amid a busy schedule with great dedication. Thanks also are due to series editors Michael Allen and Scott Swain and to Katya Covrett and Matthew Estel at Zondervan Academic for their expertise and friendship.

Gratitude should also be expressed to my brother, Larry, who first introduced me to this amazing doctrine. As always, I am grateful to my church family and to my wife, Lisa, and children for sharing with me and allowing me to share with them in the joy of being "found in him, not having a righteousness of my own that comes from the law, but that which comes through faith in Christ, the righteousness from God that depends on faith" (Phil 3:9).

ABBREVIATIONS

AB	Anchor Bible Commentary
ANF	*The Ante-Nicene Fathers*. Edited by Alexander Roberts and James Donaldson. 1885–87. 10 vols. Repr., Edinburgh: T&T Clark, 1989.
BDAG	*A Greek-English Lexicon of the New Testament and Other Early Christian Literature*. 3rd ed. Edited by Walter Bauer, Frederick William Danker, William F. Arndt, and Wilbur Gingrich. Chicago: University of Chicago Press, 2000.
CCC	*The Catechism of the Catholic Church*. New York: USCCB, 1995.
CD	*Church Dogmatics*. By Karl Barth. Edited by T. F. Torrance and G. W. Bromiley. Edinburgh: T&T Clark, 1957–77.
CO	*Ioannis Calvini opera quae supersunt omnia*. Edited by Guilielmus Baum, Eduard Cunitz, and Eduard Reuss. 10 vols. Brunsvigae: Schwetschke, 1871.
DS	*Enchiridion symbolorum definitionum et declarationum de rebus fidei et morum*. Edited by Heinrich Denzinger and Adolf Schönmetzer. Barcinone: Herder, 1973.
Haer.	*Against Heresies*. By Irenaeus.
Inst.	*Institutes of the Christian Religion*. By John Calvin. Edited by John T. McNeill. Translated by Ford Lewis Battles. Philadelphia: Westminster, 1960.
JBL	*Journal of Biblical Literature*
JSNT	*Journal for the Study of the New Testament*
LW	*Luther's Works*. Edited by Jaroslav Pelikan and Helmut T. Lehmann. Philadelphia and St. Louis: Fortress and Concordia, 1955–.

NICNT	New International Commentary on the New Testament
NPNF[1]	*The Nicene and Post-Nicene Fathers*, Series 1. Edited by Philip Schaff. 1886–89. 14 vols. Repr., Peabody, MA: Hendrickson, 1994.
NPNF[2]	*The Nicene and Post-Nicene Fathers*, Series 2. Edited by Philip Schaff and Henry Wace. 1896–1900. 14 Vols. Repr., Peabody, MA: Hendrickson, 1994.
NSBT	New Studies in Biblical Theology
PG	Patrologia Graeca. Edited by J.-P. Migne. 162 vols. Paris, 1857–1886.
PL	Patrologia Latina. Edited by J.-P. Migne. 217 vols. Paris, 1844–64.
ST	*Summa Theologica*. By Thomas Aquinas. Translated by the Fathers of the English Dominican Province. Westminster, MD: Christian Classics, 1981.
TDNT	*Theological Dictionary of the New Testament*. Edited by Gerhard Kittel. Translated and edited by Geoffrey W. Bromiley. 10 vols. Grand Rapids: Eerdmans, 1964–76.
WA	*D. Martin Luthers Werke: kritische Gesammtausgabe*. 120 vols. Weimar, 1883–2009.
WBC	Word Biblical Commentary
WUNT	Wissenschaftliche Untersuchungen zum Neuen Testament

JUSTIFICATION AND BIBLICAL-THEOLOGICAL PARADIGMS

Our beliefs not only form broader paradigms but, at least in part, are formed by them. Paradigms are resilient to challenges, which is good—otherwise we would always be reinventing disciplines from scratch. Yet this means that even noteworthy anomalies can be ignored simply because of the conviction that the reigning paradigm is the best explanation of the data. Paradigm revolutions do come, but they are rare. In spite of the grandiose advertising by advocates as well as fretful lamentations by critics, they are never complete breaks but carry the DNA of past reigning paradigms with them into the present and future.[1] The Reformation represents one such shift in the interpretation of the gospel, especially related to Paul's teaching, and we are in something like another paradigm revolution today, whose conclusions are still being worked out, refined, challenged, and revised.

Even if we could return with first naiveté to the Protestant Reformers, it would be undesirable to ignore the line of critique culminating in what has come to be called "the new perspective on Paul." Nevertheless, there is no settled consensus among scholars, and we should not regard this paradigm-shift as a fate, akin to the Copernican Revolution of the sciences. With the Reformation, we are dealing with the effective

---

1. See, e.g., Thomas Kuhn, *The Structure of Scientific Revolutions*, 4th ed. (Chicago: University of Chicago Press, 2012). This is not to accept Kuhn's entire proposal, but thus far his argument is substantiated by ample examples. As Michael Polanyi's work also documented, there are many analogies with theology, philosophy, and other disciplines in this regard.

history of texts; paradigm shifts in the humanities differ from those in the hard sciences. Another reason for caution is that in contemporary debates the Reformation interpretation of justification is typically found wanting without actually being weighed. My goal in this volume is not to vindicate the Protestant Reformers but to investigate the biblical doctrine of justification in light of contemporary exegesis. Nevertheless, something needs to be said at the outset about paradigms and the fact that, in my reckoning at least, the Reformation paradigm has been caricatured rather than genuinely engaged.

In recent debates about justification and related concepts in Scripture, scholarly acumen in biblical languages, history, criticism, and hermeneutics is not always matched by first-hand knowledge of the history, exegesis, and actual theological conclusions of the Protestant Reformers. No one expects biblical scholars to be experts in Reformation studies. However, a reasonable amount of serious engagement with the sources should be expected when one's central contention is that the Reformers fundamentally misunderstood Paul on justification. Claims abound by biblical scholars about the convictions the Reformers held, the arguments for those convictions, the role those doctrines played in their systems, and the effects of those doctrines historically.

Although there are remnants at times of primary-source research, for the most part the "old perspective" turns out to be nineteenth- and especially twentieth-century German liberalism, at far remove from the sixteenth-century Reformers. If Roman Catholic polemicists of yore sought to cut a figure of Luther from the cloth of Marcionite antinomianism, liberal Lutherans seemed to provide the needed fabric.

Read through the thick multilayered lens of Ritschl, neo-Kantian, existentialist, and in varying degrees anti-Semitic assumptions, Ferdinand Weber, Rudolf Bultmann, and others thoroughly reconstructed "Lutheranism." Familiar categories like law and gospel became ciphers for a contrast between fact and value, history and existential encounter, myth and kerygma. Justification by faith as opposed to works came to mean an attitude of surrender to the unknowable apart from evidence and reason. The "Christ-event" (at least in its redemptive significance) refers not to certain happenings surrounding the Jesus of history but to the contemporary presence of the Christ of faith through preaching. "Judaism" becomes the perfect foil for a generic moralism and a self-righteousness that clings to the "works" of an apologetics based on rational and evidential arguments. Not Luther, Melanchthon, and Chemnitz but Herrmann, Natorp, and Heidegger provided the substance of law and gospel for Bultmann's program.

But the foundations of this mislabeled "old" or "Lutheran" perspective go back further to Kant and pietism. This combination of *Aufkärung* and evangelical revival played a key role in transforming theology in anthropology and religious psychology. In contrast, it is difficult to find a movement in church history more focused on the sheer objectivity of Christ's work for us outside of us (*extra nos*) than the magisterial Reformation. All the major Lutheran confessional statements on justification tie the "chief article" to the incarnation, cross, and resurrection of Christ. Nothing could be further from an existentialist gospel than Luther's definition: "The Word is the Gospel of God concerning his Son who was made flesh, suffered, rose from the dead, and was glorified through the Spirit of holiness."[2] Scions of Renaissance humanism, the Reformers, and their "scholastic" successors into the seventeenth century were simultaneously first-order exegetes, philologists, linguists, historians, and theologians. Not only were there no territorial disputes, there were no distinct territories with identifiable borders between doctrine and exegesis.

With the advent of pietism and especially Johann Albrecht Bengel (1687–1752), however, dogmatics drifted apart from exegesis and biblical studies. One therefore returned to the Bible over against the history of theology, the creeds and confessions, and systematic theology. More often than not, the result, ironically, was something closer to Gnosticism, Arianism, and Pelagianism. Whatever it was, such biblical scholarship was adamantly insistent that it was not dogmatics and certainly not confessional theology.

Yet in much of Protestant biblical studies (including evangelical), one still detects a certain degree of reticence toward "church theology" and dogmatics. This is ironic, since biblical studies in our day often proceeds in a manner distinctive of modern dogmatics, namely, with a central dogma from which all else is deduced. If only one understands x or y, everything will fall into place, and we will finally be able to understand Jesus or Paul. It is not difficult to fill in the blank with a particular project or school set over against other projects and schools

---

2. Martin Luther, "The Freedom of a Christian," in *LW* 31:346.

in a manner that looks strikingly similar to nineteenth- and twentieth-century dogmatics.

If we are to advance at all beyond the current tangle of false choices in treatments of justification, the first binary we must deconstruct is the one between exegesis/dogma and biblical studies/theology. Together with the biblical scholars I will engage in this volume, we are all doing theology and are indebted to those who have done theology before us. Theology must always be grounded in patient exegesis of the text in the original languages, while exegesis must always be honest and explicit about its dogmatic assumptions and its ecclesial location. Some biblical scholars are familiar with Reformation theology first hand, but this seems increasingly rare even among the Lutheran and Reformed. As a result, the "old perspective" turns out to be largely a straw opponent.

JUSTIFICATION IN CONTEMPORARY BIBLICAL SCHOLARSHIP: POST-WAR PAUL STUDIES

"Put simply," David Shaw summarizes, "the doctrine of justification in the twentieth century has endured one of two fates. It has either retained its traditional meaning but been declared peripheral to Paul's concerns, or it has remained central by undergoing a degree of redefinition."[3] Often identified as the new perspective on Paul, this somewhat loose affiliation of views is united in its conviction that the Reformation fundamentally misunderstood the gospel proclaimed by the apostle to the gentiles.[4] Engaging that conclusion is beyond my interest in this volume. Nevertheless, I hope that readers with an eye for such issues will discover more to account for if they make that case. Our study encompasses the whole Bible, but the debates concerning justification continue to focus on the Pauline corpus.

---

3. David Shaw, "Romans 4 and the Justification of Abraham in Light of Perspectives New and Newer," *Themelios* 40, no. 1 (2015): 50–62.

4. I interact at length with the new perspective in Michael Horton, *Covenant and Salvation: Union with Christ* (Louisville: Westminster John Knox, 2007). The following are among the most formative works of the new perspective: E. P. Sanders, *Paul and Palestinian Judaism: A Comparison of Patterns of Religion* (Philadelphia: Fortress, 1977); Sanders, *Paul, the Law, and the Jewish People* (Philadelphia: Fortress, 1983); James D. G. Dunn, *The Theology of Paul the Apostle* (Grand Rapids: Eerdmans, 2006); Dunn, *The New Perspective on Paul*, 2nd ed. (Grand Rapids: Eerdmans, 2007); N. T. Wright, *The Climax of the Covenant: Christ and the Law in Pauline Theology* (Edinburgh: T&T Clark, 1991); Wright, *What Saint Paul Really Said: Was Paul of Tarsus the Real Founder of Christianity?* (Grand Rapids: Eerdmans, 1997); Wright, *Paul: In Fresh Perspective* (Minneapolis: Fortress, 2009); Wright, *Paul and the Faithfulness of God* (Minneapolis: Fortress, 2013); and Wright, *Justification: God's Plan and Paul's Vision* (Downers Grove, IL: IVP Academic, 2016).

Reversing the de-Judaizing program of their predecessors, Gerhard von Rad, Günther Bornkamm, Ernst Käsemann, and other post-War biblical scholars set about to ground Jesus and Paul in their Jewish milieu. W. D. Davies's *Paul and Rabbinic Judaism* (1948) launched a similar enterprise in the English-speaking world, which (along with J. Munck's 1954 monograph, *Paulus und die Heilsgeschichte*) influenced E. P. Sanders's seminal tome *Paul and Palestinian Judaism* (1977) and Krister Stendahl's *Paul Among Jews and Gentiles and Other Essays* (1977).[5] These last two works may be credited with the beginning of what N. T. Wright coined in a 1978 Tyndale Lecture as "the new perspective on Paul." James D. G. Dunn and Wright became the most prominent advocates of the proposal, though not without their own distinct emphases.

The New Perspective

Whatever the Reformation's disagreements with the medieval church over how to understand and relate law and gospel, justification and sanctification, and the forensic and transformative aspects of salvation, they pale in comparison to the shifts within modern Protestantism itself. Modernism had already grown accustomed to pitting Jesus against Paul, the former heralding the social gospel while the latter was more Hellenized (Catholic), with its idea of a divine Redeemer and obsession with personal salvation.

An entirely new paradigm especially for interpreting Paul emerged in the 1980s. This new perspective on Paul actually began as a new perspective on Judaism with E. P. Sanders's *Paul and Palestinian Judaism* (1977) and had an impact well beyond New Testament scholarship.[6] But already for decades many biblical scholars and theologians had been

---

5. The essay first appeared in Krister Stendahl, "The Apostle Paul and the Introspective Conscience of the West," *Harvard Theological Review* 56 (1963): 199–215. There have been challenges to Sanders's description of Judaism as a religion of grace, e.g., Robert H. Gundry, "Grace, Works and Staying Saved in Paul," *Biblica* 66 (1985): 1–38; Douglas Moo, "'Law', 'Works of the Law,' and 'Legalism' in Paul," *Westminster Theological Journal* 45 (1983): 73–100. Others have argued that Sanders's largely correct claims about Judaism have little bearing on Paul's view of God's righteousness. See H. Weder "Gesetz und Sünde: Gedanken zu einem qualitativen Sprung im Denken des Paulus," *New Testament Studies* 31 (1985): 357–76.

6. Sanders was hardly the first to critique modern (especially Protestant) interpretations of Judaism. The architect of Anglo-liberal Judaism, C. G. Montefiore and Sanders's doctoral supervisor, W. D. Davies, as well as C. H. Dodd and David Daube, had already laid the groundwork for Sanders's thesis in the first half of the century. Other important works of Sanders followed *Paul and Palestinian Judaism*, including *Paul* (Oxford: Oxford University Press, 1991) and *Judaism: Practices and Beliefs* (London: SCM, 1992). Sanders's principal target was Ferdinand Weber, whose portrait of Judaism had been refuted by Montefiore.

drawn to Albert Schweitzer's conviction that the center of Paul's thought was mysticism (being "in Christ"), with forensic justification as little more than "a subsidiary crater."[7] Krister Stendahl extended the critique of the Reformation as due more to Luther's introspective conscience than to exegesis of Paul.[8] Echoing Schweitzer, E. P. Sanders concluded in *Paul and Palestinian Judaism* that Paul's difference with Judaism did not turn on questions of grace and justification but on being in Christ. For Paul, he argued, the forensic is subordinated to the mystical.[9] Many other factors went into the creation of the perfect storm, but these were among the most significant. For these scholars, the culprit behind the shift from a salvation-historical to an introspective and individualistic focus was not Paul but the Protestant Reformers.

Though exhibiting a range of views, the new perspective is united by the contention that the Reformers misunderstood Paul and the type of religion he opposed. The main problem, it is argued, was anachronism. With little first-hand familiarity of the primary sources, the Reformers read early Judaism as an ancient version of medieval works-righteousness and failed to recognize that Second Temple Judaism had a robust doctrine of grace. More generally, the argument continues, Judaism was not obsessed with personal salvation but with participation in an end-time "setting-right" of this world. Thus the principal question was not, "How can I go to heaven when I die?" but "When will the exile be over?" and "How can we identify the true community of those who will share in the resurrection and rule of the just?"

In short, whereas the sixteenth-century debate turned on differences over *how* individuals are saved, the new perspective turns the focus from soteriology to ecclesiology and the role of the church in challenging worldly empire in service to Christ's transforming reign. Justification is indeed a legal verdict in the courtroom, as the Reformers argued over

---

7. Albert Schweitzer, *The Mysticism of Paul the Apostle*, trans. W. Montgomery (New York: Seabury, 1931), 225.

8. Stendahl, "The Apostle Paul and the Introspective Conscience of the West."

9. Interestingly, even before these debates, the Princetonian biblical theologian Geerhardus Vos recognized that "Paul consciously and consistently subordinated the mystical aspect of the relation to Christ to the forensic one. Paul's mind was to such an extent forensically oriented that he regarded the entire complex of subjective spiritual changes that take place in the believer and of subjective spiritual blessings enjoyed by the believer as the direct outcome of the forensic work of Christ applied in justification. The mystical is based on the forensic, not the forensic on the mystical." Vos, "The Alleged Legalism in Paul's Doctrine of Justification," in *Redemptive History and Biblical Interpretation: The Shorter Writings of Geerhardus Vos*, ed. Richard B. Gaffin Jr. (Phillipsburg, NJ: P&R, 1980), 384.

against Rome's definition of justification as a process of becoming holy. Nevertheless, it is a verdict that one is a member of the true community of God in the present, with faith (rather than circumcision and dietary laws) as the badge, and a final justification according to works. "Paul, in company with mainstream Second Temple Judaism, affirms that God's final judgment will be in accordance with the entirety of a life led—in accordance, in other words, with works."[10]

Within this new frame (which was actually part of Rome's argument against the Reformers), Paul's polemic against "the works of the law" is directed not against a false scheme of personal salvation ("works-righteousness") but against religio-ethnic superiority. Hence, "works of the law" refers not to the whole Torah (including the moral law) but merely the boundary markers such as circumcision, food laws, and Sabbaths that distinguish Jews from gentiles. As we have seen in volume 1, this was the view of Origen in contrast with Irenaeus, Chrysostom, and Augustine.

Even on this point, there is some diversity of opinion among new perspective scholars. E. P. Sanders argued that Paul experienced a total shift from "covenantal nomism" to "participation in Christ."[11] For his part, Sanders is unwilling to adjudicate between Paul's participationist eschatology and Judaism. "Paul's view could hardly be maintained, and it was not maintained. Christianity rapidly became a new covenantal nomism, but Paulinism is not thereby proved inferior or superior."[12]

James D. G. Dunn disagrees. He judges that Sanders "did not follow through this insight far enough or with sufficient consistency." His mistake is in assuming that after the Damascus road experience Paul leapt "in arbitrary fashion . . . from one system (covenantal nomism) into another (Christianity), leaving his theology, particularly in reference to the law, incoherent and contradictory."[13] Sanders's erroneous conclusion is more emphatic in the work of Heiki Räisänen.[14] In Dunn's view, however, it is not Paul who misunderstands Judaism and advances

---

10. N. T. Wright, "New Perspectives on Paul," in *Justification in Perspective: Historical Developments and Contemporary Challenges*, ed. Bruce L. McCormack (Grand Rapids: Baker Academic, 2006), 253.

11. Sanders, *Paul and Palestinian Judaism*, 543–56.

12. Sanders, *Paul and Palestinian Judaism*, 552.

13. James D. G. Dunn, introduction to *Romans 1–8*, WBC 38A (Waco: Word, 1988), lxvi-lxvii, citing Sanders, *Paul and Palestinian Judaism*, 550–52, and Sanders, *Paul and the Law* (throughout).

14. Dunn, introduction to *Romans 1–8*, lxvi-lxvii.

a contradictory system; the problem is Reformation interpretations of Paul that endure even in the assumption of scholars like Sanders. Paul's theology can only be understood in the context of a very specific first-century debate over Jew–gentile relations in the emergent community.

Few specialists today would side with Rudolf Bultmann or other representatives of what is misnamed the "Lutheran" perspective when it comes to the description of early Judaism. Yet among the scholars who lauded Sanders's groundbreaking *Paul and Palestinian Judaism* are those who are nevertheless sharp critics of the more controversial theses of the new perspective.[15] Indeed, even some architects of the New Perspective now express second thoughts, wondering if there has been an overreaction. Dunn, for example, has suggested recently concerning the thesis of gentile inclusion, "To recognize this is *not* to deny or play down the more fundamental fact that no person can stand before God except by God's forgiving, justifying grace."[16] N. T. Wright observes that the new perspective emphasizes "that every time Paul discusses justification he seems simultaneously to be talking about Gentile inclusion," yet it has "usually" failed to show "how this integrates with the traditional view that he is talking about how sinners are put right with God."[17]

The concept of covenant plays a central role in the new perspective—more central, in fact, than in the scholarship of the preceding two or three generations before Gerhard von Rad and Walther Eichrodt. Since "covenant theology" is in many ways the organizing structure of Reformed theology, one might expect this to be an important point of convergence with the new perspective. However, whereas Reformed (federal) theology distinguishes between different types of covenants

---

15. See, e.g., Peter Stuhlmacher, *Reconciliation, Law and Righteousness: Essays in Biblical Theology* (Philadelphia: Fortress, 1986); Stuhlmacher, *Paul's Letter to the Romans: A Commentary* (Louisville: Westminster John Knox, 1994); Stuhlmacher, *Revisiting Paul's Doctrine of Justification: A Challenge to the New Perspective* (Downers Grove, IL: IVP Academic, 2001); Stephen Westerholm, *Perspectives Old and New on Paul: The 'Lutheran' Paul and His Critics* (Grand Rapids: Eerdmans, 2003); Westerholm, *Justification Reconsidered: Rethinking a Pauline Theme* (Grand Rapids: Eerdmans, 2013); Douglas Moo, *The Epistle to the Romans*, NICNT (Grand Rapids: Eerdmans, 1996); D. A. Carson, ed., *Right with God: Justification in the Bible and the World* (Grand Rapids: Baker and Carlisle: Paternoster, 1992); Mark A. Seifrid, *Justification by Faith: The Origin and Development of a Central Pauline Theme* (Leiden: Brill, 1992); Thomas Schreiner, *The Law and its Fulfilment: A Pauline Theology of Law* (Grand Rapids: Baker, 1993); Schreiner, *Romans*, Baker Exegetical Commentary on the New Testament (Grand Rapids: Baker Academic, 1998); Simon J. Gathercole, *Where Is Boasting? Early Jewish Soteriology and Paul's Response in Romans 1–5* (Grand Rapids: Eerdmans, 2002).

16. James D. G. Dunn, "The New Perspective: Whence, What, and Whither?" in *The New Perspective on Paul: Collected Essays* (Grand Rapids: Eerdmans, 2005), 87.

17. Wright, *Paul: In Fresh Perspective*, 36

(law and gospel), a wide consensus of biblical scholars and theologians (including Barth and the new perspective) merges them into one covenant. The covenant motif has been not only affirmed but central to N. T. Wright's proposal since *Climax of the Covenant* in 1991. He says that "covenant theology is one of the main clues, usually neglected, for understanding Paul."[18] Yet he is quick to distance his covenant theology from sixteenth- and seventeenth-century versions.[19] Nevertheless, in a later work Wright concedes that he has not read these sources.[20] Consequently, in case after case contemporary readers of such important biblical-theological explorations only have access to caricatures.[21]

Regardless of whether one agrees with the conclusions of the sixteenth- and seventeenth-century Reformed theologians, sweeping dismissals and misrepresentations are a pity, because these older scholars were pioneering exegetes, philologists, and translators as well as theologians. In fact, they were often more deeply trained even than the Reformers themselves in the history of interpretation from the patristic era to Byzantine teaching and medieval scholasticism, as well as emerging issues in natural and political science. It is a waste to dismiss such a massive and profound body of exegetical theology without even encountering its actual arguments. Again, it is not my purpose in this volume to defend or repristinate these gains, but my indebtedness to their labors will be evident as I engage with contemporary exegetical proposals.

In any event, one cannot conclude that the new perspective represents a cohesive, much less settled, consensus. For example, Douglas Campbell questions the plausibility of N. T. Wright's return-from-exile motif,[22] and Wright questions much of Campbell's system.[23] Some insist

---

18. Wright, *The Climax of the Covenant*, xi, 1.

19. Wright, *What Saint Paul Really Said*, 117.

20. Wright, *Paul: In Fresh Perspective*, 13. "Like many New Testament scholars, I am largely ignorant of the Pauline exegesis of all but a few of the fathers and reformers. The Middle Ages, and the seventeenth and eighteenth centuries, had plenty to say about Paul, but I have not read it." With this volume, Wright distances himself in a more general way from the new perspective. He suggests that even the new perspective has been too interested in a theology of salvation rather than in the ostensibly Pauline interest in transforming society under the lordship of Christ.

21. A number of helpful surveys have appeared in recent years offering more direct access to the Reformers' interpretation of Paul. See for example Michael Allen and Jonathan Linebaugh, *Reformation Readings of Paul: Explorations in History and Exegesis* (Downers Grove, IL: IVP Academic, 2010); and Stephen J. Chester, *Reading Paul with the Reformers: Reconciling Old and New Perspectives* (Grand Rapids: Eerdmans, 2017).

22. Douglas A. Campbell, *The Deliverance of God: An Apocalyptic Rereading of Justification in Paul* (Grand Rapids: Eerdmans, 2013), 1031.

23. N. T. Wright, *Paul and His Recent Interpreters* (Minneapolis: Fortress, 2015), 187–221.

that critique of empire is a key to understanding Jesus and Paul, while critics argue that there is little in the New Testament to indicate any such critique.[24] As Wright said in 2003, "There are probably almost as many 'new' perspective positions as there are writers espousing it— and I disagree with most of them."[25] James Dunn concludes, "I am not convinced that we have yet given the proper reading of Paul from the new perspective of first-century Palestinian Judaism opened up so helpfully by Sanders himself."[26] Responding to those who suggest that resisting the new perspective is like clinging to a pre-Copernican cosmology, Donald Hagner judges, "The revolution, however, is not yet complete. Some of us, moreover, continue to believe that the evidence still points to a geocentric universe—at least as far as Paul's theology is concerned."[27] Stephen Westerholm suggests, "Students who want to know how a Rabbinic Jew perceived humanity's place in God's world will read Paul with caution and Luther not at all. On the other hand, students who want to understand Paul, but feel that they have nothing to learn from Martin Luther, should consider a career in metallurgy. Exegesis is learned from the masters."[28]

At the same time, there can be no direct route back to the Reformation perspective that is unmoved by or outright ignores the challenges of the last half-century. Any defense of the basic conclusions of the Reformation does so with a "second naiveté."

Beyond the New Perspective: Apocalyptic Liberation

A still-emerging trajectory criticizes the new perspective for not being radical enough in its rejection of the Reformation paradigm. The gospel that Paul announces should be seen less as the "climax of the covenant"

---

24. Support for this theme falls predictably along new perspective lines, with those most ardently favoring empire-critique including Richard Horsley and N. T. Wright, and those most skeptical including John M. G. Barclay (in "Why the Roman Empire Was Insignificant to Paul," in *Pauline Churches and Diaspora Jews* [Tübingen: Mohr Siebeck, 2011], 363–88) and Seyoon Kim (*Christ and Caesar: The Gospel and the Roman Empire in the Writings of Paul and Luke* [Grand Rapids: Eerdmans, 2008]). Barclay and Kim, however, are not "new perspective" scholars. Wright dubbed the emphasis on Paul's ostensible critique of empire "the fresh perspective on Paul" in his 2000 Manson Memorial Lecture, expanded upon in his *Paul: In Fresh Perspective* (Minneapolis: Fortress, 2009).

25. Wright, "New Perspectives on Paul," 246.

26. Dunn, *The New Perspective on Paul*, 95.

27. Donald Hagner, "Paul and the Matrix of Early Christianity: Issues in the Current Debate," *Bulletin for Biblical Research* 3 (1993): 111–30.

28. Stephen Westerholm, *Israel's Law and the Church's Faith: Paul and His Recent Interpreters* (Grand Rapids: Eerdmans, 1988), 173.

(*pace* Wright) than a radical in-breaking of divine action: divine rescue, liberation, and transformation on a cosmic scale. Thus Christ should be seen less as the *fulfillment* of God's covenantal promises than the *exception* to history as such, in the light of whom all of previous and subsequent history must now be reinterpreted. If the new perspective is in large measure a reaction against Bultmann, the "beyonders" are indebted to the Swiss theologian Karl Barth. This was evident already with an important source of this trajectory, Ernst Käsemann (1906–98).[29] Biblical scholars outnumber dogmaticians in this very volume, but given Barth's prominent role in the widely influential trajectory of Käsemann and his contemporary sympathizers, his account deserves greater (albeit brief) attention.

Barth represents the most extreme version of the apocalyptic emphasis, though without Schweitzer's notion that Jesus failed to inaugurate his kingdom. If the Reformers identified the Pharisees and Paul's opponents with the pope and his retinue, the *Römerbrief* expanded the lust for self-justification to the "religious man" in general. Significantly revising the first edition, Barth later noted that he had embraced a practically "Osiandrian" view of justification in the first edition of *The Epistle to the Romans*, so in the second edition he sought to understand the doctrine more in terms of Christ *for us* than *in us*.[30] Nevertheless, A. T. B. McGowan is justified in concluding that for Barth, as well as Thomas F. Torrance, "justification is not conceived of in forensic terms, involving the imputation of the righteousness of Christ and the nonimputation of sin, but, rather, in terms of the participation in, and the sharing of, Christ's righteousness."[31] Where union with Christ ("the great exchange") was seen by the Reformers as Paul's overarching term for the multifaceted gift of salvation that included both justification and sanctification, this approach tends to dissolve these distinct gifts in union.

Unlike Schweitzer, however, Barth did not think that the justification of the ungodly was a "subsidiary crater" in Paul's theology. He even

---

29. See Paul F. M. Zahl, *Die Rechtfertigungslehre Ernst Käsemanns* (Stuttgart: Calwer, 1996).

30. Karl Barth to Eduard Thurneysen, 3 December 1920, in *Revolutionary Theology in the Making: Barth-Thurneysen Correspondence, 1914–1925*, trans. J. Smart (London: Epworth, 1964), 55.

31. A. T. B. McGowan, "Justification and the *Ordo Salutis*," in *Justification in Perspective: Historical Developments and Contemporary Challenges*, ed. Bruce L. McCormack (Grand Rapids: Baker Academic, 2006), 160.

appropriated penal substitution.[32] However, his actualist ontology, especially after his new view of election, led to a radical reinterpretation of justification and related doctrines. Wary of the assimilation of Christ to history in liberal Protestantism and a pietistic focus on various stages of the believer's salvation, Barth pushed back against the idea both of a *historia salutis* (history of salvation) and an *ordo salutis* (order in the way God applies redemption to people).[33] His thought displays a general tendency to absorb every "before" and "after" into an eternal decision in which God not only elects Christ together with all of humanity but in this act determines his own being.[34] Election and justification become essentially the same event.[35] As a single action of God's reconciliation of the world in Christ, Bruce McCormack summarizes,

> "Justification" is something that takes place in Jesus Christ, in his death and resurrection. . . . Seen in this light, it is important that we should avoid setting up "a dualism between an objective procuring of salvation there and then and a subjective appropriation of salvation here and now" [*CD* IV/2:502–3]. . . . Expressed even more concretely: justification is not first made effective when the Holy Spirit awakens faith in us; rather, the Spirit awakens faith in us so that we might live from and toward the reality of a justification that is already effective for us even before we come to know of it.[36]

The "traditional dualism" between redemption *accomplished* and *applied* reflects an inadequate Trinitarian theology, Barth argues, by undermining the unity of God as the single subject, as if only Christ

---

32. See Bruce L. McCormack, "The Ontological Presuppositions of Barth's Doctrine of the Atonement," in *The Glory of Atonement: Biblical, Theological and Practical Perspectives*, ed. Charles E. Hill and Frank A. James (Downers Grove, IL: InterVarsity, 2004), 346–66.

33. See the insightful critique on this point by G. C. Berkouwer, *The Triumph of Grace in the Theology of Karl Barth,* trans. H. R. Boer (Grand Rapids: Eerdmans, 1956), 256–58.

34. See Michael Horton, "Covenant, Election, and Incarnation: Evaluating Barth's Actualist Christology," in *Karl Barth and American Evangelicalism*, ed. Bruce L. McCormack and Clifford B. Anderson (Grand Rapids: Eerdmans, 2011), 112–47.

35. Bruce L. McCormack, "*Justitia aliena*: Karl Barth in Conversation with the Evangelical Doctrine of Imputed Righteousness," in *Justification in Perspective: Historical Developments and Contemporary Challenges*, ed. Bruce L. McCormack (Grand Rapids: Baker Academic, 2006), 178: "For Karl Barth, the word 'justification' is a term that is rightly employed to describe the *whole* of the reconciling activity of the triune God (including both 'objective' and 'subjective' soteriology). Employed in this way, the only comparable terms in his theology are 'sanctification' and 'vocation.' These terms, too, describe the whole of the reconciling activity of God."

36. McCormack, "*Justitia aliena*," 179. See also *CD* IV/2, 501.

accomplished redemption and only the Spirit applies it.[37] Although we may experience these as different events, notes McCormack, "This does not mean that they are distinct in precisely the same way for God as well."[38] McCormack adds,

> Barth rejects the concept of an *ordo salutis*—or at least he does so to the extent that it is thought of as "a *temporal* succession [of acts] in which the Holy Spirit brings forth His effects . . . here and now in men." [*CD* IV/2:502] Barth would not have disagreed that *some* sequencing in the *opera trinitatis ad extra* is necessary. For him, as for the tradition, divine acts that take place in eternity (election and glorification) come "before" and "after" those which take place in time. His scruples against the concept of an *ordo salutis* are directed strictly toward those elements believed traditionally to take place in time, in the life history of the believer.[39]

"His insistence on the unitary character of the work of God in Christ, and in the Holy Spirit, means that the work of Christ *is* effective as such, that the work of the Spirit does not complete it or give to it an efficacy it does not otherwise have."[40]

Everything that is usually included under the so-called *ordo salutis*, including justification, is already accomplished in eternity objectively and realized fully in the incarnation with the humiliation and exaltation of the incarnate God.[41] "Barth defines justification materially as the act of divine judgment that restores the covenant of grace that God made with the human race in eternity past." By bearing judgment Christ restores the right of the human partner to fellowship with God.[42]

All of this proceeds from Barth's ontology, in which, at least according to McCormack, God "gives being to himself in the eternal act of entering into the covenant of grace with human beings."[43] McCormack thinks therefore that "Barth's doctrine is not only Protestant but radically so." "For he also insists that Jesus' 'history is as such our history and even our *most proper* history (in a way that is incomparably more direct

---

37. *CD* IV/2, 503.
38. McCormack, "*Justitia aliena*," 179–80.
39. McCormack, "*Justitia aliena*," 180.
40. McCormack, "*Justitia aliena*," 181.
41. McCormack, "*Justitia aliena*," 182.
42. McCormack, "*Justitia aliena*," 184, from *CD* IV/1, 516.
43. McCormack, "*Justitia aliena*," 186.

and more intimate than anything we think ourselves to know as our history).'"[44] God not only constitutes human being and history in the eternal decision of election but his own being as well.[45] Consequently, all people are already "in Christ" "by virtue of the divine election." "Barth does not make use of the language of a positive imputation of Christ's righteousness," McCormack adds. But that is because of the foregoing: there is no *distinct* act separate from the fully accomplished and effective will and work of God in Christ already. Imputation becomes superfluous since this is already accomplished in eternal election.[46] Furthermore, for Barth, justification (thus defined) is "never a completed action in my life's history" but is "new each morning." "At no point is justification my secure possession or a predicate of my existence in this world."[47]

The whole framework is forensic, McCormack insists.[48] "After all, what could be more consistent with forensic thinking than to make 'being' a function of decision and act?"[49] Yet such a thought seems to me to be the consummation of nominalism. With Barth's teaching, we lose justification (at least as the imputation of Christ's righteousness to the sinner) and along with it the other gifts of salvation distinct from election. In short, not only is there no place for any inner transformation that corresponds to God's justifying verdict (though not vice versa), but for Barth God becomes his own decision, at least if McCormack's reading is correct. McCormack's reading is controversial among Barth scholars. Those familiar with McCormack's interpretation relative to election and the Trinity will recognize just how far such nominalist logic can be taken.[50]

In any case, in Barth's thinking, "*The* transition (the movement from past to future that has actually arrived at its goal) has already taken place in the movement of Jesus from his death to his resurrection."[51]

---

44. McCormack, "*Justitia aliena*," 190, from *CD* IV/1, 548.
45. McCormack, "*Justitia aliena*," 191.
46. McCormack, "*Justitia aliena*," 192.
47. McCormack, "*Justitia aliena*," 194, quoting *CD* IV/1, 589.
48. McCormack, "*Justitia aliena*," 192.
49. McCormack, "*Justitia aliena*," 193.
50. Bruce L. McCormack, "Grace and Being: The Role of God's Gracious Election in Karl Barth's Theological Ontology," in *The Cambridge Companion to Karl Barth*, ed. John Webster (Cambridge: Cambridge University Press, 2000), 92–110. An avalanche of literature appeared pro and con in this debate in the new century's first five years. For George Hunsinger's interpretation of Barth on grace and ontology, especially in criticism of some of McCormack's basic readings of Barth, see Hunsinger, *Reading Barth with Charity: A Hermeneutical Proposal* (Grand Rapids: Baker Academic, 2015).
51. McCormack, "*Justitia aliena*," 193.

In this scenario, not even the ascension and Pentecost add anything new to God's saving act. If even the post-Golgotha events cannot add anything new to the event of redemption, then it is unsurprising that Barth rejected any relationship of God with humanity prior to the fall that was not based on grace. Hence, he strongly rejected the distinction between a covenant of works and a covenant of grace embraced by Reformed covenant (federal) theology. Barth thundered, "There can be no 'Federal Theology.'"[52] T. F. Torrance and James B. Torrance followed with a flurry of essays pitting Calvin against the Calvinists.[53]

In terms of its historical accuracy, the Torrance thesis has been refuted decisively over the last several decades.[54] Nevertheless, its impact on nonspecialists in the field continues to be felt. Repeatedly noting his dependence on the Torrance thesis, New Testament scholar Douglas Campbell devotes a section to federal theology, identifying it with his nemesis, "justification theory" or the "'Lutheran' perspective."[55]

Although Barth offered a bracing criticism of neo-Protestant moralism, his system is a highly creative retrieval of Reformation theology that nevertheless diverges from it at every major point. Thus it is highly idiosyncratic and, at key points, conceptually incoherent. Wary of "salvation-historical" approaches that assimilate the apocalyptic in-breaking of redemption to the horizontal plane of immanent development, his system is an overcorrection—as, I will argue, one that Käsemann and his contemporary followers perpetuate and even exaggerate.

---

52. Karl Barth, *The Epistle to the Romans*, trans. Edwin C. Hoskyns (New York: Oxford University Press, 1968), 423. Of course, this is a caricature of federal theology, according to which humans do nothing of the sort. Rather, God binds humanity to himself according to his love and law. It is hardly reciprocal in the sense of any symmetrical relationship (such as a contract), but it is between genuine partners. Here as elsewhere, Barth's "God is God!" threatens to reduce humanity to unreality.

53. The bibliography continues to grow, but the following represent the most seminal essays in defense of the "Calvin versus the Calvinists" thesis: T. F. Torrance, "Karl Barth and the Latin Heresy," in *Karl Barth: Biblical and Ecumenical Theologian* (Edinburgh: T&T Clark, 1990); James B. Torrance, "The Concept of Federal Theology," in *Calvinus Sacrae Scripturae Professor*, ed. William H. Neuser (Grand Rapids: Eerdmans, 1994); James B. Torrance, "Covenant or Contract," *Scottish Journal of Theology* 23, no. 1 (February 1970): esp. 53; Basil Hall, "Calvin against the Calvinists," in *John Calvin*, ed. G. E. Duffield, Courtenay Studies in Reformation Theology (Appleford: Sutton Courtenay, 1966).

54. The work of Richard Muller, Irena Backus, Willem van Asselt, Susan Schreiner, and others has recovered an early Reformed tradition based on primary sources rather than sweeping denunciations of "scholasticism." On criticism of the "Calvin versus Calvinism" thesis in particular, see especially Richard Muller, *After Calvin: Studies in the Development of a Theological Tradition* (New York: Oxford University Press, 2004); Carl Trueman and R. S. Clark, eds., *Protestant Scholasticism: Essays in Reassessment* (Carlisle: Paternoster, 1998); Paul Helm, *Calvin and the Calvinists* (Edinburgh: Banner of Truth Trust, 1982); Willem J. Van Asselt and Eef Dekker, eds., *Reformation and Scholasticism: An Ecumenical Enterprise* (Grand Rapids: Baker Academic, 2001).

55. Campbell, *The Deliverance of God*, 4.

Ernst Käsemann was not simply a "Barthian," yet his point of departure is Barth's more apocalyptic *Römerbrief* over against the approach of his doctoral supervisor, Rudolf Bultmann. Like Barth, Käsemann saw God's act of deliverance in Christ as an utterly alien penetration into history of the kingdom from above, condemning *homo religionis* with its self-righteousness and marginalization of the outcasts. Over against the existentializing individualism of Bultmann, Käsemann and his students interpret "the righteousness of God" as both deliverance and transforming power. However, if in Bultmann's hands the law-gospel contrast became a cipher for an essentially neo-Kantian antithesis between objective-historical facts and the crisis of personal decision, the Käsemann trajectory bends toward its own abstractions and generalizations that have more to do with liberation from oppressive economic and political systems than with the *justification* of the *ungodly* in advance of the final judgment. As a result, those in the Käsemann trajectory often simply champion the opposing side of Bultmann's false choices: salvation is apocalyptic and cosmic, not existential and individual. The question is not how to find a gracious God but how God has entered this present age to transform it.

If Weiss and especially Schweitzer represent a counteroffensive against Ritschl and the history of religions school, and Barth represents a similar reaction against Troeltsch and Harnack, the turn to Jewish apocalyptic in the wake of Käsemann represents a third reaction, this time against Bultmann. However, the current trend inspired by Käsemann is even more radical in its single-minded devotion to the apocalyptic irruption of divine liberation over against the salvation-historical emphasis now represented by Sanders, Dunn, and Wright. J. Louis Martyn, Martinus de Boer, Beverly Roberts Gaventa, Richard Hays, J. Christiaan Beker, and Douglas Campbell challenge theories of patterns and types that treat the Christ-event as the horizontal culmination especially of a particular history (e.g., covenantal nomism) rather than God's utterly unique and vertical-apocalyptic interruption of history. Where the new perspective emphasizes continuity, the "post-new perspective" underscores discontinuity.[56]

---

56. See Douglas Campbell, "Christ and the Church in Paul: A 'Post-New Perspective' Account," in *Four Views on the Apostle Paul*, ed. Michael F. Bird, Counterpoints (Grand Rapids: Zondervan, 2012), 113–43; Martinus de Boer, "Paul's Mythologising Program in Romans 5–8," in *Apocalyptic Paul: Cosmos and Anthropos in Romans 5–8*, ed. Beverly Roberts Gaventa (Waco: Baylor University Press, 2013), 1–20; Gaventa, "The Cosmic Power of Sin in Paul's Letter to

Beker follows Philipp Vielhauer and Klaus Koch in identifying three essential elements of apocalyptic: "historical dualism, universalism, and imminent expectation."[57] First, on historical dualism, rather than the metaphysical dualism of Greek philosophy and religion (e.g., body and soul), Jewish apocalyptic embraces a dualism between *ages* or epochs: this age (of sin, oppression, injustice, and death) and the age to come (after final judgment, unending righteousness, and peace). Second, Jewish apocalyptic is identified by its world-encompassing outlook ("universalism" here not necessarily meaning salvation). Third, in opposition to seeing history as a steady evolution from acorn to oak tree, for Jewish apocalyptic the decisive moment is God's *interruption* of world history in order to judge and deliver. The prayer of Isaiah 64:1, "Oh that you would rend the heavens and come down, that the mountains might quake at your presence," expresses well the vision of Jewish apocalyptic.

What then can it be to which Paul is objecting in his polemics? For these writers, Paul's target is "flesh" (*sarx*)—that is, this present evil age. The whole world lies under the dominion of the cosmic powers of sin and death. The age to come is breaking in on this present age through the Christ-event and the descent of the Spirit to release humanity from the powers of darkness in order to become part of the new creation. Hence, "The human dilemma consists at its base, not of guilt, but of enslavement to powers lying beyond the human being's control."[58] Accordingly, while sharing the new perspective's basic suspicion of "forensic" interpretations of Paul's theology, these scholars think that it is still too mired in debates over individual salvation rather than a radical, cosmic, and apocalyptic seizing of history by God in Christ through the liberating power of the Spirit.

For Campbell especially, much of the proposal consists of a sharp reaction against what he calls "justification theory." In fact, he has made the success of his entire program dependent to a very large extent on the

the Romans: Toward a Widescreen Edition," *Interpretation* 58, no. 3 (2004): 229–40. For a good critique of Campbell's proposal, see R. Barry Matlock, "Zeal for Paul but Not According to Knowledge: Douglas Campbell's War on 'Justification Theory,'" *JSNT* 34 (2011): 115–49.

57. J. Christiaan Beker, *The Triumph of God: The Essence of Paul's Thought*, trans. Loren T. Stuckenbruck (Minneapolis: Fortress, 1990), 64. He refers to Phillip Vielhauer, introduction to *New Testament Apocrypha*, ed. W. Schneemelcher, 2 vols. (Philadelphia: Westminster, 1963–65), 2:581–607; Klaus Koch, *The Rediscovery of Apocalyptic: A Polemical Work on a Neglected Area of Biblical Studies and Its Damaging Effects on Theology and Philosophy*, Studies in Biblical Theology 2, no. 22 (London: SCM, 1972).

58. J. Louis Martyn, *Galatians: A New Translation with Introduction and Commentary*, AB 33A (New York: Doubleday, 1997), 308.

validity of his description of the foil for his own account. Campbell's alternative theory stresses that God is fundamentally benevolent rather than just, unconditionally gracious in his relation to human beings, and saves by delivering/liberating victims from the power of sin and death. There is no salvific role for the "application of redemption" or for the engagement of individuals with Christ through repentance and faith. The Holy Spirit does not add anything to the work of salvation. Nor does personal faith play any role in whether one is justified. "The strong endorsement of God's sovereignty and eschatological action in apocalyptic readings leads inevitably to an essentially unconditional conception of salvation," Campbell insists. "This unconditionality then imparts a retrospective character to epistemology."[59] "God, therefore, is not fundamentally just and the atonement designed to assuage God's righteous anger at transgression; God is fundamentally benevolent and the atonement intended to deliver humanity from bondage to evil powers and to reconstitute it in the age to come."[60]

New Historical and Systematic Proposals

At the interstices of New Testament studies, ethics, and theology, there is a lively circle of scholarship that may be characterized as postliberal—largely Barthian, Anabaptist, and Anglo-Catholic. Whatever the differences among these proponents and schools, they are united by a common vision that sharply challenges the emphases and legacy of the magisterial Reformation.

As I observed in the first chapter of the first volume, various proposals in historical and systematic theology have tacked closely to the new perspective, including Radical Orthodoxy, the new Finnish interpretation of Luther, and a postliberal communitarian perspective inspired by Anabaptist theologian John Howard Yoder. Hans Frei's emphasis on narrative theology (easily applied to Christian ethics), Leander Keck's New Testament scholarship (especially on Romans), and other representatives of the "Yale School" produced a roster of remarkably gifted and influential students, including Stanley Hauerwas (shaped by Yoder as well as Barth and Frei) and the New Testament scholar Richard Hays.

Milbank expresses appreciation for Hauerwas, Douglas Harinck, and others in this postliberal circle who seek to wed apocalyptic theology

---

59. Campbell, *The Deliverance of God*, 191.
60. Campbell, *The Deliverance of God*, 192.

to a radical critique of political and economic liberalism. With nary a footnote Milbank makes the extraordinary claim that Calvin in particular was drawn away from his initial patristic grounding in a doctrine of participation to embrace an "extrinsicism" through his fascination with the "oriental despotism" of the Hebrew Bible.[61] If God and creation are not "individual entities," but rather creation exists as an analogical participation in God, "then there is no ontological limbo in which the divine decree of justification can hover. . . . We must indeed receive, as Aquinas taught, an infused *habitus* of *justitia.*"[62] Well, then, it seems quite settled. But one wonders if in this extreme version of Christian Neoplatonism (verging on emanation) one can even speak of *ex nihilo* creation.

As another chapter in the history of Christian Neoplatonism, Radical Orthodoxy wrestles with a nature-grace problem, as if there is something inherently unstable or even vicious about creation itself, while Reformation theology wrestles with a sin-grace problem. For the latter, the question is not how to reconcile finite and infinite, matter and spirit, time and eternity, but how to reconcile fallen sinners to God.

In various ways, these scholars locate the Reformation and its doctrine of justification as contributing to an individualist and contractualist outlook that paved the way for the modern age. Indeed, following Harink, Milbank stresses that "'justification' in Paul is the divine action of really making just, not of imputing justice."[63] Supplementing these influences, T. F. Torrance and James B. Torrance contributed the historical-theological account of the allegedly "contractual" orientation of classic Lutheran and especially Reformed theologies that drive Douglas A. Campbell's proposal in *Deliverance of God.*

That *radical* protestants would unite with *medieval* theologies of justification should not surprise us. As Anabaptist historical theologians attest, the reaction of sixteenth-century Anabaptists to Luther's

---

61. John Milbank, *Being Reconciled: Ontology and Pardon* (London: Routledge, 2003), 48–49.

62. John Milbank, "Alternative Protestantism," in *Radical Orthodoxy and the Reformed Tradition: Creation, Covenant and Participation*, ed. James K. A. Smith (Grand Rapids: Baker Academic, 2005), 32–33. See also my interaction with Milbank in the same volume ("Participation and Covenant," 107–34).

63. John Milbank, "Paul against Biopolitics," in *Paul's New Moment: Continental Philosophy and the Future of Christian Theology*, by John Milbank, Slavoj Zizek, and Creston Davis (Grand Rapids: Brazos, 2010), 55n69, drawing liberally from Douglas Harink, *Paul among the Postliberals: Pauline Theology beyond Christendom and Modernity* (Grand Rapids: Brazos, 2003).

interpretation ranged from disinterest to sharp polemics against it.[64] If anything, they were more opposed than Rome to the idea of an "external righteousness imputed." Instead, they were indebted to the Neoplatonist (indeed, almost Gnostic) ideal of *fusion with the divine* "where 'all creaturely desires are rooted out and smashed,'" such that by "crucifying the human . . . grace divinized people so fully that they passed beyond 'the creaturely.'"[65]

The Neoplatonist link may help to explain the otherwise unlikely comradery of Anglo-Catholic (John Milbank), Lutheran (Robert Jenson and Tuomo Mannermaa), Reformed (Hans Boersma and Peter Leithart), and various contemporary Roman Catholic and Orthodox (David Bentley Hart) writers with neo-Anabaptists. Over against the caricatured portrait of the Reformation as encouraging a nominalist individualism, with God relating to the world only extrinsically, these thinkers are drawn to the expansive vision of the church as an alternative *polis* that transforms the world (especially political and economic liberalism and militarism) precisely by opposing the world with a type of Christian socialism, or at least "sectarian" communitarianism.[66]

FALSE CHOICES

In the interest of providing a simple map for the journey, I have kept the footnotes to a minimum in summarizing these positions. The documentation will appear in the following chapters at the points where I interact with these views. My principal critique of the present state of the controversy is its attachment to false dichotomies, especially the following two (although I am saving fuller engagement for other chapters where these issues are especially raised).

---

64. Thomas N. Finger, *A Contemporary Anabaptist Theology: Biblical, Historical, Constructive* (Downers Grove IL: InterVarsity, 2004), 109. Finger in fact argues that Anabaptist soteriological concerns (especially deification) can bring greater unity especially between the soteriologies of marginalized Protestant groups (Pentecostals and Quakers) and those of the Orthodox and Roman Catholic traditions (110). Finger observes also that "following Jesus" has always been the center of Anabaptist piety (132–33).

65. Finger, *A Contemporary Anabaptist Theology*, 563, 474. Finger even cites (on 474) the verdict of recent Anabaptist historian Werner Packull that such views represented a Pelagian or semi-Pelagian assumption.

66. John Milbank fails to even acknowledge the extent to which his "Anglo-Catholic" vision is indebted to the radical *Protestant* tradition in England. I am convinced that Milbank's entire project is motivated by a personal project of "what genuine Christianity looks like" that is remarkably similar to the Anabaptist vision. If I am not mistaken, Stanley Hauerwas would probably agree with that appraisal.

Historia Salutis *versus* Ordo Salutis

The history of salvation (*historia salutis*) refers to the actual events of judgment and deliverance that reach their fulfillment in Christ's person and work: for example, the exodus, conquest, and exile as well as the incarnation, life, death, resurrection, and ascension of Christ. The *ordo salutis* refers to the way in which persons come to share in that redemption: for example, election, effectual calling justification, sanctification, and glorification.

Especially since Krister Stendahl, it has been customary in biblical scholarship to identify the Reformation with an interest in the latter over against the former. However, this assumption rests on a serious misunderstanding. In fact, it is not the Reformers but later pietism and neo-Protestantism that made these moves, as Herman Ridderbos points out:

> While in Luther and Calvin all the emphasis fell on the redemptive event that took place with Christ's death and resurrection, later under the influence of pietism, mysticism, and moralism, the emphasis shifted to the process of individual appropriation of the salvation given in Christ and to its mystical and moral effect in the life of believers. Accordingly, in the history of the interpretation of the epistles of Paul the center of gravity shifted more and more from the forensic to the pneumatic and ethical aspects of his preaching, and there arose an entirely different conception of the structures that lay at the foundation of this preaching.
>
> This shift acquires scholarly significance and force, however, only in the theology deriving from the Enlightenment, without which the whole story of the *Paulustorschung* during the nineteenth and twentieth centuries is inconceivable.[67]

Note especially Ridderbos's point that the individualizing, subjectivizing, and moralizing tendency took its point of departure *over against* the Reformation's focus on Christ's objective work.

In contrast with the modern development, classic Reformed theology has especially emphasized that the history of redemption is the horizon for personal salvation. In other words, the "new creation" is not

---

67. Herman Ridderbos, *Paul: An Outline of His Theology*, trans. John R. de Witt (Grand Rapids: Eerdmans, 1975), 14.

first of all a personal experience but a cosmic and eschatological event into which individuals are inserted through union with Christ.[68] To put it differently, the question of *how we are saved* is linked inextricably to the question of *what God has done in Christ* to bring cosmic redemption. The Christ-event, including his resurrection and ascension as well as his crucifixion, is the objective source of every gift that is received by such participation. Thus the *objectivity* of redemption is the primary concern. However, this objectivity may be stressed to the point of denying any determinative role for human response. This is obvious especially in Barth as seen above.

Especially among evangelical biblical scholars, one discerns a reaction—an overreaction—against a pietist-revivalist emphasis on the individual experience of "getting saved," a process of conversion that is often detached from the history of Israel and the accomplishment of redemption in the incarnation, life, death, resurrection, and ascension of Jesus the Messiah. If in pietism the corporate, ecclesial, cosmic, eschatological, and apocalyptic character of salvation was eclipsed by an emphasis on meeting certain conditions for being converted, then the more recent tendency is to eclipse the application of redemption for actual persons. The reduction of salvation to the experience of individual conversion has been criticized in Reformed circles long before the advent of the new perspective, as we will see. In short, Reformed theology refuses the false choice between the *historia salutis* and the *ordo salutis*, speaking instead in terms of salvation *accomplished* and *applied*, underscoring that both are the work of God the Father in Christ through the Holy Spirit.[69]

It is striking how frequently disparaging references to "some *ordo salutis* scheme" appear in critiques of the Reformation doctrine of justification, as if it represents an obsession with the question, "How can I be saved?" while the New Testament—and Paul especially—focus

---

68. I develop this point in part 2 of this volume. Many of N. T. Wright's criticisms of the tendency to focus only on the individual aspects of redemption and renewal rather than the cosmic and eschatological scope of the new creation, as well as of the "Platonized gospel" of "going to heaven when you die," were made in the twentieth century by Reformed biblical theologians like Geerhardus Vos and Herman Ridderbos. They are remarkably tied to exegesis (in a way that eludes so many dogmatically driven projects, including new and post-new perspectives). At some point, I think that not only Wright but others encountered Vos and Ridderbos and then went *beyond them* to imagine a situation in which Reformation theology itself provided nothing relevant for contemporary discussion. At this point, they became "radical Protestants," not just *nouvelle* critics of an "old perspective."

69. As in the title of John Murray's summary, *Redemption Accomplished and Applied* (Grand Rapids: Eerdmans, 1955; repr. 2015).

instead on the historical question, "How can God fulfill his promise to Abraham of being the father of a worldwide family?"

The tendency to regard Paul's gospel as a discourse on ecclesiology rather than soteriology is another way of stating the dichotomy between *historia* and *ordo*. This wariness of the *ordo salutis* is, I think, part of a tradition, at least since Ritschl (but initiated implicitly by Kant's proscription of constitutive knowledge of God), of attempting to drain theology of metaphysics. Thus, the antithesis of *historia* and *ordo salutis* is connected conceptually to the broader antithesis of kerygma and dogma. Paul's "purpose" in Romans "is apostolic-kerygmatic rather than dogmatic," according to Beker.[70] But what does it mean to speak of Christ being crucified and raised apart from his being, "delivered up *for our sins* and raised *for our justification*" (Rom 4:25)?

In spite of the general allergy of the new perspective to anything smacking of Western individualism, even E. P. Sanders concluded, "Käsemann, Stendahl and others are correct that the heart of Paul's theology cannot be centred on the individual, while Bultmann, Bornkamm and Conzelmann are correct in maintaining that the particular formulation 'righteousness by faith' does primarily concern the individual."[71] The opposition of personal salvation to cosmic redemption unites new perspective and post-new perspective programs. Representing the latter, Beker argues, "Moreover, Paul's apocalyptic theology challenges us to rethink our traditional conceptions of salvation and ethics. The center of Paul's thought is misunderstood when it is located in individual justification or in the equation of redemption with individual heavenly bliss or in a sectarian and elitist ecclesiology that defines itself simply *over against* the world."[72] It is not salvation history but "Jewish apocalyptic [that] forms the basis of Paul's thought."[73] So while the new perspective dispenses with the *ordo salutis* by opposing it to the *historia salutis*, the post-new perspective opposes its apocalyptic emphasis to both.

Regardless of how we negotiate this *historia/ordo* question ourselves, repeated claims that the Protestant Reformers focused on the latter to the exclusion of the former are wide of the mark. Douglas Campbell, for example, says that while the Reformers gave a prominent place to the

---

70. Beker, *The Triumph of God*, 53.
71. Sanders, *Paul and Palestinian Judaism*, 438.
72. Beker, *The Triumph of God*, xiv.
73. Beker, *The Triumph of God*, 19.

cross, the resurrection played no significant role.[74] Indeed, "Justification theory struggles to account for the soteriological value that Paul ascribes elsewhere to the aspects of Christ in addition to his death—such as his resurrection."[75] Yet Luther declares, "The *resurrection of Christ* is our righteousness and life, by virtue of its power. Apart from it, no one can rise from the dead, no matter how many good works he does. Furthermore, the Holy Spirit was given *through the resurrection of Christ.*"[76] Similarly, for Calvin, to say that "We are justified by the grace of God" is to say "Christ is our righteousness, the mercy of God is the cause of our righteousness, righteousness has been obtained for us *by the death and resurrection of Christ*, righteousness is bestowed on us through the gospel, we obtain righteousness by faith."[77] In this characteristic statement, the *historia* and *ordo* are held together: redemption accomplished by the incarnate Son and applied by the Holy Spirit. Ironically, it is not the Reformers but Karl Barth who more nearly approximates Campbell's characterization when he writes that Christ "was and is the end of the old and the beginning of the new form of this world *even without his resurrection and ascension.*"[78]

Covenantal versus Apocalyptic versus Forensic

The opposition between covenantal and apocalyptic and then of both over against forensic accounts mirrors the older dichotomy between *Christus Victor* and *Agnus Dei*—the atonement as either Christ's triumph over the powers of evil or his vicarious sacrifice for the forgiveness of sins. I have challenged this dichotomy elsewhere and will elaborate at various points in chapters 4–6.[79]

In recent years, Dunn and Wright have started to rethink some of these antitheses or at least the ways the antitheses have been framed. There is simply no reason logically to oppose covenantal and forensic categories,

---

74. Campbell, *The Quest for Paul's Gospel* (London: T&T Clark, 2005), 168; Campbell, *The Deliverance of God*, 28, 76–77, 163, 395–96, 946.

75. Campbell, *The Deliverance of God*, 77.

76. Martin Luther, *First Lectures on Galatians*, in *Reformation Commentary on Scripture*, New Testament 10, *Galatians, Ephesians*, ed. Gerald Bray (Downers Grove, IL: InterVarsity Press, 2011), 8, emphasis added.

77. John Calvin, *Commentary on Galatians*, in *Reformation Commentary on Scripture*, New Testament 10, *Galatians, Ephesians*, ed. Gerald Bray (Downers Grove, IL: InterVarsity Press, 2011), 95, emphasis added.

78. *CD* IV/2, 132–33, emphasis added.

79. Michael Horton, *Lord and Servant: A Covenant Christology* (Louisville: Westminster John Knox, 2005), 178–207.

especially when the covenant is interpreted as the context in which both God's forensic and effective speech-acts acquire their meaning and effect. What could be more central to God's covenantal acts than judging and delivering? However, as I will argue more fully, confusion results from reducing diverse covenants to a single type (e.g., covenantal nomism). For all of the renewed interest in "covenant" among biblical scholars, there has been surprisingly insufficient attention given to the actual covenants that play a determinative role in Scripture and particularly in Paul's arguments.

Eschewing the false choice between forensic and participatory themes, Dunn nevertheless surmises that the Reformation opted for the former over the latter: "For although Calvin was more successful than the Lutheran tradition in holding together both the forensic and the 'in Christ' motifs in Paul, the Reformation tradition generally has found it difficult to integrate Paul's participation in Christ ('in Christ') emphasis with 'justification by faith' as the article by which the church stands or falls."[80] Yet, as I demonstrated in volume 1 (ch. 7), the Reformers not only affirmed participatory union with Christ as well as forensic justification but conceived the former as the wider context for relating justification and sanctification. In this way, justification itself was placed within that wider framework of the "great exchange." Not since the apostle Paul has any theologian given such a wide berth and rich an account of union with Christ as Calvin.[81] Christ and the cosmic horizon of their soteriology is clearly apocalyptic and participatory.

But Dunn complains that with Käsemann's influence recent discussions add yet another dichotomy—this one between covenantal continuity and apocalyptic discontinuity of the Christ-event, choosing the latter over the former.[82] His complaint is justified. J. Louis Martyn's *Galatians* presses this dichotomy even further than Käsemann.[83] Similarly, at the heart of Richard Hays's narrative theology is the apocalyptic event in which Christ achieves victory over the power of sin and death by the Spirit rather than *torah*.[84] This school is therefore wary of any history

---

80. James D. G. Dunn, foreword to *The Faith of Jesus Christ: Exegetical, Biblical, and Theological Studies*, ed. Michael F. Bird and Preston M. Sprinkle (Milton Keynes: Paternoster, 2009), xvii.

81. See especially the expansive exploration by J. Todd Billings, *Calvin, Participation, and the Gift: The Activity of Believers in Union with Christ* (New York: Oxford University Press, 2008).

82. Dunn, foreword to *The Faith of Jesus Christ*, xvii.

83. Martyn, *Galatians*, 308–10.

84. Richard Hays, *The Faith of Christ*, 2nd ed. (Grand Rapids: Eerdmans, 2002), xxiii.

of redemption, whether old promise and fulfillment narratives or new ones, such as the "climax of the covenant."

If followers of Käsemann exaggerate the contrast between apocalyptic and historical approaches, several other scholars have raised concerns about simply fitting the Christ-event into the framework of the story of Israel as defined especially by Second Temple Judaism. Like Francis Watson, Douglas Moo warns that the approach of Frank Thielman and N. T. Wright "does not sufficiently allow for the degree to which God's act in Christ forces Paul to reevaluate and recast the story of Israel." To whatever extent Paul's Jewish contemporaries thought about personal salvation, it is clear enough that the apostle did very much. "The argument of Romans 5–8, then, suggests that the more individual, vertical-oriented, reading of Romans typical of the Reformation paradigm is to some extent justified."[85]

Just as the new perspective has helped us to understand Paul's context more fully, the apocalyptic trajectory has offered some helpful corrections to a purely horizontal interpretation that ignores the absolute *novum* of the Christ-event. J. Christiaan Beker has also reminded us of the clear importance in Paul of an expectation of *imminent* deliverance. This imminence is something that the apocalyptic emphasis recovers after a long time of embarrassment. "Ever since the Enlightenment," notes Beker, "New Testament scholars have sought to excise the imminent expectation of the end time from Paul's thought." It is "either demythologized or neutralized in some other way." "On the other hand, it is characterized as a flexible variable, while the Christ-event is regarded as the stable center of Paul's thought."[86]

Nevertheless, we are once again faced with a trend that tends to exaggerate one crucial lens of interpretation (apocalyptic) and then sets it over against equally important lenses (e.g., covenantal history) as if one must choose between them. Outlining his program, Beker writes, "Stimulated by the studies of A. Schweitzer and E. Käsemann, I am recasting Paul's theology as a theocentric theology of hope rather than as a christocentric salvation-history (O. Cullmann) or as an existentialist theology of the cross (R. Bultmann). A theology of hope views the

---

85. Douglas J. Moo, "Israel and the Law in Romans 5–11," in *Justification and Variegated Nomism*, vol. 2, *The Paradoxes of Paul*, ed. D. A. Carson, Peter T. O'Brien, and Mark A. Seifrid, WUNT 2/181 (Grand Rapids: Baker Academic, 2004), 195. Cf. Francis Watson, "Is There a Story in These Texts?" in *Narrative Dynamics in Paul: A Critical Assessment*, ed. Bruce Longenecker (Louisville: Westminster John Knox, 2002), 239.

86. Beker, *The Triumph of God*, 31.

present as the dawn of the future and the future as the full actualization of the present."[87] So now a "recasting [of] Paul's theology" in terms of a theocentric (apocalyptic) approach is set over against a christocentric (redemptive-historical) paradigm.

The dichotomies multiply. "In this respect," Beker adds, "William Wrede taught us that in Paul 'all statements about salvation as an accomplished fact are immediately transformed into statements about the future.'"[88] In apocalyptic thinking, the imminent future, and not any progress of redemption through history (*Heilsgeschicte*), is the frame of reference. So Beker argues, "Moreover Paul's churches are empowered by God to participate in redemptive praxis in the world, which aims at preparing the whole creation for its future glory."[89] Ironically, the theocentric emphasis on God's salvific interruption of history tends among all of these scholars to drift toward a suspiciously neo-Kantian, even Ritschlian, gospel of redemption and reconciliation through ecclesial programs.

Even within this apocalyptic trajectory, there are important forks in the road, with insistent demands that one be taken over the other. Given the *theocentric* (rather than christocentric) approach, Beker believes that Chalcedonian Christology and its "full immanental Trinitarian hermeneutic seems to compel an interpretation of Paul's Christology in ontological rather than functional terms and thus fuses God and Christ to the detriment of the coming final glory of God, to which, according to Paul, Christ is subordinated and for which he lived and died."[90] However, Richard Hays, J. Louis Martyn, and Douglas Campbell have no difficulty identifying this apocalyptic paradigm as christocentric.

This dichotomy between covenantal (redemptive-historical) apocalyptic (punctiliar) interpretations of redemption is taken as far as it can go in Douglas A. Campbell's *The Deliverance of God*. He is convinced that the Reformation doctrine of justification is Arian, contractual, and violent: the sharp end of a spear driven into the heart of the world. "Either we do something about it, or we face real and terrible consequences for our inaction."[91] In Campbell especially, "apocalyptic" is

---

87. Beker, *The Triumph of God*, viii.
88. Beker, *The Triumph of God*, 20, from William Wrede, *Paul*, trans. Edward Lummis (London: Philip Green, 1910), 105–6.
89. Beker, *The Triumph of God*, 20.
90. Beker, *The Triumph of God*, xiii.
91. See Douglas A. Campbell, "The Current Crisis: The Capture of Paul's Gospel by Methodological Arianism," in *Beyond Old and New Perspectives on Paul: Reflections on the Work of Douglas Campbell*, ed. Chris Tilling (Eugene, OR: Cascade, 2014), 48.

code for "unconditional, revelatory, transformational, and liberation-al."[92] Thus, any proposal that does not accept the whole package—"faith" as Christ's faithfulness (subjective rather than objective genitive), cosmic transformation *rather than* forensic justification, and that Romans 1–3 expresses the views of a false teacher rather than Paul's own—cannot be considered to be genuinely "apocalyptic" or "participatory." Campbell expresses his debt repeatedly to Barth via the Torrances. The critique of natural theology and the reduction of different covenants to a single covenant of grace, as well as the unconditional and universalistic emphases, function as dogmatic norms across Campbell's wide-ranging proposal.

The opposite of this apocalyptic view, according to Ben Myers, is "N. T. Wright's characterization of Christ as 'the climax, the denoue-ment, of a story . . . which had been steadily unfolding' throughout history."[93] On the contrary, "For Paul, the death of Jesus is the disso-lution of the cosmos, and the resurrection is sheer *creatio ex nihilo*—an event of *creatio* which now reorganizes history around itself, so that the continuities between Israel and Christ on the one hand, and nature and grace on the other, are established by the event itself."[94] At this point, Campbell turns to Barth over Torrance when the latter argues that Christ's humanity transforms our human essence. "Instead, in Barth's view there is no human essence at all—or rather, essence is *history*; it is a trajectory of action set in motion by the prevenient action of Jesus Christ" that acts retroactively on all previous history-so-called.[95]

No adjustments here and there will do, Campbell repeatedly insists. "Justification theory" (from which the new perspective fails adequately to extricate itself) rests on an "Arian" paradigm as opposed to the "Athanasian" one. There is no middle path; it's all or nothing.[96] This includes embracing Barth's actualist ontology, according to which there

---

92. Campbell, *The Deliverance of God*, 66.

93. Benjamin Myers, "From Faithfulness to Faith in the Theology of Karl Barth," in *The Faith of Jesus Christ: Exegetical, Biblical, and Theological Studies*, ed. Michael F. Bird and Preston M. Sprinkle (Milton Keynes: Paternoster, 2009), 296, from Wright, *Paul: In Fresh Perspective*, 134.

94. Myers, "From Faithfulness to Faith in the Theology of Karl Barth," 297.

95. Myers, "From Faithfulness to Faith in the Theology of Karl Barth," 303.

96. Though generally sympathetic, historical theologian and colleague at Duke Divinity School J. Warren Smith judges that "Arius and Athanasius do not work as cyphers for Brunner and Barth quite the way Campbell hopes because, as I show below, Arius and Athanasius are closer in their epistemologies than Campbell presents them" (Smith, "'Arian' Foundationalism," in *Beyond Old and New Perspectives: Reflections on the Work of Douglas Campbell*, ed. Chris Tilling [Eugene, OR: Cascade, 2014], 80).

is no such thing as a human nature logically antecedent to the incarnation. Despite the appeal to Athanasius, Barth's thoroughly modern metaphysics is required for an absolute antithesis between christocentric and anthropocentric, unconditional and conditional/contractual, apocalyptic and salvation-historical (or covenantal), backward-looking (retrospective/retroactive) and forward-looking. It is only by accepting this systematic framework wholesale that everything else falls into place. Exegesis then becomes subservient to the paradigm. Those who point up any grammatical-syntactical, exegetical, or theological anomalies are dismissed as not getting it. I suggest that what critics do not "get"—or at least accept—is the fundamental ontology of Karl Barth.

As Graham Tomlin summarizes, Campbell's description of his nemesis—"justification theory"—consists of four ideas:

> 1. That God's justice is essentially retributive justice. 2. That human beings are rational, ethical individuals, with a prior natural and objective knowledge of God as Judge. 3. That the answer to the dilemma of judgment is found in the death of Christ offered as atonement for sin. 4. That salvation is individual and conditional upon the prior exercise of faith.[97]

However, Tomlin (a Luther scholar) responds, "I would suggest that Luther's move to Reformation theology involves a questioning of much of this."[98] The first point "is a misunderstanding, fostered by later interpretations of Luther in Lutheran and pietistic circles (and perhaps some of Luther's own later reminiscences, shaped by his reading of Augustine), that focuses on his internal struggles of conscience." It was actually the view of God primarily as retributive judge that Luther moved away from rather than gravitated toward. "I did not love, yes, I hated the righteous God who punishes sinners," Luther said concerning his earlier view of God.[99]

As to the second point, Tomlin points out, "The rational, ethical, objective individual posited by Justification Theory simply cannot be

---

97. Graham Tomlin, "Luther and the Deliverance of God," in *Beyond Old and New Perspectives: Reflections on the Work of Douglas Campbell*, ed. Chris Tilling (Eugene, OR: Cascade, 2014), 26.

98. Tomlin, "Luther and the Deliverance of God," 26. I would only qualify this point; Luther never moved away from the condemning righteousness of God but rather saw it as the terror of the law that drives us to Christ.

99. Tomlin, "Luther and the Deliverance of God," 27, quoting *LW* 34:336.

found in Luther's understanding of the unredeemed self. Instead he explicitly describes the unredeemed state as 'bondage.' It was Erasmus, whom Luther took on in 1525, who posited the rational, ethical individual capable of both recognizing his or her own sin and responding with contrition and renewal of life." He quotes Hans Schwartz: "Because of the natural knowledge of God is prone to so many misunderstandings, it cannot serve as the starting point of faith for Luther."[100] Coming to know God's judgment as well as grace depends on God's gracious operation.[101] Further, God's revelation of judgment through the law is his "alien" work (*opus alienum*), while his "proper" work (*opus proprium*) is love and mercy.[102]

> The point is not, however, that an awareness of sin always precedes a knowledge of the gospel. Law and gospel are not to be considered as inevitably sequential but dialectical in Luther's thought. The tension is an ongoing one in the entire Christian life, in that we are tempted to believe (law) that we are still under the bondage of sin, and refuse to believe (gospel) the word that says that Christ has brought freedom to those who are united to him by faith. . . . As Bernhard Lohse puts it: "True repentance is effected not by the preaching of the law, but only by the preaching of the gospel. If only the law were preached, it would lead to despair, not to conversion."[103]

Regarding the third point, Tomlin judges, "Reading Campbell's description of the apocalyptic, participative understanding of justification reminds this reader, at least, more of Luther's theology than does Campbell's description of Justification Theory."[104] I can only agree with Tomlin's response. Any modestly sympathetic reader would come away from Luther's sermons and treatises with a profound sense that he was gripped by the objective realism of God's rending of the heavens to descend in our humanity and thereby to redeem it through a loving obedience that culminates at Golgotha. If one were to ask Luther when

---

100. Tomlin, "Luther and the Deliverance of God," 28, quoting Hans Schwarz, *True Faith in the True God: An Introduction to Luther's Life and Thought* (Minneapolis: Fortress, 2015), 43.
101. Tomlin, "Luther and the Deliverance of God," 28–29.
102. Tomlin, "Luther and the Deliverance of God," 29.
103. Tomlin, "Luther and the Deliverance of God," 29–30, quoting Bernhard Lohse, *Martin Luther: An Introduction to His Life and Work* (Philadelphia: Fortress, 2000), 182.
104. Tomlin, "Luther and the Deliverance of God," 30.

he was "saved," he would have replied, "About noon, AD 33, outside the center-city of Jerusalem."

Luther did indeed speak of his own spiritual experience more than the other Reformers—certainly more than Calvin, whose one line of spiritual autobiography has been debated as to whether it points to a "conversion" of sorts. Whatever moving testimonies Luther gave to his experience, they were *responses* to the sheer fact of God's gift in Christ *then and there*, which becomes ours *here and now* through the gospel. Indeed, through the word and the sacraments, what happened then and there is the objective accomplishment of our redemption *extra nos*; our conversion is not a condition of the efficacy of Christ's redeeming work.

Often in pietism, it is assumed that God has already provided the possibility of salvation and now faith supplies the believer's part in the process. But for Luther, faith "is not an independent prior capacity we have to fulfill our part in the contract of salvation. That is precisely the idea he is trying with all his might to counter."[105]

> It is precisely this nominalist, contractual understanding of salvation that Luther rejects in his Reformation theology. He does not assume it, adopt it, and find another way round it; he firmly repudiates it. In his "Disputation on Justification" of 1535, Luther writes: "Faith is a divine, not a human work."[106]

The chief target of Campbell's revulsion against "justification theory" is federal theology, which he describes at length with lavish footnotes to the idiosyncratic historiographic narrative of T. F. Torrance and James B. Torrance and not a single reference to primary sources or the withering critiques. Not only the Reformers but Augustine is included in the Torrance-Campbell sweep as the inventor of the "Latin Heresy" set over against "Athanasianism."[107]

---

105. Tomlin, "Luther and the Deliverance of God," 31–32, quoting *LW* 34:189.

106. Tomlin, "Luther and the Deliverance of God," 31–32, quoting *LW* 34:189.

107. See Campbell, "The Current Crisis," 37–48. Anyone familiar with the Torrance thesis recognizes its pervasive influence on Campbell's entire project, and in fact on all these points he appeals to various essays by T. F. and James Torrance in "The Current Crisis" (as well as throughout *Deliverance*). In the same volume, patristics scholar J. Warren Smith suggests that "Arius and Athanasius do not work as cyphers for Brunner and Barth quite the way Campbell hopes" ("'Arian' Foundationalism," 80). Far from advocating a natural theology, for Arius God is radically unknowable. Not even the Son knows him in his essence! This is why we need a mediator (the Logos) to reveal him to some extent. "The chief difference is that for Athanasius the Logos cannot properly reveal God the Father or allow us to participate in the divine nature

Campbell's theological framework is hardly novel; it is the outworking of the principles of Karl Barth's system and the Torrances' controversial reading of historical theology. "Once these differences and their implications have been clearly appreciated," he says, "it seems unlikely that many Pauline interpreters would want to deny them."[108] Indeed. But the jury is still out on whether he has adequately described the differences and their implications. Unlike some biblical scholars who seem little concerned with the proximity of their conclusions to their ecclesial tradition, Campbell says, to his credit, that "our interpretative traditions and communities will of course assist us" in understanding Paul.[109] But it is not entirely clear to me how exactly this can obtain if one believes that the whole church (with the exceptions of Athanasius, Barth, and the Torrances) have so fatally misread Scripture until the publication of his work. The stakes are even higher if it turns out (as I believe it does) that Athanasius would not know what to make of the views or the role that Campbell assigns to him.

In short, I believe that the false choice between redemptive-historical and apocalyptic approaches is resolved by recognizing the genuine character of both. The former is not a Hegelian unfolding of *Geist* with the telos of immanence within history itself and the latter is not a divine event that has no connection (or worse, an antithetical connection) to history as such. A false immanence that assimilates God's saving work to human "progress" and an equally false transcendence that implies redemption *from* history are disastrous and unbiblical.

In contrast with both, Geerhardus Vos thinks in terms of a triangle, with vertical and horizontal axes connected. Therefore, "Through the appearance or resurrection of Christ the eschatological process has been set in motion." In fact, "The horizontal movement of thought on the time-plane gives way immediately to a vertical projection of the eschatological interest" into history. "Consequently, the idea of 'heaven' and such metaphorical locally-oriented phrases as 'the things above' had to take the place of the older technical terms. 'Heaven' offered moreover the advantage of expressing that the provisionally realized final

unless the Logos is equal in divinity with the Father" (81–82). In fact, the patristic affirmation of natural law was part of an anti-Gnostic affirmation that the God of creation is also the God of redemption and that God had in fact revealed himself to some extent in the material world (86–88).

108. See Campbell, "The Current Crisis," 47.

109. Campbell, *The Deliverance of God*, 123.

state lies on a higher plane than the preceding world-development."[110] Expressions such as "seated with him in heavenly places" (e.g., Eph 2:6) are not spatial but refer to the eschatologically higher plane of existence: namely, the realities of the age to come.[111]

Vos observes that we must never confuse this "eschatological two-sidedness with the philosophical bisection of the universe into a higher and lower sphere."

> Heaven, so to speak, has received time and history into itself, no less than time has received unchangeableness and eternity into itself. Herein lies the inner significance of the repatriation of Christ into heaven, carrying thither with Himself all the historical time-matured fruit of his earthly stage of work, and now from there guiding with impartial solicitude the two lines of terrestrial and celestial development of his Church.[112]

The incarnation is the decisive factor here, and it is by the Spirit that we are united to Christ's eschatological life. All of this "stands at a far remove from Greek philosophical dualism."[113]

CONCLUSION

Especially since the nineteenth century there has been a tendency to reduce complex systems to a distinguishing central dogma.[114] Marxism can be contrasted with capitalism by the fact that the former seeks to overcome the alienation of humans from their labor and the latter seeks to maximize individual freedom and initiative. Similarly, it was argued by nineteenth-century (especially German) historical theologians that Roman Catholicism, Lutheranism, and Calvinism can be contrasted easily by attending to their central dogma: papal authority, justification by faith, and the sovereignty of God, respectively.

This methodological reductionism continues unabated in biblical studies and dogmatics. In the paradigms and dichotomies surveyed above,

---

110. Geerhardus Vos, *The Pauline Eschatology* (repr., Philipsburg, NJ: P&R, 1994), 37–39.
111. Vos, *The Pauline Eschatology*, 38–39.
112. Vos, *The Pauline Eschatology*, 40.
113. Vos, *The Pauline Eschatology*, 41.
114. See for example Richard Muller's review of how this happened in nineteenth-century Calvin scholarship in *After Calvin*, 97.

the central dogma approach is deployed in defense of one's proposal. If we can locate the core idea in Jesus or Paul, then our readers must accept as logically consequent everything we deduce from it. It is also deployed in critique of others. Once one has identified the one essential dogma of a rival system, everything else follows logically—regardless of what proponents of that system actually argue.

This method is the cause not only of many false dilemmas but of countless false descriptions of other views. Especially when the central-dogma method is combined with an antidogmatic and anticonfessional bias, what emerges are allegedly groundbreaking insights of direct exegesis advanced over against caricatured foils, circulating in a loop of gossip that suits students of particular schools but does not necessarily advance our understanding of Scripture or a doctrine's reception history.

United particularly by their criticism of Reformation theology, the various proposals that I have mentioned often draw on each other. Somehow in the midst of this collaborative critique, Barthians and Radical Orthodoxy unite despite the fact that Barth's system rather than the Reformation represents the most nominalist metaphysics of modern theology. Despite the fact that John Milbank is not a biblical exegete, footnotes to Milbank appear in Campbell's *Deliverance of God*, while Milbank asserts confidently that the new perspective confirms his demolition of the Reformation doctrine of justification. Both figures appeal to the new Finnish interpretation of Luther, while Wright relies on T. F. Torrance alone for his knowledge of the seventeenth-century covenant theology that he strongly rejects.[115]

In short, much of Pauline scholarship today is heavily influenced by twentieth-century dogmatics and highly polemical, as well as disputed, theological projects. Numerous examples could be cited to confirm that the current wave of antipathy toward the Reformation among Protestant exegetes, theologians, and other scholars expresses itself at least in part by creating an interdisciplinary echo chamber dominated by theses that specialists in each discipline find implausible but, taken together, reinforce their collective anti-Reformation bias.

Paradigms are powerful, but for that reason—especially in theology—they should be derived and tested by rigorous exegesis according to the analogy of Scripture. Theologians are hardly the only ones capable of

---

115. While this is evident in his written works so far, through personal interaction Wright has sought other sources challenging the Torrance paradigm.

building castles in the air with a priori central dogmas. If one just gets the big idea (e.g., justification, union/participation, theosis, covenantal nomism, end-of-exile, rectification, covenant faithfulness, reading retrospectively, faith of Christ, etc.), then every pericope becomes a variation on a theme and every argument a piece of the puzzle. And if the pieces do not seem to fit, perhaps some may even be replaced with a homemade piece. Paul J. DeHart's critique of Radical Orthodoxy's sweeping narrative could be extended to cover this broader landscape. "The map should ideally arise organically out of careful research into each thinker or trend," he advised. But it is easy to allow our map to *determine* the landscape. "Once in place it offers to tell readers in advance what they will find if they look closely enough."[116]

I do not pretend to escape this matrix of paradigms, presuppositions, expectations, motives, and agendas. Allow me to make mine explicit. I am a Reformed minister deeply impressed by the Trinitarian and christocentric coherence of the ecumenical creeds as this faith is interpreted especially in our confessions and catechisms. That there is no central dogma in this system is, to my mind, one of its greatest strengths. Instead of working deductively from a center outward to logically subordinate points, it pushes in a business-like way from the triune God to God's free purposes and works in the economy of grace. For a variety of reasons that I hope to explain as we go forward, this theology—whatever label we wish to give it—integrates the personal and the ecclesial, the ecclesial and the cosmic, the covenantal-historical and the apocalyptic, the forensic and the transformative, divine and human agency, and a host of other points that too often have become antitheses in modern biblical and theological scholarship.

Herman Ridderbos summarized well the basic milieu from which I am approaching these serious matters:

> Justification by faith unmistakably belongs to the very heart of Paul's preaching, and is not a secondary "polemic" directed against the Jews (Wrede), or a "side issue" within the main stream of the mystical doctrine of redemption of "being in Christ" (Schweitzer). But by approaching Paul's doctrine exclusively from the standpoint of justification by faith there is a danger of depriving Paul's

---

116. Paul J. DeHart, *Aquinas and Radical Orthodoxy: A Critical Inquiry* (New York: Routledge 2014), 13.

preaching of its redemptive historical dynamic and of making it into a timeless treatment of the vital question: how is one justified before God? Justification by faith as proclaimed by Paul is rather one *aspect*, although a very central aspect, of the great redemptive event of which Paul knew himself to be the herald, and which he described as the fullness of time in which God has sent the Son (Gal. 4:4), as the revelation of the mystery that has been hid for ages and from generations (Rom. 11:25–26; Col. 1:26), as the grace, which is given to us in Jesus Christ before the world began, but is now made manifest by the appearing of our Savior Jesus Christ (2 Tim. 1:9–10), so that it can now be said, old things are passed away; behold all things are become new (2 Cor. 5:17); behold, now is the accepted time, behold now is the day of salvation (2 Cor. 6:2).[117]

Everyone has been looking for "the real core of Paul's preaching" and matters have hardly improved since Ridderbos made that observation in 1957.

First, the contrast between flesh and spirit, then the mystical communion with Christ was conceived as the dominating motif of his preaching. Paul has been viewed as a Hegelian idealist (Tübingen school), as a preacher of the superiority of the human spirit (the liberals); as a mystic of the Hellenistic mystery-religions (Bousset); as a gnostic, par excellence (Reitzenstein). And as a result the "religion" of Paul was placed at such a great distance from that of Jesus that the cleft was apparently unbridgeable.[118]

"What was forgotten, however, in all these changing conceptions and interpretations of Paul," he says, "was the awareness that Paul's preaching was not formed by a new idea, or by a new ethos, or a new religious vital feeling or a *Seinsverständnis*, but before everything else, he was the *proclaimer of a new time*, the great turning point in the history of redemption, the intrusion of a new world aeon."[119] Only within this context can we recognize "the many facets and interrelations of his preaching,

---

117. Herman Ridderbos, *Paul and Jesus: Origin and General Character of Paul's Preaching of Christ*, trans. David H. Freeman (Philadelphia: Presbyterian and Reformed, 1958), 63–64.
118. Ridderbos, *Paul and Jesus*, 64.
119. Ridderbos, *Paul and Jesus*, 64.

e.g., justification, being-in-Christ, suffering, dying, and rising again with Christ, the conflict between the spirit and the flesh, the cosmic drama, etc."[120]

The doctrine of justification lies at the center not merely of our systematic reflection on the meaning of salvation but of our piety, mission, and life together. My interest in this volume is not simply to repeat noble maxims and formulas along with their traditional proof texts but to encounter these remarkable passages in conversation with the provocative proposals that, despite a wide range of differences, have brought the doctrine of justification once again to the forefront of contemporary debate.

120. Ridderbos, *Paul and Jesus*, 64–65.

PART 1

THE HORIZON OF JUSTIFICATION

CHAPTER 1

ADAM AND ISRAEL

The church has always struggled to avoid, on the one hand, a Marcionite temptation to pit the God of redemption and grace against the God of creation and law and, on the other hand, a tendency to assimilate the gospel to the law. Church fathers like Irenaeus, Chrysostom, and Augustine refer explicitly to the covenant with Adam and the Sinai covenant as law-covenants distinguished from the covenant of grace.[1]

Similarly, elaborating the law-gospel distinction, the Reformed tradition developed a covenant theology that distinguished between the conditional covenants sworn by the people (Adam and Israel) and the unconditional oath sworn by God (the *protoeuangelion* of Genesis 3:15 and the Abrahamic, Davidic, and new covenants). The mediatorial work of Christ is construed in this light: Jesus is the Last Adam, who by his active obedience fulfilled the covenant and won for his coheirs the right to eat from the Tree of Life. Thus the Sinai covenant was the script for a geopolitical and typological theocracy analogous to Hamlet's play-within-a-play, recapitulating Adam's original vocation. And "like Adam, they broke the covenant" (Hos 6:7). Nevertheless, the evangelical promise remained all along the basis for redemption from the curse of sin and death.

---

1. See esp. *Haer.* 3.10.4; 3.12.11–12; 4.11.2; 4.14.2; 4.25.1; 4.31.1; and 4.38.1 (*ANF* vol. 1). Irenaeus further explores the relation of these covenants in 4.25.1–26.1; 4.27.2; 4.16.2; and 5.22.2. Cf. Everett Ferguson, *Backgrounds to Early Christianity*, 2nd ed. (Grand Rapids: Eerdmans, 2003), 92, 288, 292, 405, 425, 468–69, 507–8, 524–27, 547–50; cf. J. Ligon Duncan, "The Covenant Idea in Irenaeus of Lyons: Introduction and Survey," in *Confessing Our Hope: Essays in Honor of Morton Howison Smith on His Eightieth Birthday*, ed. J. A. Pipa Jr. and C. N. Willborn (Taylors, SC: Southern Presbyterian Press, 2004). Besides Augustine's *De spiritu et littera* (*On the Spirit and the Letter*), his *Civitas Dei* (*City of God*) contained influential seeds for the two covenants: "The first covenant was this, unto Adam: 'Whensoever thou eatest thereof thou shalt die the death,'" and this is why all his children "are breakers of God's covenant made with Adam in paradise" (Augustine, *City of God*, ed. David Knowles, trans. Henry Bettenson [New York: Penguin, 1972], 16.28 [688–89]).

This narrative is not only exegetically demonstrable but also provides the best doctrinal coordinates for atonement and justification. The law at the heart of creation was not circumvented but satisfied by the self-offering of the incarnate Son. I make this case by attending, first, to the relation of Israel to Adam and, second, to the relationship of Sinai to Zion. There has been a happy renaissance of interest in the Bible's covenant theology over the last half-century, but questions hinge on the type of covenant theology we find there.

But first, allow me to sketch an outline and genealogy of monocovenantalism—that is, the widespread tendency to reduce diverse covenants to a single type. No less than in modern dogmatics has biblical scholarship been given to a priori dogmas driving exegesis. Just as the biblical phrase "the righteousness of God" has come to be construed even lexically as a purely positive concept (e.g., deliverance, deliverdict, rectification, etc.),[2] there is an a priori assumption among many biblical scholars and theologians that "covenant" is an inherently gracious concept.[3]

At one end of this spectrum is the tendency to assimilate the gospel to the law. The one relationship with God is considered basically *nomistic* but modified in a gracious direction by being *covenantal*.[4] E. P. Sanders insists that the one covenant is gracious because all along Israel "gets in" by grace; God even provides all sorts of ways for them to "stay in" by grace-assisted obedience. Sanders's own citations (e.g., of election conditioned on foreseen merits) call into question even this gracious "getting in."[5] In any case, Sanders recognizes that Paul does not agree with this position, but instead of seeing Paul as carrying forward the longing for a new and better covenant in the Hebrew prophets

---

2. This shift in definition came through the work of Diestel, Ritschl, and especially Hermann Cremer. See the masterful genealogy and critique of this trajectory in Charles Lee Irons, *The Righteousness of God: A Lexical Examination of the Covenant-Faithfulness Interpretation*, WUNT 2/386 (Tübingen: Mohr Siebeck, 2015).

3. Some conservative Reformed scholars like John Murray conclude that the original relationship between God and humankind in Adam was *not* a covenant precisely because it does not display a sufficiently gracious basis that he believes to characterize all biblical covenants (John Murray, "The Adamic Administration," in *The Writings of John Murray*, vol. 2 [Edinburgh: Banner of Truth, 1977], 48–49). However, most exegetes are happy to call it a covenant precisely because they do think that it is gracious, in spite of the obvious conditional basis (Gen 2:17).

4. E. P. Sanders, *Paul and Palestinian Judaism: A Comparison of Patterns of Religion* (Philadelphia: Fortress, 1977), esp. 75, 236, but everywhere he invokes explicitly or assumes the idea that "covenantal" as a modifier of "nomism." I explore this point more fully in *Covenant and Salvation: Union with Christ* (Louisville: Westminster John Knox), chs. 1–5.

5. I note these observations from Sanders in the following chapter.

themselves, he treats the apostle as an innovator: *"Paul in fact explicitly denies that the Jewish covenant can be effective for salvation, thus consciously denying the basis of Judaism.* Circumcision without complete obedience is worthless or worse (Rom. 2.25–3.2; Gal. 3.10)."[6] Sanders concludes, "Paul's view could hardly be maintained, and it was not maintained. Christianity rapidly became a new covenantal nomism, but Paulinism is not thereby proved inferior or superior."[7]

James Dunn demurs from Sanders's stark contrast, focusing on a more restricted scope for Paul's polemic: the ethnic exclusion of gentiles from the covenant community.[8] In fact, from Sanders's description of Second Temple Judaism, Dunn goes as far as to conclude (beyond Sanders himself) that "'covenantal nomism' can now be seen to preach good Protestant doctrine: that grace is always prior; that human effort is ever the response to divine initiative; that good works are the fruit and not the root of salvation."[9] Similarly, Walter Brueggemann: "Thus I suggest that E. P. Sanders's term covenantal nomism is about right, because it subsumes law (*nomos*) under the rubric of covenant. . . . By inference, I suggest that grace must also be subsumed under covenant."[10] N. T. Wright notes in *Climax of the Covenant*, "The overall title reflects my growing conviction that covenant theology is one of the main clues, usually neglected, for understanding Paul,"[11] and since writing that, he has developed this motif with profound insight. Nevertheless, especially in his recent study of the atonement (*The Day the Revolution Began*), he also sees the various biblical covenants as the outworking of an original "covenant of vocation" given to Adam and Eve—a commission to rule and subdue, bringing reality under the lordship of Yahweh.[12]

---

6. Sanders, *Paul and Palestinian Judaism*, 551, emphasis original. "More important," he adds, *"the covenantal promises to Abraham do not apply to his descendants, but to Christians* (Rom. 4.13–25; Gal. 3.15–29)." This is however not Paul's way of putting the matter. The covenantal promises apply especially to his descendants ("to the Jew first," as in Rom 1:16), but also (in fulfillment of the prophetic vision of an expanding of Israel's tents and the nations streaming to Zion) to gentiles who become his spiritual descendants in Christ.

7. Sanders, *Paul and Palestinian Judaism*, 552.

8. James D. G. Dunn, *Jesus, Paul, and the Law: Studies in Mark and Galatians* (Louisville: Westminster John Knox, 1990), 194.

9. James D. G. Dunn, *The New Perspective on Paul*, 2nd ed. (Grand Rapids: Eerdmans, 2007), 199.

10. Walter Brueggemann, *Theology of the Old Testament* (Minneapolis: Fortress, 1997), 419

11. N. T. Wright, *The Climax of the Covenant: Christ and the Law in Pauline Theology* (Edinburgh: T&T Clark, 1991), xi.

12. N. T. Wright, *The Day the Revolution Began: Reconsidering the Meaning of Jesus' Crucifixion* (New York: HarperOne, 2016), 23–88.

At the other end of the monocovenantal spectrum is the biblical-theological program rooted in Karl Barth and carried forward by Ernst Käsemann, J. Louis Martyn, Richard Hays, and Douglas Campbell. Here, the law is assimilated to the gospel. There is one covenant of grace that is synonymous with the eternal election of Christ and, with him, all of humanity. There can never be a reciprocal relationship with God, Barth insists.[13] Appealing to Barth (*CD* IV/1, 57), Campbell insists that "God's relationship with humanity is fundamentally unconditional and benevolent. In more biblical parlance, it is covenantal. In theological or dogmatic terms, it is elective, in the sense especially that Barth recovered so insightfully."[14] Thus, "covenantal" equals "unconditionally gracious," because of universal election. Accordingly, "God *does not conditionally act toward humanity at all.*"[15] Thus, the traditional Reformed distinction between a covenant of law (or works) and a covenant of grace represents a "contractual" system, he insists.[16] Campbell insists therefore that Sanders's "covenantal nomism" is just as dangerous as "legalism."[17] "No strings attached" is probably not the first impression that Deuteronomy 28 has on a casual reader. However, like Picasso's retort to critics who said that his portrait of Gertrude Stein did not bear her likeness, the monocovenantalist replies, "No matter, she will."

---

13. See Karl Barth, *The Epistle to the Romans*, trans. Edwin C. Hoskyns (New York: Oxford University Press, 1968), 423.

14. Douglas A. Campbell, "The Current Crisis: The Capture of Paul's Gospel by Methodological Arianism," in *Beyond Old and New Perspectives on Paul: Reflections on the Work of Douglas Campbell*, ed. Chris Tilling (Eugene, OR: Cascade, 2014), 45.

15. Campbell, "The Current Crisis," 44. See John M. G. Barclay's critique of these assumptions in *Paul and the Gift* (Grand Rapids: Eerdmans, 2015), 77.

16. Douglas A. Campbell, "Connecting the Dots," in *Beyond Old and New Perspectives: Reflections on the Work of Douglas Campbell*, ed. Chris Tilling (Eugene, OR: Cascade, 2014), 100 and 100n9. His reference is to Karl Barth, *CD* IV/1, 54–66. Campbell, "The Current Crisis," 45, emphasis added. Once more he cites James B. Torrance's "Covenant or Contract" in defense. In a volume of 1248 pages that even includes a section on "Federal Calvinism," there is not a single footnote acknowledging, much less engaging, these serious and, to my mind, devastating, criticisms (see 31n54). More problematic is not only the repetition but still more radical caricatures of this profound body of post-Reformation exegesis. Stacking the deck at the outset, he states erroneously: "Federal Calvinism (from the Latin *foedus* for 'contract')." While *foedus* could be used for contracts, it is only because of the poverty of the Latin in comparison with the Greek. Actually, *foedus* covered a host of legal relationships, translating both *berit* and *diathēkē* (covenant or testament in distinction from *synthēkē*, a mutual agreement like a contract). No major federal theologian used *foedus* and "contract" interchangeably; on the contrary, they typically distinguished the two ideas, especially when defining the covenant of grace as unilaterally gracious in its basis. The Torrance thesis has been solidly refuted by a number of specialists, including Richard Muller, Irena Backus, Paul Helm, R. Scott Clark, Carl Trueman, Willem van Asselt, and Anton Vos.

17. Douglas A. Campbell, *The Deliverance of God: An Apocalyptic Rereading of Justification in Paul* (Grand Rapids: Eerdmans, 2013), 91–106.

THE COVENANT OF CREATION

In order to demonstrate the distinctive character of the original covenant, I begin by highlighting its elements. It was (a) based on law (with the act-consequence connection), (b) federal or representative of all humanity "in Adam," (c) with the reward of confirmation in everlasting life, immortality, and righteousness.

According to the founding narrative of the Hebrew scriptures, humanity—represented by Adam—came into being as an image-son of the Creator Yahweh, an image that he shared with his partner, Eve.[18] The Westminster Confession summarizes succinctly, "The first covenant made with man was a covenant of works, wherein life was promised to Adam; and in him to his posterity, upon condition of perfect and personal obedience."[19] Reformed theologians have also designated this the covenant of creation, of law and of life.

Although the word בְּרִית (berith) never appears in Genesis 1–3, it is hard to think that Israel could have even imagined a relationship with God on the part of a creature that was not covenantal. Walther Eichrodt observes, "Even where the covenant is not explicitly mentioned the spiritual premises of a covenant relationship with God are manifestly present."[20] In addition to a preamble and historical prologue identifying the suzerain and his just claim, the text features a stipulation with a sanction: everlasting life for obedience and death for disobedience, as well as the sacramental tree of life standing as a reward for faithful fulfillment of the divine commission.[21]

First, the basis of this covenant was law rather than grace. Given the integrity of human nature as created by God, it is not surprising that grace and mercy do not enter the picture until the promise in Genesis 3:15. Assuming that law is the opposite of love, our modern culture finds it difficult to comprehend the integral relationship of law and love in ancient Near Eastern societies. In the Bible, God's moral law merely stipulates what love looks like in concrete relationships. The suzerain

---

18. Phyllis Bird, "'Male and Female He Made Them': Gen 1:27b in the Context of the Priestly Account of Creation," *Harvard Theological Review* 74, no. 2 (1981): 140, 155–58.

19. Westminster Confession of Faith 7.2, in *The Trinity Hymnal* (Atlanta: Great Commission Publications, 1990), 852.

20. Walther Eichrodt, *Theology of the Old Testament* (Philadelphia: Westminster, 1961), 36–37.

21. While we should beware of making too much of the formal comparisons with the ancient Near Eastern suzerainty treaty, the elements of such a political instrument are present in these opening narratives of Genesis.

is represented as a shepherd, father, guardian, and benefactor of the people. Nevertheless, the relationship is conditional, with the vassal swearing fealty and assuming the responsibility for carrying out the covenant's sanctions upon the penalty of death for treason against the suzerain's love, wealth, and protection. The conviction that law merely stipulates the concrete rule of love is stated explicitly in Deuteronomy 6:5 (cf. 10:12) and of course by Jesus in his famous summary of the law (Matt 22:38; cf. 1 John 4:21). As Max Stackhouse has observed, "The sociotheological idea of covenant is so rich with ethical content that it gives moral meaning to all it touches."[22] If the fall had never occurred, the relation of humanity to God, to each other, and to their fellow creatures would have been a symphony of love with each member playing his or her role in the orchestra.

The name given in biblical scholarship to this original constitution is the act-consequence connection.[23] While the gospel is a surprising and foreign announcement, this law of creation is so woven into the human consciousness that no concept is more universally recognized in the world's wisdom literatures.[24] It is the law of reaping what you sow, the Stoic idea of going with the grain of nature, of karma and samsara, getting back what you dish out. This principle dominates Israel's horizon, provoking some of the most fascinating theodicy literature in the Hebrew Bible, such as Asaph's wrestling with the prosperity of the wicked in Psalm 73 and the book of Job. The disciples assumed the principle when they asked Jesus whether a man was blind from birth because of his sin or that of his parents (John 9:2–3). Not all sickness, disease and natural disasters were signs of God's displeasure, but God sent them episodically (and restricted to certain people, places, and things) as a foretaste of the waste that would come upon the nation as a whole if God judged the covenant to be thoroughly violated. It was through this prism of the act-consequence connection at the heart of the Sinai pact that Israel interpreted the story of Adam.

---

22. Max Stackhouse, *Covenant and Commitment: Faith, Family and Economic Life* (Louisville: Westminster John Knox, 1997), 140.

23. On the act-consequence: see H.-D. Preuss, *Old Testament Theology*, trans. L. G. Perdue, vol. 1 (Edinburgh: T&T Clark, 1995), 184–94; K. Koch, "Is There a Doctrine of Retribution in the Old Testament?" in *Theodicy in the Old Testament*, ed. James L. Crenshaw (Philadelphia: Fortress, 1983), 57–87.

24. I am of course affirming both general revelation, a *sensus divinitatis* (Calvin), and natural law. For helpful accounts of this topic, see especially David VanDrunen, *Divine Covenants and Moral Order: A Biblical Theology of Natural Law*, Emory University Studies in Law and Religion (Grand Rapids: Eerdmans, 2014).

Second, the Scriptures represent this original covenant as encompassing all of humanity with Adam as the representative head. Gregory Beale notes, "Just as God, after his initial work of creation, subdued the chaos, ruled over it, and further created and filled the earth with all kinds of animal life, so Adam and Eve, in their garden abode, were to reflect God's activities in Genesis 1 by fulfilling the commission to 'subdue' and 'rule over all the earth' and to 'be fruitful and multiply.'"[25] Representatively, Adam was to imitate Yahweh's pattern of work and entrance into the Sabbath rest of glory. Surrounded by God's lush provision, the only motive for eating from the Tree of Knowledge of Good and Evil could have been sheer treason.

Walter Brueggemann observes, "As Israel believes that its own life is covenantally ordered, so Israel believes that creation is covenantally ordered; that is, formed by continuing interactions of gift and gratitude, of governance and obedience."[26] This expresses the "relentless ethical dimension."[27] He adds, "Creation has within it the sovereign seriousness of God, who will not tolerate the violation of the terms of creation, which are terms of gift, dependence, and extravagance. For those who refuse the doxology-evoking sovereignty of Yahweh, creation ends on an ominous warning."[28]

Third, this original covenant promised confirmation in everlasting life and righteousness. A stark choice is symbolized in these two trees. Understanding the probationary aspect of Adam's trial is essential if we are to grasp the meaning of Jesus's mission as recapitulating Adam's failed vocation as the representative of humanity.

All three of these elements—a covenant based on law, representing all of humanity "in Adam," with the promise of life for obedience and death for disobedience—were presupposed in in the Hebrew Scriptures and made explicit in the subsequent references to original sin (e.g., Ps 51:5; Isa 64:6; Job 9:20, 29; 15:14, etc.). Paul in fact quotes the Psalms to support his argument that "no one is righteous, no not even one" (Rom 3:10).

These three elements are present also in the two seminal passages where Paul treats the two federal heads: Romans 5 and 1 Corinthians 15.

---

25. G. K. Beale, *The Temple and the Church's Mission: A Biblical Theology of the Dwelling Place of God*, NSBT 17 (Downers Grove, IL: InterVarsity, 2004), 83.

26. Brueggemann, *Theology of the Old Testament*, 158–9.

27. Brueggemann, *Theology of the Old Testament*, 158.

28. Brueggemann, *Theology of the Old Testament*, 156.

First, Paul speaks of that original relationship as involving *a law, a representative/covenantal office* typological of Christ's mediatorial role in the covenant of grace. If there are two heads or mediators, then there must be two covenants that they mediate. Second, the *stipulations* of the moral law are said to be inscribed on the conscience of gentiles (Rom 2:14–15).[29] Paul explains this further in Romans 5: "Therefore, just as sin came into the world through one man, and death through sin, and so death spread to all men because all sinned— . . ." (5:12a). Here he breaks off in mid-sentence, and with good reason. Paul realizes that he cannot just assume this reading. Philo, for one, treated Adam merely as a bad example.[30] For Paul, however, "Death reigned . . . even over those who did *not* sin by breaking a command, as did Adam" (Rom 5:14 NIV).

So Paul breaks off his argument to explain that humanity was under a *curse* even before the arrival of *torah* at Mount Sinai: ". . . for sin was indeed in the world before the law was given, but sin is not *counted* where there is no *law*. Yet death reigned from Adam to Moses, even over those whose sinning was not like the transgression of Adam, who was a type of the one who was to come" (Rom 5:12b–14). There is no "counting" of sin apart from a law and there is no law where there is no covenant.[31] He has already argued that even the gentiles are "under the law," since God's existence and attributes as well as his moral require-

---

29. If Barth, Martyn, Hays, and Campbell regard gentiles as incapable of such knowledge, then it is not only this opening argument of Romans but the Hebrew Scriptures that assume an "Arian" foundationalism. God held the gentile nations responsible for their wickedness as well, and the gentile king Abimelech even knew enough to upbraid Abraham for doing "things that ought not to be done" (Gen 20:9).

30. Especially in *On the Creation of the World*. See Jonathan Worthington, "Philo of Alexandria and Romans 5:12–21: Adam, Death, and Grace," *Reading Romans in Context: Paul and Second Temple Judaism*, ed. Ben C. Blackwell, John K. Goodrich, and Jason Maston (Grand Rapids: Zondervan, 2015), 80. Cf. Timo Laato, *Paul and Judaism: An Anthropological Approach* (Atlanta: Scholars' Press, 1995), 146. But Adam does not actually affect us, and we can resist his example (Philo, *Legum allegoriae* 1.106–108; Philo, *Questions and Answers on Genesis* 1.81, both cited by Worthington, "Philo of Alexandria and Romans 5:12–21," 82).

31. Paul picks up his train of thought again, completing his argument about the "Two Adams." Abstracting from the rest of the sentence the clause in verse 12, "death spread to all because all sinned (θάνατος διῆλθεν, ἐφ᾽ ᾧ πάντες ἥμαρτον)," the Pelagian interpretation identifies death as a sentence for the actual sins of each person. However, this reverses the direction of the source that is established in the first clause: death is the result of sin and "sin came into the world through one man." The "and thus" (καὶ οὕτως) makes no sense if, after blaming the entrance of sin to all on Adam's transgression, Paul were to conclude that the curse is dependent instead on the sins of individuals. If the Pelagian interpretation is correct, then the entire argument that all people are condemned, corrupt, and die because of Adam's sin is negated. See Herman Ridderbos, *Paul: An Outline of His Theology*, trans. John R. de Witt (Grand Rapids: Eerdmans, 1975), 96. He refers explicitly to Rudolf Bultmann as expressing the "Pelagian" interpretation in Bultmann, "Adam and Christ in Romans 5," in *The Old and New Man in the Letters of Paul* (Richmond: John Knox, 1967), 62.

ments are known to them (1:20–32; 2:14–15). But the Jews are no better off. Paul's diatribe against his fellow Jews simply repeats the familiar prosecution of the prophets. The goal is to show them that they are arraigned with the gentiles. "For we have already charged that all, both Jews and Greeks, are under sin," since "none is righteous, no, not one" (3:9–10). "Now we know that whatever the law says it speaks to those who are under the law, so that every mouth may be stopped, and the *whole world* may be held accountable to God" (3:19). Cutting off all hope of salvation by this covenant of law, whether known by natural or special revelation, Paul prepares his readers for the announcement of the "*free gift*" of righteousness from verse 31 on.

But now Paul picks up his argument again. The conclusion, "for all have sinned" (5:12), is based on the fact that the entire human race was somehow present covenantally in and with Adam in that fatal act.[32] The repetition is striking: "many died through one man's trespass . . . one man's sin . . . one trespass [that] brought condemnation . . . because of one man's trespass, death reigned through that one man . . . one trespass led to condemnation for all men . . . by one man's disobedience the many were made sinners." Far from justifying a Pelagian view, the statement that "death spread to all because [ἐφ' ᾧ: for the reason that] all sinned" confirms that all sinned in Adam. Death is the result of sin, and "sin came into the world through one man." By contrast, he says, "The free gift by the grace of that one man Jesus Christ abounded for many," for it has "brought justification . . . the abundance of grace and the free gift of righteousness, . . . justification and life" (5:15–21). In 1 Corinthians 15, we again meet the contrast between Adam and Christ as covenant heads, and again the conclusion is that death results from sin, whose power is the law (1 Cor 15:56–57). Death is therefore a legal penalty (Rom 6:23). Thus, with respect to both plight and solution, the forensic declaration (condemnation/justification) is the basis for the ethical condition (corruption/sanctification) and its sanctions (death/life).

Generally speaking, Second Temple Judaism (especially after the destruction of the temple in AD 70) emphasizes the role of Adam as a cautionary tale (e.g., Philo) rather than the source of an intractable condition of guilt and corruption. Nevertheless, we find parallels for the New Testament view in some Second Temple texts. "I belong to

---

32. See Ridderbos, *Paul*, 96.

wicked humanity and to the assembly of perverse flesh," according to Qumran's Manual of Discipline. "My iniquities, my transgression, my sin (together with the perversities of my heart) belong to the assembly of worms and of things that move in darkness."[33] The most interesting Jewish text in this regard is 4 Ezra (2 Esdras 3–14), which is indisputably linked to official Judaism even though it is postdestruction.[34] In dialogue with the angel Uriel, Ezra protests: Since we are all guilty in Adam, sinful from birth, how can anyone hope to enter Paradise? "You gave [Adam] your one commandment to obey; and when he disobeyed it, you made both him and his descendants subject to death" (3:6–7). Thus, "Not only he [fell] but all who were descended from him. So the weakness became inveterate" (3:20–22). Uriel repeats the baseline act-consequence connection. Only those who obey will live, and the number will be few (7:30). Salvation depends on perfect obedience (7:22, 90, 95; 13:42). Deeds are stored up for reward (7:35, 77). "On the day of judgement, therefore, there can be no mercy for those who have lost their case, no reversal for those who have won" (vv. 115–126).[35]

Israel and Adam

The only place one could flee from the act-consequence connection was the temple, whose sacrifices and substitutes bore the consequences for guilt. But, of course, this was no longer possible after AD 70. Instead of a sacrifice for guilt, one's repentance and fresh obedience rendered satisfaction. The act-consequence connection is still in effect but relaxed somewhat. Rabbi Samuel Sandmel recognizes that for Paul there is no way of climbing out of the hole into which we have fallen and that we continue to dig every day. "But in the view of the rabbis," he says, "a person who sinned could, and should, regret it and make suitable amends. . . . In the Jewish tradition, man atones and, it is believed, God graciously pardons him." "In Paul's view, man cannot atone. . . . The contrasts, then, are between sins and sin, between the atonement which

---

33. 1QS 11.9–10a, trans. W. H. Brownlee, "The Dead Sea Manual of Discipline," *Bulletin of the American Schools of Oriental Research—Supplemental Studies*, no. 10–12 (New Haven, CT: American Schools of Oriental Research, 1951).

34. Over against sectarian groups, the document is nationalistic and focuses on the whole nation rather than a remnant. Bruce M. Metzger, "The Fourth Book of Ezra: A New Translation and Introduction," in *The Old Testament Pseudepigrapha*, vol. 1, *Apocalyptic Literature and Testaments*, ed. James H. Charlesworth (London: Darton, Longman and Todd, 1983), 516–59.

35. I am quoting the Revised English Bible translation, from *Sacred Writings*, vol. 2, *Christianity: The Apocrypha and the New Testament*, ed. Jaroslav Pelikan (New York: Quality Paperback Book Club, 1992).

man makes and that which is made for him."[36] It must be said that if this had been the presupposition of preexilic Israel, there would never have been a sacrificial system to deal with guilt in the first place.

Nevertheless, Sandmel is right in recognizing that Paul rejects the contemporary assimilation of the gospel to the law, of Zion to Sinai. Paul is convinced that the law is not only good but must in fact be fulfilled for the redemption of transgressors. However, for those who follow Barth's line of thinking, there is no such law-covenant in the first place. At the end of the day, law must always be a form of the gospel and wrath a form of grace.[37] Adam for Barth has no real existence, like a Platonic shadow cast by the "first and true Adam," the true representative of humanity, Jesus Christ.[38] Since Christ swallows Adam whole, there can be no place for a covenant prior to the covenant of grace. Campbell believes that the first three chapters of Romans do in fact teach a "bicovenantal" interpretation. However, since he is convinced that this inaugurates an "Arian," foundationalist, and contractualist religion, he imputes this entire argument not to Paul himself but to an anonymous Jewish-Christian false teacher.[39] Besides Adam, Israel also

36. Rabbi Samuel Sandmel, *A Jewish Understanding of the New Testament* (Woodstock, VT: Jewish Lights, 2008), 59. In the ellipses, Sandmel repeats the mistaken description of Paul's view as humans requiring transformation from a natural creature into a spiritual one. This fails to appreciate Paul's eschatological interpretation of the flesh and the Spirit. Rabbi Sandmel's description of the contrast between the rabbis and Paul is similar to that of E. P. Sanders. However, while new perspective scholars generally restrict this contrast to boundary markers, and some scholars, especially Heiki Räisänen, conclude that Paul simply misinterpreted Judaism as a legalistic system as he moved clumsily from one system (covenantal nomism) to another (participatory Christology). See Heiki Räisänen, *Paul and the Law*, 1st ed. (Philadelphia: Fortress, 1986), esp. 23–28, 42–83. There are hints of this stronger view in Sanders, *Paul and Palestinian Judaism*, 550–52.

37. *CD* IV/1, 541–46. "Whether man hears [the gospel], whether he accepts it and lives as one who is pardoned is another question" (*CD* IV/1, 568).

38. *CD* IV/1, 513, 616. See also Barth, *Christ and Adam: Man and Humanity in Romans 5*, trans. T. A. Smail (New York: Harper, 1957). As Bruce McCormack argues, one may understand Barth's view of the relation of Adam and Christ in terms of a Hegelian dialectic in which the former is sublated in the latter (Bruce L. McCormack, *Karl Barth's Critically Realistic Dialectical Theology: Its Genesis and Development 1909–1936* [Oxford: Clarendon, 1997], 266–69).

39. Campbell, "Connecting the Dots," 113, 143. Much of Romans 1–4 (the entire argument in Romans 1:18–32 and 2:2–13, and 3:19a and 3:20 with interjections in 2:25–29 and 3:19–4:4:25) is not Paul's at all, Campbell argues, but the heretical position of an unidentified source whom he designates the "Teacher." Campbell seems to be influenced by Stanley K. Stowers, who argues that Romans 1–3 represents "the 'presumptuous teacher' introduced in Rom 2:17" (Stanley K. Stowers, *A Rereading of Romans: Justice, Jews, and Gentiles* [New Haven, CT: Yale University Press, 1994], 189). With Gaston, Stowers argues that Paul's gospel is only for gentiles; the Jews had everything they needed in Torah (Stowers, *A Rereading of Romans*, 129–30, 190). Paul is "speaking in character"—a rhetorical trope known as *prosopōpeia,* he argues, representing the view that he argues against especially in chapters 5–8 (Campbell, *The Deliverance of God*, 528–42). This argument has met with blank stares from exegetes, and even Campbell has backed away from certain aspects of the argument. However, it represents the most extreme (Barthian) attempt

fades into the background; Christ does not fulfill nature and history as much as overwhelm it.

In some sense Israel did interpret its own situation under the terms of the Sinai covenant as a repetition of the original covenant with Adam. Echoing the Adamic commission, Exodus 1:7 announces, "But the people of Israel were *fruitful* and *increased greatly*; they *multiplied* and grew exceedingly strong, so that *the land was filled* with them."[40] On the basis of passages like Leviticus 20:7–8, Jacob Milgrom states frankly, "Israel can achieve holiness only by its own efforts. YHWH has given it the means: Israel makes itself holy by obeying YHWH's commandments."[41] Israel was a new Eden, the high priest a new Adam, and the people at large "a kingdom of priests" (Exod 19:6).[42] We find the same principle in the covenant code delivered to Israel at Sinai, summarized in Deuteronomy 28 with the promises of blessings for obedience and curses for disobedience extending even to the natural world, just as in Genesis 3:17–19. Employing similar language to that of Genesis 1:28, Yahweh says that he will make Israel fruitful and multiply them only if they are faithful to the covenant.[43]

With clear allusions to God's primordial temple-garden, the design of the tabernacle and temple highlighted the correspondence between

to assimilate the law to the gospel. With John Barclay, I can only conclude that this approach represents the closest position to Marcion on offer in contemporary debates concerning Pauline theology. John M. G. Barclay, *Paul and The Gift* (Grand Rapids: Eerdmans, 2015), 173.

40. Beale, *The Temple and the Church's Mission*, 106. Cf. Daniel C. Timmer, *Creation, Tabernacle, and Sabbath: The Sabbath Frame of Exodus 31:12–17; 33:1–3 in Exegetical and Theological Perspective*, Forschungen zur Religion und Literatur des Allen und Neuen Testaments (Göttingen: Vandenhoek & Ruprecht, 2009). Dominating Israel's horizon, according to Michael Morales, was "this picture of Israel as a new Adam, being delivered through the waters of death and conveyed to the mountain of God" (L. Michael Morales, *Who Shall Ascend the Mountain of God? A Biblical Theology of the Book of Leviticus*, NSBT 37 [Downers Grove, IL: InterVarsity, 2016], 95). See also Seth D. Postell, *Adam as Israel: Genesis 1–3 as the Introduction to the Torah and Tanakh* (Eugene, OR: Wipf and Stock, 2011).

41. Jacob Milgrom, *Leviticus*, 3 vols., AB 3–3B (Garden City, NY: Doubleday, 1998–2001), 2:1739–40. I am grateful to Bryan Estelle for the reference in his essay, "Leviticus 18:5 and Deuteronomy 30:1–14 in Biblical-Theological Development," *The Law Is Not of Faith: Essays on Works and Grace in the Mosaic Covenant*, ed. Bryan Estelle, J. V. Fesko, and David VanDrunen (Phillipsburg, NJ: P&R, 2009), 114.

42. Beale provides a fascinating list of passages throughout Genesis where the calling to "rule," "subdue," and "be fruitful and multiply" is repeated (*The Temple and the Church's Mission*, 94–95). He offers a very helpful summary of the echoes of the Edenic commission in Israel on pp. 116–17. Cf. R. J. Clifford, *The Cosmic Mountain in Canaan and the Old Testament* (Cambridge, MA: Harvard University Press, 1972); David Noel Freedman, "Temple Without Hands," in *Temples and High Places in Biblical Times* (Jerusalem: Nelson Glueck School of Biblical Archaeology of Hebrew Union College–Jewish Institute of Religion, 1981), 21–30; M. G. Kline, *Kingdom Prologue: Genesis Foundations for a Covenantal Worldview* (Eugene, OR: Wipf and Stock, 2006).

43. Beale, *The Temple and the Church's Mission*, 110.

heaven and earth. The basin represented the sea, restrained by God's word (as it was in creation and the exodus). Later, with the temple, the altar is "the mountain of God" (Ezek 43:15–16), and its base is "the bosom of the earth" (Ezek 43:14). "It also appears evident that the menorah was a stylized tree of life (cf. Exod 25:31–40)," L. Michael Morales notes. "The tabernacle, then, 'is a microcosm of creation, the world order as God intended it writ small in Israel.'"[44] The base, middle, and top of Mount Sinai corresponded, respectively, to the court, holy place, and most holy place.[45] In fact, in Psalm 68, which was likely composed for the inaugural entrance of the ark into the temple, we read,

> The chariots of God are twice ten thousand,
>> thousands upon thousands;
>> the Lord is among them; *Sinai is now in the sanctuary.*"
> (Ps 68:17, emphasis added)

What the priests accomplished in the sanctuary was nothing less than the perpetual restoration of ethical equilibrium of Israel surrounded by the waters of chaos (i.e., the darkness and void of the gentile world). Torah was a gift, and if Israel kept it, the land would continue to be a small-scale replica of the heavenly city filled with righteousness, justice, and peace. It would be a new Eden. But for that very reason—the conditional basis of the covenant—Torah was a burden as well. And a threat.

The concept of a universal moral law, as binding as physical laws, was well known in the ancient Mediterranean world. Especially in Stoicism, there is the idea of the "elementary principles" that produce harmony, and the human being must live with the grain of this cosmic order. Somehow, the evil that you send out into the cosmos comes back to you. It is a law written into the natural, biological, and moral code of life. But for Israel, Torah was this cosmic framework. Transgressing Torah, however, was not merely like violating the law of gravity, transgressing the principle of "do no harm," or going against the grain of nature. It was not a principle but a personal claim by Yahweh, the creator and

---

44. L. Michael Morales, *The Tabernacle Pre-Figured: Cosmic Mountain Ideology in Genesis and Exodus* (Leuven: Peeters, 2012), 251, quoting T. E. Fretheim, "Because the Whole Earth is Mine: Theme and Narrative in Exodus," *Interpretation* 50, no. 3 (1996): 238.

45. See Mary Douglas, *Leviticus as Literature* (Oxford: Oxford University Press, 2001), ch. 3. Cf. A. M. Rodriguez, "Sanctuary Theology in the Book of Exodus," *Andrews University Seminary Studies* 24 (1986): 132–34; R. E. Clements, *God and Temple* (Philadelphia: Fortress, 1965), chs. 2 and 5.

deliverer of his people.[46] Torah does not represent, symbolize, or point to reality; it *is* the real world. Only with malicious intent could one created in God's image, ordered to this order, choose to break away from it. It is the order in which freedom, love, and peaceful relationships flourish. Not all sins were equal. However, the nation could so fatally reject God's suzerainty that it would cause a tear in the cosmic fabric. This is why the temple was so essential for repairing, purifying, and restoring the order of the nation as a microcosmos, as well as for averting God's wrath from the individual and the community. Like Moses, whose arms raised brought victory and fallen brought defeat, the priests' intercession and offering of sacrifices to some extent enabled God to dwell in the midst of his people.

Given the abundant parallels between Eden and Canaan, Adam and Israel, it is not surprising that Israel also saw itself as being on trial. With the wilderness generation as a cautionary tale, the people were aware of the precariousness of their tenure in the land. To live in the precincts of God's holy land was a blessing, but it was also a threat. Just as Yahweh had driven out the pagan nations, he will expel Israel from the land—east of "Eden"—if they turn their back on his covenant.

It was not a later, largely gentile, church that universalized Israel's narrative. On the contrary, it was Israel's conviction all along that its political head of state was also the God of all nature and nations, that Adam was the representative of humanity before God, and that Eve was "the mother of all living." As the story unfolds, it becomes progressively clearer that Israel is like Hamlet's play-within-a-play, a parable of the wider history of humanity.

Although Israel appears in Second Temple Jewish writings as a second Adam and as somehow suffering because of gentile oppressors, nowhere in the Hebrew Scriptures, even in Isaiah 53, is Israel the vicarious bearer of God's punishment for the guilt of the nations as well as their own. The first Adam failed *for all* (including Jews) and the second Adam succeeded *for all* (including gentiles). The nearly seven centuries from the covenant renewal recorded in Joshua 24 to the exile is a typological subplot pointing Israel to the coming Messiah, the last Adam. Hence,

---

46. This is the burden of David Novak's argument (*Covenantal Rights: A Study in Jewish Political Theory* [Princeton: Princeton University Press, 2009]) in comparison and contrast with modern rights-theory. Jon D. Levenson explains this beautifully in *The Love of God: Divine Gift, Human Gratitude, and Mutual Faithfulness in Judaism*, Library of Jewish Ideas (Princeton, NJ: Princeton University Press, 2015), esp. chs. 1 and 2.

Paul's reference to this history of the holy nation as "our guardian until Christ came, in order that we might be justified by faith" (Gal 3:24). But again, Israel not only did not bear the guilt of the nations; its role is not described as redemptive until the rabbinical traditions. Rather, Israel is a "light for the nations" (Isa 42:6; 49:6; cf. Luke 2:32; Acts 13:47; 26:23), the firstfruits of the world harvest, a choir to "sing . . . his praise from the end of the earth" to the "islands" (Isa 42:10 NIV) and to "declare with a shout of joy" and to "send it out to the end of the earth" that God has brought redemption (Isa 48:20).

In N. T. Wright's account, "The covenant is there to solve the problems with creation." Evidently, this single covenant of creation is the same as the one that Yahweh swore to Abraham. "God called Abraham to solve the problem of evil, the problem of Adam, the problem of the world."[47] However, this interpretation fails on two counts.

First, where do we find—in the Abraham cycle, in the Prophets, or in the New Testament—any mention of this messianic role of the father of faith? The biblical plot is bounded by two Adams, not three, so how can Abraham be the one through whom God would solve "the problem of Adam"? A multiplication of "Adams" tends to reduce the unique significance of the two who bound Paul's horizon. Further, as appears especially in *The Day the Revolution Began*, Wright's plotline may suggest that Adam was merely one who, with Eve, dropped the ball, and Jesus picked it back up and passed it on to us for the score. Yet this account appears to be challenged by Wright's own qualifications.

Acknowledging a covenant and commission with Adam and Eve to multiply, rule, and subdue as God's viceroys, Wright further observes that the tragedy, according to Paul, is that "Israel too is in Adam."[48] He also says that according to Romans "the long entail of Adam's sin and death can be undone (5.12–21) through his obedience."[49] In spite of Israel's unfaithfulness, "God must stick to the plan. . . . But that means that sooner or later he will require a representative Israelite who *will* be faithful, who will be obedient to God's purpose not only for Israel but through Israel for the world."[50] He even affirms that, again, *somehow*, this righteous status is communicated to them:

47. N. T. Wright, *Paul: In Fresh Perspective* (Minneapolis: Fortress, 2009), 24.
48. Wright, *Paul: In Fresh Perspective*, 36.
49. Wright, *Paul: In Fresh Perspective*, 47.
50. Wright, *Paul: In Fresh Perspective*, 47.

"The Messiah represents his people so that what is true of him is true of them."[51]

However, what Wright's account lacks is a bicovenantal framework in which Christ's unique fulfillment of the covenant of vocation can be adequately appreciated. Instead, seminal moments in redemptive history, such as Abraham, Sinai, David, and the new covenant, become mere sequels to a single covenant that begins in Eden. In an earlier work, he says, "Thus at key moments—Abraham's call, his circumcision, the offering of Isaac, the transition from Abraham to Isaac and from Isaac to Jacob, and in the sojourn in Egypt—the narrative quietly makes the point that Abraham and his family inherit, in a measure, the role of Adam and Eve." But Wright's own caveats—"quietly makes the point" and "in a measure"—betray the tenuous character of the claim that Abraham is picking up the ball that Adam dropped and continuing the covenant of vocation. In fact, Wright adds, "The differences are not, however, insignificant." In Genesis 17, "*The command* [to Adam and Eve] *('be fruitful . . .') has turned into a promise ('I will make you fruitful . . .'),*" and "most importantly, possession of the land of Canaan, and supremacy over enemies, has taken the place of the dominion over nature given in 1.28. We could sum up this aspect of Genesis by saying: Abraham's children are God's true humanity, and their homeland is the new Eden."[52]

But can a single covenant survive such inner contrasts? These important differences that Wright himself points up challenge his initial suggestion that Abraham is another Adam. Abraham is therefore not picking up where Adam left off as a representative head in a covenant of law but is the recipient of the promise already announced in Genesis 3:15. In fact, Adam was a unique figure in biblical history: until Jesus, the only representative and covenant head of the human race under a covenant of works. After the fall, however, this approach to the Tree of Life is forever barred—until finally the Last Adam appears who wins that right and gives the fruit of immortality to his brothers and sisters.

Second, Wright's argument conflates the covenants of law and promise, Sinai and Abraham. "When Israel is in trouble," he says, "and the covenant promises themselves seem to have come crashing to the ground, the people cry to the covenant God precisely as the creator."

51. Wright, *Paul: In Fresh Perspective*, 113.
52. Wright, *The Climax of the Covenant*, 21–23, emphasis added.

Yet again we search in vain for any instance of the prophets invoking the covenant of creation as the basis for deliverance from the curse of exile and the problem of evil. On the contrary, it is the promise made to David and his seed that is likened to God's unbreakable covenant with day and night. In that day the city of God will be called "The LORD is our righteousness" (Jer 33:16–21). The new promise echoes the Abrahamic covenant: "As the host of heaven cannot be numbered and the sands of the sea cannot be measured, so I will multiply the offspring of David my servant, and the Levitical priests who minister to me" (33:22). In Wright's view, the Sinai covenant is the answer to humanity's failure to fulfil the covenant of vocation: "Something is deeply amiss with creation, and within that with humankind itself, something to which the covenant with Israel is the answer. Something is deeply amiss with the covenant, whether Israel's sins on the one hand or Gentile oppression on the other, or perhaps both—and the answer to this is a re-invoking of creation, or rather of God as creator."[53] However, for anyone in breach of the law-covenant, to *appeal* to it is to invoke God's wrath. If Israel stands condemned "under the law," then surely gentiles have no reason to think that they will have a better turn at the wheel. While calling on the name of the LORD who is also creator as well as redeemer, the last thing that we would want to invoke is the *covenant* of creation or of Sinai in order to grant us mercy or for the strength to fulfill our vocation. And, in fact, the prophets never appeal to Sinai for mercy but only as the basis for judgment. Instead of Sinai, it is the promise that God swore to "the fathers" (Abraham, Isaac, and Jacob) and to David, the new covenant that is "not like" the one that Israel broke (Jer 31:32), that becomes the only hope beyond exile. The Messiah will win the right for his coheirs to eat from the Tree of Life because he will be their righteousness (Rev 2:7). This is an unbreakable covenant in contrast with Sinai (Heb 6:17–18; 8:6–7).

Third, Wright's proposal universalizes the Sinai covenant, despite the fact that, according to numerous passages, the pact established a unique relationship between Yahweh and the people and nation of Israel. The Sinai covenant never included gentiles (Eph 2:12; cf. Deut 4:8; 7:6; 29:14; Rom 9:4). Therefore, they cannot appeal to it. This is why Paul repeatedly directs believers, Jew and gentile, to Abraham and

---

53. Wright, *Paul: In Fresh Perspective*, 24.

his faith in the promise *rather than* the Sinai covenant as the basis for their shared inheritance in Christ.

Ben Witherington is correct, I think, when he demurs from N. T. Wright's interpretation of 1 Corinthians 10. Wright says that "when Paul appeals (for instance) to the exodus story in 1 Corinthians 10.1–13 he does so not simply to pick out an example from long ago but in order to stress that the erstwhile pagan converts in Corinth are part of the same, single family that was once rescued from Egypt."[54] Witherington says, "This is where I personally find Wright least convincing." Paul bases his exhortation on the fact the Corinthians are dealing with *the same God*, not *the same story*. "*The Corinthians were never part of the Mosaic story or covenant. They were grafted into the patriarchal story and the Abrahamic covenant now fulfilled in Christ and in the new covenant.*"[55]

The fall has already barred any return to the covenant of creation, with cherubim guarding clever trespassers from entrance to the Tree of Life (which would only confirm them everlastingly in their present state—namely, death). Instead, God opens space in history for the fulfillment of his promise of redemption. He will send his Messiah to win the right for his coheirs to eat from the Tree of Life because he will be their righteousness (Rev 2:7).

In short, Abraham is not another Adam, and Israel is not the Redeemer but the mother of the Redeemer. Nevertheless, like a theme in a symphony, Israel's history repeats Adam's creation-exodus from darkness and void, God's gift of a land with vineyards it did not plant and wells it did not dig, and, tragically, Adam's failure to cling to every word that comes from the mouth of God and instead demand the food he craved. The eastward exile confirms this association. But it is the true and faithful Israel, the promised seed of Abraham, who, instead of repeating this dreary cycle, recapitulated the story of Adam and Israel faithfully. And by his obedience he has won for his coheirs the title to his estate.

The stakes could not be higher with the two Adams: everlasting life, confirmed in righteousness and glory, or everlasting judgment, confirmed in injustice. The entire Mosaic economy is typological, pointing

---

54. Wright, *Paul and His Recent Interpreters*, 260–61.
55. Ben Witherington, "Paul and his Recent Interpreters by N.T. Wright—Part Nine," *Patheos*, September 10, 2015, www.patheos.com/blogs/bibleandculture/2015/09/paul-and-his-recent-interpreters-by-n-t-wright-part-ten/, emphasis original.

back to Adam and forward to Christ, plight and solution. Salvation comes from the Jews because it comes from Jesus Christ and for no other reason. Israel is the twelve-star-crowned mother in Revelation 12 giving birth to the child who will rule the nations. The Sinai covenant explicitly restricted God's special relationship with humanity to the nation of Israel. In every episode of the play-within-a-play, Israel finds, as N. T. Wright says, that it too is in Adam. Its kings are parodies of David, much less of his greater Son. And yet, God cherishes Israel as his bride, anticipating the day when he sends his Son to save her and expand her tents. Precisely because Israel too is "in Adam," God can show mercy upon all, Jew and gentile, on equal terms (Rom 11:32).

In addition, rabbinic tradition held that all of humanity is "under the law" in the sense of obligation to the commands that God gave to Noah, which are essentially what Christians identify as the moral law—the Ten Commandments.[56] On the basis of this covenant, Yahweh even makes pagan nations his "servant" in the drama of redemption, notes Brueggemann. "The entire world of creation is in covenant with Yahweh."[57] Thus, Paul is not improvising or innovating but explaining the plotline in light of where we are now because of the Christ-event. We soon discover the contrasting views of the plight upon closer examination of implicit syllogism in which Romans 2:6 is placed:

- He will judge everyone according to their works: gentiles by the covenant of law written on the conscience in creation, Jews by the written Torah (2:6–16).[58]
- But no one is righteous, no not one (3:9–18).

---

56. See Novak, *Covenantal Rights*, 48, 65–71, 84, 86, 101, 172–75, 215.

57. Bruegemann, *Theology of the Old Testament*, 494.

58. These verses have been interpreted frequently as justifying the possibility of attaining justification by moral effort. Richard N. Longenecker surveys these views with a thorough exegetical rebuttal (Richard N. Longenecker, *Paul, Apostle of Liberty*, 2nd ed. [Grand Rapids: Eerdmans, 2015], 78–107). It is increasingly thought, even among more traditional scholars, that the gentiles mentioned here are Christians (the strongest argument perhaps being Simon Gathercole, *Where Is Boasting? Early Jewish Soteriology and Paul's Response in Romans 1–5* [Grand Rapids: Eerdmans, 2001], 127). However, I remain unpersuaded. Paul has been speaking of these gentiles as a class of idolaters who "suppress the truth in unrighteousness," refuse to retain knowledge of God, and give their bodies over to unnatural lusts (Rom 1:18–32). He points out that gentiles have access to God's moral by natural law even though they do not possess Torah. However, gentile *Christians* certainly had Torah as well as the moral instruction of Jesus and the apostles that confirmed the Decalogue's precepts. Further, the point of his argument up to 3:19 is to imprison everyone under the law and its condemnation. Whatever we make of any verse in these chapters, the interpretation must fit into that larger argument arraigning all Jews and gentiles together (summed up in 3:10–20).

- Therefore, the law (whether known by creation or by Torah) condemns all people, Jew and gentile alike, and according to it, no one can be justified (3:19).

Not only is this argument consistent with chapters 5–8, but apart from it these chapters are suspended in midair. And the hinge on which the two parts turn is Romans 3:21–4:25, anticipated already in 3:21: "But now the righteousness of God has been manifested apart from the law, although the Law and the Prophets bear witness to it."

SINAI AND ZION

On the national-typological level, Israel saw itself in some sense as a new Adam, but the people knew that their only hope of redemption and justification before God was found in the Abrahamic promise and elaborated by the Davidic and new covenants. In the 1970s, Moshe Weinfeld argued that the Abrahamic and Sinai covenants fit the form and content of a royal grant and a suzerainty covenant, respectively.[59] A host of specialists have argued similarly.[60] It may well be that Weinfeld placed too much weight on the form rather than content to determine the nature of biblical covenants for his comparisons.[61] Even so, it is important to note the widespread recognition of differences between covenants of law and promise. Of course, there are commands and promises in both types of covenant, but in the former, personal fulfillment of the stipulations is the *basis* for the promised blessing, while in the latter obedience is the fruit of God's fulfillment of his own unilateral oath.[62]

---

59. Moshe Weinfeld, "The Covenant of Grant in the Old Testament and the Ancient Near East," *Journal of the American Oriental Society* 90 (1970): 109–97. There are various forms for royal grants. According to Delbert R. Hillers, "A typical brief example, runs as follows: 'From this day forward Niqmaddu son of Ammistamru king of Ugarit has taken the house of Pabeya [. . .] which is in Ullami, and given it to Nuriyana and to his descendants forever. Let no one take it from the hand of Nuriyana or his descendants forever. Seal of the king'" (Hillers, *Covenant: The History of a Biblical Idea* [Baltimore: Johns Hopkins University Press, 1969], 105.)

60. George E. Mendenhall, *Law and Covenant in Israel and the Ancient Near East* (Pittsburgh: Biblical Colloquium, 1955) lent further support, followed by many others, including Hillers, *Covenant*; Steven L. McKenzie, *Covenant* (St Louis: Chalice, 2000); Dennis J. McCarthy, SJ, *Treaty and Covenant: A Study in Form in the Ancient Oriental Documents and in the Old Testament* (Rome: Biblical Institute, 1963); McCarthy, "Three Covenants in Genesis," *The Catholic Biblical Quarterly* 26 (1964): 184; Meredith G. Kline, *Treaty of the Great King* (Grand Rapids: Eerdmans, 1963); and Kline, *By Oath Consigned* (Grand Rapids: Eerdmans, 1968).

61. So David Noel Freedman, "Divine Commitment and Human Obligation," *Interpretation* 18 (1964): 419–31.

62. This point provides crucial nuance against exaggerated contrasts that have been criticized in recent decades by Gary N. Knoppers, Noel Weeks, David Noel Freedman, and others.

It is clear enough that Israel "gets in by grace"—on the basis of God's promise to Abraham. In fact, upon entering the land the people are warned against imagining that they merited it (Deut 9:4–6). Israel was *not* to imagine Yahweh saying, as the Yalkut Shimoni puts it: "In the merit of Jerusalem I split the sea for them."[63] Thus, Paul is not, from his Damascus road experience, introducing a novel theology but correcting his contemporaries' assimilation of Zion to Sinai. Paul is challenging the view expressed in rabbinical texts in which Israel's election and gift of the land are treated as a reward for the righteousness, at least, of the patriarchs.[64]

The Abrahamic promise stands in contrast with the original (Adamic) covenant. Furthering the promise of Genesis 3:15, God alone swears to bless the families of the earth through a single offspring of Abraham and Sarah and confirms this oath by passing in a self-maledictory oath between the pieces of animal carcasses (Gen 15:1–17). This was a common way of confirming secular treaties, where the suzerain, having liberated a helpless people, annexed them to his kingdom and caused the vassal-ruler to pass through the pieces.[65] Yet what is astonishing in Genesis 15 is that rather than causing Abraham—the vassal—to pass between the parts, Yahweh passes *alone* through the pieces.[66] The promise—of an earthly people and land and of blessing for all nations in one offspring of Abraham and Sarah—was unconditional, an outright gift, with God himself as the mediator.[67] After Abraham believes the promise and is justified, the obligations that God places on him are a reasonable response to the inheritance rather than its basis. The same is true of the

---

63. Yalkut Shimoni, Isaiah 473, https://www.jewishvirtuallibrary.org.

64. See the quotations in Sanders, *Paul and Palestinian Judaism*, 84–106, 257–69, 329–33, 362–64.

65. Hillers, *Covenant*, 40–41. "'Just as this calf is cut up, so may Matiel be cut up,' is the way it is put in the text of an Aramaic treaty from the eighth century B. C.," notes Hillers. Hillers adds, "From this ceremony is derived the Hebrew idiom for making a treaty, *karat berit*, 'to cut a treaty,'" a formula also found in Homer. Dennis J. McCarthy, SJ, notes that the political idiom "to cut a covenant" was used as early as the 1400s BC in Aramaic and Phoenician as well as Hebrew records (McCarthy, *Treaty and Covenant: A Study in the Ancient Oriental Documents and in the Old Testament* [Rome: Biblical Institute, 1963], 52–55).

66. Mendenhall, in *Law and Covenant in Israel and the Ancient Near East*, points out that the Decalogue and Joshua 24 fit these forms of a suzerainty treaty, but "it can readily be seen that the covenant with Abraham (and Noah) is of completely different form." Not even circumcision is a condition. On the contrary, Abram believed and was justified, with circumcision as a sign and seal of God's promise, like the rainbow in Genesis 9 (p. 36).

67. Instead of making a name for themselves by their own achievements, as the Promethean builders of Babel attempted (Gen 11:4), Abram is given a new name by Yahweh and this becomes paradigmatic for the covenant of promise to the end of the age (Gen 35:10; Isa 45:4; 62:6; Rev 2:17).

covenant with David (2 Sam 7). Even "if we are faithless, he remains faithful—for he cannot deny himself" (2 Tim 2:13). We "get in" and "*stay in*" by grace alone, in Christ alone, through faith alone.

After Yahweh cleanses the land and hands it over to the twelve tribes, God's promise concerning a typological inheritance of land and genetic descendants was fulfilled. Joshua announces to the people, "Not one word of all the good promises that the LORD had made to the house of Israel had failed; all came to pass" (Josh 21:45). And now it was Israel's turn to swear an oath. If she pollutes the land, then the same curses will come upon her as fell upon the wicked whom God dispossessed.

As with the Adamic covenant, the tenure in the land was conditional; the Sinai covenant now established the basis for "staying in." Joshua stresses this point, even warning them of the oath's dangers in light of their straying heart (Josh 24:19–27). This oath was a renewal of the Sinai pact in which Israel swore the terms with Moses as its mediator, and Moses "took the blood and threw it on the people and said, 'Behold the blood of the covenant that the LORD has made with you in accordance with all these words'" (Exod 24:8). Here, the blood was on the people's head if they should violate their oath, "All this we will do."

Accordingly, when God threatened the exile, he declared, "Those who transgressed my covenant and did not keep the terms of the covenant *that they made before me*, I will *make them* like the calf that they cut in two and passed between its parts" (Jer 34:18). And yet, the second part of the Abrahamic promise—of a worldwide family and inheritance of the whole earth—was yet to be fulfilled not through the nation's obedience but through that of the single offspring of Abraham.

So Paul is not rejecting the Hebrew Scriptures in favor of a theology of his own devising. He is simply carrying out the bicovenantal teaching of the prophets. In Galatians 4:21–26, Paul refers explicitly to "two covenants," identified as "promise" (the Abrahamic covenant) and "law" (Sinai). It was the prophets who said that the new covenant would not be like the Sinai covenant but would rest instead on God's immutable oath and sovereign grace (Jer 31:32). Failing to discern that the Sinai theocracy was a parenthesis within the history of the covenant of grace, Paul's agitators had subordinated the covenant of grace to the national covenant based on Israel's oath, "All this we will do" (Exod 19:8). In short, Galatians 3:3 suggests that Paul's critics embraced a "covenantal nomism" even as E. P. Sanders defines it ("getting in by grace, staying in by obedience").[68] But the law (i.e., the Sinai covenant mediated by Moses) was never intended as a means of anyone's justification before God (Gal 3:21).

It is important to stress that this distinction between covenants of law and promise is so self-evident in Scripture that it can hardly be called a Reformed distinctive. We have noted its appearance in patristic sources, but this view is well-represented in contemporary scholarship, including Jewish and Roman Catholic. For example, Jon Levenson and Joseph Cardinal Ratzinger (Pope Benedict XVI) recognize the sharp contrast between the covenants of promise (Abrahamic, Davidic, and new) and the Sinai covenant, even to the point of correlating them with a suzerainty treaty and royal grant, respectively.[69] Remarkably, Pope Benedict even acknowledges,

> The rediscovery of Pauline theology at the Reformation laid special emphasis on this point: not works, but faith; not man's achievement, but the free bestowal of God's goodness. It emphatically under-lined, therefore, that what was involved was not a "covenant" but a "testament," a pure decision and act on God's part. This is the context in which we must understand the teaching that it is God alone who does everything. (All the *solus* terms—*solus Deus, solus Christus*—must be understood in this context.)[70]

Contradicting their own exegesis, however, both scholars finally assimilate the gospel to the law when it comes to theological conclusions. Levenson even says that the Abrahamic-Davidic covenant "displaced the Sinaitic . . . in the New Testament" and identifies this as the crux of the difference between Christianity and Judaism.[71] "There is, therefore, no

---

68. Sanders, *Paul and Palestinian Judaism*, 93; cf. 178, 371. For "covenantal nomism," see 75, 543–56.

69. Jon D. Levenson, *Sinai and Zion: An Entry into the Jewish Bible* (San Francisco: HarperSanFrancisco, 1985), 45, 56–57, 194, 210, 216, 286; Joseph Cardinal Ratzinger, *Many Religions, One Covenant: Israel, the Church, and the World* (San Francisco: Ignatius, 1999), 16, 50–51, 66–67.

70. Ratzinger, *Many Religions, One Covenant*, 67. However, the Reformers (certainly the covenant theology that arose in the Reformed tradition) did not contrast *covenant* and *testament*, as the writer suggests, but recognized that the specific type of *berit* that the Abrahamic-Davidic-new covenant was a promised inheritance (testament) rather than a mutual contract, and so could only be served by the Greek *diathēkē* rather than *synthēkē*. On this point, see Geerhardus Vos, "Hebrews: The Epistle of the Diatheke," *Princeton Theological Review* 13 (1915): 587–632; and 14 (1916): 1–61; repr., in Richard B. Gaffin Jr., ed., *Redemptive History and Biblical Interpretation: The Shorter Writings of Geerhardus Vos* (Phillipsburg, NJ: Presbyterian and Reformed, 1980), 161–233.

71. Levenson, *Sinai and Zion*, 216.

voice more central to Judaism than the voice heard on Mount Sinai."[72] In fact, "The covenant without stipulations, the Abrahamic covenant of Genesis 15 and 17, is only a preparation for the Sinaitic covenant, *into which it is absorbed.*"[73] At just this point, he says, Christianity parted ways with Judaism.[74] Similarly, in spite of his exegesis, Pope Benedict XVI too absorbs the promise to the law.[75] In fact, he says, "The Law itself is the concrete form of grace. For to know God's will is grace."[76] The new covenant that is ratified at the Last Supper "is *the prolongation of the Sinai covenant, which is not abrogated, but renewed*" (emphasis added).[77]

In contrast with Levenson and Benedict, Richard N. Longenecker carries through consistently the exegesis to its logical conclusion. Reflecting especially on Romans 1–3, he says, "The best explanation is that Paul saw two strands running throughout the Old Testament and the New: (1) the law of God, which promised life but because of man's sin and inability brought only judgment and death, and (2) righteousness based on faith." These are obvious contrasts in Galatians 3:11–12 and Romans 10:5–13 as well. He continues, "Martin Luther probably best understood and most adequately represents Paul's emphasis at this point in saying: 'All the Scriptures of God are divided into two parts— commands and promises. . . . Suffice it here to say that the contrast we see between Romans 2:6ff. and 3:21ff. is the same as that between Law and Gospel."[78] It is difficult to imagine the comparison of old covenant saints to being "kept under law (*hypo nomon*)" like "a pedagogue in relation to a child" without thinking in contractual terms, he adds.[79] But then there is the promise. There are not two contracting parties in this covenant of promise; God himself is the guarantor as well as promise-maker (Gal 3:20).[80] The choice then is whether one will be "in Christ" or "under the law" (*hypo nomon*; see 1 Cor 9:20; Gal 4:21, 5:18); whether one will attempt (in vain) to achieve the inheritance as a reward for personal obedience or receive it as a gift (in Christ).[81]

---

72. Levenson, *Sinai and Zion*, 86.
73. Levenson, *Sinai and Zion*, 45, emphasis added.
74. Levenson, *Sinai and Zion*, 194.
75. Levenson, *Sinai and Zion*, 194.
76. Levenson, *Sinai and Zion*, 68–71.
77. Levenson, *Sinai and Zion*, 62
78. Longenecker, *Paul, Apostle of Liberty*, 110.
79. Longenecker, *Paul, Apostle of Liberty*, 114.
80. Longenecker, *Paul, Apostle of Liberty*, 115, from J. B. Lightfoot, *Saint Paul's Epistle to the Galatians*, 10th ed. (London: Macmillan, 1890), 146–47.
81. Longenecker, *Paul, Apostle of Liberty*, 115.

THE REIGN OF TORAH: ACT-CONSEQUENCE CONNECTION

In the Bible's unfolding plot, the Sinai covenant seems to hit the pause button of redemptive history, but it is a productive interim. In the age of Torah, we are reminded of the precariousness of a relationship with God based on its fickle human partner. It is the breach of this covenant that keeps grinding history to a halt until God renews *his* unconditional and unilateral oath. It is another covenant, the one with Abraham, which itself continues the promise to Eve in Genesis 3:15, that keeps history moving. In some sense, the age of Torah is a parable of the larger plot with Adam and Christ as the main characters and the Abrahamic promise as the plot device that keeps history moving forward even when the nation's covenant breach has stopped it in its tracks. The Sinai covenant was never intended to bring the plot to its denouement but to serve as a temporary parenthesis, foreshadowing the person and work of the one who would.

The reign of Torah is based on a specific type of covenant: a relationship of love that is stipulated by laws. Like the original covenant with humanity in Adam, it is based on the principle of conditional blessing and curse (i.e., the "action-consequence connection" mentioned in the introduction). It appears in Genesis 2:15–17 with the stipulation and sanction. The Tree of Life stood before them as the reward for obedience. Nevertheless, they were as yet without sin, confirmed by verse 25: "And the man and his wife were both naked and not ashamed."

We find the same principle in the covenant code delivered to Israel at Sinai, summarized in Deuteronomy 28 with the promises of blessings for obedience and curses for disobedience. All of nature—the elements of the sky, sun, rain, land, vegetation, and animals—will be drawn into this blessing or curse. Like Genesis 3:17–19, if Israel sins, the land itself will become resistant to Israel's prosperity until the nation is finally exiled from God's earthly homeland (Deut 28:16–24). The blessing of entering a land that they did conquer, living in houses they did not build, and eating the fruit of vines and trees that they did not plant (Deut 6:11) will be reversed: "You shall build a house, but you shall not dwell in it. You shall plant a vineyard, but you shall not enjoy its fruit" (v. 30).[82]

---

82. In fact, God could justly have exiled the people as soon as the conquest, since he judged them for failing to drive out the nations fully from the land (Judg 1–3).

Just as Adam and Eve sinned against God's love, expressed in his liberal provision ("from all the trees you may freely eat," except one), Yahweh pledges, "Because you did not serve the LORD your God with joyfulness and gladness of heart, because of the abundance of all things, therefore you shall serve your enemies whom the LORD will send against you, in hunger and thirst, in nakedness, and lacking everything. And he will put a yoke of iron on your neck until he has destroyed you" (28:47–48). And like the consequences of Adam's sin on humanity, Israel's offspring will suffer the curses for their fathers' sins. "And you shall be plucked off the land that you are entering to take possession of it" (vv. 58–60, 63).

Like Eden, Canaan was claimed by Yahweh as his sacred temple-garden, not to be enjoyed by God for its own sake (as if he needed fruitful vineyards) but as the place of covenantal communion with his people. As holy, the whole land was under the direct governance of Yahweh. While God reigned over the whole earth—"east of Eden"—in providence and common grace, he was Lord in Israel by his special grace. Therefore, if there was drought or disease, Israel rightly concluded that it was guilty of some national sin. Even physical infirmities (e.g., blindness, deformity, and, above all, scale disease) could be visible signs of God's displeasure, while fruitful wombs and prosperity signaled God's delight. Because of the conditionality of this national covenant, Israel was reminded on every hand that obedience brought blessing and disobedience yielded thorns and thistles.

But this Deuteronomic (act-consequence) logic was questioned at various points especially by the empirical fact that the righteous sometimes suffer while the wicked flourish. In Psalm 73, Asaph participates in a long tradition of wrestling with this apparent contradiction of God's design: "Truly God is good to Israel, to those who are pure in heart," he says. "But as for me, my feet had almost stumbled . . . when I saw the prosperity of the wicked." It does not seem that they struggle, even as "pride is their necklace" and "violence covers them as a garment." They are "always at ease, they increase in riches" (vv. 1–13). So it led him to wonder,

> All in vain have I kept my heart clean
> and washed my hands in innocence.
> For all the day long I have been stricken
> and rebuked every morning. (vv. 13–14)

He did not gain his perspective "until I went into the sanctuary of God" and discovered that there is a final judgment after all (vv. 16–23). And now, instead of professing his innocence, he finds his confidence in God's mercy:

> You hold my right hand.
> You guide me with your counsel,
>   and afterward you will receive me to glory.
> Whom have I in heaven but you?
>   And there is nothing on earth that I desire besides you.
> My flesh and my heart may fail,
>   but God is the strength of my heart and my portion forever.
>   (vv. 23–26)

Of course, the most extensive piece of Hebrew "theodicy" is the book of Job.[83] Job's friends express the baseline "action-consequence connection" inherent in Israel's covenant with Yahweh. Searching for some hidden sin that Job has either willfully ignored or suppressed in his subconscious, they suppose that they are aiding Job in recovering his prosperity by repenting and returning to the wheel of obedience and reward. But Job protests his innocence—until he comes to realize that even if he is not aware of any particular transgression that would merit his suffering, he is in fact a sinner. Once more, the resolution is neither philosophical nor moral but eschatological. He no longer appeals to God to defend his righteousness but to accept him as righteous through a mediator.

> For I know that my Redeemer lives,
>   and at the last he will stand upon the earth.
> And after my skin has been thus destroyed,
>   yet in my flesh I shall see God,
> whom I shall see for myself,
>   and my eyes shall behold, and not another.
> My heart faints within me! (vv. 25–27)

---

83. I put this in scare quotes because most scholars doubt that this is the right category for Job. I am calling it "theodicy" here only in the widest sense, as literature in which God's inscrutable ways with humankind are explored.

As in the prophets, any appeal to one's innocence according to the law is going to fail; only by looking beyond the law to Yahweh's fulfillment of his oath is joy restored.

In short, whenever this question ("Why do the righteous suffer?") is raised, the conclusion is that the premise is mistaken. This is true not only in Paul (especially Rom 9–11) but throughout Israel's pilgrimage. The righteous do not suffer; no one is righteous in the sense that they qualify for God's unmitigated blessing and favor. Thus, the only thing to do is to cast oneself on God's mercy. This is precisely what David did in Psalm 51 after committing two capital crimes. Acknowledging not only his sins (first, against Yahweh, and secondarily, against Bathsheba and Uriah) but his sinful condition from conception, David does not appeal to any mechanism in the law but to a direct pardon from the King of Heaven.

As we will see, these exceptions are expanded when the whole nation is found to have so thoroughly transgressed the covenant that the curses of Deuteronomy 28 are finally pronounced by Yahweh through his prophets. God had been a faithful husband. "But like Adam they transgressed the covenant; there they dealt faithlessly with me" (Hos 6:7). From the law, Israel could expect nothing but sorrow; only on the basis of another covenant could the prophets bring good news of a future that is not conditioned on the obedience of the people but is an outright gift based on the obedience, death and resurrection of the Lord's faithful Servant.

Thus, the act-consequence connection at the heart of the Sinai covenant is akin to the natural law that I highlighted in the introduction. Just as Yahweh commanded Israel to "show no mercy" to the idolatrous corrupters of God's land in Deuteronomy 7:2, Yahweh warns that he will show no mercy if the nation that he has called to holiness casts off his yoke:

> And if you forget the LORD your God and go after other gods and serve them and worship them, I solemnly warn you today that you shall surely perish. Like the nations that the LORD makes to perish before you, so shall you perish, because you would not obey the voice of the LORD your God. (Deut 8:19–20)

According to this act-consequence connection at the heart of the law-covenant, Israel has no mediator who can step into the breach.

Interestingly, Moses cannot stand in for Israel in the golden calf episode: "Only the one who has sinned against me will I blot out of my book" (Exod 32:30–33). The consequences must come back on the doer. This was the principle that Job's counselors assumed in their advice, which was entirely justified in view of the blessing-curse formulas of the Sinai covenant. So too in Ezekiel 18 the principle is repeated: "Only the person who sins shall die." Fathers and sons cannot bear each other's guilt (Ezek 18:20). The act-consequence connection brings the consequences back on the doer of the sin. This is the principle of the law that Paul recounted in Romans 2:13: "For it is not the hearers of the law who are righteous before God, but the doers of the law who will be justified." So, obviously, no one will be justified on this basis (Rom 3:20).

Jeremiah and Ezekiel eventually are forbidden by God even to intercede for the nation; they suffer, but their suffering cannot affect the outcome. The act-consequence connection is in play. But with Isaiah 52–53, as Hermann Spieckermann points out, "*Prophetic suffering acquires a new sense.*"[84] "At the same time vicarious suffering is limited to and concentrated upon the fate of a single person whose guilt has the power to wipe out guilt once for all." There is something strikingly new in Isaiah 53, Spieckermann says. "*By leaving room for one Servant to remain righteous, God makes the Servant's righteousness a part of the vicarious event.* The Servant makes the many righteous and thereby breaks the bounds of previous conceptions of individual retribution and prophetic intercession."[85] With the temple gone, having fulfilled its typological purpose, the one place now, finally and forever, for sinners to avoid the consequences of their actions is the cross.

After the advent of Christ, Paul seems to identify even Torah itself with the "elementary principles of the world" (στοιχεῖα τοῦ κόσμου) in Galatians 4:3, 9 and Colossians 2:8, 20. Sarah and Hagar represent "two covenants," Paul says. "One is from Mount Sinai, bearing children for slavery; she is Hagar. But the Jerusalem above is free, and she is our mother" (Gal 4:24, 26). The act-consequence wisdom of the world— στοιχεῖα τοῦ κόσμου—ingrained in our nature as God's image-bearers, and repeated in Torah, is that God will not acquit the guilty (Exod 23:7).

---

84. Hermann Spieckermann, "The Conception and Prehistory of the Idea of Vicarious Suffering in the Old Testament," in *The Suffering Servant: Isaiah 53 in Jewish and Christian Sources,* ed. Bernd Janowski and Peter Stuhlmacher, trans. Daniel P. Bailey (Grand Rapids: Eerdmans, 2004), 13.

85. Spieckermann, "The Conception and Prehistory of the Idea of Vicarious Suffering," 14.

However, Christ is now our "wisdom from God," "who became to us wisdom from God, righteousness and sanctification and redemption" (1 Cor 1:24, 30). Christ has fulfilled the act-consequence principle at the heart of wisdom traditions, including Torah, becoming our righteousness. And now, the only sacrifice left *for us* is the nonbloody, living sacrifice of praise and thanksgiving.[86]

Now, at last, the vocation for which we were created has been recovered, but it does not come through our fulfillment of the Adamic covenant of law. Rather, it comes by being united to Christ through faith for both justification and renewal according to his image. Through union with Christ we can now love and serve our neighbors in joyful freedom, released from bondage to the act-consequence connection. What Jesus endured faithfully and joyfully was the vocation for which humanity was created—the complete love of God and fellow humans that won the right for him, and for us in him, to eat from the Tree of Life. And now the Holy Spirit unites us to Christ through faith so that, with Abraham and Sarah, we are *judicially restored* to the status of covenant-keepers and *gradually conformed* to the image of the faithful Son, sharing in his vocation as prophets, priests, and kings. It is therefore not in our fulfillment of the covenant of vocation but in our participation in his faithful execution of that calling through faith that we are led in triumphal procession into the everlasting Sabbath, spreading the fragrance of life as we go (2 Cor 2:14).

JESUS AND SINAI: THE PRIORITY OF THE ABRAHAMIC COVENANT

If I am not mistaken, the absorption of the Abrahamic covenant into the Sinaitic is precisely the target of Paul's sharp polemic—but not Paul alone. Already with John the Baptist there is the incendiary announcement that a coming division within the house of Israel is coming, and the true Israel will be defined by faith in Christ. As N. T. Wright puts it, Jesus redraws the boundaries of Israel around himself, and this lies at the heart of Paul's teaching.[87]

---

86. On this comparison of the believer as a "living sacrifice" to the cereal or wave offering in Leviticus, see Laura Smit, "Justification and Sacrifice," in *What Is Justification About? Reformed Contributions to an Ecumenical Theme*, ed. Michael Weinrich and John P. Burgess (Grand Rapids: Eerdmans, 2009), 145.

87. Wright, *Paul: In Fresh Perspective*, 115–22.

The history of both covenants is in view when John the Baptist appears on the scene. He upbraids the religious leaders for imagining that they have an unconditional and inviolable *national* covenant with Yahweh and that, consequently, they are true children of Abraham simply because they are his *physical* descendants (Matt 3:7–10). Even before Jesus takes up his ministry, then, the religious leaders are targeted: "You brood of vipers! Who warned you to flee from the wrath to come?" (v. 7). The last judgment is on the horizon, dividing Israel from the gentile world, vindicating them as God's people, but separating the house of Israel itself. They must repent and receive John's baptism in preparation for the Messiah. "And do not presume to say to yourselves, 'We have Abraham as our father,' for I tell you, God is able from these stones to raise up children for Abraham. Even now the axe is laid to the root of the trees. Every tree therefore that does not bear good fruit is cut down and thrown into the fire" (vv. 9–10). And then all attention turns to "the Lamb of God who takes away the sin of the world" (John 1:29), for "he who is coming after me is mightier than I" and "will baptize you with the Holy Spirit and fire." "His winnowing fork is in his hand, and he will clear his threshing floor and gather his wheat into the barn, but the chaff he will burn with unquenchable fire" (Matt 2:11–12).

John the Baptist himself seems more like an Old Testament prophet—or an Essene defender of Torah—in comparison to Jesus. According to the evangelists, he distinguishes explicitly between his and Jesus's ministry and baptism. Hartmut Stegemann observes that while there are many reasons why it would have made more practical sense for John to have baptized on the right bank of the Jordan—or in the many flowing streams, private homes, or public baths—he baptizes on the left bank of the Jordan because it is explicitly reenacting the crossing of the Jordan from the east, from the desert to the Promised Land.[88] "'Preservation' from annihilation in the coming Last Judgment was John's specific salvific stamp, his baptism its visible side. . . . Never before had there been anyone who performed a baptismal rite."[89] And John was undoubtedly of priestly birth. Hence, "John did not lead the people of Israel *through* the Jordan into the Holy Land, as Joshua once had (Joshua 3–4). Instead,

---

88. Hartmut Stegemann, *The Library of Qumran: On the Essenes, Qumran, John the Baptist, and Jesus* (Grand Rapids: Eerdmans, 1998), 214.
89. Stegemann, *The Library of Qumran*, 219.

he led them *to the border* of this crossing."[90] Even Josephus found interesting enough to emphasize (*Antiquities* 18.117) that the Baptizer never forgives sins; he only declaims the sins of the people and calls them to repentance. John's baptism was "only *unto* the forgiveness of sins."

Here we may also note that there is a sense in which John corresponds not only to Elijah but to Moses, with Jesus foreshadowed by Joshua. Jesus himself marks the difference between his and John's ministries. Matthew 11 records Jesus as telling his audience,

> But to what shall I compare this generation? It is like children sitting in the marketplaces and calling to their playmates,
>
> > "We played the flute for you, and you did not dance;
> > we sang a dirge, and you did not mourn."
>
> For John came neither eating nor drinking, and they say, "He has a demon." The Son of Man came eating and drinking, and they say, "Look at him! A glutton and a drunkard, a friend of tax collectors and sinners!" Yet wisdom is justified by her deeds. (vv. 16–19)

Jesus's answer to the Pharisees concerning why his disciples abstained from the fast is also illustrative: "And Jesus said to them, 'Can the wedding guests fast while the bridegroom is with them? As long as they have the bridegroom with them, they cannot fast'" (Mark 2:19). John's ministry was clearly on the fasting and mourning side of things, but Jesus, the bridegroom, has arrived for his wedding day.

Already with the Baptist, then, the critique is that the religious leaders have assimilated the Abrahamic promise to Sinai: a single covenantal nomism that is gracious in the sense of God's superabundance and priority but not in terms of incongruity. They presume that they are children of Abraham because of their ancestry and covenant fidelity instead of becoming children of Abraham through faith in Christ. The religious leaders have not read the turning of the times. "For the law was given through Moses; grace and truth came through Jesus Christ" (John 1:17).

---

90. Stegemann, *The Library of Qumran*, 220. He adds, interestingly, that in Jesus's context "Nazarene" meant not someone who comes from Nazareth but someone from John's circle: Nazarene (Mark 1:24; 10:47; 14:67; 16:6; Luke 4:34; 24:19) or Nazaroean (Matt 2:23; 26:71; Luke 18:37; John 18:5, 7; Acts 2:22; 3:6; 4:10; 6:14; 22:8; 24:5; 26:9).

It is crucial to observe that John does not challenge the religious leaders for trying to keep the law but, as Paul will say also, for *failing* to keep it—not for excluding gentiles but for exiling themselves and fellow Jews. This is the problem in light of God's coming judgment. The leaders assume quite mistakenly that they have kept Torah and that by tightening the screws on the nation's obedience to it, God's gracious intervention will be even more fitting. But they have a shallow diagnosis and, consequently, a shallow cure. If the messianic era were in fact a revival of the Sinai covenant, then the Pharisees would have been doing precisely what was called for in that moment: doubling down on the pure/impure distinction and excluding the latter from everything belonging to the former. The last thing one would have expected in a renewal of the Sinai covenant is precisely what Jesus was doing in associating with sinners. Like Paul, John the Baptist already begins the gospel by announcing that the word of God has not failed, for not all who are Abraham's physical descendants are his true offspring. Jesus continues this message throughout his ministry.

Everything that Jesus is doing in his ministry is fulfilling what the prophets had announced concerning the Abrahamic covenant: a world-wide family through the promised seed. Rather than an abstract contrast between faith and works, the Messiah's works are contrasted with ours. Christ is the fulfillment of the law as well as the promises, so to be united to him is to be a true child of Abraham. God himself would transfer the guilt of his people to the Suffering Servant and transfer to them the righteousness of this obedient Son (Isa 53). In the new covenant, Yahweh himself will mediate, judge, and justify, bringing salvation to the earth (Isa 59; Jer 23:5–6; 33:16; 1 Cor 2:30–31; 2 Cor 5:21). Therefore, not by setting aside the covenant of works but by fulfilling all righteousness and bearing the sanctions on our behalf, the Last Adam wins the right for himself and for his posterity to eat from the Tree of Life. Jesus's vocation is to "fulfill all righteousness" (Matt 3:14–15; cf. Matt 5:17; John 4:34; 8:29; Heb 10:8–10; Ps 40:7–8).

Jesus faces the serpent in the wilderness in a temptation that virtually repeats the seducer's script in Genesis 3. This time, however, Jesus answers Satan as Adam should have: responding with God's Word to the blandishments of power and glory. The same account is given in Matthew 4:1–11 and Luke 4:1–13, both echoing Moses's receiving of the words of the law while fasting forty days and forty nights (Exod 34:28).

We are led by the evangelists to see Jesus as recapitulating Adam's trial as well as that of Israel in its forty-year wandering, in order that he might fulfill all righteousness. As the covenant servant, he is bringing the human order back into alignment with the righteous word of Yahweh, answering, "Here I am," instead of fleeing God's voice.

It is true that Jesus criticized the Pharisees for their externalism (Matt 5:21–48) and hypocrisy (Matt 6:1–18; 15:1–20; 23:1–31) and their propensity to observe their own traditions ("oral Torah") over Scripture itself (Mark 7:9). However, that is not the center of his critique. Jesus may have been criticized by the religious leaders for not observing oral Torah (Matt 15:2), yet when it came to Torah itself, Jesus raised the bar:

> Do not think that I have come to abolish the Law or the Prophets; I have not come to abolish them but to fulfill them. For truly, I say to you, until heaven and earth pass away, not an iota, not a dot, will pass from the Law until all is accomplished. Therefore whoever relaxes one of the least of these commandments and teaches others to do the same will be called least in the kingdom of heaven, but whoever does them and teaches them will be called great in the kingdom of heaven. For I tell you, unless your righteousness exceeds that of the scribes and Pharisees, you will never enter the kingdom of heaven. (Matt 5:17–20)

The rest of Jesus's sermon drives home the point that the moral commands are violated in the heart even if the hands have not carried out the act (viz., lust is adultery, hatred is murder, etc.).

Jesus was hardly a kinder Moses. No one loved Torah more than Jesus, the Word incarnate. Jesus was convinced that the religious leaders—representatives of Second Temple Judaism—had simultaneously *relaxed* the requirements of Torah and *imposed* their own strict regulations (Matt 23:4). Furthermore, they prided themselves on being biblical scholars but failed to recognize the clear testimony of Moses and the prophets about him (John 5:46). Seeking their life in Torah, they refused to embrace the Word incarnate (John 5:39). So once again the issue is not an abstract "legalism," but the failure to recognize in Jesus the Messiah the *telos* of redemptive history. When Jesus adds, "My yoke is easy, and my burden is light" (Matt 11:28–30), he is not merely saying that he is a more lenient Moses. As Larry R. Helyer points out,

"Jesus' criticism went much deeper than specific religious practices, which are ineffectual to deal with the real problem facing humanity (Mk 7:20–23)."

> Already Mark's Gospel preserves a saying of Jesus that points in a different direction: "For the Son of Man came not to be served but to serve, and to give his life a ransom for many" (Mk 10:45; cf. Mt 20:28). The NT presentation of Jesus' death as an atonement for the sins of the world (cf. Jn 3:16; Rom 3:25; Gal 1:3–4; 1 Jn 2:2) differs sharply from all other expressions of Judaism during the Second Temple period. It insists that acceptance before God is received as a gift *through faith in Jesus Christ alone.* In theological terms, salvation is rooted in Christology (i.e., the person and work of Christ).[91]

If Paul misunderstood Second Temple Judaism, then Jesus did as well, at least according to the well-attested reports of the evangelists.

Jesus has not come to give the Sinai covenant an extension but to fulfill it and bring it to an end. He repeatedly pressed the religious leaders (and the crowds listening in) with the demands of the law, which they had not kept. So it was not merely that they were going beyond Torah or interpreting it in a superficial manner but that they had in fact become "blind guides" who lead others astray (Matt 15:14); in fact, they had become wicked tenants of the Lord's estate (Matt 21:33–46). Dawning in his ministry and sealed by his death, the new covenant renders the old covenant obsolete. Rather than sacrifices, God delights to show mercy, Jesus says. "For I came not to call the righteous, but sinners" (Matt 9:13). The time for fasting is over, for the groom has come. To confuse these two covenants Jesus says, is analogous to sewing a new patch on an old garment or pouring new wine in old wineskins (vv. 14–17).

Given this background in Jesus's own teaching, it is not surprising that as Donald Hagner puts it, "Paul's Christianity is christocentric, not nomocentric."[92] Yet these should not be set in abstract opposition. As christocentric, Paul's message highlights the goodness and inviolability of the law. Only by cherishing, keeping, and fulfilling the law and

---

91. Larry R. Helyer, *Exploring Jewish Literature of the Second Temple Period* (Downers Grove, IL: InterVarsity, 2002), 40.

92. Donald Hagner, "The Law of Moses in Matthew and Paul," *Interpretation* 51 (1997): 27.

bearing its curse did Jesus redeem and justify its violators. Whatever quibbles I have with Sanders's description of early Judaism and its gracious character, I concur with his conclusion that what Paul found wrong with Judaism ultimately was that it lacked Christ. But of course, that is everything.

In Jesus's actions and speeches, he highlights the good news of the gospel to "sinners," while he emphasizes the law with the Pharisees. In Luke 10, Jesus is tested by a scribe:

> And behold, a lawyer stood up to put him to the test, saying, "Teacher, what shall I do to inherit eternal life?" He said to him, "What is written in the Law? How do you read it?" And he answered, "You shall love the Lord your God with all your heart and with all your soul and with all your strength and with all your mind, and your neighbor as yourself." And he said to him, "You have answered correctly; do this, and you will live. (vv. 25–28)

The conclusion, "do this, and you will live," should be familiar by now. It is the formula for a law-covenant. It appears in the covenant with Adam, as the threat, "You shall surely die" (Gen 2:17), and the promise of eating from the Tree of Life. This sanction-formula lies at the heart of the covenant at Sinai. It is not a covenant of mercy but of personal, perfect, and perpetual obedience. If one seeks to be justified on these terms, then one must love in a wholly self-sacrificial manner. Pure love of God and neighbor has always been the summary of God's law. Surely the scribe knew this. "But he, desiring to justify himself, said to Jesus, 'And who is my neighbor?'" (v. 29).

Luke makes it evident that the scribe was not a sincere inquirer; Jesus turns the tables and puts his interlocutor to the test. Jesus did not come to be a new and improved Moses, revealing a new rule or condition that had been hidden in past ages, but to be the Last Adam and faithful Israel. If the scribe is determined to have eternal life by the law, then he should know what it requires: perfect love of God and neighbor. Justification cannot be secured apart from the fulfillment of the law. No one can accomplish this, even with God's gracious assistance. The scribe, "desiring to justify himself" (v. 29), found Jesus's interpretation of the law impossible. It is clear from Jesus's statement, "Do this and you shall live," that Jesus was not proclaiming the gospel but leading the scribe to despair by illuminating the Torah he thought he kept. Compare this with the argument in Romans 2:

> Do you suppose, O man—you who judge those who practice such things and yet do them yourself—that you will escape the judgment of God? Or do you presume on the riches of his kindness and forbearance and patience, not knowing that God's kindness is meant to lead you to repentance? But because of your hard and impenitent heart you are storing up wrath for yourself on the day of wrath when God's righteous judgment will be revealed. He will render to each one according to his works. (vv. 3–6)

To those who trust in the law, Jesus says in effect what Paul does in Galatians 4:21: "Tell me, you who desire to be under the law, do you not listen to the law?" Indeed, Paul's exposure of hypocrisy and self-righteousness in Romans 2 mirrors that of Jesus at various points in his interchanges with the Pharisees, especially his "woes" in Matthew 23. "But woe to you, scribes and Pharisees, hypocrites! For you shut the kingdom of heaven in people's faces. For you neither enter yourselves nor allow those who would enter to go in" (Matt 23:13). The religious leaders are accused of tying down loads that they themselves do not keep, of refusing to enter the messianic kingdom, apart from any question about boundary markers.

The same point is made in Jesus's parable of the publican and the Pharisee in Luke 18: "He also told this parable to some who trusted in themselves that they were righteous, and treated others with contempt" (v. 9). Under the guise of praising God's grace, the Pharisee was parading his superior righteousness over against the publican who was crying out, "Lord, be merciful to me, a sinner!" "I tell you," Jesus says of the publican, "this man went down to his house justified, rather than the other. For everyone who exalts himself will be humbled, but the one who humbles himself will be exalted" (vv. 13–14). Luke therefore emphasizes Jesus's critique of the Pharisees as self-justification: "desiring to justify himself," "you seek to justify yourselves before men" (16:15), and "he spoke this parable to certain people who trusted in themselves that they were righteous" (18:9–11).

It is significant that the religious leaders are characterized as those "who trusted in themselves that they were righteous." There is no controversy yet about gentile inclusion. Everyone—at least the targets of Jesus's rebukes—is circumcised and keeps the feasts, Sabbath, and dietary laws. Jesus never upbraids the religious leaders for failing to keep kosher, and the Pharisees' consternation with Jesus and the disciples over certain rituals concerned the tradition of the elders rather than Torah itself (Matt 15:1–9). While ethnic superiority and ceremonial purity were no doubt involved, the focus of Jesus's critique is that they *trusted in themselves that they were righteous* and therefore did not cry out to Jesus for mercy.

> And the Pharisees and their scribes grumbled at his disciples, saying, "Why do you eat and drink with tax collectors and sinners?" And Jesus answered them, "Those who are well have no need of a physician, but those who are sick. I have not come to call the righteous but sinners to repentance." (Luke 5:30–32)

The religious leaders should have taken their place alongside the prostitutes and tax collectors, clinging to Christ for mercy, but instead they wanted to exclude these very people from the holy places so that God would look favorably on them and send his Messiah to deliver them. Circumcision was not for them a sign and seal of the justification that they had through faith but a badge of false security. According to this interpretation, then, circumcision plays a large role, indeed (especially with the gentile mission) as a badge of exclusion. But, as we see in these Lukan narratives, this desire to justify themselves *before others* went hand-in-hand with their desire to justify themselves *before God*. After all, Jesus said nothing to the rich young ruler about ceremonies yet pressed the claims of the moral law.

But after exile, God's promise of election still stands. Although it is not correlative with Abraham's physical offspring, this election to everlasting life by no means excludes them. Paul's argument in Romans 9–11 begins with the "remnant chosen by grace" even "at the present time," with Jews like Paul himself as examples of the fulfillment of this pledge. Yet the argument grows to include a wider regathering of the ethnic descendants after the era of calling the gentile elect into the vine of Israel is completed.

Just as the Pharisees and Paul's opponents had conflated the two covenants, they had conflated the two elections: the physical seed, identified by circumcision, and the spiritual seed of Abraham, identified by faith. It is one thing to make this identification when the people of God (i.e., the church) is identified with one nation, but now that Christ has come and the word of the prophets is being fulfilled, that which has been true all along (viz., that justification through faith makes one a true child of Abraham) becomes tested by the reality of gentile inclusion. "In Adam" Israel stands condemned along with the gentiles (Rom 3:9–20; 5:12–14), yet "in Christ" Jew and gentile are justified together through faith (Rom 3:21–26; 5:15–21). Given this conflation of covenants in the days of Jesus and Paul, it is not surprising that the type of religion that one finds in Second Temple Judaism can be characterized as "covenantal nomism." However, it is just at this point where Christianity parted ways with Judaism—and continues to part ways with every confusion of the law and the gospel.

Therefore, we ought to find implausible any interpretation of the Bible's "covenant theology" that cannot account for Paul's contrast between these "two covenants" (Gal 4:24). Similarly, Hebrews 6 interprets Genesis 15 as the anchor for new covenant believers:

> For when God made a promise to Abraham, since he had no one greater by whom to swear, he swore by himself, saying, "Surely I will bless you and multiply you." And thus Abraham, having patiently waited, obtained the promise. For people swear by something greater than themselves, and in all their disputes an oath is final for confirmation. So when God desired to show more convincingly to the heirs of the promise the unchangeable character of his purpose, he guaranteed it with an oath, so that by two unchangeable things, in which it is impossible for God to lie, we who have fled for refuge might have strong encouragement to hold fast to the hope set before us. (vv. 13–18)

Consequently, we have come not to Sinai, which provoked such terror

> that Moses said, "I tremble with fear." But you have come to Mount Zion and to the city of the living God, the heavenly Jerusalem, and to innumerable angels in festal gathering, and to the assembly of the firstborn who are enrolled in heaven, and to God, the judge of all, and to the spirits of the righteous made perfect, and to Jesus, the mediator of a new covenant, and to the sprinkled blood that speaks a better word than the blood of Abel. (Heb 12:21–24)

CHAPTER 2

"WORKS OF THE LAW" IN PAUL

"Get in by grace, stay in by obedience." This definition of covenantal nomism by E. P. Sanders fits perfectly well with Israel's national status in the land. But Israel knew also of a covenant that God swore to Abraham concerning a promised offspring who would bring redemption to the world. Following Abraham, they believed that promise and were justified.

These two covenants, one governing "long life in the land," and the other guaranteeing an unconditional gift of grace, coexisted in the consciousness of the people. Remarkably, the identification of these distinct covenants appears already in the Covenant Code of Sinai itself. In Deuteronomy 10:16, the Israelites are commanded to circumcise their hearts, while Yahweh promises in Deuteronomy 30:6 that after the nation's failure to keep the covenant, he will circumcise their hearts.[1] Confusing these covenants is the basic problem of Paul's agitators, and it provides the specific context for Paul's polemic against "works of the law" (ἔργων νόμου).

The new perspective on Paul has delivered us from sweeping and erroneous caricatures about early Judaism associated especially with Bultmann. Paul does not set out to describe Judaism as "a religion of x" (i.e., legalism, self-righteousness, or even ethnic superiority). At the same time, we should not assume that Paul either exaggerated the

---

1. Obviously, one's interpretation depends on one's view of whether Deut 30:6 is part of a postexilic interpolation rather than predictive prophecy original to the code itself. I take the latter view, but either way it is the case that postexilic Israel possessed what it took to be a uniform covenantal document in which these two covenants were distinguished.

"legalism" of his Jewish contemporaries or that his polemics have nothing to do with relying on one's own righteousness for salvation from the wrath of God.

Based on the last chapters of Acts, one could conclude that Paul considered himself the true heir of Pharisaic Judaism.[2] With respect to Paul's Jewish contemporaries, E. P. Sanders is correct in saying that what the apostle found wrong with Judaism was that it was not Christianity. But he—and the new perspective generally—too frequently assume that Second Temple Judaism was in fundamental continuity with the Law and the Prophets and thus judge Paul by comparison with its "pattern of religion." Jesus, however, upbraided the disciples themselves for failing to recognize him as the central character in Israel's story (Luke 24:27). Jesus and his apostles saw themselves as the nucleus of the true Israel in continuity with the prophets and in considerable contrast with their contemporaries.

After Pentecost, the apostles' christological interpretation of Israel's Scriptures underscores the fact that at least they believed they were the faithful rabbis. Although Sanders and others are correct to contrast Paul's "pattern of religion" (viz., being in Christ) with the Judaism of his day, Paul grounds everything that he says in the Hebrew Scriptures (especially the Psalms and Prophets). Thus he remains a rabbi, not an innovator but an exegete of Israel's sacred texts—albeit one with the advantage of having encountered Israel's enthroned Messiah in person. His "brothers according to the flesh" are ignorant of the righteousness that comes by faith and instead pursue justification by works (Rom 10:1–5). Regardless of what anyone makes of that claim vis-à-vis Second Temple Judaism, that is how things look from the vista of the gospel that Paul proclaimed.

WORKS OF THE LAW IN PAUL AND SECOND TEMPLE JUDAISM

There are very few references in the ancient Jewish literature to "works of the law" in the formulaic way that Paul employs it. A section of 4QMMT titled Some Works of the Law exhorts recipients who "have aptitude and knowledge regarding the law." It even adds, "And it will

---

2. I am grateful to my colleague Zach Keele for this insight.

be reckoned to you as righteousness when you do what is upright and what is good in his presence, for the good of yourselves and for Israel" (4Q398 ii:2–3, 7).[3] Here, as in Paul, "works of the law" are things to be *done*. Further, drawing upon the example of Phinehas (Num 25:6–13; Ps 106:28–31) and Genesis 15:6, 4QMMT interprets justification as "finally based on one's observance of the Torah," Jason Maston and Aaron Sherwood observe. God's aid is needed in understanding it. "Nevertheless, . . . one must not downplay the emphasis here on obeying the Torah as the means to righteousness."[4] Fitzmyer also points out that the "righteousness of God" is inextricably related to the "works of the law" in early Judaism. Referencing 4QMMT, he says, "In these writings it clearly means things prescribed by the Mosaic Law, and in the latter passage [4QH—Thanksgiving Hymn], it occurs in a context that speaks of 'righteousness.'"[5]

It is in the context of the anticipation of final judgment that the question, "Who is the true Israel?" becomes especially acute, eliding any dichotomy between ecclesiology and soteriology. To belong to the true Israel *is* to escape the coming wrath. Answers were given along a broad spectrum. Not all spoke of only a few being saved, as Qumran or 4 Ezra did, but even the Pharisaic elites in Jerusalem were anxiously enforcing ritual cleanness to ensure that as much of the nation as possible would be among the resurrection of the just and enjoy the messianic age.

The Hebrew prophets had already provided an inner critique of externalism and hypocrisy. But this prophetic element appears in the law itself (Deut 10:16; 30:6–10; cf. Jer 4:4), Qumran (1QpHab 11.13), and Philo (*On the Special Laws* 1.305). The more sectarian groups like Qumran align themselves with the prophetic tradition over against the Deuteronomic school with its various Jerusalem-centered rabbis. When it comes to suffering, Qumran's Community Rule identifies with the prophets' indictment of Jerusalem's and its temple's wicked leadership. But it is important to note that while Qumran shared the prophets' criticism of merely external religion, their alternative was to greater and deeper personal devotion to Torah. Qumran was "scrupulous for

3. Jason Maston and Aaron Sherwood, "4QMMT and Romans 3:1–20: Works of the Law and Justification," in *Reading Romans in Context: Paul and Second Temple Judaism*, ed. Ben C. Blackwell, John K. Goodrich, and Jason Maston (Grand Rapids: Zondervan, 2015), 52.
4. Maston and Sherwood, "4QMMT and Romans 3:1–20," 55.
5. Joseph A. Fitzmyer, SJ, *The Dead Sea Scrolls and Christian Origins* (Grand Rapids: Eerdmans, 2000), 30.

purity," obedient to the letter, and deeply committed to inward piety and devotion.[6]

So the rabbis in Jerusalem and the sectarians in the desert were equally convinced that preparation for the Messiah required more intense devotion to the law.[7] An important part of Tannaitic Midrashim is Sipre Deuteronomy. "*Sipre* sees the covenant in legal-contractual terms as an agreement entered into freely by two parties in the presence of witnesses."[8] According to *pisqa* 343, the Lord offered the Torah first to the children of Esau, who rejected its commands, and then to the other nations. So he came to Israel, which happily embraced it, and God saw that Israel was able to bear the burden. "The blessings of the covenant are conditional," Philip S. Alexander observes. "The gift of the Land is, apparently, not absolute. If the terms of the covenant are not fulfilled then Israel is handed over to the nations and exiled from her own Land."[9]

Hypocrisy was a major charge of the Qumran exiles (the Yahad) against the Jerusalem leadership. "By aligning themselves with the prophetic tradition, the Yahad associates their wicked opponents with those who have the appearance of righteousness due to their prosperity but are actually in breach of covenant faithfulness (cf. 1 En. 96:4)."[10] Hence the transgressors in the community itself were dealt with strictly. As the end-time regathering of the twelve tribes, the Qumran community could not tolerate any impurity. Jubilees "follows Genesis 17 quite closely," Sarah Whittle observes, picking up on "this idea of

---

6. Richard N. Longenecker, *Paul, Apostle of Liberty*, 2nd ed. (Grand Rapids: Eerdmans, 2015), 74.

7. Recently, some specialists have called into question the entire notion of a Qumran community establishing itself outside of Jerusalem. They argue instead that the sectarians were Jerusalem based and merely fled with their scrolls with the advance of Roman troops. See David Stacey and Gregory Doudna, *Qumran Revisited: A Reassessment of the Archaeology of the Site and Its Texts*, BAR International Series 2520 (Oxford: Archaeopress, 2013). Regardless, the teachings and practices of this group remain in some tension with aspects of the official Jerusalem regime. (Thanks to my colleague, S. M. Baugh for this reference.)

8. Quoted in Philip S. Alexander, "Torah and Salvation in Tannaitic Literature," *Justification and Variegated Nomism*, vol. 1, *The Complexities of Second Temple Judaism*, ed. D. A. Carson, Peter T. O'Brien, and Mark A. Seifrid, WUNT 2/140 (Grand Rapids: Baker Academic, 2001), 289–90.

9. Quoted in Alexander, "Torah and Salvation in Tannaitic Literature," 293.

10. Mark D. Matthews, "*Community Rule* and Romans 5:1–11: The Relationship between Justification and Suffering," *Reading Romans in Context: Paul and Second Temple Judaism*, eds. Ben C. Blackwell, John K. Goodrich, and Jason Maston (Grand Rapids: Zondervan, 2015), 75; cf. Moshe Weinfeld, *Deuteronomy and the Deuteronomic School* (Oxford: Clarendon, 1972). One can almost hear Troeltsch whispering his famous contrast of church-consciousness and sect-consciousness in such descriptions of early Judaism, but there does appear to be a remarkable family resemblance among sectarian religious movements across time and place. By definition, they are outside the mainstream—yet only because they believe that they are more truly the heir to the ongoing "mainstream" heritage than those presently in power.

'internalizing' circumcision as an eschatological category in 1:23–24."[11] The text also follows Jeremiah 31, in which God alone promises to circumcise hearts in the new covenant.[12]

As we saw in the previous chapter, the angel Uriel in 4 Ezra relates that God will circumcise the hearts of the elect in the age to come so they will no longer sin, but only *after* the final judgment; the only way of surviving that judgment is by circumcising one's own heart and keeping all of God's rules, as Deuteronomy 10:16 commands. Sanders points to the conclusion of the conversation between Ezra and Uriel in 4 Ezra: "It is better for transgressors to perish than for the glory of the law to be besmirched by having mercy on them."[13]

Richard Bauckham discovers the same emphases in 1 Enoch, dating from before the middle of the second century BC.[14] The Book of Watchers warns of the coming separation of elect and nonelect, with doom for the latter, but interestingly the judgment takes place at Mount Sinai, not Zion. The unfaithful among Israel are very much included in the destruction of the wicked gentiles.[15] A much later (late first-century AD) text, 2 Enoch has "no reference whatever to the mercy of God" across its 72 chapters. "As Andersen justifiably puts it: 'A blessed afterlife is strictly a reward for right ethical behavior.'"[16] The scales will be just on that great day, and "each [person] will be weighed in the balance, and each will stand in the market" to be measured, "and in accordance with that measurement each will receive his reward." Bauckham adds, "In the *Testament of Abraham* (A12–14; B9) it is clear that people are assigned according to whether their sins outnumber their righteous deeds. . . . It is clear that for 2 Enoch all of Adam's descendants have the same free choice as Adam had."[17]

---

11. Sarah Whittle, "*Jubilees* and Romans 2:6–29: Circumcision, Law Observance, and Ethnicity," in *Reading Romans in Context: Paul and Second Temple Judaism*, ed. Ben C. Blackwell, John K. Goodrich, and Jason Maston (Grand Rapids: Zondervan, 2015), 47.

12. See *The Book of Jubilees*, in *The Apocrypha and Pseudepigrapha of the Old Testament in English: With Introductions and Critical and Explanatory Notes to the Several Books*, 2 vols., ed. R. H. Charles (Oxford: Clarendon, 1913); cf. N. T. Wright, "The Law in Romans 2," in *Paul and the Mosaic Law*, ed. James Dunn (Grand Rapids: Eerdmans, 2001), 131–50.

13. Quoted in E. P. Sanders, *Paul and Palestinian Judaism: A Comparison of Patterns of Religion* (Philadelphia: Fortress, 1977), 416.

14. Richard Bauckham, "Apocalypses," in *Justification and Variegated Nomism*, vol. 1, *The Complexities of Second Temple Judaism*, ed. D. A. Carson, Peter T. O'Brien, and Mark A. Seifrid, WUNT 2/140 (Grand Rapids: Baker Academic, 2001), 137.

15. Bauckham, "Apocalypses," 140–46.

16. Bauckham, "Apocalypses," 156, quoting F. I. Andersen, "2 (Slavonic Apocalypse of) Enoch: A New Translation and Introduction," in *The Old Testament Pseudepigrapha*, 2 vols., ed. J. H. Charlesworth (New York: Doubleday, 1983), 1:96.

17. Bauckham, "Apocalypses," 154–55.

The Dead Sea Scrolls reveal a community that, while invoking divine grace, made works the basis for acquittal at the day of judgment.[18] The wicked fathers were justly exiled, according to the Damascus Document, but God raised up a few who held to Torah. "But God considered their deeds" and delivered them. Yet even after this, many followed the "Man of Mockery" and "were handed over to the sword that avenges the breach of his covenant." God "annihilated the lot of them, because all their deeds were uncleanness to him."[19]

For everyone, and especially the Yahad, "Who is the true Israel?" meant, "Who will be saved when the Lord comes to judge in his wrath?" "A striking parallel between Qumran and the NT," says Larry R. Helyer, "lies in the conviction of both communities that the new covenant prophesied by Jeremiah (cf. Jer 31:31–34; cf. Ezek 16:60–62) had been established between God and a repentant remnant."[20] But far from the obsolescence of the Sinai covenant (2 Cor 3:4–18 and Heb 8:6–13), for Qumran it is doubling-down on the law.[21] Helyer concludes,

> Though both stressed the priority of grace, for the Teacher, "works of the law" were essential for obtaining final salvation. For the NT, "works of the law" result in condemnation (Gal 2:16; 3:10–14). Instead, one needs to be liberated from the "works of the law" and united with Jesus Christ in his death, burial and resurrection (Rom 6:1–4, 15–19; 7:1–11). This, paradoxically, results in a true fulfillment of the law (cf. Rom 8:1–8). Union with Christ brings about justification and sanctification (Rom 8:1–17).[22]

Paul's encounter with Christ caused him to relinquish his "confidence in the flesh" (Phil 3:5), but a view of humanity as deeply corrupt was not unknown in Second Temple literature, as we have seen already from 4 Ezra. Paul's stark view of human sinfulness echoes the Old Testament (e.g., Pss 51, 103, 143), Joseph Fitzmyer observes, but such a

---

18. Michael Wise, Martin Abegg Jr., and Edward Cook, trans., *The Dead Sea Scrolls: A New Translation* (NY: HarperCollins, 1999). The group's literary remains date between 150 BC and AD 68.

19. Wise, Abegg, Cook, trans., *Dead Sea Scrolls*, 52 (A 1–1–2:1).

20. Larry R. Helyer, *Exploring Jewish Literature of the Second Temple Period* (Downers Grove, IL: InterVarsity, 2002), 205.

21. Helyer, *Exploring Jewish Literature of the Second Temple Period*, 206.

22. Helyer, *Exploring Jewish Literature of the Second Temple Period*, 261; cf. 235.

view also appears in Qumran's Manual of Discipline, as we have seen.[23] Particularly striking here is the stark awareness of one's own sharing in a "wicked humanity."

So too "Paul's teaching about *dikaiōsis*, 'justification,' as an effect of the Christ event," according to Fitzmyer, "is also derived from his Old Testament and Jewish background" as "above all a judicial relationship." Josephus seeks "to achieve that status of rectitude before God the Judge" by obeying the commandments (*Against Apion* 2.41.293), and a similar piety appears in the Qumran literature. However, one also finds reflections like the following from 1QS 11.11–15:

> If I stumble because of a sin of the flesh, my judgment is according to God's righteousness. . . . In His mercy He has drawn me close (to Him), and with His favors will He render judgment of me. He has judged me in His righteous fidelity; in His bounteous goodness He expiates all my iniquities, and in His righteousness He cleanses me of human defilement and of human sinfulness, that I may praise God for His righteousness and the Most High for His majesty.[24]

Similarly, according to 1QH 12.35–37,

> And I said, It is because of my transgression that I have been abandoned far from Your covenant. But when I recalled Your mighty hand along with the abundance of Your mercy, then I was restored and I stood up; my spirit strengthened my stance against blows, because [I] have based myself on Your grace and on the abundance of Your mercy. For You expiate iniquity to clean[se a human b]eing from guilt by Your righteousness.[25]

So it is certainly true that appeals to God's mercy and forgiveness in view of an intractable sinfulness exist alongside the weighing of merits. The difference is that Paul sees this as the effect of the Christ-event: "'By grace' and 'through faith in Christ Jesus' (Rom 3:22) are the Pauline

---

23. "As for me, I belong to wicked humanity, to the assembly of perverse flesh; my iniquities, my transgressions, my sins together with the wickedness of my heart belong to the assembly doomed to worms and walking in darkness" (1QS 11:9–10), as quoted in Joseph A. Fitzmyer, SJ, "Paul's Jewish Background and the Deeds of the Law," in *According to Paul: Studies in the Theology of the Apostle* (New York: Paulist, 1993), 24.

24. Quoted by Fitzmyer, "Paul's Jewish Background and the Deeds of the Law," 25–26.

25. Quoted by Fitzmyer, "Paul's Jewish Background and the Deeds of the Law," 25–26.

specifications added to the early Christian teaching about Christ as our righteousness (1 Cor 1:30) that he may have inherited."[26] Hence, there is no tension between God's mercy and our works in justification. Christ alone has merited it for us.

Paul clearly uses the phrase "works of the law" critically, as the antithesis to faith, Christ, and grace. However, it is not an abstract antithesis (*pace* Bultmann and, to a certain extent, Barth and Käsemann). For Paul, the law is good when used properly (1 Tim 1:8). Torah is a gift, Moses said, that demonstrated God's intimate and discriminating love for Israel (Deut 4:7). When the fourth gospel announces, "For the law was given through Moses; grace and truth came through Jesus Christ" (John 1:17), there is no intimation of a contrast between bad and good, only of good and better—marvelously, qualitatively, astonishingly better. It is the same argument from lesser to greater that we meet in 2 Corinthians 3 and throughout the Letter to the Hebrews. Paul teaches in many places, in fact, that the gospel liberates us to obey the law from the heart, in the Spirit, for the first time. Good works are only antithetical to faith as the means of both getting in and staying in the covenant; relying only on Christ, faith bears the fruit of love and good works.

The question therefore is not whether grace is intrinsically opposed to law but which one forms the basis for the inheritance of immortal life, eating and drinking—and reigning—with God in Christ. In other words, we have to understand Paul's meaning of "works of the law" in his own context, in terms of the role that those works play in the story of the "two covenants," law, and promise (Gal 4:24).

GRACE OR RACE? ETHNIC BADGES VERSUS "WORKS-RIGHTEOUSNESS"

"What, then, can it be to which Paul is objecting?"[27] This question, put by James Dunn, lies at the heart of the historical and contemporary debates over Paul's theology in general and justification in particular.

The Argument

Despite the diversity among scholars identified with the new perspective on Paul, one central tenet commonly argued (or, increasingly,

---

26. Fitzmyer, "Paul's Jewish Background and the Deeds of the Law," 26.
27. James D. G. Dunn, introduction to *Romans 1–8*, WBC 38A (Waco: Word, 1988), lxvi.

merely assumed) is the thesis that Paul's polemic against "works of the law" targets *exclusion*, not *works-righteousness*. William Wrede launched this new interpretation in his 1904 work, *Paulus*.[28] Wrede's work was followed by C. G. Montefiore's rebuttals of portrayals of "Jewish legalism" and by G. F. Moore's monumental study in 1927.[29] Judging by the footnotes, it is not Luther and Calvin who represent the "old perspective," but F. Weber, Bousset, Billerbeck, and Bultmann. Not Melanchthon and Chemniz but Herrmann and Heidegger were Bultmann's muses for this so-called "Lutheran perspective."

Krister Stendahl revived Moore's thesis and added what would become another essential plank in the new perspective: the distancing of Paul from Augustine, Luther, Calvin, and modern culture. The apostle displays no signs of their "introspective conscience." It is not "works" in general that Paul is opposing, much less a timeless "legalism," but the circumstances related specifically to the gentile mission.[30] It is not Greek (gnostic) mysticism that pervades Paul's thought, Ernst Käsemann argued against his doctoral supervisor Bultmann, but Jewish apocalyptic. In justification "God establishes his right over the earth," inserting a new power that overcomes the cosmic forces of evil.[31]

Then in 1970 W. D. Davies's landmark *Paul and Rabbinic Judaism* countered the thesis of the history of religions school (culminating in Bultmann) that Paul was more Hellenistic than Jewish, but perhaps at the expense of making him more rabbinical than he really was (as if "rabbinical" is easily defined). Blending law and gospel, Davies interpreted Paul as proclaiming Jesus as the "New Torah."[32] "Paul was the preacher of a

---

28. In *Paulus* (1904), William Wrede argued that Paul's interest in justification and critique of "works of the law" was provoked by a purely intramural Jewish and Jewish-Christian dispute revolving around gentile inclusion. Continuing the tradition of Bauer and the history of religions school, Wrede also emphasized that in his more important ideas the apostle to the gentiles was a key figure in the transition to a Hellenized theology—indeed, even the "second founder of Christianity" (Wrede, *Paul*, trans. Edward Lummis [London: Green, 1907], 179).

29. G. F. Moore, *Judaism in the First Centuries of the Christian Era: The Age of the Tannaim*, 3 vols. (Cambridge, MA: Harvard University Press, 1927–30). Cf. C. G. Montefiore, *Judaism and St. Paul: Two Essays* (London: Goshen, 1914).

30. Krister Stendahl's famous essay, "The Apostle Paul and the Introspective Conscience of the West," appeared first in the *Harvard Theological Review* 55, no. 4 (1963): 199–215, and later in *Paul Among Jews and Gentiles* (Philadelphia: Fortress, 1976).

31. Käsemann wrote this rather spunky missive to his doctoral supervisor asserting that the motif "that unites the New Testament writings in all their diversity" is that "God establishes his right over this earth" rather than "what you call our new understanding of being." "You doubtless will only be able to call this message mythological. But the message stands and falls precisely with this mythological message, at least in my view!" Quoted and translated by John Riches, *Galatians Through the Centuries* (Oxford: Wiley-Blackwell, 2013), 169.

32. W. D. Davies, *Paul and Rabbinic Judaism: Some Rabbinic Elements in Pauline Theology* (London: SPCK, 1970), 323.

New Exodus wrought by the 'merit' of Christ who was obedient unto death," Davies argued, "but this New Exodus like the Old was constitutive of community, it served to establish the New Israel; it also led to the foot of a New Sinai," with Paul delivering "new demands" for the church that were no less "Torah" than the law of Israel.[33] Continuity, not discontinuity, marks the relation of Judaism and Paul in this trajectory.

Another way of challenging the sweeping accounts of the Jews as mired in legalism was to shift this problem of "boasting" to everyone. But in this way, the particularity of Judaism—and of Paul's highly contextualized argument—was eclipsed.[34] Partly in reaction against to this tendency of Barth and Käsemann, and fortified by the Dead Sea Scroll discoveries in the 1940s and 50s, a new era was born, focusing more concretely on the Jewish context of Paul's message.

Building on these trajectories, the text that launched this "new perspective on Paul" was E. P. Sanders's *Paul and Palestinian Judaism* (1977). Like Davies, Sanders concluded that Paul's difference with Judaism is not "works versus grace," and following Schweitzer, Sanders asserts that the difference is Paul's "participationist eschatology."[35] The difference between Sanders and subsequent new perspective scholarship is larger than is often acknowledged. For Dunn, Wright, and others, the traditional Protestant contrast of Judaism and Paul in terms of works and grace exaggerates differences. But for Sanders, the contrast does not go far enough. It is not a minor difference but "the change of 'entire systems,'" Sanders says. "Since salvation is only by Christ, the following of *any* other path is wrong."[36] In any case, according to Dunn, "Works of the law" refers to a "badge of membership," not to works in general, much less to "merit-amassing" ones.[37]

---

33. Davies, *Paul and Rabbinic Judaism*, 323.

34. Barth goes so far as to say that "Abraham's path of faith is *not* the way of the Jew *but* the way of the Gentile, of Abraham as a human being." Karl Barth, *Der Römerbrief*, 2nd ed. (Munich: Kaiser, 1922), 19, quoted in Markus Bockmuehl, "Aquinas on Abraham's Faith in Romans 4," in *Reading Romans with St. Thomas Aquinas*, ed. Matthew Levering and Michael Dauphinais (Washington, DC: The Catholic University of America Press, 2012) 47n25; cf. 107–8; Bockmuehl's italics and translation.

35. Sanders, *Paul and Palestinian Judaism*, 502–7. In the line of Diestel, Ritschl, Cremer, Von Rad, and Käsemann, Sanders considers "righteousness" in Paul to be a transfer term, not a description of behavior (i.e., conformity to a norm); it is not being transferred from condemned to justified or unconverted to converted (544–48). Albert Schweitzer, *The Mysticism of Paul the Apostle*, trans. William Montgomery (London: A&C Black, 1931).

36. Sanders, *Paul and Palestinian Judaism*, 550.

37. James D. G. Dunn, *Jesus, Paul, and the Law: Studies in Mark and Galatians* (Louisville: Westminster John Knox, 1990), 194.

At this point, the traditional doctrine of justification (whether Catholic or Protestant) had indeed become a subsidiary crater, or even a subterranean well, in large swaths of Paul scholarship. The basic difference between old and new covenants is that gentiles are now included, so "works of the law" must obviously be restricted to the ceremonies that excluded them.[38] "In standard Christian theological language," says N. T. Wright, "it wasn't so much about soteriology as about ecclesiology; not so much about salvation as about the church."[39] In other words, "We see the meaning of 'justified,' not as a statement about how someone becomes a Christian, but as a statement about who belongs to the people of God, and how you can tell that in the present."[40] "Faith, not the possession and/or the practice of Torah, is the badge which marks out this family."[41] Galatians 2:1–11 is where we find "the first ever statement of Paul's doctrine of justification by faith, and, despite the shrill chorus of detractors, it here obviously refers to the way in which God's people have been redefined."[42]

Evaluating the Argument

We should be grateful to Sanders and his predecessors for dispelling many of the distortions and, frankly, dangerous misrepresentations of Judaism. We have seen that God's mercy and forgiveness play an important role in Judaism. Furthermore, there is much to be said in favor of some of his conclusions concerning Paul's teaching, particularly (with Schweitzer) his recognition of the importance of participation in Christ for Paul and the way Paul interprets plight in the light of the solution.[43] And although he may exaggerate the prominence of the "end-of-exile" motif in Paul (conquest-exodus seems to me more obvious), Wright's insights into the Abrahamic narrative offer essential components for interpreting Paul.

However, neither Sanders nor new perspective scholarship has convinced me that Judaism is a religion of grace *in the sense that Paul understood that term.*

---

38. Dunn, *Jesus, Paul, and the Law*, 11; cf. 192, 194, 198, 200, 202, 222.
39. N. T. Wright, *What Saint Paul Really Said: Was Paul of Tarsus the Real Founder of Christianity?* (Grand Rapids: Eerdmans, 1997), 119.
40. N. T. Wright, *Paul: In Fresh Perspective* (Minneapolis: Fortress, 2009), 112.
41. Wright, *Paul: In Fresh Perspective*, 113.
42. Wright, *Paul: In Fresh Perspective*, 111.
43. Sanders, *Paul and Palestinian Judaism*, 442–46.

ECCLESIOLOGY VERSUS SOTERIOLOGY

Justification is not about how people are saved, says Wright. "It has to do with the questions, 'Who now belongs to God's people?' and 'How can you tell?'"[44] However, the coming judgment was not upon an abstract world or nation but upon every individual. It is not just Israel but every member who swore allegiance to Yahweh according to the Sinai covenant, by whose stipulations their works will be weighed at the final assize. There is no doubt that the Platonic version of "going to heaven when you die" has infected the popular piety of Christians throughout the centuries, not least in more pietistic and revivalistic circles. Familiar to many biblical scholars, this evangelical heritage has been home to Davies (Congregationalist), Sanders and Dunn (Methodist), and Wright (Anglican). It is not surprising that the ultimate target identified by Douglas Campbell for his own project is Billy Graham and the Four Spiritual Laws (a popular evangelistic tract).[45] But these are hardly better representatives than, for example, Bultmann of the "Lutheran" perspective or "justification theory."

It is surely an overreaction to downplay the question of *personal* election, redemption from sin, condemnation and death, union with Christ, and final resurrection and glorification as anything but central in the entire biblical narrative, and especially in Paul. And in this, the apostle hardly stands alone. The concern with personal salvation is evident throughout the Gospels, as it is also in Second Temple Judaism (especially in its more apocalyptic texts). Wright says that Romans is not "a detached statement of how people get saved, how they enter a relationship with God as individuals, but as an exposition of the covenant purposes of the creator God."[46] I am not sure what he means by "a detached statement" (perhaps detached from the story of Israel, which is surely correct), but it is difficult to take the rest of his description at face value as a legitimate construal of the epistle. The wealthy Jewish ruler had not just been reading Plato's *Timaeus* when he asked Jesus, "Good Teacher, what must I do to inherit eternal life [ζωὴν αἰώνιον]?" (Luke 18:18). The Philippian jailer was not chided for asking the wrong question: "Sirs, what must I do to be saved?" Paul and Silas said, "Believe in the Lord Jesus, and you will

---

44. Wright, *Paul: In Fresh Perspective*, 121.

45. Douglas A. Campbell, *The Deliverance of God: An Apocalyptic Rereading of Justification in Paul* (Grand Rapids: Eerdmans, 2013), 337.

46. Wright, *What Saint Paul Really Said*, 131.

be saved, you and your household" (Acts 16:30–31). The few examples I cited from Jewish sources above indicate that these questions were very much alive in the world known to Jesus and Paul.

GRACE AND COVENANTAL NOMISM

It has become standard, especially since Hermann Cremer, to see the "righteousness of God" as only a positive saving deliverance (i.e., covenant faithfulness) and, since Sanders, to see "covenantal" as a gracious modifier of "nomism."[47] Campbell presses this further by making "covenantal" equivalent to "unconditional and benevolent" without a nomistic element.[48] Hence, righteousness now means covenant faithfulness, covenantal now means gracious, and for some at least, gracious means (a) singularity ("God is *only* gracious, not just") and (b) noncircularity ("no strings attached"). According to Sanders, Paul mostly discarded covenantal nomism in favor of participation in Christ.

For whatever it is worth, I think that Sanders is closer to the truth than most subsequent new perspective proposals in recognizing the radical difference in paradigms between Paul and Judaism provoked by the advent of Christ.[49] However as I noted in the introduction, Dunn and Wright follow Sanders in seeing "covenantal" as a gracious modifier of nomism, while Campbell thinks that Second Temple Judaism was inimical to his normative picture of a God who never relates unconditionally to human beings—Sanders's "covenantal nomism" is just as fearful as "legalism."[50] In other words, for the new perspective the one covenant is nomistic and gracious while for Campbell it is "without any strings attached," based solely on God's universal and unconditional election. As we have seen, Campbell exonerates Paul from this error of affirming any legal-covenantal relationship by making the source of the main argument in Romans 1–3 a false teacher rather than the apostle himself.

Both attempts to accommodate Paul to "covenantal nomism" and to reject any "conditionalism" in Paul result from a conflation of covenants.

---

47. Sanders, *Paul and Palestinian Judaism*, 236.

48. Douglas A. Campbell, "The Current Crisis: The Capture of Paul's Gospel by Methodological Arianism," in *Beyond Old and New Perspectives: Reflections on the Work of Douglas Campbell*, ed. Chris Tilling (Eugene, OR: Cascade Books, 2014), 45, emphasis added.

49. To this point, see Francis Watson, *Paul and the Hermeneutics of Faith* (New York: Bloomsbury T&T Clark, 2004), esp. 14–15; Jonathan A. Linebaugh, *God, Grace, and Righteousness in the Wisdom of Solomon and Paul's Letter to the Romans* (Leiden: Brill, 2013), and John M. G. Barclay, *Paul and the Gift* (Grand Rapids: Eerdmans, 2015), 156–57.

50. Campbell, *The Deliverance of God*, 91–106.

Accordingly, Sanders says, "*obedience maintains one's position in the covenant, but it does not earn God's grace as such.* It simply keeps an individual in the group which is the recipient of God's grace."[51] He says that "works are the condition of remaining 'in,' but they do not earn salvation."[52] But is this a distinction without a difference? Further, if, as Sanders says, Paul "presents an *essentially different type of religiousness from any found in Palestinian Jewish literature*,"[53] then why cannot the apostle think that Judaism falls short of affirming grace in *his* sense of the term? I think that Sanders allows for this possibility more than Dunn and Wright, although he thinks it rests on Paul's misunderstanding of what Jews actually believed.[54]

But leaving aside the methodological issues, let us focus for a moment on the facts of the case that Sanders has set before us. First, he bases his entire case for Judaism's affirmation of "getting in by grace" on the doctrine of election, which establishes the *priority* of grace. Sanders emphasizes the fact that "election and ultimately salvation are considered to be by God's mercy rather than human achievement."[55] This ensures, says Wright, that even though "staying in" depends on obedience, "'being in' in the first place was a gift."[56]

However, there was hardly a consensus in Second Temple Judaism that election was unconditional. Election is clearly conditioned on foreseen merits according to Philo and the Qumran community, for example.[57] In fact, Philo also "assumes that 'covenants are drawn up for those who are worthy of gift.'"[58] Larry Helyer also points to the sharp contrast between Paul's interpretation of election in Romans 9 and that of the Qumran community.[59] Indeed, Sanders himself says that there are basically three answers to the question, "Why did God choose Israel?"

---

51. Sanders, *Paul and Palestinian Judaism*, 420.
52. Sanders, *Paul and Palestinian Judaism*, 543.
53. Sanders, *Paul and Palestinian Judaism*, 543.
54. See Barclay, *Paul and the Gift*, 151–65.
55. Sanders, *Paul and Palestinian Judaism*, 442.
56. Wright, *What Saint Paul Really Said*, 19.
57. Barclay, *Paul and The Gift*, 230, from Philo, *De Specialibus Legibus* 1.303. Philo held clearly to election based on foreseen merits. "The comment encapsulates Philo's understanding of the status of his people," Barclay says. "Israel is a special nation because it is the highest form of humanity, properly aligned to the truth of the cosmos (worshipping the one transcendent God) and supreme in its receipt and exercise of virtue." He has migrated from the land of the senses (Haran) to the realm of spirit. He is "chosen out of all on the grounds of his excellence" (from Philo, *De Abrahamo* 830, quoted by Barclay at 232).
58. Barclay, *Paul and The Gift*, 227.
59. Helyer, *Exploring Jewish Literature of the Second Temple Period*, 261, citing Philo, *De Mutatione Nominum*, 52 (on Gen 17:1–2). Cf. 58 (on Gen 17:2).

One answer is that God offered the covenant (and the command-ments attached to it) to all, but only Israel accepted it. The second answer is that God chose Israel because of some merit found either in the patriarchs or in the exodus generation or on the condition of future obedience. The third answer is not really an answer at all: that is it does not in fact give a reason beyond God's own will: it is that God chose Israel for his own name's sake.[60]

Sanders reveals his own sympathies, as in other places, where he too suggests that unconditional election would be arbitrary. God "chose Israel because of some merit found either in the patriarchs or in the exodus generation or on the condition of future obedience."[61] If the third is "not really an answer at all," the first two are not doctrines of *election* at all. In the first view Israel elected Torah, and in the second God merely knew that Israel would deserve it.

The first two "answers" are precisely what Israel was warned against in Deuteronomy 9:5. In fact, the prophets confirm this after Israel vio-lates the covenant. God will save, but it is neither Israel's righteousness nor that of the patriarchs but "for the sake of the promise I made to Abraham, Isaac and Jacob," that Yahweh continually restrains his wrath. In God's promises of the new covenant in the prophets after exile, there are frequent statements like the following: "not because of you, but because of the promise I swore to Abraham/the fathers," and the only reason that is given for this is "for the sake of my own name" (e.g., Ezek 20:9, 14, 22; cf. Ezek 36:21–22; 39:7; Ps 106:8; Isa 48:11). If this is not sufficient justification for God's mercy, then, to quote Paul, "grace is no longer grace" (Rom 11:6). In any case, Sanders's frequent claim that Judaism generally affirmed the priority of grace via election ("getting in by grace") seems to be unfounded even according to his own analysis. He even agrees that, theologically, unconditional election makes little sense.

Second, ancient Judaism taught a doctrine called the "merit of the fathers," with which I interact in chapter 8. Arthur Marmorstein's mag-isterial study of this rabbinic doctrine documents how singularly devoted saints "benefit not merely themselves, but also their posterity, their fellow-creatures, their ancestry, their whole generation, not merely during their life, but even after their departure from the land of the living. Even in

---

60. Sanders, *Paul and Palestinian Judaism*, 87–88.
61. Sanders, *Paul and Palestinian Judaism*, 87.

the hereafter their merits protect and heal others."[62] Sanders elaborates this point as well with ample citations but insists that Palestinian Judaism was gracious also, because, besides the sacrificial system, repentance and renewed obedience could make up for past sins. He speaks of various strategies in the rabbinic tradition for dealing with sin and even compares them to the medieval doctrine of penance.[63] He even finds rudiments of something like the doctrine of purgatory.[64] Sanders acknowledges the widespread motif of final salvation by a "weighing of merits" on a scale.[65] He tries to exonerate rabbinic teaching from teaching that salvation is merited outright, though he acknowledges that it generally taught that final acquittal depended on the merit of works. So too medieval theology devised elaborate arguments distinguishing between condign and congruent merit. It is difficult to resist the conclusion that, in comparison with the gospel, the covenantal nomism of Paul's day was similar in principle to the type that was summarized by the medieval thesis: "God will not deny his grace to those who do what lies within them."[66]

The new perspective has wisely cautioned against reading the Reformation debate into Paul's polemic. Nevertheless, the summary that I have just offered—drawn largely from Sanders's descriptions—demonstrates that there are striking similarities between the views of Second Temple Judaism and the late medieval church. Acknowledging the danger of anachronism, we nevertheless cannot fail to see that there are some universal human questions and at least some questions that have been provoked by the parts of the biblical narrative that are shared by both religions. Appealing to Barclay's taxonomy, one might say that it is the *incongruity* of grace that the idea of conditional election cannot perfect. Indeed (as Thomas Aquinas insisted), without unconditional election, not even the *priority* of grace can be maintained. In terms of substance, the medieval and Reformation debates are quite similar to the issues raised in ancient Judaism.[67]

---

62. Arthur Marmorstein, *The Doctrine of Merits in the Old Rabbinical Literature*, Jewish College Publication 7 (London: Jews' College, 1920), 4, emphasis added.

63. Sanders *Paul and Palestinian Judaism*, 285, where the texts he cites even use the term.

64. Sanders *Paul and Palestinian Judaism*, 148.

65. Sanders, *Paul and Palestinian Judaism*, 87–88.

66. With earlier roots, this was a common formula for the "covenantal nomism" of late medieval (especially Franciscan) soteriology, as I explain in vol. 1, ch. 5.

67. Years ago I came to Sanders's text prepared to be more fully chastened. Yet it actually had the opposite outcome. The more of *Paul and Palestinian Judaism* I read, the more convinced I became that the type of "covenantal nomism" he was describing did in fact resemble the medieval

In neither case (Second Temple nor medieval) can it be said that a doctrine of grace was absent, but these examples demonstrate that whatever it is, it is not Paul's doctrine of grace. In a 2009 essay, John M. G. Barclay argued that in the ancient world gifts were given to those who were worthy of them. A gift it may still well be—it did not have to be given. But there was something in the recipient that made him or her worthy of it. (This, by the way, was the distinction drawn in medieval theology between condign and congruent merit.)[68] This, Barclay points out, was assumed also in Second Temple Judaism. What is utterly distinctive about Paul's understanding, Barclay argues, is his stress on the unworthiness of the recipient of God's grace in Christ.[69]

In addition to teaching that sinners are unworthy of God's favor, Paul emphasizes an absolute contrast between *wages* and *gift* (Rom 4:4). There is no fine print about different types of merit. No amount of grounding in God's gracious operations in improving the sinner's moral condition will bring Paul to acknowledge the slightest human contribution to salvation. Even faith is a gift (Eph 2:8–9). Abraham was circumcised *after* he was justified (from Gen 15 to Gen 17, about 13–24 years). "It was not *through the law* that Abraham and his offspring received the promise that he would be heirs of the world, but *through the righteousness that comes by faith*" (Rom 4:13 NIV, italics added).[70] This is the opposite of the teaching in ancient Judaism that we find in texts such as Sirach, Miriam J. Kamell explains in detail. "Thus, in 4:16 Abraham is not the father merely of those who by blood and circumcision are his offspring, but rather, of those who share his *faith*."[71]

For Paul, Abraham is not a meritorious reason for Israel's election. On the contrary:

---

theology against which the Reformers reacted. Across a broad spectrum, medieval theologians bent over backwards to avoid any taint (much less charge) of "Pelagianism," but none perfected grace as wholly incongruous. On a host of topics related to the concept of grace in salvation, corollaries between ancient Judaism and medieval theology present themselves at every turn.

68. According to medieval theology, *condign* merit is required by divine justice (merit in the strict sense), while the status of *congruent* merit is bestowed graciously by God over and beyond what God's justice demands (for example, the awarding of a soldier with a medal). I elaborate with sources in vol. 1, ch. 4.

69. John Barclay, "Grace within and beyond Reason: Philo and Paul in Dialogue," in *Paul, Grace, and Freedom: Essays in Honour of John K. Riches*, ed. Paul Middleton, Angus Paddison, and Karen Wenell (London: T&T Clark, 2009), 1–21.

70. Mariam J. Kamell, "Sirach and Romans 4:1–25: The Faith of Abraham," in *Reading Romans in Context: Paul and Second Temple Judaism*, ed. Ben C. Blackwell, John K. Goodrich, and Jason Maston (Grand Rapids: Zondervan, 2015), 70–71.

71. Kamell, "Sirach and Romans 4:1–25," 71.

> For if Abraham was justified by works, he has something to boast about, but not before God. For what does the Scripture say? "Abraham *believed God*, and it was counted to him as righteousness." Now to the one who works, his wages are not counted as a gift but as his due. And to the one who does not work but believes in him who justifies the ungodly, his faith is counted as righteousness. (Rom 4:2–5)

He is "an example for us" not in his ethical obedience but as one who, even while a gentile, trusted in God's promise. Nor are Isaac and Jacob candidates for merit-based election: "Before they [the twins Jacob and Esau] were born or had done anything good or bad—in order that God's purpose in election might stand; not of works but by him who calls" (Rom 9:11–12). Therefore, "It does not depend on human desire or effort but on God's mercy" (v. 16). The opening line of Romans 4—"What then shall we say was gained by Abraham, our forefather according to the flesh?"—announces a bold departure from contemporary interpretation, even if it accorded better with the patriarchal narratives and the prophets.

Dunn writes, "So Israel's righteousness was not so much something to be achieved by self-effort; rather it was understood and measured in terms of obedience to the law of the covenant, faithfulness to the terms of the covenant."[72] "Achieved by self-effort" may be the wrong way to put it, but "measured in terms of obedience to the law of the covenant" hardly softens that idea. I happily grant that everlasting life was never "achieved by self-effort": Abraham believed the same gospel (Rom 4:22–25; Gal 3:8), as did Moses and other Jewish luminaries (Heb 11:1–40). However, the terms for the national covenant (Sinai) contrast sharply with this Abrahamic covenant. Abraham's descendants were given the land by grace, yet whether they kept or lost the estate depended on their fulfillment of the vow. They have not only lost this national estate, Paul argues, but join the gentiles under the coming wrath of God.

Wright says that according to Paul, Jews were "guilty not of 'legalism' or 'works-righteousness' but of what I call 'national righteousness,' the belief that fleshly Jewish descent guarantees membership of God's

---

72. Dunn, "Paul, Grace and ERGA NOMOU," in *Ancient Perspectives on Paul*, ed. Tobias Nicklas, Andreas Merkt, and Joseph Verheyden (Göttingen: Vandenhoeck & Ruprecht, 2013), 267.

covenant people."[73] However, how can such a distinction hold when the national covenant was based on the law? Furthermore, this confidence in "national righteousness" *was* a form of legalism to the extent that the national covenant (Sinai) had absorbed the promise in the thinking of an individual, school, or circle that Paul confronted in his polemics.

Westerholm, who praised *Paul and Palestinian Judaism* in one of the earliest reviews, nevertheless judges that there is simply no way to square what Paul says about grace with Jewish texts of the period.[74] Jews certainly did believe that grace and forgiveness were necessary. But qualifications are in order.[75] According to Sanders, the rabbis did not contrast grace and works as Paul did.[76]

> At this point, the head-scratching begins: How can his view of grace be the same as that of a Judaism that did *not* consider "grace and works" to be "opposed to each other in any way"? If Jews did not distinguish grace and works as paths to salvation, then the old view that they believed in salvation by works, not grace, can hardly be right. But must it not be equally wrong, and for precisely the same reason, to maintain that Jews thought they were saved by grace, not works?[77]

Debates over whether the Judaism of the first century was legalistic depend finally on the interpreter's normative theological commitments. Sanders sympathizes with the critique of unconditional election as arbitrary and thinks that divine assistance is enough to qualify a type of religion as "gracious." Philip S. Alexander concludes, "Tannaitic Judaism can be seen as fundamentally a religion of works-righteousness, and it is none the worse for that. The superiority of grace over law is not self-evident and should not simply be assumed."[78] But the relevant question is whether Paul considered unconditional election arbitrary. It seems evident that he did not. On the contrary, being gracious (and therefore by definition undeserved), election secured the utterly prior, superabundant, and incongruous character of grace.

---

73. N. T. Wright, "The Paul of History and the Apostle of Faith," *Tyndale Bulletin* 29 (1978): 65.

74. Stephen Westerholm, *Justification Reconsidered: Rethinking a Pauline Theme* (Grand Rapids: Eerdmans, 2013), 29.

75. Westerholm, *Justification Reconsidered*, 29.

76. Sanders, *Paul and Palestinian Judaism*, 4, 100, 297.

77. Westerholm, *Justification Reconsidered*, 30–31.

78. Alexander, "Torah and Salvation in Tannaitic Literature," 300.

Grace, of course, will have to suffer the consequences of so many suitors. But perhaps one might suggest a temporary moratorium on the use of the word "legalism" until some generally recognized definition could be given to it. We have become accustomed to accepting statements like "Salvation is by works; righteousness comes through Torah as a reward for our faithfulness. But this isn't legalism." If "legalism" is voided wherever God and his assistance are invoked, then there is hardly a religious context in which it is relevant. Of course, Second Temple Judaism was "legalistic" in the sense that observance of Torah was considered a condition of surviving the final judgment, as is any system that makes final salvation dependent on one's works—even with divine assistance. But this too is a normative theological judgment, based on what I take to be Paul's insistence upon *solus Christus, sola gratia, sola fide*, the latter merely reinforcing the first "sola."

Richard N. Longenecker comes closest to a useful definition, by distinguishing between *acting nomism* and *reacting legalism*.[79] There are examples of obsession with externals, especially the wrangling over the tiniest matters in the Mishnah and the Gemaras.[80] There are various (even pre–AD 70) expressions that seem to justify "a purely commercial view of righteousness," such as the saying that "a man shall always regard himself as though he were half guilty and half meritorious: if he performs one precept, happy is he for weighting himself down in the scale of merits; if he commits one transgression, woe to him for weighting himself down in the scale of guilt."[81] But he notes that the Talmud itself "distinguishes between the 'reckoning Pharisee' and 'God-loving Pharisee.' . . . The Gospels speak of the Pharisees as hypocrites and lacking the love of God, and yet commend a Pharisaic scribe for realizing that love of God and neighbor is basic to all spirituality."[82] He adds,

> The distinction in these contrasts often falls between what I shall call an "acting legalism" and a "reacting nomism"; i.e., between an ordering of one's life in external and formal arrangement according to the Law in order to gain righteousness and/or appear righteous,

79. Longenecker, *Paul, Apostle of Liberty*, 70.
80. Longenecker, *Paul, Apostle of Liberty*, 60, quoting F. V. Filson, *St. Paul's Conception of Recompense* (Leipzig: Hinrichs, 1931), 7.
81. Longenecker, *Paul, Apostle of Liberty*, 62, quoting B. Qid. 40b and M. Aboth 2.14.
82. Longenecker, *Paul, Apostle of Liberty*, 71, quoting B. Sot. 22b.

and the molding of one's life in all its varying relations according to
the Law in response to the love and grace of God. To both classes,
the Law was of great importance, but it was important for different
reasons. To both "the joy of the commandment" was very real, but it
sprang from different sources.[83]

In principle, I have suggested the same distinction in terms of a *law-
covenant*, in which law functions as the basis for reward, and a *promissory-
covenant*, in which God's gift comes first (as Christ's reward) and obedience "in view of God's mercies" is our "reasonable service" (Rom 12:1).

We are well aware that Jesus criticized the religious leaders of his
day for being hypocrites obsessed with externals rather than genuine
love of God and neighbor. However, Jesus's critique, and Paul's, cuts
much deeper than this distinction. The gospel is opposed to both acting
nomism and reacting legalism. The fact is (even according to Deut 30
and Jer 31) Abraham's descendants cannot circumcise their own hearts.
Even if outward conformity to Torah is possible, the inner disposition
to love is not in the power of those who are "dead in trespasses and sins"
(Eph 2:1). The fly in the ointment is the *nomism*. From the perspective
of someone relying on the Sinai covenant as the charter for personal
salvation from the coming judgment, Paul's position could only be seen
as absurd. Everything he says goes against the act–consequence principle at the covenant's core. But Paul is grounding his arguments in the
covenant of grace.

This interpretation is less susceptible to any anti-Jewish construal.
First of all, Paul is not writing an encyclopedia entry on Judaism; he
is diagnosing Israel's plight in light of the solution he discovered in
Christ over against a Jewish-Christian party that has conflated the Sinai
covenant (which never promised justification in the first place) and the
Abrahamic covenant (which did). Second, according to the new perspective, Jews were confident in their ethnic superiority, which can only
be a Jewish problem. However, in the view that I am defending, some
Jews had turned the gift of Torah into a means of confidence in their
moral superiority, which is a perennial temptation for Christians also
and indeed for humanity in general. According to Dunn, the problem
according to Paul was

---

83. Longenecker, *Paul, Apostle of Liberty*, 72.

dividing Jew from non-Jew, the haves from the have-nots, those within from those without ([Rom] 2:12–14); the law as a source of ethnic pride for the typical devout Jew (2:17–23); and circumcision as the focal point for this sense of privileged distinctiveness (2:25–29). Paul regularly warns against "the works of the law," not as "good works" in general or as an attempt of the individual to amass merit for himself, but rather as that pattern of obedience by which "the righteous" maintain their status within the people of the covenant, as evidenced not least by their dedication on such sensitive "test" issues as Sabbath and food laws.[84]

But how is the *not peculiarly Jewish trait* of moral self-reliance more critical of Judaism per se than "ethnocentricity" and arrogant, exclusionary practices toward outsiders? There are disconcerting phrases such as the following by Dunn:

> Paul's negative thrust is against the law *taken over too completely by Israel*, the law misunderstood by a misplaced emphasis on boundary-marking ritual, . . . the law *sidetracked into a focus for nationalistic zeal*. Freed from *that too narrowly Jewish perspective*, the law still has an important part to play in "the obedience of faith."[85]

Thus Paul's target is "the Law misunderstood in too distinctively Jewish terms."[86] But Romans 2 does not complain about the law being "taken over too completely by Israel," but—quite the contrary—that those who are boasting in it *have not done* what the law requires. Paul is not chastising his interlocutor for being too narrowly or distinctively Jewish but for having failed to be what Israel was called to be all along. Ironically, Dunn's position is closer to Billerbeck's and Bultmann's, viewing Paul's problem with Judaism in terms of trying to be too Torah-centered, when my argument is that the apostle's polemic is directed at a *failure* to keep the law.

Paul's "world" is not "religion," but the richly textured world of a specific narrative and context with a Jewish-Christian attempt to keep believers from coming wholly and exclusively under the mediatorial

---

84. Dunn, *The New Perspective on Paul*, 150.
85. Dunn, *The New Perspective on Paul*, 150–51.
86. Dunn, *The New Perspective on Paul*, 151.

reign of Christ rather than Moses. *From the perspective of Christ's advent,* it seems hardly provocative to call this "legalism."[87] In any case, Paul called it "confidence in the flesh" (Phil 3:1), and perhaps this is a better way to characterize his view of Judaism.

Rabbi Samuel Sandmel suggests as much when he resists the idea that Paul basically shared the outlook of Judaism with respect to works, grace, and final judgment and differed merely on the boundary markers:

> Commentators have frequently explained Paul's negative attitude towards the Law as stemming from the difficulties and inconvenience of the Orthodox Jewish regimen. Paul has not one word to say of such difficulty; indeed, this commentary must be ascribed to a mixture of condescension towards Judaism and of unfamiliarity with it. Moreover, this explanation deprives Paul of any profundity, for it would mean that principle was not at stake for him, but only ease and convenience.[88]

Paul's difference was more significant, namely, a total rejection of self-dependence:

> The rabbis, who urged reliance on God, did not deny large areas of man's self-dependence. Paul sees man as completely dependent on God. God, through Christ, provided Paul with the salvation which the Law could not provide. A prerequisite for that salvation was the possession of Abraham's unique quality, faith. Faith and works of the Law are, for Paul, a set of contradictory and opposing principles.[89]

Sandmel goes so far as to say that Paul was opposing those for whom "the Christ was an addition to their Judaism." "For Paul, the Christ is a replacement of that which was central in Judaism. Paul is not content that a person should both observe the Law and have 'faith in Christ'; the choice, he insists, is exclusive; 'if you receive circumcision, Christ will be of no advantage to you' (Gal. 5:2)." It is the whole law that must

---

87. On genuine legalism in early Judaism, see Donald Hagner, "Paul and Judaism: The Jewish Matrix of Early Christianity: Issues in the Current Debate," *Bulletin for Biblical Research* 3 (1993): 117–19; and Paul Schreiner, *The Law and Its Fulfillment: A Pauline Theology of Law* (Grand Rapids: Baker, 1993), 114–21.

88. Rabbi Samuel Sandmel, *A Jewish Understanding of the New Testament*, 3rd ed. (Woodstock, VT: Jewish Lights, 2005), 68.

89. Sandmel, *A Jewish Understanding of the New Testament*, 69.

not be observed for salvation.[90] He adds, "Paul's writings are such that the literature which explains them is often more difficult than Paul himself."[91] From a Jewish perspective, says Sandmel, this argument is easy to understand. "The part of the Old Testament which Paul is declaring obsolete is only the Mosaic law; the rest is still valid for him."[92]

> Paul begins first with the assertion that the Gospel which he preaches is a living power of God to bring man to salvation. One receives this salvation through believing it; faith, indeed, is the only way to righteousness and salvation. Gentile and Jew alike have pursued the wrong way, the Gentile pursuing 'wisdom,' and the Jew the Law of Moses. What God truly requires is obedience to His higher Law, the Law of nature, yet neither the wisdom of the Gentiles nor the Jewish Law of Moses reaches the level of the higher Law. Indeed, he contends, Jews do not fully observe the Law of Moses; obviously, then, they are not at all obeying the higher Law. . . . If even Jews, then, possessing the Law, are unrighteous and are under the power of sin, the Law surely does not bring salvation.[93]

For Paul, according to Sandmel, there is an either-or choice that must be made here with respect to justification: obedience versus gift, the law versus Christ. "Salvation comes apart from the Law, in the gift of the Christ. And man, whether Jew or Gentile, believing in Christ, attains salvation." He can even say that for Paul "faith therefore upholds the intent and basic purpose of the Law." "In [Abraham's] case circumcision was not an act of obedience to the Law, but rather a sign or seal of that faith which he had prior to circumcision."[94]

Besides summarizing Paul in terms recognizable to anyone sympathetic to the Reformers' interpretation, Sandmel offers brilliant insight into the fact that the apostle's argument is hardly new. Paul's "break with legalism [!]" is already present in Amos and other prophets, he observes, so there is already a critique within Judaism itself.[95] Legalism and "prophetism" characterize all religions, including Christianity, he observes:

---

90. Sandmel, *A Jewish Understanding of the New Testament*, 70.
91. Sandmel, *A Jewish Understanding of the New Testament*, 77.
92. Sandmel, *A Jewish Understanding of the New Testament*, 89.
93. Sandmel, *A Jewish Understanding of the New Testament*, 91.
94. Sandmel, *A Jewish Understanding of the New Testament*, 92.
95. Sandmel, *A Jewish Understanding of the New Testament*, 166.

It is somewhat strange to Jewish ears, to hear Catholics, with their elaborate canon law, or Anglicans with theirs, or Methodists with their Discipline, ascribe to Jews exclusively a tendency equally persistent in themselves. Protestants have been acutely aware of the legalism in Catholicism, but apparently not nearly so vividly alert to it in peculiarly Protestant forms. Denomination after denomination in Protestantism has extolled Paul for breaking the shackles of narrow legalism; and denomination after denomination has felt compelled to devise its own, equally necessary, legalism.[96]

At the same time, it is important to distinguish Paul's interest from a mere "type": prophetism versus legalism. Sectarianism of all stripes typically criticizes officialdom for external piety, going through the motions, while the heart is not quite in it. But such introspective piety can be just as intensely "legalistic" in the sense of self-confident, self-righteous, and piteously censorious of those who do not keep up. If we accept the traditional interpretation of Jesus's dialogue with the rich young ruler, Jesus was not simply trying to shift his interlocutor from focusing on externals to a more inner-motivated piety. Rather, he was pushing him to recognize that he had not in fact kept all these laws from his youth as he professed (Luke 18:21–23). For Paul, as for the Hebrew prophets, the alternative is not only between an inward versus merely outward circumcision but even more basically between the responsibility to fulfill conditions (whether external or internal, public or private, formal or informal) and the announcement that they have been fulfilled and are granted *gratis*.

Davies said of Qumran that "the community is aware of itself as under 'the Law' and yet as a 'household of the spirit'; it reveals no sense of an essential incompatibility or essential tension between life under 'the Law' and life under 'the Spirit.'"[97] Yet this tension is precisely what they *should* have seen, according to Paul's message. Longenecker makes the point precisely when he suggests that "the essential tension" of Hebraic Judaism after the destruction of the temple in AD 70 "especially of the nomistic element . . . was not primarily that of legalism versus love, or externalism versus inwardness, but fundamentally that of promise versus fulfillment."

---

96. Sandmel, *A Jewish Understanding of the New Testament*, 167.
97. Longenecker, *Paul, Apostle of Liberty*, 75.

Suffice it here to insist that the change which took place in the conversion experience of at least many early Jewish Christians was not necessarily in the abandonment of an acting religion for a reacting faith; not necessarily the change from outward to inward piety and motivation. The primary tension of Judaism, which dominates all Old Testament and Jewish thought, is that of promise and fulfillment. And this was what the earliest Christians found resolved in Christ.[98]

But here is where similarities with Judaism end, says Longenecker. "At the heart of the Apostle's teaching is his conviction that the Law in its contractual aspect—and that means especially Jewish nomism—has come to its full completion and terminus in Christ."[99] Quoting C. G. Montefiore, he says, "The major Jewish objection to Paul's teaching regarding abrogation of the Law is that 'the Law gives no indication of its own transitoriness.' Its enactments are to be 'statutes for ever throughout your generations.'"[100] Judaism after AD 70 was committed to the idea that in the Messianic era Torah would be *more* closely studied and followed.

The Qumran community considered the Pharisees in Jerusalem compromising hypocrites, false brethren who would be excluded from the Messiah's kingdom. But both groups were convinced that the answer to the coming judgment is doubling down on law-observance. According to the fourth gospel, John the Baptist offered many criticisms with which the Qumran exiles would sympathize, but he also said much that they, no less than the Pharisees, could only have heard as blasphemy. Pointing to an approaching young man, he declares, "Behold, the Lamb of God, who takes away the sin of the world" (John 1:19). The external-versus-internal critique binds the sectarians and Jesus, but the similarities end there. "For the law was given through Moses; grace and truth came through Jesus Christ" (John 1:17). Such words could never have been spoken by a Jewish person of any school. Sanders was closer than Dunn and Wright to seeing that for Paul the break with Judaism was total—not because of a doctrine here or there but because of *Christ*.

---

98. Longenecker, *Paul, Apostle of Liberty*, 77.
99. Longenecker, *Paul, Apostle of Liberty*, 116.
100. Longenecker, *Paul, Apostle of Liberty*, 117, quoting C. G. Montefiore, *Judaism and St. Paul*, 170.

"In short, *this is what Paul finds wrong with Judaism: it is not Christianity.*"[101] The question now for Paul is not whether a theory in one's soteriological system is more or less affirmed; it is whether salvation is to be found only in Christ. To seek even part of it somewhere else—anywhere else—is to cut oneself off from the only hope of standing in the final judgment.

From a Christian perspective, the plight is also different—precisely in view of the solution, Christ. Although we have seen some early Jewish testimonies to something close to original sin, this was not the majority view. Rabbi Sandmel notes that Judaism does not really have a soteriology because it does not really have a doctrine of sin.[102] Everyone sins, of course. "But this is not the same as being born in a state of sinfulness from which liberation is necessary," Stendahl notes. "Sin comes only when man actually disobeys; if he were not to disobey he would not be a sinner."[103] However, Westerholm counters,

> But it is no caricature of Judaism to say, *with Sanders*, that it lacked a doctrine of the "essential sinfulness" of humankind; no Jew would regard *that* claim as an insult. For Paul, on the other hand, it is precisely the "essential sinfulness" of humankind that requires a salvation based on grace alone, apart from human "works." Judaism was not ignorant of divine grace, but that is no reason to deny that Paul could have understood justification in terms of an exclusive reliance on grace in a way that was foreign to the thinking of contemporary Jews.[104]

The problem, as Barclay notes, is that everyone is *assuming* a normative definition of grace rather than arguing for it explicitly.[105] He applies his taxonomy to Sanders's description of Palestinian Judaism as

---

101. Sanders, *Paul and Palestinian Judaism*, 552.
102. Sandmel, *A Jewish Understanding of the New Testament*, 59.
103. Krister Stendahl, *Paul Among Jews and Gentiles* (Philadelphia: Fortress, 1976), 115.
104. Westerholm, *Justification Reconsidered*, 34.
105. Barclay, *Paul and the Gift*, 66–74. To remind ourselves, Barclay says that views of grace differ depending on which element is "perfected" (taken to an extreme). These perfections of grace are (1) superabundance, (2) priority, (3) singularity, (4) incongruity, (5) noncircularity and (6) efficacy. When (1) is perfected, the essence of grace is seen primarily as its ineffable lavishness over and beyond what we could expect. The perfection of (2) locates the essence of grace in its divine initiative, before anything that the recipient does, while (3) refers to the idea of grace as the sole or exclusive motive (over against justice or other divine attributes). Noncircularity (5) means that the gift is given without strings attached and with no expectation of anything in return, while those who perfect efficacy (6) understand grace as a divine gift that achieves its intended effect in the recipient.

"a religion of grace." Sanders rendered a great service by challenging caricatures.

> Nonetheless, at the heart of his project is a lack of clarity concerning the very definition of grace. . . . It also led Sanders to homogenize Second Temple texts that arguably advance *differing* conceptions of divine mercy or grace. . . . Finding grace everywhere, he gave the impression that grace is everywhere the same, and that one perfection (priority) necessarily entails another (incongruity).[106]

"As with Sanders," he says, for Dunn, "the issue might be clarified if a distinction were made between the *priority* of grace and its *incongruity*."[107] I question the priority of grace in a system that makes election dependent on merit. Nevertheless, even if we granted this belief in the priority of grace, is there any branch of Second Temple Judaism that affirms that salvation, from beginning to end, is granted as a gift apart from every human work? If not, then, at least from Paul's perspective, such a view denies salvation by grace alone. The question for him is not whether there is some grace mixed in with the nomism; the slightest nomism vitiates the gospel.

For Paul, grace does not exist on a spectrum. Unlike a dimmer switch, it is binary: "grace would no longer be grace" if works played any role as the ground or instrument of justification (Rom 11:6). Barclay is correct when he says that the *incongruity* of grace is central for Paul: "It is because *this* is the core of Israel's identity and history that it is also the hope for the salvation of the world."[108]

Yet still, Paul is not developing an abstract theology of *sola gratia*. Rather, his thinking is tethered to the redemptive-historical fulfillment of the promises made to Adam and Eve, to Abraham and to Israel. "But when the fullness of time had come, God sent forth his Son, born of woman, born under the law, to redeem those who were under the law, so that we might receive adoption as sons" (Gal 4:4–5). It is *solus Christus* that measures the gulf between Paul and every other system. With respect to the everlasting inheritance, this apocalyptic event renders all human striving worthless in comparison with Christ:

---

106. Barclay, *Paul and the Gift*, 157–58.
107. Barclay, *Paul and the Gift*, 165.
108. Barclay, *Paul and the Gift*, 558.

But whatever gain I had, I counted as loss for the sake of Christ. Indeed, I count everything as loss because of the surpassing worth of knowing Christ Jesus my Lord. For his sake I have suffered the loss of all things and count them as rubbish, in order that I may gain Christ and be found in him, *not having a righteousness of my own* that comes from the law, but *that which comes through faith in Christ*, the righteousness *from* God that depends on faith. (Phil 3:7–9, emphasis added)

This righteousness depends on faith, not works, so that it may be *from God*, not from himself. The mother of all contrasts for Paul, then, is "my own righteousness" attained by works of the law versus "Christ's righteousness" received through faith.

Barclay is exactly right: "If Paul cannot here make sense of the Christ-event without reference to Israel's creation and sustenance by God's elective call, neither can he make sense of Israel without reference to Christ."[109] Thus Paul especially perfects grace as "the incongruity of the gift of Christ."[110] He adds,

Paul rejects "works (of the Law)" as a ground of "boasting" not because they might form a basis for salvation *alternative* to grace, but because they would figure God's grace as *fitting* to the recipient's worth. Because the Christ-gift was unfitting, Paul redefines "grace" as an incongruous gift and thus creates the antithesis of 4:4–5. But nothing here suggests that other Jews, or Jews in general, thought that "working" was a sufficient route to salvation, without the need for grace.[111]

It is therefore beside the point to dispute whether Jews believed in grace. A thousand quotes about the importance of grace would fly right by Paul. Even grace given to the undeserving (which we have seen in some texts) is not yet what Paul has in mind. For Paul, grace is not merely a divine attribute but an act. "God's grace *has appeared* in Christ" (Titus 2:11). Of course, it is grounded in his moral character, but wrath and grace are divine acts. This is why Paul can speak of God's wrath

---

109. Barclay, *Paul and the Gift*, 559.
110. Barclay, *Paul and the Gift*, 569.
111. Barclay, *Paul and the Gift*, 484.

being revealed (Rom 1:18). In fact, Titus 2:11 and Romans 1:18 have a similar construction:

Romans 1:18	Titus 2:11
Ἀποκαλύπτεται γὰρ ὀργὴ Θεοῦ	Ἐπεφάνη γὰρ ἡ χάρις τοῦ Θεοῦ

God *expresses* his wrath and his grace freely as he pleases, when and where he pleases. In both cases it is an event, and for Paul the event of grace is Christ. Barclay states the issue succinctly:

> Within this debate, what is distinctive about Paul is not that he believed in the possibility of God's incongruous grace, but that (a) he identified this phenomenon with a very specific event (the love of God *in Christ*), that (b) he developed this perfection for the sake of his Gentile mission (founding Jew-Gentile unity on novel terms), and that (c) he thereby rethought Jewish identity itself, tracing from Abraham onwards a narrative trajectory of the power of God that creates *ex nihilo* and acts in gift or mercy without regard to worth.[112]

And I would argue that this is because Paul recognized, unlike his fellow Jews and others in the church, that the inheritance of everlasting life, the resurrection from the dead, and peace with God in this age and in the age to come were granted according to the covenant of grace rather than on the terms of the Sinai covenant.

"WORKS OF THE LAW":
SOMETHING TO BE DONE IN ITS ENTIRETY

Another characteristic shared by Jewish texts and Paul (as well as references elsewhere in the New Testament to "the law") is that the works of the law are something one does. Circumcision is done to a person, but Torah is something to be fulfilled in its entirety. Richard N. Longenecker notes that one cannot separate out "the ethical kernel and the ceremonial husk."[113]

With his contemporaries, Paul viewed Torah as undivided.[114]

---

112. Barclay, *Paul and the Gift*, 491.
113. Longenecker, *Paul, Apostle of Liberty*, 108.
114. Longenecker, *Paul, Apostle of Liberty*, 108.

But it should be at least noted here that his insistence, in Galatians 3:10 and 5:3, that anyone who takes upon himself the outward physical sign of obligation to the Law with the intention of bringing upon himself the benefits of it is under obligation to the *whole* Law, is in conformity with Jewish thought and stands as a warning to those who would see Paul narrowly defining the Mosaic Law or separating it into unequally valid parts.[115]

Several texts from Qumran (that preserve documents from Palestinian Judaism) refer to "men of fidelity," described as such because they are "doers of the law."[116] Fitzmyer notes, "It has recently been restricted by J. D. G. Dunn to mean *'particular observances of the law like circumcision and the food laws,'* i.e., those observances *'widely regarded as characteristically and distinctively Jewish.'"*[117] "In this view," says Fitzmyer, "Paul would be attacking a 'basic Jewish self-understanding.'"[118]

Yet it is now seen in the light of this Qumran text that "works of the law" cannot be so restricted. The text of 4QMMT does single out about twenty halakhot, but they are not limited to circumcision and food laws; they are moreover associated by the Jewish leader who wrote this letter with the status of "righteousness" before God. . . . In fact, it makes explicit mention of study of "the Book of Moses and the words of the prophets and David." Given such a broad outlook, it is difficult to see how the restriction of the phrase that Paul uses can be understood in Dunn's sense.[119]

Dunn's restriction does not adequately appreciate his retrospective outlook, Fitzmyer says.[120]

---

115. Longenecker, *Paul, Apostle of Liberty*, 109.

116. Fitzmyer, "Paul's Jewish Background and the Deeds of the Law," 20–21. In 1QpHab 7:11, "'men of fidelity' are described as *'wsy htwrh*, 'doers of the law.' The same phrase occurs again in 1QpHab 8:1; 12:4; 4QpPs^a 1–2 ii 14, 22. A significant variant of the phrase is found in 11QTemple 56:3: *w'syth 'lpy htwrh*, 'and you shall do according to the law.'"

117. Fitzmyer, "Paul's Jewish Background and the Deeds of the Law," 23, from Dunn, "The New Perspective on Paul," *Bulletin of the John Rylands University Library of Manchester* 65, no. 2 (1982–83): 95–122, esp. 107, italics original. See also Dunn, "Works of the Law and the Curse of the Law (Gal 3.10–14)," *New Testament Studies* 31 (1985): 523–42; and Dunn, "Yet Once More—'The Works of the Law': A Response," *JSNT* 46 (1992): 99–117.

118. Fitzmyer, "Paul's Jewish Background and the Deeds of the Law," 23, quoting Dunn, "The New Perspective," 110.

119. Fitzmyer, "Paul's Jewish Background and the Deeds of the Law," 23.

120. Fitzmyer, "Paul's Jewish Background and the Deeds of the Law," 24.

Once again we see that when it comes to justification, Paul's contrast is not between some works (e.g., external rites and rules) and others (e.g., spiritual obedience from the heart), but between *doing* (the law) and *receiving* (Christ). Unlike the gospel, the law is not an announcement of what someone else has accomplished, but an imperative: "You shall therefore keep my statutes and my rules; *if a person does them, he shall live by them*: I am the LORD" (Lev 18:5). Of course, it is this verse that Paul cites in Romans 10:5, contrasting "the righteousness based on the law" with "the righteousness based on faith." Paul thinks of "works of Torah" as an all-encompassing covenant that one indwells. It is the world of "Do-this-and-you-will-live," the action-consequence reality. What you do comes back to you. Justice will win out. As his earlier citation of Habakkuk indicates, it is in contrast with the world of the gospel, which reveals, "the righteous by faith will live" (Ὁ δὲ δίκαιος ἐκ πίστεως ζήσεται, Rom 1:17 NET, quoting Hab 2:4).

The translation of Habakkuk 2:4 (and Paul's use of it) is controversial, to say the least, but Romans 10:5 illumines it. "For Moses writes about the righteousness that is based on the law, that the person who does the commandments shall live by them." There is a covenant that promises life by works—by *doing the commandments*—and there is a covenant that promises life by Christ—through *faith in him*. In Sirach (Ecclesiasticus), dated 200–175 BC, Abraham is said to have moved from *obedience* to *faith*. For Paul, it is the other way around; in fact "from faith to faith."[121] Whether Paul had this precise formula from Ben Sira in mind or not, he was correcting a familiar Jewish version of the story (especially when he comes to focus on Abraham in chapter 4).

Further, in Galatians 3:12 he says, "But the law is not of faith, rather 'The one who does them shall live by them.'" In all of these instances, Paul is alluding to the Sinai covenant (Lev 18:5; Deut 4:1; Ezek 20:11, 13; Neh 9:29). "Do this, and you will live" is the formula for a covenant of law. There is no need to speculate about messianic interpretations in Second Temple texts in order to force Habakkuk and Paul to say, "The Messiah will live by his covenant faithfulness."[122] According to Paul, the righteousness of God (δικαιοσύνη Θεοῦ) is being revealed through the gospel. He never uses the phrase to refer to Jesus. God is the revealer

---

121. Kamell, "Sirach and Romans 4:1–25: The Faith of Abraham," 71.
122. For this interpretation see Richard Hays, *The Faith of Jesus Christ*, 2nd ed. (Grand Rapids: Eerdmans, 2002), 132, 166, 173; and Campbell, *The Deliverance of God*, 613–15.

and the revealed, while the subject of the action of believing is assigned to those, Jews and gentiles, who trust in Christ.

This gift of righteousness is "from faith for (or better, *to*) faith." From beginning to end (both in terms of the *historia salutis*, old to new covenants, and the *ordo salutis*, from the beginning of faith to the day when it becomes sight), justification is through faith alone. This is why Paul is "not ashamed of the gospel" (Rom 1:16). Paul *should* be ashamed of the gospel he preaches, according to his detractors, because he is saying in effect, "let us do evil that good may result" (3:8 NIV). Further, Paul himself anticipates that the doctrine of grace he has pressed upon the minds of his hearers may well provoke questions like, "What shall we say then? Are we to continue in sin that grace may abound?" (6:1). "What then shall we say? That the law is sin?" (7:7). "What shall we say then? Is there injustice on God's part?" (9:16). "You will say to me then, 'Why does he still find fault? For who can resist his will?'" (9:19). Of course, the answer in every case is a resounding μὴ γένοιτο! But if the new perspective interpretation is correct, then it seems doubtful that these questions would have been provoked in the first place.

Based on my argument so far in this section, there is no contradiction between Romans 2:13 ("the doers of the law . . . will be justified") and 3:20 ("For by works of the law no human being will be justified in his sight, since through the law comes knowledge of sin."). The διότι (for/therefore) of 3:20 underscores that it is the conclusion of the argument. Only the *doers* will be justified, but nobody has *done* it, and *therefore*, no one will be justified (in the present or the future) according to it. The law will still be the standard of righteousness by which God judges on the last day, but believers have already heard the verdict. Justification is a fully realized eschatological gift.

One cannot simply define legalism in general religious terms and insert it into Paul's glossary. Seeing Paul's argument in Romans 1–3 as targeting either ethnic superiority or generic legalism requires a superficial reading. Both may play a role, but both remain on the surface. The real issue is that people insist on boasting about walking a path that they themselves had not completed, taking pride in a race that they fatally imagine that they have won, and being faithful to a covenant that they have thoroughly violated. If Paul can get them to see that the "no one righteous" includes them, then the gospel that he is eager to unpack will be seen as the singular light at the end of the tunnel.

Hence, the argument in Romans 10. If one appeals to the law as a way to life, especially after Christ has come, one gets a covenant of ascending, climbing, trying to find God, but instead only finding a "consuming fire." To *receive through faith* the God who in Christ has descended to us is righteousness and life. This gospel is "the word of faith that we proclaim," so that "if you confess with your mouth that Jesus is Lord and believe in your heart that God raised him from the dead, *you* will be *saved*" (vv. 8–9), precisely the "desire and prayer" that he has for his fellow Jews in verse 1. The contrast is between *hearing* the gospel ("the word of faith that we preach") and *doing* the law for righteousness (vv. 3–5).

Bryan Estelle argues persuasively that Romans 10:6 is a *gezerah shawa*, "making lexical analogies through linking verbal phrases between various texts."

> But the righteousness based on faith says, "*Do not say in your heart*, 'Who will ascend into heaven?'" (that is, to bring Christ down). (Rom 10:6)

> *Do not say in your heart*, "My strength and the power of my hand did for me this great mighty deed." (Deut 8:17 LXX)

> *Do not say in your heart* when the LORD your God destroys these nations from your face, "Because of my righteousness the LORD led me in to inherit this good land." (Deut 9:4–5 LXX)[123]

Notice that all three warn against trusting in one's own righteousness. If both of the Deuteronomy instances of "Do not say in your heart" (and a third in 7:6–7) warn against self-righteousness, then that is probably the point of Paul's allusion. To try to "ascend into heaven" is to take salvation into one's own hands. Christ has done all, even descending into the depths and ascending to the heights, so there is nothing more to be accomplished.[124] The only appropriate response is to hear this

---

123. Pointed out in Bryan Estelle, "Leviticus 18:5 and Deuteronomy 30:1–14 in Biblical-Theological Development," in *The Law is Not of Faith: Essays on Works and Grace in the Mosaic Covenant*, ed. Bryan Estelle, J. V. Fesko, and David VanDrunen (Phillipsburg, NJ: P&R, 2009), 143.

124. Estelle, "Leviticus 18:5 and Deuteronomy 30:1–14 in Biblical-Theological Development," 145.

message and embrace it. "For with the heart one believes and is justified, and with the mouth one confesses and is saved" (Rom 10:10).

Noting Paul's quotation of Leviticus 18:5 in Romans 10:5, Dunn observes, "This attitude Sanders characterized by the now well known phrase 'covenantal nomism.'"[125] Yes, but Paul has now shifted the near-to-hand, present, not-impossible message from the law (Lev 18:5) to the gospel (Rom 10:15). "Boasting in God cannot be glossed as 'boasting in Torah,'" Simon Gathercole notes, since "there is room only for boasting through Christ."[126] Torah (works of the law) and Christ (faith) are not two emphases to keep balanced, but two worlds that cannot coexist in the new creation that has dawned in Christ. One must belong to Torah-world or Christ-world, this fading age or the age to come.

We find the same formula in Ezekiel 20, with the cycle of "I gave them my statues," "But they rebelled against me," "I poured out my wrath," "Then I sent them fresh statues, but they rebelled again," and so on. Each cycle ends with their abandonment of the commandments "which, if a person does them, he shall live" (vv. 13, 21). Finally, the cycle is broken in verses 33–44 with the unilateral promise of a new covenant: "You shall know that I deal with you for my name's sake, not according to your evil ways, nor according to your corrupt deeds, Oh my Israel, says the Lord GOD" (v. 44). The principle of "Do this and you shall live" can only provide death to sinners, not life. The only hope for life is through a different covenant founded on better promises.

Returning to the pre-Cremer view of God's righteousness as norm (the righteousness by which God judges), Gathercole says,

> The principal difficulty concerns understanding "righteousness" in terms of *membership* within the covenant rather than as *doing what God requires* within the covenant. I would propose "doing what God requires" as the basic sense of righteousness in the Old Testament and early Judaism. The classic statement of this comes in Deuteronomy 6:24–25: "Then the Lord commanded us to observe all these statutes, to fear the Lord our God, for our good always, so as to keep us alive, as is the case today. If we are careful to

---

125. Dunn, introduction to *Romans 1–8*, lxv.
126. Simon Gathercole, *Where Is Boasting: Early Jewish Studies and Paul's Response in Romans 1–5* (Grand Rapids: Eerdmans, 2002), 261.

observe all these commandments before the Lord our God, as he commanded us, *that will be our righteousness.*"[127]

Gathercole's point may be supported by a cursory survey of references in the Hebrew scriptures.[128] The Old Testament refers to works or deeds (*huqqot*), but does not use the phrase "works of the law"—presumably because *huqqot* occurs ordinarily as the stipulations of Torah itself. For example, Israel is warned, "You shall not do as they do in the land of Egypt, where you lived, and you shall not do as they do in the land of Canaan, to which I am bringing you. You shall not walk in their statutes" (Lev 18:3). The Hebrew phrase in this sentence, "after the doings" (*kema'aseh*), here underscores that the works of Egypt and Canaan are a norm—equivalent to walking "in their statutes" (*ubekhuqqotehem*). In many passages, Israel is called to "do/perform/fulfill the law" with reference to the entire Torah (Deut 28:58; Josh 1:7; Neh 9:34; 2 Chr 14:3; 33:8). But of course, this swims against the grain of the "covenant faithfulness" interpretation of δικαιοσύνη Θεοῦ ("righteousness of God)") that we have seen to have become an established (if highly dubitable) theory assumed by the new perspective. Citing several examples, Gathercole notes that in early Judaism, "righteousness is something that is 'done': 'everyone who does righteousness shall receive his reward' (Sir. 16:14)." "The cash value of this for the interpretation of Paul is that when he speaks of the reckoning of righteousness, it is not just that Christians stand before God as members of the covenant but, rather, that *it is as if they have done everything that God requires.*"[129]

Once more we see that the problem is not with the law but with the failure of the covenant people to *do* what it requires. Maston and Sherwood observe that both Qumran (4QMMT) and Paul quote Psalm 143:2 (LXX Ps 142:2): "For no one living is righteous before you."

---

127. Simon Gathercole, "The Doctrine of Justification in Paul and Beyond," in *Justification in Perspective: Historical Developments and Contemporary Challenges*, ed. Bruce L. McCormack (Grand Rapids: Baker Academic, 2006), 237, emphasis added. See further the first part of Gathercole's *Where Is Boasting?*

128. See Mark Seifrid's catalogue of every such reference in "Paul's Use of Righteousness Language Against its Hellenistic Background," in *Justification and Variegated Nomism*, vol. 2, *Paradoxes of Paul*, ed. D. A. Carson, Peter O'Brien, and Mark Seifrid, WUNT 2/181 (Grand Rapids: Baker Academic, 2004), 39–74.

129. Gathercole, "The Doctrine of Justification in Paul and Beyond," 237. "The righteous are 'all those who walk in the way of righteousness, and do not sin like the sinners' (*1 Enoch* 82:4). *Jubilees* puts it similarly, in the mouth of Jacob: 'And Jacob said: "I will do everything just as you have commanded me because this thing is an honor and a greatness for me and a righteousness for me before the Lord, that I should honor them"' (*Jubilees* 35:2)."

Yet when Paul does so (Rom 3:10), he adds, "by works of the law." "The point is no longer a comparison between sinful humans and the righteous God," as it is for the psalmist and 4QMMT; "rather, the focus is now on the way in which one attains (or cannot attain) a righteous verdict from God. . . . Paul highlights the human act of *doing* the Torah, and he rejects this as a means to attaining righteousness."[130]

With Galatians 2:15–21 in mind, John Barclay makes a significant point for my argument:

> Although the Gentile mission threw certain of these practices into special relief (e.g., circumcision and dietary laws), there is no reason to restrict the referent of ἔργα νόμου "primarily" or "in practice" to those rules that created boundaries between Jews and Gentiles (*pace* Dunn). Rather, Paul uses the Antioch incident to speak about Torah-observance in general: the issue is the validity of the Torah in grounding and defining "righteousness." In this context, it becomes clear that the issue is *not* the subjective value of "works" as a miscon-strued means of eliciting God's favor (Luther), nor "human enter-prise" that depends on human rather than divine initiative (Martyn), but the practice of the Torah as though it were the authoritative cultural frame of the good news.[131]

Therefore, "'Not by works of the Law' means, quite concretely, 'not by the practice of the Torah.'"[132] Righteousness comes through Christ, not the law. "To be 'considered righteous by faith in Christ' is thus the result of the Christ-gift, not the condition for it. But with 'righteous-ness' thus redefined, a key definition of worth—the main currency of the old symbolic capital—has been recalibrated by 'the truth of the good news.'"[133]

CIRCUMCISION COUNTS FOR NOTHING

It is not merely that circumcision is not enough; *it does not count*, just as being a Pharisee of the tribe of Benjamin and blameless according to its outward precepts do not count (Phil 3:3–11). And for anyone who

---

130. Maston and Sherwood, "4QMMT and Romans 3:1–20," 57.
131. Barclay, *Paul and the Gift*, 347.
132. Barclay, *Paul and the Gift*, 375.
133. Barclay, *Paul and the Gift*, 378.

takes it as a sign and seal of their righteousness, it is a death warrant (Gal 5:2). Circumcision is therefore a sign and seal of a covenant with many conditions; "works of the law" cannot be reduced to its entrance requirement. How can those who rely on circumcision and dietary laws be "under the curse of the law"? Only if they have not *done* them.

But one can hardly say that the "teachers" failed regarding circumcision or dietary laws when that was the whole point of their demand upon the gentiles. Paul's point is not that they have failed to keep the identity markers but that, having received circumcision, they have failed to keep "the whole law" to which it obligates them (Gal 5:3). And if "works of the law" mean boundary markers, how can those who boast in their circumcision be considered *hypocrites* through whom God's name is blasphemed among the gentiles (e.g., Rom 2:5–29)? Paul tells us, and it is by referring to the moral law.

With Galatians we meet for the first time the Jew-gentile debate, provoked by the circumcision-party: "A person is not justified by works of the law but through faith in Jesus Christ" (2:16).[134] He quotes the Hebrew text of Psalm 143:2: "Do not enter into judgment with your servant; for no one living is found righteous in your sight."[135] As Stephen Westerholm observes, "It is not clear why he would even have thought of Psalm 143:2, let alone deemed it proof of his claim," if his point "had been that circumcision and other 'boundary markers' are not requirements for sitting at the table of God's people." "The verse from the Psalms was the perfect one to quote, however, if he wanted to say that human beings (Jews like Peter and Paul no less than Gentiles like the Galatians) are sinners who can never be deemed righteous before God by anything they do: 'before you no one living is found righteous.'"[136]

"For Gentile believers in Christ," Westerholm argues, "to be circumcised now would be a disaster not because they would be unnecessarily taking on requirements binding only Jews, but because they would be abandoning Christ, whose death is the sole means by which Jews and Gentiles alike can find righteousness, and they would be embracing the life under a covenant that can only condemn them. Such is the

---

134. Westerholm, *Justification Reconsidered*, 12.
135. Westerholm, *Justification Reconsidered*, 14.
136. Westerholm, *Justification Reconsidered*, 77.

thrust of Galatians."[137] When Paul discusses justification in Galatians and elsewhere, he treats it as the solution to a universal problem. He sees "the law" as a principle of "Do this and you shall live." But the goal of the law was to "imprison" everyone in sin until Christ should come.[138]

Regardless of whether he is consistent with early Judaism (if he were, then he would hardly have clashed with its defenders), Paul views the Sinai covenant now on this side of Christ's advent as a ministry of death and condemnation (2 Cor 3:7–9). "When Paul declares, then, that 'a person is not justified by works of the law' (Gal 2:16), he is, to be sure, denying that Gentiles should be circumcised; but the point of the formula, and the reason *why* Gentiles ought not to be circumcised, is that God's favor cannot be enjoyed by *sinners* under a covenant whose condition for blessing is compliance with its laws."[139] It is not that if they do this they will be exclusive, but will be "under a curse" (3:22).[140] Surely Jews are not under a curse for failing to be circumcised. And why are *gentiles* "under the curse" as well? Again, Paul tells us: "For all have sinned and fall short of the glory of God" (Rom 3:23).

Westerholm continues: "By the time we reach Romans, the terminology and formulas Paul invoked in response to the Galatian crisis have been fully assimilated into his repertoire."[141] He is writing to a church that he did not plant, summarizing the gospel he has been proclaiming everywhere, and its theme is that "the righteous shall live by faith" (Rom 1:17, from Hab 2:4). "Unrighteous people can be found righteous only by extraordinary means, and God has provided that means in the gospel."[142] The same contrast between "the righteousness that is by faith" and "the righteousness that is by works" appears in Philippians 3.[143]

No one questions whether the ceremonies of the law are included, but how do circumcision, dietary laws, and the Sabbath regulations *bring wrath*? Furthermore, how do they bring wrath *upon Jews* and Jewish Christians who not only keep these codes but require them as entrance requirements? And how do these ceremonies bring God's wrath upon gentiles who were never given Torah in the first place? Jewish scholars observe that, according to rabbinic teaching, gentiles are accountable to

137. Westerholm, *Justification Reconsidered*, 14–15.
138. Westerholm, *Justification Reconsidered*, 15.
139. Westerholm, *Justification Reconsidered*, 16.
140. Westerholm, *Justification Reconsidered*, 17.
141. Westerholm, *Justification Reconsidered*, 19.
142. Westerholm, *Justification Reconsidered*, 19.
143. Westerholm, *Justification Reconsidered*, 21.

the moral laws that God gave to Noah.[144] I am not aware of any stream of Judaism that claims that gentiles are condemned on the last day by failing to keep the rules that were given uniquely to Israel as God's special nation.

It is therefore a mistake to assume that the Jews were too wrapped up in their Jewishness (as Dunn argued above) or that their "meta-sin," as Wright calls it, was claiming ethnic or national privilege.[145] Israel *had a claim* to a privileged relationship with God: the covenant (Sinai) and the promises (Abrahamic/Davidic/New), as Paul says (Rom 3:1–3). The problem, from Paul's perspective, is not that his opponents were merely exclusionary and ethnocentric but that *Jews too had failed to keep God's law* even though they had it written down and were in a special covenant with God, while gentiles merely had it inscribed on the conscience (as a remnant of the Adamic covenant in which humanity was created). In other words, the plight is not that Jewish Christians are not Jewish enough, nor that they are too exclusive, but that they are essentially gentiles—cut off from Christ and therefore from God's covenant of promise. The only hope of Jews and gentiles alike is the Abrahamic/ new covenant with Christ as mediator.

Note the subtle difference in the questions and answers:

> Then what *advantage* has the Jew? Or what is the value of circumcision? *Much in every way.* To begin with, the Jews were entrusted with the oracles of God. (Rom 3:1–2)

> What then? Are Jews any *better off*? *No, not at all.* For we have already charged that all, both Jews and Greeks, are under sin. (3:9)

According to the new perspective, it would seem that Paul should have reversed his answers to the same questions: his interlocutors should *not* have thought that they were privileged over gentiles but that they are in the covenant and have the problem of excluding gentiles from it. No, Paul says, they *are* privileged and should have recognized the responsibility that goes with it. But now, it is a moot point. Everyone is

---

144. Michael Wyschogrod, *Abraham's Promise: Judaism and Jewish-Christian Relations* (Grand Rapids: Eerdmans, 2004), 54–60, 188–201; cf. David Novak, *Covenantal Rights: A Study in Jewish Political Theory* (Princeton: Princeton University Press, 2009), 48, 65–71, 84, 86, 101, 172–75, 215.

145. N. T. Wright, *The Climax of the Covenant: Christ and the Law in Pauline Theology* (Edinburgh: T&T Clark, 1991), 240; cf. Wright, *Paul: In Fresh Perspective*, 36.

"under sin"—including Jews. This is the problem, not merely that they are excluding gentiles from the covenant but that they are condemning themselves by that very covenant. It is dangerous to be in a covenant based on law when one is found to be *a transgressor*. To be in the covenantal sphere is to be under martial law—under *herem*, devoted (holy) to God either for life or destruction based on ethical and ritual purity.

Thus, everything now depends on who is swearing the oath and on the covenant's stipulations and sanctions. It is hard to imagine anything more perverse than turning the old covenant sacrament of the covenant of grace—circumcision—into a badge of superiority, except that Christians too take pride in their baptism or their having "made a decision for Christ." There are myriad ways of turning a sacrament of grace into a self-righteous boast. But even so, the main point again is that they have not done what the law requires. Instead of being a light to the nations and guide to the blind, they have failed themselves to keep the covenant in which they boast (Rom 2:17–24). Specifically, they had violated the core commandments (i.e., the moral law) to which even gentiles are obligated according to the law written on their conscience. Paul specifically mentions theft, adultery, and blaspheming God's name among the gentiles in verses 21–24, and in 7:7 he adds coveting with no mention of failing to be circumcised or keep kosher.

But Paul's critics also fail to realize that Abraham is not their father—in terms of justification before God (with reference to final judgment)—unless they enter the covenant of grace as he did, through faith alone. Paul's "solution" is not that they double down on Torah-observance but that they accept God's verdict of condemnation for sin and of justification in Christ. Their most basic failure is not seeing faith rather than circumcision as the badge of membership, but turning a gift into a reward (Rom 4:4–5). If Paul's focus in Romans is ecclesiological boundary markers, then the gist of his argument up to that point (and indeed, on into chapter 5) seems quite beside the point.

We have seen that Campbell skips over Romans 4. Similarly, Wright says that Paul refers to Abraham's faith in Christ leading to justification, but these issues "are not its main subjects." Rather, it is Abraham as father of worldwide family.[146] This seems to run roughshod over the role that Paul gives the patriarch. Abraham is *not* our father according

---

146. N. T. Wright, "The Letter to the Romans," in *The New Interpreter's Bible*, vol. 10 (Nashville: Abingdon, 2002), 497.

to the law, which he himself could not boast before God in keeping, but according to the promise. The "works" by which no one will be justified cannot be limited to Torah when the prime example is a patriarch who lived five centuries before its advent: "If he had been justified by works, he would have something to boast about, but not before God" (Rom 4:2). We do not become united to Abraham (through his merits) but to Christ (through his). Abraham is an example not of someone who attained God's blessing by his obedience but of a gentile who believed and was justified even before he was circumcised. One simply cannot draw a line between soteriology and ecclesiology here.

John Barclay sounds precisely the right note: "Our task is to integrate Paul's dual portrayal of Abraham, as both *believer* in God and *father* of a multinational family."[147] It is precisely because this family is not based on worthiness that it is open to all, including Jews who have not kept the law they profess. "This incongruity between divine action and human status is the unifying theme of Paul's argument: it is the *theological rationale* for the calling of Gentiles, and also the calling of Jews, into the single Abrahamic family."[148] In fact, "What Abraham 'discovered' is what Scripture itself says (Gen 15:6), and what Paul has also discovered in the wake of the Christ-event: that what counts before God has nothing to do with works, whether of the Law or of any other sort."[149]

Paul's charge that "no one does good, not even one" (Rom 3:10) is a verdict pronounced on all alike, Jew and gentile.

> Now we know that whatever the law says it speaks to *those who are under the law*, so that *every* mouth may be stopped, and *the whole world* may be held accountable to God. For by works of the law *no human being* will be justified in his sight, since through the law comes knowledge of sin. (Rom 3:19–20)

Paul draws upon Psalm 53:1 (in Rom 3:20) to show that this is as true of Israel as of the nations. Even if one interprets this diatribe (in the classical sense) against the gentiles as referring to *Christian* gentiles, the point that Paul makes is the same. Tragically, Jews are in the same sinking boat as the gentiles, and gentiles, like Jews, are "under the law,"

---

147. Barclay, *Paul and the Gift*, 481.
148. Barclay, *Paul and the Gift*, 481.
149. Barclay, *Paul and the Gift*, 483–84.

which of course cannot include circumcision. Does it make any sense to see Paul's appeal to Psalm 53:1 in Romans 3:10 as insinuating that "there is no one who is a covenant member"? If we simply search for "righteous/righteousness" and plug in "covenant faithfulness," we can see how unlikely this interpretation is over against the ordinary and straightforward idea of "good works." For example, how can "our sinful passions" be said to be "aroused by the law"—identified as "the written code" (Rom 7:5–6)—if the law consists merely of ceremonies? In fact, the one example Paul cites is "you shall not *covet*" (v. 7).

Paul's frame of reference is the coming wrath, not against Israel but against the whole world; it is not just a question of how gentiles get into Israel's covenant, but how sinful Jews and gentiles can get out of the covenant of works altogether. "Now we know," says Paul, "that whatever the Law says, it speaks to those who are under the Law, so that every mouth may be closed and all the world may become accountable to God" (Rom 3:19). According to Sanders, this simply does not follow logically: if the law speaks to *those under the law*, then it speaks only to Jews.[150] But this widely assumed thesis (that Paul is no longer talking about gentiles but only Jews) is itself the problem. Paul has been arguing that everyone is guilty, that no one is righteous. Francis Watson is exactly right: "The solution to this apparent *non sequitur* is to see that the argument is also based on the *content* of what the law says, which is that 'no one is righteous' (Rom 3.10)."[151] If the law is given "so that *every* mouth may be closed and *all the world* may become accountable to God," then Paul can hardly be referring to Jewish rites; in this instance, "the Law" is the moral law summarized in the Decalogue. This is why in chapter 5 Paul moves from the play-within-a-play (Abraham and Torah) to the two overarching covenants and their respective mediators that identify the larger plot: Adam (the covenant of works) and Christ (the covenant of grace). The world is not absorbed into Israel; Israel is mapped onto the history of humanity as determined by these two federal heads.

Torah and faith do not function merely as badges of membership, but as different bases of inheritance of everlasting life and salvation. "The law is not based on faith [*ek pisteōs*]; on the contrary, it says, 'The person who does these things will live by them'" (Gal 3:12 NIV, quoting

---

150. E. P. Sanders, *Paul, the Law, and the Jewish People* (Philadelphia: Fortress, 1983), 82.
151. Watson, *Paul and the Hermeneutics of Faith*, 59n74.

Lev 18:5). In other words, the principle of inheritance ("long life in the land") according to the law is "do this, and you will live," but the covenant of grace is based on Christ's mediation in his active and passive obedience with the inheritance of everlasting life through faith in him. This *doing of the law* is what Paul contrasts with *believing the promise*, just as Peter did in Acts 15.

In the Gospel of John as well, there is a recurring indictment of "the Jews" as seeking salvation in the law rather than the gospel. This critique begins in John 1:17: "For the law was given through Moses; grace and truth came through Jesus Christ." "Do not think that I will accuse you to the Father," Jesus says. "There is one who accuses you: Moses, on whom you have set your hope" (John 5:45). Obviously, then, the restoration of the entire Sinaitic dispensation is the intention of the religious leaders.

But while Jesus brings this indictment to the Pharisees (and zealots of various stripes), Paul lodges it against professing Jewish-Christian "teachers of the law," who are in fact using the law unlawfully (1 Tim 1:6–11). Westerholm explains that for Paul "the law *as given by God* cannot be set aside by, or combined with, the promise to Abraham as a condition of divine blessing ([Gal] 3:17–18); the law *as given at Sinai*, whose validity—and the period of whose 'guardianship'—was limited to the time between Sinai and the coming of Christ (3:17–25)." There can be no mixture or golden mean between law and gospel when it comes to the basic principle of inheritance, no covenantal nomism. "Believers are 'redeemed,' not from distortions of the law, but from the law itself (4:5), its 'yoke' (5:1), and its curse (3:13). . . . Paul is not attacking Judaism *per se*, but showing why the law, whose observance Paul's opponents are demanding of his converts, cannot in fact lead to the righteousness God requires of all human beings."[152]

There is no doubt that Paul is contrasting law and promise in terms of doing and receiving. The works of the law are not only badges of membership but actions that conform to a specific norm. Again, I appeal to Westerholm: "To 'do the law' is to do 'what is good.' That 'doers of the law' need not be confined to Jews is then shown by the argument that when Gentiles observe things commanded in the law, they show themselves to be aware of its requirements ([Rom] 2:14–15)."[153] It is the

---

152. Westerholm, *Justification Reconsidered*, 79–80.
153. Westerholm, *Justification Reconsidered*, 81.

law that is therefore binding on gentiles and Jews alike: namely, the moral law, from which Paul's explicit examples are taken in the passage.

THE LAW BRINGS WRATH

If Paul reads the plight in light of the solution, he nevertheless sees the law as the revealer of sin. One way of getting around the straightforward meaning of "works of the law" as the standard or norm of God's judgment (and thus condemnation resulting from failing to *do* all that is commanded) is to turn the law into the gospel. Turning a valid observation—namely, that Paul addresses the plight from the vantage point of the solution—into a dogma, Sanders, Martyn, Campbell, and Leithart assign to the *gospel* the role of revealing sin. This despite Paul's repeated statements that the *law* reveals sin (in Romans alone, see 3:19, 20; 4:15; 5:13, 20; 7:7, 8, 11) with no mention of the gospel doing so. Paul writes, "For all who rely on works of the law are under a curse; for it is written, 'Cursed be everyone who does not abide by all things written in the Book of the Law, and do them'" (Gal 3:10).

In fact, Sanders maintains that for Paul it is not the law itself that pronounces a curse, but the absence of faith. Changing his earlier position (*Paul and Palestinian Judaism*, 137, 484), as Timo Laato points out, Sanders "emphatically challenged the assumption that this verse presents a requirement that cannot be fulfilled."[154] "According to him, the Mosaic Torah does not pronounce the curse because everyone at least occasionally violates its commands or prohibitions, but rather because only faith can bring the blessing. Therefore, everything else results in principle in alienation from God."[155] But this runs counter to a host of statements from Paul that we have already encountered: the *law* brings wrath, condemns all, exposes sin, and places everyone under its curse. Laato offers a compelling rebuttal of Sanders's argument, concluding, "Galatians 3:10, especially when it is interpreted in the light of 5:3 (note: this is not a quote from the Old Testament, but Paul's *own* words), expresses that everyone who relies on the works of the law must fulfill all the commandments (without exception!) down to the smallest detail. It is self-evident that this requirement, sharpened *ad absurdum*,

---

154. Timo Laato, "Paul's Anthropological Considerations," in *Justification and Variegated Nomism*, vol. 2, *The Paradoxes of Paul*, ed. D. A. Carson, Peter T. O'Brien, and Mark A. Seifrid, WUNT 2/181 (Grand Rapids: Baker Academic, 2004), 354.

155. Laato, "Paul's Anthropological Considerations," 354, citing Sanders, *Paul and the Law*, 20–23.

transcends human ability."[156] To repeat: Paul nowhere arraigns his Jewish interlocutors for *trying* to keep the law (here Sanders ironically approaches Bultmann's argument) but for *failing* to keep the law that they think they have kept.

According to Romans 4:15, "the law brings wrath" precisely because the law is the norm of God's righteousness. The law brings wrath not inherently but as much as it reveals covenant-breaking (Rom 3:20). When Paul speaks of the works of the law, then, he has in mind the law that must be fulfilled (*lex implenda*) and the law that has been fulfilled in Christ (*lex impleta*). Brevard S. Childs notes, "Thus, when Luther spoke of the law both as *lex implenda* and *lex impleta*, he was not reflecting an allegedly 'tortured subjectivity,' but seeking to deal critically with the biblical material both exegetically and theologically."[157]

If the law brings wrath, however, then it is still in effect until the end of the age. But new perspective scholars emphasize the fact that circumcision and food laws are abrogated as necessary for entrance into the community. How then can the law as boundary markers be the arbiter of God's final judgment? "Paul has a clear and positive view of Torah," Wright properly notes. "Even when it is performing a negative task, it remains God's Law, holy and just and good. What it cannot do—and, in the mysterious purposes of God, what it was never actually intended to do—was to give the life it had promised."[158] This is exactly right: the law is not a means of anyone's justification before God—never has been—but merely of measuring whether we have kept covenant with God. Since none of us keep it, "the law brings wrath." Paul's critics have not understood the proper use of the law. He warns Timothy,

> Certain persons, by swerving from these [sound doctrines], have wandered away into vain discussions, desiring to be teachers of the law, without understanding either what they are saying or the things about which they make confident assertions.
>
> Now we know that the law is good, if one uses it lawfully, understanding this, that the law is not laid down for the just but for the lawless and disobedient, for the ungodly and sinners, for the

---

156. Laato, "Paul's Anthropological Considerations," 356.

157. Brevard S. Childs, *Biblical Theology of the Old and New Testaments: Theological Reflections on the Christian Bible* (Minneapolis: Fortress Press, 1993), 533.

158. Wright, *Paul: In Fresh Perspective*, 103.

unholy and profane, for those who strike their fathers and mothers, the sexually immoral, men who practice homosexuality, enslavers, liars, perjurers, and whatever else is contrary to sound doctrine in accordance with the gospel of the glory of the blessed God with which I have been entrusted. (1 Tim 1:6–11)

What can this mean but that the law (a) is the norm that defines the "righteousness of God," (b) arraigns all who transgress as "unholy and profane," and (c) consists of the moral commandments rather than the ceremonies?

Finally, since the law brings wrath, Paul says that it is clear that "by the works of the law no human being will be justified in his sight" (Rom 3:20a). To use the law as the solution to sin's guilt and corruption is foolish, "since through the law comes knowledge of sin" (Rom 3:20b). How would "boundary markers" make sense of Romans 3:20? Simon Gathercole argues,

> Wright explains the statement as follows: "Paul's point here is that the verdict of the court, i.e., of God, *cannot be* that those who have 'works of Torah' on their record will receive the verdict righteous." The big question here, however, is whether Paul would concede the point that his fellow Jews *do* "have" works of the law on their record. Wright has too minimal a view both of the nature of works of the law and of their function.[159]

Taken at face value, Paul in Romans 4 is setting whole systems in opposition. "Here I see no problem with the idea that Paul is contrasting two soteriologies," says Gathercole, "his own and that of Judaism." "Those who are unhappy with this do not sufficiently appreciate that verbs of repayment and recompense are frequently used in Judaism in connection with the eschatological reward for obedience."[160]

Of course, bringing wrath is not the only function of the law according to Paul or the New Testament generally. For Paul the law of Christ is not different in content from the moral law. The Decalogue is not simply obsolete; instead, the *covenant of law* makes fulfillment a necessary condition of everlasting blessing. Paul upholds the moral commands

---

159. Gathercole, "The Doctrine of Justification in Paul and Beyond," 238–39.
160. Gathercole, "The Doctrine of Justification in Paul and Beyond," 240.

as obligatory for Christians despite their no longer being "under the law."[161] Like Jesus (Matt 22:37–40) and Moses (Deut 6:4; 10:12), Paul summarizes this moral law as love. After repeating the commands of the second table, he says, "The one who loves another has fulfilled the law" (Rom 13:8). The description of the fruit of the Spirit in Galatians 5 basically highlights the inner motives of love, "against which there is no law" (Gal 5:18–23). So the content of "works of the law" has not changed; the moral law, not the ceremonies, are mentioned. Rather, it is only from justifying faith that genuine love and good works can spring.

CONCLUSION: JESUS CAME TO FULFILL AND THEN BRING AN END TO THE AGE OF TORAH-FLESH

"It is in view of the person and work of Christ that Paul rejected nomism as well as legalism, both being now classed as forms of legality," Longenecker notes.[162] "The illustration of Luther at this point is entirely within the Pauline framework of thought: he who would gain righteousness by faith *and* works is as 'the dog who runs along the stream with a piece of meat in his mouth, and, deceived by the reflection of the meat in the water, opens his mouth to snap at it, and so loses both the meat and the reflection.'"[163]

First, Christ has come not to abolish but to establish the law (Matt 5:17–19). Surely he did not come to establish circumcision and the dietary laws. If he had, then the course that Christianity took at the Jerusalem council was a repudiation of the purpose of his mission. Second, he came to *fulfill* the law. And even Matthew, the most Jewish gospel, agrees at 11:13 with Luke 16:16 and Paul: Christ was the end of the law.[164] Jesus says repeatedly that he has come to fulfill the law in his life of obedience, ministry, and death (Matt 3:15; 5:17; 26:54; Mark 1:15; 14:49; Luke 4:21; 24:44). Interestingly, he never says this in reference to the resurrection, for this event lies beyond the law, for he has entered the heavenly Sabbath as the pioneer of the new creation.

---

161. The language of the Westminster Confession is very helpful on this point: ". . . not as a covenant of works, but . . ."

162. Longenecker, *Paul, Apostle of Liberty*, 140.

163. Longenecker, *Paul, Apostle of Liberty*, 141, from "Treatise on Christian Liberty," *LW*, 2:313–14.

164. Longenecker, *Paul, Apostle of Liberty*, 126.

Second, while the Gospels present Jesus as establishing and fulfilling the Law, they also insist that he set himself and his purpose as being more important than the Law. "He recognized the legitimate authority of the rabbinic succession, yet he did not seek rabbinic ordination for His ministry but claimed to have a higher authority than that contained in the Law—namely, 'from heaven.'"[165] Everything, even rules about separation, became subservient to *his* mission.[166]

Whatever Paul knew of all of this—Christ's teachings while on earth—other than the fact that he had been crucified and therefore cursed of God, *everything* changed on the Damascus road. There was no steady development, a slow conversion, since he was on his way to persecuting Christians at the moment. "For him, 'futuristic eschatology' had become to a large extent 'realized eschatology'—or, better yet, inaugurated eschatology."[167] It was his life's turning point.

Hence, we read in Romans 10:4: "For Christ is the end of the law in its connection with all righteousness to all who believe." Barclay compares "works of the law" to banking with outdated currency.[168] It is not one aspect but the entire law as a system that was abrogated. Understandably, *eis dikaiosynēn* ("for righteousness") is often ignored especially by those who insert a distinction between moral and ceremonial aspects of the law. Longenecker suggests,

> There is no reason to doubt that he viewed the Law, as did Judaism, as one indivisible whole. Yet there are many indications that he did distinguish between the two purposes of the Law in the old Covenant; i.e., between "the Law as the standard and judgment of God" and "the Law as a contractual obligation"—between "the standard of God" and "the covenant of works." It is that latter purpose that the Apostle has in mind when he says: Christ is the end of the law "unto righteousness" (ASV), "for righteousness" (AV), or "in connection with righteousness."[169]

What has ended is "the Law in its contractual obligation—i.e., 'in its connection with righteousness' (*eis dikaiosynēn*)," Longecker notes.

---

165. Longenecker, *Paul, Apostle of Liberty*, 127.
166. Longenecker, *Paul, Apostle of Liberty*, 128.
167. Longenecker, *Paul, Apostle of Liberty*, 130–31.
168. Barclay, *Paul and the Gift*, 383.
169. Longenecker, *Paul, Apostle of Liberty*, 132.

It has died [Rom 7:1–6], been "torn down" [Gal. 2:18]. Not because it has evolved into something new, but because God has established a new covenant wherein "commandments" and "ordinances" are ended and the distinction between Israel under contract and the Gentiles outside the covenant is abrogated. . . . "'It is finished' is just as much a cry of Paul as of Christ." Yet we must be careful to note that in all of the Pauline expressions there is no hint that the Law as the standard and judgment of God is also ended.[170]

Longenecker's conclusion is crucial to my argument:

Basic to Paul's teaching regarding the abrogation of the Law in its contractual aspect, and thus in its association with righteousness, is his realization that the antagonism between God and man has been removed and the contractual obligation of the Law has been fulfilled by Christ. . . . Paul does not proclaim a salvation that only wipes out the curse of the Law, presenting the individual to God as neutral. He insists that Christ has also fulfilled the legal demands of the contractual obligation established in the Old Covenant, thus presenting before the Father a positive righteousness for all of those who are "in Him."[171]

The "one act of obedience" in Romans 5:18–19 is his active as well as passive obedience, with the cross as a synecdoche. "Christ stood in the place of humble submission and complete obedience to the Law, as Adam and all his descendants had not done."[172]

Indeed, now that Christ has fulfilled the law, those who seek to obtain the inheritance by their own righteousness are actually being *lawless*, refusing to "submit to God's righteousness" (Rom 10:3). Similarly, the phrase εἰς σωτηρίαν ("for salvation") in verse 1 is often overlooked. Paul's heart breaks for his fellow Jews, praying "that they may be *saved*," not that they may merely become more open to gentile inclusion in God's worldwide family. "For being ignorant of the righteousness of God, and seeking to establish their own, they did not submit to God's righteousness" (v. 3). If "seeking to establish their own [righteousness]"

170. Longenecker, *Paul, Apostle of Liberty*, 133–34.
171. Longenecker, *Paul, Apostle of Liberty*, 134–35.
172. Longenecker, *Paul, Apostle of Liberty*, 135.

is not something close to "works-righteousness," it is hard to know how else one might describe it. In any case, it is consistent with what we have seen in the Gospels: Jesus tells the parable of those "who trusted in themselves that they were righteous," in which the publican rather than the Pharisee "went home *justified before God*" (Luke 18:9, 14). "You are the ones who justify yourselves before men," Jesus said, "but God knows your hearts" (Luke 16:15). The rich young ruler, "desiring to justify himself," would not submit to the righteousness that God *is* in the law, much less even wait around to receive the righteousness that God *gives* in the gospel (Luke 10:29).

Across the spectrum of ancient Judaism, there was the urgency of preparing for the Messiah precisely by ratcheting up obedience to Torah (and much else besides). "Yet it is ironic," says Fitzmyer, "that that gospel should turn out to be, not a proclamation of strict observance of 'the deeds of the law' (Rom 3:20) in the Pharisaic sense, but of justification by grace through faith 'apart from deeds of the law' (Rom 3:28), apart from that which meant so much to the Pharisee of his day."[173]

Christ is therefore the end of the law in a far deeper sense than there no longer being a need for circumcision, dietary laws, and Sabbath regulations. And yet, the importance of the boundary markers is not thereby denied. On the contrary, the issue of inclusion becomes crucial, but only because it is provoked by the particular practice of demanding that gentiles come to Christ by way of Moses. As Peter proclaims to the Jews at the Jerusalem council (Acts 15:10), *they* have failed to do this, so why would they place this yoke on gentiles? And by equating Torah with the στοιχείων τοῦ κόσμου (Gal 4:3, 9; Col 2:20), Paul indicates a radical caesura in history, utterly incongruous grace.[174]

Torah is not inherently evil or semidemonic. "What then shall we say? That the law is sin? By no means!" (Rom 7:7). But now that Christ has come, Paul says, turning back to the law is tantamount to turning back to the pagan "elements" that determine one's fate according to the

---

173. Joseph A. Fitzmyer, *According to Paul: Studies in the Theology of the Apostle* (New York: Paulist, 1993), 4.

174. Commenting on Galatians 4:8–9, Jerome, I think, gets as close as we can to Paul's intention: "When we speak of the law of Moses as 'weak and destitute elements,' the heretics find an occasion to disparage the Creator who founded the world and sanctioned the law. We will respond to them with what we said above: the 'elements' are 'weak and destitute' to those who revert to them after the grace of the gospel. But before the time pre-ordained from the Father came, the 'elements' were not so much called 'weak and destitute' as 'of the world.'" St. Jerome, *Commentaries on Galatians, Titus, and Philemon*, trans. Thomas P. Scheck (South Bend, IN: University of Notre Dame Press, 2010), 163.

logic of act-consequences ("do this, and you will live," "break this and you will die").[175] "Since Christ has brought to an end the possibility of a valid nomistic piety," writes Richard Longenecker, "even Jewish nomism now is relegated to the position of one of 'the elements (*ta stoicheia*) of the world.' Therefore, any return to the Law for either justification or, as in the case of the Galatians, for sanctification is a return to 'the weak and beggarly elements' and a renunciation of Christ."[176] Torah equals Karma. Grace is a break in the cosmic "reap what you sow" order revealed in nature and in Scripture. For the rabbis, Torah may be the sun, but for Paul all now revolves around Christ. Paul is not interested in a general critique of Judaism. What Paul does want Jews to know is that they are no better off than gentiles, "so that every mouth may be stopped, and the whole world may be held accountable to God" (Rom 3:19).

Interestingly, Jewish theologian Michael Wyschogrod sees the way Christ changes everything for Paul, the former rabbi, and gives rise to his classic emphasis on justification. In Judaism, says Wyschogrod, merit is still a live category, and it is hoped that humanity will come to deserve redemption. If not, however, "only God justifies and he justifies far more on the basis of mercy than on the basis of rewards earned by good deeds."

> This being so, how could Paul have so misunderstood things? Part of the answer is his fixation on Jesus. The Jesus event so absorbed his theological attention that nothing could be permitted to compete with Jesus including the Torah, which had the deep loyalty of most Jews.[177]

Paul's "problem," from a Jewish perspective, is "his fixation on Jesus." If we are not similarly and fixed stubbornly on Christ, we will hardly wrestle with the problems that Paul considered primary.

---

175. Joseph R. Dodson, "Wisdom of Solomon and Romans 6:1–23: Slavery to Personified Powers," in *Reading Romans in Context: Paul and Second Temple Judaism*, ed. Ben C. Blackwell, John K. Goodrich, and Jason Maston (Grand Rapids: Zondervan, 2015), 87–92.

176. Longenecker, *Paul, Apostle of Liberty*, 141.

177. Wyschogrod, *Abraham's Promise*, 232.

PART 2

THE ACHIEVEMENT
OF JUSTIFICATION

CHAPTER 3

THE GOD WHO JUSTIFIES THE UNGODLY

Theology over the last century has been rife with candidates for the starting point and unifying center of theology: Christology (Barth), New Being (Tillich), the crucified God (Moltmann), a new exodus (theologies of liberation), and Spirit-Baptism (Pentecostalism). This approach is problematic for several reasons. First, as I have argued, to deduce an entire system from a single doctrine leads necessarily to reductionism; key doctrines are left out or marginalized, while others are exaggerated. Second, for the most part, such central-dogma projects are anthropocentric, placing the redemption, liberation, experience, or piety of creatures at the center of the metaphysical universe. This cannot fail to distort our doctrine of God, as the greatest need of humans (as perceived by the theologian) is allowed to determine the sort of God we are dealing with. The method itself, like the question itself, is flawed. Following the pattern of biblical revelation, theology begins with God—the Holy Trinity: God's being, persons, and acts *intra* (e.g., the processions) and *extra* (the missions). God's eternal decrees are logically antecedent to and distinguished from their execution in time. Further, one cannot decide the meaning of redemption apart from a sound doctrine of creation and fall. To be sure, the Christ-event governs our interpretation of these "earlier" topics, but the incarnation both logically and temporally follows the history of creation and Israel. Any Christology that ignores, hovers above, or dissolves this history in an eternal moment, or by any other route, is not the Christology of the Bible.[1]

Therefore, we must beware of reading the Reformers' insistence on justification as the "chief article"[2] anachronistically, as if they were adopting a nineteenth-century central-dogma theory. They were not suggesting like Eberhard Jüngel that it is the "hermeneutical category" by which all other doctrines are judged.[3] Justification does not determine who God is, since it is a free act of his loving mercy. He could have chosen otherwise, but he cannot be other than the triune God of an immutable, eternal, and simple essence. This freedom *from* the world only serves to fill us with wonder at his incomprehensible choice of being free *for* the world. As John Webster wisely reminds us, "The origins of the saving act of God lie wholly within the being of God," rooted in grace, which itself is based on the "spontaneous, uncaused, . . . eternal sufficiency of God."[4] My scope here is more restricted to God's moral attributes, particularly love, righteousness, and justice, as we seek to apprehend the mystery of the God who justifies the wicked.

---

1. On this point, see John Webster, *God without Measure: Working Papers in Christian Theology*, vol. 1, *God and the Works of God* (London: Bloomsbury T&T Clark, 2016), 159–76; Michael Allen, *Justification and the Gospel: Understanding the Contexts and Controversies* (Grand Rapids: Baker Academic, 2013), chs. 1–2.

2. Of the article of justification Luther famously declared, "The church stands, if this article stands, and the church falls, if it falls" (*WA* 40/III:352). Bucer called it the "chief article of religion" (quoted in Frank A. James III, introduction to *Predestination and Justification: Two Theological Loci*, trans. and ed. Frank A. James III, Peter Martyr Library 8 (Kirksville, MO: Sixteenth Century Essays & Studies, 2003], xxxiii). According to Calvin, it is "the primary article of the Christian religion," "the main hinge on which religion turns," and "the principal article of the whole doctrine of salvation and the foundation of all religion" (*Inst.* 3.2.1, 3.11.1). "For unless you first of all grasp what your relationship to God is, and the nature of his judgment concerning you, you have neither a foundation on which to establish your salvation nor one on which to build piety toward God," Calvin warns (*Inst.* 3.11.1). All of the other abuses—pilgrimages, merits, satisfactions, penances, purgatory, tyranny, superstitions and idolatry—flow from this corruption of the faith at its source. According to Peter Martyr Vermigli, "This doctrine is the hand, fountain, and mainstay of all religion. Therefore, we should be most sure and certain of this above all" (Peter Martyr Vermigli, *Locus on Justification*, in *Predestination and Justification: Two Theological Loci*, trans. and ed. Frank A. James III, Peter Martyr Library 8 [Kirksville, MO: Sixteenth Century Essays & Studies, 2003], 96–97). When Luther speaks of the doctrine as the judge of other doctrines, he is suggesting that doctrines of free will, merit, etc. must surrender to this article. It would be anachronistic to impute a nineteenth-century historical method of "central dogma theory" to the Reformer.

3. Eberhard Jüngel, *Justification: The Heart of the Christian Faith*, trans. Jeffrey F. Cayzer (Edinburgh: T&T Clark, 2001), 47.

4. John Webster, "*Rector et iudex super omnia genera doctrinarum?* The Place of the Doctrine of Justification," in *What Is Justification About? Reformed Contributions to an Ecumenical Theme*, ed. Michael Weinrich and John P. Burgess (Grand Rapids: Eerdmans, 2009), 39.

"*GOD* WAS IN CHRIST"

"Father, if you are willing, remove this cup from me. Nevertheless, not my will, but yours, be done" (Luke 22:42). We need not speculate about the necessity of the cross. It is enough to know from the Father's deafening silence that it was the path that God chose, as Father, Son, and Spirit, in order to be both just and justifier of the ungodly. If Christ's death was not in some sense (relatively) necessary in order to achieve the salvation of the wicked, then surely the death of Christ is a wasteful act. There are less horrific ways of God telling the world that he loves it, how seriously he takes sin, or how great earth would be if we simply did what Jesus did. Only a divine rescue requires a divine rescuer.

Modern theology is replete with examples demonstrating that a Pelagian anthropology and soteriology engenders an Arian Christology. Based on his axiom of the nonrepresentability of the subject, Immanuel Kant insisted that guilt is "not a *transmissible* liability which can be made over to somebody else, in the manner of a financial debt."[5] For Kant, Christ's death can only offer a motive to repentance, but it is our own repentance that finally effects our redemption.[6] This appears to be the most characteristic doctrine of liberal theology with respect to the atonement, as indeed of Pelagian, Abelardian, and Socinian teaching before it. However, it is not only modern Pelagians who reduce theology to anthropology. There is always a danger, even in evangelical theology, for ostensibly "christological" and "christocentric" proposals to end up finally as a discourse on human beings and their need for salvation. Hence, especially since Ritschl, Protestants have often relegated theology proper to "metaphysical speculations" that fail to address the self in its moral and existential quest. Among the many casualties of this approach is God's freedom from the world that makes his freedom for the world all the more an act of love rather than inner necessity.

---

5. Guilt is "not a *transmissible* liability which can be made over to somebody else, in the manner of a financial debt (where it is all the same to the creditor whether the debtor himself pays up, or somebody else for him), but the *most personal* of all liabilities, namely a debt of sins which only the culprit, not the innocent, can bear, however magnanimous the innocent person might be in wanting to take the debt upon himself for the other." Kant, "Religion within the Boundaries of Mere Reason," in *Religion and Rational Theology*, in *The Cambridge Edition of the Works of Immanuel Kant*, ed. Allen W. Wood and George di Giovanni (Cambridge: Cambridge University Press, 1996), 6:72 (113). Kant does not actually demonstrate this axiom but rather assumes it as taken for granted. In more popular terms, the same argument is made by the evangelical revivalist Charles G. Finney in *Systematic Theology*, ed. L. G. Parkhurst Jr. (Minneapolis: Bethany, 1994), 206–9.

6. Kant, *Religion and Rational Theology*, 76–97, 104–45.

As central as the *pro nos* of atonement and justification are, it is only when we begin with the Trinitarian being of God that we find a proper grounding for soteriology itself.

First, the atonement is an act of the triune God that expresses his total (or better, *simple*) being. While there is for us a conceptual difference between, for example, justice and love, these are not really different attributes in God. Robert Sherman puts it better: "God does not *have* attributes. . . . God *is* these attributes."[7] Unlike us, therefore, God does not negotiate various attributes. In fact, at the cross God acts both as gracious and righteous simultaneously (vv. 24–26). Neither those for whom God is "fundamentally benevolent" nor those for whom God is "fundamentally just" should even bother with the apparent conundrum that Paul sees resolved by justification.

God must be good and therefore just not only in himself but in his works. God is not picking at a peccadillo here or there. The transgression of Adam and Eve was not a trivial mistake but a fatal decision to hand over themselves and creation to God's archenemy. Since Adam and Eve, we have exercised our calling and rich endowments as lords under the Lord God to wage war against God and his glorious purposes for creation. We have turned our God-like capacity for rule into treason, for loving service into tyranny, for acuity of reason into plots against him and each other. N. T. Wright expresses the point vividly: "When God looks at sin, what he sees is what a violin maker would see if the player were to use his lovely creation as a tennis racquet."[8] Given the realities of this world and its history, if God is "fundamentally benevolent" and not also righteous and just, then God is not good or loving. "Even a man would not be sufficiently zealous for the good if he thought only of his own good but was indifferent to the victory or defeat of the good outside him," I. A. Dorner notes. "How much more in God must it belong to his ethical self-affirmation that he will the good outside himself with the same holy zeal as he will it in himself."[9] If God eschews all forms of violence, even in defense of the good, then he is not the defender of the oppressed, including a creation that groans for

---

7. Robert Sherman, *King, Priest, and Prophet: A Trinitarian Theology of Atonement* (New York: T&T Clark, 2004), 56.

8. N. T. Wright, *The Day the Revolution Began: Reconsidering the Meaning of Jesus' Crucifixion* (New York: HarperOne, 2016), 132.

9. I. A. Dorner, *Divine Immutability: A Critical Reconsideration*, trans. and ed. Robert R. Williams and Claude Welch (Minneapolis: Fortress, 1994), 183.

its redemption from the curse of human violence (Rom 8:19–24). This point is understood better by our neighbors suffering under regimes where the pressure point of trust in God's love and goodness is not his judgment but his patience and long-suffering.[10]

Taken to its logical conclusion, pitting the benevolent God against the just God leads to Gnosticism, specifically of the Marcionite stripe. In this case, we would have to choose the Christ who redeems us *from* the Creator and law-giver of the world rather than acknowledging the Christ who *is* the Creator and law-giver and who, together with the Father and the Spirit, reconciled the world to himself. This world, with its beautiful design, with physical and moral laws that stipulate his loving will and order, must simply be rejected in favor of a benign deity who can never have a conditional relationship with creatures. If this is so, then righteousness is required neither in God the archetype nor in the ectype-creature he made in his image. A significant trajectory in contemporary theology veers in this Marcionite direction of rejecting the God of Israel—the God of creation, law, justice, and righteousness—as someone other than the "Father of our Lord Jesus Christ" (Eph 1:3).[11]

In contrast with this stark opposition between love and justice, Scripture assures us that God takes us and his world as seriously as he takes himself. Death, the penalty for violation, is announced in the covenant of creation and throughout Scripture (viz., Ezek 18:4; Rom 6:23). Because God is free, immutable, and in no way obligated to show mercy (obliged mercy being an oxymoron at the outset), atonement lies simply in his pleasure (Isa 53:10) and love (John 3:16). In other words, atonement is in God's nature and not simply in an arbitrary will. God would remain the God of love and righteousness even if he had not chosen to redeem any of his rebels, but he did choose it in his eternal councils, and this is the absolutely unconditional and certain basis of the covenant of grace.

Second, in addition to being simple, God is impassible. Change cannot be predicated of his eternal nature or decree. Scripture's representations of God in terms of wrath (as well as pity) are anthropomorphic.

---

10. This point is made elegantly and informed by personal experience in Miroslav Volf, *Exclusion and Embrace: A Theological Exploration of Otherness, Identity and Embrace* (Nashville: Abingdon, 1994).

11. Examples include C. S. Cowles, "Radical Discontinuity," in *Show Them No Mercy: Four Views on God and Canaanite Genocide*, ed. Stanley N. Gundry (Grand Rapids: Zondervan, 2003); and Gregory A. Boyd, *Crucifixion of the Warrior God: Interpreting the Old Testament's Violent Portraits of the Cross* (Minneapolis: Fortress, 2017).

The biblical God is nothing like the Babylonian or Greek gods who fly into rages, depending on what happens in the world. Calvin speaks for the broader catholic tradition when he says that Scripture sometimes (e.g., Col 1:20–22) represents our redemption as if we were under God's wrath until the atonement. "Expressions of this sort," he says, "have been accommodated to our capacity that we may better understand how miserable and ruinous our condition is apart from Christ."[12] Paul wants to focus our faith on Christ alone, since it is only in him that we find shelter from the coming wrath.[13] In short, the transition from wrath to propitiation is not something that happens *in God* or *in us* but *between us* in the covenantal relationship. One evangelical writer says that prior to the cross "God was not my Father. He was my judge and executioner."[14] However, such expressions are easily misinterpreted to imply that the cross changed God's disposition toward us rather than expressed it. Calvin cites Augustine's comment against this way of thinking:

> God's love is incomprehensible and unchangeable. For it was not after we were reconciled to him through the blood of his Son that he began to love us. Rather, he has loved us before the world was created, that we also might be his sons along with his only-begotten Son—before we became anything at all. The fact that we were reconciled through Christ's death must not be understood as if his Son reconciled us to him that he might now begin to love those whom he had hated. Rather, we have already been reconciled to him who loves us, with whom we were enemies on account of sin. The apostle will testify whether I am speaking the truth: "God shows his love for us in that while we were yet sinners Christ died for us" [Rom. 5:8].[15]

Third, the atonement is rooted not only in the attributes of the one God's simple being, but in the unity of the Son with the Father. Though a distinct person, there is no distinction from the Father with respect to the essence. Sherman wisely stipulates that there must not be any separation of Christ's humanity from his divinity, "the divine-human

---

12. *Inst.* 2.16.2.
13. *Inst.* 2.16.3–4.
14. John Piper, foreword to *Pierced for Our Transgressions: Rediscovering the Glory of Penal Substitution*, by Steve Jeffrey, Michael Ovey, and Andrew Sach (Wheaton, IL: Crossway, 2007), 14.
15. *Inst.* 2.16.4, citing Augustine, *Homilies on the Gospel of John* 110.17.21–23 (*NPNF*[1] 7:411).

Christ . . . from the other two persons of the Trinity," or the "last Adam" from the "first Adam." "Should a separation be supposed in any of these connections, then one could readily construe the Son's priestly sacrifice as somehow forced upon him by the Father and of no possible connection or benefit to humanity."[16]

The subject of the incarnation is God the Son who assumed our humanity. A properly ecumenical doctrine of the Trinity therefore will not allow any image of an angry God who punishes a mere human being for other human beings. As truly as the Father sent the Son out of love, the Son embraces his mission in love for the Father and for his bride. Once more Calvin offers illuminating comment. Our Lord's descent into hell, he says, occurred on the cross.

> Yet it is not to be understood that the Father was ever angry toward him. For how could he be angry toward his beloved Son, "in whom he was well pleased"? Or how could he appease the Father by his intercession, if the Father regarded him as an enemy? But it is in this sense that he is said to have borne the weight of divine severity, since he was "stricken and afflicted" by God's hand, and experienced all the signs of a wrathful and avenging God, so as to be compelled to cry out in deep anguish: "My God, My God, why hast thou forsaken me?"[17]

A mere mortal could have served as a moral example or deterrent to other mortals and a prophetic goad to repentance and obedience. However, only God can reconcile the world to himself. No mere mortal could have borne the guilt of many, as Yahweh told Moses when he begged to be "blotted out" of God's book instead of the Israelites, who had made the golden calf (Exod 32:32–33).

In short, we do not read that "God was so angry with the world that he found a suitable human substitute" but that "God so loved the world that he sent his only-begotten Son" (John 3:16). In fact, Calvin adds, "Because the Lord wills not to lose what is his in us, out of his own kindness he still finds something to love."[18] Far from passive, therefore,

---

16. Sherman, *King, Priest, and Prophet*, 195.

17. I. John Hesselink, *Calvin's First Catechism: A Commentary* (Louisville: Westminster John Knox, 1997), 23–24. Calvin repeats his argument in *Inst.* 2.16.11.

18. *Inst.* 2.16.2–4.

Jesus is the Lord who commands as well as the human servant who obeys, the offended party as well as the one who out of love voluntarily bore the guilt for the offender.[19] It was by bearing their judgment that he fulfilled this loving purpose. Jesus says repeatedly that it is his decision to go to the cross. "No one takes my life from me," he said, "I lay it down. I have the authority to lay it down and to take it up again" (John 10:18–19). Not even the Father took his life from him; much less did the Jewish and Roman authorities. The volitional character of Christ's sin-bearing is underscored by the fact that he was given a people by the Father from the foundation of the world and willingly assumed the role of mediator for them. Therefore, the cross establishes not God's love for us but the ground upon which God can justly accept those whom he has already loved in Christ "from the foundation of the world" (Eph 1:4).

Finally, a Christian anthropology will eschew the Pelagian auton-omy at the heart of modernity. As God has his own being in himself, we have our being in God. We are creatures of his word, defined and normed by his speech. Whether we like it or not, even in a state of treason we remain God's office-bearers. The fall has not stripped us of any natural endowment, which is why God still holds us responsible for our participation in Adam's willing captivity to sin and death. Yet original sin has so corrupted our heart, mind, and will that "the flesh" (i.e., nature in its fallen condition) cannot be reformed. It can only be crucified and buried in order to be reborn in the new creation of which Christ is the firstfruits, and as a baptized member of the body of which Christ is the head. Yet we cannot participate in this crucifixion and resurrection unless these are real events in history in which Christ bears our curse and is justified in his resurrection, beyond the reach of condemnation, unrighteousness, Satan, death, and hell.

If God's immutable nature challenges any attempt to treat the cross as an inner process of divine therapy, it also opposes modern rehabil-itations of Abelardian "subjective" theories that lodge the efficacy of Christ's death in the change that it brings about within us. That it *does* effect such change one can hardly doubt, but this is the effect rather than

---

19. John Murray puts the matter well in *The Atonement* (Philadelphia: Presbyterian and Reformed, 1962), 16: "The doctrine of propitiation is precisely this: that God loved the objects of His wrath so much that He gave His own Son to the end that He by His blood should make provision for the removal of this wrath. It was Christ's so to deal with the wrath that the loved would no longer be objects of wrath, and love would achieve its aim of making the children of wrath the children of God's good pleasure."

redemption itself. *In short, the atonement's efficacy lies not within any change that it produces in God or in us but in the change that it produces between God and human beings in their covenantal relationship.*

THE "RIGHTEOUSNESS OF GOD"

Of central importance in contemporary debates over justification is the meaning of the phrase the "righteousness of God." The sheer number of references in the Hebrew scriptures to God's righteousness underscores the importance of this concept.[20] The habitat of "righteousness" in the Old Testament is the covenant with Yahweh.[21] Until the late nineteenth century, all sides in the debate over justification understood God's righteousness in Scripture to refer to an objective norm. It is the righteousness of God, a divine attribute, by which God defines human relationships to himself, each other, and creation and judges moral beings. In the Hebrew Scriptures, righteous conduct, character, or standing is almost always in view, as in Psalm 112:9:

> They have distributed freely, they have given to the poor;
> their righteousness endures forever. (NRSV)

Righteousness consists of deeds that conform to an objective norm.

However, many biblical scholars today—and certainly those associated with the new perspective on Paul—consider it a settled consensus that in the Bible "righteousness" is defined not by a *norm* but by a *relationship.*

---

20. John Reumann, *"Righteousness" in the New Testament: "Justification" in the United States Lutheran-Roman Catholic Dialogue, with Responses by Joseph A. Fitzmyer and Jerome D. Quinn* (Philadelphia: Fortress; New York: Paulist, 1982), 12–13. Reumann observes, "The verb root involved in Hebrew, sdq, occurs 41 times in the Kittel OT text, meaning 'to be righteous,' or (hiphil) 'declare to be in the right.' The adjective *saddiq,* 'righteous,' 'just,' 208 times; the nouns *sedequ and sedaqa,* 'righteousness,' 'justice,' 115 and 158 times respectively. Of these more than 500 cases, about 90 percent are rendered in Greek by a form of *dikaios.* . . . Statistically, therefore, the term is a major one in the OT." See also K. I. Onesti and M. T. Brauch, "Righteousness, Righteousness of God," in *Dictionary of Paul and His Letters: A Compendium of Contemporary Biblical Scholarship,* ed. Gerald Hawthorne, Ralph P. Martin, and Daniel G. Reid (Downers Grove, IL: InterVarsity, 1993), 827–37. Onesti and Brauch point out that in the LXX *sedeq* is rendered *dikaiosyne* 81 times, *sedaqa* 134 times, and 6 times for the adjective *saddîq* ("just," "righteous," "honest"). There are also 8 instances of *hesed* being rendered *dikaiosyne.* "The common Hebrew word for righteousness is *sedeq* or its feminine form *sedaqa* which occurs in the OT 117 and 115 times respectively" (827–37). See also Mark Seifrid, "Paul's Use of Righteousness Language Against its Hellenistic Background," in *Justification and Variegated Nomism,* vol. 2, *The Paradoxes of Paul,* ed. D. A. Carson, Peter T. O'Brien, and Mark A. Seifrid, WUNT 2/181 (Grand Rapids: Baker Academic, 2004), 39–74.

21. Reumann, *"Righteousness" in the New Testament,* 13, 16.

Specifically, it refers to loyalty or faithfulness in a relationship. This antithesis between norm and relationship rests on a broader contrast that is drawn between Hellenistic (legal and norm-centered) and Hebraic (relational-covenantal) habits of thought. Proponents of the new view argue that in the covenantal relationship that Israel knew, it is not conformity to some ethical standard but relational obligations that are determinative. Others drew the same contrast in content but with the grid of Greek (Eastern Orthodox) versus Latin (Roman Catholic and Reformation) approaches to the atonement and justification. Tracing the genealogy of this thesis helps us come a long way toward understanding many of the biblical-theological objections to the traditional doctrine of justification.

Genealogy of the New Definition of "Righteousness"

The most important lexical study of "righteousness" to appear in recent decades is Charles Lee Irons's *The Righteousness of God.*[22] In detail, Irons documents the genealogy of the paradigm-shift of "righteousness" and offers an overwhelmingly persuasive lexical rebuttal of the its central theses.

Ludwig Diestel (1825–78) argued that the *dikaiosynē theou* refers not to *iustitia distributiva* (an external norm) but to the salvation of the godly (an inner norm).[23] On this basis, Albrecht Ritschl (1822–89), a close friend of Diestel, argued that only love (revealed in Jesus) is God's inner motive for action.[24] Any notion that righteousness is judicial or punitive comes from paganism, not from Scripture.[25] God's righteousness is his love and grace.[26] Consequently, "The righteousness of God stands accordingly in the nearest analogy with his faithfulness."[27]

So far, this helps to explain some of the factors involved in Ritschl's

---

22. Charles Lee Irons, *The Righteousness of God: A Lexical Examination of the Covenant-Faithfulness Interpretation*, WUNT 2/386 (Tübingen: Mohr Siebeck, 2015).

23. Irons, *The Righteousness of God*, 29. See Ludwig Diestel (1825–1878), "Die idee der Gerechtigkeit, vorzüglich im Alten Testament, bibischtheologisch dargestellt," *Jahrbücher für deutsche Theologie* 5 (1860): 173–253.

24. Irons relates, "In fact, Ritschl was close friends with him [Diestel] and explicitly acknowledged his dependence on Diestel's 1860 article" (Irons, *The Righteousness of God*, 31, referring to Albrecht Ritschl, *Die christliche Lehre von der Rechtfertigung und Versöhnung: Der biblische Stoff der Lehre*, 3rd ed. [Bonn: Marcus, 1889], 2.103n1).

25. Irons, *The Righteousness of God*, 31.

26. Irons, *The Righteousness of God*, 30, quoting Ritschl, *Die christliche Lehre von der Rechtfertigung und Versöhnung*, 2:102–13.

27. Irons, *The Righteousness of God*, 31, from Ritschl, *Die christliche Lehre von der Rechtfertigung und Versöhnung*, 2.111.

attempt to evacuate any and every judicial concept related to the gospel.[28] Ritschl took Diestel's thesis to the edges of a Marcionite interpretation of justification and reconciliation.[29] When push comes to shove, love wins out over God's justice and righteousness.[30] As John M. G. Barclay points out, with respect to the definition of grace Marcion perfected superabundance and especially singularity, even to the point of identifying wrath and judgment with a putatively evil creator god in contrast with Jesus. This view is evident, Barclay rightly observes, in liberal theologies as well.[31] If God is personal at all, then love is God's constitutive attribute. God may also be just, holy and righteous, but at the end of the day these must yield to eternal love.

Of great importance in this development was Hermann Cremer (1834–1903).[32] Ironically, Cremer and Adolf Schlatter, friends who thought along similar lines, were conservatives, critical of the Ritschlian school. Nevertheless, in the wake of Ritschl's questioning of the identification of righteousness with distributive justice, Cremer "was the first biblical scholar to identify 'righteousness' in biblical language as a relational concept (*Verhältnisbegriff*)."[33] God's righteousness is the act of his saving deliverance, as in Isaiah 56:1: "My salvation is about to come and my righteousness to be revealed."[34] Despite his criticism of the liberals, Cremer "agrees with Ritschl that righteousness is 'thoroughly positive' (*durchaus positiver*) and does not include any thought of punishment." "Righteousness, which someone possesses or which he exercises, always comes to the good of those with whom he stands in relationship (*Verhältnis*)."[35] Schlatter argued that the righteousness of God is not

28. This is evident especially in Ritschl's magnum opus, *Die Christliche Lehre von der Rechtfertigung und Versöhnung* (1870–74), published in English as *The Christian Doctrine of Justification and Reconciliation* (Edinburgh: T&T Clark, 1900). After devouring the works of Kant and Schleiermacher, he became increasingly skeptical of all so-called "scholastic" approaches to theology and attempted to empty Christianity of metaphysics, focusing on the moral, practical, and experiential needs of the individual and the Christian community.

29. Ritschl was familiar with Marcion. In fact, one of Ritschl's earlier works, *Das Evangelium Marcions und das kononische Evangelium des Lukas* (1846), argued that Luke based much of his gospel on the apocryphal gospel of Marcion.

30. In the helpful taxonomy of John M. G. Barclay, *Paul and The Gift* (Grand Rapids: Eerdmans, 2015), 185–86, this is the perfection of grace as *singularity*—that is, that God is only gracious.

31. Barclay, *Paul and the Gift*, 81–85.

32. Hermann Cremer, *Die paulinische Rechtfertigungslehre im Zusammenhange ihrer geschichtlichen Voraussetzungen*, 2nd ed. (Gütersloh: Bertelsmann, 1900).

33. Irons, *The Righteousness of God*, 32.

34. Irons, *The Righteousness of God*, 33.

35. Irons, *The Righteousness of God*, 35, from Cremer, *Die paulinische Rechtfertigungslehre im Zusammenhange ihrer geschichtlichen Voraussetzungen*, 37.

"the static attribute of righteousness but . . . 'God's salvific work.'"[36] As is often the case in pietism, says Irons, justification and sanctification blur in Schlatter's treatment.[37] Instead of imputation, justification is God's powerful saving activity within the believer. "The [Reformation] interpreter began with his own self," Schlatter judged, "while Paul began with God."[38]

Schlatter mediated the new concept to Ernst Käsemann.[39] "The widely-held view that God's righteousness is simply a property of the divine nature can now be rejected as misleading," said Käsemann. "It derives from Greek theology." Instead, God's righteousness is God's "faithfulness in the context of community."[40] A theocentric, cosmic, and apocalyptic emphasis is set over against the individualistic and anthropocentric orientation especially of Bultmann.[41] The canvas of the righteousness of God is wider than an existential crisis; in fact, it is nothing less than "God's cosmic act of making creation right again."[42] Justification is not just gift, but power that transforms. "Paul knows no gift of God which does not convey both the obligation and the capacity to serve."[43] Irons points out that neither antagonist distinguished properly between sense and reference. To be sure, the gift comes with obligation, but "the righteousness of God" does not *mean* cosmic transforming-saving power.[44]

The great Heidelberg Old Testament scholar Gerhard von Rad declared that Cremer's view "has so far been rightly accepted as proven, in its basic thesis at least." The "righteousness of Yahweh is 'always' a gift that brings salvation. 'It is inconceivable that it should ever menace Israel.'" Not only are there no references to "the concept of a punitive צְדָקָה [tsedaqah]," Cremer pronounced, but the very idea is a contradiction

---

36. Adolf Schlatter, *Romans: The Righteousness of God*, trans. Siegfried S. Schatzmann (Peabody, MA: Hendrickson, 1995), 21, cited by Irons, *The Righteousness of God*, 39.

37. Irons, *The Righteousness of God*, 50.

38. Schlatter, *Romans*, 22, quoted in Irons, *The Righteousness of God*, 41.

39. Irons, *The Righteousness of God*, 39. See Käsemann's 1961 lecture, "Gottesgerechtigkeit bei Paulus," in *Zeitschrift für Theologie und Kirche* 58 (1961): 367–78. ET: "'The Righteousness of God' in Paul," in *New Questions of Today* (Philadelphia: Fortress, 1969), 168–82.

40. Ernst Käsemann, "Righteousness of God," 174, quoted in Irons, *The Righteousness of God*, 42

41. See especially Rudolf Bultmann, *Theology of the NT*, trans. K. Grobel (New York: Scribner, 1955), 1:270–329.

42. Irons, *The Righteousness of God*, 41.

43. Ernst Käsemann, "Righteousness of God," 170, quoted in Irons, *The Righteousness of God*, 41.

44. Irons, *The Righteousness of God*, 44.

of terms.[45] Von Rad's colleague, Walter Eichrodt (1890–1978), adopted the thesis explicitly, as did Elizabeth R. Achtemeier (1926–2002), in her 1962 article, "Righteousness in the OT," for the *Interpreter's Dictionary of the Bible*," which Dunn said influenced him as well.[46]

All of the major writers in the loose circle affiliated with the new perspective follow "the Schlatter/Käsemann/early Stuhlmacher school" in interpreting it as "God's covenant faithfulness."[47] Irons summarizes, "First, there is the claim that the Hebraic usage differs significantly from the typical Hellenistic Greek usage."[48] This claim became a settled thesis in New Testament scholarship, especially through Kittel's *TDNT*.[49] This was the era before James Barr, Martin Hengel, and others began to question the opposition between Hebrew and Hellenistic thinking.

> Second, once the Hebraic/relational interpretation of 'righteousness' has been put on the table as an accepted fact, the theory then exercises a controlling influence on the New Perspective interpretation of Paul's thematic statement in Rom 1:17. "The righteousness of God" is interpreted in Hebraic terms as "the covenant faithfulness of God."[50]

N. T. Wright says,

> All this builds up intense pressure for us to accept the normal biblical and post-biblical reading of the phrase "God's righteousness." The phrase does not denote a human status which Israel's God gives, grants, imparts or imputes ("a righteousness *from* God" as in Philippians 3.9), or a human characteristic which "counts" with God ("a righteousness which avails before God"). . . . It retains its primary scriptural meaning, which is that of God's *covenant faithfulness*.[51]

---

45. Irons, *The Righteousness of God*, 36, from Von Rad, *Old Testament Theology* (repr., Louisville: Westminster John Knox, 2001), 1.371.

46. James D. G. Dunn, "The New Perspective: Whence, What and Whither," in *The New Perspective on Paul: Collected Essays*, ed. James D. G. Dunn, WUNT 2/185 (Tübingen: Mohr Siebeck, 2005), 2.

47. Irons, *The Righteousness of God*, 56.

48. Irons, *The Righteousness of God*, 56. E.g., James D. G. Dunn, *The Theology of Paul the Apostle* (Grand Rapids: Eerdmans, 1998), 341.

49. Irons, *The Righteousness of God*, 57.

50. Irons, *The Righteousness of God*, 57.

51. Irons, *The Righteousness of God*, 58, from Wright, *Paul and the Faithfulness of God* (Minneapolis: Fortress, 2013), 996. See also 796–804 where Wright especially treats this.

"Third, having redefined 'the righteousness of God' as God's covenant faithfulness, both Dunn and Wright go on to apply this to the terminology for 'justification,' both the verb and the noun."[52] For example, Wright asserts,

> The point is that the world "justification" does not itself denote the process whereby, or the event in which, a person is brought by grace from unbelief, idolatry and sin into faith, true worship and renewal of life. Paul, clearly and unambiguously, uses a different word for that, the word "call." The word "justification," despite centuries of Christian misuse, is used by Paul to denote that which happens immediately after the "call": "those whom God called, he also justified" (Romans 8.30). In other words, those who hear the gospel and respond to it in faith are *then* declared by God to be his people, his elect, "the circumcision," "the Jews," "the Israel of God." They are given the status of *dikaios*, "righteous," "within the covenant."[53]

Unlike effectual calling, then, justification never "happens." It is not a judicial event in its own right but simply a status of existing within the covenant community.[54] So stressing the "apocalyptic" aspect highlighted by Käsemann, Douglas Campbell argues that Paul's phrase "righteousness of God" "refers to Christ's enthronement by God and denotes 'a singular, saving, liberating, life-giving, eschatological act of God in Christ' but that it does not have the added meaning of 'God's covenant faithfulness.'"[55] However, for most biblical scholars today (certainly those associated with the new perspective), the "righteousness of God" refers not to God's character by which he judges and justifies but his saving deliverance, which simply *is* his covenant faithfulness. Similarly, the believer's righteousness or justification is his or her covenant membership.

---

52. Irons, *The Righteousness of God*, 58.

53. N. T. Wright, *Paul: In Fresh Perspective* (Minneapolis: Fortress, 2009), 121–22, quoted by Irons, *The Righteousness of God*, 59. It is important to interject at this point that this is most certainly "doing theology" in the manner of systematic theologians. It is not simply lexical study. Second, it is not necessarily good systematic theology: Wright is not engaging responsibly with the history of doctrine. He assumes that he has introduced a new *ordo salutis* of effectual calling before justification, apparently unaware that this is the classic Reformed position.

54. Dunn acknowledges H. Cremer (*Die paulinische Rechtfertigungslehre im Zusammenhange ihrer geschichtlichen Voraussetzungen*) as the source of the shift to understanding "the righteousness of God" as a relational concept (i.e., God's own faithfulness) in "The Justice of God: A Renewed Perspective on Justification by Faith," *Journal of Theological Studies* 43, no. 1 (1992): 16.

55. Irons, *The Righteousness of God*, 59, quoting Douglas Campbell, *The Deliverance of God: An Apocalyptic Rereading of Justification in Paul* (Grand Rapids: Eerdmans, 2009), 208–11.

Irons challenges the lexical methodology of this trajectory. First, he raises the charge of *illegitimate totality transfer.* James Barr coined this phrase in criticizing Kittel's *TDNT*: "The attempt to relate the individual word directly to the theological thought leads to the distortion of the semantic contribution made by words in contexts; the value of the context comes to be seen as something contributed by the word, and then it is read into the word as its contribution where the context is in fact different."[56] For example, the word *ekklesia* is used in Acts 7:38 and Ephesians 5:23, but they have totally different meanings as determined by their contexts.[57]

Second, the new trajectory places considerable weight on the argument that biblical writers would not repeat themselves. This is a rather surprising assertion, since Hebrew parallelism has long been recognized. There are all sorts of "parallels": not just synonyms but hyponyms. For instance, Isaiah 3:8 says, "Jerusalem has stumbled, and Judah has fallen."

> Faithfulness (keeping one's word or promise) is an important subcategory within the larger domain of righteousness. As Mark Seifrid points out, faithfulness is covenant-righteousness. The way God is "righteous" within the terms of a (promissory) covenant is by being faithful to keep his promises and delivering his people. But this does not mean that the lexical denotation of "righteousness" *is* "faithfulness to the promissory covenant." Just as everyone who is in Jerusalem is in Judah but not everyone who is in Judah is in Jerusalem, so all instances of faithfulness to a promissory covenant may be termed "righteousness," but not all "righteousness" is faithfulness to a promissory covenant.[58]

Third, Irons challenges Cremer's leap from stereotypes to calques: that is, assuming that the translated word means exactly what it meant in the original language. "This, in my opinion, is the Achilles' heel of the Cremer theory," he says, though this leap has become quite

---

56. Irons, *The Righteousness of God*, 64, quoting James Barr, *The Semantics of Biblical Language* (Oxford: Oxford University Press, 1961), 233 and 218.

57. Irons, *The Righteousness of God*, 64.

58. Irons, *The Righteousness of God*, 67, quoting Mark Seifrid, "Righteousness Language in the Hebrew Scriptures and Early Judaism," in *Justification and Variegated Nomism*, vol. 1, *The Complexities of Second Temple Judaism*, eds. D. A. Carson, Peter T. O'Brien, and Mark A. Seifrid, WUNT 2/140 (Grand Rapids: Baker Academic, 2001), 423.

common among biblical scholars. The result is the assumption that by ordinary use over time, the Greek word δικαιοσύνη (righteousness) came to acquire (for Jews at least) the meaning that צְדָקָה had in the Hebrew Bible.[59] However, this is precisely where the Cremer thesis falls apart. In detail, Irons shows that δικ-terms are not in fact "used with a Hebraic/relational meaning in *compositional* Koiné Greek literature written by Greek-speaking Jews (e.g., The Wisdom of Solomon; 4 Maccabees; The Testament of the Twelve Patriarchs; the *Sentences* of Pseudo-Phocylides; *The Letter of Aristeas*; The Sibylline Oracles; Philo; Josephus; and so on)."[60]

The Cremer thesis fails to distinguish meaning (sense) from reference (overtones, allusions, connotations, etc.). For example, ἱλαστήριον is probably not a calque. It is a Greek word meaning "expiatory or propitiatory object." That is, it does not *mean* "mercy seat" simply because it was used to translate the Hebrew term; rather, "mercy seat" is its *reference*.[61] Irons asks, "Is something similar going on with the ΔΙΚ-group? Is it possible that they are Greek words with Greek meanings *and* with Hebraic allusions, connotations, and echoes?"[62]

Fourth, the undergirding assumption of a Hebrew-versus-Hellenistic mind among biblical writers has been refuted. Martin Hengel, for example, observes, "From about the middle of the third century BC all Judaism must really be designated 'Hellenistic Judaism' in the strict sense."[63] "Even extra-biblical Greek recognizes that keeping one's promises is a subset of 'righteousness.'"[64] Faithfulness can be seen as righteous, but righteousness can't be seen exclusively as faithfulness.[65]

Next, Irons surveys "righteousness" in the Old Testament.[66] Cremer went so far as to claim that because God's righteousness equals salvation, "righteousness and faithfulness are synonyms."[67] However, Cremer fails

---

59. Irons, *The Righteousness of God*, 73.

60. Irons, *The Righteousness of God*, 74.

61. Irons, *The Righteousness of God*, 75.

62. Irons, *The Righteousness of God*, 75.

63. Martin Hengel, *Judaism and Hellenism: Studies in their Encounter in Palestine during the Early Hellenistic Period* (repr., Eugene, OR: Wipf and Stock, 2003), 1.104, quoted by Irons, *The Righteousness of God*, 78.

64. Irons, *The Righteousness of God*, 84.

65. Irons, *The Righteousness of God*, 106.

66. Irons, *The Righteousness of God*, 109. The *zadik* root "occurs 523 times in the Hebrew OT, including the adjective (206 times), the two nouns together (276 times), and the verb in its various forms (41 times)."

67. Irons, *The Righteousness of God*, 78, 133, from Cremer, *Die paulinische Rechtfertigungslehre im Zusammenhange ihrer geschichtlichen Voraussetzungen*, 23.

to show how relationship and distributive justice are distinguished in all of these passages. On the contrary, they indicate that God saves the godly *by means of* punishment and judgment and that there is a distinction between those whom he saves and those whom he condemns.[68] Cremer, however, assumes that "righteousness" is always positive, and "then from this he makes the logical leap that righteousness is fundamentally relational and that 'righteousness and faithfulness are synonymous.'" Hence, "Cremer has not fundamentally distanced himself from the Ritschlian assault on the notion of God's distributive justice."[69]

The key to Irons's work is his examination of the "righteousness of God" in Paul. "The righteousness of God in Jewish Greek can be used with three main meanings: (1) God's distributive justice; (2) his punitive judicial activity which results in the deliverance of his people from their oppressors (*iustitia salutifera* in the proper sense); and (3) the status of divinely-approved righteousness before/from God."[70] Scholars who defend the "covenant faithfulness" interpretation (especially N. T. Wright) appeal to Romans 3:1–8 and 3:25–26, along with 2 Corinthians 5:21.[71] Irons focuses on each of these passages.[72] Paul never uses dik-group words when speaking of God's covenant faithfulness, instead using *pistis*, *aletheia*, and *bebaioō*.[73]

> There is also a perfectly good word for "faithfulness" in the Greek (*pistotes*) that Paul could have used. Paul does not use this exact word, but he comes close. He speaks of "the faithfulness of God" (Rom 3:3). Three times he says that "God is faithful" . . . (1 Cor 1:8; 10:13; 2 Cor 1:18), and on other occasions he uses the adjective *pistos* in reference to God or Christ (1 Thess 5:24; 2 Thess 3:3; 2 Tim 2:13). In addition, Paul uses a variety of phrases and idioms to affirm that God keeps his promises, but none of them involves the use of "righteousness" terminology.[74]

If Paul not only had faithfulness-terms at hand but in fact employed them, why would he not use them if he *meant* faithfulness instead of

68. Irons, *The Righteousness of God*, 133.
69. Irons, *The Righteousness of God*, 134.
70. Irons, *The Righteousness of God*, 272.
71. Irons, *The Righteousness of God*, 273.
72. Irons, *The Righteousness of God*, 273–94.
73. Irons, *The Righteousness of God*, 295.
74. Irons, *The Righteousness of God*, 295.

righteousness or saw them merely as synonymous? If the "righteousness of God" *means* "God's covenant faithfulness," Irons asks, "why does Paul not use the lexeme in Romans 11, the one place where Paul explicitly addresses the question of God's covenant faithfulness in maintaining his promises to Israel based on his divine election?"[75]

Irons also examines the many uses of the righteousness and the wrath of God as subjective genitives.[76] There are also intertextual allusions, the most notable being Habakkuk 2:4 and Genesis 15:6. In both cases, God's righteousness is a gift that God gives.[77] In the principal passages adduced (besides Romans, 2 Cor 5:21, and Phil 3:9) by new perspective scholars, righteousness as covenant faithfulness is far from obvious. Just as diverse covenants must be reduced to a covenant of grace in their view, the righteousness of God must mean God's covenant faithfulness, which always means saving deliverance.

Others besides Irons have questioned the Cremer thesis. According to Joseph Fitzmyer, SJ, the claim that God's righteous deeds are *always* salvific and "always positive" is semantically and exegetically implausible. He argues that "it is not possible to leave it [*tsedaqah*] merely as 'relationship' (*pace* Cremer et al.); it needs further specification, be it societal, or even judicial."[78] For example, it is often related to "the idea of Yahweh's *rib*, 'lawsuit,' with Israel (Jer 12:1, etc.) and is not therefore always saving deliverance but judgment" as well.[79] He adds, "What I am concerned about in this regard is the tendency in some modern discussions of either God's 'righteousness' or of 'justification' in both the OT and the NT to sever the relationship (rightly found in those concepts) from its judicial moorings." Especially in the turn of the prophets from doom to the reality of the exile and hope beyond it, God does indeed emphasize his righteousness as fidelity to his saving purposes. However, "It is still something that he exercises in a judicial setting; it is his salvific bounty *or* activity manifested in a just judgment—and that differs from a manifestation of his power in creation or in governing the universe."[80]

---

75. Irons, *The Righteousness of God*, 296.
76. Irons, *The Righteousness of God*, 297–300.
77. Irons, *The Righteousness of God*, 304–11. On the many places where "the gift of righteousness" appears, see 311–36.
78. Fitzmyer, response to John Reumann, 198.
79. Fitzmyer, response to John Reumann, 199.
80. Fitzmyer, response to John Reumann, 200, emphasis added.

Righteous Judgment

In Tannaitic literature, *tsedaqah* means almost exclusively proper behavior, often in connection with almsgiving.[81] The Septuagint almost always translates *tsdq*-root words with *dik*-root words. In the few exceptions, the word for alms/mercy is used.[82] Not once is a *tsdq*-word translated with a *pist*-word (i.e., faithfulness); rather, it is the Hebrew word *hesed* that means covenant faithfulness and is therefore rendered with *pist*-vocabulary. Consequently, whatever connotations they may have in different contexts, *tsdq*-root words *mean* "righteous," "righteousness," "justify," or "justified." It is the *covenant member's* just act and status. For example, Judah identifies Tamar as "more righteous than I" in Genesis 38:26. Righteousness is not *merely* an external norm because it is the righteousness *of God*. But it is indeed an external norm:

> Righteous are *you*, O LORD,
>   and right are your *rules*. (Ps 119:137)

Here we see, laconically expressed, both meanings of the "righteousness of God" that are excluded by the Cremer thesis.

It is always crucial to identify which covenant is in view. God's righteousness in a conditional covenant involves judgment for violation, while God expresses his faithfulness and righteousness in a covenant of grace by keeping his promises. I need not repeat the argument that the terms of the Sinai covenant are life and death. Can there be any legitimate reading of Torah—particularly Deuteronomy 28—as an unconditional promise "with no strings attached"? The answer must be no. God's righteousness is not an unconditional pledge to deliver the nation no matter what. On the contrary, Yahweh says that if Israel does not keep the covenant, he will do to Israel what he did to the nations that he drove out of his land before them. God's justice will not surrender to his love; on the contrary, his love is expressed in his defense of the defenseless. Israel, too, is "in Adam"—not only judicially but in practice, oppressing the widow, orphan, poor, and sojourner. God will deliver the nation to the sword for this. There is no basis in the Sinai

---

81. Benno Przybylski, *Righteousness in Matthew and His World of Thought* (Cambridge: Cambridge University Press, 1980), 75.

82. J. A. Ziesler, *The Meaning of Righteousness in Paul: A Linguistic and Theological Enquiry*, Society for New Testament Studies Monograph Series 20 (Cambridge: Cambridge University Press, 2004), 59–60.

covenant for blessing apart from righteousness—that is, deeds of justice that conform to Torah.

As great as the blessings for obedience, the danger of being in covenant with God on the terms of Sinai were voiced by Joshua in his sober warning before the people renewed the covenant. "But Joshua said to the people, 'You are not able to serve the LORD, for he is a holy God. He is a jealous God; he will not forgive your transgressions or your sins'" (Josh 24:19). If one seeks to be justified on the terms of Torah, he or she must know that "it is not the hearers of the Law who are righteous before God, but the doers of the Law will be justified" (Rom 2:13). God regulates his actions toward human beings according to specific covenants and according to the covenant of law, whether known by nature or by Torah, "no flesh will be justified in his sight" (Rom 3:20).

Of course, all of God's covenants with human beings establish a *relationship*. Marriage and adoption also establish a relationship. Yet they are first of all legal instruments through which covenants are made and publicly ratified. Thus, the relationship rests on a secure basis. It would have surprised the prophets to have heard that the covenant lawsuit (*rib*) they were commissioned to prosecute had nothing to do with external norms (i.e., Torah, with its 618 laws). They would have had an entirely different career if they had been sent to announce only God's saving deliverance.

Covenant faithfulness is *not* always merciful. It is the context within which God executes his righteous judgment, including deliverance to destruction (see Isa 1:26; 16:5; 26:9; 42:6; 45:8, 13, 19; 51:1, 5, 8; 62:1–2; Hos 2:19; 10:12; Mic 6:5; 7:9). God is a righteous judge (Pss 7:11–12; 11:4–7; 50:3–7; 129:1–4). And God is just in his judgment of the ungodly (Exod 9:27; 2 Chr 12:1–6; Ezra 9:15; Neh 9:32–33; Isa 5:15–16; 10:22–23; 28:17; 42:21–25; Lam 1:18; Dan 9:7, 14). In the vision of the bowl of wrath in Revelation 16 the angel says,

> "Just are you, O Holy One, who is and who was,
>   for you brought these judgments.
> For they have shed the blood of saints and prophets,
>   and you have given them blood to drink.
> It is what they deserve!"

And I heard the altar saying,

> "Yes, Lord God the Almighty,
>> true and just are your judgments!" (Rev 16:4–7)

But this leads to salvation for one group (the godly/oppressed) and wrath for another (the ungodly/oppressors). Von Rad says of God's righteousness, "It is inconceivable that it should ever menace Israel."[83] But this can hardly be a conclusion based on exegesis since God's righteousness is routinely presented as a threat against Israel should the nation violate the terms of the treaty. God is faithful to his covenant, but which covenant? Each covenant has a norm (stipulations) by which judgments are determined (sanctions); without a *norm* there is no concrete *relationship*. Unlike our modern Western ideas, there is no antithesis of love and law in the world of the ancient Near East; law stipulates the relationships of love between the suzerain and fellow subjects. Jesus summarized the *law* as *loving God and neighbor* (Matt 22:38).[84]

If Yahweh is faithful to the terms of the Sinai covenant, then because Israel has become ungodly alongside the rest of the world, it must be judged. This is the tragedy that the exile demonstrates. "Like Adam, Israel broke the covenant," *in spite of* Yahweh's faithfulness (Hos 6:7) and, according to Jeremiah 34:18–20, now must be made to pass between the pieces (i.e., to undergo the actual curse that they assumed when they swore, "All this we will do"). Yet, as with Adam and Eve, God promises deliverance on the basis of a *promise* that is guaranteed *through faith, to all who believe in Christ Jesus.* Yahweh himself passed between the pieces in the theophany of Genesis 15, assuming full responsibility for the terms of the Abrahamic covenant. In Christ, not in the Israelites or in the gentile world, those promises are fulfilled (2 Cor 1:20).

We could know the basic trajectory of this interpretation even without the Pauline epistles. It is already there in the prophets. The new covenant "will not be like the covenant" that Israel swore at Sinai (Jer 31:32). God will unilaterally save by forgiving sins and circumcising hearts. Nations will stream not to Sinai but to Zion for worship. In the national covenant, Yahweh is the suzerain and Israel the vassal; in the Abrahamic covenant fulfilled in the new covenant, Yahweh is "just and

---

83. Irons, *The Righteousness of God*, 36, from Von Rad, *Old Testament Theology*, 1.371.

84. Jon D. Levenson explains the covenantal notion of love well in *The Love of God: Divine Gift, Human Gratitude, and Mutual Faithfulness in Judaism* (Princeton: Princeton University Press, 2015), ch. 1. "Love, so understood," he writes, "is not an emotion, not a feeling, but a cover term for acts of obedient service" (4).

the justifier" of the ungodly who believe in Christ (Rom 3:26). It is certainly true that in Greco-Roman ethics, justice/righteousness can be seen as conforming to an abstract norm (virtue), independent of the divine-human relationship. Especially in Stoicism, self-control is its own reward. Living with the grain of nature is different from living before the face of Yahweh. But the covenantal character of Israel's relationship with Yahweh does not change the *meaning of the words*, given the fact that even in this relational context Yahweh's righteousness is his just decrees in view of the inherent justice of the accused. Only on the basis of a better covenant, based on better promises, with a better mediator and priesthood, is life possible beyond the exile of Adam and Israel.

The Psalms that Cremer adduced do speak of deliverance and righteousness in the same breath (e.g., Ps 31:1: "in your righteousness deliver me"). But rather than a tautology ("in your deliverance deliver me"), the Psalmist is pleading for deliverance *on the ground* of God's righteousness. Because it is in his righteousness (*betsidqateka*) that God acts, in this case the Psalmist pleads that the form such action takes is deliverance (*palleteni*)—precisely because it could be otherwise. Convinced that he is in the right and therefore is qualified to invoke Yahweh to rescue him, the Psalmist anchors his claim in God's justice. Those who invoke God for his mercy, on the basis of God's promise, are asking God to act righteously. This is also true in the New Testament, where forgiveness is based on God's righteousness and justice, since Christ has fulfilled all righteousness. Thus, the justified have a right to final salvation. God is not only merciful but "*faithful and just* to forgive us our sins and to cleanse us from all unrighteousness" (1 John 1:9).

The same can be said of Cremer's other proof texts (e.g., Pss 36:10; 51:14; 69:27–28; 71:1–2, 15–16; 98:2–3), including Psalm 143:1–2, 11–12, which says:

> Hear my prayer, O LORD;
>> give ear to my pleas for mercy!
>> In your faithfulness answer me, in your righteousness!
> Enter not into judgment with your servant,
>> for no one living is righteous before you. . . .
> For your name's sake, O LORD, preserve my life!
>> In your righteousness bring my soul out of trouble!

> And in your steadfast love you will cut off my enemies,
>   and you will destroy all the adversaries of my soul,
>   for I am your servant.

Here the Psalmist is invoking God's faithfulness and righteousness, not on the basis of his integrity according to Torah but on the basis of his mercy. It becomes evident that the interpretation of these pleas depends on which covenant is being invoked. On the basis of Torah, David himself could have suffered capital punishment for either or adultery or murder, so quite understandably he appeals not to God's faithfulness to the Sinai covenant in Psalm 51 but to God faithfulness to his promise to save in mercy those who call on his name.

On the basis of the Sinai covenant, God's covenant love (חֶסֶד) is upon generations that keep his commandments (Ps 103:17–18). This remains true in the new covenant, but it does so on a different basis. Instead of being the condition for God's covenant love, keeping the commandments becomes the inevitable course of life for those who have been given a new heart, have been justified, and are being sanctified (Jer 31:31–35). On the basis of the Sinai covenant (and the covenant of creation), however, the ungodly *cannot* be justified (Exod 23:7; Prov 17:15; Nah 1:3). It is worth noting that the Hebrew verb in all of these verses is the H stem (*hiphil*) of צֶדֶק (*tsedeq*), which means "to declare righteous." This is the exact equivalent of δικαιόω in the New Testament when Paul says that God justifies the wicked. For the guilty, God's faithfulness to his righteousness demands condemnation, not deliverance. Hence, in the psalmist's invocation of God's wrath on the wicked and deliverance of the righteous, distributive justice is clearly in view (Pss 7:9; 58:11). There is no contradiction between these verses and the justification of the ungodly, since they pertain to two different covenants.

There are many laws that are contingent, commanded by God for a particular time in a unique context with his special nation. These precepts are designed to separate Israel from the nations. Yet the core, the moral law delivered in the Decalogue, is the revelation of God's eternal and unchanging character. God did not have to create the world with sentient moral creatures made in his image. But if he did choose to do so, he could not have done otherwise than to give them these laws. Therefore, the moral law is an intimate expression of the *relational* terms of God's covenant with human beings.

Paul refers to the "righteousness of God" in some places as a divine attribute (Rom 1:17; 3:5, 21, 22; 10:3), notes Fitzmyer, "and the phrase sounds like a frequently used slogan." "Yet it is never found *verbatim* in the Old Testament," he adds, "which otherwise often calls God 'righteous' and speaks of his 'righteousness.'" "It has now, however, turned up verbatim in the Dead Sea Scrolls, either as *sedeq 'el* (1QM 4:6) or as *sidqat 'el* (1QS 10:25; 11:12). Clearly, then, Paul was echoing a phrase current in the Judaism of his day."[85] For Paul and Qumran, the "righteousness of God" was an attribute and a norm.

Another weakness in the trajectory that we have explored is the tendency sometimes to marginalize ontology in favor of apocalypticism. In other words, the "righteousness of God" comes to be understood exclusively as an activity rather than referring also to God's inherent attribute. This was the case, I believe, with Karl Barth actualist ontology.[86] Scott Hafemann sees this problem in Käsemann and Campbell:

> The righteousness of God is not the activity *per se*, but an inextricable organic *expression* of God's character in saving, life-giving, eschatological acts of deliverance that express both God's sovereignty and his power, which in turn can be evaluated or described as a characteristic of God in view of God's right actions (i.e., the abstraction, δικαιοσύνη Θεοῦ). . . . God is righteous because, as the expression of his being, he does what is right.[87]

While Hafemann thinks that "Cremer's classic study pointed in the right direction," he says that "it failed to incorporate the entire scope of God's being-action."

> This led to the one-sided interpretation of God's righteousness only in terms of its salvific action that is typical of German scholarship. Indeed, as Campbell observes, it is "'right' for the king to save his people when they are in extremity"; but there is a strong, albeit

---

85. Joseph A. Fitzmyer, SJ, *The Dead Sea Scrolls and Christian Origins* (Grand Rapids: Eerdmans, 2000), 28–29.

86. Michael Horton, "Covenant, Election, and Incarnation: Evaluating Barth's Actualist Christology," in *Karl Barth and American Evangelicalism: Friend or Foes?*, ed. Bruce L. McCormack and Clifford B. Anderson (Grand Rapids: Eerdmans, 2011), 112–47.

87. Scott Hafemann, "Reading Paul's ΔΙΚΑΙΟ-Language: A Response to Douglas Campbell's 'Rereading Paul's ΔΙΚΑΙΟ-Language,'" in *Beyond Old and New Perspectives on Paul: Reflections on the Work of Douglas Campbell*, ed. Chris Tilling (Eugene, OR: Cascade, 2014), 216.

secondary emphasis in the biblical tradition that it is also right for the king to judge those in rebellion against his rightful authority. Both are equally "ethical action," and both are demanded by the "underlying relationship" with his people that exists in accord with the king's responsibilities.[88]

Hafemann refers to several passages confirming his point that in Scripture the king judges the rebellious.[89] In Romans 1:17 and 18, the wrath of God in the law and the mercy of God in the gospel are both exercises of God's righteousness, and "no wedge" can be placed between these verses. "Instead, it is possible to take up the γὰρ of Romans 1:18 seriously as grounds for the argument of the revelation of God's righteousness in 1:16–17 (is Paul following the flow of the argument from Psalm 98/97:2 to 97:9 in his own move from Romans 1:16–17 to 1:18?)."[90] Campbell suggests that righteousness *is* saving deliverance and that such deliverance is "intrinsic to God as a divine King," but Hafemann counters that it depends on God's covenantal stipulations and sanctions.[91]

> In Psalm 97:3 LXX God makes known his righteousness before the peoples by mightily saving his people not because he is a "king," but as a result of the fact that God "remembered his mercy to Jacob and his truth to the house of Israel." . . . What obligates God is not the fact that he is a king *per se*, but the fact that he is King *over Israel* as a result of his own covenant-creating and covenant-sustaining actions in fulfillment of his promises to the patriarchs. It is not kingship *qua* kingship, but the king's role in the covenant that provides the key explanatory concept canonically for Paul's understanding of righteousness.[92]

Further, Hafemann does not see any basis for setting "covenantal" over against "forensic." "A covenantal notion of righteousness, with its

---

88. Hafemann, "Reading Paul's ΔΙΚΑΙΟ-Language," 202.
89. Hafemann refers to "Isa 5:16; 10:22; Lam 1:18; Neh. 9:33; Dan 9:14; cf. Rev 9:11; and in relationship to God's 'righteousness,' see Deut 33:21; Judg 5:11; 1 Sam 12:7; Pss 31:1–3; 51:14; 89:15–17; 103:16; 143:1–2, 11–12; Isa 26:8–10; Dan 9:7, 13–19," in "Reading Paul's ΔΙΚΑΙΟ-Language," 216–17.
90. Hafemann, "Reading Paul's ΔΙΚΑΙΟ-Language," 217.
91. Hafemann, "Reading Paul's ΔΙΚΑΙΟ-Language," 217.
92. Hafemann, "Reading Paul's ΔΙΚΑΙΟ-Language," 218.

forensic implications, is therefore integral to the righteousness of God expressed in his apocalyptic acts of deliverance."[93] It is "God's unconditional grace creating the keeping of the new covenant conditions."[94]

It is important to remind ourselves that the driving force for the apocalyptic school is Barth's doctrine of election. David Hilborn observes that Campbell's *unconditionalism* seems to be dependent on a "soteriological *universalism*," especially when he invokes "Barth's famous recasting of election in universalist terms in the *Church Dogmatics*" in defending unconditional benevolence.[95]

But besides running into insuperable exegetical obstacles, Barth's position is ultimately incoherent as well. Let me explain why I think this is the case. By saying that everyone is elect in Christ, Barth thinks that he has eliminated the anxiety over the question, "Am I among the elect?" Yet his confidence in God's sovereign freedom presses him in the end to draw back from the conclusion that everyone will be saved in the end.[96] At least in the traditional Reformed view, we find our election in Christ. *All* who look to Christ are chosen, redeemed, justified, being sanctified, and will be glorified (Rom 8:30–31). But in Barth's view, it is at least possible that some of the elect, who are already redeemed and justified, will finally be lost. This is the Achilles heel of his doctrine, which creates deeper anxiety. What could account for one whom God has chosen, redeemed, and justified being finally lost? If it is not arbitrary, then it must be due to the persistent refusal to accept God's grace. So faith is, after all, a necessary condition of salvation. Campbell says, "Like Barth, however, I tend to prescind from a definitive answer to this question, since it rests in the hands of a God who knows more than I do and will do a better job of finally unraveling history into its appropriate destinies."[97] Given Campbell's dire warnings about the consequences of such a conclusion, his decision to "prescind from a definite answer to this question" is tantamount to a greater conditionalism

---

93. Hafemann, "Reading Paul's ΔΙΚΑΙΟ-Language," 219.

94. Hafemann, "Reading Paul's ΔΙΚΑΙΟ-Language," 228.

95. David Hilborn, "A Response to Campbell's 'Connecting the Dots,'" in *Beyond Old and New Perspectives on Paul: Reflections on the Work of Douglas Campbell*, ed. Chris Tilling (Eugene, OR: Cascade, 2014), 121, citing *CD* II/1, 274, 373, 553; II/2, 2, 27, 92, 164, 265, 496; III/2, 562, 602–40.

96. *CD* III/2, 186–88, 602–40. Cf. *CD* II/1, 274, 373, 553; II/2, 2, 27, 92, 164, 265, 496; III/2, 562, 602–40.

97. Campbell, "Douglas Campbell's Response to David Hilborn," in *Beyond Old and New Perspectives on Paul: Reflections on the Work of Douglas Campbell*, ed. Chris Tilling (Eugene, OR: Cascade, 2014), 115.

THE GOD WHO JUSTIFIES THE UNGODLY

than traditional "justification theory." Anyone who looks to Christ is assured of everlasting life, according to the Reformation perspective. But in Barth's conception, the objectivity of redemption is finally left in question.

This refusal to affirm universal salvation calls into question Barth's entire soteriology. Is wrath *really* a form of grace? Does no one finally experience rejection and judgment? In spite of his emphatic answer in the affirmative, he succumbs to agnosticism on these questions. At least Ritschl was logically consistent, excluding wrath at the outset as a possible expression of God's righteousness.

Similarly, taking for her example the *Joint Declaration on the Doctrine of Justification* (1999) between representatives of the Lutheran World Federation and the Vatican, Katherine Sonderegger observes that most contemporary conversation partners among mainline Protestants and Catholics have embraced some version of "universalism," particularly that of Karl Barth. Daringly but incontestably, she judges that despite its brilliance, "we may well wonder if Barth's doctrine is not *sui generis*," although it is "more modern than his sources may suggest—indeed, a fitting companion to Schleiermacher's."[98] It goes without saying that the older Reformed *ordo salutis*—the so-called "golden chain" of Romans 8:30—has now vanished from the consciousness of modern theology.[99] Sonderegger says,

> A Reformed theologian might well ask whether the doctrine of justification, shorn of its relation to the doctrine of predestination, can successfully ward off both the confident striving and the anxious insecurity of our age. . . . When universalism forms the backdrop of Christian teaching, faith is vulnerable to becoming a work of the human will with little at stake. We may no longer be able to see why justification became church-dividing in the first place.[100]

These days, she concludes, "justification has little work to do for our easy consciences."[101] "Can the Lord's mighty arm—strong to save—comfort,

---

98. Katherine Sonderegger, "Called to Salvation in Christ," in *What Is Justification About? Reformed Contributions to an Ecumenical Theme,* eds., Michael Weinrich and John P. Burgess (Grand Rapids: Eerdmans, 2009), 134.

99. There are other reasons for Barth's criticism of the very idea of an *ordo salutis*, as I point out in my essay, "Covenant, Election, and Incarnation," as referenced above (174n86).

100. Sonderegger, "Called to Salvation in Christ," 137.

101. Sonderegger, "Called to Salvation in Christ," 137.

177

restore, justify, and beat down Satan under our feet when there is and has always been nothing but election that awaits us?"[102]

However, Campbell's construal is even more self-contradictory than Barth's. On the one hand, he says absolutely, "God, therefore, is not fundamentally just and the atonement designed to assuage God's righteous anger at transgression; God is fundamentally benevolent and the atonement intended to deliver humanity from bondage to evil powers and to reconstitute it in the age to come."[103] "God's fundamental posture toward humanity," says Campbell, "evident in Father, Son, and Spirit, is unconditionally benevolent."[104] Obviously, in the "Lutheran" system, one must believe, so "grace, so defined, does not and cannot denote *unconditional* divine action or salvific initiative. . . . It is 'unmerited,' or 'undeserved,' rather than 'unconditional' (at which point one wonders whether it really is 'grace' in the way that the signifier is usually defined theologically)."[105] At this point he is closer to Ritschl than to Barth: God is gracious *rather than* just. This in contrast to the retributive "Lutheran" view according to which God "must reward the righteous inevitably and punish the guilty implacably."[106] Further, he assumes that retributive justice is simply *unjust* in the case of God. "It is not just to hold individuals accountable for acts that they cannot help committing."[107]

On the other hand, Campbell not only leaves the door open to God's justice having the last word in some cases but qualifies his absolute contrast of divine love with justice and wrath considerably. Recall his critique of the "Lutheran" view that God "must reward the righteous inevitably and *punish the guilty implacably*." Yet in leaving open the possibility of some being lost, Campbell himself declares, "There is no anger deeper or *more implacable—or more appropriate*—than the anger of a fundamentally loving God confronted with the evils of a humanity committed to hate instead of love, and to vicious relationships of exploitation and violence instead of relationships of fidelity, affirmation, and peace."[108]

So is God's response to *some* people finally conditioned on their behavior? And how is this response—"no anger deeper or more implacable"—consistent with the idea of a God who is *fundamentally* benevolent and

102. Sonderegger, "Called to Salvation in Christ," 137–38.
103. Campbell, *The Deliverance of God*, 192.
104. Campbell, *The Deliverance of God*, 71.
105. Campbell, *The Deliverance of God*, 27.
106. Campbell, *The Deliverance of God*, 16.
107. Campbell, *The Deliverance of God*, 48–49.
108. Campbell, "Response to David Hilborn," 115.

unconditional rather than just? Campbell himself has insisted with great vigor that his thesis must be taken as a whole without exceptions or qualifications. Yet he offers his own qualifications, and they threaten to bring down the logical system that Campbell (and Barth) have constructed. Campbell concedes that Paul does talk in places about God's wrath, but "it might be more akin to a surgical action—the wrath of aggrieved love," he says, "not the anger of affronted justice."[109] But in this case, the "violence" has merely shifted from "affronted justice" to a crime of passion, which is hardly more "benevolent." In any event, unlike Ritschl, Campbell so prevaricates on his central thesis that his final answer becomes unclear.

Campbell makes everything turn on conditional (contractual) versus unconditional salvation.[110] The gift requires no response, "with no strings attached, as pure gift."[111] Noting Campbell's dependence on Thomas and James Torrance, Barclay judges, "In perfecting the singularity of grace, Campbell sounds most like Marcion (deploying some of the same vocabulary)." Only if grace (not justice) is God's only way of relating to human beings is it truly grace.[112] The biblical narrative—the specific shape that it takes and the actions that God takes to bring it to its denouement—is filled with unnecessary and trivial twists and turns if benevolence is God's only attribute. Furthermore, as Westerholm reminds us, "A god who chose to overlook the disfigurement of a good creation would be neither good nor just."[113]

Campbell rests his case for universal benevolence not only on God's nature but on the inability of sinners, which apparently renders them nonculpable for their response to God. "Non-Christians are fundamentally *incapable* of any such reasoning or activity." In fact, "The more radical view of human sinfulness is—again—arguably the dominant opinion of Paul's other texts."[114] However, none of this matters when God is more primordially benevolent than anything else. To whatever extent Campbell rearranges the pieces, his *description* of the "justification

109. Campbell, *The Deliverance of God*, 93.

110. Barclay, *Paul and the Gift*, 100–105.

111. Barclay, *Paul and the Gift*, 100.

112. Barclay, *Paul and the Gift*, 173. Stephen Westerholm also draws the connection of Campbell's view to Marcion in *Justification Reconsidered*, 90. Campbell expresses his dependence on the Torrances throughout *The Deliverance of God* but especially on the following pages: xxiv, 14–15, 212, 939–40n10.

113. Stephen Westerholm, *Justification Reconsidered: Rethinking a Pauline Theme* (Grand Rapids: Eerdmans, 2013), 91.

114. Campbell, *The Deliverance of God*, 75.

theory" (in its anthropology and doctrines of God, the atonement, justification, and even the role of faith) belongs to a trajectory of criticism that leads from Ritschl through Cremer via Käsemann and casts its shadow across much of theology and biblical scholarship today.

The new perspective and the apocalyptic school share the trajectory up to Käsemann. God's righteousness *is* his covenant faithfulness, which *is* positive deliverance—a relationship and not conformity to a norm. With the exception of Dunn, they hold that Paul's phrase πίστις Χριστοῦ (Rom 3:22, 26; Gal 2:16; 2:20; 3:22; Phil 3:9) means "the faith(fullness) of Christ" rather than "faith in Christ" (see ch. 10). But it is at this point—Käsemann—that they part ways. For Dunn and Wright, God's righteousness means his saving faithfulness to Israel, while for Käsemann, Martyn, and Campbell it means his faithfulness to deliver the world from the evil powers of sin and death.

Yet neither of the current wings of the Cremer trajectory (especially with Campbell's perfection of singularity) can account for the question that Paul took for granted as the heart of the topic: How can God be just *and* justify the ungodly? (Rom 3:26). If this is not a real question—indeed, conundrum—for us as well, then we have probably not wrestled yet with Paul's doctrine of God.

THE WRATH OF GOD REVEALED FROM HEAVEN

Saved from what? If God is only gracious, then what are we to make of the urgent warning of John the Baptist, Jesus, and the apostles, including Paul, concerning the coming wrath? Our concept of salvation in general and justification in particular will be in large part determined by what we consider to be the threat from which we are rescued.

Scripture indicates that the plight is many-sided. In Adam, we are heirs of death, subject to the evil powers, and destined finally for exclusion from God's everlasting peace and glory. In short, we are "under the law," "under the dominion of the flesh," and, as transgressors of the covenant, subject to God's wrath. In Christ, we are heirs of immortal life, sharing in Christ's everlasting triumph over Satan and evil, and are destined finally for being raised bodily and glorified with Christ by the Spirit in the presence of the Father forever.

Although the plight is many-sided, Scripture frequently identifies the *basis* of all our woes in condemnation. Death is a legal sentence, a covenantal sanction, imposed for treason (Rom 6:23; 1 Cor 15:56). We are the plaything of evil powers and captive to Satan because the charges that he brings against us before God are well-founded, and we are corrupt because we are guilty from conception by union with Adam (John 8:44). Our exclusion from God's presence is demanded by God's goodness, justice, and holiness (John 3:18). But when the basis of the law's condemnation is removed—that is, when we are justified—death no longer has a claim on us; we are released from the powers. Christ by his cross triumphed over these powers precisely by cancelling the debt that stood against us (Col 2:13–15). And we *must* be raised in the likeness of Christ on the last day, since he is the firstfruits of the whole harvest (1 Cor 15:20). As I argue in the following two chapters, God's deliverance of human beings—and the wider creation—from bondage to sin, death, the powers, and the flesh are nuclear to Paul's soteriology. But we have still not plumbed the depth of the plight according to Paul until we have discovered what he considers the root cause of these enemies: namely, the condemnation of the law that renders death a just sentence in the first place (e.g., Rom 5:12, 14; 6:23; 1 Cor 15:22, 56).

The core agreement among those identified with the new perspective is expressed well by James D. G. Dunn. He says, "The leading edge of Paul's thinking was the conviction that God's purpose embraced Gentile as well as Jew, not the question of how a guilty man might find a gracious God."[115] If this is so, Stephen Westerholm replies, "then it must be said that Paul's message to the Thessalonians left them in the dark about the core of his thinking while pointlessly answering a question that they were born in quite the wrong time and place to even dream of raising. The answer Paul gave to the question he is no longer allowed to have raised was that God had provided, through his Son Jesus, deliverance from the coming wrath (1:10; 5:9)."[116] This constitutes "salvation," and its announcement is "the gospel."[117]

The importance of this argument lies in the fact that 1 Thessalonians, probably the earliest Pauline letter, does not mention anything about gentile inclusion. Like the prophets, he warns of imminent judgment: "the coming wrath." Westerholm continues,

---

115. James D. G. Dunn, "Works of the Law and the Curse of the Law (Gal. 3:10–14)" in *The New Perspective on Paul*, 2nd ed. (Grand Rapids: Eerdmans, 2007), 130.
116. Westerholm, *Justification Reconsidered*, 6.
117. Westerholm, *Justification Reconsidered*, 6.

We may well wonder whether [Krister] Stendahl can be right in suggesting that the question "How am I to find a gracious God?" has occupied people in the modern West, but it is inconceivable that he is right in denying such a concern to the people of antiquity— particularly if we think of those who responded to Paul's message of pending doom. Whether or not it induced a harbinger of the introspection characteristic of later times is, in this regard, a red herring. With or without an introspective conscience, anyone who takes seriously a warning of imminent divine judgment must deem it an urgent concern to find God merciful.[118]

Even by the time that Paul comes to Corinth, there is apparently no mention of the issue of gentile inclusion. He does refer to being sensitive to both Jews and gentiles, yet "so that by all means I might save some (1 Cor 9:20–22; cf. 10:33)." However, in both letters, "salvation" is "deliverance from God's wrath and judgment."[119] By the time that Paul writes Romans, the wrath of God is still the central problem, but justification has become more fully articulated as the heart of its solution.

For I am not ashamed of the gospel, for it is the power of God for salvation to everyone who believes, to the Jew first and also to the Greek. For in it the righteousness of God is revealed from faith for faith, as it is written, "The righteous shall live by faith." For the wrath of God is revealed from heaven against all ungodliness and unrighteousness of men, who by their unrighteousness suppress the truth. (Rom 1:16–18)

The Gospel of John opens with the incarnation of the Word precisely because of God's imminent judgment, not only on the world but on Israel, dividing the people into "wheat" and "chaff." Indeed, it is often noted that Jesus had more to say about hell and judgment than the apostles. Unsurprisingly, this too is Paul's immediate concern.

Much of the contemporary criticism of the Reformation doctrine of justification is propelled by the dislocation of the many effects of the fall from its basis in our condemnation according to God's law. This generates a host of false choices that I mentioned in the introduction:

118. Westerholm, *Justification Reconsidered*, 5–6.
119. Westerholm, *Justification Reconsidered*, 7.

Christus Victor versus *Agnus Dei*, salvation-historical versus apocalyptic, cosmic and ecclesial versus personal, transformative versus forensic, and so forth. Rather than this guilt, one or another of guilt's effects operates as the determinative problem that the gospel solves. However, a biblical view does not reduce the plight to guilt any more than it reduces the solution to justification. Rather, it teaches us that once the guilt and condemnation of sin are removed, forgiveness and justification lead to adoption (reconciling enemies and making them coheirs with Christ), sanctification (breaking the bondage of sin and the powers of the flesh), and glorification (transformation of this lowly body into the glorious likeness of Christ's deified humanity).

The approaching day of the Lord's wrath was the eschatological horizon that first-century Jews and Christians shared. In the light of the interweaving of the distinct Sinai and Zion traditions that we have encountered, it should be little surprising that the contemporaries of Jesus and Paul should have been ambivalent at least about whether the messianic age would be one of unmitigated deliverance. In any case, the religious leaders were set straight on this account by John the Baptist (Matt 3:7–12). More than seven centuries earlier, Amos had warned Israel against assuming that the coming "Day of the LORD" is going to be a saving deliverance for the nation (Amos 5:18–24). All the prophets of Israel and Judah prophesy the messiah's advent as simultaneously a regathering of Yahweh's scattered people and a division within the nation itself. The "Israel according to the flesh" would be sifted, and only those who are circumcised in heart would remain.

This message, which is the heart of Paul's argument in Romans 9–11, was carried by Jesus from the beginning of his ministry. It is certainly true that their contemporaries were not inclined to meditations on the so-called afterlife. They were looking for God to make things right and to vindicate them as his people publicly before the eyes of the nations on the earth. The dominant eschatology at least of the Pharisees turned on the resurrection of the just, not on the flight of the soul from its bodily prison house. However, the question, "Who is Israel" was also not simply an abstract question about ecclesiology but provoked personal anxiety about whether one belonged or would in fact be subject to the wrath to come. The scribe was not stirred by a fresh reading of Plato or a modern evangelist when he asked Jesus, "Teacher, what good deed must I do to have eternal life?" (Matt 19:16). Especially since it would be the resurrection of the *just*, there was much pondering of the precise identity of "the just" and the conditions for being in that number. It is therefore not a reflection of the tortured subjectivity of an early modern Luther that Jesus's auditors were concerned about their place in the kingdom of God. It was about ecclesiology *and* soteriology, tangled in an inextricable web of assumptions, hopes, and fears.

Jon Levenson points out that the concern with personal salvation was always very real for the informed person in early Judaism. How can Judaism go on affirming the inviolability of the national covenant in the face of exile, not to mention the destruction of the temple? After all, the temple was the place of removing the sinner's guilt. Levenson says that this could only be maintained—in the absence of land, temple, and kingdom—by redefining the whole faith of Israel. In "a world without a Temple," one's piety and good deeds replace sacrifices.[120] The question for a Jewish person then becomes one of personal, ethical ascent. In view of Psalms 15 and 24, "How does one climb that mountain? What must one do to move from profane space to sacred space, from this world to the world-to-come? The question is a large one in rabbinic theology."[121]

The major break with Judaism occurred precisely at the point where Jesus was proclaimed as "the end [*telos*] of the law for righteousness to everyone who believes" (Rom 10:4). Recognizing the "Mosaic/Sinaitic and the Davidic/Zionistic orientations" as contrasting categories, Levenson says that the priority of the former over the latter is precisely where Judaism and Christianity part ways. "In fact, the Davidic theology is the origin of Jewish messianism and the christology of the church."[122] The Sinai legacy, according to Levenson, rather than being the "schoolmaster" to lead us to Christ, is integrated into the Zion tradition in that the messiah will come with "Israel's observance of the stipulations of Sinai."[123] "If the Davidic covenant never displaced the Sinaitic in the Hebrew Bible," he says, "it did, in a sense, in the New Testament."[124]

---

120. Jon D. Levenson, *Sinai and Zion: An Entry into the Jewish Bible* (San Francisco: HarperSanFrancisco, 1985), 180–81.

121. Levenson, *Sinai and Zion*, 183.

122. Levenson, *Sinai and Zion*, 194.

123. Levenson, *Sinai and Zion*, 209.

124. Levenson, *Sinai and Zion*, 216. I would only add that in the New Testament, Sinai is not displaced, but fulfilled. It is rendered obsolete not because it was wrong, but because it was always a temporary regime and reached its goal despite Israel's failures. In fact, precisely because Israel's representative servant has kept his Father's word, even in this deeper (legal, not just typological) sense, the law-covenant has been fulfilled.

Composed probably in Alexandria between 200 BC and AD 50, Wisdom of Solomon (or Book of Wisdom) was included in the Septuagint.[125] Comparing this text with Romans 1:18–2:5, J. A. Linebaugh observes, "'The Wrath of God is being revealed from heaven' (Rom 1:18). . . . Paul's proclamation, however, does not begin with a revelation of saving righteousness; the first word is a word of *wrath*. The divine wrath that is revealed in Paul's preaching (1:18) will be fully enacted at the revelation of God's 'righteous judgment' (2:5)—a judgment in which the conclusion that 'Jews and Gentiles alike are all under the power of sin' (3:9) can only have one consequence: 'No one will be declared righteous' (3:20)." Wisdom of Solomon 13–15, like Romans 1:18–2:5, "considers the relationship of Jews and Gentiles before God within the human history of idolatry."[126] As God judged the Egyptians, this coming wrath (according to Wisdom of Solomon) is "the 'fitting judgment of God' (12:26)."

Linebaugh explains,

> Wisdom unleashes this rhetorical attack in three stages, moving from (1) the folly of nature worship (13:1–9) to (2) the origins of idolatry and the ethical corruption it causes (13:10–15:17) and finally on to (3) the particularly foolish and debased cultic practices of the Egyptians (15:18–19). . . . "If they had the power to know so much as to try to understand the material world, how did they not find the Lord of these things?" (13:8–9; cf. 13:1).[127]

Idolatry is the heart of immorality "and the theological conclusion": "the ungodly and their ungodliness are equally hateful to God" (14:9). But Israel is innocent: "For neither has the evil intent of human art deceived us, nor the fruitless toil of painters" (15:4). "Such potential sin, however, is an actual impossibility: 'we will not sin' (Wis 15:2)."[128]

Linebaugh continues, Romans 1:18–2:5 starts in Eden, with the same "argumentative sequence" as well as "themes and vocabulary."[129] Wisdom says that Israel will escape, and the judge in Romans 2:3

---

125. Jonathan A. Linebaugh, "Wisdom of Solomon and Romans 1:18–2:5: God's Wrath against *All*," in *Reading Romans in Context: Paul and Second Temple Judaism*, ed. Ben C. Blackwell, John K. Goodrich, and Jason Maston (Grand Rapids: Zondervan, 2015), 39.

126. Linebaugh, "Wisdom of Solomon and Romans 1:18–2:5," 38.

127. Linebaugh, "Wisdom of Solomon and Romans 1:18–2:5," 40.

128. Linebaugh, "Wisdom of Solomon and Romans 1:18–2:5," 41.

129. Linebaugh, "Wisdom of Solomon and Romans 1:18–2:5," 41.

"appears to presume that he 'will escape God's judgment' . . . because God is *patient and kind*—an echo of Exod 34 that echoes Wisdom's appeal to LXX Exod 34:9 (Rom 2:4; cf. Wis 15:1)." Yet in spite of the golden calf episode, Wisdom insists on "Israel's innocence in relation to idolatry." In contrast, "Paul's reminder that 'you who pass judgment' also 'do the same things' (Rom 2:1, 3) serves to *include* Israel within the human story of sin. . . . The revelation of wrath is connected to the revelation of *righteousness* by the repeated use of the word *for* in 1:16–18."[130] The "righteousness of God," therefore, cannot refer exclusively to God's deliverance.

> The progression of Paul's logic suggests that the word of wrath is the first word of a two-part proclamation: wrath and righteousness, death and life. . . . For Wisdom, God could have been reasoned to from creation, but this potential has gone unrealized. Paul, however, says that "what may be known about God is plain . . . because God has made it plain" (Rom 1:19). Thus, in contrast to Wisdom, people "knew God" (1:21), and their error is not stupidity, but sin— the failure to honor God "as God" (1:21) and the corresponding idolatry of worshiping the creature (1:25; cf. 1:21–24).[131]

Whereas for Wisdom "the movement from idolatry to immorality is a *natural devolution*," Linebaugh observes, "Paul presents this as an enactment of *divine judgment*: idolaters are *handed over* to immorality."[132]

The situation is not one of unbelievers going about their daily business unaware of God, arguments for his existence, evidence of his providence and miracles, and so forth. Rather, the situation is more like that of a selfish husband who knows his wife but dislikes her and, consequently, perversely interprets every evidence of her noble character—kindness, love, wisdom, and so forth—as intolerable oppression and cruelty.

But this analogy is especially true of Israel, Yahweh's bride. Linebaugh adds, "Romans 3:22–23 provides a perfect summary of Rom 1:18–2:5:

---

130. Linebaugh, "Wisdom of Solomon and Romans 1:18–2:5," 42–43. Linebaugh observes that the LXX Psalm 105:20 is almost identical to Romans 1:23: "And they exchanged the glory that was theirs for the likeness of a grass-eating ox." "Wisdom's presentation of an idolatry-free Israel deletes this episode [golden calf] from Israel's history in order to preserve this distinction between the unrighteous (non-Israel) and the righteous (Israel). Paul, however, faces the canonical facts: Israel's original sin at Sinai includes Israel in the history of idolatry and immorality announced in Rom 1:18–32."

131. Linebaugh, "Wisdom of Solomon and Romans 1:18–2:5," 43.

132. Linebaugh, "Wisdom of Solomon and Romans 1:18–2:5," 44.

'There is no difference between Jew and Gentile, for all have sinned.' But for Wisdom, there is a difference."[133] This is the radical assessment of the situation that marks Paul's departure from Judaism, but it is the same verdict found in the prophets, John the Baptist, and Jesus. Like Jesus, Jewish texts like 2 Enoch interpret the prophets as warning of an imminent judgment, a separation of sheep and goats. "How can I share in the resurrection of the just?" is not a question merely of ecclesiology.

Before AD 70, the question was apocalyptic: judgment is imminent, and we need to be on the right side. The Pharisees thought that they were on the right side, trying to reform the cultic and ethical purity of the nation under the precarious conditions of Roman occupation and a thoroughly compromised pseudo-Jewish king. The Qumran exiles were convinced that the *wrong* side was the perverted cult of the Jerusalem temple and its priesthood.

But after the destruction of the temple, it was a moot point. Philonic Judaism had to become more attractive in this situation, with everything in the Hebrew Bible—including eschatology—radically allegorized. Philo is a lodestar for anyone looking for a Platonized gospel of salvation as "going to heaven when you die." In order to be a faithful Jew, one needs no temple, no legitimate priesthood and sacrifices, no literal land. Interestingly, where the departure at the ascension of Jesus allowed for a literal historical fulfillment of the prophecies, Judaism did not. The ascension of Jesus did not end Christianity, as the destruction of Jerusalem and its temple brought an end to traditional Judaism. The incarnate Christ, raised and enthroned at the Father's right hand, is present *bodily* (though in heaven and through the work of the Spirit) in preaching and sacrament. And Jesus—the true temple—will return bodily.

Levenson's characterization of the concern for personal salvation from God's judgment in Second Temple Judaism is supported by the fact that the question is put to Jesus, "How can I be saved?" The young ruler, well-versed in Torah, asked Jesus, "Good Teacher, what must I do *to inherit eternal life?*" (Luke 18:18). After Jesus spoke at length of salvation from the coming judgment only through him, "They said to him, 'What must we do, to be doing the works of God?' Jesus answered

---

133. Linebaugh, "Wisdom of Solomon and Romans 1:18–2:5," 44. See also John M. G. Barclay, "Unnerving Grace: Approaching Romans 9–11 from The Wisdom of Solomon," in *Between Gospel and Election*, ed. F. Wilk and J. R. Wagner, WUNT 257 (Tübingen: Mohr Siebeck, 2010), 91–110. Cf. Westerholm, *Justification Reconsidered*, 32.

them, 'This is the work of God, that you believe in him whom he has sent'" (John 6:28–29). When the Philippian jailer asked, "Sirs, what must I do to be saved?" Paul and Silas did not challenge the question as presupposing a Platonic worldview. Rather, assuming that it was the right question, "They said, 'Believe in the Lord Jesus, and you will be saved, you and your household'" (Acts 16:30–31).

For Sanders, everything in early Judaism hinged on "how getting in and staying in are understood."[134] It seems to me that Sanders's mistake is one of omission. The broader new-perspective dichotomy between a covenantal (ecclesiological) question and a soteriological question proves reductionistic. What does it mean to be "in"? For Jesus, Paul, and their Jewish contemporaries, being "in" meant salvation from the coming judgment and everlasting joy in the presence of Yahweh. If the quest for personal salvation is the imposition of much later gentile interests, why are there so many ancient Jewish texts and rabbinical debates over the weighing of merits in the hope of finding acquittal? *To be within the true Israel is to be saved from that wrath.* In a covenantal worldview, there is no space between these two questions. Belonging to the true church and being justified are roughly equivalent.

The uncircumcised, those outside the community, are already under God's wrath. The New Testament shares that conviction with early Judaism. What is new, astonishingly and offensively new, in the former is the belief that Israel is *not* sheltered from the wrath of God by being "under the law." On the contrary, all people are "under the law" and thereby condemned. By transgressing the covenant, one's circumcision has been annulled (Rom 2:25). Romans is of course concerned in large part with answering the question, "How can we trust God's promise if God has failed to keep his covenant with Israel?" If the wicked are on top and the righteous are subjected to horrible oppression, then either Yahweh or the nation has been unfaithful. The canonical prophets are unified in designating the people as the party in breach, but the people protest their innocence. This follows much of the early Jewish literature as well. Ezra especially dares to ask the most poignant questions of Uriel, the high angel of Yahweh in 4 Ezra.

Paul's point is that God has not been unfaithful. On the contrary, if he were to be faithful merely to the Sinai covenant, there would be

---

134. E. P. Sanders, *Paul and Palestinian Judaism: A Comparison of Patterns of Religion* (Philadelphia: Fortress, 1977), 17.

no Israelites left. But he has been faithful to the Abrahamic covenant, which *he* swore. It will be a greater fulfillment than anything that Israel could have expected had they been obedient to the covenant that *they* swore at Sinai. Already, "wild branches" are being grafted onto the vine of Israel; the word—specifically the gospel—has *not* failed, even though the people of Israel, along of course with the gentile world, have failed thoroughly (Rom 9–11). The breach of Sinai cannot annul God's faithfulness to Abraham and his seed forever: "He who calls you is faithful, and he will do it" (1 Thess 5:24); "God, by whom you were called into the fellowship of his Son, Jesus Christ our Lord, is faithful" (1 Cor 1:9; 2 Cor 1:18). Can Israel's unbelief "nullify the faithfulness of God? By no means! Let God be true though every man a liar" (Rom 3:3–4). God promised through the prophets that he would save his people not because of their righteousness but because of his name and the promise that he made to Abraham (Ps 143:11–12; Ezek 36:22–28; 39:25, etc.) and to David (1 Kgs 11:12, 13, 34; 15:4–5, 19:34; 2 Chr 6:42; Ps 132:10; Isa 37:35; Hos 3:5).

The parable of the tax collector and Pharisee is explicit (Luke 18:14), but in sharing fellowship with the moral outcasts, the entire ministry of Jesus is the enactment of the justification of the ungodly. This is how God is fulfilling his promise to Abraham in and through his single offspring. Almost all of Jesus's sharp run-ins with the Pharisees turned on such actions, since purity (ethical and ceremonial) was the sine qua non of justification. God judges *rightly*, which means that the violators are condemned and those who are righteous in themselves are acquitted. Jesus turns this thinking on its head. But on what basis? He is either flaunting Torah, and therefore contradicting his claim to be fulfilling rather than dispensing with the law, or he is making *himself* the temple where he dispenses forgiveness. Further, Jesus's repeated imperative for entering the kingdom is "repent and believe in the gospel" (Mark 1:15). The kingdom is, more than anything else, God's righteousness ("seek first . . .") and yet, simultaneously, the "forgiveness of sins" (Luke 1:77; 7:47–50). Even the outpouring of the Holy Spirit, the other attorney (ἄλλον Παράκλητος), is associated with the courtroom trial, bringing about within us the conviction of sin and righteousness (John 14:16).

This correlation of the gospel of the kingdom with the forgiveness of sins is carried forward in Acts (3:19; 5:31; 10:43; 13:38). Bultmann is correct when he says, "Jesus looks to the future, to the *coming* kingdom of God—which is coming or dawning *now*. But Paul looks back . . . to an event which enables him to maintain that in Jesus the eschaton has occurred."[135] As a sign of salvation, it is not surprising that Jesus placed so much weight on faith as the instrument of being healed. "One can go further," according to John Reumann, "and say that precisely in the words of Jesus, 'Only believe!' (*monon pisteue*, Mark 5:36) one has in essence Paul's phrase, 'faith alone'!"[136] Even the miraculous healings were signs of the kingdom as, more than anything else, the forgiveness of sins (Luke 5:23–24). As Fitzmyer observes, justification becomes more central after its eschatological basis occurred in Jesus's resurrection.[137]

THEODICY AND THE WRATH OF GOD: DEUTERONOMY DOESN'T WORK?

Why do the righteous suffer and the wicked prosper? The answer for Asaph and Job, among other figures in the Old Testament, is eschatological vindication for the former and judgment for the latter. Yet this only intensifies the question, "How can I be sure that I am among the former?" which is inextricable from the question, "What must I do to be saved?" Yahweh will spread his dominion around the world. But right now, precisely in the context of exile and oppression, the real question is the coming wrath of God. Interpreting *this* is primary. No less for Qumran and 4 Ezra than for John the Baptist, Jesus, and the apostles is "the coming wrath," which includes unfaithful Jews as well as the gentiles. While the continuing exile plays its role, the coming wrath is the headline for all parties in first-century Palestine.

The Greek king Antiochus IV Epiphanes (Ἀντίοχος Δ΄ ὁ Ἐπιφανής, *Antíochos D' ho Epiphanēs*, meaning "God manifest") ruled the Seleucid Empire from 175 to 164 BC. By sacking Jerusalem and profaning the temple, he provoked the Maccabean revolt. It was in this context apparently that the Qumran sect formed, and they gained popularity when the Hasmonean heirs of the Maccabean heroes became embroiled in political infighting and cultic compromise.

Even though some—probably even the majority—were scattered

---

135. Rudolf Bultmann, "The Significance of the Historical Jesus for the Theology of Paul," in *Faith and Understanding I*, ed. Robert Funk (New York: Harper & Row, 1969), 233.

136. Reumann, *"Righteousness" in the New Testament*, 25.

137. Fitzmyer, response to John Reumann, 202.

throughout Jerusalem and the Diaspora, only about three hundred formed the Qumran community. For these "true believers," the change of the cultic calendar rendered the entire sacrificial system null and void, since for Torah the precise time of the sacrifices was inseparable from their efficacy. Hartmut Stegemann observes,

> On the basis of the Essenes' messianic concept, it was necessarily reserved to the *future* that there would be high priests and kings in Israel. And this future could only begin with the coming Last Judgment of God. . . . God had revealed this fixed term through the biblical prophets. The Essenes had at first counted on the year 70 B.C.; then they had recognized their error and, on the basis of a new exegesis of the book of Daniel, had established that the Last Judgment would come only in A.D. 70.[138]

So the appearance of John the Baptist and Jesus around AD 30 "was of no importance," since the announcement of an *imminent* judgment contradicted the AD 70 "expectation." They were divided over whether to wait or act, but most were patient and even endured martyrdom without physical resistance."[139]

For the Qumran sect, as for John the Baptist, the coming judgment will not only divide Israel and the nations but will separate Israel itself.

> It is simply in their strict connection of all salvation for Israel to its *presence in the Holy Land* that the Essenes are to be distinguished from many of their Jewish contemporaries. The Essenes regarded Jews living in the worldwide Diaspora as rejected by God unless they returned to the Holy Land before the Last Judgment. Likewise, the Essenes believed that all of those Jews within the Holy Land who failed to follow the will of God revealed in the Torah with that clarity and earnestness which characterized the Essenes themselves were about to be struck by God's punishment in the Last Judgment. Outside the pan-Israelite union of the Essenes in the Holy Land, there could ultimately be no salvation, neither for Jew nor for Gentile.[140]

---

138. Hartmut Stegemann, *The Library of Qumran: On the Essenes, Qumran, John the Baptist, and Jesus* (Grand Rapids: Eerdmans, 1998), 158.

139. Stegemann, *The Library of Qumran*, 159, citing Josephus, *Jewish War* 2.152–58.

140. Stegemann, *The Library of Qumran*, 201.

The central figure of the group, the Teacher of Righteousness, died around 110 BC. He could not therefore be a messianic figure. The group calculated in any case that "the time of the Last Judgment revealed that there were still 'some forty years' to pass before the end of days, the Essenes dispensed with choosing a successor and instead expected the future to bring a priestly messiah in addition to a royal messiah."[141]

If the Qumran community is illustrative, Second Temple Judaism had a prominent place for a righteousness of God that demands and condemns violators (with a sober view of human depravity and failure to keep Torah) *and* a righteousness that God gives by grace alone, pardoning sins and accepting as righteous those who trust in his mercy.[142] In fact, according to the community's commentary on Habakkuk 2:4 (cited by Paul), we read that "God will deliver from the House of Judgment" those who have sinned "because of their faith in the Teacher of Righteousness."[143]

J. Christaan Beker is therefore correct when he explains,

In Jewish apocalyptic the faithfulness and vindication of God is primarily directed to the vindication of those in Israel who are obedient to the Law of God. . . . Although Israel can conceive of a new covenant with God in the messianic era, it finds the notion of a new Torah or its abrogation abhorrent. . . . Paul modifies this apocalyptic motif at its very foundation. He does not draw a dividing line between those faithful to the Torah and gentile "sinners" (Gal. 2:15), but marks the death of Jesus Christ as the focal point of God's universal wrath and judgment.[144]

There is no division in biblical or Jewish sources between "loving the sinner" and "hating the sin." "For the ungodly and their ungodliness are equally hateful to God" (Wis 14:9). Although God loves and cares providentially for all he has made, God's redemptive love is directed to his elect. The Epistle of Enoch (composed by multiple authors between 300 BC and the first century) complains, "Having hoped to become the

141. Stegemann, *The Library of Qumran*, 207, quoting the Damascus Document 20:15.
142. See especially the Manual of Discipline (col. 11), reproduced by Reumann, *"Righteousness" in the New Testament*, 19.
143. Quoted in Reumann, *"Righteousness" in the New Testament*, 19.
144. J. Christiaan Beker, *The Triumph of God: The Essence of Paul's Thought*, trans. Loren T. Stuckenbruck (Minneapolis: Fortress, 1990), 25.

head, we have become the tail" (103:11; cf. Deut 28:13, 44). However, as J. A. Linebaugh observes, God's justice will be revealed.

> The question is whether this upside-down existence, implying as it does the inversion of the Deuteronomic pattern of blessings and curses, reflects reality or is simply a temporary aberration of injustice. The sinners express one opinion: "The pious die according to fate, and what is gained for them by their works?" (102:6). Enoch offers an alternative: at the judgment the righteous "will not be found as sinners" (104:5). The apparent righteousness of the rich (96:4) and the assumed disobedience of the downcast (103:9–15) will both be exposed as illusions of injustice in an eschatological reversal of fortunes (104:5–6).[145]

God will balance the scales. "The *Epistle* is a revelation that the righteousness of God will be disclosed."[146] Linebaugh adds,

> Paul, by contrast, locates the revelation of divine righteousness in the *now*: "But *now* apart from the law the righteousness of God has been made known" (Rom 3:21). To Enochic ears, these words can only be heard as an announcement that what was promised to happen at the future judgment has occurred in the event Paul calls "the redemption that came by Christ Jesus" (3:24). Like the *Epistle*, Romans describes "the day . . . when [God's] righteous judgment will be revealed," when "God will repay each person according to what they have done" (2:5–6). The time preceding this judgment is a period of "forbearance" (3:25). But rather than seeing this period as the present, Romans 3:21–26 puts it in the past. For Paul, the period of forbearance—the time when God "left the sins committed beforehand unpunished" (3:25)—ended in the enactment of divine righteousness that is the death of Jesus Christ. What the *Epistle* promises as an end-time judgment, Paul proclaims as apocalypse now: God's act of "present[ing] Christ as a sacrifice of atonement"

---

145. Jonathan A. Linebaugh, "The *Epistle of Enoch* and Romans 3:21–31: The Revelation of God's Righteousness," in *Reading Romans in Context: Paul and Second Temple Judaism*, ed. Ben C. Blackwell, John K. Goodrich, and Jason Maston (Grand Rapids: Zondervan, 2015), 60. See James C. VanderKam, *1 Enoch: A New Translation* (Minneapolis: Fortress, 2004).
146. Linebaugh, "The *Epistle of Enoch* and Romans 3:21–31," 61.

(3:25) is the revelation of God's "righteous judgment" (2:5)—the judgment of God against sin.[147]

Further, like other texts that we have seen, the Epistle of Enoch draws a sharp contrast between "the righteous and the sinners," while Paul says, "there is no difference . . . for all have sinned" (3:22–23; cf. 3:9). For the Epistle of Enoch, such a claim can lead to only one conclusion: condemnation. "And this is exactly what Paul concludes within the closed circle of the law in Romans 3:20: 'No one will be declared righteous in God's sight by the works of the law.'"[148] From an Enochic perspective, the death of Christ can hardly be seen as salvific, as if two wrongs make a right (see 1 En. 99:15; 102:4–11; 103:3, 9–10, 15). The unjust death of Jesus ("the righteous") can hardly be a means of finally dealing with sin; the "cursed one" could hardly be the means of undoing the curse.[149]

But this is precisely where Judaism and Christianity part ways. God has not been unfaithful; Israel has. The curses have fallen on the nation. But all who enter the covenant of grace through Christ ("the door," "the narrow way," "the gate to the sheepfold," etc.) are saved because the ultimate curse of sin and death that encompasses all of humanity has been borne by him. Objectively, for the elect, the last judgment has occurred at Golgotha, just as the beginning of the resurrection of the dead and the age to come begins at Easter. The eschatological vindication of the righteous and the judgment of the wicked have been brought forward into the middle of history. Now we know the end of things, not by entering the typological sanctuary with Asaph but by viewing the incarnate God on the altar, stripped and hanging as the curse-bearing "sinner." We recognize that *we* are the wicked, who are declared righteous for his sake. Not by suspending the law or because God is fundamentally loving rather than just, but because of Christ's obedience, to the point of death on a cross and his resurrection-vindication, God has cancelled our debts and credited us with the righteousness of Christ. "It was to show his righteousness at the present time, so that he might be just and the justifier of the one who has faith in Jesus" (Rom 3:26).

---

147. Linebaugh, "The *Epistle of Enoch* and Romans 3:21–31," 62.
148. Linebaugh, "The *Epistle of Enoch* and Romans 3:21–31," 62.
149. Linebaugh, "The *Epistle of Enoch* and Romans 3:21–31," 63.

CHAPTER 4

JUSTIFIED BY HIS BLOOD

Agnus Dei *and* Christus Victor

"When were you saved?" Many Protestants who ask that question might be as flummoxed as traditional Roman Catholics by the Reformers' answer, roughly paraphrased: "On Easter weekend, around AD 33." Strictly speaking, we are not justified *by faith* any more than by works. It is the apostle Paul himself who declares that we are "justified by his blood" (Rom 5:9) and that Jesus was "raised for our justification" (Rom 4:25).

While Roman Catholic and many Protestant systems treat justification under the third article (i.e., the Holy Spirit and his work of regenerating), early Lutheran and Reformed confessions see justification as a second-article (i.e., christological) doctrine.[1] Jesus's death and resurrection did not make salvation possible but accomplished it. Therefore, one cannot talk about justification as anything other than the realization here and now of what happened objectively in Christ's life, death, and resurrection.

---

1. "The *first and chief article*," Luther writes in the Smalcald Articles (1537), is the *atonement*, which includes justification (*Book of Concord: Confessions of the Evangelical Lutheran Church*, ed. and trans. Robert Kolb and Timothy Wengert [Minneapolis: Fortress, 2000], 295–328). The Belgic Confession (1561) of the Reformed churches testifies to Christ's atonement (art. 21) and its sufficiency which leads to a statement of justification through faith in Christ alone (art. 22–23). Both statements raise the issue of justification *sola fide* as the answer to the question as to whether Christ's death is sufficient for salvation. I do not intend by this comment to suggest that whenever it is treated under the third article justification is misunderstood. The order of instruction should not be given undue significance. It is entirely possible to offer a faithful confession of justification under the locus of the Spirit's *application of redemption*. However, in this case I think that it is important to ground justification in the atonement rather than in the Spirit's work, even though the latter is the essential sine qua non of embracing Christ and therefore being justified.

THE ACHIEVEMENT OF JUSTIFICATION

In the words of the Heidelberg Catechism, "During his whole life on earth, but especially at the end, Christ sustained in body and soul the wrath of God against the sin of the whole human race. This he did in order that, by his suffering as the only atoning sacrifice, he might deliver us, body and soul, from eternal condemnation, and gain for us God's grace, righteousness, and eternal life."[2]

Apart from the atonement, justification either hovers above history as an eternal decision or becomes assimilated to the inner experience of conversion. In fact, Yale theologian George Lindbeck argues that many people find justification incomprehensible because there is a deeper inability to comprehend the atonement. He surmises that even in evangelical circles, exemplary (subjective) theories have become dominant in popular preaching and piety. In any case, "The atonement is not high on the contemporary agendas of either Catholics or Protestants."[3] Though continuing to use *sola fide* language, "deciding for Christ" turns faith "into a meritorious good work."

> Everyone is thus capable of being "born again" if only he or she tries hard enough. Thus with the loss of the Reformation understanding of the faith that justifies as itself God's gift, Anselmic atonement theory became culturally associated with a self-righteousness that was both moral and religious and therefore rather nastier, its critics thought, than the primarily moral self-righteousness of the liberal Abelardians. In time, to move on in our story, the liberals increasingly ceased to be even Abelardian.[4]

Indeed, Lindbeck suggests, much of popular preaching especially in the United States today is a type of "Pelagianism" that is beyond anything propounded at the Council of Trent.[5] "Where the cross once

---

2. Heidelberg Catechism, LD 13, Q 37.
3. George Lindbeck, "Justification and Atonement: An Ecumenical Trajectory," in *By Faith Alone: Essays on Justification in Honor of Gerhard O. Forde*, ed. Joseph A. Burgess and Marc Kolden (Eerdmans, 2004), 205. I would qualify this observation today by noting that several monographs and symposia have displayed a fresh awareness both of the problem that Lindbeck noted and of the importance of the doctrine to the gospel itself.
4. Lindbeck, "Justification and Atonement," 207.
5. Lindbeck, "Justification and Atonement," 209. Arminian theologian Roger Olson agrees: "The gospel preached and the doctrine of salvation taught in most evangelical pulpits and lecterns, and believed in most evangelical pews, is not classical Arminianism, but semi-Pelagianism, if not outright Pelagianism." *Arminian Theology: Myths and Realities* (Downers Grove, IL: InterVarsity, 2006), 30.

stood is now a vacuum."[6] In light of these facts, the Lutheran-Vatican agreements (in which Lindbeck played a large hand) seem irrelevant. "It seems that the withdrawal of the condemnations under these circumstances is not wrong, but vacuous."[7] In addition to the challenge of therapeutic individualism, modern Pelagianism reduces redemption to sociopolitical action. George Hunsinger judges that in much of modern Christianity "the social or horizontal aspect of reconciliation . . . eclipses its vertical aspect."[8]

It is the grounding of justification in Christ's life, work, and ministry that subverts the charge of "legal fiction": that is, an arbitrary decree that has no basis in reality. This chapter labors toward an integrated interpretation of Christ's work that I will call "Vicarious Victor." Like forensic justification, substitution is not the whole story, but without it the other chapters are left blank.[9] The cluster of commercial and legal terms I will be collecting fall under the rubric *Agnus Dei*, while the terms that focus on military conquest I will refer to as *Christus Victor*.

A NEW MAP: THE PROBLEM WITH "THEORIES OF THE ATONEMENT"

The usual method associated with "atonement theories" is more susceptible to distortion than illumination. Distinguishing between objective and subjective theories can be helpful.[10] Less helpful—even distorting—is the typology of *Christus Victor* versus "the Anselmian

---

6. Lindbeck, "Justification and Atonement," 211. Lindbeck's description does not quite do justice to conservative evangelical theology, which has tended to depend considerably on Protestant orthodoxy. However, in actual practice, the pietist-revivalist roots of the movement often work against this theology. As James D. Hunter notes, in popular evangelical speech, salvation is often reduced to steps, procedures, and principles that one takes. One sees this in the title of Billy Graham's best-seller, *How to Be Born Again* (1989). The late nineteenth-century revivalist Charles G. Finney rejected the doctrines of original sin, the substitutionary atonement, justification, and the supernatural character of the new birth, which instead he considered nothing more than the result of following the correct procedures.

7. Lindbeck, "Justification and Atonement," 216.

8. George Hunsinger, *Disruptive Grace: Studies in the Theology of Karl Barth* (Grand Rapids: Eerdmans, 2001), 21.

9. I expand on atonement and justification in *Lord and Servant: A Covenant Christology* (Louisville: Westminster John Knox, 2005), 176–205.

10. Subjective theories teach that the purpose of Christ's death was to effect some change within us: to provide a demonstration of God's love (moral influence) and/or sober warning of God's righteousness (governmental) that might move us to repentance or to offer an example for us to follow of selfless love (moral example). These theories are in fact adopted explicitly by various modern groups. Formulated by the Dutch Arminian Hugo Grotius, the governmental view is favored by many Arminians, while Socinianism and liberal Protestantism have generally adopted exemplary interpretations.

view." The former cannot be sustained apart from substitution, and the latter is a caricature drawn by critics rather than a responsible representation of Anselm's view. Unfortunately, this stereotype is often also promoted by defenders of substitution.

Especially with the dawn of Gustaf Aulén's *Christus Victor* (1931), the theme of Christ's victory over the powers, which he called the "classic" view, has received renewed interest.[11] Far from a dispassionate survey, Aulén held that "the work of Christ is first and foremost a victory over the powers which hold mankind in bondage: sin, death, and the devil."[12] Aulén brought renewed and needed attention to the patristic emphasis on victory (coinciding with the apocalyptic interpretation of justification as deliverance from evil powers, especially by Käsemann). Furthermore, as I will argue, he is correct to emphasize that deliverance from these powers and everlasting communion with the triune God are in fact the goal of redemption. Yet his thesis trades on various false dichotomies, many of which we have already encountered: Hebrew versus Hellenistic, covenantal relationship versus legal norm, ecclesial/cosmic/apocalyptic versus soteriological/individual. The ultimate antithesis is East versus West, with the Orthodox fathers providing a timely alternative to both moralistic (exemplary) and more traditional (substitutionary) interpretations exemplified, Aulén argues, in Anselm's ostensibly feudalistic theory of satisfaction. In addition to criticisms by historical theologians, biblical scholars have questioned Aulén's handling of the biblical material on the subject.[13] His was not the first attempt at pitting the Eastern fathers against the West.[14] Nevertheless, his approach seems to have stuck.

---

11. Gustaf Aulén, *Christus Victor: An Historical Study of the Three Main Types of the Idea of the Atonement*, trans. A. G. Herber (London: SPCK, 1931; repr., New York: Macmillan, 1969).

12. Aulén, *Christus Victor*, 20.

13. Alan Richardson contends that Aulén's theory is not a doctrine of atonement at all, since it focuses exclusively on alien powers and eclipses any notion of the reconciliation of sinners to God (Richardson, *An Introduction to the New Testament* [New York: Harper & Row, 1958], 205). Eugene Fairweather observes, "This is ingenious, but it is not accurate exegesis either of St. Irenaeus or St. Paul. The latter's meaning, reproduced by the former, is quite clearly that the gift of justification is won for sinners through the total human obedience of the righteous Christ" (Fairweather, "Incarnation and Atonement: An Anselmian Response to Aulén's *Christus Victor*," *Canadian Journal of Theology* 7 (July 1961): 174. See also Leonard Hodgson's critique of Aulén's Christology in *The Doctrine of the Atonement* (New York: Scribner, 1951), 147.

14. One of many examples from the nineteenth and twentieth centuries includes H. N. Oxenham's (1865) work in which he asserted astonishingly yet confidently that only with the Reformation was Christ's death "for the first time viewed as a vicarious punishment, inflicted by God on Him instead of on us" (*The Catholic Doctrine of the Atonement* [London: Longman, Green, Longman, Roberts, and Green, 1865], 119). He states earlier (112–13), "There is no trace,

Aulén himself was careful to stipulate that he is describing a "classic idea" rather than a theory.[15] However, many who appeal to Aulén fail to heed his important qualification. For many, one of the attractions of Aulén's approach is that it eschews the choice between penal substitution and an antisupernaturalistic and subjective moralism, which can be illustrated by Adolf von Harnack's remark, "It is not a question of angels and devils, thrones and principalities, but of God and the soul, the soul and its God."[16]

The "theories of atonement" approach, especially when governed by the dichotomy between *Christus Victor* and the Anselmian view, is unhelpful on both historical and theological-exegetical grounds.

As for the historical grounds, this approach assumes that the ancient church had a well-defined theory of the atonement or central motifs they identified as *Christus Victor* and penal substitution. And as for Anselm, his "theory" has been more caricatured than read at first hand. Furthermore, the magisterial Reformers were as interested in Christ's victory over the powers as they were in vicarious sacrifice.[17] While

---

as we have seen, of the notions of vicarious satisfaction, in the sense of our sins being imputed to Christ and His obedience imputed to us, which some of the Reformers made the very essence of Christianity; or, again, of the kindred notion that God was angry with His Son for our sakes, and inflicted on Him the punishment due to us; nor is Isaiah's prophecy interpreted in this sense, as afterwards by Luther; on the contrary, there is much which expressly negatives this line of thought. There is no mention of the justice of God, in the forensic sense of the word; the Incarnation is invariably exclusively ascribed to His love; the term satisfaction does not occur in this connection at all, and where Christ is said to suffer for us, *huper* (not *anti*) is the word always used, it is not the payment of a debt, as in St. Anselm's *Cur Deus Homo*, but the restoration of our fallen nature, that is prominent in the minds of these writers, as the main object of the Incarnation. They always speak, with Scripture, of our being reconciled to God, not of God being reconciled to us." To this may be added J. F. Bethune-Baker, *An Introduction to the Early Christian History of Christian Doctrine to the Time of the Council of Chalcedon* (London: Methuen, 1903), 351–52, for the extraordinary claim that the patristic consensus sided with what we today call "subjective" theories (e.g., moral influence).

15. Aulén, *Christus Victor*, 174–75. Unlike the sacrificial-substitutionary and subjective views, Aulén said, *Christus Victor* was never "put forward . . . as a rounded and finished theological doctrine . . ." but rather as "an idea, a motif, a theme, expressed in many different variations."

16. Adolf von Harnack, *What Is Christianity?*, trans. Thomas Saunders (Philadelphia: Fortress, 1986), 56. Furthermore, Aulén himself (belonging to the "Lundensian school") shared the popular opposition between Luther and Lutheranism. According to Aulén, Luther represents the greatest *Christus Victor* theologian since the apostles, but Lutheran orthodoxy emphasized forensic justification (138). George O. Evenson provides a helpful general review and especially a good analysis of Aulén's "Luther" in his essay, "A Critique of Aulén's *Christus Victor*," *Concordia Theological Monthly* 28 (October 1957): 738–49; cf. Gordon Rupp, *The Righteousness of God: Luther Studies* (London: Hodder and Stoughton, 1953), 16. This assumption of a Luther-versus-Lutheranism dichotomy is carried forward in the new Finnish school and finds its parallel in the Calvin-versus-Calvinism thesis of T. F. and James B. Torrance (T. F. Torrance, "Karl Barth and the Latin Heresy," *Scottish Journal of Theology* 39 [1986]: 451–82; cf. Torrance, "Karl Barth and Patristic Theology," in *Theology Beyond Christendom: Essays on the Centenary of the Birth of Karl Barth May 10, 1986*, ed. John Thompson [Allison Park, PA: Pickwick, 1986], 215–39).

17. It is commonly supposed that the Reformers mediated Latin legalism to modernity, over against the East's emphasis on victory. Examples of this point of view are legion. The argument is

N. T. Wright thinks that Luther was singularly obsessed with legal categories (in the context of purgatory and penance),[18] Aulén himself goes so far as to say that Luther "stands out in the history of Christian doctrine as the man who expressed the classic idea of the Atonement with greater power than any before him."[19] Calvin's interest in the cross as Christ's victory over the powers is well-known.[20] So too is his treatment of the cross in terms not only of his priestly sacrifice but of his threefold office (*munus triplex*), which many have offered as a good way of integrating the motifs.[21] Yet the same can be said of the Reformed orthodox theologians and the confessions, which organize their treatment of Christ's work around the threefold office.[22]

All of this suggests that the pitting of *Christus Victor* against *Agnus Dei* is overdrawn and misleading. As for the theological-exegetical problems with the *Christus Victor* thesis, these will be pointed out in the following argument. First, let me update the map to the present day.

---

made throughout Denny Weaver's *The Nonviolent Atonement*, 2nd ed. (Grand Rapids: Eerdmans, 2011). Mark D. Baker and Joel B. Green refer to a putative shift from a gentler satisfaction theory to "the Luther-Calvin . . . penal substitution model" in *Recovering the Scandal of the Cross* (Downers Grove, IL: IVP Academic, 2011), 169.

18. N. T. Wright, *The Day the Revolution Began: Reconsidering the Meaning of Jesus' Crucifixion* (New York: HarperOne, 2016), 28–33.

19. Aulén, *Christus Victor*, 138. While Calvin scores higher marks in considering Christ's death as restoring the royal and priestly vocation of humanity (49, 76), Luther is seen by Wright as mired still in the medieval world of penance and purgatory and therefore emphasizing Christ's death in almost exclusively propitiatory terms (28–33). Swirling together in the same air, these contradictory theses create a cloud of suspicion that hovers around the Reformation (either Luther or Calvin or both or neither reformer but their successors), justifying in the minds of many a general antipathy to the movement even though there is little first-hand engagement with the sources.

George O. Evenson provides a helpful general review and especially a good analysis of Aulén's "Luther" in his essay, "A Critique of Aulén's *Christus Victor*," *Concordia Theological Monthly* 28 (October 1957): 738–49; cf. Gordon Rupp, *The Righteousness of God: Luther Studies* (London: Hodder and Stoughton, 1953), 16.

20. Robert Peterson notes, "One of Calvin's favorite themes of the atonement was Christ as victor, who conquers the foes of his people" (*Calvin's Doctrine of the Atonement* [Philipsburg, NJ: P&R, 1983], 46).

21. Gabriel Fackre argues as much in "The Lutheran *Capax* Lives," *Trinity, Time, and Church: A Response to the Theology of Robert W. Jenson*, ed. Colin E. Gunton (Grand Rapids: Eerdmans, 2000), 100. Calvin was not the originator of the "threefold office," but, following Martin Bucer (the first to adopt it as a motif), he made it an organizing atonement rubric. See Geoffrey Wainwright, *For Our Salvation: Two Approaches to the Work of Christ* (Grand Rapids: Eerdmans, 1997), 103–4.

22. For a good summary, see Robert J. Sherman, *King, Priest, and Prophet: A Trinitarian Theology of Atonement* (New York: Bloomsbury T&T Clark, 2004), 65–70. Thus there is no basis for the caricature that the Reformers focused exclusively on sacrifice or that they avoided this fate while their followers did not. So we may lay to rest the caricature that the Reformers focused exclusively on sacrifice ("the Anselmian theory") *or* that while they elude this charge, it was their successors who returned to a supposedly medieval "legalism."

Recent Criticism of Agnus Dei

Going well beyond Aulén, *Christus Victor* has become the banner for more radical critiques of substitution that, in the end, repristinate the subjective interpretation of Christ's work. Traditional accounts of Christ's death as the propitiation of God's wrath and satisfaction of God's justice are treated as valorizing—indeed deifying—violence. Joanne Carlson Brown and Rebecca Parker complain, "Divine child abuse is paraded as salvific and the child who suffers 'without even raising a voice' is lauded as the hope of the world."[23] "We must do away with the atonement, this idea of a blood sin upon the whole human race which can be washed away only by the blood of the lamb."[24] Rosemary Radford Ruether argues, "Jesus did not 'come to suffer and die,'" but to liberate the oppressed.[25] He never conceived of his death as redemptive, although he knew that his political mission might lead to that end. What is redemptive is Jesus's undoing of injustice as a singular example and martyr. "The means of redemption is conversion."[26] Thus, redemption is not found in Christ, what he did, or what happened to him, but in us and what we do: our repentance and acts of reconciliation in the world.

Of course, the rejection of all forms of violence has been the center of Anabaptist faith and practice since the failure of the peasant wars. The early Anabaptists advanced a nearly Marcionite hermeneutic over against the magisterial Reformers' stress on the unity of the covenant of grace and by often expressing wariness of the God of the Old Testament's holy wars.[27] Anabaptists preferred a soteriology based on the idea of *Gelassenheit*—surrender to God's will that brings unity between the human and divine spirit—to vicarious substitution and justification. As we will see below, many early Anabaptists exhibited a radical spirit-matter and God-world antithesis that proscribed the belief that Christ assumed our true humanity, thereby provoking the Belgic Confession's condemnation (art. 18). Not surprisingly, it is especially among contemporary representatives (whether of the peace churches or

---

23. Joanne Carlson Brown and Rebecca Parker, "For God So Loved the World?" in *Christianity, Patriarchy, and Abuse: A Feminist Critique*, ed. Joanne Carlson Brown and Carole R. Bohn (New York: Pilgrim, 1989), 2.

24. Brown and Parker, "For God So Loved the World?" 26.

25. Rosemary Radford Ruether, *Introducing Redemption in Christian Feminism* (Sheffield: Sheffield Academic Press, 1998), 104.

26. Rosemary Radford Ruether, *Women and Redemption: A Theological History* (Minneapolis: Fortress, 1998), 279.

27. I am not suggesting that any argument against infant baptism is implicitly Marcionite but only that the temptation to Marcionite hermeneutics emerged in that polemical context.

of some Baptist traditions that identify with this heritage) that we find renewed challenges to substitution.

Some evangelical scholars in recent years have followed this general trend. C. S. Cowles defends a "radical discontinuity" view of the relation between Old and New Testaments, opposing Christ to the God of the holy wars.[28] God had nothing to do with Jesus's crucifixion, argues Brian Zahnd; rather, it was the injustice and wrath of civilization that he bore.[29] Jesus could freely criticize or reject parts of the law and the prophets, argues Gregory A. Boyd.[30] "The Old Testament is responsible for more atheism, agnosticism, disbelief—call it what you will—than any book ever written," he says.[31] In fact, "To be perfectly honest," he adds, "I have a certain respect for Marcion and his followers who decided it was better to 'cast away the Old Testament than tarnish the image of the Father of Jesus Christ by mixing in traces of a warlike God.'" He says, "I admire their bold choice."[32] Like the other scholars mentioned, Boyd takes the Anabaptist side. Luther and Calvin concentrated on "the work and offices of Christ," while "the Anabaptists focused on the person of Christ, with an unparalleled emphasis on the call to obey his teachings and follow his example."[33] Douglas Campbell places himself within this Anabaptist ambit in his own demand that we choose the God of love over the God of justice.[34]

Fortified by René Girard's theory of the "scapegoat mechanism," many such critiques maintain that Jesus died "not as a sacrifice, but in order that there be no more sacrifices," as Girard himself says.[35] Instead of imitating the violence of the scapegoat mechanism, Jesus calls us to imitate his nonviolence. Girard's theory at least in relation to biblical

---

28. C. S. Cowles, "Radical Discontinuity," in *Show Them No Mercy: Four Views on God and Canaanite Genocide*, ed. Stanley N. Gundry (Grand Rapids: Zondervan, 2003), 13.

29. Brian Zahnd, *Sinners in the Hands of a Loving God* (Colorado Springs: Waterbrook, 2017).

30. Gregory A. Boyd, *Crucifixion of the Warrior God: Interpreting the Old Testament's Violent Portraits of the Cross* (Minneapolis: Fortress, 2017), 344.

31. Boyd, *Crucifixion of the Warrior God*, 1005. For example, he describes Elijah's act of calling down fire to consume the soldiers sent by the Baal-worshiping King Ahaziah (2 Kgs 1:10) "the diabolical miracle" that the prophet performed "without the help of the Holy Spirit" (1005).

32. Boyd, *Crucifixion of the Warrior God*, 1, quoting A. A. Milne.

33. Boyd, *Crucifixion of the Warrior God,* 123.

34. See Curtis W. Freeman, "The Faith of Jesus Christ: An Evangelical Conundrum," in *Beyond Old and New Perspectives on Paul: Reflections on the Work of Douglas Campbell*, ed. Chris Tilling (Eugene, OR: Cascade, 2014), 253–54, 258–59, with Campbell's response, 260.

35. Rebecca Adams and René Girard, "Violence, Difference and Sacrifice: A Conversation with René Girard," *Religion and Literature* 25, no. 2 (1993): 21–23, quote on 21. See also René Girard, *Violence and the Sacred* (Baltimore: Johns Hopkins University Press, 1977), 2.

studies has been criticized.[36] However, it continues to play a key role in views of Christ's death as exemplary and locate its efficacy in conversion, repentance, and obedience to our call to redemptive action in the world.

In short, Girard reinterprets the New Testament as a radical critique of the scapegoat mechanism, which, as Christopher Schroeder indicates, "follows the well-known tracks of Marcion."

> Eventually, the labeling of the God of the Old Testament as the "God of scapegoats, the barbaric God of the tribe," as the "God of lynchers" and the "God of executioners," supports the view of the Old Testament as "pre-christian" and fosters the latent anti-Judaism of Christianity. The main reason for this gloomy view of the Hebrew scriptures is that Girard sees divine wrath as inseparable from human violence against a scapegoat.[37]

In recent decades Anabaptist theologians have drawn upon Girard's theory to critique atonement doctrine and construct an alternative "narrative *Christus Victor*" view. J. Denny Weaver considers even the classic *Christus Victor* view too violent.[38] The atonement can only be "saved" if it is stripped of all violent implications associated with traditional views.[39] "Common to this family of views in any of its versions is that the death of Jesus involved a divinely orchestrated plan through which Jesus' death could satisfy divine justice or divine law in order to save sinful humankind."[40] According to Anthony Bartlett, the New Testament really has no place for wrath and its propitiation.[41] So finally, he adopts a line from Peter Lombard: "The death of Christ therefore

36. A helpful critique of Girard's application of his theory to the Bible is provided in Paul Dumouchel, ed., *Violence and Truth: On the Work of René Girard* (Palo Alto, CA: Stanford University Press, 1988). A good argument for righteous violence as necessary for divine hospitality, engaging with Girardian theories is Hans Boersma, *Violence, Hospitality, and the Cross: Reappropriating the Atonement Tradition* (Grand Rapids: Baker Academic, 2006), esp. 25–62, 80–97, 133–152. Divine hospitality proves to be a robust motif for integrating the various aspects of the atonement. In addition, I share his interest in recovering recapitulation as an overarching theme (115–204).

37. Christopher Schroeder, "Standing in the Breach," *Interpretation* 52, no. 1 (January 1988): 17.

38. J. Denny Weaver, *The Nonviolent Atonement* (Grand Rapids: Eerdmans, 2001), 5.

39. Anthony Bartlett, *Cross Purposes: The Violent Grammar of Christian Atonement* (New York: Bloomsbury T&T Clark, 2001), 189.

40. Weaver, *The Nonviolent Atonement*, 16–17. He cites H. D. McDonald, who misinterprets A. A. Hodge. Weaver's description of this view that constitutes the major position he wishes to refute is largely based on secondary research, and not very good research at that.

41. Bartlett, *Cross Purposes*, 203–16.

justifies us, inasmuch as through it charity is excited in our hearts."[42] God cannot be in Christ, reconciling the world to himself through Christ's death, but only in us, reconciling us to each other by exciting us to redemptive repentance through the example of Jesus's nonviolent martyrdom. Weaver says, "The crucifixion of Jesus cannot be interpreted as a divinely sanctioned or divinely willed sacrifice."[43] In fact, "God did not send Jesus to die, but to live, to make visible and present the reign of God."[44] Even the Epistle to the Hebrews "treats Jesus' death as exemplary rather than substitutionary."[45]

Weaver insists that the cross does not affect God's attitude toward us but our "perception of God."[46] No more can the true God be found at work in Israel's holy wars than at the cross. Rather, "Through the *resurrection*, God in Christ has in fact defeated these powers 'for us.'"[47] And the church is not only the ambassador but the agent of this redemption by its enactment of nonviolence. "Paul's church is not an aggregate of justified sinners or a sacramental institute or a means for private self-sanctification but the avant-garde of the new creation in a hostile world, creating beachheads in this world of God's dawning new world and yearning for the day of God's visible lordship over his creation, the general resurrection of the dead."[48]

Not surprisingly, the critique extends to Chalcedonian Christology.[49] Despite the novelty of some of the arguments, it is difficult to resist the impression that these critics simply repeat the trajectory of the *Aufklärung*, with a merely human Jesus who becomes the archetype and pioneer of God's moral kingdom, however this is envisioned.[50]

---

42. Citied by Bartlett, *Cross Purposes*, 221.

43. Weaver, *The Nonviolent Atonement*, 49.

44. Weaver, *The Nonviolent Atonement*, 74.

45. Weaver, *The Nonviolent Atonement*, 64, quoting Loren L. Johns, "'A Better Sacrifice' or 'Better Than Sacrifice'? Michael Hardin's 'Sacrificial Language in Hebrews,'" in *Violence Renounced: René Gerard, Biblical Studies, and Peacemaking*, ed. Willard M. Swartley (Telford: Pandora; Scottdale: Herald, 2000), 121.

46. Weaver, *The Nonviolent Atonement*, 78.

47. Weaver, *The Nonviolent Atonement*, 76, emphasis added.

48. Weaver, *The Nonviolent Atonement*, 49, quoting J. Christiaan Beker, *Paul the Apostle: The Triumph of God in Life and Thought* (Philadelphia: Fortress, 2000), 155.

49. See, e.g., Weaver, *The Nonviolent Atonement*, 93–173.

50. It must be emphasized, however, that such arguments do not seem to be derived in any direct way from the Enlightenment but from a logic that is indigenous to Anabaptist faith and practice. While the *Aufklärung* assimilated the church to the world, Anabaptism has always practiced in varying degrees radical separation with the notion of the church as an alternative *polis*. However, there were debates early on about the Trinity and Chalcedonian Christology as well as a marked antipathy toward penal substitution and forensic justification. Though beyond our scope, the influence of Anabaptist and radical pietist communities on Spinoza, Hobbes, Kant,

Significantly, Judaism took a similar turn after the destruction of the temple; the Jewish family becomes the altar, and each person's repentance the sacrifice.[51] Also, as we have seen in volume 1, medieval theology developed a similar system according to which inner sorrow and resolve to improve forms the heart of the sacrament of penance, culminating in the Pelagianizing emphases of the nominalists. In different ways, the humanist, Anabaptist, and Socinian emphasis on the imitation of Christ's example helped shape the Enlightenment moralism of Kant and later Protestant liberalism, as exemplified by the work of Schleiermacher, Ritschl, and Harnack. The common concept in all these very different approaches is inner repentance rather than external satisfaction.

But where Christianity found the sacrificial system fulfilled in Christ's atoning work, this modern trajectory eschews both the temple cult and the reality to which it pointed. With this context of contemporary discussion in mind, the rest of this chapter focuses on the biblical-theological case for an integrated view of Christ's work.

THE LORD WHO IS SERVANT: RECAPITULATION AND THE OBEDIENCE OF CHRIST

Christus Victor and *Agnus Dei*, victory and sacrifice, are woven together from the very beginning. Christ's victory and vicarious self-offering begin with the incarnation itself. Drawing from a significant patristic vein, Calvin argues, "In short, from the moment when he assumed the form of a servant, he began, in order to redeem us, to pay the price of deliverance."[52]

Already with the theme of recapitulation we discern the integrated threads of the gospel narrative under the rubric of the "great exchange."

and later thinkers (e.g., Schelling and Hegel) is well-documented and suggests that contemporary Anabaptist critiques are less directly influenced by modernity than the other way around. Among the many helpful treatments of the rise of exemplarist theories of the atonement in the wake of the Enlightenment, see Colin Gunton, "The Sacrifice and the Sacrifices: From Metaphor to Transcendental?," in *Trinity, Incarnation and Atonement: Philosophical and Theological Essays*, ed. Ronald J. Feenstra and Cornelius Plantinga Jr., Library of Religious Philosophy 1 (Notre Dame, IN: University of Notre Dame Press, 1989), 211.

51. As we observed in the previous chapter, repentance could take the place of the sacrificial system in certain cases (especially misdemeanors). "And by the compliance of his soul with all the laws of God [one's] flesh is cleansed by being sprinkled with cleansing waters and being made holy with the waters of repentance" (1QS III 6–9). After the destruction of the temple, repentance replaced sacrifices. In one way or another, all of these systems make our repentance propitiatory.

52. *Inst.* 2.15.5.

The "summing-up (ἀνακεφαλαιώσασθαι) of all things in Christ"—or literally "reheadshiping"—in Ephesians 1:10 is behind the idea, and as far as I can tell, the first reference to the Son's work of recapitulation appears in Justin Martyr's *Contra Marcion*.[53] Associated especially with the second-century bishop Irenaeus (in his fifth book of *Against Heresies*), recapitulation became an important patristic motif.

Over against the Gnostics (especially Marcion and Valentinus), the early fathers stressed the unity of God as creator and redeemer. Instead of saving individual souls from their bodies and this world, these ancient Christians taught that God becomes flesh in order to restore it—and more than restore, to raise it to the plane of eschatological glory that Adam's treason aborted. With this emphasis on the two Adams and the covenantal history and eschatological effects that each mediates, it is not surprising that Calvin and other Reformed theologians display considerable appreciation for Irenaeus in general and his account of recapitulation especially.[54] According to John Owen, "Nothing greater than the recapitulation of all things in Christ can be conceived."[55]

Irenaeus was, unsurprisingly, drawn to the two Adams in Romans 5 and 1 Corinthians 15.[56] He writes of Christ,

---

53. In *Contra Marcion* Justin Martyr declared, "I would not have believed the Lord Himself, if He had announced any other than He who is our framer, maker, and nourisher. But because the only-begotten Son came to us from the one God, who both made this world and formed us, and contains and administers all things, *summing up His own handiwork in Himself*, my faith towards Him is steadfast, and my love to the Father immoveable, God bestowing both upon us." Quoted in *Haer.* 4.6.2.

54. Calvin quotes Irenaeus at length in the *Institutes*, particularly on points related directly to recapitulation. See my contrast between Irenaeus and Origen and comparison of the Reformed tradition with the former in Michael Horton, "Ascension and Atonement," in *Locating Atonement: Essays in Constructive Dogmatics*, ed. Fred Sanders and Oliver Crisp (Grand Rapids: Zondervan Academic, 2015), 226–50; cf. Douglas Farrow, *Ascension and Ecclesia: The Significance of the Doctrine of the Ascension for Ecclesiology and Cosmology* (London: T&T Clark, 2009); Irena Backus, *The Reception of the Church Fathers in the West: From the Carolingians to the Maurists* (Leiden: Brill, 1997); Julie Canlis, *Calvin's Ladder: A Spiritual Theology of Ascent* (Grand Rapids: Eerdmans, 2010). Besides Calvin and Owen, other Reformed theologians, such as Peter Martyr Vermigli, seem particularly appreciative of Irenaeus.

55. John Owen, *Works of John Owen*, vol. 1, *The Glory of Christ*, ed. William H. Goold (London: Banner of Truth, 1965), 372. Owen devotes a lengthy chapter to this topic (ch. 11) in this volume.

56. See J. T. Nielsen, *Adam and Christ in the Theology of Irenaeus of Lyons: An Examination of the Adam-Christ Typology in the Adversus Haeresis of Irenaeus against the Background of the Gnosticism of His Time* (The Netherlands: Konninkliijke Van Gorcum, 1968), 11. In fact, Irenaeus defines recapitulation by a nearly verbatim quotation of Rom 5:19: "For as by the disobedience of the one man who was originally molded from virgin soil, the many were made sinners, and forfeited life; so was it necessary that, by the obedience of one man, who was originally born from a virgin, many should be justified and receive salvation." *Haer.* 3.18.7 (*ANF* 1:448).

He has therefore, in His work of recapitulation, summed up all things, both waging war against our enemy, and crushing him who had at the beginning led us away captives in Adam. . . . The enemy would not have been fairly vanquished, unless it had been a man [born] of woman who conquered him. . . . And therefore does the Lord profess Himself to be the Son of man, comprising in Himself that original man out of whom the woman was fashioned, in order that, as our species went down to death through a vanquished man, so we may ascend to life again through a victorious one; and as through a man death received the palm [of victory] against us, so again by a man we may receive the palm against death.[57]

In this view, Christ—not only by his death and resurrection but also by his incarnation and obedient life—undoes the work of the first Adam and fulfills his commission representatively on our behalf. From Adam we receive death; from Christ we receive life.

The *life of Jesus* was of no consequence to the Gnostics since the eternal *Christ* alone saves our inner-divine *nous* from contamination by the body, the world, and history. While for the Gnostics the bodily history of Jesus is but the husk that hides the true Christ of faith, for Irenaeus it is precisely the incarnation, life, ministry, death, resurrection, ascension, and bodily return of Jesus that constitute salvation. Jesus "became what we are that He might bring us to be even what He is Himself."[58] Of crucial significance in Irenaeus's thought is his emphasis on Christ's humanity as his link with us and our bond with him (and therefore with God). In his headship, everything we lost in Adam is comprehensively recovered in Christ.[59]

According to Aulén, unlike vicarious satisfaction, the "classic view" constitutes "a veritable revolution" by declaring that God has "broken through the order of justice and merit, triumphed over the powers of evil, and created a new relation between the world and God."[60] But if Christ has "broken through the order of justice and merit," then he has not honored the order of creation that has been violated and that he himself, as God, demands be restored. Irenaeus explains it differently.

---

57. *Haer.* 5.21.1 (*ANF* 1:548–49).
58. *Haer.* preface to bk. 5 (*ANF* 1:526).
59. *Haer.* 3.18.1 (*ANF* 1:445–46).
60. Aulén, *Christus Victor*, 79.

First, for Irenaeus, none of the elect in either Testament has ever been justified by merit, and second, they are justified by Christ's fulfillment of the order of justice and merit. While "the law of works occupied the intervening period" between Abraham and Christ, he says, in both Old and New Testaments justification is through faith alone. The covenant of grace unites the whole of Scripture. "Christ is the treasure which was hid in the field . . . since He was pointed out by means of types and parables."[61] "For 'all men come short of the glory of God,' and are not justified of themselves, but by the advent of the Lord—they who earnestly direct their eyes toward His light."[62]

Recapitulation and justification affirm that God did not—could not—circumvent creation (the covenant of works) and the law (Sinai) in order to reconcile us to himself; instead he had to become what we were and be born "under the law" to fulfill that justice we owed and bear the curse that was ours (Gal 4:4), to win the victory over Satan and the powers of the flesh (human capacity under sin and death) and take our glorified humanity with him to the right hand of the Father in grand conquest (Heb 2:9–13). By itself, the defeat of evil powers does not require the incarnation. Yahweh could easily have *destroyed* Satan and his hosts, but *humanity* would not have been redeemed. The defeat of the powers requires atonement: the guilt offering, purification offering, and peace offering. By becoming the Last Adam, faithfully enduring the trial, and winning the right for his posterity to eat of the Tree of Life, the incarnate Son is the source not only of forgiveness but of life, justification, glorification, and communion with the triune God in a regenerated cosmos.

Christ's recapitulation of Adam's ruined headship begins already in his incarnation. "How does the holy conception and birth of Christ benefit you?" asks the Heidelberg Catechism. It answers: "He is our mediator and, in God's sight, he covers with his innocence and perfect holiness my sinfulness in which I was conceived."[63] The incarnation was not merely a prelude to redemption but an essential part of it (Heb 4:15). Not only at Jesus's death but in his incarnation and obedience, the inscription above Jesus's whole existence says "for you." Especially for this reason, Calvin and other Reformers such as Jan Łaski

---

61. *Haer.* 4.25.1–26.1 (*ANF* 1:495–96).
62. *Haer.* 4.27.2 (*ANF* 1:499).
63. Heidelberg Catechism, LD 15, Q. 37.

so strongly denounced the doctrine of the "celestial flesh" taught by some Anabaptists.[64] The Reformers echoed the words of Gregory of Nazianzus against Apollinaris: "That which he did not assume, he did not heal."[65] Thinkers like Irenaeus and Calvin realized that only by becoming everything that we are and going through the trial of justice could Jesus cancel our guilt and heal our wounds.

Recapitulation continues through Jesus's entire life of obedience as our representative. Even in the opening scenes of Jesus's ministry, he is found recapitulating the trial of Adam and Israel in his temptation by the serpent. At each seminal moment of Jesus's suffering obedience, the Father announces his benediction with the Spirit signaling his approval: "This is my beloved Son in whom I am well-pleased" (Matt 3:17 with Isa 42:1; Matt 17:5). Repeatedly, we read that specific actions were performed not to break the chains of the Creator and Law-Giver but "to fulfill all righteousness" (Matt 3:15; John 4:34; 8:29, etc.). It is not enough to be *forgiven*; we must be restored and obtain the status of the righteous Son-image of God. In Christ's active obedience, this demand becomes a reality.

However, even though Christ's vicarious self-offering begins with his incarnation and active obedience, Irenaeus underscores that it culminates in his vicarious sacrifice: "And truly the death of the Lord became the means of healing *and* remission of sins."[66] "Abraham himself," along with the other patriarchs, "were justified . . . without the law of Moses" but only "through faith in God's promise."[67] It also represents, according to Irenaeus, "crushing him who had at the beginning led us away captives in Adam."[68]

There were two broad types (with of course many variations) of sacrifice in the old covenant: thanksgiving and guilt offerings. Thanksgiving

---

64. Instead of receiving his humanity from the Virgin Mary, as Menno Simons, following Melchior Hoffman and Dirk Philips, argued, Jesus had taken his humanity from heaven. See Menno Simons, "Brief Confession on the Incarnation (1544)," "Reply to Micron (1556)," and "Epistle to Micron," in *Menno Simons: The Complete Writings*, ed. J. C. Wenger, trans. Leonard Verduin (Scottsdale, PA: Herald, 1984), 422–54, 835–952. In criticism, see *Inst.* 2.13.3.

65. Gregory of Nazianzus, Epistle 101, "To Cledonius," in *NPNF*[2] 5:438. As Leonard Hodgson observed long ago, Gustav Aulén's Christology is practically docetic (or at least Apollinarian); Christ's humanity is little more than a vehicle for his victorious deity—in this case, a trap set for the devil. Hodgson, *The Doctrine of the Atonement* (New York: Scribner, 1951), 147; cf. H. E. W. Turner, *The Patristic Doctrine of Redemption* (London: Mowbray, 1952), 62.

66. *Haer.* 4.27.2 (*ANF* 1:499), emphasis added.

67. *Haer.* 4.16.2 (*ANF* 1:481).

68. *Haer.* 5.21.1 (*ANF* 1:561).

implies recognition of dependence, the opposite of autonomy.[69] But since the fall, not only is a life of thanksgiving necessary, but a guilt offering as well. Both are offered freely by Jesus in his active and passive obedience. Offering a bull, ram, or goat for violations is one thing. But what delights the Father is living wholly, perfectly, and personally with palms outstretched to the Great King, saying, "Here I am, O LORD." It is precisely this sacrifice of thanks—a living sacrifice—that Jesus offered and that Hebrews 10:5–18, interpreting Psalm 40, regards as superior to the burnt sacrifices that never removed sins but only reminded the conscience of guilt. Hebrews 5:7–9 illumines the point:

> In the days of his flesh, Jesus offered up prayers and supplications, with loud cries and tears, to him who was able to save him from death, and he was heard *because of his reverence*. Although he was a son, he *learned obedience* through what he suffered. And *being made perfect*, he became the *source of eternal salvation* to all who obey him, being designated by God a high priest after the order of Melchizedek.

Because of Christ's active obedience, we have not only forgiveness (the guilt offering), but justification (crediting his complete obedience in offering his life as a thank offering). Having been justified, all who are united to him must be glorified. What then is left for us? Nothing but a *responsive* life of grateful praise as recipients of and participants in his victorious entrance into the Sabbath enthronement. "But thanks be to God, who in Christ always leads us in triumphal procession, and through us spreads the fragrance of the knowledge of him everywhere" (2 Cor 2:14).

THE SUFFERING SERVANT: VICARIOUS SACRIFICE

Christ's recapitulation and obedience culminated in his death. In addition to being grounded in a Trinitarian theology of God's being and

---

69. Cain and Abel both brought offerings. Presumably, they both brought regular offerings of thanksgiving or tribute, acknowledging Yahweh's lordship and bounty. Yet after the fall, a sacrifice for sin was also required. Genesis 4 does not tell us much, but it does indicate that Cain brought only the tribute offering while Abel brought a guilt offering (the firstfruits of his flock) and that God was not pleased with Cain or his offering, leading to the first religious war. Evidently, Cain was the first Pelagian, denying his sinful condition and that he could be redeemed and reconciled to God only by looking in faith to "the Lamb of God who takes away the sin of the world" (John 1:29).

works, an adequately Christian doctrine of Christ's atoning work must correspond fittingly to the types of the old covenant sacrificial system. This system itself broadens our horizon with its various categories and effects while substitution is the sine qua non of all else.

Political and Judicial Practices

Before we come to the sacrificial system, it is worth mentioning briefly some of the other aspects of Torah touching on the political and judicial life of Israel. First, the kinsman redeemer (הַגֹּאֵל; haggo'el) assumes responsibility for providing for a relative.[70] The "avenger of blood" (גֹּאֵל הַדָּם; go'el haddam) is the one who tracks down and executes just vengeance on the murder of his near relative (Num 35:9–34). In other cases, the kinsman redeems the relative's life or property (Lev 25:47–55; 27:9–25).

Isaiah 51:10 describes Yahweh as Israel's avenger and the people as the "redeemed" (גְּאוּלִים; ge'ulim). In fact, if one were to ask an Israelite what redemption meant, they would have told the story of God's deliverance of his people from Egyptian bondage. As Joseph A. Fitzmyer argues, many New Testament references to Christ echo "Yahweh as go'el, redeemer,' acquiring his people as he freed them from Egyptian bondage (Isa 41:14; 43:14; 44:6; 47:4; Ps 19:15; 78:35)."[71] Throughout the Psalms, Yahweh is praised as the redeemer not only of the nation but of the psalmist personally (Pss 7:8; 19:14; 26:1; 35:24). The writer to the Hebrews refers to Jesus as our nearest relative who has come to redeem and vindicate his brothers and sisters (Heb 2:11, 16–18; 4:14–16).

Second, the practice of offering a *ransom* became an important type on which the New Testament draws. Torah prescribed the giving of a ransom (כֹּפֶר; koper), often in exchange for one's own life.[72] In Job 33,

---

70. D. A. Leggett, "The Levirate Goel Institutions in the Old Testament," in *Theological Dictionary of the Old Testament (TDOT)*, ed. G. Johannes Botterweck, Helmer Ringgren, and Heinz-Josef Fabry (Grand Rapids: Eerdmans, 2003), 2:350–55. In fact, just as Boaz served as kinsman-redeemer so that Ruth and Naomi would not be "the name of the dead may not be cut off from among his brothers and from the gate of his native place" (Ruth 4:10). The narrative climaxes in the announcement of Boaz's marriage to Ruth with emphasis on the offspring that will come from this sorrowful event in the past. All of the people give their blessing, praying that this offspring will be "renowned in Bethlehem" (Ruth 4:11–12). Then follows the genealogy leading to David.

71. Joseph A. Fitzmyer, *According to Paul: Studies in the Theology of the Apostle* (New York: Paulist, 1993), 13–14.

72. In the case of a negligent owner of an ox who has gored someone, "If a ransom is imposed on him, then he shall give for the redemption of his life whatever is imposed on him" (Exod 21:30). Further, "When you take the census of the people of Israel, then each shall give a ransom

Elihu encourages Job to look for a merciful mediator who will say, "Deliver him from going down to the pit; I have found a ransom," and God "accepts him." For God "has redeemed my soul from going down to the pit and my life shall look upon the light" (Job 33:23–28).

The New Testament refers to Christ's work as a ransom (λύτρον). Jesus said that "the Son of Man came . . . to give his life as a λύτρον for many" (Matt 20:28; Mark 10:45). The "one mediator," Jesus Christ, "gave himself as a ransom [ἀντίλυτρον] for all, which is the testimony given at the proper time" (1 Tim 2:5–6). Peter exhorts believers to new obedience on the basis of Christ's deliverance, "knowing that you were ransomed [ἐλυτρώθητε] from the futile ways inherited from your forefathers, not with perishable things such as silver or gold, but with precious blood of Christ, like that of lamb without blemish or spot" (1 Pet 1:18–19). "You were bought [ἠγοράσθητε] with a price," Paul says (1 Cor 6:20).

Thus the language of "dying for" becomes prominent.[73] Bernd Janowski notes, "It always means that one person, by taking action or suffering, takes the 'place' of others who are not willing or able to take it up themselves."[74] Based on incidents such as Stephen's stoning for "attacking" the temple, Martin Hengel concludes that the heart of the church's earliest proclamation was "the death of the crucified Messiah, who had vicariously taken upon himself the curse of the Law, had made the Temple obsolete as a place of everlasting atonement for the sins of Israel. . . . Therefore the ritual Law had lost its significance as a necessary institution for salvation."[75] Similarly, N. T. Wright reminds us that Jesus aroused the greatest ire of the religious leaders when he presumed to forgive sins directly, bypassing the temple.[76] Whatever he was doing, it was a replacement for what had been done through

---

for his life to the LORD when you number them, that there be no plague among them when you number them" (Exod 30:12).

73. In Greek, substitution is intended with prepositions such as ἀντί (instead of/for), διά (through/because/on account of), περί (for), ὑπέρ (on behalf of), and nouns such as ἀντάλλαγμα (an exchange/price), ἀντίλυτρον (a ransom), etc. Analogous in the Old Testament are prepositionally qualified verbs like וְאֶתֵּן תַּחַת, to give *in place of/offer* (e.g., Isa 43:4) or with the help of the expressions סְבָלָם or נָשָׂא plus a term for sin or sickness, to bear sin(s)/sickness(es) (e.g., Isa 53:4, 11–12).

74. Bernd Janowski, "He Bore Our Sins: Isaiah 53 and the Drama of Taking Another's Place," in *The Suffering Servant: Isaiah 53 in Jewish and Christian Sources*, ed. Bernd Janowski and Peter Stuhlmacher, trans. Daniel P. Bailey (Grand Rapids: Eerdmans, 2004), 53–54.

75. Martin Hengel, *The Atonement in New Testament Teaching* (Philadelphia: Fortress, 1981), 36–8, 49.

76. N. T. Wright, *Jesus and the Victory of God* (Philadelphia: Fortress, 1997), 130, 605.

the temple cult. Because Christ died *for us*, we have peace with God (Rom 5:1). Thus, *reconciliation* is not first of all subjective but objective (Rom 5:10). We are reconciled to God only because he is reconciled to us, having found us actually acceptable because of Christ (2 Cor 5:19–20).

Third, there are also noncultic references to *making atonement*. In these cases, Yahweh's wrath against the whole congregation is withdrawn because someone has acted in their stead or acted in a way (viz., "jealous for my name") that reestablished Yahweh's righteous government.[77]

Covenant Ratification: Passover and Circumcision

Themes of *Christus Victor* and *Agnus Dei* blend already in the deliverance of Israel from Egypt by God's mighty hand and outstretched arm. Even before the redemption from Egypt, there is the redemption from God's judgment through the blood of a lamb. L. Michael Morales observes,

> The theology of Israel's redemption is brought out by the distinct elements of the Passover ritual found in Exodus 12:6–11, 21–22, related to *atonement*, *purification* and *consecration*, respectively: (1) the slaying of a lamb or young goat as a sacrifice, (2) the smearing of its blood on the doorposts and (3) the eating of its meat. Apart from the slaying of the lamb, it is evident that the firstborn sons of Israel would have died, no less than those of the Egyptians. The sacrifice therefore involved the concept of substitutionary atonement, the animal's death being regarded as "in the stead of" the firstborn male within each Israelite household, atoning for sin.[78]

---

77. After the people made the golden calf, Moses pleaded with God to "make atonement" for their sins (Exod 32:3), which he does by fasting and prayer for forty days. God's wrath is stayed (Deut 9:13–29; Ps 106:19–23). When later Israel sinned, Aaron offered up incense and "made atonement," which turned back the plague (Num 16:41–50). When Israelites were marrying Moabites and bowing down to their gods, Yahweh sent a plague, but Phinehas drove a spear through Zimri and his Midianite wife as they flaunted their relationship. It stopped the plague and Yahweh pledged a "covenant of peace," with Phinehas's children serving before him as priests from generation to generation. "Phinehas . . . has turned back my wrath from the people of Israel," Yahweh told Moses, and "was jealous for his God and made atonement for the people of Israel" (Num 25:1–12). Reciting this event, Psalm 106: 30–31 declares, "That was counted to him as righteousness [וַתֵּחָשֶׁב לוֹ לִצְדָקָה] from generation to generation forever."

78. L. Michael Morales, *Who Shall Ascend the Mountain of the Lord? A Biblical Theology of the Book of Leviticus*, NSBT 37 (Downers Grove, IL: InterVarsity, 2015), 80.

In fact, "Early Jewish interpretation, such as the *Mekilta deRabbi Ishmael*, Pisba' 7 and *Exodus Rabbah* 15.11, links the Passover sparing of the firstborn son with the near-sacrifice of Isaac in Genesis 22."[79]

This threefold act in Passover (slaying, smearing, eating) will correspond to the three stages of the sacrificial system (atonement, purification, consecration) prescribed in Leviticus: the sin offering, followed by the well-being offering, and finally the peace offering that is eaten together with God by priests and people alike. Even the smearing of the blood on the gate of the sanctuary will reenact the blood on the lintels of each home in Egypt.[80]

As the first Passover climaxed with the eating of the lamb, so too the annual reenactment (Lev 12:8–11, 43–47). In fact, "The sacrificial meat was holy, making those who ate it holy as well" (12:10). "Through the Passover ritual each Israelite household functions in a priestly manner and Israel itself is being prepared to become 'a kingdom of priests and a holy nation' (Exod. 19:6). Indeed, through the Passover rites, 'the whole nation became a priesthood for one day.'"[81] Atonement, purification, and consecration are the pathway to eating and drinking (i.e., fellowship) with God.

It appears that God's act of clothing Adam and Eve in animal skins represents typologically clothing new humanity in Christ's righteousness. In any case, after the fall, something more than a tribute or thank offering is required; now human beings must sacrifice an animal and call on the name of the Lord. Cain's violence against Abel resulted from his jealousy for God accepting Abel and his sacrifice (the firstborn of his flock) rather than Cain and his offering of the fruit of his field (a tribute or thank offering).

In Israel, the shedding of blood began with circumcision, which was a partial cutting off of the flesh to keep the whole person from being sacrificed.[82] As Paul underscores, the command to circumcise was given to Abram after he believed and was justified (Rom 4:10). To whatever extent it had been taken into the Sinai covenant (much less

---

79. Morales, *Who Shall Ascend the Mountain of the Lord?*, 80. The book of Jubilees even has the redemption of Isaac take place on the date of Passover as its original commemorative event (17:15; 18:3, 18–19). Some rabbinic texts, such as Targum Neofiti to Leviticus 22:27, understand all sacrificial lambs to symbolize Isaac, including the daily morning and evening ascension offerings (Leviticus Rabbah 2.11).

80. Morales, *Who Shall Ascend the Mountain of the Lord?*, 81.

81. Morales, *Who Shall Ascend the Mountain of the Lord?*, 81, quoting G. B. Gray, *Sacrifice in the Old Testament: Its Theory and Practice* (Oxford: Clarendon, 1925), 374.

82. M. G. Kline, *By Oath Consigned: A Reinterpretation of the Covenant Signs of Circumcision and Baptism* (Grand Rapids: Eerdmans, 1968), 45.

been abused in the first century as a form of "boasting in the flesh"), this original identification with the covenant of grace—of inclusion rather than exclusion—was never lost.

Passover, too, was not a sacrament of Sinai but of God's deliverance of his people from judgment simply by identifying with him as their savior-suzerain. The new covenant actually originates in Jesus's sacrifice at Passover (Matt 26:28). Whereas after the destruction of the temple, Judaism exchanged the temple sacrifices into repentance and good deeds, Christians proclaimed, "For Christ, our Passover lamb, has been sacrificed" (1 Cor 5:7). Circumcision and Passover could only point forward to a future reality. As good as it gets under the regime of "flesh," these sacraments nevertheless could not influence the reality to which they pointed. As Paul adds in Romans 8:3, "For *God has done* what *the law*, weakened by the flesh, *could not do*. By sending his own Son in the likeness of sinful flesh and for sin, he condemned sin in the flesh." As Peter Leithart puts it, "In Jesus, God himself lives a human life *in* flesh that was not constituted *by* flesh."[83] Fallen Adam—flesh—had to die in order for the subject of this death to participate in the death and resurrection of the Last Adam.[84]

The partial cutting off of the flesh in order to save the life of the whole person marks the key significance of circumcision. However, Paul contrasts this partial "cutting off" with Christ's whole-body "circumcision," in which we participate through faith and is sealed in baptism (Col 2:11–15). Christ's whole self was handed over to death. He did not merely receive circumcision on the eighth day but was circumcised—cut off—completely for us. In baptism, we participate in Christ's circumcision-death to be raised with Christ in newness of life (Rom 6:1–14).[85]

Cultic Sacrifice

While Mesopotamian religion was basically "the care and feeding of the god," Jacob Milgrom notes that Israel's priests "banned all food

---

83. Peter J. Leithart, *Delivered from the Elements of the World: Atonement, Justification, Mission* (Downers Grove, IL: IVP Academic, 2016), 136.

84. Leithart raises an intriguing thesis from Nicholas Perrin's *Jesus the Temple* (Grand Rapids: Baker Academic, 2010). Perrin argues that all of Jesus's practices are "essentially . . . temple practices" (79). Perrin argues, for instance, that Jesus's ministry of healing (154), his table fellowship (168–70), and his insistence that his disciples give up their wealth to support the poor (147) are all integrated parts of a new-temple program" (137n20).

85. Kline, *By Oath Consigned*, 45.

rites inside the shrine."[86] God is pleased by the sweet-smelling aroma of sacrifices, but the only time he "eats" is *with his people* at his table in the peace offering that follows the guilt offering. God does not long to be fed, but to provide and share food and drink with his covenant people at his table. But for this intimate communion in joy and peace, there must be the satisfaction for guilt.

GUILT OFFERINGS

At Moriah, Yahweh kept Abraham from offering Isaac on the altar of sacrifice by substituting a ram caught in a thicket: "So Abraham called the name of that place, 'The LORD will provide'; as it is said to this day, 'On the mount of the LORD it shall be provided'" (Gen 22:14). It was here where Solomon was instructed to build the temple (2 Chr 3:1–2).

Once at Sinai, the question is who may ascend God's holy hill—in this case, Sinai—and the answer comes back in no uncertain terms in Exodus 19: Moses alone is called to ascend as mediator. His mediation comes in handy for the people; he returns from receiving the law only to find Israel engaging in adultery on its wedding night in the golden calf episode (Exod 32). On one hand, God wants to dwell in the midst of his people. On the other hand, his holiness is too dangerous for their approach. God is, as it were, anxiously looking for ways to commune with his people without their being consumed by his holy presence. Even Moses had to learn this. When he begged to see God's glory (his face), Yahweh responded, "No one can see me and live" (Exod 33:20).

The sacrificial system, with the mediation of the high priest, becomes the only way of approaching the holy God safely: namely, at a distance.[87] Through the cult God found a way to dwell with his sinful people safely. Therefore, as important as the tribute offering is for acknowledging one's dependence on the suzerain, the writer to the Hebrews summarizes the old covenant well when he says, "Indeed, under the law almost everything is purified with blood, and without the shedding of blood, there is no forgiveness of sins" (Heb 9:22). Atonement, purification, and consecration are the only pathway to God that does not end in death. Atonement removes the guilt, purification removes the pollution,

---

86. Jacob Milgrom, *Leviticus: A Book of Ritual and Ethics*, Continental Commentary (Minneapolis: Fortress, 2004), 21. For this prohibition, see Exod 30:9.

87. T. H. Gaster, "Sacrifice and Offerings, OT," in *Interpreter's Dictionary of the Bible* (New York: Abingdon, 1962), 4:148–53.

and consecration establishes a positive relationship of communion with God and each other.

The various sacrifices are spelled out in Leviticus 1:1–6:7, including voluntary and mandatory offerings. The important point is that an expiatory sacrifice "would precede the triad of ascension, tribute and peace offerings."[88] Before there can be purification and communion, there must be substitution. The sin and trespass offerings (Lev 4:1–5:26) are mandatory and "expiate for sin." The "sin offering" (חַטָּאת; *khattat*) must be distinguished from all other offerings (Lev 5:11), Milgrom observes.[89]

There are other important sacrifices associated with the festivals that led up to the all-important Day of Atonement. One animal would be sacrificed on the altar and burned entirely, while another would be a scapegoat. "He shall lay his hand on the head of the burnt offering, and it shall be accepted for him to make atonement for him" (Lev 1:4). The priest then sent the animal off into the wilderness (vv. 16–22). In this way, "The impurity of the sanctuary is purged."[90] These animals went into the presence of God and were consumed *in the place of* human beings who would have experienced such destruction if they had violated his holy space. It is the layman who performs much of this sacrifice, each individual Israelite. The priests only take over at the altar.

In the sacrifices of animals, Israel was given a substitute. As Baruch J. Schwartz observes, the formula of Leviticus 17:11, 14, "the life is in the blood," derives from נֶפֶשׁ הַבָּשָׂר בַּדָּם and נֶפֶשׁ plus כַּפֵּר, meaning "to act as a ransom for your lives, a payment in place of your lives, which would otherwise be forfeit." The animal's blood, representative of its life, takes the place of that of the one making the offering with respect to God's wrath.[91] "What the sprinkling of the ark of the covenant with the blood of animals by the high priest each year on *Yôm Kippûr* symbolized for Israel (Lev 16:14–20)," notes Fitzmyer, "that Christ Jesus has obtained for all humanity by his own blood and by his death (Rom 3:25)."[92]

---

88. Morales, *Who Shall Ascend the Mountain of the Lord?*, 122–23.

89. Milgrom, *Leviticus: A Book of Ritual and Ethics*, 28–29.

90. Milgrom, *Leviticus: A Book of Ritual and Ethics*, 38.

91. Baruch J. Schwartz, "The Prohibition Concerning the 'Eating' of Blood in Leviticus 17," in *Priesthood and Cult in Ancient Israel*, ed., Gary A. Anderson and Saul M. Olyan, Journal for the Study of the Old Testament Supplemental Series 125 (Sheffield: Sheffield Academic Press, 1991), 55. I am grateful to Jason Vartanian for pointing out this reference to me.

92. Fitzmyer, *According to Paul*, 13. See also Jay Sklar, *Sin, Impurity, Sacrifice, Atonement: The Priestly Conceptions*, Hebrew Bible Monographs 2 (Sheffield: Sheffield Phoenix, 2005), 163–65.

THE ACHIEVEMENT OF JUSTIFICATION

The Qumran community boycotted the temple as polluted by the reigning authorities. Consequently, they invoked Psalm 40 to argue that repentance will atone in the place of sacrifices.[93] It would be just this move—repentance better than sacrifice—that most Jews would be forced to make after the temple's destruction in AD 70. However, the writer to the Hebrews replaces the temple (and the priesthood) with Christ, not only in his sacrificial death but in his vicarious life and continuing priesthood.

There is no victory without propitiation. In Hebrew a כִּפֶּר (kippur; piel) is a covering of sin. The Septuagint and New Testament translate כִּפֶּר by ἱλάσκομαι or ἱλασμός. The meaning of the verb, "to render propitious," or its nominal form, "an appeasing," in the contexts in which it appears, affirms beyond all doubt that the atonement is something that turns away God's wrath. Only on this basis can God be reconciled to us and we be reconciled to God. Paul declares that the way God reconciled the world to himself in Christ was by "not counting their sins against them [μὴ λογιζόμενος αὐτοῖς τὰ παραπτώματα αὐτῶν]" (2 Cor 5:19), which indicates no moral change in us but rather a reckoning by God on account of Christ. Apart from the notion of appeasement of God's wrath, the joyful announcement, "Behold, the Lamb of God who takes away the sin of the world" (John 1:29) is inconceivable. The sinless substitute for the sinful people is central to the biblical doctrine of atonement (Matt 26:28; 2 Cor 5:21; Gal 3:13; Heb 9:28; 1 Pet 2:24; 3:18, etc.).

Paul says, "God put [Christ] forward as a propitiation by his blood, to be received by faith. This was to show God's righteousness, because in his divine forbearance he had passed over former sins" (Rom 3:25). According to BDAG, ἱλαστήριον is "that which serves as an instrument for regaining the goodwill of a deity; concr. a 'means of propitiation or expiation, gift to procure expiation,' . . . the initiative taken by God to

---

93. Hartmut Stegemann, *The Library of Qumran: On the Essenes, Qumran, John the Baptist, and Jesus* (Grand Rapids: Eerdmans, 1998), 175. Stegemann says, "The Essenes took their orientation in the situation at hand from indications from God such as his word through Solomon: 'The sacrifice of the wicked is an abomination to the Lord, but the prayer of the upright is his delight [Prov. 15:8; '. . . is a pleasing sacrifice' in CD 11:21]" (CD 11:20–21). "Instead of the flesh of burnt offerings and the fat of slain offerings, the prescribed sacrifice of the lips [liturgically correct prayer services] will be accounted as an adequate odor of sacrifice and perfect conduct [a manner of life in conformity with the Torah], as well-pleasing [to God], a freely offered sacrifice,' which will 'atone for [all] guilt through the transgression [of God's commands] and the [other] sinful deeds, and [win God's] benevolence for the [Holy] Land' (1QS 9:4–5; similarly, 1QS 8:6–7, 9–10)." The community still slaughtered red heifers for the ashes to be used in purification rituals and they prayed toward the temple, Stegemann observes (176).

effect removal of impediments to a relationship with God's self." The place of propitiation and expiation was the mercy seat.[94] This "mercy seat" (הַכַּפֹּרֶת *hakkapporet*; Gk: ἱλαστήριον) was the gold lid with two cherubim of gold covering it. Once a year, on the Day of Atonement, the high priest was allowed to enter the Holy of Holies and sprinkle the blood of the bull on this covering. Thus, it was considered the place where God covered over the sins of his people.

In the New Testament Jesus is described as the place or means of ἱλαστήριον: "[We] are justified by his grace as a gift, through the redemption that is in Christ Jesus, whom God put forward as a propitiation by his blood, to be received by faith" (Rom 3:24–25). "He is the propitiation for our sins, and not for ours only but also for the sins of the whole world" (1 John 2:2; cf. 4:10). The writer to the Hebrews explains, "Therefore he had to be made like his brothers in every respect, so that he might become a merciful and faithful high priest in the service of God, to make propitiation for the sins of the people" (Heb 2:17). In fact, the publican's prayer, "Lord, be merciful to me, the sinner!" (Luke 18:13) could be rendered, "Lord, be propitiated [ἱλάσθητί] for me, the sinner!"

Considering 1 John 2:2 and 4:10, C. H. Dodd famously declared, "The common rendering 'propitiation' is illegitimate here as elsewhere."[95] Westcott and Dodd demonstrate that the pagan idea of placating and angry God is absent from the Old Testament, Leon Morris observes.[96] However, when they say in effect that "when the LXX translators used 'propitiation,' they do not mean 'propitiation,' it is surely time to call a halt." No sensible person "uses one word when he means another, and in view of the otherwise invariable Greek use it would seem impossible for anyone in the first century to have used one of the ἱλάσκομαι group without conveying to his readers some idea of propitiation."[97]

In Dodd's widely influential view, God's wrath is not really wrath at all; it is no more than allowing human beings to suffer the consequences of their own sin—or, in the more recent statement of Joel B. Green and Mark D. Baker, it is simply "letting us go on our own way."[98]

---

94. BDAG, 473–74.

95. C. H. Dodd, *The Bible and the Greeks* (London: Hodder and Stoughton, 1935), 95.

96. Leon Morris, *The Apostolic Preaching of the Cross*, 3rd ed. (Grand Rapids: Eerdmans, 1955), 155.

97. Morris, *The Apostolic Preaching of the Cross*, 155. See also Roger R. Nicole, "C. H. Dodd and the Doctrine of Propitiation," *Westminster Theological Journal* 17, no. 2 (May 1955): 117f. Though dated, Nicole's essay remains incisive.

98. Joel B. Green and Mark D. Baker, *Recovering the Scandal of the Cross: Atonement in New Testament and Contemporary Contexts* (Downers Grove, IL: InterVarsity, 2000), 55.

Similarly, Christopher Schroeder argues that Christ "stands in the breach" not by *bearing* God's wrath but by *turning it away*—and this opens new possibilities for us to stand in the breach with him.[99] But this contradicts the explicit verbs of Isaiah 53 as well as its New Testament interpretation. Further, can this thesis explain the cry of dereliction: "My God, my God, why have you forsaken me?" Jesus did not ask to be relieved of the vocation to *turn away* the cup of wrath but of *drinking* it. In fact, this cry is impossible to reconcile with the any of the alternative views.

According to Douglas Campbell, Christ "*rescues*" sinners and "also *judges* [the] sinful situation, terminating and executing it."[100] Notice that human beings are subjects only of rescue, but only a "sinful situation" is judged. "We also learn at this point that the atoning death of Christ is not fundamentally a penal act."[101] With respect to Romans 3:25, Campbell asserts that Paul is not saying that God held back his wrath (which has been the apostle's subject since 1:18) until the cross. Rather, God's "forbearance" here is "an act of respite in which God holds back something oppressive—here the enslaved human condition, which is decisively liberated in Christ."[102] Campbell eliminates anything like propitiation at the outset as a violation of the "no strings attached" relationship that constitutes all of God's dealings with humanity. In short, the problem are the oppressive powers, not God's wrath. Whatever ills befall us, according to Campbell, they cannot be inflicted *by God*. For Campbell, the governing *a priori* norm is "that God *does not conditionally act toward humanity at all*."[103] This unconditionality—"no strings attached"—is what "covenantal" *means*, he insists, contrary to every lexicon and the obvious counterevidence of countless passages, most obviously Deuteronomy 28.[104] Next, Campbell inserts the Cremer thesis on "God's righteousness" and a subjective-genitive reading of πίστις Χριστοῦ ("the faith/faithfulness of the Messiah" rather than "faith in the Messiah"), joined to a martyrological reading of Habakkuk 2:4 in

---

99. Schroeder, "Standing in the Breach," 18–22.

100. Douglas A. Campbell, "The Current Crisis: The Capture of Paul's Gospel by Methodological Arianism," in *Beyond Old and New Perspectives: Reflections on the Work of Douglas Campbell*, ed. Chris Tilling (Eugene, OR: Cascade Books, 2014), 45.

101. Campbell, "The Current Crisis," 45.

102. Douglas A. Campbell, *The Deliverance of God: An Apocalyptic Rereading of Justification in Paul* (Grand Rapids: Eerdmans, 2013), 671.

103. Campbell, "The Current Crisis," 44.

104. Campbell, "The Current Crisis," 45. Once more he cites James B. Torrance's "Covenant or Contract" in defense.

Romans 1:17.[105] Consequently, the cross loses its splendor as the place where God found a way to be "just *and* the justifier of the one who has faith in Jesus Christ" (Rom 3:26).[106]

Over against Ritschl, Barth at least speaks of Christ's "bearing of the eternal wrath of God." "For the terrible thing, the divine No of Good Friday," Barth says, "is that there all the sins of Israel and of all men, our sins collectively and individually, have in fact become the object of the divine wrath and retribution."[107] Barth further adds,

> But the real judgment of God is alone the crucifixion of Christ, and the terror of this event is that it is the reality which all other judgments upon Israel, the world and mankind can only foreshadow or reflect. . . . The only correct view, i.e., in harmony with the biblical interpretation, is that expressed in the 14th article of the Heidelberg Catechism that "no mere creature can bear the burden of the eternal wrath of God against sin." In face of a real outbreak of God's avenging wrath, the creature would be annihilated.[108]

But Campbell turns Barth's paradoxical dialectic of the Good Friday "No" and Easter "Yes" into a monotone "Yes" that could not be otherwise because God is love, not justice.

Regardless of one's appraisal of Barth's account, it was of central importance to him that the one who was "no other than God's own Son, and therefore the eternal God Himself in the unity with human nature that he freely accepted" was the one "who on the cross took upon Himself and suffered the wrath of God."[109] Barth concludes beautifully,

> For in Him who took our place God's own heart beat on our side, in our flesh and blood, in complete solidarity with our nature and constitution, at the very point where we ourselves confront Him, guilty before God. Because it was the eternal God who entered

---

105. Campbell, *The Deliverance of God*, 708.

106. The interpretation is reminiscent of Origen's contention that Jesus's reference to the separation of the sheep and the goats on the last day pertains to *ideas* rather than *persons*, on the basis that God is without wrath and that punishment can therefore never be retributive but merely remedial. See Origen, *On First Principles* 4.4.5n1 and 4.9.2; cf. Joseph W. Trigg, *Origen: The Bible and Philosophy in the Third Century* (London: SCM, 2012), 101.

107. *CD* II/1, 395.

108. *CD* II/1, 396.

109. *CD* II/1, 397.

in in Jesus Christ, He could be more than the Representative and Guarantor of God to us. . . . He could also be our Representative and Guarantor towards God.[110]

All of this marvelous paradox is voided in Campbell's account, which is closer to Ritschl and even to Marcion in its elimination of justice from God's attributes and works. Recognizing this paradox, R. Barry Matlock calls for "a satisfactory account of the interdependence of 'justification' and 'participation.'"[111] Without the removal of the legal curse that keeps the powers of death, hell, Satan, and demonic forces in the game, participation in God in any form would be a terrifying prospect since "our God is a consuming fire" (Heb 12:29). To be united to God as the ungodly through our own action (however passive) rather than to be justified through Christ's mediatorial work is to be consumed in his wrath.

Central to Paul's thinking is the juxtaposition of condemnation and justification as problem and solution and both the condemnation and justification are of *persons*, not just *situations*. "For the judgment following one trespass brought condemnation [κατάκριμα], but the free gift following many trespasses brought justification [δικαίωμα]" (Rom 5:16). It is not only Paul's way of thinking but John's: "*Whoever* [an individual person] does not believe is condemned already, because *he* has not believed in the name of the only Son of God" (John 3:18). But it is this entire way of "legalistic" thinking—namely, juxtaposing condemnation and justification—that many biblical scholars and dogmaticians find repulsive. Repeatedly, we are told in Scripture that God cannot simply clear the guilty—letting bygones be bygones (Exod 34:7; Num 14:13; Nah 1:3). He cannot just love the sinner and hate the sin (Ps 5:4–6; Nah 1:2). "For the wrath of God is revealed from heaven against all ungodliness and wickedness of those who by their wickedness suppress the truth" (Rom 1:18).

Yet in the alternatives to sacrificial atonement, we are left with possibilities for transformation, when a more radical analysis of the human condition suggests that this will not do. Nothing short of Christ's curse-bearing will establish the basis on which genuine liberation and

---

110. *CD* II/1, 402.
111. R. Barry Matlock, "Zeal for Paul but Not According to Knowledge: Douglas Campbell's War on 'Justification Theory,'" *JSNT* 34 (2001): 147.

communion are possible. There is no path to the fellowship meal without the propitiatory sacrifice.

Attempts to purge the cross of any residue of a once-and-for-all act of *divine* propitiation leaves us with something like an exemplary view that makes mimetic violence all the more tempting. On the contrary, Jesus did not ask us to stand in the gap with him, even when James and John begged for it, not knowing that it meant crucifixion (Matt 20:22). He stood in the trench alone while the disciples fled and Peter denied him three times to a young girl. But this was something that Jesus had to do alone. Nor will it do to say, with James Dunn and others, that Jesus bore this judgment as a representative rather than a substitute, since, as Hans-Jürgen Hermisson notes in relation to Isaiah 53, it is quite clear that "he has brought the many back into a right relationship with God by surrendering his life for the sins of many."[112]

Nor can the *penal* aspect be removed from propitiation, thereby converting it to mere expiation, as Dodd prefers. As T. H. Gaster explains, the *guilt* offering (especially as offered on the Day of Atonement) was utterly unique. If other sacrifices expressed thanks and restored the people to God's table, the sin offering was required by the individual beyond mere compensation. "Its purpose was punitive, not compensatory."[113] It is impossible to avoid this interpretation in the New Testament. "Since, therefore, we have now been *justified by his blood*, much more shall we be saved by him *from the wrath of God*" (Rom 5:9). "Christ redeemed us *from the curse* [ἐξηγόρασεν ἐκ τῆς κατάρας] of the law *by becoming a curse* [κατάρα] *for us*—for it is written, 'Cursed [ἐπικατάρατος] is everyone who is hanged on a tree'—so that in Christ Jesus the blessing of Abraham might come to the Gentiles, so that we might receive the promised Spirit through faith" (Gal 3:13–14).

We do need to be careful to articulate this propitiation in a biblical rather than pagan frame, grounding it in God's attributes (including simplicity and impassibility) and a fully Trinitarian and covenantal reference. Take away simplicity, and we are prone to press a false choice between God's justice and love. Remove impassibility, and we can

---

112. Hans-Jürgen Hermisson, "The Fourth Servant Song in the Context of Second Isaiah," in *The Suffering Servant: Isaiah 53 in Jewish and Christian Sources*, ed. Bernd Janowski and Peter Stuhlmacher, trans. Daniel P. Bailey (Grand Rapids: Eerdmans, 2004), 39–41.

113. T. H. Gaster, "Sacrifices and Offerings, OT," *Interpreter's Dictionary of the Bible* (New York: Abingdon, 1962), 4:152; cf. Roland de Vaux, *Ancient Israel*, vol. 2, *Religious Institutions* (New York: McGraw-Hill, 1965), 451–54; Jacob Milgrom, "Atonement in the Book of Leviticus," *Interpretation* 52 (Jan 1998): 8–11.

easily imagine that God's wrath is a fit of rage in reaction to an injury rather than the goodness of the Creator in upholding justice in his world. Take away Christ's deity, and we are left with the horrifying image of God punishing a helpless victim of his anger rather than God incarnate willingly offering himself to remove the curse. Together, the Father and the Son were moved by love, not by anger, and the Son willingly embraced the cross "for the joy set before him" (Heb 12:2). No one, not even the Father, takes Jesus's life; he lays it down and takes it back up again (John 10:18). In fact, Christ's death was foreordained from the foundation of the world, when the Father, the Son, and the Spirit entered into the covenant of redemption. The cross lay in the heart of the Father, the Son, and the Spirit before the creation of the world.

Take away the covenantal context and we fail to see that wrath, punishment, slavery to the powers of corruption (the flesh), death, Satan, and hell are grounded in the *sentence* that God delivered with respect to humanity in Adam. Miroslav Volf brings together nicely these themes of covenant and cross: "On the cross we see what God has done to renew the covenant that humanity has broken."[114] Jesus inaugurates the new covenant in his blood, not the blood splashed on the people, "in accordance with all the words you have spoken, 'All this we will do'" (Exod 24:8). After referring to the sacrificial ceremony in which God passed through the halves, Volf says, "For the narrative of the cross is not a 'self-contradictory' story of a God who 'died' because God broke the covenant, but a truly incredible story of God doing what God should neither have been able nor willing to do—a story of God who 'died' because God's all too human *covenant partner* broke the covenant."[115] "God's self-giving on the cross is a consequence of the 'eternality' of the covenant," Volf adds, "which in turn rests on God's 'inability' to give up the covenant partner who has broken the covenant."[116]

Finally, the Day of Atonement's sacrifice for guilt comes to its fullest expression in the Suffering Servant of Isaiah 53. The language is unmistakably sacrificial, especially in verses 5–12. The Servant

---

114. Miroslav Volf, *Exclusion and Embrace: A Theological Exploration of Otherness, Identity and Embrace* (Nashville: Abingdon, 1994), 153.

115. Volf, *Exclusion and Embrace*, 155.

116. Volf, *Exclusion and Embrace*, 155.

was pierced for our transgressions;
> he was crushed for our iniquities;
upon him was the chastisement that brought us peace,
> and with his wounds we are healed. (v. 5)

In one sense, he is the sacrificial victim, like the scapegoat: "The LORD has laid on him the iniquity of us all." He was "silent" and "opened not his mouth."

If Isaiah 53 speaks ultimately of the Messiah, then it is impossible to conclude that Yahweh, the Father of Jesus Christ, played no role in his violent death: "The LORD has laid on him the iniquity of us all" (v. 6). He was crushed.

> Yet it was the will of the LORD to crush him;
>> he has put him to grief;
> when his soul makes an offering for guilt,
>> he shall see his offspring; he shall prolong his days;
> the will of the LORD shall prosper in his hand. (v. 10)

Nevertheless, the Servant is not a passive victim but offers himself freely.

> Out of the anguish of his soul he shall see and be satisfied;
> by his knowledge shall the righteous one, my servant,
>> make many to be accounted righteous,
>> and he shall bear their iniquities. (v. 11)

Furthermore, the cross was not the end but the means to his reward:

> Therefore I will divide him a portion with the many,
>> and he shall divide the spoil with the strong,
> because he poured out his soul to death
>> and was numbered with the transgressors;
> yet he bore the sin of many,
>> and makes intercession for the transgressors. (v. 12)

This is why we fix our eyes on Jesus, "who for the joy that was set before him endured the cross, despising the shame, and is seated at the right hand of the throne of God" (Heb 12:2).

N. T. Wright stipulates that any legitimate view of Christ's cross should be willing, at a minimum, to see Jesus as fulfilling Isaiah 53.[117] Whatever remaining questions, Hermann Spieckermann argues, there are obvious and incontrovertible conclusions that a sound reading of Isaiah 53 demands: a "sinless and righteous" substitute intercedes for "the many," he does so freely, and "God brings about the vicarious action of the one for the sins of the other intentionally."[118]

Jesus interprets himself as the Suffering Servant of Isaiah 53.[119] Instituting the Supper, Jesus says, "And he took a cup, and when he had given thanks he gave it to them, saying, 'Drink of it, all of you, for this is my blood of the covenant, which is poured out for many for the forgiveness of sins'" (Matt 26:27–28; cf. Matt 20:28). Throughout the Gospel of John, Jesus emphasizes that he has come to do the will of his Father—namely, to save all that the Father has given him. And he does so both in obedience to the Father and of his own free will (John 10:18).

The apostles also interpret Jesus as the Suffering Servant (Matt 7:17; Luke 22:37; Rom 4:25; 5:1; 2 Cor 5:21; Gal 3:13; 1 Tim 1:15; Heb 9:28; 1 Pet 1:10–11; 2:21–25; 3:18; 1 John 1:28, 36). Isaiah 53 reverberates in the statement, "Christ suffered once for all to make atonement for sins, the righteous for the unrighteous, in order to bring you to God" (1 Pet 3:18).

What Christ bore on the cross was that justice that Christ himself demanded as the eternal Son and fulfilled as the incarnate Son. It was not a cathartic release of anger but a just satisfaction of God's cosmic and covenantal righteousness that provided the basis for both our forgiveness and rectitude—legal rectitude in justification, moral rectitude in sanctification, and consummate rectitude of body and soul in glorification. In this way, Christ is victor even as he is the sacrificial victim. The picture in Revelation 7:17 expresses this paradoxical unity of *Christus Victor* and vicarious substitution, with the Lamb seated on a throne.

Thus the settling of accounts, as it were, is not a matter of legalistic bookkeeping, but of God himself settling the accounts by paying the bill himself (like the Good Samaritan). Augustine expresses this point vividly:

---

117. N. T. Wright, *Evil and the Justice of God* (London: SPCK, 2006), esp. ch. 3.; Wright, *Jesus and the Victory of God* (Minneapolis: Fortress, 1996), esp. ch. 12.

118. Hermann Spieckermann, "The Conception and Prehistory of the Idea of Vicarious Suffering in the Old Testament," in *The Suffering Servant: Isaiah 53 in Jewish and Christian Sources*, ed. Bernd Janowski and Peter Stuhlmacher, trans. Daniel P. Bailey (Grand Rapids: Eerdmans, 2004), 5–6.

119. Peter Stuhlmacher, "Isaiah 53 in the Gospels and Acts," in *The Suffering Servant: Isaiah 53 in Jewish and Christian Sources*, ed. Bernd Janowski and Peter Stuhlmacher, trans. Daniel P. Bailey (Grand Rapids: Eerdmans, 2004), 160–61.

Desperately sick indeed is the one who in a frenzy beats the doctor. So what sort of frenzy must possess the person who kills the doctor? And on the other hand, what must the goodness and power of the doctor be, who from his own blood made a medicine for his crazy killer? After all, the one who had come to seek and to save what had got lost didn't say in vain as hung there, *Father, forgive them, because they do not know what they are doing* (Luke 23:24). "They are in a frenzy, I'm the doctor; let them rave and rage, I bear it patiently; it's when they've killed me that I will heal them." So let us be among those whom he heals.[120]

The point can hardly be more clearly than as follows by James Denney:

> God is love, say [some], and therefore he does not require a propitiation. God is love, say the Apostles, and therefore he provides a propitiation. . . . Nobody has any right to borrow the words "God is love" from an apostle, and then to put them in circulation after carefully emptying them of their apostolic import. . . . But this is what they do who appeal to love against propitiation. To take the condemnation out of the Cross is to take the nerve out of the Gospel. . . . Its whole virtue, its consistency with God's character, its aptness to man's need, its real dimensions as a revelation of love, depend ultimately on this, that mercy comes to us in it through judgment.[121]

PURIFICATION AND PEACE OFFERINGS

We are not changing topics when we declare that the sacrifices foreshadowing Christ's work produce purification and consecration so that we may eat and drink with God. The sacrifices themselves included not only the guilt offering but purification and peace offerings.

The peace offering (*shelamim*) was a meal shared together with God and the priest (Lev 3:1–5). God considered it a "pleasing aroma to God" in his nostrils (Lev 3:5). The best rendering for this *shelamim* is "saving

---

120. Jesse Couenhoven, *Stricken by Sin, Cured by Christ: Agency, Necessity and Culpability in Augustinian Theology* (Oxford: Oxford University Press, 2013), 4, quoting Augustine, *Works of Saint Augustine* III/5, ed. John E. Rotelle, OSA, trans. Edmund Hill, OP (New Rochelle: NY: New City, 1992), 261 (sermon 174.6).

121. James Denney, "The Second Epistle to the Corinthians," in *Expositor's Bible* (London: Hodder, 1894), 221–22. I am grateful to Derek Rishmawy for this reference.

offering."[122] Each worshiper laid hands on the animal and then cut its throat; the priest then laid the peace offering on top of the meal offering, which was itself laid on top of the burnt offering. All the meat was to be eaten right away and nothing was to be left of it on the third day (Lev 7:11–18). The fellowship offering is only possible because the sacrifice for guilt has been made. This was quite literally the case, since the gate of entrance to the temple itself was daubed with blood. The sacrifices take into account everything that was needed for Israel to come near to Yahweh: being ransomed/redeemed, purified, consecrated, and united to him in communion. "The common denominator of all three categories is joy," Milgrom observes. "'You shall sacrifice the well-being offering and eat them, *rejoicing* before the LORD your God' (Deut 27:7)."[123]

As the small-scale replica of the whole cosmos, every inch of the sanctuary must be purified with blood. Just as the worshiper has been purified, so now must be the diseased miniature cosmos. Unless the pollution is removed "by a purification offering, the community is in danger that their God will be forced to abandon the sanctuary." Blood is daubed on the horns of the altar: in this case, to purify the altar, not the person. "The act is described by the word *kippur*, 'purge' (as in Yom Kippur: the Day of Purgation)."[124] The altar is contaminated. "Since the offerer must bring the sacrifice, the offerer must in some way be implicated in the contamination of the altar. Thus the first principle: Blood is the ritual cleanser that purges the altar of impurities inflicted on it by the offerer."[125] On Yom Kippur, the whole sanctuary is purged with blood from top to bottom, and the High Priest daubs the blood on the mercy seat itself on behalf of the whole community, which has rendered the sanctuary contaminated by its collective sin.[126]

This displays the covenantal emphasis on *solidarity* rather than individualism. "Israel's neighbors also believed that impurity polluted the sanctuary," Milgrom notes. "For them, however, the source of impurity was demonic. Therefore, their priests devised rituals and incantations to immunize their temples against demonic penetration." However, Israel "abolished the world of demonic divinities."

---

122. C. F. Keil and Franz Delitzsch, *Commentary on the Old Testament* (Grand Rapids: Hendrickson, 2006), 1:298.
123. Milgrom, *Leviticus: A Book of Ritual and Ethics*, 28.
124. Milgrom, *Leviticus: A Book of Ritual and Ethics*, 30–31.
125. Milgrom, *Leviticus: A Book of Ritual and Ethics*, 31.
126. Milgrom, *Leviticus: A Book of Ritual and Ethics*, 31.

Only a single being capable of demonic acts remained—the human being. The humans were even more powerful than their pagan counterparts: they could drive God out of God's sanctuary. . . . To be sure, the Merciful One would tolerate a modicum of pollution. But there is a point of no return. If the pollution levels continue to rise, the end is inexorable. God abandons the sanctuary and leaves the people to their doom.[127]

The complicated details of this system may seem strange, as if God is keeping his people at arm's length. However, in truth, God is actually clearing a safe path into his presence when the easier course would be simply to destroy Israel and begin afresh, as he did in the flood and threatened to do after the golden calf incident until Moses's intercession prevailed. Leithart explains that there were no sacrificial meals (the "peace offering") with God prior to Sinai. "The first use of *shelamim* is in Exodus 20:24, at the beginning of Israel's covenant-cutting wedding ceremony." The tabernacle now "becomes a place of continuous feasting." "Yahweh has moved into his house in the midst of Israel, and he makes it a house of hospitality (see Deut 12)."[128]

It is significant that when Asaph's "feet almost slipped" over this apparent inequity, he regained his equilibrium when he entered the sanctuary (Ps 73). Jeremiah's question, "Why do the wicked prosper?" looms large in the Hebrew Bible. "We know now where to find their answer—not in words but in rituals," says Milgrom, "not in legal statutes but in cultic procedure—specifically, in the rite with the blood of the purification offering."[129] There is a sense of collective guilt: "Sinners may go about apparently unmarred by their evil, but the sanctuary bears the wounds, and with its destruction, all the sinners will meet their doom."[130] Since the earthly sanctuary reflects heaven and earth, its pollution bears cosmic significance.

The "good" people who perish with the evildoers are not innocent. For allowing brazen sinners to flourish, they share the blame. Indeed, they, the involuntary sinners, have contributed to the pollution of the

---

127. Milgrom, *Leviticus: A Book of Ritual and Ethics*, 31–32.
128. Leithart, *Delivered from the Elements of the World*, 109.
129. Milgrom, *Leviticus: A Book of Ritual and Ethics*, 32.
130. Milgrom, *Leviticus: A Book of Ritual and Ethics*, 32.

sanctuary. What of the "silent majority" of every generation—the Germans who tolerated the Nazi rise to power and territorial aggression, and the peoples of the free world who acquiesced in silence?[131]

Jesus brings a similar message to the scribe through the parable of the good Samaritan, and the scribe sloughs off his collective responsibility. "But he, desiring to justify himself, said to Jesus, 'And who is my neighbor?'" (Luke 10:29). Am I really responsible for slavery, sex-trafficking, and other moral evils committed by others? Have I calculated my willful complicity as well as my sins of omission in this collective narcissism? Can things get so bad that God abandons the earth and us to ourselves? For God to abandon the sanctuary was, for Israel, equivalent to his deserting the cosmos. We are all responsible, collectively and individually, for the corruption of God's house. Even the ground cries out against us (Gen 4:10), and the whole creation is in bondage because of us (Rom 8:20–21). As Milgrom reminds us, the worshiper offering guilt offerings "seeks more than forgiveness." "If God will accept his sacrifice he will be once again restored to grace, at one with his Deity."[132]

In short, then, Christians believe that it is through the sacrifice for guilt—"the Lamb of God who takes away the sin of the world" (John 1:29)—that we can enter into communion with God, feasting with him at his table as justified heirs in a purified cosmos. Forgiveness and justification are the basis for this communion, but it is fellowship with God together as his holy people that is the goal of it all. Substitution is not only the answer to guilt but to pollution, the desecration not only of ourselves but of God's cosmos. Only because an animal dies *in place of the offerer*, the creation may be purified for the time being at least until the incarnate God shed his blood and enters the heavenly sanctuary through it to purify the whole cosmos, "thus securing an eternal redemption" (Heb 9:11–12, 23–28). "For if the blood of goats and bulls, and the sprinkling of defiled persons with the ashes of a heifer, *sanctify for the purification of the flesh*, how much more will the blood of Christ, who through the eternal Spirit offered himself without blemish to God, *purify our conscience from dead works to serve the living God*" (vv. 13–14). In the sin offering the bull was killed outside the camp, while the fat and

---

131. Milgrom, *Leviticus: A Book of Ritual and Ethics*, 32.
132. Milgrom, *Leviticus: A Book of Ritual and Ethics*, 44.

blood were offered on the altar. "So Jesus also suffered outside the gate in order to *sanctify* the people through his own blood" (Heb 13:12).

Yet much more is involved. With the transition-word διὸ in Hebrews 10:5, the writer is about to tell us why these animal sacrifices fall short. In the process, he changes the original Hebrew of Psalm 40:6 ("but you have given me an open ear"—or, literally, "you have dug out ears for me") to "but a body have you prepared for me." "When he said above, 'You have neither desired nor taken pleasure in sacrifices and offerings and burnt offerings and sin offerings' (these are offered according to the law), then he added, 'Behold, I have come *to do* your will'" (10:8–9). The speaker is no longer David, delighting in God's redemption and asking, as a needy sinner, for an open ear; it is "Christ" who "came into the world" in the flesh that was prepared for him. "He does away with the first [sacrificial offerings under the law] in order to establish the second [living sacrifices under the gospel]. And *by that will we have been sanctified through the offering of the body of Jesus Christ once for all*" (vv. 9–10, emphasis added). Unlike the priest who is always standing and working, offering repeated sacrifices "which can never take away sins," Christ offered himself once and for all and then, entering his Sabbath victory, "sat down at the right hand of God, waiting from that time until his enemies should be made a footstool for his feet" (vv. 11–12). At this point, the writer reminds them of the promise of the new covenant in Jeremiah 31, underscoring verse 34: "and then he adds, 'I will remember their sins and their lawless deeds no more.' Where there is forgiveness of these, there is *no longer any offering for sin*" (vv. 15–18). Hebrews 10 encapsulates Christ's entire ministry from incarnation to ascension as an offering of thanksgiving, of guilt, and of cosmic purification so that his coheirs may join him at the everlasting feast.

Christ is also the peace offering, reconciling all things, "making peace by the blood of his cross" (Col 1:20). This peace is therefore objective, because it is established not in the fickle repentance of worshipers but in the perfect righteousness of Christ and his sacrifice. "For our sake he made him to be sin who knew no sin, so that in him we might become the righteousness of God" (2 Cor 5:21). "Therefore, since we have been justified by faith, we have peace with God through our Lord Jesus Christ. Through him we have also obtained access by faith into this grace in which we stand, and we rejoice in the hope of the glory of God" (Rom 5:1–2). In Christ, we have moved from purification (sin offering) to consecration and ascent (ascension offering) to the peace offering (communion).

Jesus explodes the typology even as he fulfills it. First, he is not only the sacrifice but the high priest. Second, he is not a helpless animal but the incarnate God whom death cannot hold. Third, the resurrection completes his deliverance, which has no parallel in the sacrificial system. Fourth, as Hebrews 6 remind us, Jesus is a better mediator than Moses and the covenant that he mediates is better precisely because it is founded on "two unchangeable things": first, the immutable nature of the God himself and his "Melchizedek priesthood" grounded in eternity and, second, the unilateral oath that he made to Abraham apart from the law, apart from the mediation of Moses, the Aaronic priesthood, and the fickle promises of the people at Sinai (Heb 6:13–20). The sacrifices were offered to God by the worshiper, but in the new covenant, God has offered the sacrifice for them once and for all. "The one who, according to the old dispensation, received the sacrifice, now became the giver," notes Gunton.[133] Therefore, access is obtained into the Holy of Holies, indeed to the throne of grace, not only typologically and not just for the high priest once a year but for every believer at all times.

God could not be the God of creation and covenant—loyal not only to himself and his purposes but to his creation—apart from dealing with the cosmic effects of sin in corrupting creation's original purpose. When we take a closer look at the civil laws of the Old Testament theocracy, a common theme emerges: the transgressor must make restitution. This is not a matter of chivalry but of justice—and not merely retributive but restorative justice, *rectitudo*. We are again in the realm of the act-consequence connection. Neither punishment nor reform is central in Israel's Torah. What is central is *tsdq*, "righteousness," the righting of wrongs and the consequent placement of enemies in the relation of friends, restoring the fruitfulness of the fallow earth by lifting the curse. Sometimes the righting of wrongs comes about by repaying a neighbor for the damage caused by one's bull. Other times, because every person is God's image-bearer, restitution meant that a life had to be exchanged for a life taken (Exod 21:23). In both cases, the judgment is more than

---

133. Colin Gunton, "The Sacrifice and the Sacrifices: From Metaphor to Transcendental," in *Trinity, Incarnation, and Atonement: Philosophical and Theological Essays*, ed. Ronald J. Feenstra and Cornelius Plantinga Jr., Library of Religious Philosophy 1 (Notre Dame, IN: University of Notre Dame Press, 1989), 217.

punitive. It is certainly not a matter of revenge. However, it is also not simply done for the reform of the criminal. Rather, it is done to set things right: not only to bring about the sense that justice has been done but to actually mend the fences broken by violence.

But no mere mortal can set this world right. Establishing objective rectitude before God by his death, Christ begins, by his word and Spirit, to reconcile and restore the *imago Dei*—not according to its original archetype (Adam) but according to its glorified archetype (Christ) (1 Cor 15:45). He has made our peace; he *is* the everlasting peace offering. And by sharing sacramentally in his death and resurrection through baptism and in his body and blood in the Supper, we are enjoying the true Passover feast. "The cup of blessing that we bless, is it not a participation in the blood of Christ? The bread that we break, is it not a participation in the body of Christ?" (1 Cor 10:16). The old covenant meal offering seems to be fulfilled in two ways: in Christ's active obedience, since the bread consisted of fine flour, oil, frankincense, and—crucially—no leaven (symbolizing sin). But through the unleavened bread we feed together on the unblemished lamb in a covenantal meal (1 Cor 10:16). Jesus is the true bread from heaven, and to eat his flesh and drink his blood is to have everlasting life (John 6:25–59). Therefore, the holy meal is called the Eucharist, "thanksgiving," rather than a repeated sacrifice for sin. The guilt sacrifice has been once offered, and all that remains is the Eucharist and the offering of our bodies as *living* sacrifices of praise (Rom 12:1–2).

CHAPTER 5

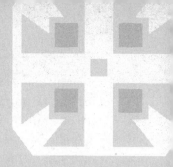

VICARIOUS VICTOR

An Integrated Account

It is in fact impossible to see Christ's incarnation, life, and death as anything but vicarious—indeed, vicarious suffering *and at the same time* his conquest over Satan, death, hell, and the evil powers that stalk the earth.[1] Vicarious substitution is not the whole story, but there is no story apart from it. As Oliver Crisp points out, the motifs of ransom or victory can be an aspect of Christ's work but not an encompassing doctrine. The mechanism is missing for *how* such victory is secured. "One is left wondering how it is that Christ's work achieves the reconciliation of human beings."[2] This chapter integrates recapitulation and propitiatory sacrifice with the theme of victory.

One can hardly pit sacrificial against conquest images when the sacrifices themselves included offerings of thanksgiving, purification, and fellowship as well as guilt. As Laura Smit observes, Jesus fulfills all of these offerings in various ways. "He offers himself completely to his Father, as a burnt offering, and yet he also offers himself in a way that leads to a shared meal with his disciples, as a grain offering. The book of Hebrews particularly emphasizes that in Christ we have fulfillment for the Day of Atonement."[3] Specifically, the sacrifices pointed to *atonement*, *purification*, and *consecration*.[4] Under these headings we may loosely place

---

1. On this point, see Jeremy R. Treat, *The Crucified King: Atonement and Kingdom in Biblical and Systematic Theology* (Grand Rapids: Zondervan, 2014).

2. Oliver Crisp, "Is Ransom Enough?" *Journal of Analytic Theology* 3 (2015): 3.

3. Laura Smit, "Justification and Sacrifice," in *What Is Justification About? Reformed Contributions to an Ecumenical Theme*, ed. Michael Weinrich and John P. Burgess (Grand Rapids: Eerdmans, 2009), 150.

4. I draw these elements from L. Michael Morales, *Who Shall Ascend the Mountain of the Lord? A Biblical Theology of the Book of Leviticus*, NSBT 37 (Downers Grove, IL: InterVarsity, 2015), 80.

recapitulation and substitution (atonement), victory and restoration of God's moral government (purification), and communion with God and each other in a living sacrifice of praise and thanksgiving (consecration).

In the patristic sources as well, Christ stands as both vicarious sacrifice and victor. The following could be taken by critics as a crass statement of a "commercial theory": "But because Christ, erasing this IOU with his own blood, affixed it to his own cross, we ought to be crucified according to the old man, who was subject to sin, so that 'the body of sin may be destroyed and we might no longer be enslaved to sin.'"[5] However, the author is Origen. Further, Origen argues that Christ's legal satisfaction of justice for sin's guilt is the basis for liberation from sin's tyranny.[6] Indeed, he says, "All the Scriptures testify to the fact that Christ became a sacrifice for the sake of sin and was offered for the cleansing of sins," citing various passages concerning his sin-bearing for us.[7] Christ's victory over the devil was based on his substitutionary atonement, Athanasius argued.[8] "Christ, though guiltless, took our punishment," said Augustine, "that he might cancel our guilt, and do away with our punishment."[9] Yet he also wove this theme without difficulty into the idea of a ransom paid to the devil.[10] Chrysostom considered "nothing greater" than this exchange of guilt for righteousness and curse for blessing at the cross.[11] The Spirit could not be sent until Christ's death "since the curse had not yet been lifted, the original sin had not yet been forgiven, but all men were still subject to the penalty for it."[12]

These early writers wove together the various strands into a beautiful tapestry of atonement doctrine that modern theology has pulled apart and set in separate heaps. Leon Morris states the point succinctly:

---

5. Origen, *Commentary on the Epistle to the Romans*, vol. 1, *Books 1–5*, trans. Thomas P. Scheck (Washington, DC: Catholic University of America Press, 2001), 364.

6. Origen, *Commentary on the Epistle to the Romans, Books 1–5*, 364. Admittedly, his statements in the commentary contradict his treatment in *On First Principles*.

7. Origen, *Commentary on the Epistle to the Romans, Books 6–10*, 49–50.

8. Athanasius, *On the Incarnation*, in *The Christology of the Later Fathers* (Philadelphia: Westminster Press, 1954), 64, 74.

9. Augustine, "Contra Faustus Manicheaus," 14.4 (*NPNF*[1] 4:208).

10. Augustine, *De trinitate* 13.14.18.

11. For only one example of the theme turned over several times in one homily, see John Chrysostom, *Homilies on Ephesians* 1:7, hom. 1 (*NPNF*[1] 12:53).

Leon Morris, *The Cross of Christ* (Grand Rapids: Eerdmans, 1965), 381.

12. Chrysostom, *Commentary on Saint John the Apostle and Evangelist*, vol. 41, *Fathers of the Church*, trans. Sister Thomas Aquinas Goggin (Washington, D. C.: The Catholic University of America Press, 1959), hom. 78, 345 (see also 338–52).

"The Fathers at times use expressions compatible with several later theories. They did not so much evolve a precisely defined theory, as give vigorous expression to the thought of Christ's triumph which Aulén was able to work into a theory."[13] Let us then see how Christ as *vicar* upholds Christ as *victor*.

Christus Victor

It is at the cross where God is vindicated as "just and the justifier of those who believe in Christ" (Rom 3:26). Aulén argued that Christ's victory over the powers ignored the claims of justice, going around the demands of law.[14] But if Christ has "broken through the order of justice and merit," as Aulén puts it, then he has not honored the order of creation that has been violated and that he himself, as God, demands to be restored.

Campbell presses still further into Marcionite territory when he says, "God, therefore, is not fundamentally just and the atonement designed to assuage God's righteous anger at transgression; God is fundamentally benevolent and the atonement intended to deliver humanity from bondage to evil powers and to reconstitute it in the age to come."[15] "We also learn at this point," he says, "that the atoning death of Christ is not fundamentally a penal act."[16] Here the cross loses its splendor as the place where God found a way to be "just *and* the justifier of the one who has faith in Jesus Christ" (Rom 3:26) precisely because he has fulfilled the law and borne the consequences for our actions.[17]

However, substitution and justification are the mechanism, not the goal, of Christ's victory. Käsemann observes that Paul's cosmic interpretation of righteousness and anthropology set "the church *over against* the world in several ways: it is the battle of the Spirit (*pneuma*) against the flesh (*sarx*; Gal. 5:17), of faith in Christ against the dominion of the

---

13. Morris, *The Cross of Christ*, 381.

14. Gustaf Aulén, *Christus Victor: An Historical Study of the Three Main Types of the Idea of the Atonement*, trans. A. G. Herber (London: SPCK, 1931; repr., New York: Macmillan, 1969), 79.

15. Douglas A. Campbell, *The Deliverance of God: An Apocalyptic Rereading of Justification in Paul* (Grand Rapids: Eerdmans, 2013), 192.

16. Douglas A. Campbell, "The Current Crisis: The Capture of Paul's Gospel by Methodological Arianism," in *Beyond Old and New Perspectives on Paul: Reflections on the Work of Douglas Campbell*, ed. Chris Tilling (Eugene, OR: Cascade, 2014), 45.

17. The interpretation is reminiscent of Origen's contention: the separation of the sheep and the goats on the last day pertains to *ideas* rather than *persons* because God is without wrath and that punishment can therefore his justice can never be retributive but merely remedial. See Origen, *Commentary on Matthew* 10.2.3 (*ANF* 10:411–512).

law (Gal. 2:15–21), of the foolishness of the cross against the wisdom of the world (1 Cor. 1:18–25) and, last but not least, the battle between the powers of life against the powers of death (Rom. 8:38–39)."[18] Christ purchased us from Satan's power, to which we had willingly enslaved ourselves, but did so by cancelling the debt we owed to God's justice. Christ's victory over the powers of sin and death are as essential to the atonement as vicarious substitution. However, three points must be kept in mind.

First, a biblical concept of Christus Victor *is grounded in Christ's satisfaction of God's justice.* The key *Christus Victor* passages are Colossians 2:13–15, 1 Corinthians 15 (esp. vv. 25–28), and the passages in the Gospels that highlight Jesus's ministry of healing and casting out demons. Yet in all these instances, the victory over the powers is the consequence of the cancelling of debts. On the basis of passages like Colossians 2:13–15, Douglas Campbell concludes that "the atonement is intended to deliver humanity from bondage to evil powers" *rather than* "to assuage God's righteous anger at transgression."[19] However, these verses say explicitly that God made us alive in Christ "by canceling the record of debt that stood against us with its legal demands. This he set aside, nailing it to the cross." Therefore, "He disarmed the rulers and authorities and put them to open shame, by triumphing over them in him." This passage is reminiscent to the Apocalypse of Zephaniah. As usual in the Second Temple literature, the final judgment is according to the weighing of deeds. In this case, God and Satan make the calculations, and Zephaniah pleads successfully, "May you wipe out my manuscript [i.e., the record of his sins] because your mercy has come to be in every place and has filled every place" (7:8).[20] However, in Colossians 2, the manuscript is wiped out not because of Zephaniah's arguments in his favor, in addition to an appeal to God's mercy, but on the basis of Christ's death.

According to 1 Corinthians 15, all things are put under Christ's feet until the final enemy, death, is vanquished subjectively as it already has been objectively in Christ. But death cannot be the root problem solved by the cross and resurrection; rather, it is a symptom. "The sting of death is sin, and the power of sin is the law. But thanks be to God, who

---

18. Ernst Käsemann, *Perspectives on Paul* (Philadelphia: Fortress, 1971), 29.
19. Campbell, *The Deliverance of God*, 192.
20. Richard Bauckham, "Apocalypses," in *Justification and Variegated Nomism*, vol. 1, *The Complexities of Second Temple Judaism*, ed. D. A. Carson, Peter T. O'Brien, and Mark A. Seifrid, WUNT 2/140 (Grand Rapids: Baker Academic, 2001), 157–58.

gives us the victory through our Lord Jesus Christ" (1 Cor 15:56–57). Once the *sentence* is removed, death no longer has a legal claim on us. A similar relationship between *Christus Victor* and *Agnus Dei* can be found in Romans 8. Through Christ, "we are more than conquerors." "For I am sure that neither death nor life, nor angels nor rulers, nor things present or things to come, nor powers, nor height nor depth, nor anything else in all creation, will be able to separate us from the love of God in Christ Jesus our Lord" (Rom 8:37–39). But why? Because, through Christ's offering, no one can "bring any charge against God's elect." "It is God who justifies. Who is to condemn?" (vv. 31–34).

And the ministry of Jesus of healing and casting out demons in the power of the Spirit is the sign that the kingdom has dawned. Why is Satan bound? So that he can no longer deceive the nations and blind them to the glory of the gospel. Christ's healing miracles attest to his power to forgive sins, a forgiveness that they receive (along with the healing) through faith (Luke 5:20–25; Matt 9:2–8, etc.). And what is the result? Not only as God but as the faithful Last Adam, he restores the human vocation, cleansing God's garden-temple from all that defiles and binds us. All along the way to Golgotha, Jesus anticipates this victory, with Satan falling from heaven like lightning (Luke 10:17–20). In fact,

> The seventy-two returned with joy, saying, "Lord, even the demons are subject to us in your name!" And he said to them, "I saw Satan fall like lightning from heaven. Behold, I have given you authority to tread on serpents and scorpions, and over all the power of the enemy, and nothing shall hurt you. *Nevertheless, do not rejoice in this, that the spirits are subject to you, but rejoice that your names are written in heaven.*" (emphasis added)

In the next chapter, Jesus introduces the Lord's Prayer with the petition, "Your kingdom come, your will be done on earth as it is in heaven" (Luke 11:2). He follows this by fulfilling his prayer, casting out a demon, and sparking a controversy about the source of his power. "But if it is by the finger of God that I cast out demons, then the kingdom of God has come upon you. When a strong man, fully armed, guards his own palace, his goods are safe; but when one stronger than he attacks him and overcomes him, he takes away his armor in which he trusted and divides his spoil" (vv. 20–22).

Referring to patristic ideas of a ransom to the devil and deceiving Satan with the "bait" of Christ's humanity, Aulén observes, "Behind all the seemingly fantastic speculations lies the thought that the power of evil ultimately overreaches when it comes in conflict with the power of good, with God Himself. It loses the battle at the moment when it seems victorious."[21] This is a beautiful statement of the thesis that I have been defending. This is indeed what the fathers meant by their sometimes extravagant analogies. However, if with Aulén we make this the alternative to substitution, then the fish is let off the hook. It is not by going around the law and the covenant of creation that Jesus accomplishes redemption, but by fulfilling it, bearing its curse, and being raised as the beginning of the new creation. "God made him who had no sin to be sin for us, so that in him we might become the righteousness of God" (2 Cor 5:21).

So we sing with the saints in heaven that new song, where reigning in victory is grounded in the Lamb's triumph: "By your blood you ransomed people for God from every tribe . . . and you have made them a kingdom and priests to our God, and they shall reign on the earth" (Rev 5:9–10). In fact, throughout the book of Revelation the motifs of *Agnus Dei* and *Christus Victor* wind their way in and out of each other freely. There is no greater *Christus Victor* vision than the one in Revelation 12. There the cosmic victory of the seed of the woman over the serpent is captured in a single snapshot with this central announcement:

> And I heard a loud voice in heaven, saying, "Now the salvation and the power and the kingdom of our God and the authority of his Christ have come, *for the accuser* of our brothers has been thrown down, who accuses them day and night before our God. And they have conquered him *by the blood of the Lamb* and by *the word* of their testimony, for they loved not their lives even unto death. (Rev 12:10–11, emphasis added)

Volf is exactly right: "No doubt, there is more to divine judgment than setting the records straight; the One who judges at the end of history is the same One who 'justifies sinners' in the middle of history. But can

---

21. Aulén, *Christus Victor*, 54–55.

divine judgment be anything less than setting the records straight?"[22] Consequently, "The attempt to transcend judgment—whether it be judgment of reason or of religion—does not eliminate but enthrones violence. The escape from the castle of (judging) conscience lands one in the castle of murderers."[23]

Martyn, Campbell, Leithart, and others who follow after Käsemann highlight important Pauline emphases (especially apocalyptic accents) that are sometimes left out. It is not that their canvas is too broad, but that it is too narrow. And, to change metaphors, their version of *Christus Victor* has become a central dogma—a "Grand Theory"—that drowns out the Pauline symphony with a single melody. But we have seen that Scripture links these aspects to Christ's blood and the proclamation of the gospel as that which overcomes Satan's legal accusations in the divine courtroom. To be sure, we must beware of making the reverse mistake by turning substitution into the central dogma. But as Wright observes in his critique of Martyn's interpretation of Galatians 1:4 and elsewhere,

There is of course far more to say about that highly contested passage, but Paul seems happy to affirm *both* the redemptive curse-bearing of the Messiah *and* the larger effect of that death, linking them as achievement and purpose (i.e. the Messiah bore the curse *in order that* the Abrahamic blessing might flow to the gentiles), just as in 1.4 the Messiah "gave himself for our sins" *in order to* liberate us from the present evil age. We might suggest . . . that a similar sequence is visible in the crucial passage 4.4–7, and on into 4.7–11. The redemptive act of God in the Messiah, redeeming those "under the law," was accomplished *in order that* those so redeemed might receive adoption, might receive the spirit [sic], might be made "heirs," and might thus be liberated from the "elements," whatever they are, that had formerly enslaved them (4.8–11).[24]

"'Delivering from sins' is exactly the way by which God 'rescues us from the evil age,'" he says. "The two belong together."[25]

22. Miroslav Volf, *Exclusion and Embrace: A Theological Exploration of Otherness, Identity and Embrace* (Nashville: Abingdon, 1994), 242.
23. Volf, *Exclusion and Embrace*, 290.
24. N. T. Wright, *Paul and His Recent Interpreters: Some Contemporary Debates* (Minneapolis: Fortress, 2015), 175.
25. Wright, *Paul and His Recent Interpreters*, 177.

Second, any scriptural interpretation of Christus Victor *must affirm the simplicity of the divine nature according to which God's goodness and love are not set over against his judgment and wrath but are seen as integrally related.*

As we have seen, some advocates of *Christus Victor* have pushed the theory into Marcionite territory, separating the God of creation, justice, and law from the God of redemption, love, and mercy.[26] However, this dissolving of the paradox between love and justice renders the cross a meaningless tragedy and horrifying waste. Jesus Christ did not go around the Creator and his law, as if it were the work of an alien god. Jesus, who *is* the Creator together with the Father and the Spirit, did not criticize, much less reject, the righteous law that God delivered to Moses. On the contrary, he was the one human being in history who cherished it with the fullness of his heart, acknowledging its goodness, and delighting to follow it in perfect submission. "For truly, I say to you, until heaven and earth pass away, not an iota, not a dot, will pass from the Law until all is accomplished" (Matt 5:18). He allowed the law to have the last word even upon his mortal life. He was judged as a sinner because of us in the joyful knowledge that his Father had another word after this one: namely, the resurrecting-justifying word of vindication as his reward.

We have encountered repeated suggestions to the effect that God's love has conquered his justice, his grace has swallowed his law, and by his triumph over the evil powers Jesus has subverted the law's powers. However, Paul teaches, "Do we then overthrow the law by this faith? By no means! On the contrary, we uphold the law" (Rom 3:31). At the cross, Christ triumphs *not by destroying* this good and natural order of creation but by bearing the curse for our violation *so that a new order* based on Christ's resurrection will emerge. "So the law is holy, and the commandment is holy and righteous and good" (Rom 7:12). In fact, with Christ's resurrection there is a *restoration of the law* in its deepest intent. And because he has fulfilled it and borne its consequences, we receive justification *apart from the law.* Far from pitting law against love, it is the law that stipulates what it means to love God and neighbor

---

26. As we have seen, some contemporary scholars go so far as to dismiss the God of the Old Testament entirely. Douglas Campbell provides a terse formula for this view: "God, therefore, is not fundamentally just and the atonement designed to assuage God's righteous anger at transgression; God is fundamentally benevolent and the atonement intended to deliver humanity from bondage to evil powers and to reconstitute it in the age to come" (Campbell, *The Deliverance of God*, 192).

(Matt 22:37–38). Only in Christ can this good law be restored among us (1 John 2:7–8).

Third, the powers of darkness from which Christ has delivered us are chiefly "in heavenly places," and the weapons are spiritual. According to Ephesians 6, these weapons are forged from the objective work of Christ: the helmet of salvation, "the breastplate of righteousness," and the "sword of the Spirit, which is the word of God" (Eph 6:12–18). Of course, evil powers infect and enslave nations, empires, and global structures as well. From Cain and Lamech to Nimrod and Pharaoh, from Queen Athaliah all the way to Herod, Caesar, Pilate, and the Sanhedrin, Satan has used human emissaries to carry out his plan to remain the god of this present evil age. There is no pristine landing place for the Son of Man when he appears in glory to judge. And it is part of the believer's vocation to be alert to the attempts of Caesar to claim ultimate power to save and to rule.

In this situation, Satan is in some sense holder of the title deed that we have surrendered to him. There is something not only salvageable but significant in the "ransom" idea that we find in some of the early fathers.[27] Significantly, we are never told that Christ paid a ransom to Satan but rather that Christ bound him and recovered his stolen property (Mark 3:26–27), hinted at by the restoration of Job's fortunes beyond any prior wealth after his intercession for his friends (Job 42:10). Even from the biblical passages we have already encountered, it is clear that a redemption—a buying back—has been accomplished through a price that is nothing less than Christ's blood. These passages indicate that we are redeemed or ransomed *for* God *from* sin and "from the empty

---

27. Unfortunately, it is beyond this project's scope to examine the patristic sources on this theme, but it suffices to say that there is no single "ransom theory" among the church fathers any more than there is a single theory of the atonement. Although Origen sees the ransom as paid to the devil (Origen, *Commentary on the Epistle to the Romans, Books 1–5*, 161, 297), Irenaeus interprets it as having been paid to God. Athanasius and Augustine offer a more complex view: the devil held us justly because we had surrendered ourselves to his lordship, but God outwitted him at the cross. Yet in their interpretations, as in Irenaeus's, Satan's title deed to us depended on God's just sentence, which could only be removed by the vicarious sacrifice of Christ (Athanasius, *On the Incarnation of the Logos*, 6–7, 9; Athanasius, "Orations Against the Arians," 2:69; Augustine, *De trinitate* 13.19). Peter Lombard also, summarizing Augustine (*De trinitate* 13.14.18), says "We were *taken away from the power of the devil by the remission of sins*, and so the devil is overcome by Christ through justice, and not through power" (Peter Lombard, *The Sentences*, 4 vols., trans. Giulio Silano [Toronto: Pontifical Institute of Mediaeval Studies, 2010], 86, emphasis added). In short, far from establishing antitheses, theologians of East and West alike moved easily back and forth between ransom, recapitulation, and victory themes—yet with Christ's sacrifice on behalf of sinners as the basis. The result of all of this is reconciliation (*katallage*) with God, rendered in Tyndale's 1526 translation as "atonement."

way of life" that we have inherited. But none of these texts indicate a person to whom a ransom was paid. This fact alone should caution against speculation. Paul laments being "sold to sin" (Rom 7:14), but surely this is a personification. In Adam, humanity has sold itself to sin leading to death. However, death is the sentence for sin, and "the power of sin is the law" (1 Cor 15:56). Therefore, Satan holds us in his power, but only because he knows that we are condemned to death by God's own righteous law.

Cast out of heaven, the serpent and his minions were already at work in the world before Adam's creation, setting up shop to repeat on earth the disaster that he has accomplished in heavenly places. As N. T. Wright puts it, Adam and Eve handed over their vice-regency and transferred their fealty to the father of lies. They surrendered their calling to rule, subdue, and multiply on God's behalf and became false witnesses along with Lucifer.[28]

So there is a sense in which Satan owns us. But lacking any original and proper rights, he works parasitically on God's. He cannot claim sovereignty, so he must work cleverly to use God's rule against him, as it were. Satan did not even *win* the title to humanity; we willingly gave it to him, just as Esau sold his birthright for a pot of stew. It was God's covenant, which we broke, that placed us under the curse. And yet, it was precisely this debt to God that Satan could justly invoke as the basis for his making us captive to his empire of death.

Ever since God promised the offspring who will crush the serpent's head (Gen 3:15–16), Satan had been trying to intercept the Messiah. The slaughter of Abel, the firstborn in Egypt, the royal family (2 Kgs 11:1–12:11), and the firstborn in Bethlehem were failed strikes at the heart of God's promise. And now the Son in whom the Father is well-pleased has arrived, and even in his ministry, three years before the cross, the war to end all wars began. This ministry is itself part of the gospel, essential to the narrative that we identify as "redemption."

Considering the earth his own realm, Satan presumes to offer Jesus all the kingdoms of the world if he would simply yield fealty to him (Matt 4:9). Paul says that "the god of this world has blinded the minds of the unbelievers, to keep them from seeing the light of the gospel of the glory of Christ, who is the image of God" (2 Cor 4:4). Satan must

---

28. N. T. Wright, *The Day the Revolution Began: Reconsidering the Meaning of Jesus' Crucifixion* (New York: HarperOne, 2016), 73–88.

have recourse to *God's* courtroom, to *his* law, and *his* sentence in order to press his own charges and claims. But our treason is bound up with his since we both incurred the judgment *and* transferred our allegiance from God to Satan. Lucifer is a dangerous prosecutor in the heavenly courtroom not because of any original dominion or right to judge but because he has access to *Yahweh's* evidence against us. He appeared in the divine court to accuse and harass God's people in the Old Testament (e.g., Job 1:6–12; Zech 3:1–10, etc.). Hence, the significance of his being cast out of heaven (Luke 10:18).

Throughout Jesus's confrontations with Satan and his demonic hosts, we encounter marshal imagery with Jesus binding Satan and looting his empire, casting him out of heaven and out of people. The demons clearly fear this appearance of the one who will crush their master's head. In Mark 1:24, the demon that Jesus casts out is, ironically, the first witness to Jesus's identity: "What have you to do with us, Jesus of Nazareth? Have you come to destroy us? I know who you are—the Holy One of God." Only this access to the courtroom, with its legal records that demand our death, makes it bearable for the saints that he has been cast down to the earth. He cannot prosecute but instead persecutes the saints. "Therefore, rejoice, O heavens and you who dwell in them! But woe to you, O earth and sea, for the devil has come down to you in great wrath, because he knows that his time is short!" (Rev 12:12). All of these passages focus on defeating Satan precisely at the point where he claims us on the basis of God's just sentence. Once this sentence is lifted, he knows that his attempt at the divine throne has been thwarted and his time is short. With the justification of the ungodly, the palaces and prisons of darkness come crashing down into a heap.

To accomplish this feat, the serpent-crushing Messiah had to be not only a human sage, martyr to nonviolence, or moral example, but "very God of very God." This is where we may insert that famous "Christus Victor" passage from Gregory of Nyssa's *Great Catechism*: "The Deity was hidden under the veil of our nature, so that, as with ravenous fish, the hook of Deity might be gulped down with the bait of flesh, and thus, life being introduced into the house of death, and light shining in darkness, that which is diametrically opposed to light and life might vanish."[29] As we have seen, the humanity of Christ is essential—not

---

29. Gregory of Nyssa, *The Great Catechism* 24 (NPNF² 5:494).

merely as bait hiding the hook of divinity but as the recapitulating-life and obedience of the Last Adam. Yet any account of the atonement that does not require a *divine rescuer* for its Christology should be excluded at the outset.

The deeper point of the ransom argument, at least as expressed by Gregory of Nyssa, is that God in Christ has outwitted Satan. After centuries of wanton violence, with a river of blood from Abel to Zechariah and Herod's raving infanticide of Bethlehem's newborn males, the devil imagined that he had finally nailed his would-be slayer to a cross. Yet he did not know that it was impossible for the grave to hold him, and through what seemed like the greatest example of divine weakness and injustice, God actually triumphed in merciful power and justice (1 Cor 2:8).

Even though there is an important emphasis in the New Testament on our being victims of the evil powers, the emphasis falls on the conquering King breaking the power of *our* lawlessness. He not only atones but purifies each living stone of his end-time sanctuary and consecrates them for fellowship with him and with each other. Guilt-bearing and justification are not the only achievements of this King; he releases us from bondage and sanctifies us as those who are now baptized into his death and resurrection (Rom 6:1–23; Col 2:8–15).

Christ's kingdom is not a power alongside other powers, vying for control through sociopolitical action. Rather, it is for the sake of the "unshakable kingdom" that the fragile and temporary regimes of this age continue to exist. We are not building a kingdom by brick and mortar programs and relevance-craving agendas of the left and the right, imagining that we are redeeming and reconciling the world alongside Jesus. Rather, "We are *receiving* a kingdom that cannot be shaken" (Heb 12:28). "Fear not, little flock," Jesus says, "for it is your Father's good pleasure to *give you* the kingdom" (Luke 12:32). From the world's perspective, the church is trivial and insignificant (in the West) or a dangerous threat (in many other parts of the world), but because it is the communion of God's elect, redeemed, and justified people, "we are more than conquerors through him who loved us" (Rom 8:37), gathering guests for the end-time banquet (Luke 14:12–24).

It is for this that the King keeps history open, even through the fragile and oppressive rulers of the age, to keep a parody of that ultimate peace while he extends his everlasting peace with God throughout the world by the proclamation of the gospel. Only at Christ's second advent will it be consummated in glory. "The God of peace will soon crush Satan under your feet" (Rom 16:20). Until then, the gospel flourishes under the sign of the cross. "And this gospel of the kingdom will be proclaimed throughout the whole world as a testimony to all nations, and then the end will come" (Matt 24:14).

MORAL GOVERNMENT

In a treatise against Socinianism in 1617, the great Arminian jurist and theologian Hugo Grotius devised the governmental theory as a refutation of this heresy with which he and other followers of Arminius had been charged. Over against Socinianism, Grotius argued that God cannot simply overlook sin since this would throw into question his moral government of the universe. Yet, rather than demand full exaction of justice, God makes Christ's death a sufficient cause for offering salvation to us on easier terms than full, perfect, personal, and perpetual obedience to the whole law. According to this view, Christ did therefore suffer punishment for sin, but not an exact payment for particular transgressions.[30]

As subsequent advocates explain the theory, the cross displays God's displeasure with sin and serves as a deterrent, since those who continue in their sins will suffer the same fate.[31] Christ's death therefore serves a general and public justice rather than a commutative or distributive type.[32] Christ did not endure the penalty for particular sins, but his

---

30. Hugo Grotius, *Defensio fidei catholicae de satisfaction Christi adversus Faustum Socinum* (Johannes Patius, 1617). See Alan W. Gomes, "Hugo Grotius' Defensio fidei Catholicae de satifactione Christi adversus Faustum Socinum: An Interpretative Reappraisal," lecture, Evangelical Theological Society, Far West Regional Meeting, Spring 1988, *Conference Papers*, 260. http://place.asburyseminary.edu/trenpapers/260.

31. H. Orton Wiley, *Christian Theology* (Kansas City, MO: Beacon Hill, 2013), 241; John Miley, *Systematic Theology* (New York: Hunt and Eaton, 1889; repr., Peabody, MA: Hendrickson, 1989), 2:246; J. Kenneth Grider, *A Wesleyan-Holiness Theology* (Kansas City: Beacon Hill, 1994), 12. Grider says, "While Calvinists teach boldly that Christ paid the penalty for us—that He took our punishment—and believe their view to be biblical, it is altogether opposed to the teaching of Scripture." Like Grotius and later advocates of the theory, including Jonathan Edwards Jr., Nathaniel Taylor, Samuel Hopkins, and others associated with the New England Divinity, as well as Charles G. Finney's *God's Moral Government*, Grider leans heavily on a logical inference more than exegesis: "One cannot both punish and forgive, surely. . . . Neither a human being nor God, surely, can accept payment for a debt and still forgive the debt." In both instances, the "surely" only works if the same party is being forgiven and paying the debt. This overlooks the key point of the traditional doctrine: namely, that God forgives *"the many"* because *he* (the incarnate Son) bears the debt himself.

32. Edwards Amasa Park, "The Rise of the Edwardsian Theory of the Atonement," in *The Atonement: Discourses and Treatises Rise of the Edwardsean Theory of the Atonement* (Boston: Congregational Board of Publications, 1859), iii; see Jonathan Edwards Jr. on p. 38 of the same

death is sufficient to punish it publicly in such a way that the world knows that God remains in charge of his government and that the sinner who persists in his sins will suffer the same fate. Faith, repentance, and new obedience are adequate now as the basis for God's forgiveness. Although Arminius and Wesley did not embrace this theory, it has been favored by many Arminian theologians as an alternative to Socinian and traditional perspectives of substitution.[33]

As with the other models, the governmental theory fails to provide a satisfactory atonement doctrine when treated as an alternative to substitution, though it contributes an essential aspect when integrated into the latter. In addition to its exegetical implausibility as a stand-alone theory, God's moral government is hardly upheld by a *relaxation* of God's law.

First, the law drifts away from God's moral character, becoming an arbitrary norm. The nominalist influence is apparent at this point.[34] According to this view, God's upholding of his moral government does not require the satisfaction of his full claims of justice. At the end of the day, all moralistic theories fail to uphold God's law but lower its standards to a level that seems more attainable. Second, the cross is not, according to this view, the place where the paradox of divine justice and love embrace. On the contrary, it is a demonstration of God's justice and wrath that this view highlights. Third, as with the moral influence theory, the governmental theory—by itself—leaves nothing actually restored by Christ's death. A relaxed law evacuates divine righteousness and therefore hardly serves as a moral deterrent, while the gospel is reduced to an easier form of salvation by works. Redemption is lodged not in Christ's bearing the full consequences of sin's sentence but in the believer's decision to repent and begin in new obedience out of fear for suffering the same fate as Jesus. As in Aulén's version of *Christus Victor*, Christ triumphs only by going around justice rather than by fulfilling it. And once again, there is the anthropological assumption that human beings can essentially redeem themselves by repentance if simply presented with an adequate demonstration of God's anger at sin.

volume. See Brandon J. Crawford, *Jonathan Edwards on the Atonement* (Eugene, OR: Wipf and Stock, 2017).

33. Roger Olson, *Arminian Theology: Myths and Realities* (Downers Grove, IL: InterVarsity Press, 1994), 224.

34. I am referring to the late medieval school that emphasized the absolute will of God to the point (among some representatives at least) where God can arbitrarily violate his own moral order.

This idea that good will and fresh obedience can procure absolution belongs to a long history in Christian theology, particularly in the doctrine of penance, and it is an important element in the governmental view. In fact, it is typically assumed or argued explicitly when *Christus Victor* is treated as an alternative to *Agnus Dei*: Christ liberated us from the powers so that now we may, in imitation of him, take up our calling of redeeming and reconciling the world. When separated from substitution, *Christus Victor* defenses mistake the symptoms (the evil powers death, injustice, violence, etc.) for the disease (the curse). Hence, they mistake the effects (liberation) for the cure (abolition of the curse, i.e., justification) and the redeemed for the Redeemer.

A mere demonstration of justice can render us just in neither a forensic nor analytic sense. Yet when it is part of an integrated account with Christ's substitutionary sacrifice, the important truth in the governmental theory is not only affirmed but settled on a better foundation: a *full and complete satisfaction of God's justice*. This is where the motif of *restoration-purification* enters the picture, as it finds its basis in the forgiveness of sins and justification (Jesus's life as thank offering and guilt offering).

Paul brings together both sacrifice and restoration of government especially in Romans 3:24–26: "Christ Jesus, whom God put forward as a propitiation by his blood, to be received by faith. This was *to show God's righteousness* . . . at the present time, so that he might be just and the justifier of the one who has faith in Jesus." It is precisely as "a sacrifice of atonement" that God's justice is revealed. As such it achieves a restoration of God's world: the purification of the cosmic sanctuary that follows the offering for guilt.

Ironically, this is the emphasis of Anselm without the miscontruals associated with "the theory of Anselm." Mired in feudalism, Anselm saw Christ's death as analogous to the satisfaction required by one who has offended a prince's dignity. Criticisms along these lines are offered not only by critics of substitution but in Reformed summaries as well.[35]

While generally described over against *Christus Victor* and moral government theories, Anselm's actual treatment of the atonement in *Cur Deus Homo* (Why the God-Man) in fact *focuses* on restoration. Anselm does not reduce the atonement to the idea of a monarch requiring

---

35. Louis Berkhof, *Systematic Theology* (Grand Rapids: Eerdmans, 1996), 385–86.

satisfaction to restore his offended dignity. On the contrary, Anselm denies that the impassible God's dignity and glory can be diminished or threatened in any way.[36] Rather, the central reason why God cannot justly overlook sin is because it is a corruption of "the beauty and order of the universe itself."[37] This fits well with the theme that we have encountered above, in considering the importance of the purification and holiness of God's temple-cosmos. It must be purified with blood just as the earthly temple, as a microcosm, is purified with blood.

"One may refuse to submit to the Divine will and appointment, yet he cannot escape it," Anselm warns.[38] Even in sinning one remains "subservient, under infinite wisdom, to the order and beauty of the universe." Notice the similarity with the moral government view:

> For if Divine wisdom were not to insist upon things, when wickedness tries to disturb the right appointment, there would be, in the very universe which God ought to control, an unseemliness springing from the violation of the beauty of arrangement, and God would appear to be deficient in his management. And these two things are not only unfitting but consequently impossible; so that satisfaction or punishment must needs follow every sin.[39]

God, in other words, maintains his honor *for the sake of* "the beauty and order of the universe" as its Lord and governor. Even if we wish to associate Anselm's argument with medieval feudalism, as Colin Gunton

---

36. Anselm, *Cur Deus Homo*, trans. Sidney Norton Deane (repr., Andesite/Beloved, 2014), 220, 223.

37. Anselm, *Cur Deus Homo*, 223. This, by the way, is quite different from John Milbank's version of the impassibility argument vis-à-vis the atonement. Similar to Origen, Milbank asserts that "God does not forgive, since he cannot be offended, but only continues to give, despite our rejection of his gift" (Milbank, *Being Reconciled: Ontology and Pardon* [London: Routledge, 2003], 60). For Milbank, there are only two options: a change in God (unacceptable in the light of immutability) or a change in us. What is lacking is a third—covenantal—category: a change in the relation *between* God and creatures with respect to God's purpose for "the beauty and order of the universe." "Therefore," says Milbank, "divine redemption is not God's forgiving us, but rather his giving us the gift of the capacity for forgiveness" (62). Christ's cross is therefore emptied of its most cherished vocabulary: reconciliation, redemption, forgiveness, justification, propitiation, and substitution. "Hence, the New Testament does not speak of Jesus's death as a sacrifice in the rabbinic sense of a death atoning for sins." "*Nothing can be taken from the impassible God*," so there is no need for compensation for injustice (99). In contrast, Anselm appeals to impassibility to show (contrary to the usual characterization of his "theory") that the atonement is required not because God has suffered any personal loss but because he must care for his creation and exercise justice on behalf of the good that he is. This entire piece is missing in Milbank, for whom any lack of personal injury renders the atonement unnecessary.

38. Anselm, *Cur Deus Homo*, 223–24.

39. Anselm, *Cur Deus Homo*, 224.

notes, "It was the duty of the feudal ruler to maintain the order of rights and obligations without which society would collapse. Anselm's God is understood to operate *analogously* for the universe as a whole as the upholder of universal justice."[40]

At this point, Anselm explains why the debt that humanity owes cannot be paid by a mere human being. "Repentance, a broken and contrite heart, self-denial, various bodily sufferings, pity in giving and forgiving, and obedience"—these are what we owe, and therefore they cannot satisfy for past sin.[41] Boso wonders why his faith "working by love" cannot be sufficient to warrant forgiveness and Anselm famously replies, "You have not as yet estimated the great burden of sin."[42] Crimes against an infinite God require infinite punishment and humans have no way to repay this debt.[43] Far from "conquering the devil," we continue in his grip. A human being must do this, "but a sinful man can by no means do this, for a sinner cannot justify a sinner."[44] Consequently, "His salvation must necessarily be by Christ."[45]

The rest of the argument explains why Christ must therefore be both God and human, so that he could conquer the devil, first of all, by rendering "a complete expiation of sin, which no sinner can effect for himself."[46] God does this precisely by becoming human. "This restoration can only be made from human beings, since there is no other source" of the responsibility for disorder, and yet only God *could* accomplish this.[47]

After reasoning from this need for redemption and restoration to the incarnation, Anselm explains how Christ's death not only liberated us from guilt but from the devil (with the payment made to God rather than Satan) and restored "the beauty and order of the universe."[48] It was not divine lust for personal satisfaction of offended dignity that moved God to send his Son, Anselm reminds us, but the consideration of the human situation, motivated by both his love and justice.

---

40. Colin Gunton, *The Actuality of Atonement: A Study of Metaphor, Rationality, and the Christian Tradition* (Edinburgh: T&T Clark, 1988), 89–90.
41. Anselm, *Cur Deus Homo*, 240.
42. Anselm, *Cur Deus Homo*, 242.
43. Anselm, *Cur Deus Homo*, 243.
44. Anselm, *Cur Deus Homo*, 246.
45. Anselm, *Cur Deus Homo*, 251.
46. Anselm, *Cur Deus Homo*, 256–60.
47. Anselm, *Cur Deus Homo*, 46.
48. Anselm, *Cur Deus Homo*, 300: "But whatever was demanded of man, he owed to God and not to the devil."

God made the satisfaction. He did not simply mete out punishment for his personal satisfaction but "gave his only-begotten Son." "*God* was in Christ reconciling the world to himself" (2 Cor 5:19). The term that Anselm uses repeated throughout his argument is *restitutio*, or restitution. Christ's work is required not only to cancel the debt of sin but to restore the creation to its proper condition. The goal of Christ's death is not punishment but restoration. Like the microcosmic temple, the whole cosmos must be purified and brought into right relation; its disordered condition both of individuals and of creation itself must be set right. At the cross, God justifies himself as well as sinners.[49] Colin Gunton observes, "In face of a tendency to mythologize the metaphor of ransom, Anselm's achievement is immense."[50]

Critics of substitution often refer to the example of the Prodigal Son, where the father embraces the son without any payment or demand for restitution. It is the paradigm of "unconditional forgiveness."[51] Similar to Douglas Campbell's argument, Gregory Boyd says that he cannot imagine how adherents of substitution can "reconcile the idea that the Father needs to exact payment from or on behalf of his enemies with Jesus' teaching (and example) that we are to love unconditionally and forgive without payment."[52] However, the parable of the prodigal son does not explain the atonement generally. It is a parable of how the Father receives us now into his loving fellowship in spite of our guilt, not of how the guilt was covered. Furthermore, as Gunton notes, in the parable the offence is only against the father, while in the case of the cross, the whole world is corrupted by human treason. "Were the offense actually against someone else, however, or against a group, it would hardly be the father's prerogative to excuse or ignore it. Indeed, in such a circumstance, it would be egregiously unjust for the father to grant forgiveness if the actual injured party had not first done so or actually refused to."[53]

Similarly, Volf reasons, a God who ignores the claims of justice is neither good nor loving toward his creation. "If Jesus had done nothing

---

49. Gunton, *The Actuality of Atonement*, 106. Referring to P. T. Forsyth's *The Justification of God*, Gunton says, "The theme of the book is that the justice of God can be found only where he justifies himself, and that is in the act of atonement on the cross."

50. Gunton, *The Actuality of Atonement*, 87.

51. Gunton, *The Actuality of Atonement*, 190–91.

52. Gregory Boyd, "Christus Victor," in *The Nature of the Atonement: Four Views*, ed. J. Beilby and P. R. Eddy (Downers Grove, IL: IVP Academic, 2006), 104.

53. Gunton, *The Actuality of Atonement*, 190–91.

but suffer violence, we would have forgotten him as we have forgotten so many other innocent victims."[54] He adds, "A nonindignant God would be an accomplice in injustice, deception, and violence. . . . A 'nice' God is a figment of the liberal imagination, a projection onto the sky of the inability to give up cherished illusions about goodness, freedom, and the rationality of social actors."[55] In fact, Volf goes so far as to suggest that "the practice of nonviolence requires a belief in divine vengeance."

> To the person who is inclined to dismiss it, I suggest imagining that you are delivering a lecture in a war zone (which is where a paper that underlies this chapter was originally delivered). Among your listeners are people whose cities and villages have been burned and leveled to the ground, whose daughters and sisters have been raped, whose fathers and brothers have had their throats slit. The topic of the lecture: a Christian attitude toward violence. The thesis: we should not retaliate since God is perfect noncoercive love. Soon you would discover that it takes the quiet of a suburban home for the birth of the thesis that human nonviolence corresponds to God's refusal to judge. In a scorched land, soaked in the blood of the innocent, it will invariably die. And as one watches it die, one will do well to reflect about many other pleasant captivities of the liberal mind.[56]

Given the sacrificial system and the New Testament's interpretation, it is impossible to conclude that God forgives "unconditionally" and "without payment." Drawing upon Jesus's exhortation to imitate God, who sends rain upon the just and the unjust alike (Matt 5:45), Boyd engages in a category mistake, treating God's act of judgment and our acts of judgment on the same level.[57] Jesus is describing God's common grace, not the final judgment, which is quite different (Matt 25:31–46). In fact, when we are treated unjustly, we are not to respond in kind— not because God is unconditionally benevolent, but for precisely the opposite reason: "Beloved, never avenge yourselves, but leave it to the wrath of God, for it is written, 'Vengeance is mine, I will repay, says the Lord'" (Rom 12:19).

---

54. Volf, *Exclusion and Embrace*, 293.
55. Volf, *Exclusion and Embrace*, 297–98.
56. Volf, *Exclusion and Embrace*, 304.
57. Gregory Boyd, *God at War: The Bible and Spiritual Conflict* (Downers Grove, IL: InterVarsity, 1997), 240.

MORAL EXAMPLE/INFLUENCE

Because Christ is "the Lamb of God who took away the sins of the world" (John 1:29), he is the revelation and example of God's love. Jesus himself tells us repeatedly that his purpose of coming into the world was to save sinners, to die for his friends, to judge Satan once and for all, and to usher in the Jubilee, the hour of God's favor. It is also true that "God shows his love for us" in the cross. But how? Paul answers, "While we were still sinners, Christ died for us" (Rom 5:8).

As with the moral government theory, subjective theories that reduce the efficacy of Christ's death to its moral effects on us are exegetically untenable and logically inconsistent—for the reasons considered above. However, Christ's example and influence are fully accounted for on the basis of his objective work of reconciling the world to the Father.

First, subjective views assume a weak—even Pelagian—anthropology, according to which human beings are regarded not as enemies of God, subject to his wrath and dead in sins, but as basically good people who get blown off course at times and need a little direction and motivation. Jesus helps us to brush ourselves off and take up our role with him in redeeming and reconciling the world. Volf correctly judges that modernity "is predicated on the belief that fissures of the world can be repaired and that *the world can be healed*" through "the twin strategies of *social control* and *rational thought*." "It expects the creation of paradise at the end of history and denies the expulsion from it at the beginning of history." But the inner logic of the cross "underscores that evil is irremediable." "Before the dawn of God's new world, we cannot remove evil so as to dispense with the cross. None of the grand recipes that promise to mend all the fissures can be trusted."[58] We require more than a good example and moral uplift. "To claim the comfort of the Crucified while rejecting his way is to advocate not only cheap grace but a deceitful ideology."[59] There must be exclusion before there can be embrace, yet Christ has borne the former so that, with him, we may receive the latter without reserve from the Father of the prodigal son.

Second, reducing the cross to its moral influence on us not only fails to account for the arguments rehearsed above but offers little hope to victims of injustice. Only those of us removed from the daily despair over whether there will be a righting of wrongs can live with

---

58. Volf, *Exclusion and Embrace*, 27–28.
59. Volf, *Exclusion and Embrace*, 24.

the idea of a new creation without judgment and restoration.

Third, God's love cannot be demonstrated merely in the death of an innocent man. Any victim who obeyed such a command would be suicidal, and anyone who forced him to do it would be demonic.[60] If Jesus were merely the passive victim of Jewish or Roman power, the cross would not be a *revelation* of anything at all, at least concerning God, but would be nothing more than another example of the dreary headlines of this passing evil age. Furthermore, instead of being outwitted by God, the sinful powers would have succeeded, and we would be left in our sins. In any of these cases, the cross would be a revelation of fruitless violence rather than love.

Only if Christ's death *for us*—as our substitute—actually saves us from the curse, then it is a demonstration of God's love. Indeed, this is the way Jesus described it: "Greater love has no one than this, that someone lay down his life for his friends" (John 15:13). When Jesus struggled in Gethsemane and asked, "If it is possible, let this cup pass from me; nevertheless, not my will but yours be done" (Matt 26:39), the silence gave him his answer. There is no use in speculating about the metaphysics involved over the necessity of Christ's death. It is sufficient to observe from the Scriptures that God determined that there was no other way to be "just and the justifier."

Further, in view of Girard's analysis of the scapegoat mechanism, we can say that because Christ's death is propitiatory (and therefore unique), it is impossible to imitate (Heb 10:10). "In this is love, not that we have loved God but that he loved us and sent his Son to be the propitiation for our sins" (1 John 4:10). We are exhorted to imitate the humility and love revealed in Christ's passion (e.g., Phil 2:3–11) but never to enact his atoning death. We are saved not by imitating Christ's offering for guilt but by receiving his. Thus we do not become guilt sacrifices, offering our works to God for atonement, but thank offerings as Christ leads us in triumphal procession, spreading the aroma of life (2 Cor 2:14). As the scapegoat, Christ carries away our guilt. "Yet Christ's sacrifice does not return us to this 'original' state and then simply leave us to our own devices," Robert Sherman reminds us. He is also the firstfruits of the new creation.[61] This brings us to the resurrection as the basis for our justification.

---

60. The "offering of Isaac" is not in this category for a variety of reasons, most of which I cannot take up here. Notably, however, God never intended to take Isaac's life by Abraham's hand and, far from an arbitrary object lesson in demonstrating God's love (which, by itself, it could hardly be), the event pointed to Christ's sacrifice for sin, symbolized in the ram provided by Yahweh and sacrificed in Isaac's place.

61. Robert Sherman, *King, Priest, and Prophet: A Trinitarian Theology of Atonement* (New York: T&T Clark, 2004), 193–94.

CHAPTER 6

RAISED FOR OUR JUSTIFICATION

Besides the tidy division between *Agnus Dei* and *Christus Victor*, I have challenged the tendency to identify, respectively, the former as the site of Christ's death and resurrection. Christ's whole life was a vicarious suffering that culminated in the cross, but it was simultaneously his triumph over the powers of darkness. It is not surprising therefore that Paul attributes justification to both events (Rom 4:25; 5:9).

At the same time, Good Friday and Easter do not blur into one event. The crucifixion was the climax of the raging powers and principalities led by Satan against Yahweh and his Anointed, but the resurrection inaugurated the new creation, the age to come. Jewish eschatology already had taught the distinction between "this age" and "the age to come" but saw them as exclusive periods.[1] According to the New Testament, however, the age to come has indeed broken into this present evil age, even though it seems hardly noticeable to the world. Jesus has been raised as the beginning of the general resurrection, and the verdict of the last judgment is the ungodly's justification, which is being rendered already for those who believe in Jesus. Having completed his six-day labor, he has entered his triumphant rest at the Father's right hand, reigning by his Word and Spirit "until all his enemies are made a footstool for his feet" (1 Cor 15:25). Satan is bound so that he can no longer deceive the nations (Rev 20:3; cf. Matt 12:28–30). The perfecting Spirit has

---

1. This is one of the reasons why a Jewish scholar like Pinchas Lapide, though persuaded that Christ rose from the dead, nevertheless cannot acknowledge him as Messiah, since he did not usher in the final resurrection of the dead, judge the world, and restore Israel. Pinchas Lapide, *The Resurrection of Jesus: A Jewish Perspective* (repr., Eugene, OR: Wipf and Stock, 2002).

been sent to make the elect sharers in Christ's achievement. The final "regeneration of all things" has begun already in the regeneration of the inner self from spiritual death (2 Cor 4:16; cf. John 3:3; Eph 2:1–5).

Thus, the two ages are not airtight compartments; they intermingle. "Salvation" is both a present and future reality.[2] "According to Romans 5.9, 10," Ridderbos points out, "after and because being justified by Christ's blood, the readers *shall* be saved from the wrath of the judgment through Him, and that particularly through his (resurrection-) life."[3] In 1 Thessalonians 5:8–9 we are told that "God has appointed believers unto the obtaining of salvation and that this is said with reference to the end appears from the opposite, 'not unto wrath,' the latter term having eschatological meaning throughout with Paul."[4] So "this present age" is not only the age of flesh but, as such, the age of wrath. This is why Paul can say that "the wrath of God is being revealed from heaven against all ungodliness" (Rom 1:18). Everything that is outside Christ is under wrath, exposed to the "elements" (στοιχείων τοῦ κόσμου; Col 2:20), under the law, awaiting arraignment, sentencing, and the final purification of the cosmic sanctuary from all that defiles (Rev 21:27). Justification does not consume the whole horizon of this new creation, but without it we remain under the power of the law, the flesh, sin, death, and condemnation.

Unfortunately, when Jesus speaks of "the regeneration of all things" (Matt 19:28), the ESV translates τῇ παλιγγενεσίᾳ "the new world." The NIV is closer: "the renewal." And the NASB is closer still: "the regeneration." If the ESV errs on the side of *discontinuity* (the idea that this final judgment and final liberation of the cosmos occurs in a different world from ours), the NIV errs in favor of *continuity* (assuming that the "renewal" referred to here is merely a recovery of this world and return to its pristine state). In the former (ESV) view, our individual regeneration now has little to do with the regeneration spoken of here, while in the latter (NIV) view, "renewal" seems like a weak term for the complete change that occurs. My point is this: the "regeneration" about which Jesus speaks is the same event as the resurrection of Christ, the regeneration and rebirth of the individual and the resurrection-regeneration

---

2. Herman Ridderbos, *Paul: An Outline of His Theology*, trans. John R. de Witt (Grand Rapids: Eerdmans, 1975), 51.

3. Ridderbos, *Paul*, 52.

4. Ridderbos, *Paul*, 53.

of our bodies in Christ's likeness at the end of the age in a regenerated cosmos. Each of these is a facet or aspect of the one event of cosmic regeneration lodged in Jesus's resurrection from the dead.

Consequently, these facets belong to the "new creation," not to the powers of this present age. The word for regeneration, παλιγγενεσία (Matt 19:28) was used in Greco-Roman mystery religions, Plato, and Neoplatonism to refer to the transmigration of souls. "With Philo it signifies the life after death, individual conceived, but also is applied to the future world collectively," notes Ridderbos. "Subsequently, however, the metaphorical meaning developed, even in Philo. Cicero calls his return from banishment his *palingenesia*."[5] But for Paul it means the new creation that begins with the inner regeneration and finally shares in Christ's bodily resurrection (2 Cor 5:1–5; cf. 4:16), and it is first of all cosmic—a total restoration of all things—though individuals are included in its liberating sweep.

Justification is not the only gift of salvation, but apart from it, the announcement "Jesus is Lord" can hardly be good news. Left under the curse of the law and its sentence of death, Christ's sovereignty and kingdom can only threaten with the fear that we must be swept away in the tide of his judgment. But the world wears a new face because Christ has been "raised for our justification" (Rom 4:25)—for much else, to be sure, but certainly for that unspeakable gift. The resurrection marks the point at which the Spirit, who gave his benediction along with the Father at Jesus's baptism, now raises up the ruins, exalts the fallen sanctuary, and ends the exile of his people Israel. Together, that astonishing weekend of the cross and the resurrection constitutes the greater exodus and conquest.

CHRIST'S HISTORY AND OURS

We have seen that there are two major trajectories leading from Origen and Irenaeus, respectively. The former offers a contemplative and moral ascent away from this world, the body, and history, returning to the One from whom our soul fell away in a world before this one. The latter announces a redemption of the world, including our whole persons, with our bodies, and history. With this gospel, the emphasis

---

5. Ridderbos, *Paul*, 50.

falls on Christ's historical pattern of descent, ascent, and return, and our union with him so that we may share in his glorified humanity. The resurrection and ascension are not allegories for the soul's release from its bodily carapace, but they instead assure us that as goes the head, so go the members.

Yet, at least in terms of its salvific import the resurrection has been marginalized in various ways. First, the resurrection is often treated merely as an exclamation point in the cry, "It is finished!" For example, Barth states that instead of being a new episode in the event of redemption, "His resurrection revealed Him as the One who reigns in virtue of His death." The resurrection reveals and perhaps certifies but does not complete Christ's saving work, he says.[6] However, recall the categories of the old covenant sacrifices that we have been invoking: the guilt sacrifice leading to atonement, sacrifices of purification, and sacrifices of consecration. Christ's "It is finished" refers to his work of atonement and purification, not to the further work of consecration. For this we require the raising and exalting of our representative head so that as he is, we will be also. Evangelicals have maintained a faithful witness and extraordinary body of scholarly defense of the resurrection. This is of inestimable value to the church's testimony. However, with Richard Gaffin, I wonder if the resurrection "for the most part has been restricted to its apologetic value and as a stimulus to faith."[7] The resurrection proves that Jesus is God and that the atonement was successful, but it is not always clear how our history is caught up into his.

A second way of marginalizing the eschatological significance of the resurrection is quite different from the first. Especially through the influence of pietism and revivalism, there is a tendency to allow the history of Jesus to drift apart from "my history." In this case, the resurrection becomes muted by an emphasis on "Jesus in my heart." It is easy to return to an Origenist narrative in which the wider historical narrative of the redemption and regeneration of the cosmos is subordinated to what happens in the individual soul. Rather than mapping

---

6. *CD* IV/2, 291. Thus it is all the more ironic that Douglas Campbell (*The Quest for Paul's Gospel* [London: T&T Clark, 2005], 168) and Peter Leithart (*Delivered from the Elements of the World*, 331n33) would characterize the Reformation as displaying little interest in the resurrection. For his case, Leithart in fact quotes selectively from the Augsburg and Westminster Confessions, as well as the Heidelberg Catechism, omitting the clear references to the relationship of justification to the resurrection.

7. Richard B. Gaffin Jr., *Resurrection and Redemption: A Study in Paul's Soteriology* (Phillipsburg, NJ: P&R, 1987), 11.

our personal history to Christ's, we map Christ's onto our individual, inner experience. This tendency is as evident in Protestant liberalism (Rudolf Bultmann springs to mind) as in conservative circles. However, the resurrection is not our own "Easter experience"; it is something that happened to Jesus. Pointing to the examples of Bultmann and Harry Emerson Fosdick, J. Christiaan Beker observes that this "spiritualist interpretation of the resurrection" is very much alive in the modern age.[8] But this is closer to the "Greek-Platonic thought world" than to "Paul's apocalyptic worldview."[9] Christ's resurrection and the general resurrection "stand or fall together." "Whenever apocalyptic categories are demoted or degraded, as if they are purely culturally determined or an obsolete survival, Paul's resurrection theology is transmuted into something else, such as the immortality of the soul or our heavenly ascent, or an existential possibility or the renunciation of the created order."[10] Only if Jesus is really raised—regenerated bodily as the pattern and forerunner of the new age—will we be as well.

There is a third threat: an overreaction to the gnostic-Platonic worldview. Many, including Ridderbos, but especially new perspective scholars reared in the evangelical heritage, rush to the other extreme by downplaying the reality of individual salvation. However, one can hardly read a page of Paul's letters without being impressed with his interest in how we are saved—and from what we are saved. The resurrection is not only the epistemological justification for believing in Christ; it is the justification *of Christ himself* and therefore of us as well. Everything that happened to Christ must happen to those who are united to him. Therefore, "He was . . . raised *for our justification*" (Rom 4:24–25). "The resurrection of Christ is therefore not so much an event *in the midst of* history as an event that inaugurates *the end of* history."[11] Furthermore, Gaffin adds, "The resurrection of Christ is no isolated or 'completed' event. Although the death of Christ is a 'once and for all' event, the same cannot be said of the resurrection. The resurrection is not 'completed' in its full meaning and consequence until the future resurrection of the dead takes place."[12] This is a crucial point. There are not two resurrections:

---

8. J. Christiaan Beker, *The Triumph of God: The Essence of Paul's Thought*, trans. Loren T. Stuckenbruck (Minneapolis: Fortress, 1990), 77.

9. Beker, *The Triumph of God*, 74–75.

10. Beker, *The Triumph of God*, 77.

11. Beker, *The Triumph of God*, 73.

12. Beker, *The Triumph of God*, 72–73.

Christ's and ours, but one resurrection with Christ as the firstfruits. In Jesus, the final resurrection of the dead *has* begun. And because he has been raised, all who are united to him by faith *must* be raised with him.

So one could say that the subjectivizing approach (e.g., Bultmann and pietism) downplays the cosmic-eschatological horizon of the new creation, focusing on the *ordo salutis* (individual salvation), while the opposite reaction downplays the latter. But instead of sidelining the *ordo salutis*, the proper approach is to ground it in the *historia salutis*.

With respect to the resurrection in particular, this is to say that the new creation is not first of all the individual's transition from death to life through the new birth but rather Christ's objective transition from wrath to grace, death to life, the old age of the flesh to the new age of the Spirit. Plato's "two worlds" provide a completely different metaphysical map from the "two ages" assumed by Second Temple Judaism, Jesus, and Paul. Ridderbos explains,

> When [Paul] speaks here of "new creation," this is not meant merely in an individual sense ("a new creature"), but one is to think of the new world of the re-creation that God has made to dawn in Christ, and in which everyone who is in Christ is included. This is also evident from the neuter plural that follows: "the old things have passed away, the new have come," and from the full significance that must be ascribed here to "old" and "new." It is a matter of two worlds, not only in a spiritual, but in redemptive-historical, eschatological sense. The "old things" stand for the unredeemed world in its distress and sin, the "new things" for the time of salvation and the re-creation that have dawned with Christ's resurrection.[13]

"He who is in Christ, therefore, is new creation: he participates in, belongs to, this new world of God."[14]

ORDAINED AS THE SON OF GOD IN POWER

Having made the point that whatever happened to Christ as a result of his victory must happen to us, I turn to the significance of the resurrection for Christ (and consequently, for us).

---

13. Ridderbos, *Paul*, 45.
14. Ridderbos, *Paul*, 45–46.

So anxious is the apostle to get to the purpose of his famous epistle that he exchanges his customary greeting for a plot summary of the gospel (Rom 1:1–7). Even if it is a pre-Pauline Jewish-Christian formula, it is no less Paul's message than his appeal to an earlier formula in 1 Corinthians 15:3. The death, burial, and resurrection of Christ "according to the Scriptures," he himself says, is "of first importance." It is not a polite introduction but a thesis statement. As Wright points out contra Martyn, Paul could hardly have begun in this manner simply to appease a partly Jewish-Christian audience by mentioning "Jesus's Davidic Messiahship," which did not interest him personally. "No, the gospel message, for Paul, is the message about Jesus the Messiah. All that follows in terms of the revelation of God's righteousness means what it means in that context."[15]

"The gospel of God . . . concerning his Son"

As in 1 Corinthians 15:3, so also here Paul considers it essential first to ground his gospel in the prophetic scriptures (Rom 1:2). Paul is no innovator, the "second founder of Christianity" (Wrede), or inventor of "catholic Christianity" (Harnack). Paul is an *apostle* (one sent) of God bringing the *gospel of God*, which was *promised in his Word*.

It is "the gospel of God . . . *concerning his Son*." According to his humanity, this Son is of Davidic lineage "and was declared [constituted] to be the Son of God in power according to the Spirit of holiness by his resurrection from the dead, Jesus Christ our Lord" (Rom 1:2–4). He could only redeem those "in the flesh" (ἐν τῇ σαρκί, Rom 7:5)— that is, those under sin and death—by descending "according to the flesh" (κατὰ σάρκα, Rom 1:3) and could only have been the Messiah by having been of David's seed (ἐκ σπέρματος Δαυὶδ). As Barth puts it in his striking opening to his *Römerbrief*, "Because Jesus is Lord over Paul and over the Roman Christians, the word 'God' is no empty word in the Epistle to the Romans."[16]

No gnostic redeemer myth or docetic descent of the Logos in "celestial flesh"—a sort of human space suit—will do. As in Isaiah 53,

15. N. T. Wright, *Paul and His Recent Interpreters: Some Contemporary Debates* (Minneapolis: Fortress, 2015), 118. Here, especially, he has Martyn in his sights, who (in the "post-Bauer tradition") attributes this unique opening, as well as Gal 1:4, to a pre-Pauline Jewish-Christian formula that Paul tacked on for the sake of getting on the right foot with his audience (174, from Martyn, *Galatians: A New Translation and Commentary*, AB 33A [New York: Doubleday, 1997], 90).

16. Karl Barth, *The Epistle to the Romans*, trans. Edwin C. Hoskyns (New York: Oxford University Press, 1968), 30–31.

the exalted God joyfully assumed our humanity under the curse in humiliation and was "highly exalted." In fact, he was the descendant of David, just as Israel had expected the Messiah to be. He not only descends into death but is raised in glory.

". . . declared [constituted/ordained] to be the Son of God in power according to the Spirit of holiness by his resurrection from the dead, Jesus Christ our Lord."

Jesus was "*declared* [ὁρισθέντος] to be *the Son of God in power*."[17] It is important to understand the force of this verb, ὁρίζω, which means to mark off, appoint, designate, or determine. Jesus was not merely "shown to be the Son of God," as some translations render it. On the other hand, as John Murray argues, "declared" is probably not the right word either. In its use elsewhere (Luke 22:22; Acts 2:23; 10:42; 11:29; 17:26, 31; Heb 4:7) it means determine, appoint, or ordain. Some may worry that "declared" undermines the fact that Christ is the eternal Son. "But," as Murray suggests, "this objection has validity only as we overlook the force of the expression 'with power.'"[18] This in addition to the fact that he has been speaking of Christ's humanity ("descended from David according to the flesh"). Murray adds, "The apostle is dealing with some particular event in the history of the Son of God incarnate by which he was *instated* in a position of sovereignty and invested with power, an event which in respect of investiture with power surpassed everything that could previously be ascribed to him in his incarnate state." It is not that he was appointed Son of God but Son of God *in power*—in a condition and position of eschatological significance that he had not held before. The resurrection did not affect Christ's deity, so once again the concern is a transition in his messianic lordship. No longer in a condition of humiliation and weakness, he is raised in victory. It is not his humanity and deity that are being contrasted but his humiliation and exaltation.[19] There is something more in view than the resurrection merely proving that he is the Son of God.

First Corinthians 15 illuminates what Paul means. "Thus it is written, 'The first man [ὁ πρῶτος ἄνθρωπος] Adam became a *living being*'

---

17. On this point, see Geerhardus Vos, *The Pauline Eschatology* (repr., Philipsburg, NJ: P&R, 1994), 228–30.

18. John Murray, *The Epistle to the Romans*, 2 vols., NICNT (Grand Rapids: Eerdmans, 1965), 1:9.

19. Murray, *The Epistle to the Romans*, 1:11.

[ψυχὴν ζῶσαν]; the last Adam [ὁ ἔσχατος Ἀδὰμ] became a *life-giving spirit"*
[πνεῦμα ζωοποιοῦν] (v. 45). Ἐγένετο ("became") becomes the head
verb shared by the two Adams, who are separated by the first Adam
becoming alive at creation and the Last Adam becoming life-giving
at his resurrection. "So as in Adam all die, so in Christ are all made
alive" (v. 22). Adam was a living being, but he forfeited eschatological
exaltation for himself and his posterity and thus became the source of
condemnation and death. Jesus, by contrast, recapitulated Adam's trial
and in his resurrection *became* not only a living being again but the
source of eschatological life. In Romans Paul contrasts the two Adams
as two covenant heads from whom issue radically different forms of
existence (Rom 5:12–19).

With Romans 1:3–4, we are in the courtroom atmosphere: Christ
being *appointed* or *ordained* the Son of God *in power*. I take this to mean
at least that at his resurrection he became not the Son of God (see, e.g.,
Col 1:15) but the eschatological, life-*giving* Adam. All that we inherit
from Adam is fleshly existence (i.e., the powers of nature, corrupted by
sin), but from Christ we inherit a pneumatic existence (i.e., the powers
of the age to come, in the Spirit). Just as the work of Christ consists of
the interweaving of forensic-substitutionary and apocalyptic-victory
aspects, the new creation that dawns with Christ's resurrection encompasses forensic and transformative facets that must be distinguished but
never separated. And just as the legal act of nailing our list of violations
to the cross is the basis for the victory over the powers (Col 2:13–15),
Jesus's own justification—being declared the Son of God in power—is
the legal basis for our being justified by his resurrection from the dead.

In our proper defense of Christ's deity, we sometime miss the significance of Paul's point.[20] He is not thinking of ontological preexis-
tence but of eschatological attainment: specifically, a forensic verdict.
According to his formula in 1 Timothy 3:16,

---

20. For example, Charles Hodge interprets "according to the flesh" to refer to Christ's
humanity and "according to the Spirit of holiness" to his divinity (as Paul were contrasting κατὰ
σάρκα with πνεῦμα). Thus, the resurrection is the incontrovertible proof that Jesus is the Son of
God (Hodge, *Commentary on the Epistle to the Romans* [repr., Grand Rapids: Eerdmans, 1977], 20).
According to this view, however, the resurrection does not actually contribute to redemption but
merely proves it—particularly, it proves Christ's claim. The wonderful truth that Paul presents,
however, is not simply that a proposition has been proved but that a new creation has been born.
Of course, Hodge does not deny that a new creation has emerged from the resurrection, but he
neglects to discern that Paul is making that point here.

Great indeed, we confess, is the mystery of godliness:

He was manifested in the flesh,
vindicated by the Spirit,
seen by angels,
proclaimed among the nations,
believed on in the world,
taken up in glory.

There is no good reason not to translate the phrase ἐδικαιώθη ἐν πνεύματι as "*justified* by the Spirit," and in so doing we recognize the continuity with Romans 1:4. Having become human and recapitulated Adam's trial (echoed in Israel's), the *incarnate* Son has also been adopted as the Father's true and faithful son that Adam and Israel failed to be. "I glorified you on earth," Jesus prayed, "having accomplished the work that you gave me to do" (John 17:4). Having done so, he has merited justification for himself and for us. Who else could dare to say, much less to pray, "And for their sake I sanctify myself [ἁγιάζω ἐμαυτόν], that they also may be sanctified [ἡγιασμένοι] in truth" (John 17:19)?

Gaffin observes, "The resurrection is the salvation of Jesus as the last Adam; it and no other event in his experience is the point of *his* transition from wrath to grace."[21] The perspective from which Paul views the believer's resurrection, then, is nothing less than cosmic.[22] The verses in Romans 1:3–4 "form a contrast," he says. "Christ's manifestation" in the flesh" and "his justification" in the Spirit.[23] The concern is not the two natures but the one person crossing the threshold from one age to the other.[24] "The unexpressed assumption [of 4:25] is that Jesus's resurrection is his justification. His resurrection is his justification as the last Adam, the justification of the 'firstfruits.' This and nothing less is the bond between his resurrection and our justification."[25] Christ's "resurrection is not simply a guarantee; it is a pledge in the sense that it is the actual beginning of the general event."[26] As Paul explains in Colossians 1:15–18, "Only as he himself is one 'from the dead' is Christ

---

21. Richard B. Gaffin Jr., *Resurrection and Redemption: A Study in Paul's Soteriology* (Phillipsburg, NJ: P&R, 1987), 116.
22. Gaffin, *Resurrection and Redemption*, 83.
23. Gaffin, *Resurrection and Redemption*, 119.
24. Gaffin, *Resurrection and Redemption*, 120.
25. Gaffin, *Resurrection and Redemption*, 123.
26. Gaffin, *Resurrection and Redemption*, 35.

'first-born.' Only as he is part of that group which is (to be) raised does he enjoy this exalted status."[27]

Murray puts it well: "The thought of [Rom 1] verse 4 would then be that the lordship in which he was instated by the resurrection is one all-pervasively conditioned by pneumatic powers."[28] Vos writes,

> Not only a new status had been acquired through the resurrection: new qualities amounting to a reconstructed adjustment to the future heavenly environment had been wrought in Him by the omnipotent power of God: He had been determined (declared effectually) the Son of God with power according to the Spirit of Holiness, by the resurrection from the dead. It is self-evident that these words do not refer to any religious or ethical transformation which Jesus in the resurrection had to undergo. Such a thought nowhere finds support in Paul's Christology, nor in his general teaching.[29]

"This comprehensive change," he adds, "was inseparable from the resurrection itself; it was not an additional element, but an integral part of the first and only act required."[30]

"For the history of Christ is the gospel in a nutshell," says Gaffin, which is why Romans 1:3–4 is more than an epistolary salutation.

> Not Christ the God-man, but Christ, the eternal Son of God become incarnate in the present evil age with the humiliation, suffering, and death this sarkic existence involved, and as the incarnate Son of God raised up to be the source for others of the eschatological power and life this pneumatic existence of the coming age involves—that is the gospel to which Paul goes on to give such unsurpassed development in the body of Romans.[31]

It is, therefore, Christ's history that remains fundamental. Our personal history cannot generate an ecclesial body but only a collection of individuals with their similar religious experiences, interests, and commitments. However, Jesus as the eschatological head of the covenant of

---

27. Gaffin, *Resurrection and Redemption*, 38.
28. Murray, *The Epistle to the Romans*, 1:11.
29. Vos, *The Pauline Eschatology*, 209.
30. Vos, *The Pauline Eschatology*, 209–10.
31. Gaffin, *Resurrection and Redemption*, 113.

THE ACHIEVEMENT OF JUSTIFICATION

grace creates a body by his word and Spirit. Only by belonging to that history are we justified and made part of God's new creation, members of his justifying and life-giving existence.

In Acts 13 Paul preaches the same message in Antioch, quoting Psalm 2:7, and featuring the same Abrahamic-Davidic story line. He declares, "Brothers, sons of the family of Abraham, and those among you who fear God," he announces, "to us has been sent the message of this salvation." In judging Jesus guilty, the rulers in Jerusalem "did not recognize him nor understand the utterances of the prophets, which are read every Sabbath" (vv. 26–27). After relating the crucifixion and resurrection (vv. 28–31), he says,

> And we bring you the good news that what God promised to the fathers, this he has fulfilled to us their children by raising Jesus, as also it is written in the second Psalm,
>
>> "'You are my Son,
>> today I have begotten you.'
>
> And as for the fact that he raised him from the dead, no more to return to corruption, he has spoken in this way,
>
>> "'I will give you the holy and sure blessings of David.'
>
> Therefore he says also in another psalm,
>
>> "'You will not let your Holy One see corruption.'
>
> For David, after he had served the purpose of God in his own generation, fell asleep and was laid with his fathers and saw corruption, but he whom God raised up did not see corruption. Let it be known to you therefore, brothers, that through this man forgiveness of sins is proclaimed to you, and by him everyone who believes is freed from everything from which you could not be freed by the law of Moses. (vv. 32–39)

On the basis of these arguments, we can be fairly confident that Paul in Romans 1:4 was interpreting Psalm 2:7 not in ontological terms—as if Jesus somehow became the Son of God at his resurrection—but in eschatological-pneumatic terms, as the pioneer of the new creation. Jesus was "constituted/ordained to be the Son of God in power . . . by his resurrection from the dead" in terms of the raising and glorification of the Last Adam as the firstfruits of the whole new-creation harvest. Jesus did not by the resurrection attain a new unity with the Father, but he did attain a new status and condition as human, not only for himself but for all who are united to him.

Yet we have not fully grasped Paul's plot summary in Romans 1:2–4 apart from the clause "according to the Spirit of holiness." In fact, it is the culmination of this opening argument of Romans. There are two points worth noting about the Spirit regarding this clause in particular.

First, the Spirit is often identified with judicial operations in Scripture, especially bringing about within creation itself the proper "amen" to all that the Father has "worded" to be, in the Son. This may seem counterintuitive at first since we tend to identify Jesus with judgment. Typically, we expect to find the Spirit not in courtrooms but in comforting and renovating hearts. This expectation is deepened by the fact that ever since Origen, translators have preferred "Comforter" for Παράκλητος in John 14:16 and 16:7–11 in order to distinguish the Spirit from Jesus, who is "properly" designated advocate or defense attorney.[32] However, there is no reason to render Παράκλητος "Advocate" only when Jesus is the subject (as in 1 John 2:1).[33]

The Spirit sets apart servants, designating them at their investiture with special dignity, signified by anointing with oil. This anointing is nuclear to the ordination of Israel's prophets (1 Kgs 19:16; 1 Chr 16:22; Ps 105:15), priests (esp. the high priest; Exod 29:29; Lev 4:3; 16:32; 40:15; Num 3:3), and kings (1 Sam 9:16; 10:1; 1 Kgs 1:34, 39). Messiah means "anointed" (Ps 2:2; Dan 9:25–26; Isa 61:6). In the first Servant Song, Yahweh declares, "Behold my servant, whom I uphold, my chosen, in whom my soul delights; I have put my Spirit upon him; he will bring forth justice to the nations" (Isa 42:1).

As at Jesus's baptism, the Spirit's anointing designates his chosen one. His first public act was to read Isaiah 42:1 and announce himself as its fulfillment (Luke 4:16–21). He is the Anointed One on whom the Spirit

---

32. Origen, *On First Principles*, trans. G. W. Butterworth (Gloucester, MA: Peter Smith, 1973), 119.

33. See BDAG, 519.

rests (John 1:32–33, 41; Acts 4:27; 9:22; 10:38; 17:2–3; 18:4, 28). Jesus focused on the judicial aspect of the Spirit especially in his farewell discourse. Jesus calls the Spirit "the Advocate" (Παράκλητος, "attorney") whom he will send to "convict the world of sin and of righteousness and of judgment" (vv. John 16:7–11). After the ascension, they will trade places: Jesus will be the Advocate in heaven and the Spirit will be the Advocate on earth, bringing sinners to accept God's righteous verdict against them and to receive his justifying pardon.

The Spirit united God the Son to us in the incarnation, and now the Spirit, sustaining and confirming the Last Adam in his trial of active obedience, raises the Son in eschatological glory as the *Son of God in power*. Finally, the Holy Spirit unites *us* to his glorified humanity so that his historical existence becomes ours. But before the Spirit can clothe *us* with Christ, he must clothe *Christ* with glory, immortality, and confirmation in righteousness. He has saved us "not because of our works" but by his eternal purpose in grace, "which now has been manifested through *the appearing* [ἐπιφανείας] of our Savior Christ Jesus, who *abolished death and brought life and immortality to light through the gospel*" (2 Tim 1:10). Geerhardus Vos observes, "It has been not implausibly held that this forensic aspect of the resurrection as a declarative, vindicatory, justifying act, forms a very old, if not perhaps the oldest, element in Paul's doctrine on the subject. To Judaism the belief largely bore this meaning."[34] Since death is "the penalty for sin imposed by the Law, . . . the resurrection is the final removal of the condemnation of sin."[35] Since God "made him who knew no sin to be sin on our behalf" (2 Cor 5:21), it is reasonable to surmise that Jesus's resurrection not only vindicated him publicly but justified him before God his Father. Having been under condemnation three days beforehand, he is now not only the spotless Lamb he was before Good Friday but also the righteous King of heaven. Hence, as Vos notes, "Paul could truthfully say that in preaching the resurrection he defended the Pharisaic position, not merely through insistence upon the fact, but also so far as this fact amounted to a vindication of the people of God."[36]

Something has happened to Jesus. All along, even from eternity, he is the Son of God. But now he has become the source of eschatological

---

34. Vos, *The Pauline Eschatology*, 152.
35. Vos, *The Pauline Eschatology*, 152.
36. Vos, *The Pauline Eschatology*, 152, referencing Acts 23:6.

justification and life for all who will be united to him. The regeneration that the Spirit brings because of Christ is first inward and then confirmed publicly, visibly, bodily, and completely when we are raised from the dead. At Jesus's resurrection-coronation on earth, he is anointed with the oil of the Spirit in order for his messianic humanity to become ours in him. The language of the Heidelberg Catechism (LD 12, Q. 31–32) is helpful in connecting Christ's anointing to ours, even alluding to Romans 1:4:

> Q. Why is he called "Christ," meaning "anointed"?
>
> A. Because he has been ordained by God the Father and has been anointed with the Holy Spirit to be our chief *prophet* and teacher who fully reveals to us the secret counsel and will of God concerning our deliverance; our only *high priest* who has delivered us by the one sacrifice of his body, and who continually pleads our cause with the Father; and our eternal *king* who governs us by his Word and Spirit, and who guards us and keeps us in the freedom he has won for us.

> Q. But why are you called a Christian?
>
> A. Because by faith I am a member of Christ and so I *share in his anointing.* I am anointed to confess his name [prophet], to present myself to him as a living sacrifice of thanks [priest], to strive with a free conscience against sin and the devil in this life, and afterward to reign with Christ over all creation for eternity [king].[37]

So the resurrection definitively carries Jesus from the present age, which culminated in his death, to the age to come, which was inaugurated by his life. Objectively, it does the same for us in him, even though for us there is an "already" and "not yet" aspect. Our regeneration (inwardly now and outwardly in the future) is baptism into his regeneration-resurrection. Our justification and deliverance from wrath is a participation in his justification and deliverance from wrath. Our transition from judgment to favor here and now is a sharing in Christ's transition. The preacher to the Hebrews emphasizes the fact

---

37. Heidelberg Catechism, LD 12, Q. 31–32.

that everything in the earthly sanctuary had to be constantly purified with blood. Yet Jesus entered heaven through his own blood.[38] His atoning work on the cross constituted the basis for everything that he now performs in the heavenly sanctuary. "Similarly," says Bavinck, "as a result of the resurrection of Christ, the water of baptism is the ruin of the ungodly and the salvation for believers. For Christ, who arose from the dead and instituted baptism and gives power to it, after subduing all angels, authorities, and powers by his ascension, now sits at God's right hand."[39]

Thus Jesus is not just a model or paradigm for us, but everything that is applied to us now by the Spirit is a baptism into everything that he accomplished then. As primary as the *historia salutis* certainly is, however, Gaffin wisely reminds us, "This does not mean that Paul obscures the distinction between justification and sanctification."[40] In fact, the resurrection "is itself a forensically constitutive declaration." "This does not at all mean that Paul qualifies the synthetic character of the justification of the ungodly." But "the justification of the ungodly is not arbitrary but according to truth; it is synthetic with respect to the believer only because it is analytic with respect to Christ (as resurrected). Not justification by faith but union with the resurrected Christ by faith (of which union, to be sure, the justifying aspect stands out perhaps most prominently) is the central motif of Paul's applied soteriology."[41]

Beginning with the eternal covenant of redemption (*pactum salutis*), Bavinck summarizes beautifully the priority that belongs to that objectivity of Christ's person and work which becomes ours subjectively in time:

> Christ became human and acquired salvation for his people in virtue of that pact. He could do this precisely because he already was in communion with them and was their guarantor and mediator. And the whole church, comprehended in him as its head, has objectively been crucified, has died, been resurrected, and glorified with him.

---

38. As Bavinck observes of Heb 9:12, "The author of this letter nowhere says that Christ entered heaven with his blood, the way the Old Testament high priest on the great Day of Atonement entered the holy of holies with blood to sprinkle it on and before the mercy seat. He only says that Christ once for all entered the sanctuary *through* his blood" (Bavinck, *Reformed Dogmatics*, 4 vols., ed. John Bolt, trans. John Vriend [Grand Rapids: Baker Academic, 2008], 3:477, emphasis added).

39. Bavinck, *Reformed Dogmatics*, 3:481.

40. Gaffin, *Resurrection and Redemption*, 131.

41. Gaffin, *Resurrection and Redemption*, 132.

All the benefits of grace therefore lie prepared and ready for the church in the person of Christ. All is finished: God has been reconciled; nothing remains to be added from the side of humans. Atonement, forgiveness, justification, the mystical union, sanctification, glorification, and so on—they do not come into being after and as a result of faith but are objectively, actively present in Christ. They are the fruits solely of his suffering and dying, and they are appropriated on our part by faith. God grants them and imputes them to the church in the decree of election, in the resurrection of Christ, in his calling by the gospel.

In God's own time they will also become the subjective possession of believers. For though it is true that we humans need not add anything to the work of Christ, Christ himself, by having acquired salvation, is very far from having completed the work assigned to him. He took on himself the task of really and fully saving his people. He will not abdicate as mediator before he has presented his church—without spot or wrinkle—to the Father.[42]

ASCENSION AND JUSTIFICATION: ENTHRONEMENT OF ADAM

"The justification by faith perspective on Christ's work, while placing a satisfactory emphasis on the cross, evacuates his incarnation, much of his life, his resurrection, and his ascension of all soteriological value."[43] From what we have seen thus far, and from numerous sources that could be culled from Reformed and Lutheran confessions, this is a seriously uninformed judgment. Drawing on these (as well as patristic) sources, I have already demonstrated the soteriological significance of the incarnation and life of Christ (recapitulation/active obedience) as well as his resurrection. And the Reformed have had a distinctive interest in the soteriological value of the ascension.

Nevertheless, in modern theology and witness generally, the ascension is rarely included in summaries of the gospel. How many sermons might a regular church member hear on the saving effects of Christ's ascension? And because of this, we (especially in the West) tend to be stuck at Good Friday or Easter without appreciating the "more" that

---

42. Bavinck, *Reformed Dogmatics*, 3:523.
43. Douglas A. Campbell, *The Quest for Paul's Gospel* (London: T&T Clark, 2005), 168.

Christ's further work of redemption accomplished. While there are biblical references to being "justified by his blood" (Rom 5:9) and "raised for our justification" (Rom 4:25), there is no such explicit connection drawn in relation to Christ's ascension. Nevertheless, justification is related to the ascension in important ways.

As with the resurrection, we inquire here: What are the actual effects of Christ's ascension for us here and now? Again the Heidelberg Catechism provides a useful introduction, so useful in fact that I will appropriate its three points below.

> Q. How does Christ's ascension to heaven benefit us?
>
> A. First, he is our advocate in heaven in the presence of his Father. Second, we have our own flesh in heaven as a sure pledge that Christ our head will also take us, his members, up to himself. Third, he sends his Spirit to us on earth as a corresponding pledge. By the Spirit's power we seek not earthly things but the things above, where Christ is, sitting at God's right hand.[44]

Advocate in Heaven

The incarnation is more glorious than our first creation. Christ's active obedience assures us that we are not only forgiven but justified—righteous before God. Christ's death is the guilt offering and the purification offering. But his resurrection and ascension belong to the sacrifice of consecration, restoring fellowship and communion. The goal of our salvation is communion with the Trinity, through Christ's mediation, along with our brothers and sisters.

It is not only that *those whom he justified* will also *be glorified*, but that they will be glorified *because* they are justified. There is a direct connection between the ascension and justification. William Ames can say that glorification "is actually nothing but the carrying out of the sentence of justification. . . . In glorification the life that results from the pronouncement and award given to us: We have it in actual possession."[45] A reheadshiping has taken place that includes the repatriation of the Last Adam to claim his reward in Sabbath enthronement. On Colossians 3:1, Calvin writes, "Ascension follows resurrection: hence if we are

---

44. Heidelberg Catechism, LD 18, Q. 49.
45. William Ames, *The Marrow of Theology*, trans. John D. Eusden (Boston: Pilgrim, 1968; repr., Durham, NC: Labyrinth, 1983), 172.

members of Christ we *must* ascend into Heaven, because He, on being raised up from the dead was received up into Heaven that He might draw us with Him."[46]

Particularly when we recognize that our subjective glorification, like Christ's, occurs with our resurrection from the dead, Ames's point becomes all the clearer. In our proper enthusiasm for eschatology, we should beware of the notion that there is an "already" and "not-yet" to every element in the *ordo salutis*. For example, the cleavage opened by this assumption of a "not yet" aspect to justification leads N. T. Wright to conclude that justification has two poles present and future. "The whole point about 'justification by faith,'" he says, "is that it is something which happens *in the present time* (Romans 3.26) as a proper anticipation of the eventual judgment which will be announced, on the basis of the whole life led, in the future (Romans 2.1–16)."[47] Whatever legitimate protestations he can make against being drawn into sixteenth-century disputes, at this point he does in fact tie justification to the question of "how one is saved," and he makes the Roman Catholic move: a first justification by grace alone and a final justification by works. But Paul does not make this move, as I argue in the final chapter.

Applying the "already but not yet" distinction to justification either unhelpfully cracks the door open between justification and the final judgment or is simply irrelevant. Instead, we should see justification as *the future verdict of the last day brought forward into the present* by the Spirit through the gospel proclaimed and sealed in the sacraments. One may truly say that our sanctification, as freedom from the dominion of sin, will be realized fully in the freedom from the very presence of sin, that our liberty for righteousness now is an anticipation of a fully realized confirmation in righteousness. However, there is no "not yet" or unrealized aspect to justification any more than there is to election or atonement. We have been chosen and we have been reconciled. The aorist active indicative leaves no room for a further realization of these objective fact. While these accomplished facts do not have a "not-yet" aspect, they do provide the basis for the progressive realization of all the benefits that we have in Christ.

---

46. Calvin, *The Epistles of Paul the Apostle to the Galatians, Ephesians, Philippians, and Colossians*, ed. David W. and Thomas F. Torrance, trans. T. H. L. Parker (Grand Rapids: Eerdmans, 1965), 345 (Col 3:1).

47. Wright, *Paul: In Fresh Perspective*, 57.

In the ascension, Christ takes his seat, no longer performing the work of redemption but assuming the throne of glory for us and expanding his empire of grace by his word and Spirit on earth. Because Christ is beyond the reach of Golgotha, so are we. "There is therefore now no condemnation for those who are in Christ Jesus" (Rom 8:1). How do we know this? "And those whom he predestined he also called, and those whom he called he also justified, and *those whom he justified he also glorified*" (Rom 8:30, emphasis added). In fact, Paul goes on to ask how we can even wonder about God's favor in the light of this gift. "Who is to condemn? Christ Jesus is the one who died—more than that, who was raised—who is at the right hand of God, who indeed is interceding for us" (8:34). The fact that we can never be condemned (contradicting many interpretations of Romans 2:6, 12–13) depends not only on the finality of Christ's death and his justifying resurrection but on his ascension into heaven to continue his high priestly ministry on our behalf.

We have an insight into this present intercession when we recall Jesus's "high priestly prayer" in John 17: "I am praying for them. I am not praying for the world but for those whom you have given me, for they are yours. . . . Father, I desire that they also, whom you have given me, may be with me where I am, to see my glory that you have given me because you loved me before the foundation of the world" (vv. 9, 24). All of those given to the Son by the Father before the foundation of the world will be called, justified, and glorified. "All that the Father gives me will come to me," Jesus says, "and whoever comes to me I will never cast out. For I have come down from heaven, not to do my own will but the will of him who sent me. And this is the will of him who sent me, that I should lose nothing of all that he has given me, but raise it up on the last day" (John 6:37–39). Only if Jesus's intercession could fail is there a possibility that one could be lost of those given to him by the Father and sealed by the indwelling Spirit as the legal deposit guaranteeing their final salvation.

Sure Pledge

Second, as the catechism has it, "We have our own flesh in heaven as a sure pledge that Christ our head will also take us, his members, up to himself." This sentence encapsulates my opening point in this chapter that our story must be inserted into his story; the *historia salutis* is the wide cosmic and eschatological horizon for the *ordo salutis*.

By grounding our subjective reception of Christ and his benefits in the successive events of his life and work, we can now be called ones raised up with Christ and seated "with him in heavenly places" (Eph 2:6; cf. Col 3:1–5). The objectivity here is striking: because of Christ's career (now ascended), it is appropriate for us even now to be spoken of as "glorified" and "seated with [Christ] in heavenly places." Jesus is not only "God with us," but "we with God": true humanity seated on the victorious throne in communion with the Father and the Spirit.

Even more glorious than the first creation, John Owen argues, "this new relation of the creation unto the Son of God" is "more beautiful than it was before."[48] As incarnate, the Son "is near us, indeed touches us, since he is our flesh."[49] It is not just in his divinity that Christ is life-giving, Calvin says. As the eschatological firstfruits, his humanity is "pervaded with fullness of life to be transmitted to us" and this is why "it is rightly called 'life-giving.'"[50] Since he did not leave this humanity behind but raised and glorified it at the Father's right hand, we have a future with him. There is no daylight peeking through between Christ's salvation and ours:

> If then you have been raised with Christ, seek the things that are above, where Christ is, seated at the right hand of God. Set your minds on things that are above, not on things that are on earth. For you have died, and your life is hidden with Christ in God. When Christ who is your life appears, then you also will appear with him in glory. (Col 3:1–4)

The only difference comes between firstfruits and harvest, head and body, vine and branches. Because the root is holy—that is, justified, sanctified, and glorified—so are the branches (Rom 11:16). Christ is ahead of us but one with us—or rather, we are one with him.

Consequently, in the exaltation of "his humanity," observes Bavinck, "our humanity was exalted beyond all prior dignity . . . so that same person is the subject of the exaltation in both his natures."[51] In fact, John Owen observes of the ascended Christ, "He it is in whom *our nature,*

---

48. John Owen, "The Person of Christ," in *Works of John Owen,* vol. 1, ed. William H. Goold (London: Banner of Truth Trust, 1965), 373.

49. *Inst.* 2.12.1.

50. *Inst.* 4.17.9.

51. Bavinck, *Reformed Dogmatics,* 3:432, 435.

which was debased as low as hell by apostasy from God, *is exalted* above the whole creation. . . . In him the relation of our nature unto God is eternally secured. . . . Heaven and earth may pass away, but there shall never be a dissolution of the union between God and our nature any more."[52] It is the weakness and mortality that will be changed "and not the very substance of the flesh," said Francis Turretin.[53] "For what [Christ] took he never laid aside (Ps. 16:10; Jn.2:19; Acts 2:31). . . . Our bodies ought to be no other than those which were deposited in the earth, as no other body was given to Christ than that which he had before."[54]

The Sending of the Spirit

"Third," the catechism reminds us, "he sends his Spirit to us on earth as a corresponding pledge. By the Spirit's power we seek not earthly things but the things above, where Christ is, sitting at God's right hand."

We cannot ascend to God, but he descended to us. Yet beyond this, the Spirit raised us up with him in glory (Eph 2:6). How can this be, when we are on earth, living in the realities of corruption and death, and Christ has ascended to the Father's right hand? The hinge between Jesus-history and our history is the work of the Holy Spirit. He who united the Son to our humanity and raised him as the eschatological Lord of life now unites us to him. A weak pneumatology is evident wherever the *historia salutis* (what Christ accomplished for us) and the *ordo salutis* (how his achievement becomes ours) drift apart. In addition to Christ's intercessory ministry in the heavenly courtroom, his ascension has opened a fissure in history for the descent of the Spirit at Pentecost, to bring inward conviction of sin *and* of justification. In this time between the times, the indwelling Spirit "is the *guarantee* of our inheritance until we acquire possession of it, to the praise of his glory" (Eph 1:14).

Notice that with the Spirit we have not left the legal domain; on the contrary, he is the attorney at work in the inner courtroom of our heart while Christ is the attorney in the heavenly sanctuary. And when Christ

---

52. John Owen, "Preface to the Reader," in *Works of John Owen*, vol. 1, ed. William H. Goold (London: Banner of Truth Trust, 1965), 276–77, 281.

53. Francis Turretin, *Institutes of Elenctic Theology*, ed. James T. Dennison, Jr., trans. George Musgrave Giger (Phillipsburg, NJ: P&R, 1997), 569.

54. Turretin, *Institutes*, 3:572–73.

returns, the Spirit, who now guarantees our final glorification inwardly and personally, will endow it visibly, completely, and publicly on the last day as he did at Christ's resurrection. The connection between Christ's ascension and the Spirit's ministry of uniting sinners to Christ through faith by the ministry of the gospel is the theme of Christ's farewell discourse in John 14–16 and is spelled out beautifully in Ephesians 4:1–16.

Only with Easter morning does the "age to come" truly dawn even in what is still for us "this present age." According to the fourth gospel, Jesus declared on "the last day of the feast [of booths], the great day," that he is the source of the "living water." "Whoever believes in me, as the Scripture has said, 'Out of his heart will flow rivers of living water.'" Significantly, the evangelist explains, "Now this he said about the Spirit, whom those who believed in him were to receive, *for as yet the Spirit had not been given, because Jesus was not yet glorified*" (John 7:39). Jesus himself must be glorified by the Father in the Spirit before he can be the eschatological source of glorification for our humanity as well. The Spirit then unites us to the glorified Son of Man so that we share in his perfect humanity. Kathryn Tanner puts the point well: "Jesus' human life exhibits the Word's relationships with the other members of the Trinity."[55] His eternal generation from the Father, in the unity of the Holy Spirit, now finally has its ectypal, human counterpart in his mission, and those who are united to him now participate analogically (by adoption) in this human relation to the Father, in the Son, by the Spirit. The Son, who from eternity possesses the Spirit now, in time, possesses the Spirit "without measure" *in his humanity* (John 3:34). It is by this same Spirit that the obedient human Adam loves the Father even to the point of death. For this reason, he is raised and exalted by the Father in the Spirit and, at Pentecost, anoints his own with the Spirit so that they share in his justified and deified humanity, which brings them finally into communion with the Father.

Because of his ascension, the eschatological boundary between heaven and earth is porous. As Jesus ascends, he opens a hole in history for the Spirit's descent, to unite us even here and now to the Christ and his history. Through Word and sacrament, the Spirit brings the powers of the age to come into this present age (Heb 6:4–5), "bringing life and immortality to light through the gospel" (2 Tim 1:10).

---

55. Kathryn Tanner, *Christ the Key* (Cambridge: Cambridge University Press, 2010), 147.

There is much else to say about the ascension's relationship to the Spirit's work through preaching and the sacraments. In summary, Christ's ascension assures us that this world and our bodies and history have not been and will not be left behind but have been raised already to the right hand of the Father, objectively, in our forerunner and head. It also assures us that our present justification is being confirmed, defended, and secured by Christ's ongoing intercession. And finally, it assures us that the Spirit has been sent so that the one who united Christ to us and justified and glorified him is now uniting us to him for our justification and glorification.

PART 3

THE GIFT OF RIGHTEOUSNESS

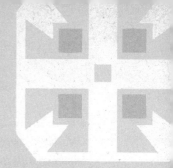

CHAPTER 7

WHAT JUSTIFICATION MEANS

Defining the Roman Catholic position on justification, Karl Adam wrote, "We have not only the certainty of forgiveness, but also the severe imperative, the commandments, and the doctrine of merit."[1] Indeed, forgiveness itself depends on this inward sanctification.[2] Regardless of the variety among schools and individuals in interpreting questions related to justification, according to the *Catechism of the Catholic Church*, justification is both a declaration and transformation effected by the infusion of grace through the sacraments, enabling final justification according to merits. Further, quoting the Council of Trent, the Catechism declares, "Justification is not only the remission of sins, but also the sanctification and renewal of the interior man."[3]

According to the Protestant Reformers, the heart of the gospel is that justification is a gift only because it is the righteousness of Christ credited or imputed to the believer. This righteousness is alien in the sense that it does not belong inherently to the believer. With the advantage of being a half-century later than the first Reformation confessions and seeing the debates that arose within Protestantism itself, the Westminster Confession excludes several errors in a lapidary statement:

---

1. Karl Adam, *The Spirit of Catholicism*, trans. Dom Justin McCann, OSB (1924; repr., New York: Crossroad, 1977), 101, 149.
2. Adam, *The Spirit of Catholicism*, 180. As I pointed out in volume one, medieval theology in the line of Lombard, Bonaventure, and Aquinas understood justification as a process (tied closely to penance) of restoring the dominance of the higher soul (reason) over the lower soul (the passions).
3. *CCC*, para. 1989, quoting the Council of Trent (1574): DS 1528.

Those whom God effectually calls, He also freely justifies; *not by infusing righteousness into them*, but by pardoning their sins, and by accounting and accepting their persons as righteous; *not for any thing wrought in them*, or *done by them*, but for Christ's sake alone; *nor by imputing faith itself*, the act of believing, or any other evangelical obedience to them, as their righteousness; but by imputing the obedience and satisfaction of Christ unto them, they *receiving and resting* on Him and His righteousness by faith; *which faith they have not of themselves, it is the gift of God*.[4]

However, since the Enlightenment modern Protestantism and Roman Catholicism have been shaped to a large extent by reactions against even the more Augustinian assumptions that both traditions shared. Despite the continuing witness of confessional churches, the same presuppositions that aroused antipathy toward dogmas like original sin and substitutionary atonement brought the doctrine of justification into disrepute as undermining moral effort in the vain hope of a rescue outside of the self.

Further, as we have seen, traditional (patristic and medieval as well as Reformation) interpretations of crucial phrases such as the righteousness of God (i.e., God's covenant faithfulness rather than divine attribute and norm) and works of the law (i.e., exclusionary ceremonies) as well as faith (i.e., faithfulness) and faith in Christ (i.e., faithfulness of Christ) have been radically redefined, especially since Hermann Cremer, with a strong dichotomy between ostensibly Hebrew and Hellenistic (as well as Eastern and Latin) mentalities.[5] Despite powerful criticisms from

---

4. Westminster Confession of Faith, in *The Book of Confessions* (Louisville: PCUSA General Assembly, 1991), ch. 11.

5. The Hebrew-Hellenism dichotomy first took the form of an opposition between Jesus and Paul. Then some said no; Jesus and Paul are unified, and the source of the problem is the (mis)reading of Paul through a Western (Latin) lens (which is ironic, since the Greek Christian tradition can hardly be conceived as less Hellenistic). Then the Reformers became the Hellenizing culprits. But in the time of Barth, Karl Holl, and the Torrances, it was in fact the successors who swung the pendulum away from Luther and Calvin's Athanasian-Eastern habits of thought and toward the dregs of Latin scholasticism. The same pressures that were brought to bear on the classic formulation of Christ's atonement as involving a propitiatory sacrifice have challenged forensic categories altogether. Rather than a legal declaration, justification came to be seen (in Socinian and liberal Protestant programs) in terms of an exclusively transformative act of divine deliverance or a subjective change in the sinner to open him or her to God's love and so become an active participant in the moral kingdom of God. More recently, the Reformation interpretation of justification has been challenged in Protestant circles especially through the new perspective on Paul but also through the influence of movements like Radical Orthodoxy, *nouvelle théologie*, and the new Finnish interpretation of Luther.

some prominent biblical scholars (e.g., James Barr, Martin Hengel, and Troels Engberg-Pedersen), this paradigm-shift has played a prominent role in setting the terms in advance for even the range of possibilities for interpreting justification.

"Put simply, the doctrine of justification in the twentieth century has endured one of two fates," notes David Shaw. "It has either retained its traditional meaning but been declared peripheral to Paul's concerns, or it has remained central by undergoing a degree of redefinition."[6] Although the upshot of contemporary discussions of justification generally fall out into recognizable patterns of the sixteenth-century debate, the terms of the debate are quite different.

Ironically, the question on which the whole Reformation turned—namely, whether justification is a process of making just or declaring just—is rather moot today at least among biblical scholars, if not theologians. Leading Roman Catholic exegetes take it as a settled conclusion that justification means "to declare righteous" rather than "to make righteous."[7] As we will see, this is the conclusion of new perspective scholars as well, although they challenge the Protestant doctrine at other points. Most basically, the view that I am defending here is that justification is simply "the gift of righteousness" in contrast with the righteousness by which God condemns and the righteousness that one may acquire by his or her deeds.

INTRODUCTION: FRAMING PAUL'S ARGUMENT

Those united with Christ receive many gifts (see ch. 11). However, justification establishes the forensic basis of a new relationship by answering the problem of the coming "wrath of God" that will be poured out on the ungodly. This doctrine assumes that the problem is far deeper than mere externalism and impotency to carry out the requirements of the law or, if one prefers, to live obediently in the Spirit. Justification cancels guilt and credits the believer with the status of Christ as righteous in the heavenly court.

---

6. David Shaw, "Romans 4 and the Justification of Abraham in Light of Perspectives New and Newer," *Themelios* 40, no. 1 (2015): 50–62.

7. See, e.g., Joseph A. Fitzmyer, SJ, "The Letter to the Romans," and "The Letter to the Galatians," in *The Jerome Biblical Commentary*, ed. Raymond S. Brown, SS, Joseph A. Fitzmyer, SJ, and Roland E. Murphy, O.Carm. (Englewood Cliffs, NJ: Prentice Hall, 1968), esp. 241–44 and 303–15; and Brendan Byrne, *Romans*, Sacra Pagina (Collegeville, MN: Liturgical, 1996), 57.

Again, as I emphasized in relation to the Protestant Reformers' understanding of justification in volume 1, the issue is not the virtue of faith versus works, divine versus human action, in the abstract, but the concrete alternative between *Christ* and *everything else*.[8] Surely if any law could be given that would give life and justification, it would be Torah (Gal 3:21). There is nothing wrong with Torah, but it is incapable of justifying because of the weakness of sinful flesh (Rom 7:14). It can only justify those who have fulfilled it (Rom 2:13). In comparison with Christ, Paul now sees his "righteousness" as worthless with respect to God's searching judgment. Regardless of how far advanced one might be in comparison with others, no one has fulfilled it (Rom 3:10). Therefore, no one will be justified by it (v. 20). As we have seen, Paul (and the Reformers) had a generous appreciation of the civic virtue that even gentiles are capable of. But all human righteousness, gentile and even Jewish, is cast into the bin in comparison with being found in Christ, clothed in his righteousness (see Phil 3:9). The church father Jerome puts it this way: "Therefore one who thinks that he 'is justified' by some observance of the law destroys the grace of Christ and loses the gospel that he had held." And "the law" here "embraces the whole law universally."[9]

Of fundamental importance in the justification debates, new and old, is the interpretation of Romans 3:21–26:

> But now the righteousness of God has been manifested apart from the law, although the Law and the Prophets bear witness to it— the righteousness of God through faith in Jesus Christ for all who believe. For there is no distinction: for all have sinned and fall short of the glory of God, and are justified by his grace as a gift, through the redemption that is in Christ Jesus, whom God put forward as a propitiation by his blood, to be received by faith. This was to show God's righteousness, because in his divine forbearance he had passed over former sins. It was to show his righteousness at the present time, so that he might be just and the justifier of the one who has faith in Jesus.

---

8. On this point, see especially Jonathan A. Linebaugh, "The Christo-Centrism of Faith in Christ: Martin Luther's Reading of Gal 2.16, 19–20," *New Testament Studies* 59, no. 4 (2013): 535–44; cf. Allen, *Justification and the Gospel*, 113 (see also, in criticism of Campbell, 102).

9. Jerome, *Commentaries on Galatians, Titus, and Philemon*, trans. Thomas P. Scheck (Notre Dame: University of Notre Dame Press, 2010), 201.

Paul is working with a problem that is intrinsic to Israel's history and Torah itself. However, with Israel's history as a "play within a play"—the wider "play" being the story of humanity in Adam—the problem of being "under the law" and found guilty is universal. His answer is that God cannot justify the ungodly according to a covenant sworn by the people with clearly conditional terms of blessing and curse. If God were to justify the ungodly on this basis, he would cease to be God. If under the terms of the old covenant it is unjust for a judge to justify the ungodly (Exod 23:7; Isa 5:23; Prov 17:15), then how can God—the purest judge of all—do the same? So God justifies the ungodly on the basis of another covenant, one with a different mediator and founded on better promises. Surely the accused agree that God "will by no means leave the guilty unpunished" (Exod 34:7), but they insist on their innocence, imagining that they stand approved according to these terms.

Paul's opening argument attempts to dissuade them of this fatal misunderstanding, preparing them for his transition to the good news in Romans 3:21: The righteousness *of* God (which condemns all as law-breakers) is not the end of the story; the righteousness *from* God justifies the ungodly. Christ's death provides propitiation (*hilastērion*; Rom 3:25), which turns away the wrath of God that is coming upon all of humanity (1:18) and brings objective peace with God (5:1). Everyone has fallen short of God's glory, but everyone—Jew and gentile alike—can now be "justified freely by his grace" (3:24). Peter makes the same argument *in nuce* in Acts 3:25–26.

Every Israelite was directed by the sacrificial and ceremonial system of Torah to faith in Christ. Israel's tenure in the land as God's geopolitical kingdom depended on the nation's keeping of Torah, but justification before God was never attained (or intended to be attained) by works of the law. This was a misunderstanding of many of Paul's contemporaries, both Jewish and Jewish-Christian. Never in the New Testament are believers directed to imitate the faith of those who swore allegiance at Sinai; rather, they are exhorted to imitate Abraham's faith in the promise through which he was justified.

This contrast between the "two covenants"—law and promise, Sinai and Abraham, earthly and heavenly Jerusalem, Hagar and Sarah (Gal 4:21–31)—is central to Paul's letter to the Galatians. It is significant that Paul describes his critics in the Galatian church as "enemies of the gospel." Those who are perverting the faith of the church in Galatia are not merely ultraconservatives who need to become more liberal and open to outsiders but are "false brethren" and the church itself is in danger of being declared anathema (Gal 1:8). "You are severed from Christ, you who would be justified by the law; you have fallen away from grace" (Gal 5:4). They are not in danger of cutting off *others* from Christ but of cutting off *themselves*. Their ultimate problem is not that they are too rigid or hold to ceremonies that no longer matter since Christ has come; it is that they *fail to do* what the law says but refuse to flee to Christ alone. While requiring circumcision of gentiles, they fail to realize that circumcision obligates them to keep the whole law, which they have not done (Gal 5:3). This is why they are accounted "hypocrites." If this claim is accurate, then the central plank of the new perspective's construal of justification is eliminated. With the Reformation perspective you get the "worldwide family" (including gentiles) in the bargain. Because God justifies the ungodly, unfaithful Jews as well as pagan gentiles can be saved *and included together* in one body, one family, promised to Abraham.

The writer to the Hebrews confirms that *because* the Abrahamic promise (based on Gen 3:15, along with the Davidic and the promise of a new covenant) always remained alive and well—secured by God's oath and his Son as the mediator—the promise of entering the everlasting rest to which the temporal rest merely pointed was always left open (Heb 4:1). The true, ultimate rest is entered through faith in the gospel (v. 2), "for whoever has entered God's rest has also rested from his works as God did from his" (v. 10). And *because* this door is open wide to everyone, entered through faith rather than works, not only Jews but also gentiles find themselves passing into the land of peace arm in arm. Believers are not returning to Mount Sinai, with its terrifying words, but have finally arrived at Mount Zion through a better covenant, with better promises and a better mediator (Heb 12:18–24).

This brief summary of the context of justification in Scripture prepares us now for its definition.

DEFINING JUSTIFICATION

"And those whom he called he also justified" (Rom 8:30). Understanding what Paul meant by justification depends on whether we can come to terms with his anthropology (universal human depravity)[10] and therefore his compelling interest in, as Peter Stuhlmacher puts it, "whether Jews and Gentiles will or will not survive before God's throne of judgment."[11] The gospel is not simply that Jesus was crucified and raised, or that these events demonstrate his lordship, but that he "was crucified *for our sins* and was raised *for our justification*" (Rom 4:25, emphasis added).

As we have seen, there are a few striking parallels between Jewish texts and New Testament teaching. The Qumran scrolls have references to "the justification of human beings by God's 'mercy' and 'grace.'" Particularly striking in this regard is the closing hymn of the Manual of Discipline, where the author confesses, "As for me, I belong to a wicked humanity," "doomed" to "walking in darkness." And yet, "I, if I stagger, God's grace is my salvation forever" (1QS 11.9–12).[12] The author of the Thanksgiving Psalms also proclaims, "As for me, I know that righteousness belongs not to a human being, nor perfection of way to a son of man. To God Most high belong all the deeds of righteousness, whereas the path of a human is not set firm. . . . I have based myself on Your grace and on the abundance of Your mercy. For You expiate iniquity to clean[se a human be]ing from guilt by Your own righteousness.' (1QH 12:30–38)."[13]

"In a very similar way," says Fitzmyer, "Paul insisted that all human beings 'have sinned and fall short of the glory of God' (Rom 3:23), that is, because of their sins they fail to attain the glorious destiny planned by God for them."

The one big difference between the Essene teaching on justification and the Pauline is that the Apostle insists that human beings appropriate this status of righteousness and acquittal in God's sight through faith in Christ Jesus. For Paul, the vicarious death and the resurrection of Jesus of Nazareth have made a difference, and the important difference is "faith" (*pistis*) in Christ, by which one appropriates that status of righteousness. Nevertheless, the Qumran

---

10. See Timo Laato, *Paul and Judaism: An Anthropological Approach* (Atlanta: Scholars' Press, 1995).

11. Peter Stuhlmacher, *Revisiting Paul's Doctrine of Justification: A Challenge to the New Perspective* (Downers Grove, IL: InterVarsity, 2001), 43.

12. Joseph A. Fitzmyer, SJ, *The Dead Sea Scrolls and Christian Origins* (Grand Rapids: Eerdmans, 2000), 28–29.

13. Fitzmyer, *The Dead Sea Scrolls and Christian Origins*, 29.

tenet in this matter is clearly transitional, for it shows how the Old Testament teaching about righteousness could develop and be used by a Christian writer like Paul.[14]

Yet no community, including Qumran, would have agreed that this gift of righteousness—justification—can come *apart from works of the law* (4QMMT C 27; 4Q348 ii:2–3). Once again, we see that for Paul, and the other New Testament writers, the contrast is to be drawn not on a spectrum (texts that more or less affirm the need for grace) but between *solo Christo* and whatever deeds may be said to justify a person on the last day.

Lexical Analysis

In the Hebrew Scriptures, the verb *hitsdiq* (in the hiphil, along with its piel form *tsiddeq*) is generally used for a judicial declaration that one is in the right according to the law (Exod 23:7; Deut 25:1; Prov 17:15; Isa 5:23; Jer 3:11; Ezek 16:50–51). In the New Testament, the two words—justification and righteousness—are linked lexically, belonging to the same δικ- word group. This follows the LXX, showing that the *tsedeq* concept was regarded as equivalent to the δικ- family in early Jewish thought. The noun δικαιοσύνη (righteousness/justice) and adjective δίκαιος (righteous/just) are straightforward enough in English translation. So also is the meaning of the noun δικαίωμα clear enough: a legal verdict (of acquittal or condemnation). The verb δικαιόω therefore means "to justify." The lexical definition of justification is "to be cleared in court."[15]

The LXX translators could have used words like ἀρετή (virtue, uprightness, moral perfection) but instead chose the forensic δικαιοσύνη. It is also obvious that in the patristic sources of the Christian East, justification meant "to declare righteous."[16] Although he interpreted the doctrine in a more transformative direction, it is striking that even Origen acknowledge the semantic meaning of justification as forensic.[17] If native Greek-speakers understood justification in this way, then surely the Vulgate represents a divergence from the original sense.[18]

---

14. Fitzmyer, *The Dead Sea Scrolls and Christian Origins*, 29.
15. See BDAG, 246–50.
16. See my first volume, chs. 2–3.
17. See my first volume, chs, 2–3.
18. Significantly, while Jerome translated the Gospels from the Greek, the Pauline Epistles were translated by his contemporaries (and students) from the Old Latin. There is evidence that even Pelagius had a hand in translating the Pauline epistles: see Eric W. Scherbenske, *Canonizing Paul: Ancient Editorial Practice and the Corpus Paulinum.* (Oxford: Oxford University

Substantiating this lexical definition is the fact that in the divine κρίμα (judgment), the opposite of δικαίωμα/δικαίωσις (justification) is κατάκριμα (condemnation), as in Romans 5:16, 18. These are the opposing verbs that are used in Matthew 12:37 and John 3:17–18. For Paul as well, this δικαίωμα is "justification," set in opposition not to φθορά (corruption) but to κατάκριμα (condemnation), as in Romans 4:6–7; 5:16–18; 8:1, 14, 33–34 and 1 Corinthians 5:19.

Simply on lexical grounds, therefore, at least two alternatives may be excluded. First, δικαιόω cannot mean "to make righteous," as the Latin Vulgate translated it (as *iustificare*) and centuries of great Christian minds understood it at least until humanists such as Jacques Lefèbvre D'Étaples, Erasmus, and the Reformers rediscovered its original meaning.[19] This is not to preclude the possibility that the verdict is rendered toward those who have done something to merit it. Those are doctrinal questions that require exegetical argumentation. However, the verb itself does not *mean* "to make just" but "to declare just." To be justified in Christ is to "stand before God's tribunal acquitted or vindicated," notes Joseph Fitzmyer, SJ, "that they might stand before him as righteous persons." He continues, "In his experience near Damascus Paul realized the truth that all human beings have sinned and have failed to attain the share of divine glory destined for them," which is now given "through what Christ Jesus has obtained for them vicariously (Rom 3:21–26)." Whether Paul understood all of this on the Damascus road or subsequently, he is certainly correct in his interpretation of the apostle's teaching. "Thus, Paul realized that the righteousness that he and other Christians have is not their own; it is a 'righteousness from God' (Phil 3:9; cf. Rom 10:3), a gift freely bestowed by God because of what Christ Jesus has done for humanity."[20] E. P. Sanders also notes that in both Hebrew and Greek, justification is a forensic, courtroom term meaning "to be cleared in court."[21]

Press, 2013), 183; H. A. G. Houghton, *The Latin New Testament: A Guide to Its Early History, Texts, and Manuscripts* (Oxford: Oxford University Press, 2016), 36.

19. A similarly portentous mistranslation occurred with respect to the imperative "Repent" (*metanoeite*) being rendered as "Do penance," thus serving as the prompt for the medieval doctrine of penance. See Alister E. McGrath, *Iustitia Dei: A History of the Christian Doctrine of Justification* (Cambridge: Cambridge University Press, 1986), 11–14.

20. Fitzmyer, *According to Paul*, 12.

21. E. P. Sanders, *Paul and Palestinian Judaism: A Comparison of Patterns of Religion* (Philadelphia: Fortress, 1977), 198–99: "In the *qal*, the verb [*tsadaq*] usually means 'to be cleared in court' and is not really distinguishable from the use of the *zakah* root to mean 'innocent.' . . . It may also mean to make something correct, as in the phrase 'make the scales just.' The hif'il, 'to justify,'

Nevertheless, dogmatic commitments continue to trump exegesis among those who are committed to the medieval definition. Officially, the Roman Catholic Church remains committed to the definition of justification as a process of becoming holy. Anglo-Catholic scholar John Milbank (following Douglas Harink) insists that "*dikaiosynē* always meant 'justice' or a 'binding together in justice' in the contemporary Greek or Judeo-Greek context and never 'imputed salvation,'" and that the "Hebrew equivalents . . . never implied anything imputational."[22] Thus, "'Justification' in Paul is the divine action of really making just, not of imputing justice."[23] As we will see, justification based on inner and cosmic transformation is becoming increasingly popular among Protestant (including some evangelical) scholars, just at the time when there is such wide consensus among exegetes, including Roman Catholic and new perspective scholars, on the original meaning of the term. We are hardly witnessing the demise of a forensic doctrine of justification on lexical and exegetical grounds.

Second, on lexical grounds, δικαιόω cannot mean "to be covenant-ally faithful." The same is true of the Hebrew Scriptures. There is a perfectly good word for "covenant faithfulness": אֱמוּן (*emun*). Closely related is חֶסֶד (*khesed*), often rendered "covenant faithfulness" but actually a narrower term meaning mercy or lovingkindness. Neither אֱמוּן (*emun*) nor חֶסֶד (*khesed*) has any lexical connection with צֶדֶק (*tsedeq*). As discussed in chapter 3, the covenant faithfulness interpretation of the "righteousness of God" emerges from a particular history of nine-teenth and twentieth-century theology. This "Cremer thesis" rejects the traditional (ostensibly Hellenistic) idea of justice or righteousness as conformity to an external norm, in spite of the fact that the latter is what *tsedaqah* meant for the Hebrew prophets.[24] To be sure, faithful-ness to covenant promises is obviously involved, but the *meaning* of the word "righteous/righteousness" is not covenant faithfulness; rather, it is synonymous with justice, as is seen in Amos 5:7 ("O you who turn

---

also has a forensic connotation. When the passage in Ex. 23.7 says 'I will not justify the wicked,' it is clearly understood to mean 'hold innocent.'"

22. John Milbank, "Paul against Biopolitics," in *Paul's New Moment: Continental Philosophy and the Future of Christian Theology*, by John Milbank, Slavoj Zizek, and Creston Davis (Grand Rapids: Brazos, 2010), 56.

23. Milbank, "Paul against Biopolitics," 55n69, drawing liberally from Douglas Harink, *Paul among the Postliberals: Pauline Theology beyond Christendom and Modernity* (Grand Rapids: Brazos, 2003).

24. See ch. 3 in this volume.

justice [*mishpat*] to wormwood and cast down righteousness [*tsedaqah*] to the earth!"), repeated in 5:24 ("But let justice [*mishpat*] roll down like waters, and righteousness [*tsedaqah*] like an ever-flowing stream"), and again in 6:12. The Suffering Servant makes "many to be *accounted righteous* [*yatsdiq*], and he shall bear their iniquities" (Isa 53:11)

In a landmark study J. A. Ziesler explained, "Bultmann says that justification means to be put 'in a right relationship,' not 'ethically right,'" and Ziesler adds that this is "very similar to the usual Protestant one."[25] While it is true that most Protestant exegetes (including Bultmann) have adopted Cremer's view (opposition to the idea of the righteousness of God as an ethical norm), this dichotomy was unknown to Paul as well as the Reformers (and everyone else until Cremer). Whatever its broader connotations, justification does not *mean* "to be put 'in a right relationship,'" especially set in opposition to being declared "ethically right." Justification itself is a judicial category, not a relational one. Of course, justification changes the relationship, but that is not what justification *means*. The judicial justification of a criminal can hardly be considered anything other than declared "ethically right," since the verdict is based on whether the demands of the law have been fulfilled. Many things issue from such a verdict, but justification itself is declaratory. (If we say "*merely* declaratory" in criticism of the doctrine, then we do not yet appreciate the power of God's speech.)

It is significant that Ziesler himself says, "The theologian might assume that justification is more than this, and be right in so arguing, but he must recognize that Paul does not include this 'more' in his use of the verb."[26] He concludes,

> The debate about whether on *a priori* grounds δικαιόω can mean "declare righteous" must surely be regarded as closed. Not only is it clear that it *does* mean this in Biblical Greek, but the parallel with ἀξιόω, and the fact that in secular Greek there is only one place when it has been discovered to mean 'make righteous,' show that a declaratory force ought to be given to it unless there are strong reasons to the contrary.[27]

---

25. J. A. Ziesler, *The Meaning of Righteousness in Paul: A Linguistic and Theological Enquiry*, Society for New Testament Monograph Series (Cambridge: Cambridge University Press, 1972), 4.

26. Ziesler, *The Meaning of Righteousness in Paul*, 5.

27. Ziesler, *The Meaning of Righteousness in Paul*, 48.

Ziesler's point has been made by many biblical scholars, especially since James Barr's critique of the Cremer thesis. The tendency in new perspective scholarship is to pour connotations into denotations, entailments into definitions, implications of a meaning into the meaning of the term itself. For example, Wright translates 2 Corinthians 5:21, "The Messiah did not know sin, but God made him to be sin on our behalf, so that in him we might *embody God's faithfulness to the covenant.*"[28] Obviously, one cannot become *God's* faithfulness to the covenant, so Wright supplies "embody." In the semantic world of the new perspective, righteousness means covenant fidelity, faith means faithfulness, and faith rather than circumcision is the badge of knowing who belongs to the covenant. Once we accept these as "assured results" of biblical scholars, the puzzle pieces of the new perspective fall into place. Wright says, "Justification . . . is not a matter of how someone enters the community of the true people of God, but of how you tell who belongs to that community."[29] But justification means neither "how one enters" nor "how we know who is in" the community. With the Cremer thesis as its point of departure, the new perspective creates a series of theological postulates. None is tenable on lexical-semantic grounds, but together they form an apparently impregnable fortress.

To dispose of any possibility of progressive-justification readings (viz., "making righteous"), I might prefer that Paul had said "*declared to be* the righteousness of God," but he did not. Stepping from definition to exegesis, I would interpret Paul as saying that in justification those who are ungodly become righteous judicially by the imputation of Christ's righteousness. However, the verb γίνομαι does not *mean* "to embody" or "to declare." It means "to become." Paul did not say, "embody *God's faithfulness to the covenant.*" The rendering of the object depends on an *interpretation* of the phrase "righteousness of God" that is in dispute. In any case, it is not a translation of the clause itself. The verbal phrase γενώμεθα δικαιοσύνη Θεοῦ *means* "become the righteousness of God."

In an earlier work, Wright offered a completely different translation of 2 Corinthians 5:21—even the subject of the verb is different. It is not believers who embody God's faithfulness; rather, *Christ became*

28. N. T. Wright, *The Day the Revolution Began: Reconsidering the Meaning of Jesus' Crucifixion* (New York: HarperOne, 2016), 81.
29. N. T. Wright, *What Saint Paul Really Said: Was Paul of Tarsus the Real Founder of Christianity?* (Grand Rapids: Eerdmans, 1997), 119.

"righteousness, that is, God vindicated him."[30] However, the sentence cannot be read this way either. The ESV translates it well enough: "For our sake he made him to be sin who knew no sin, so that in him we might become the righteousness of God." Whether we define it as a declaration or a process, imputation or infusion, *Christ* is the one who became sin, and *believers* are the ones who become righteous because of it.

Unlike other defenses of Cremer's thesis, Wright's account gives more attention to the courtroom context. This only serves to make matters more confusing, however, since it is difficult to imagine a courtroom relationship that does not depend on conformity to certain norms. Furthermore, Wright introduces the familiar dichotomy (from Bultmann!—with deeper roots in Diestel and Cremer) between moral and relational. The language of righteousness and justification is covenantal, not moral, Wright says. The "righteous acts" of God are not "virtuous acts," we are told, but "acts in fulfillment of God's covenant promises." In the same way, the "righteousness" of believers is "not a moral quality" but membership in the community.[31]

What, then, is covenant faithfulness or a final justification "on the basis of the entire life" apart from "a moral quality" that involves at least some "virtuous acts"? "'Righteousness' and its cognates, in their biblical setting, are in this sense 'relational' terms, indicating how things stand with particular people *in relation to the court*."[32] Helpfully, this avoids the familiar dichotomy between forensic and relational categories, but it only makes things more confusing: How can one be related to the court as righteous without a moral judgment?

Considering Galatians 2:11–16, Wright says, "We are forced to conclude, at least in a preliminary way, that 'to be justified' here does not mean 'to be granted free forgiveness of your sins,' 'to come into a right relation with God' or some other near-synonym of 'to be reckoned "in the right" before God,' but rather, and very specifically, 'to be reckoned by God to be a true member of his family, and hence with the right to share table fellowship.'"[33] The *context* is indeed table fellowship, which displays the practical import of justification for Jewish-gentile communion, but Wright is reading these implications into the meaning of the

---

30. N. T. Wright, *Justification: God's Plan and Paul's Vision* (Downers Grove, IL: InterVarsity, 2009), 157.

31. Wright, *Justification*, 63, 121, 133–34.

32. Wright, *Justification*, 69.

33. Wright, *Justification*, 116.

word itself, contradicting the lexical definition of the verb "to justify." It *means* precisely, as we have seen, "to be reckoned 'in the right' before God" *and therefore grants* "the right to share table fellowship." Instead, Wright simply makes the effect the definition of the cause itself.

Stephen Westerholm challenges Wright's definition, first by citing a raft of passages that state explicitly that righteousness *is* a moral quality: something done or not done that furthers God's good intentions expressed in his law. "The 'righteous' are thus those who *do* what they *ought to do* (i.e., righteousness)."[34] One clear example is Ezekiel 3:20: "Again, if a righteous person turns from his righteousness and commits injustice, and I lay a stumbling block before him, he shall die. Because you have not warned him, he shall die for his sin, and his *righteous deeds* [righteousness] *that he has done* shall not be remembered, but his blood I will require at your hand" (emphasis added). "For starters," Westerholm continues, "the language of 'righteousness' can hardly designate membership in God's covenant people." "On the negative side, Israel was a stubborn, *not* righteous, nation (a *moral* judgment) after as well as before they entered the covenant at Sinai."[35] "On the positive side, Noah was declared 'righteous' before any covenant is mentioned in Scripture (Gen 6:9)," and Abraham believed that there might be at least fifty people "in the *Canaanite* city of Sodom . . . though, in the event, these expectations of Canaanite righteousness, too, were not met."[36]

> So "righteousness" does not mean, and by its very nature *cannot* mean, membership in a covenant. Likewise, it does not mean, and by its very nature *cannot* mean, a status conveyed by the decision of a court. . . . People are what they are—innocent or guilty—based on the rightness or wrongness of what they have done.[37]

What the court does is to render a verdict on the guilt or innocence of the defendant. "'Acquitted' and 'righteous' are *not* synonyms, even in a legal setting," he adds. "If 'righteousness' *were* so conveyed, the injunction to declare 'innocent' those who *are* innocent would require judges to declare 'innocent' people *made* innocent by their declaration; and judges would

---

34. Westerholm, *Justification Reconsidered*, 61.
35. Westerholm, *Justification Reconsidered*, 62, referring to Deut 9:6–7.
36. Westerholm, *Justification Reconsidered*, 62.
37. Westerholm, *Justification Reconsidered*, 63.

be required to declare 'guilty' those *made* guilty by their declaration. Not even 'in the biblical context' does that make sense."[38]

In short, Westerholm judges,

> The word "justify" cannot mean what Wright wants it to mean; no Galatian would have heard "justified" and thought "entitled to sit at the family table"; nor would Paul (who elsewhere uses *dikaio-* terms in their ordinary sense) have used *this* word here if *that* was what he wanted to say. To the simplest answer we need add only that nothing in the context in Galatians 2 compels us to add fresh categories to the lexical definition of "justify." Paul's point . . . is that the law that requires circumcision prescribes a path to righteousness (i.e., recognition by God as one who is righteous) on which no human being can succeed; righteousness (in this ordinary sense) is not possible on the law's terms (2:21; cf. 3:10). Why, then, would anyone submit to its regime?[39]

Justification cannot therefore mean gradual transformation, recognition of membership in the people of God, or anything else other than the courtroom declaration that someone is deemed righteous before God. The court finds the defendant not only innocent but as one who has fulfilled the righteousness commanded in the law. This fact by itself does not indicate the basis on which or the means by which one is justified before God. At this stage it might be argued that one is declared to have fulfilled all righteousness personally and is therefore, on that basis, declared to be righteous. That question will be addressed later. For now, it is sufficient to conclude that justification means that *the demands of the law have been fully met* (Acts 13:39; Rom 5:1, 9; 8:30–33; 1 Cor 6:11; Gal 2:16; 3:11) so that the person is reckoned to be righteous.

The apocalyptic school, especially as represented by J. Louis Martin and Douglas Campbell, also expands the meaning of justification to its theological entailments. Martyn says that δικαίωσις (justification) *means* "rectification or liberation."[40] Similarly, Peter Leithart *defines* justification as "deliverdict," a combination of powerful deliverance

---

38. Westerholm, *Justification Reconsidered*, 65.
39. Westerholm, *Justification Reconsidered*, 68.
40. J. Louis Martin translates justification as "rectification" in Galatians 5–6; for "freedom" or "liberation," see Douglas A. Campbell, *The Deliverance of God: An Apocalyptic Rereading of Justification in Paul* (Grand Rapids: Eerdmans, 2013), 90, 657.

and a declaration of some sort (but not that the guilty are righteous in Christ by imputation).[41] He says, "'Condemnation' *means* 'condemned to be under the mastery of sin and death.'"[42] Since they are not set free from God's *condemnation*, the only "forensic" act is to "declare set free [from the evil powers]." But once again, δικαίωμα does not *mean* "to set free." And, as noted above, John and Paul do not contrast justification (δικαίωμα) with *bondage* but with *condemnation* (κατάκριμα; John 3:17; Rom 5:16). The idea of liberation is certainly biblical, but there are perfectly good New Testament verbs for this, such as διασώζω (to save), ἀπολύω (to set free), or ἐλευθερόω (to make free), the last of which Paul in fact uses several times (Rom 6:18, 22; 8:2, 21; Gal 5:1). There may be all sorts of connotations and implications of "justification," but these are not the same as the denotative meaning. It is even more amiss to choose a definition that actually contradicts or replaces the denotative meaning.

As we move from semantics to exegesis, it is clear that Martyn and Leithart miss a crucial step: being condemned under the mastery of sin and death is itself the result of a curse-sanction of the law. Such condemnation is the consequence of the law's verdict: "The sting of death is sin, and the power of sin is the law" (1 Cor 15:56). We are freed from the powers, Paul says, *because of* God's "having forgiven us all our trespasses, by canceling the record of debt that stood against us with its legal demands. This he set aside, nailing it to the cross" (Col 2:13–14). Why did Christ become incarnate? asks Leithart. "Answer: To justify humanity from *ta stoicheia tou kosmou*, because only if humanity is brought out from these childhood restrictions can there be just, mature human societies, and only God can perform this deliverance."[43] Whatever important truths may be included in Leithart's description of Paul's message, this is not what justification *means* in a single instance of his use of the term. There are many effects, but justification itself *means* "declared righteous."

The loading-down of the word "justification" with freight reaches its apogee in Douglas Campbell's proposal. "*There will in fact be no future retributive judgment*; there will be instead a triumphant realization for all of what the elect already know," Campbell declares. "So there is

41. Peter J. Leithart, *Delivered from the Elements of the World: Atonement, Justification, Mission* (Downers Grove, IL: IVP Academic, 2016), 333–54.
42. Leithart, *Delivered from the Elements of the World*, 346, emphasis added.
43. Leithart, *Delivered from the Elements of the World*, 180.

no need for the Roman Christians to feel intimidated by the threats emanating from the Teacher's rhetoric about their putative fate on the day of judgment."[44] Besides revoking his Barthian policy of prescinding from any absolute judgment on this question, Campbell *defines* the word justification only after he has already established what it can and cannot mean according to his nonretributive doctrine of God. Paul says nothing like this, of course, and much to the contrary, but the latter doctrine Campbell has already tidily imputed to a false teacher rather than the apostle; for the positive argument, Campbell is able to imagine what Paul would have said instead. Later, Campbell is willing to concede that there is a forensic aspect to justification, but it is no more than a decree *to set free*. "His decisive forensic act—his judgment—is that they be released in Christ from their ontological prison; in Christ, he has set them free. God's 'justification' is consequently a forensic-liberative act."[45] Campbell has imported his entire theological scheme into the *sense* of the word.

Regaining Focus: Letting Justification Be Justification

Undisciplined accounts of justification's semantic meaning give rise to unfocused accounts of the doctrine itself and its relation to related ones. This tendency is apparent in two directions.

On the one hand, there is the tendency to *inflate* justification to cover essentially what we mean by the word "salvation." The alternatives to the Reformation interpretation of justification resolve these two expressions of God's righteousness into one, whether defined as intrinsic conformity to a moral norm or as covenant membership. What Luther describes as "Two Kinds of Righteousness"—righteousness before God (alien) received through faith in Christ and righteous acts (proper) performed for the benefit of the neighbor—are combined by alternative paradigms into covenant faithfulness, thereby assimilating justification to sanctification.[46]

For the medieval church as well, justification had to include sanctification; for Orthodoxy, it included deification, and for many in the

---

44. Campbell, *The Deliverance of God*, 668.
45. Campbell, *The Deliverance of God*, 669.
46. In addition to the 1519 sermon, "Two Kinds of Righteousness" (*LW* 31: 293–306), Luther treated the distinction in his Galatians commentary (1535) and the *Bondage of the Will*. It was included also in Melanchthon's Apology of the Augsburg Confession and in the third article of the Formula of Concord.

pietist-revivalist traditions, conversion. If justification is purely forensic, then it seems to many that there must be no sanctification, no deification, no conversion, no other benefits of union with Christ—hence, "a conception of redemption from which no ethic could logically be derived" (Schweitzer).[47] If the Reformation view is correct, however, *justification* is only forensic, but *salvation* is not only justification. Not only does the Reformation view affirm sanctification and glorification; it demonstrates exegetically why a purely forensic justification must be their basis.

The problem of conflating justification with its effects is evident also in Wolfhart Pannenberg's treatment. He wonders how justification can be synthetic (that is, not based on any state of affairs in believers) if Paul compares it to creation *ex nihilo* in Romans 4:17.[48] However, Paul's point is that when God says, "Let there be *x*!" there *is x*. Where God speaks his unbidden and unbound mercy, the ungodly cease to be ungodly, both judicially (apart from any moral transformation) and relationally (with the effect of gradual conformity to Christ). But here in Romans 4:17 Paul does not even mention transformation or good works. His point here at least is that just as there was nothing for God to work with when he summoned the cosmos into existence, and nothing in Sarah but barrenness when God declared, "Let her be pregnant!" there is no basis in the ungodly themselves for God's verdict, "Let this ungodly person be justified!" Hence, Abraham was justified through faith alone, "fully convinced that God was able to do what he had promised" (v. 21). "But the words 'it was counted to him' were not written for his sake alone, but for ours also. It will be counted to us who believe in him who raised from the dead Jesus our Lord, who was delivered up for our trespasses and raised for our justification" (vv. 23–25). Like many other contemporary Protestant theologians, Pannenberg appears to presuppose a Roman Catholic frame of reference, with its infusions of medicinal grace, while Paul is working with the familiar covenantal concepts of a ruler-judge declaring fiats that change the status of his subjects.

E. P. Sanders says that justification "is a term indicating getting in . . . the body of the saved" or to "transfer to the body of the saved."[49]

---

47. Albert Schweitzer, *The Mysticism of Paul the Apostle* (Baltimore: Johns Hopkins University Press, 1998), 223–25.
48. Wolfhart Pannenberg, *Systematic Theology*, trans. G. W. Bromiley (Grand Rapids: Eerdmans, 2009), 3:223–24.
49. Sanders, *Paul and Palestinian Judaism*, 544.

At least Sanders uses terms like "indicating," "suggesting," and "amounting to" rather than saying something as lexically impossible as *justification means to transfer to the church*. Subsequent new perspective scholarship has not followed such caution. Yet Sanders fails to convince me that justification even has a remote connotation of "to transfer to the body of the saved." It is clearly *related* to ecclesiology via union with Christ, but justification itself says nothing about belonging, getting in, staying in, joining, transferring, or anything else other than "to declare righteous."

Douglas Campbell says that the reference to "life" in Habakkuk 2:4 (quoted by Paul in Romans 1:17 and Galatians 3:11) "seems to require the equation of 'life' and 'justification.'" So now justification is "resurrection."[50] Given the semantic cluster that I have identified with the "great exchange," it is not at all surprising that Paul here would regard justification and life as related benefits. But they are not the same. Death has been mentioned in the immediate context, so it makes sense that life would be its antithesis. The resurrection of Christ brings justification *and* life, as he says elsewhere (Rom 4:25). Peter Leithart says, "*Justification* describes how God fulfills the prophetic promise to set the world right."[51] However, Paul never constructs a sentence in which the object of justification is the world. That Paul *does* promise that God will set the world right I do not doubt for a minute (Acts 17:31; Rom 8:18–24; 1 Cor 15:20–28), but it is strange to place in the background what Paul places explicitly in the foreground and to conclude that what he really means in these instances is something that he uses different words to describe.

God's powerful word has myriad effects. There are many terms for this salvation, not all of them "justification." As Westerholm reminds us, "The terms in Paul's writings are neither synonymous nor interchangeable: sinners are declared righteous (not reconciled), enemies are reconciled (not declared righteous), and so on."[52] Whether justification is assimilated to election (Barth), redemption (Campbell and Leithart), sanctification (Trent), or glorification (Orthodoxy and the new Finnish interpretation of Luther), or these other elements of the *ordo* are assimilated to justification, the result is similar: the *difference that*

50. Campbell, *The Deliverance of God*, 863.
51. Leithart, *Delivered from the Elements of the World*, 169.
52. Westerholm, *Justification Reconsidered*, 11.

justification makes—its decisive role—is lost.[53] Simon Gathercole points out that Paul frequently treats justification as the sum of salvation.[54] "On the other hand, these aspects cannot simply be jumbled up under the general umbrella of justification."[55] As an example of this tendency, he refers to James Dunn's four summary statements concerning the doctrine:

(a) "Justification means acceptance by God, the God who justifies the ungodly who trust as Abraham trusted"; (b) "If justification means God accepting the sinner (5:8), it also means bestowing the blessing of peace on those who were formerly enemies (5:10)"; (c) "Justification by faith means Gentiles experiencing the blessing promised to Abraham, being granted a share in Israel's inheritance"; (d) "Justification means liberty."[56]

But here, Gathercole observes, "Referent and implication are all subsumed under the vaguer verb 'mean.'"[57]

On the other hand, there is the tendency to *minimize* the meaning of justification in Scripture and in Paul especially. For Dunn and Wright, for instance, faith is merely a badge of membership, and justification is a criterion for distinguishing true membership. However, first, Paul does not say anywhere that faith replaces circumcision as a badge, but he does say frequently that faith is the means of being justified rather than "works of the law" (Rom 1:17; 3:22; 4:5, 11, 16; 9:30; 10:6; Gal 2:16; 3:11, 24; Phil 3:9, etc.). Strictly speaking, baptism has replaced circumcision as the sign and seal of membership in God's community (Col 2:12; 6:1–5), and both sacraments are "a seal of the righteousness" that believers have through faith alone (Rom 4:11). The Lord's Supper is the place where the many grains are baked into one loaf, and all participate in Christ's body and blood together so that the church comes to visible expression at his table (1 Cor 10:16–17). For John, love is the chief badge of belonging (John 13:35; 1 John 3:14).

53. See the excellent warnings along this line in Allen, *Justification and the Gospel*, 6–15.

54. Simon Gathercole, "The Doctrine of Justification in Paul and Beyond," in *Justification in Perspective: Historical Developments and Contemporary Challenges*, ed. Bruce L. McCormack (Grand Rapids: Baker Academic, 2006), 230.

55. Gathercole, "The Doctrine of Justification in Paul and Beyond," 231, referring to N. T. Wright, *The Resurrection of the Son of God* (London: SPCK, 2003), 719.

56. Gathercole, "The Doctrine of Justification in Paul and Beyond," 231.

57. Gathercole, "The Doctrine of Justification in Paul and Beyond," 231.

Second, what does it mean to say that *justification* is merely a criterion for distinguishing true disciples? To put it bluntly, in this view justification does not *do* anything. Wright is not entirely consistent on this point, however. He affirms that justification is a verdict ("a *declaration that*") rather than a transformation ("Not 'God's bringing it about that'").[58] However, it is a verdict that something is already the case—namely, that one is a covenant member, not a verdict that actually changes one's status before God. "Justification is not how someone becomes a Christian," Wright emphasizes, but God's declaration about someone who is already a Christian.[59] In justification God declares that the one who has turned from idols to the living God is a member of the covenant. "But Paul does not say that God sees us clothed with the earned merits of Christ."[60]

Despite different routes, both of these tendencies blur the meaning of justification and its distinct role in the application of redemption. Wright insists that he does not reject the intention in the Reformation doctrine of justification. He even says that "one of the great truths of the gospel" is "that the accomplishment of Jesus Christ is *reckoned* to all those who are 'in him.'"

> This is the truth which has been expressed within the Reformed tradition in terms of "imputed righteousness," often stated in terms of Jesus Christ having fulfilled the moral law and thus having accumulated a "righteous" status which can be shared with all his people. As with some other theological problems, I regard this as saying a substantially right thing in a substantially wrong way, and the trouble when you do that is that things on both sides of the equation, and the passages which are invoked to support them, become distorted. . . . The mistake, as I see it, arises from the combination of the Reformers' proper sense of something being accomplished in Christ Jesus which is then reckoned to us, allied with their overemphasis on the category of *iustitia* as the catch-all, their consequent underemphasis on Paul's frequently repeated theology of our participation in the Messiah's death and resurrection,

---

58. N. T. Wright, "New Perspectives on Paul," in *Justification in Perspective: Historical Developments and Contemporary Challenges*, ed. Bruce L. McCormack (Grand Rapids: Baker Academic, 2006), 258.

59. Wright, "New Perspectives on Paul," 260, emphasis added.

60. Wright, "New Perspectives on Paul," 261.

and their failure to locate Paul's soteriology itself on the larger map of God's plan for the whole creation. A proper re-emphasis on "God's righteousness" as God's *own* righteousness should set all this straight.[61]

Wright misunderstands the Reformers' view, as if it had nothing to do with being united to Christ (particularly, sharing in his death and resurrection), when in fact it lies at the heart of their teaching on the subject (see ch. 11). In addition, as I demonstrated in volume 1, the Reformers did certainly locate Paul's soteriology on the larger map of God's plan for the whole creation. Their revolutionary insight, however, was that justification is the declaration that the sinner as sinner is righteous in Christ through faith. Their critics expanded the term to include actual transformation, being a member in good standing (in a state of grace), and a final justification based on one's entire life, thereby conflating justification and sanctification, faith and works, law and gospel. Ironically, Wright's criticism, that the Reformers make justification a catch-all term, is more accurately leveled at his and other new perspective treatments. In any case, I often find it difficult to determine whether for Wright there is after all an imputation of righteousness to believers, even if he prefers not to call it justification.

For those in Käsemann's wake, justification must be liberation, deliverance, and cosmic restoration (rectification)—essentially, Christ's consummation of his kingdom. Martyn's "rectification" and Leithart's "deliverdict" conflate a judicial verdict with its transformative effects much like the Tridentine view, although in a more apocalyptic-cosmic account.

> Justification happens to the whole human race as God condemns sinful flesh and enables humans in flesh to live, as Jesus did, by the Spirit. . . . It happens to the church, and it happens to individuals in the church as they are justified from sin in baptism and raised to live lives of justice, as they keep *nomos* by living according to the *nomos* of the Spirit.[62]

---

61. Quoted in John Piper, *The Future of Justification: A Response to N. T. Wright* (Wheaton, IL: Crossway, 2007), 122, from N. T. Wright, "Paul in Different Perspectives: Lecture 1: Starting Points and Opening Reflections," lecture, Auburn Avenue Presbyterian Church, Monroe, LA, January 3, 2005, http://www.ntwrightpage.com/Wright_Auburn_Paul.htm.
62. Leithart, *Delivered from the Elements of the World*, 188.

In fact, Leithart is convinced (accurately, I think) that his view of justification as *deliverdict* "is reflected in ecumenical documents such as the 'Joint Declaration on the Doctrine of Justification' produced by the Roman Catholic Church and the Lutheran World Federation" and "'The Gift of Salvation,' a statement produced by the American ecumenical group Evangelicals and Catholics Together, which hints at a transformational view of justification."[63]

In short, justification is inflated and minimized, often at the same time. But is it impossible to believe that justification is a purely forensic declaration based on the imputation of Christ's righteous status and *also* to believe that salvation involves more than justification?

DEFINITION TO EXEGESIS

Paul interprets everything from the nature of God, Christology, anthropology, soteriology, ecclesiology, and eschatology in a radically new way because of his perspective of being "in Christ." The apocalyptic school is right to emphasize this point. Yet it overreacts against the emphasis on salvation history shared by traditional Reformed and new perspective approaches. For post-Damascus Paul, the gospel is not like an unread novel; instead, the gospel is like one he thought he knew backwards and forwards but never really understood. He misunderstood because he misidentified the central character and what he had come to do—and therefore the plight. And after Damascus, the whole plot looks different, even though, as his copious Old Testament citations demonstrate, the characters and basic line of development were there to see all along. The Law and the Prophets (i.e., the Old Testament) prophesy that great day when Israel's gates will be opened and gentiles will at last stream to Zion rather than seek its destruction. Had Paul's critics forgotten the promise of a "new covenant" that would fulfill the promise of full pardon and a circumcised heart for gentiles and Jews together as one people through faith alone? Case in point: Abraham.[64]

---

63. Leithart, *Delivered from the Elements of the World*, 181n4.

64. However, Paul insists that he is preaching no new gospel, but the fulfillment of the gospel proclaimed by the Law and the Prophets (Rom 3:21). Richard Hays underscores the unity of the Old and New Testaments especially in relation to Abraham in *Echoes of Scripture in the Letters of Paul* (New Haven, CT: Yale University Press, 1993), 54–55. This is one place where differences appear between Lutheran and Reformed exegesis. While both emphasize the continuity of the covenant of grace in principle, Reformed exegetes would not regard law and gospel as equivalent to Old and New Testaments as Luther seems to have done: "The New Testament, properly

Romans 4

"What shall we say about Abraham?" How Paul answers this question—and we interpret his answer—determines much of what we have to say about the nature of justification. Romans 4 is the lodestar for Paul's transition from plight to solution (recognizing that the former is viewed in the light of the latter). The transition actually begins at 3:21, but it reaches its summit in the argument about Abraham before extrapolating this story of Israel as the "play within a play" of humanity in Romans 5.

The new perspective reads Romans 9–11 into the early chapters. This is understandable. After all, the question "Has God failed to keep his promises to Israel?" not only hovers in the background; it is raised already in 3:3: "What if some were unfaithful? Does their faithlessness nullify the faithfulness of God?" However, Paul himself designed the order of the epistle, and if he had intended to treat the question of postexilic Israel directly in Romans 1–4, he would have done so. The apocalyptic school would like to bring Romans 5–8 into these earlier chapters, or, in Douglas Campbell's case, write off these early chapters altogether as the misanthropic speculations of a false teacher.

Romans 1–4 in fact makes perfect sense as the opening argument to an epistle that centers on the justification of the ungodly. Far from claiming that gentiles attain justification by following natural law,[65] Paul only refers to the civil virtue of gentiles in sometimes following commands of the moral law while the covenant people imitate their vices. The important thing to bear in mind is Paul's conclusion that *no one*, Jew or gentile, is righteous before God. Having established that no one slips through the net of God's judgment, Paul announces the gift of righteousness through faith in Christ (3:21ff) and launches into chapter 4 by challenging the usual Second Temple view of Abraham as having in some sense merited not only his own covenant status but that of Israel as a whole and individual Jews, which can be imputed. According to the Damascus Document 3.2–4, Abraham "was *accounted* a friend of God because he kept the commandments of God," and, given Paul's argument here, his interlocutors must have shared this general—and widespread, according to Mormerstein, Davies, and Sanders—view.

---

speaking, consists of promises and exhortations, just as the Old, properly speaking, consists of laws and threats" (Luther, *The Bondage of the Will*, trans. J. I. Packer and O. R. Johnston [New York: Revell, 1957], 180).

65. As Milbank argues. See the quote in 326n14.

In contrast with this teaching, Paul says that Abraham could not boast before God (Rom 4:2). God justifies those who do not work but trust in him who justifies the ungodly (v. 4). Instead of boasting, Abraham trusted in the God who fulfills his saving promises even though they seem empirically impossible (vv. 18–22). David is another example of someone who, according to the law, should have been executed for his crimes. Instead, he was given a free and full pardon by God apart from any sacrifice or rite (vv. 6–8). Once more, there is a very clear logical progression in this argument: God justifies the wicked apart from works, from the covenant of promise rather than the covenant of law. Therefore, it is by grace *and* comes to gentiles as well as Jews (vv. 9–12), and all of the glory goes to God alone (v. 20). If Paul is not appealing to Abraham for an account of how people are saved, then why does he buttress it with a reference to David being forgiven of his sins?

Markus Bockmuehl has discovered one early rabbinic commentary on Exodus 14:31 "that according to Genesis 15:6 'our father Abraham inherited this world and the world to come only by virtue of his faith in the Lord.'"[66]

> Taken at face value, however, Paul's argument does certainly run dangerously close to denying what most Jews in the first century would have believed about Abraham—and what, we may presume, most of the Jerusalem church may well have believed. At least in that sense Protestant commentators are perhaps not far from the mark when they see Paul agitated by the Jewish Christian suggestion that full incorporation into the promise of Abraham required emulating his Torah observance as well as his faith.[67]

The Qumran author substantiates this reading when, as Bockmuehl suggests, he suggests that the rival priestly authorities "observe his interpretation of 'a few of the works of Torah' so that this may be 'reckoned to you as righteousness'—a position that would appear to be pretty clearly counter to what Paul has in mind here."[68]

66. Markus Bockmuehl, "Aquinas on Abraham's Faith in Romans 4," in *Reading Romans with St. Thomas Aquinas*, ed. Matthew Levering and Michael Dauphinais (Washington, DC: Catholic University of America Press, 2012), 41.

67. Bockmuehl, "Aquinas on Abraham's Faith in Romans 4," 41–42, referring to 4QMMT C 27, 31 (4Q398 ii:2–3, 7).

68. Bockmuehl, "Aquinas on Abraham's Faith in Romans 4," 41–42.

Surely any reasonably informed Jew would know that Abraham was justified before he was circumcised, but Paul builds an argument on it. What would make Paul's statement implausible to a first-century Jew? That they no longer had to be circumcised in order to belong to God's people? This would certainly be a reasonable inference, and a bold one. But the only way that Paul's use of the example of Abraham could have been radical and jarring is the claim that God would declare someone to be righteous through faith even at the moment that he or she is inherently unrighteous. Bockmuehl himself seems to draw this conclusion: "Paul's expansion of the principle here perhaps reflects Jesus's attitude that he came not for the righteous but for sinners (Mt 9:13). God justifies even the ungodly; that paradox shows how powerfully and exclusively it is grace that is at work."[69] Furthermore, that he brings David into the scene underscores the fact that Paul is talking about the remission of sins and not merely how one knows who belongs to the community.

The traditional Protestant reading of Romans 4 is substantiated by other references. As Westerholm notes, "That Christ *is* 'our righteousness,' as 1 Corinthians 1:30 declares, makes the point in the most succinct way possible." "The verb 'to justify' is used in 1 Corinthians 6:11, in a context where those said to be 'justified' (or 'declared righteous') are explicitly the 'unrighteous.'"[70] This is on the heels of warning that "the unrighteous will not inherit the kingdom of God" (v. 9). "And such were some of you," Paul continues. "But you were washed, but you were sanctified, but you were *justified* in the name of the Lord Jesus Christ and by the Spirit of our God" (v. 11).[71] In 2 Corinthians 5:19–20, God's act of "reconciling the world to himself" is equivalent to "not counting their offenses against them," just as in Romans 5:10: "When we were enemies, we were reconciled to God through the death of his Son." Christ became sin so that we may become the righteousness of God (2 Cor 5:21).

We still must wrestle with the mechanism for this (viz., infusion, imputation, or something else), but it is clear that *something* is being transferred from the believer to Christ (viz., the wages of sin) and from Christ to the believer (a status of righteousness). If so, then in Paul's

---

69. Bockmuehl, "Aquinas on Abraham's Faith in Romans 4," 43–44.
70. Westerholm, *Justification Reconsidered*, 9.
71. Westerholm, *Justification Reconsidered*, 9.

argument the *ordo salutis* (application of redemption) remains as important as the *historia salutis* (accomplishment of redemption); how we are saved is as essential as how we know who belongs. In fact, soteriology is the ground of ecclesiology.

Romans 4 and the New Perspective

Given the significance of Romans 4 for this question, it is disappointing when Wright reduces it to a footnote in Paul's argument: "Yes, Paul does then develop a very brief book-keeping metaphor in verse 4 . . . but this embroidery carries no weight in the passage as a whole."[72] The bookkeeping metaphor can be so easily dismissed only if one has decided in advance that Paul's narrative is about renewing the vocation given to Adam and Eve and then to Abraham, which has been temporarily derailed by the exile—that it is not about soteriology but ecclesiology. But Romans 4 is not Romans 9–11, and the argument here must be allowed to have its own integrity.

Against the notion of the merit of Abraham, Paul is saying that it is Christ's merits that are imputed to believers. To receive Christ's righteousness is to inherit a reward won by someone else, in contrast to working for a salary. It is understandable that this crucial argument is considered either irrelevant or even an obstacle to the new perspective. It demonstrates that Paul is contrasting a relationship of an employer to an employee—the vassal-suzerain relationship of the Sinai covenant—to a saving justification of individuals before God. As I have argued, faithful Israelites did not make this mistake; they realized that their only hope for personal salvation was always the covenant of promise. For them, circumcision was the sign and seal of their justification, not of their oath, "All this we will do." Circumcision anticipated the new covenant when a new heart and forgiveness would be granted by God's free grace. For these saints, the sacrifices did not themselves atone but directed their faith to the one who would accomplish their redemption. But Paul's interlocutors have assimilated that covenant of promise to the national covenant and its terms, "do this, and you will live." Therefore, the bookkeeping metaphor is essential to the main argument of the Epistle to the Romans. They are living as slaves, not sons as he had argued in Galatians 3 and 4.

---

72. N. T. Wright, "Paul and the Patriarch: The Role of Abraham in Romans 4," *JSNT* 35 (2013): 216.

The basic problem, as Paul sees it in Romans 4 and elsewhere, is that the Jews and Jewish Christians he has in mind have turned justification into a prize that is "their due" (Rom 4:4; "according to debt," κατὰ ὀφείλημα). It is not only that they are excluding gentiles but that they think that they have in fact kept the law and should be repaid. But it seems like God is ignoring his obligations, and instead of rewarding their covenant faithfulness is turning to the gentiles. Romans 9–11 is anticipated here, but that passage is subservient to the argument in Romans 4, not vice versa. If justification is by grace alone, on the basis of Christ's imputed righteousness alone, received through faith alone, then the Abrahamic promise can encompass both unfaithful Jews and the godless gentiles who place their faith in Christ (Rom 4:11–17). That is why Abraham is an example, not by his putatively meritorious obedience but because as a sinner—even as a gentile (before circumcision)—he was justified through faith alone (vv. 23–24).

According to Wright, faith is not how one is "saved," but "is the badge of the sin-forgiven family."[73] Consequently, "The emphasis of the chapter [Rom 4] is therefore that covenant membership is defined, not by circumcision (4:9–12), nor by race, but by faith."[74] However, this faith is now also redefined as faithfulness—our covenantal obedience, which is the basis for final justification.[75] Crucially absent from Wright's list is Paul's clause, "nor by works," or the apostle's statement that this justification comes to the one (notice the individual-personal reference) "who *does not work* but *trusts in the one who justifies the ungodly*" (v. 5). Paul contrasts working and trusting, not circumcision and Spirit-led obedience. Wright's claim is tantamount to saying that we are justified by some works (our covenant faithfulness) but not by others (ethnic purity). This takes us back to Origen and the Council of Trent (see my previous volume).

David Shaw notes that Wright caricatures the traditional reading of Romans 4, which Wright himself held in his Romans commentary:

---

73. For a good critique of Wright's argument on this point, see Mark A. Seifrid, *Christ, Our Righteousness: Paul's Theology of Justification* (Downers Grove, IL: IVP Academic, 2001), 176n13.

74. Wright, *What Saint Paul Really Said*, 129.

75. Wright, *What Saint Paul Really Said*, 160. See also Shaw, "Romans 4 and the Justification of Abraham," 56n32. Shaw notes, "One might have thought he would have taken more care not to caricature a view that *he himself once held*. See e.g. Wright, *Justification*, 193: 'Yes, of course he is arguing that Abraham was ungodly when God called him, and that it was his faith in 'the one who justifies the ungodly' . . . that simply clung on to the promise despite that ungodliness.' Clearly Wright once took a more traditional line in Romans 4 but now that reading is caricatured in order to push the reader toward his new interpretation."

"One may summarize this view point by saying that Abraham is justified because he believes in justification by faith."[76] Instead, Wright insists, the reward is a worldwide family. He argues that Abraham did not believe in his own justification but in "the God who has made this promise to him about his 'ungodly' descendants." Thus, "God reckoned this in terms of covenant membership."[77] Shaw judges, "The irony alluded to a moment ago is that while the opposing view of Rom 4 is caricatured as justification by believing in justification by faith, Wright's view of Abraham's justification is that he was justified for believing in someone else's justification by faith (namely, his future Gentile children)!"[78]

Over against Wright's interpretation, Shaw observes, "As many commentators note, God is here said to do what he forbids judges to do" (Isa 5:23; Prov 17:15; Exod 23:7). It is "farfetched to say that the justification of the ungodly in Rom 4 is a reference to the inclusion of Gentiles." On the contrary, "The clear context of the phrase is of the forensic acquittal of the guilty. To justify the ungodly in Isaiah and Proverbs and Exodus is not to extend the boundaries of the covenant community but to allow an injustice to occur within it."[79] He adds,

> That his faith becomes the model for us in these respects tells strongly against N. T. Wright's proposal. In Rom 4 Abraham and David do not stand on the solid rock of their own covenant membership and look beyond themselves to anticipate the granting of the same for Gentiles. Rather, they regard their own footing as far from secure, casting themselves on the God who, in the absence of works and the presence of sin, answers with forgiveness and justification. And those are the blessings under discussion in Rom 4.[80]

Also, in Luke's version of the Great Commission, the content of the gospel is forgiveness, not extension of covenant membership.[81] "If Wright's earlier reading is correct, as I believe it is, his more recent exegesis has it backwards. Abraham is not justified for believing a promise

---

76. Shaw, "Romans 4 and the Justification of Abraham," 56.

77. Wright, "Paul and the Patriarch," 219, quoted in Shaw, "Romans 4 and the Justification of Abraham," 57.

78. Shaw, "Romans 4 and the Justification of Abraham," 57.

79. Shaw, "Romans 4 and the Justification of Abraham," 58.

80. Shaw, "Romans 4 and the Justification of Abraham," 60.

81. Shaw, "Romans 4 and the Justification of Abraham," 60n47.

about someone else. He is justified for believing that God can do the impossible for him."[82]

The central assumption in Wright's argument is that Romans 4 has nothing to do with "how one gets saved."[83] This rests on deeper assumptions: the Cremer thesis concerning God's righteousness and covenant faithfulness, along with the new perspective dichotomy between ecclesiology and soteriology. Consequently, Wright interprets Genesis 15:6 as "God counted Abraham's faith as constituting covenant membership."[84] Only with these pieces in place, he regularly insists, can we understand what Paul is saying. However, besides assuming a series of contestable moves, this interpretation ignores the clearly soteriological import of the whole argument as irrelevant "embroidery."

First, Abraham cannot be a member of the covenant that Israel swore at Sinai. In fact, this is a large part of Paul's thesis: that the patriarch was never under the Sinai covenant, since it came more than three centuries later (see Gal 3:17), which is why he is also an example of gentile inclusion.

Second, even if Wright were correct about Paul's point regarding Abraham, why is the nonimputation of David's transgressions now a part of the argument? Is he not *saved* by this merciful forgiveness of his crimes? Wright's view also fails to reckon with the fact that even the rabbis were talking about "how one is saved" when they treated justification-related matters. Key strands of Second Temple Judaism and Paul could not disagree more over the role of Abraham in the story of the people of God. But the disagreement could only arise because they shared some basic assumptions about the story line. For Paul's Jewish contemporaries, there was hardly a barrier between soteriology and ecclesiology: many Jews were relying on Abraham's merits *for personal salvation* from God's judgment (see ch. 8). In spite of the "warts and all" description of Abraham in Genesis, Second Temple texts unanimously assign meritorious status to his obedience (along with that of Isaac and Jacob, no less).[85] It is confirmed by Mariam J. Kamell's analysis of Sirach (i.e., Ecclesiasticus), which was composed shortly before Maccabean Revolt in 167 BC:

---

82. Shaw, "Romans 4 and the Justification of Abraham," 61.
83. Gathercole, "The Doctrine of Justification in Paul and Beyond," 236.
84. N. T. Wright, *Romans*, in *The New Interpreter's Bible*, vol. 10, *Acts, Romans, 1 Corinthians* (Nashville: Abingdon, 2002), 491.
85. Even E. P. Sanders documents this amply in *Paul and Palestinian Judaism*, 87–88.

In Sirach, Abraham's faithfulness is at the center: he was faithful to the law in all ways—most particularly through his circumcision and his willingness to sacrifice his son—and, as a result, God blessed him. Included among the heroes, Abraham illustrates the point with which the entire book of Sirach concludes: "Do your *work* with integrity and he will give you your *wages* in his time" (Sir 51:30, italics added). Ben Sira's reading is not unique: "Judaism insisted that Abraham's faith as referred to in Gen 15:6 must always be coupled with Abraham's acceptance of circumcision in the covenant of Gen 17:4–14, so that the two matters of believing and keeping the covenant must be constantly brought together when one speaks of the righteousness of Abraham."[86]

It is no wonder that Paul contrasts justification through faith with justification through the law in terms of earning a wage and receiving a gift. The dichotomy is not *some works* (ceremonies) versus *other works* (obedience to the moral commands) but between working and believing, earning and receiving.

And, as usual in programs that teach salvation as the reward for one's own obedience, the bar of what the law actually requires must be lowered. How righteous do you have to be? There is no single rabbinical teaching on this point. "The righteous person is not necessarily perfect: as *m. 'Abot* 3:16 puts it: 'all is according to the *majority* of works.'" Yet, another source says (similar to James 2:10) that a disobedience to a single command disinherits (m. Qidd. 1:10).[87] According to m. 'Abot 4:11, "Repentance and good deeds are a shield against retribution." In fact, "May my death be an expiation for all my iniquities' (*m. Sanh.* 6:2)."[88] Philip Alexander summarizes, "This idea persisted into Tannaitic thought: 'For light transgressions, whether of commission or omission,

86. Mariam J. Kamell, "Sirach and Romans 4:1–25: The Faith of Abraham," in *Reading Romans in Context: Paul and Second Temple Judaism*, ed. Ben C. Blackwell, John K. Goodrich, and Jason Maston (Grand Rapids: Zondervan, 2015), 59, quoting Richard N. Longenecker, "The 'Faith of Abraham' Theme in Paul, James and Hebrews: A Study in the Circumstantial Nature of New Testament Teaching," *Journal of the Evangelical Theological Society* 20 (1977): 205.

87. Quoted in Philip S. Alexander, "Torah and Salvation in Tannaitic Literature," *Justification and Variegated Nomism*, vol. 1, *The Complexities of Second Temple Judaism*, ed. D. A. Carson, Peter T. O'Brien, and Mark A. Seifrid, WUNT 2/140 (Grand Rapids: Baker Academic, 2001), 284.

88. Quoted in Alexander, "Torah and Salvation in Tannaitic Literature," 287. Bruce W. Longenecker, *Eschatology and the Covenant: A Comparison of 4 Ezra and Romans 1–11*, Journal for the Study of the New Testament Supplemental Series 57 (Sheffiled: Sheffield Academic, 1991); and Longenecker, *2 Esdras*, Guides to the Apocrypha and Pseudepigrapha (Sheffield: Sheffield Academic, 1995).

repentance atones; for the serious transgressions repentance holds the matter in suspense until the Day of Atonement comes and brings expiation' (*m. Yoma* 8:8)."[89]

It is little wonder if someone who took the rabbinical teaching seriously, with all of its quite radically diverse answers to the most urgent question, "How can I be saved?" simply despaired of having any doctrinal or existential assurance on the matter. But the main point to bear in mind is that the question of earning enough merits by one's good works to gain eternal life was a very deep concern in Second Temple Judaism. A straightforward (and traditional) reading of Romans 4 can be confirmed, then, by the fact that the passage takes radically different positions on questions that were familiar to Jewish and Jewish-Christian readers. This would have been a direct rejection of these rabbinical teachings. But if the new perspective's interpretation is accepted, then both Paul and the rabbis were missing the point.

Wright has already determined, by his exegesis of Romans 1:17, what the rest of Paul's argument could be. Interpreting "the righteousness of / from God" (*dikaiosynē gar theou*) as a subjective genitive, Wright paraphrases Romans 1:17: "The gospel, he says, reveals or unveils God's own righteousness, his covenant faithfulness, which operates through the faithfulness of Jesus Christ for the benefit of all those who in turn are faithful ('from faith to faith')."[90] However, does this make adequate sense of the rest of the verse: "As it is written, 'The one who is righteous will live by faith'"?

Paul's citation of Habakkuk 2:4 refers to the human partner in the covenant rather than to God. It seems more consistent with Paul's wider argument in Romans 1–3 to say, in agreement with Luther, that the law reveals God's essential righteousness (his justice that condemns us),

---

89. Quoted in Alexander, "Torah and Salvation in Tannaitic Literature," 288.

90. Wright, *What Saint Paul Really Said*, 109. Related to this debate over the righteousness of God is the question of whether "faith in Christ" should also be given the subjective genitive construction (as "the faith of Christ"). This does not seem to make sense of the ordinary way Paul describes the relation of faith and justification, however. For example, Paul speaks of "the righteousness of God through faith in Jesus Christ for all who believe" (Rom 3:22); the last clause repeats the same idea as the middle (*dia pisteōs Iesou Christou*) and in verse 25 adds that his propitiatory death is "to be received by faith." This debate is beyond our scope here, but for a defense of the subjective genitive construction, see Bruce W. Longenecker, "Contours of Covenant Theology in the Post-Conversion Paul," in *The Road from Damascus: The Impact of Paul's Conversion on His Life, Thought, and Ministry*, ed. Richard N. Longenecker (Grand Rapids: Eerdmans, 1997), 133; cf. Richard Hays, *The Faith of Jesus Christ: An Investigation of the Narrative Substructure of Galatians 3:1–4:11* (Chico: Scholars' Press, 1983); Hays, "Justification," in *The Anchor Bible Dictionary*, ed. D. N. Freedman et al. (New York: Doubleday, 1992), 268–90.

while the gospel reveals God's gift of righteousness that saves us. After establishing the point that everyone, Jew and gentile, is condemned by the law and will never be justified by it because of their sin, Paul adds, "But now, apart from law, the righteousness of God has been disclosed, and it is attested by the law and the prophets, the righteousness of God through faith in Jesus Christ for all who believe." They are "now justified by his grace as a gift, through the redemption that is in Christ Jesus, whom God put forward as a propitiation by his blood, effective through faith" (Rom 3:21–25). God indeed reveals his covenant faithfulness, but by itself this is not good news—unless God reveals that the righteousness he is and requires by his law has been *given to us* as a *gift* in Jesus Christ.

Reformation exegesis distinguished the essential righteousness of God (which condemns all) from the gift of righteousness from God (which justifies everyone who believes). In fact, Luther's "breakthrough" occurred when he recognized this distinction in Romans 1–3. So Wright's repeated assertion that in the Reformation view, God's essential righteousness is transferred to the believer demonstrates a significant misunderstanding in his polemic. The only figure who taught that was Andreas Osiander, and it was rejected by Lutheran and Reformed theologians alike. Whereas the Reformation interpretation recognizes that Paul speaks of the righteousness of God as his essential justice and faithfulness to the covenant (which, obviously, he cannot give anyone) *and* as the gift of righteousness (i.e., God as "just and the justifier of those who have faith in Christ Jesus"), Wright reduces all references to the former. Yet the dialectical play between these two— just (the righteousness that God *is*) and justifier (the righteousness that God *gives*)—lies at the heart of Paul's argument in Romans 1–3.

It makes little sense, especially in the sweep of Paul's argument, to say that *God's* covenant faithfulness is disclosed through *our faith* in Christ. Rather, Paul begins, God's righteousness is disclosed first in his wrath (Rom 1:18–3:20) but then also in his grace (3:21ff.). God's righteousness as revealed by the law—"so that every mouth may be silenced, and the whole world may be held accountable to God" (3:19)—differs from God's righteousness that is revealed in the gospel "apart from law" through faith in Christ (v. 21). The law reveals that God is just (and therefore must condemn all transgressors), but the gospel reveals that God is just and justifier (v. 26).

The closest that Wright comes to allowing for justification as a gift of right-standing given to individuals is in the statement that believers "are declared, in the present, to be what they will be seen to be in the future, namely the true people of God." But then he adds immediately, "Present justification declares, on the basis of faith, what future justification will affirm publicly (according to 2:14–16 and 8:9–11) *on the basis of the entire life.*"[91] We meet the traditional Roman Catholic distinction between present and future justification, as well as the claim that final justification depends on the believer's works. For Paul the verdict of the last day has already been rendered in favor of those who have faith in Christ—through faith alone—yet according to Wright, this future verdict is merely anticipated in faith but on the basis of the believer's faithfulness.

As we have seen above, Wright emphatically opposes any notion of justification involving God's moral judgment. This is part of a long history of Protestant exegesis that opposes relationship to moral norm. But if it is simply a declaration of the court, apart from any regard for a moral norm, then is not justification a "legal fiction" indeed? Wright properly recognizes that when Paul says that God "justifies the ungodly" (Rom 4:5), "ungodly" means the same thing as it does in the Greek translation of Deuteronomy 25:1, Exodus 23:7, and Isaiah 5:23, "for the guilty whom judges are *not* to 'justify.'" "The apostle is using language of 'righteousness' *in ordinary ways* to speak of the extraordinary divine answer to the human predicament, here stated in terms of universal human culpability before God."[92] But how can God justify according to his righteousness without moral warrant for his judgment? Would that not make God the unjust judge warned against in those very passages?

Justification clearly refers to conformity to a moral norm, which should not be opposed to the divine-human relationship but considered essential to it. Paul asks in Romans 8:33, "Who shall bring any charge against God's elect? It is God who justifies. Who is to condemn?" "Justifies" here is sandwiched between two legal terms: charge and condemn. When God is justifying someone, no charge can be brought against him or her. The result is peace with God. There is simply no room here for "identified as a member of the covenant" as the *meaning*

---

91. Wright, *What Saint Paul Really Said*, 129, emphasis added.
92. Westerholm, *Justification Reconsidered*, 67.

of this action. While Paul certainly believes that justification *entitles* one "to sit at the family table," justification never *means* "table fellowship" in Paul's letters or anywhere else in the Bible.

ROMANS 4 AND THE APOCALYPTIC SCHOOL

Where the promise of a worldwide family of Abraham is crucial to both Reformation and new perspectives, for Käsemann's followers, the patriarch plays a minimal role given the absolute novum of the Christ-event. To be sure, faith is an epoch that arrives. "Now before faith came, we were held captive under the law, imprisoned until the *coming faith* would be *revealed*" (Gal 3:23). However, Jesus arrived "in the fullness of time" (Gal 4:4–5). Israel's pangs in giving birth to the Messiah are integral to the identity of the Christ himself. If apocalyptic means "the end of *Heilsgeschichte*" (history of salvation), with faith appearing for the first time with the advent of Christ, then Abraham could hardly have been "the father of all who believe" (Rom 4:16; cf. Gal 3:7, 14, 16).[93] Indeed, the promise was first announced to Adam and Eve, and Abel begins Hebrews 11's list of those who trusted in Christ (Heb 11:4).

First, Martyn, Campbell, and Leithart insist that the gospel reveals sin, since the solution always reveals the plight; everything, including Israel's history, becomes submerged in the utter novelty and uniqueness of Christ's advent.[94] The revelation of the wrath of God is "gospel," Peter Leithart argues. In fact, the *law* is the revelation of God's saving deliverance. "Luther to the contrary, Paul follows the Psalms and Prophets in viewing God's punitive justice to be *good* news."[95] This claim (made repeatedly through his book) is odd simply on exegetical grounds. Paul never refers to God's punitive judgment as good news, but everywhere identifies the revelation of God's wrath with the law and the revelation of the gift with the gospel. I am sure that we could

---

93. Quotation from J. Louis Martyn, "Events in Galatia: Modified Covenantal Nomism versus God's Invasion of the Cosmos in the Singular Gospel: A Response to J. D. G. Dunn and B. R. Gaventa," in *Pauline Theology*, vol. 1, ed. J. M. Bassler (Minneapolis: Augsburg Fortress, 1991), 174.

94. Campbell in fact acknowledges as much in *The Deliverance of God*, 1118n68: "That is, 'the salvation of God,' or 'the redemption of God.' At this point my recommendations overlap with an insightful study, Peter Leithart, 'Justification as Verdict and Deliverance: A Biblical Perspective,' *Pro Ecclesia* 16 (2007): 56–72." In my estimation, Leithart's *Delivered from the Elements of the World* is the coherent and genuinely "apocalyptic" narrative that is missing from *The Deliverance of God*. However, the latter not only acknowledges but emphasizes the wrath of God as essential—as part of the gospel, in fact. "God the Judge condemns by destroying the guilty and justifies by delivering the righteous," Leithart says. Leithart, *Delivered from the Elements of the World*, 169.

95. Leithart, *Delivered from the Elements of the World*, 334.

find passages (especially in Revelation) that see the cleansing of God's kingdom from all that corrupts as good news, but it is not *the* good news that Paul proclaims in these passages. This is simply not how the law works in Paul's arguments.

Second, according to this perspective, Romans 4 cannot be relating Abraham's being credited and righteousness before God since righteousness only becomes available with the cross and resurrection of Christ, "and we participate in that historical deliverdict, die to sin and rise to life, as we are united to Christ in baptism and faith."[96] In fact, Leithart conjectures that Abraham "did not enjoy the blessing of justification, and that because justification was not yet *available* to be enjoyed."[97] So Abraham was apparently a godly but uncircumcised man who was not yet justified because justification was not yet obtainable. If Leithart's thesis had any plausibility, then Paul's argument not only has to be revised significantly to make that point, it actually has no historical grounding. The *ordo salutis*, including justification, is swallowed whole by the *historia salutis*, and Abraham is excluded from any argument for the justification of the ungodly since he was never justified! "Christ's liberating redemption," he says, is not "the *ground* or *basis* of an act of justification that takes place at a later time," but the act of justification itself.[98] Consequently, Leithart misses Paul's use of Abraham in Romans 4. "It would be best to abandon the attempt to force Abram into the *ordo* paradigm," he says. In fact, "Given the context of Gen 15, it seems very odd to describe Abraham as 'ungodly.' He has left his home and his father's house in obedience to Yahweh's promise; he has been establishing altars throughout the land. How exactly is he ungodly?"[99]

But Leithart is arguing with the apostle at this point, since Abraham is Paul's "exhibit A" of "one who does not work but believes in him who justifies the ungodly" (Rom 4:5). Furthermore, David's "lawless deeds" are not "counted" because of this merciful justification (vv. 6–8). So Paul is clearly appealing to two central, and highly revered, figures in Israel's history to demonstrate that no one can be justified by works (and in neither case can this refer to ceremonies) but only through faith in Christ. It is ironic that many Protestant scholars today are as eager as

---

96. Leithart, *Delivered from the Elements of the World*, 333.
97. Leithart, *Delivered from the Elements of the World*, 341n21.
98. Leithart, *Delivered from the Elements of the World*, 335.
99. Leithart, *Delivered from the Elements of the World*, 341n21.

Paul's critics to defend these great exemplars of faith from taint of sin. But the whole argument depends on the fact that Abraham was ungodly.

Leithart is not alone in wondering how one could consider Abraham ungodly. Bockhmuehl says, "And it is perhaps only the polemical context of Romans 4 that causes Paul conveniently to sidestep Scripture's own statement in Genesis 26:5 that 'Abraham obeyed my voice and kept my charge, my commandments, my statutes and my laws' (using both the resonant Hebrew words *mitzvah* and *torah*)."[100] If by "ungodly" Käsemann interprets Abraham as a "scoundrel," Bockmuehl takes the opposite view. "Abraham was not in any obvious sense ungodly; nor of course, despite scholarly claims to the contrary, does this passage make Paul say so," Bockmuehl insists.[101] At this point, he appeals to the new perspective contention emphasized by Sanders that good works are necessary not for getting but "to *maintain* the covenant—the point where the Torah was the key to life."[102] Yet he allows that it is difficult to verify this clear distinction between entering and maintaining, especially since Friedrich Avemarie's *Tora und Leben*. Regardless, "The notion that God justifies the *ungodly* is indeed a radical and jarring idea, and might well be unwelcome in a Jewish context."[103]

However, both Käsemann and Bockmuehl fail to see how Abraham's ungodliness works in the argument. It would frustrate Paul's soteriology to suggest that Abraham was *not* obedient, since faith produces obedience, but Bockmuehl is quoting a verse that comes eleven chapters after the declaration that Abraham believed and was justified (Gen 15:6). Already in chapter 17, Abraham has the males of his entire household circumcised according to God's command (vv. 22–27). Following this story closely, Paul is simply saying that Abraham's subsequent obedience was the effect rather than the cause of his justification. Regardless of whether rabbinical tradition more generally had assimilated circumcision to the Sinai covenant (which seems likely), Paul's critics had certainly done so. Or so I have argued in previous chapters.

Placing Abraham in the category of "ungodly" along with the rest of us was only radical and jarring because Paul's critics could not imagine

---

100. Bockmuehl, "Aquinas on Abraham's Faith in Romans 4," 41–42.
101. Bockmuehl, "Aquinas on Abraham's Faith in Romans 4," 43.
102. Bockmuehl, "Aquinas on Abraham's Faith in Romans 4," 43.
103. Bockmuehl, "Aquinas on Abraham's Faith in Romans 4," 43, citing Friedrich Avemarie, *Tora und Leben: Untersuchungen zur Heilsbedeutung der Tora in der frühen rabbinischen Literatur*, Texte und Studien zum antiken Judentum 55 (Tübingen: Mohr Siebeck, 1996).

the patriarch to have been justified apart from works. After all, according to the Jewish interpretation of the day, Abraham had merited God's covenant faithfulness not only for himself but for the nation and for individual Israelites. From the Genesis narrative itself, it is evident that Abraham was not always faithful. Lying to a king about Sarah being his sister to get out of a difficult spot and trying to achieve a son by Hagar in spite of God's promise are hardly exemplary moments. Yet it is noteworthy that Paul never mentions these episodes. He hardly represents Abraham as a "scoundrel"; in fact, he praises his unwavering faith. The point is not whether the patriarch was on balance a "good person" but that he was in the same boat as the rest of humanity: a sinner needing to be justified. He is only "ungodly" from the perspective of (a) justification before God (no right to boast; Rom 4:2) and (b) Torah. The patriarch was justified while uncircumcised four hundred and thirty years before Sinai. And circumcision was a sign and seal of the covenant of grace, not of the Sinai covenant. Bockmuehl insightfully points out that not even "a few of the works of Torah" can play a role in justification according to Paul. "That is indeed a radically new statement for a first-century Jewish audience."[104]

It seems strange that Romans 4 typically plays a small role in new perspective and apocalyptic treatments of justification and Paul's theology. After all, there is hardly any event more apocalyptic than the justification of the ungodly. It is odd also for the new perspective, given the proper importance that it gives (especially in Wright's version) to the narrative of Abraham's worldwide family. That narrative does indeed lie at the heart of Romans 4, but gentile inclusion is grounded in the deeper solution to the plight of all human beings. Only because of justification is there a worldwide family. Abraham is Paul's example of one who was justified through faith not only apart from circumcision but apart from anything by which he might boast before God. "But the words 'it was counted to him' were not written for his sake alone, but for ours also. [Righteousness] will be counted to us who believe in him who raised from the dead Jesus our Lord, who was delivered up for our trespasses and raised for our justification" (Rom 4:23–25). What Paul means by this "counting to us" is the subject of our next chapter.

---

104. Bockmuehl, "Aquinas on Abraham's Faith in Romans 4," 42, referring to Ernst Käsemann, *Commentary on Romans* (London: SCM, 1980), 111–12.

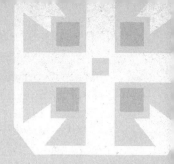

CHAPTER 8

IMPUTATION

The Mechanism of Justification

If we are "justified by his blood" (Rom 5:9), and Jesus was "delivered up for our sins and was raised for our justification" (Rom 4:25), then how do we now receive the benefits of this accomplishment? Paul answers, "Therefore, since we have been justified by faith, we have peace with God through our Lord Jesus Christ" (Rom 5:1). Faith therefore links us to Christ with all of his benefits, including justification. This chapter focuses, then, on *how* we are justified.

I proceed, first, by introducing Second Temple Jewish teaching on merit and imputation, demonstrating that these concepts are not interpolations of sixteenth-century debates into New Testament interpretation. Second, I briefly set the doctrine in the context of that Reformation debate (as I did more fully in vol. 1). Third, I interact at greater length with contemporary exegetical challenges to the Reformation view.

IMPUTATION: DEFINITION AND DEFENSE

Is imputation in fact a biblical concept, or is it an unnecessary and untenable appendage that distracts us from Paul's teaching on justification? Does imputation render justification a "legal fiction" or does it in fact save justification from that charge? Having been oppressed by failing to merit God's favor, we are told that Luther merely shifted the locus of merit from himself (and Mary and the saints) to Christ in the doctrine of imputed righteousness. At least since Ritschl, this narrative has been repeated in numerous and otherwise learned tomes.[1] However, this is far from the case.

Merit and Imputation in Ancient Judaism

Nowhere is the inextricability of ecclesiology and soteriology clearer than in the Jewish doctrine of merit. It is just this concept that we are told is the imposition of medieval categories onto Paul. Besides the sacrificial system, in which guilt was imputed symbolically to the animal, the concept of imputation was well-known in ancient Judaism. The doctrine of the merits of the fathers (*Zekut Abot*), based on the assumption of covenant solidarity, taught that not only one's own merits but the merits of others (especially Abraham) could be credited to contemporary individuals as well as to the nation.

This doctrine of the merit of the fathers, which is found in many places in the Mishnah (oral Torah) was fully elaborated in recent times by Solomon Schechter (1909) and Arthur Marmorstein (1920).[2] According to Marmorstein, "These sages taught, with few exceptions, that one is able to acquire merits before God." He observes that this is quite different from the views of the church fathers who believed, following Paul, that "man is justified by faith alone, without works of the law (Rom 3.28)."[3] Such merits, the rabbis believed,

> benefit not merely themselves, but also their posterity, their fellow-creatures, their ancestry, their whole generation, not merely during their life, but even after their departure from the land of the living. Even in the hereafter their merits protect and heal others. Judaism further teaches, as a supplement to the doctrine of *imputed merits*, the law of *imputed sin*. . . . This is nothing else but *the law of the solidarity of mankind*, of the brotherhood of all peoples and nations.[4]

Notice that Marmorstein calls this the "law of the solidarity of *mankind*," not just of Israel. It is this idea that classic Reformed theology affirms with the covenant of creation. With "the law of imputed sin"

---

1. Most recently, it is repeated in N. T. Wright, *The Day the Revolution Began: Reconsidering the Meaning of Jesus' Crucifixion* (New York: HarperOne, 2016), 27–31.
2. Solomon Schechter, *Some Aspects of Rabbinic Theology* (London: 1909; Berkeley: University of California Libraries, 1909), digital edition; Arthur Marmorstein, *The Doctrine of Merits in the Old Rabbinical Literature*, Jewish College Publication 7 (London: Jews' College, 1920).
3. Marmorstein, *The Doctrine of Merits*, 2.
4. Marmorstein, *The Doctrine of Merits*, 4, emphasis added.

we have original sin, and with "the doctrine of imputed merits" we find the category for justification (at least in principle) in the ancient Jewish texts.

After reviewing various debates between the rabbis as to the question, "What merit did the Israelites possess that God divided the sea before them?" W. D. Davies concludes that "there were many in Israel who were tempted to rely on the merit of their father Abraham for their salvation."[5] As great as the sacrifices were, even Moses "ran and relied on the merits of the Fathers."[6] Reacting against the apparent laxity of resting in Abraham's imputed merits, "many Rabbis," says Davies, "only recognized the value of self-acquired merits, as did Abtalion." "Hillel tried to take up a mediating position, which is, possibly, expressed for us in the famous saying: 'If I am not for myself, who is then for me? And if I am for myself what am I?'"[7] (This forms an intriguing antithesis to Paul's "If God is for us, who can be against us?" [Rom 8:31].)

In any case, Davies says that after AD 70, the general tendency was understandably to look to the merits of the faithful in the past as the hope for the present and future. But there was still a place for contemporaries to merit, as in the "rather boastful words of R. Simeon b. Yohai (A.D. 140–64): 'If Abraham likes to justify [by his merits] all people from his time up to my time, my merits will justify them from now up to the time of the Messiah, if not I join with Achiah, ha-shîlônî, and we will justify by our merits all creatures from Abraham up to the time of the Messiah.'"[8] With the Maccabean period, heroic martyrs could atone for Israel, and their righteousness could be imputed to the nation.[9] In Pisikta 8 (184, 319, and 325) the merit of the fathers may be expected to aid considerably.[10] However, in a text such as 4 Ezra, it is every man for himself.

The role that mercy plays also falls on a spectrum of belief. There is no mention of grace or mercy in the seventy-two chapters of 2 Enoch. However, in the Apocalypse of Zephaniah, the prophet receives mercy

5. W. D. Davies, *Paul and Rabbinic Judaism: Some Rabbinic Elements in Pauline Theology* (London: SPCK, 1970), 269, quoting Strack-Billerbeck, 1:116, ET: *Commentary on the New Testament from the Talmud and the Midrash* (Bellingham, WA: Lexham, 2013); cf. M. Baba Metzia 7.1.

6. Davies, *Paul and Rabbinic Judaism*, 271, quoting R. Haninah b. Hama, Gen. Rabba 1.

7. Davies, *Paul and Rabbinic Judaism*, 270, quoting P. 'Aboth 1.14

8. Davies, *Paul and Rabbinic Judaism*, 270–71, quoting Gen. Rabba 35.2.

9. Davies, *Paul and Rabbinic Judaism*, 271–72.

10. Philip S. Alexander, "Torah and Salvation in Tannaitic Literature," *Justification and Variegated Nomism*, vol. 1, *The Complexities of Second Temple Judaism*, ed. D. A. Carson, Peter T. O'Brien, and Mark A. Seifrid, WUNT 2/140 (Grand Rapids: Baker Academic, 2001), 295.

even before his good deeds are read out from the book. Richard Bauckham observes that the three intercessors through whom the prophet obtains mercy are Abraham, Isaac, and Jacob, and "the appearance of the patriarchs suggests that they are pleading for the sinners among their descendants *on the basis of the covenant God made with them.*"[11] Again, the Old Testament invokes the Abrahamic covenant for mercy rather than the Sinaitic. Rabbinical teaching seems to have some memory of this distinction in the prophets.

Regardless of whatever merits are supplied by others, it is clear from the Mishnah that one stands at the last day on his or her own. One will not fall into transgression if he or she keeps in mind "your deeds written in a book. . . . Faithful is your taskmaster who shall pay you the reward of your labor" (m. 'Abot 2:1, 14). The courtroom, scales, and bookkeeping dominate descriptions of final justification in ancient Judaism; they are not simply metaphors drawn from Roman jurisprudence and medieval penance projected back onto Judaism. As Hermann Lichtenberger observes, close study of these texts leads one to resist the urge to reduce ancient Judaism to a single type, whether "total self-redemption" (the tendency of P. Billerbeck, E. Schürer, and Bultmann) or Sanders's sometimes "exaggerated interpretations and doubtful systematizations."[12]

In any case, what is striking about these sources is that, in spite of all the diversity, there is a consensus affirming the imputation of both sin and merits from one person to another. For Paul, the believer's righteousness is "alien," that is, "not having a righteousness of my own that comes from the law, but that which comes through faith in Christ, the righteousness from God that depends on faith" (Phil 3:9).

Definition and Initial Defense

I draw two conclusions from these details in relation to Paul. First, the contemporary debate is often framed by a proscription on comparisons between ancient Judaism and late medieval teaching. One may surely be alert to the danger of anachronism—that is, of seeing the Reformation as a mere replay of Paul's controversy with the "Judaizers"—without being

---

11. Bauckham, "Apocalypses," 159.

12. Hermann Lichtenberger, "The Understanding of the Torah in the Judaism of Paul's Day," in *Paul and the Mosaic Law*, ed. James D. G. Dunn, Third Durham-Tübingen Research Symposium on Earliest Christianity and Judaism, 1994 (Tübingen: Mohr Siebeck, 1996; Grand Rapids: Eerdmans, 2001), 10–11 (including n12).

forced to ignore obvious parallels. Here the new perspective claims not only to be a new reading of Paul but of Paul *over against* the Reformation reading. Such a thesis would ordinarily require (a) some familiarity with the Reformation reading (which is often lacking), (b) no connection in substance between ancient Jewish and medieval teaching, and therefore (c) the Reformers' fundamental misunderstanding of Paul due to their failure to recognize (b).

Regardless of one's conclusion about whether Paul affirmed the imputation of Christ's meritorious righteousness to believers, we may put to rest at the outset the canard that the very idea is the product of a Western legalistic mentality over against an equally stereotyped "covenantal" outlook that emphasizes relationship over norm—or that the Reformation doctrine of justification is a decadent offspring of late medieval nominalism. In principle at least, the idea of sin and righteousness being imputed is as Jewish as it is Christian. When Marmorstein speaks of "the law of the solidarity of mankind," "imputed sins," and "imputed merits," Reformation theology can hardly be dismissed as belonging to a discourse that was alien to Jesus, Paul, and their Jewish contemporaries.

We have seen even from Sanders's description that ancient Judaism held several prominent beliefs that resemble late medieval teaching: for example, election based on foreseen merits, the weighing of merits, the emphasis on obedience as the condition for remaining in God's favor, notions of penance (repentance cancelling sin), and purgatory. And now we even find the doctrine of a treasury of merits: supererogatory deeds of obedience performed especially by the patriarchs that can be imputed to individuals or the nation. Indeed, the merits and intercession of departed saints, says Marmorstein, "benefit not merely themselves, but also their posterity, their fellow-creatures, their ancestry, their whole generation, not merely during their life, but even after their departure from the land of the living. Even in the hereafter their merits protect and heal others."[13] At what point were the Reformers (and are we) wrong to see parallels between their controversy with Rome and Paul's with his contemporaries?

Similarly, in the contemporary debate, it is not beside the point to observe the similarity between certain positions and the sixteenth-century debate. The new perspective argument for "works of the law"

---

13. Marmorstein, *The Doctrine of Merits*, 4, emphasis added.

as merely referring to boundary markers, so that other works may still play some role in "staying in" and final justification, is exactly the same as Origen's view as well as Luther's critics. N. T. Wright affirms a present justification through faith and a final justification by works. The new Finnish interpretation of Luther attempts to assimilate the German reformer's teaching on justification to an Orthodox doctrine of deification. John Milbank rarely engages in scriptural exegesis, but follows Bruno Blumenfeld's interpretation of Paul, defending an essentially Pelagian interpretation of Romans 1 and 2.[14] It is hardly illicit to appeal to historical maps in current debates, particularly when (a) there are clear parallels and (b) the target of critics *is* the "Reformation doctrine" of justification.

We do engage in anachronism if we simply assume that whatever contemporary interpreters of Paul propose finds some parallel in the sixteenth century debates or that the latter must be anticipated in Paul's polemics. Nonetheless, it is part of a historian's task to discern similarities in positions and arguments across various times and places, especially when they belong to the same reception history—namely, the interpretation of Paul's epistles. James Denney's observation proves valuable here: "Even in a day of overdone distinctions, one might point out that interpretations are not properly to be classified as historical or dogmatic, but as true or false. If they are false, it does not matter whether they be called dogmatic or historical; and if they are true, they may quite well be both."[15]

The second conclusion I draw from the data is a stronger claim: namely, that unless otherwise indicated we should assume a shared framework especially in arguments where significant overlap in understanding is required. If rabbinical Judaism and Paul's theology are incommensurable systems, then there never would have been a rupture

---

14. John Milbank, "Paul against Biopolitics," in *Paul's New Moment: Continental Philosophy and the Future of Christian Theology*, by John Milbank, Slavoj Zizek, and Creston Davis (Grand Rapids: Brazos, 2010), 55–56. Milbank says here that "all people everywhere should have been able (and by implication have sometimes been able) to acknowledge the true God and that all people everywhere are saved according to their obedience to the unwritten justice of God—in other words, according to ethical works (!) in the broadest sense." The focused meaning of justification becomes completely blurred in Milbank's suggestion that, according to Paul, "it is indeed by faith that one is essentially able to be just, that is to say, ethical under the governance of the law of nature" (56). Reference is made throughout this essay (and here) to Bruno Blumenfeld, *The Political Paul: Justice, Democracy, and Kingship in a Hellenistic Framework* (London: Continuum, 2001).

15. James Denney, *The Atonement and the Modern Mind* (London: Hodder and Stoughton, 1903), 7.

between the two religions. They would simply have talked past each other, like people speaking two different languages unknown to each other. Instead, the spirited clashes occurred precisely because there was significant overlap in worlds of discourse.

In fact, Davies, one of the forerunners of the new perspective, concludes in his landmark study that Paul's solution to the problem of sin "has clearly grown out of that world of thought revealed to us in the Apocrypha and Pseudepigrapha and in the Rabbinic literature which gave birth to the Rabbinic doctrine of merit and of imputed sin." "That doctrine derives from that vivid conception of the solidarity of all members of the community of Israel."[16] Indeed, as Marmorstein would add, the doctrine pertains not only to Israel's solidarity but the covenantal solidarity of humankind.

Davies judges that the merit of the fathers "did form a well-defined element in the religious thought of that milieu into which Paul came, and that Paul was familiar with the Doctrine of the Merits of the Fathers would appear to be proved by his reference in Rom. 9.5 and particularly in Rom. 11.28."[17] I would add Romans 4 and 5 to the list since that is where Paul's argument for the gift of righteousness (justification) is extrapolated in terms of the double-imputation: Adam's sin and Christ's righteousness. "Although Paul does not use the word *zakûth* [merit], Davies concludes, "nevertheless we cannot doubt that he is there [in Rom 5] governed by those conceptions of solidarity which the doctrine of merits implied."[18]

The burden of proof seems to rest on those who deny that Paul thought in terms of merit and imputation in Romans 4–5 and 1 Corinthians 1:30. A highly trained rabbi, who obviously knew such a widely held doctrine of the imputation of Abraham's merits, took aim at the patriarch's candidacy for such a role and in fact attributed Abraham's justification to a gracious "crediting" of righteousness rather than to his obedience. Why would he have done this unless he believed concerning Christ what they believed concerning Abraham?

Crucially, Paul never criticizes the concept of merit and imputation. On the contrary, Romans 5 assumes it with the imputation of sin in

---

16. Davies, *Paul and Rabbinic Judaism*, 268–69, quoting M. Makkoth 3.16. Also P. 'Aboth 6.11.; cf. Marmorstein, *The Doctrine of Merits*, 11; Schechter, *Some Aspects of Rabbinic Theology*, 170f.

17. Davies, *Paul and Rabbinic Judaism*, 272.

18. Davies, *Paul and Rabbinic Judaism*, 273.

Adam and the imputation of righteousness in Christ. What Paul rejects in Romans 4 is not the category but the donor of meritorious righteousness. Obviously, the major difference between Jewish and Christian interpretation at this point is *Christ*. Consequently, making sense of justification by the imputed merits of Christ would only require one to be convinced that Jesus is in fact the Messiah. It is the imputed guilt and inherited corruption of everyone from Adam, including Abraham, that renders all "ungodly" and therefore incapable of being meritorious agents in their own salvation, much less that of others. If Paul believed that Jesus is the Messiah, Abraham's greater son, then it should not surprise us if Paul thought that Jesus, rather than the patriarch, could justify others by his merit.

So Paul does not have to introduce a new paradigm, something other than the categories of work and faith, wages and gift, or merit imputed. The pieces are already in place—except for the fact that Abraham is the beneficiary rather than benefactor. Abraham's greater son is the meritorious redeemer whose righteousness is imputed to all who believe. If a Jewish person operating within this framework *were* to come to believe that Jesus is God, the sinless substitute, and risen Lord, then it would be natural to believe, retrospectively, that sinners cannot merit anything except judgment from God and that the imputation of Christ's righteousness is one's only hope. Such a person, I believe, was Paul. But of course, not every Jewish convert to Christianity did so. Such people, I believe, are those whom Paul is trying to persuade.

As noted above, the ancient rabbis tried to balance the merit of the fathers with personal responsibility in order to discourage moral laxity. The main issue for Paul, however, is neither laxity nor legalistic fear but the sheer fact that everyone lacks the righteousness God requires for justification. Whatever its effects, Paul's gospel is not that we can be free of libertinism or legalism but that we can be *saved from the wrath of God and united to Christ* for justification, sanctification, and glorification. Human beings can merit only condemnation. Christ alone "is our righteousness, holiness and redemption" (1 Cor 1:30). Sinful human beings can only merit judgment. Not even Abraham had any basis for boasting before God (Rom 4:1–3). Here, Paul uses the term λογίζομαι (to count, credit, reckon or impute). "For what does the Scripture say? 'Abraham believed God, and it was counted [ἐλογίσθη] to him as righteousness'" (Rom 4:3, quoting Gen 15:6). Thus, whatever it means to be justified by Christ's righteousness, it is an *imputed* (credited) righteousness that Paul intends.

As far as I have been able to find, nothing comes as close to these references to crediting of righteousness in Romans 4 as the Qumran text 4QMMT, which includes a letter from the Teacher of Righteousness to a pupil or group of pupils. The "works of the law" are things to be done, "this being counted to you for righteousness if you do what is true and good before God for the salvation of yourself and of Israel" (C 25–32; 4Q398 ii:7–8).[19] In one fell swoop, the text violates the false dichotomies of the new perspective: righteousness as a relationship rather than judicial conformity to a moral norm ("for righteousness if you *do* what is true and good before God"), ecclesiology rather than soteriology and corporate versus individual ("for the salvation of yourself and of Israel"), and belonging versus the imputation of meritorious deeds ("this [doing] being counted to you for righteousness"). These various "doings" of the law are credits, as it were, and this is precisely how ancient Judaism saw them:

> All is given against a pledge, and the net is cast over all the living; the shop stands open and the shopkeeper gives credit and the account book lies open and the hand writes and every one that wishes to borrow let him come and borrow; but the collectors go round continually every day and exact payment of men with their consent or without their consent, for they have that on which they can rely; and the judgment is a judgment of truth; and all is made ready for the banquet. (m. 'Abot 3:17)[20]

Paul follows the same commercial analogy but once again turns it against the traditional rabbinical interpretation: "Now to the one who works, his wages are not counted [imputed] as a gift but as his due. And to the one who does not work but trusts him who justifies the ungodly, his faith is counted [imputed] as righteousness" (Rom 4:4–5). While Roman Catholic critiques of the evangelical doctrine substitute infusion for imputation, the more recent (new perspective) challenges express wariness of any sort of transfer from Christ to the believer, as if Paul could be talking about salvation. However, both views fail to reckon

---

19. Lichtenberger, "The Understanding of the Torah in the Judaism of Paul's Day," 16.
20. Quoted in Alexander, "Torah and Salvation in Tannaitic Literature," 283.

with the categories of early Judaism and with Paul's argument that righteousness is credited as a gift while the recipient is still ungodly and without meritorious work. David is another example of one "against whom the Lord will not count his sin" (v. 8), which surely has some bearing on personal salvation. Abraham could not even count his circumcision as the instrument of his justification before God (vv. 9–12). "But the words 'it was counted to him' were not written for his sake alone, but for ours also. It will be counted to us who believe in him who raised from the dead Jesus our Lord, who was delivered up for our trespasses and raised for our justification" (vv. 23–25). Righteousness is counted or imputed to all who believe in Christ. They are justified at that moment by appealing to God's mercy in Christ, just like the tax collector in Jesus's parable (Luke 18:14), as one who has passed immediately from condemnation to justification (John 3:18).

In Galatians 3, with the contrast between "the works of the law" and "hearing with faith," Paul repeats the quotation from Genesis 15:6. "Counting as" or "being counted as," λογίζομαι εἰς, is found throughout the New Testament (Acts 19:27; Rom 2:26; 9:8; 2 Cor 12:6; Jas 2:23). Although λογίζομαι does not appear in Romans 5, the idea is evident throughout Paul's comparison and contrast between Adam (condemnation and death) and Christ (justification and life). These passages unmistakably teach that the righteousness by which the believer stands worthy before God's judgment is *alien*: that is, belonging properly to someone else. It is Christ's righteousness imputed, not the believer's inherent righteousness—even if produced by the gracious work of the Spirit.

Far from being antithetical paradigms, covenant and imputation are interdependent. In ancient Near Eastern cultures generally, the suzerain is the head and each subject is a member of his corporate body. This corporate-covenantal perspective is evident throughout the Hebrew Bible, especially in instances where a transgression of one member is imputed to the whole community. For example, Daniel offers a prayer in the persona of Israel, as if he were the whole nation in its transgression and justly earned exile (Dan 9:5–7). God also brings judgment on the whole camp of Israel for Achan's theft in Joshua 7. Besides the corporate aspect, it is clear from the narrative of Joshua 7 that the guilt is both incurred by an act of covenant unfaithfulness and measured against a moral norm.

As we have seen time and time again, the Old Testament affirms the principle that God only justifies those who are actually righteous, which is plainly conformity to a moral norm (Exod 23:7; Prov 17:15; Nah 1:3). There is no doubt that Paul also understands "righteousness" in terms of conformity to a norm: "the righteous requirement of the law" (δικαίωμα τοῦ νόμου)" (Rom 8:4). "But now the righteousness of God has been manifested apart from the law, although the Law and the Prophets bear witness to it—the righteousness of God through faith in Jesus Christ for all who believe" (Rom 3:21–22). Jesus has not resumed Moses's mediation of the Sinai covenant. Jesus is the mediator of the new covenant, and the promise of Genesis 3:15 has reached us through the seed of Abraham and David.

The whole notion of a covenant mediator assumes that one person may represent the whole people, which is assumed already in the substitutionary character of the atonement (see John 11:49–52). In fact, substitution and justification by imputation stand or fall together, since the former is the imputation of the sinner's guilt to Christ, and the latter is the imputation of Christ's righteousness to the sinner. So we have come full circle: the idea of a covenantal solidarity that includes the imputation of sin as well as righteousness is not the invention of Latin legalism but is an ancient Near Eastern—and specifically biblical—conception. If the rabbis saw it so clearly from their own Scriptures, why should we be surprised that Paul saw it even more clearly in reference to Christ?

If in principle Christ's righteousness cannot be imputed to believers, then the believer's sins cannot be imputed to Christ. Furthermore, Adam's guilt cannot be imputed to humanity, which strikes at the heart of the doctrine of original sin. In Paul, however, just as justification answers to imputed guilt, sanctification answers to imparted corruption—hence his contrast of justification with *condemnation*, not corruption. If the imputation of *unrighteousness* works this way under Adam as head, then the imputation of *righteousness* under Christ's mediation is analogous, as Paul in fact argues in Romans 5. In short, without the active obedience of Christ—his status as righteous covenant servant—we are forgiven but not righteous.

That which is credited or imputed to sinners is "the righteousness of God through faith in Jesus Christ for all who believe." They are "justified by his grace as a gift, through the redemption that is in Christ Jesus, whom God put forward as a propitiation by his blood, to be received by faith, . . . so that he might be just and the justifier of the one who has faith in Jesus" (Rom 3:22–26). This is the Reformation formula: "justified by grace on the basis of Christ's redemption, received through faith alone." Justification means "not having a righteousness of my own that comes from the law, but that which comes through faith in Christ, the righteousness from God that depends on faith" (Phil 3:9). Christ bore our sins "so that in him we might become the righteousness of God" (2 Cor 5:21). Christ *is* our righteousness and holiness (1 Cor 1:30), and we are clothed with Christ (3:27). This is the grand vision that Isaiah prophesied:

> I will greatly rejoice in the LORD;
> > my soul shall exult in my God,
> for he has clothed me with the garments of salvation;
> > he has covered me with the robe of righteousness,
> as a bridegroom decks himself like a priest with a beautiful
> > headdress,
> > and as a bride adorns herself with her jewels. (Isa 61:10)

United to Christ through faith, we possess his status as faithful covenant servant, credited even to those who are in themselves ungodly. "Since, therefore, we have now been justified by his blood, much more shall we be saved by him from the wrath of God" (Rom 5:9).

Merit and Imputation in Christianity

Paul upholds God's law in the most inflexible manner. It is not an arbitrary list of rules but the covenantal revelation of his essential character as righteous, loving, holy, and good. If God saves, he must do so justly—the law cannot be set aside. The apostle is in good company when he affirms Psalm 62:12: "He will repay each person according to what they have done" (Rom 2:6). He could also cite various warnings from the prophets:

> I the LORD search the heart
> > and test the mind,
> to give every man according to his ways,
> > according to the fruit of his deeds. (Jer 17:10)

The "goats" will be separated from the "sheep," Jesus warns. "And these will go away into eternal punishment, but the righteous into eternal life" (Matt 25:46). Only the righteous will be saved. This is Paul's baseline as well. The problem however is that "none is righteous, no, not one" (Rom 3:10, quoting Ps 14:1), and "a few works of the law" (4MMQT) or basic balance of good over bad will not make one righteous. Abraham's merits cannot tip the scales; he himself had to be justified by grace alone, through faith in his coming offspring. Jesus himself said that he did not come for the "righteous but for sinners" (Luke 5:32). No one can come to Christ by their own free will (John 6:44). When asked, "What must we *do*, to be *doing the works* of God?" (compare with "a few works of the law" in 4MMQT), Jesus answered, "Jesus answered them, "This is the work of God, that you believe in him whom he has sent" (John 6:28–29).

Beginning as early as John's ministry, and in full view with Jesus's ministry, is the concern that the religious leaders do not take the law and their own sin seriously enough. Unlike the gentiles, they do not need to be reconciled to God; they are already children of Abraham. John and Jesus push the people and their leaders to recognize their need not for more bulls and rams but for "the Lamb of God who *takes away the sin of the world*" (John 1:29, emphasis added). Those who seek to be justified by works of the law will indeed be judged by it, and none will escape its death sentence. Therefore, anyone who reads Psalm 62 or Nahum 1:3 imagining that it is bad news only for outsiders is gravely mistaken. And if I am not mistaken, bringing people to that realization is his motivation throughout the argument of Romans 1:17–3:20. The baseline theology that we have recognized in the ancient rabbinical literature is completely opposed to this argument, even as the basic framework remains visible. This is explained largely by the fact that they were operating within the act-consequence logic of the Sinai covenant as if the new covenant in the Messiah were merely its renewal. Even for some Jewish Christians, evidently, Jesus was a new Moses; it was too jarring to imagine that the old covenant is "obsolete" (Heb 8:13) and that those who wish to remain in it "are severed from Christ" (Gal 5:4). So it becomes even clearer that the main biblical-theological divide over justification appears in the conflation of covenants, of law and gospel, just as the apostle says explicitly throughout that epistle. And it is this same conflation that lies at the heart of divisions in contemporary interpretations of justification.

Significantly, Roman Catholic theologian Michael Schmaus acknowledges that Jesus and the apostles rejected any notion of an equivalence of deed and reward but that "the expression 'merit' originated with Cyprian and Tertullian and spread rapidly."[21] This point is confirmed by analyzing the apostolic fathers and Irenaeus, where the concept of either condign or congruent merit is absent. As we have seen in volume 1, however, merit attains an important status in Origen's writings. By the third century the word "merit" was being used interchangeably with "reward." Tertullian writes, "Again, we affirm that a judgment has been ordained by God according to the merits of every man."[22] "A good deed has God for its debtor," he writes elsewhere.[23] We are therefore once again in the ambiance of the Second Temple texts but in a Christian context. Through Rufinus (the Latin translator of Origen), Pelagius, and Julian of Aeclanum, the emphasis on merit became quite pronounced. Besides contradicting passages that we have covered, this statement contrasts sharply with Augustine's statement, "The Lord made himself a debtor not by receiving something, but by promising something. One does not say to him, 'Pay for what you received,' but 'Pay what you promised.'"[24] Augustine's *Spirit and Letter* extrapolated this Pauline contrast between law and promise. Augustine's influence continued, but even by the time of Lombard Christ had become a new Moses and the gospel was the "New Law."

According to Rome's official teaching, Schmaus says, "Man can produce acts worthy of salvation because, and insofar as, God produces them through him." Merits are excluded *before* the initial justification (in baptism), but after this conversion begins the believer does merit an increase of grace (and justification) and eventually final justification.[25] As the Reformers acknowledged repeatedly, Rome even held that Christ's merits are imputed to believers, but along with the merits of Mary and the saints as well as the believer's own merits. Calvin says, "True, he is called a Redeemer, but in a manner which implies that men also, by their own free will, redeem themselves from the bondage of sin and death. True, he is called righteousness and salvation, but

---

21. Michael Schmaus, *Dogma*, vol. 6, *Justification and Last Things* (London: Sheed and Ward, 1977), 139.
22. Tertullian, *To the Nations* 19.7 (*ANF* 3:127).
23. Tertullian, *On Repentance* 2 (*ANF* 3:658).
24. Augustine, *Explanations of the Psalms* 84:16 (*NPNF*[1] 8:404).
25. Schmaus, *Dogma*, 6:141.

so that men still pursue salvation for themselves, by the merit of their works."[26] However, the Reformer counters, "The apostle does not say that [Christ] was sent to help us attain righteousness but himself to be our righteousness."[27] Christ is either the only mediator (1 Tim 2:5), or he is not; his righteousness and merits alone suffice, or they do not. "There is nothing intermediate between . . . being justified by faith and justified by works."[28]

As for Paul, for the Reformers the matter is binary: either we are saved by grace *alone* on the basis of Christ *alone*, or not. They are not satisfied with any formula that gives *most* of the glory to God and makes salvation hinge *mostly* on Christ. Every link in the chain is pure gift, and *whatever* part of our salvation is dependent on our merits is sure to lead to despair of attaining reconciliation and final glory. "Whatever mixture men study to add from the power of free will to the grace of God," says Calvin, "is only a corruption of it; just as if one should dilute good wine with dirty water."[29] "Therefore," he says, "we explain justification simply as the acceptance with which God receives us into his favor as righteous. And we say that it consists in the remission of sins and the imputation of Christ's righteousness."[30]

The question was whether salvation is entirely to be found in Christ, apart from the meritorious deeds of believers. So, like Augustine in the quote above, the Lutheran Book of Concord confesses,

> We are not putting forward an empty quibble about the term "reward." . . . We grant that eternal life is a reward because it is something that is owed—not because of our merits but because of the promise [of God]. We have shown above that justification is strictly a gift of God; it is a thing promised. To this gift the promise of eternal life has been added.[31]

The gift is owed not only because of God's promise but because Christ has fulfilled the law on our behalf. The Protestant Reformers did

26. Calvin, "The Necessity of Reforming the Church," in *Selected Works of John Calvin: Tracts and Letters*, ed. Henry Beveridge and Jules Bonnet, 7 vols. (Grand Rapids: Baker, 1983), 1:192.
27. *Inst.* 3.15.5.
28. Calvin, *Calvin's Commentaries*, vol. 6, *Commentary on Psalms 93–150*, trans. James Anderson (Grand Rapids: Baker, 1996), 251 (on Ps 143).
29. *Inst.* 2.5.15.
30. *Inst.* 3.11.2.
31. Theodore G. Tappert, ed. and trans., *The Book of Concord* (Philadelphia: Fortress, 1989), 162.

not object to the idea of merit. Given the dignity in which God created humankind, it is neither beneath God nor above humans to conclude that a vocation could be given the fulfillment of which would have merited life. What the Reformers rejected was the possibility of meriting anything but damnation after the fall. Vermigli notes that the late medieval teaching that even the unregenerate may merit the beginning of grace contradicts Jesus's express statements in Matthew 7:17–18, 12:33–35, and Luke 17:7–10. "Therefore, since Christ denies that this can happen, how dare they claim that it may be and assert that men may be justified by works?"[32] Further, "They say that works before justification deserve it in one sense, while those works that follow are the most profitable."

> Therefore, men would in one sense enter into a business transaction with God, and count with beads how many prayers they have said. What else could they mean by this except that they would recite a certain number of Paternosters, or so many Ave Marias, thinking that by such repetition they will surely bring God under obligation to themselves?[33]

Jesus teaches us to pray "forgive us our debts" (Matt 6:12), not "acknowledge our merits." "Therefore, if our works, which we do after our regeneration, need purging by the merit of Christ, and we pray for this, how can they be propitiatory?" says Vermigli.[34]

> David cries out in the Psalms, "If you O Lord should mark iniquities, Lord who could stand?" (Ps 51). Isaiah calls the thirsty to the waters and commands those without money to purchase [Isa 55:1], but our opponents want to be justified both by merits and works, and also by money. . . . He affirms the same thing also in chapter 64, where he says that "all our righteousness is as filthy rags."[35]

The sole exception is Christ, the Last Adam. In fact, Calvin devotes an entire section of his *Institutes* (2.17) to the heading, "Christ Rightly

---

32. Peter Martyr Vermigli, *Locus on Justification*, in *Predestination and Justification: Two Theological Loci*, trans. and ed. Frank A. James III, Peter Martyr Library 8 (Kirksville, MO: Sixteenth Century Essays & Studies, 2003), 111.

33. Vermigli, *Locus on Justification*, 112.

34. Vermigli, *Locus on Justification*, 113.

35. Vermigli, *Locus on Justification*, 114.

and Properly Said to Have Merited God's Grace and Salvation for Us." Merit and grace are not contradictory in this one instance, since it is by Christ's fulfillment of the conditions of the law that he possesses the reward that he now dispenses to us by grace. As there is nothing intermediate between justification by works and by faith, there is no middle ground between being justified by Christ's merits and our own. At least in the view of the Reformers, it is either one or the other.[36] The chief article is *solo Christo*.

So far, then, this much is clear: merit *and* imputation are not innovations of the Reformation but are integral to both the Judaism of Paul's day and continued throughout the course of Christian history. The Reformers interpreted Paul as teaching that Christ's merits alone justify by being imputed to believers through faith alone.

CONTEMPORARY EXEGETICAL CHALLENGES TO IMPUTATION

Many criticisms of the Reformation view of justification have focused on imputation. Many, following Schweitzer, wonder what role imputation could serve that is not already included in mystical union with Christ. Others argue that Paul regards faith rather than Christ's righteousness as the basis of justification. These and other critiques will be treated in this section, but we begin with N. T. Wright's argument because of its significance in contemporary discussion.

Once More: Covenantal, Not Soteriological

Wright has distanced himself from other new perspective scholars, particularly James Dunn, on several points. He helpfully explains his move away from the traditional view of justification.[37] He says that he agrees with Dunn on the fundamental conviction that when "Paul talks about justification, it's in the context of the Gentile-Jewish debate."[38] "'The gospel' is not, 'You can be saved, and here's how'; the gospel, for Paul, is, 'Jesus Christ is Lord.' . . . It is a royal summons to submission,

---

36. Among the best historical studies of the Reformation and post-Reformation thinking about imputation is the following: John V. Fesko, *Death in Adam, Life in Christ: The Doctrine of Imputation*, Reformed Exegetical Doctrinal Studies (Ross–shire, UK: Mentor, 2016).

37. N. T. Wright, "New Perspectives on Paul," in *Justification in Perspective: Historical Developments and Contemporary Challenges*, ed. Bruce L. McCormack (Grand Rapids: Baker Academic, 2006), 246.

38. Wright, "New Perspectives on Paul," 247.

to obedience, to allegiance; and the form that this submission and obedient allegiance takes is faith."[39]

> I became convinced many years ago, and time and exegesis have confirmed this again and again, that Paul always uses this phrase [*dikaiosynē theou*] to denote not the status that God's people have from God or in God's presence but the righteousness of God himself. This is not to say that there is no such thing as a righteous status held by believers. There is. But it is to deny that the latter is the referent of Paul's phrase, *dikaiosynē theou*. . . . What God's righteousness never becomes in the Jewish background that Paul is so richly summing up is an attribute that is passed on to, reckoned to, or imputed to God's people. Nor does Paul treat it in this way.[40]

"What, then, about the 'imputed righteousness'?" he asks. "This is fine as it stands; God does indeed 'reckon righteousness' to those who believe," he says. "But this is not, for Paul, the righteousness either of God or of Christ except in a very specialized sense."

> Only two passages can be invoked in favor of the imputed righteousness being that of God or Christ. The first proves too much, and the second not enough. The first is 1 Corinthians 1:30–31, where Paul says that Christ has become for us wisdom from God, and righteousness, and sanctification, and redemption. . . . [However] I doubt if this will sustain the normal imputation theology, because it would seem to demand equal airtime for the imputation of wisdom, sanctification, and redemption as well. The second passage is 2 Corinthians 5:21, which is not, as a matter of good exegesis, a statement of soteriology but of apostolic vocation. The entire passage is about the way in which Paul's new covenant ministry, through the death and resurrection of Jesus, is in fact God's appointed means for establishing and maintaining the church.[41]

---

39. Wright, "New Perspectives on Paul," 249.
40. Wright, "New Perspectives on Paul," 250.
41. Wright, "New Perspectives on Paul," 252; cf. Wright, "On Becoming the Righteousness of God: 2 Corinthians 5:21," in *Pauline Theology*, ed. D. M. Hay, 4 vols. (Minneapolis: Augsburg Fortress, 1991–97), 2:200–208.

Already we begin to see a discounting of the relevance of these passages for justification due to a false choice between ecclesiology (covenant) and soteriology. Wright fails to see how these two passages function as proof texts. Those who defend imputation appeal to 1 Corinthians 1:30 not as a direct proof of righteousness being imputed (admittedly, λογίζομαι doesn't appear here), but only to point out that *Christ is our righteousness*. It is not proving too much, since the point drawn from the verse is that Christ is our righteousness as well as our wisdom from God, sanctification, and redemption. Yet Christ is each of these things "for us" in different ways.

For Israel wisdom is Torah, and for gentiles, philosophy. But Paul says that Christ is our wisdom. Christ is our wisdom from God in that we only know God the Father in his Son, "in whom are hidden all the treasures of wisdom and knowledge" (Col 2:3; cf. John 17:3). Furthermore, Christ is our sanctification, since we are not only justified but definitively consecrated as holy in him. This is why Paul can refer to the Corinthians as "having been sanctified [ἡγιασμένοις] in Christ Jesus" (1 Cor 1:2) in spite of the church's moral disarray that he addresses later in the letter. Similarly, Jesus prayed, "And for their sake I consecrate myself, that they also may be sanctified in truth" (John 17:19). But Christ is our sanctification neither by revelation nor imputation but by participation in his eschatological life as the source of the new creation. And Christ is our redemption by dying and rising for us and by no other way. We appeal to 1 Corinthians 1:30 simply to point out that Christ is our righteousness, not to explain how. And arguably, from the passages that we have explored, imputation is the best explanation of how Christ is our righteousness.

As for Wright's handling of 2 Corinthians 5:21, I am more perplexed. The entire passage is a combination of references to Paul's ministry and to its saving message, explaining how anyone who is in Christ "is a new creation," with the old passing; "behold, the new has come."

> All this is from God, who through Christ reconciled us to himself and gave us the ministry of reconciliation; that is, in Christ God was reconciling the world to himself, not counting their trespasses against them, and entrusting to us the message of reconciliation. Therefore, we are ambassadors for Christ, God making his appeal through us. We implore you on behalf of Christ, be reconciled to

God. For our sake he made him to be sin who knew no sin, so that in him we might become the righteousness of God. (vv. 18–21)

Surely it is grasping at straws to say that the concluding statement (v. 21) "is not, as a matter of good exegesis, a statement of soteriology but of apostolic vocation." Paul cannot think of his vocation apart from soteriology, and this verse demonstrates the point clearly by referencing God in Christ reconciling the world, not imputing sins, as well as the great exchange of sin and righteousness.

Wright continues,

> Is there, then, no "reckoning of righteousness" in, for instance, Romans 5:14–21? Yes, there is; but this is not God's own righteousness or Christ's own righteousness that is reckoned to God's redeemed people but, rather, the fresh status of "covenant member," and/or "justified sinner," which is accredited to those who are in Christ, who have heard the gospel and responded with "the obedience of faith."[42]

As we will see below, this idea is similar to Wright's thinking on Romans 2:14, which he interprets as a final justification by works.

In every passage in question, Wright presupposes the Cremer thesis and repeats the additional new perspective contention that justification equals covenant membership. Frequently, Wright insists that once the pieces are properly arranged, the puzzle is obvious. It appears that in Wright's view a "covenantal" interpretation of Paul's theology is equivalent to adopting all of Wright's theses.[43] But the pieces consist of a retranslation of "righteousness of God" as God's faithfulness to the covenant (interpreted as "return from exile"), faith as faithfulness, and therefore the identification of "works of the law" as boundary markers rather than works of obedience in general. Only with the importation of these exegetical and dogmatic assumptions can he conclude, "The phrase does not denote a human status which Israel's God gives, grants,

---

42. Wright, "New Perspectives on Paul," 253.
43. "Despite the strong covenantal theology of John Calvin himself, and his positive reading of the story of Israel as fulfilled in Jesus," Wright says, "many who claim Calvinist or Reformed heritage today resist applying it in the way that, as I argue in this book, Paul himself does, in line with a solid biblical foundation for the 'continuing exile' theme" (N. T. Wright, *Justification: God's Plan and Paul's Vision* [Downers Grove, IL: IVP Academic, 2009], 12. Yet, Wright later observes, not even Calvin got the ecclesiological center of Paul's thought (23).

imparts or imputes ('a righteousness *from* God' as in Philippians 3.9), or a human characteristic which 'counts' with God ('a righteousness which avails before God'). . . . It retains its primary scriptural meaning, which is that of God's *covenant faithfulness.*"[44] Once it is taken for granted that "its primary *scriptural meaning*" is "God's covenant faithfulness," the pieces do indeed fall into place. But what if that is not its primary scriptural meaning? The fact that he includes a key verse—Philippians 3:9—in what cannot be meant indicates the extent to which this approach appears to engage in question begging.

Justification in the first century was not about how one is saved, or in other words, "it wasn't so much about soteriology as about ecclesiology," Wright again stipulates.[45] Consequently, "Justification is the judge's verdict that someone is in the right. Righteousness is the status before the court which results from that declaration."[46] I fail to see how the conclusion follows from the premise: surely if one obtains the status before God's court of "righteous," that would have something to do with salvation. In any case, instead of imputation, the basis of this declaration, Wright says, is God's covenant faithfulness.[47]

We have already seen how thoroughly immersed the ancient Jewish sources are in the question of how to be saved. The apocalyptic emphasis on the coming judgment drove them to it in such a way that any bifurcation of soteriology and ecclesiology is impossible. Much of Christian (especially evangelical) piety today incontestably and lamentably sets "getting saved" over against "belonging to the church" (i.e., to the actual, visible, living people of God rather than a Platonic idea). However, ancient Jews did not think that way, nor did Paul—or the magisterial Reformers for that matter. Contemporary biblical scholarship engages in the same historical anachronism that it accuses the Reformers of when it interpolates pietistic individualism into the first century or into the sixteenth. No one on either side of these debates conceived of a soteriology-ecclesiology dichotomy. The Jewish doctrine of merits, including imputation of both sins and righteousness, was not simply about who you could tell was "in"; it was about whether the

---

44. N. T. Wright, *Paul: In Fresh Perspective* (Minneapolis: Fortress, 2009), 121–22.

45. N. T. Wright, *What Saint Paul Really Said: Was Paul of Tarsus the Real Founder of Christianity?* (Grand Rapids: Eerdmans, 1997), 119.

46. N. T. Wright, "Justification: Its Biblical Basis and Contemporary Relevance," in *The Great Acquittal: Justification by Faith and Current Christian Thought*, ed. Gavin Reid (London: Collins, 1980), 13–37.

47. Wright, *What Saint Paul Really Said*, 110, 127, 129.

scale-pans would tip in their favor on the last day, which strikes me as bearing a decidedly soteriological interest. If Wright is correct, then it is not only the Protestant Reformers but the ancient rabbis who confused matters by talking about merits, imputation, and personal salvation.

According to Wright, God's righteousness can only refer to his own faithfulness to the covenant.[48] And although righteousness is certainly "a forensic term, that is, taken from the law court," it cannot be transferred from God to us. Nor can it mean that the defendant is inherently righteous and therefore deserving of acquittal. Rather, "For the plaintiff or defendant to be 'righteous' in the biblical sense *within the law-court setting* is for them to have that status *as a result of the decision of the court.*"[49]

Since this is central to Wright's account, it is important to engage his argument as it unfolds.

First, Wright seems to conflate imputation with declaration. According to the traditional view, the declaration that the defendant is righteous before the court is not itself imputation. Rather, imputation is the reason why he or she is declared righteous. In other words, believers are declared righteous because they are righteous—not in themselves but because Christ's righteousness is credited to them.

Second, Wright misunderstands the Reformation interpretation when he says that it makes no sense for the judge to give his own righteousness to the defendant.[50] God's people will be "justified," he says. "*But the righteousness they have will not be God's own righteousness. That makes no sense at all. God's own righteousness is his covenant faithfulness.*"[51] He adds, "If we use the language of the law court, it makes no sense whatever to say that the judge imputes, imparts, bequeaths, conveys or otherwise transfers his righteousness to either the plaintiff or the defendant. Righteousness is not an object, a substance or a gas which can be passed across the courtroom."[52] But it has never been the Reformation position that *God's righteousness* is imputed, much less that it is a substance or a commodity (like a "gas"!) that is transferred from one person to another, rather than a legal status. Not even Rome held that infused righteousness was God's essential righteousness; rather, it is "created grace." Even this idea of justification

48. Wright, *What Saint Paul Really Said*, 96.
49. Wright, *What Saint Paul Really Said*, 97–98.
50. Wright, *What Saint Paul Really Said*, 98.
51. Wright, *What Saint Paul Really Said*, 99, emphasis original.
52. Wright, *What Saint Paul Really Said*, 98.

as a created substance of righteousness was rejected by the Reformers. Calvin explicitly criticized the medieval view for teaching that grace is something (i.e., a substance) rather than Christ's act of clothing his people with his merits (see, e.g., *Inst.* 3.1.1; 3.1.4; 3.2.24; 4.17.11). In fact, the mature Reformation doctrine of justification was articulated against both Rome's understanding of justification as an infused quality of righteousness and Andreas Osiander's notion of the believer's participation in the essential righteousness of Christ's deity.[53]

Crucially missing from Wright's courtroom setting is the third party: the mediator who, as representative head, fulfills the law and merits for himself and his covenant heirs the verdict of "righteous" or "just" before God. Although the one who fulfilled the terms of the law-covenant as the human servant is also the divine Lord, it is his active and passive obedience rather than the essential divine attribute of righteousness that is credited to believers. In this covenantal interpretation, Christ becomes the believer's righteousness both in justification (by imputation) and in sanctification (by impartation), just as Adam's federal headship yielded both condemnation and corruption. Wright may not agree with this conclusion, but we must recognize that it was at least the Reformers' view.

Richard N. Longenecker reminds us, "It is through both the sacrifice and the obedience of Christ that reconciliation has been made possible; through both His death and His life."[54] He extrapolates, "That which the contractual obligation of the Law demanded, Christ has provided. He stood for mankind in offering the perfect righteousness, so that all who stand in Him stand before the Father not in their own righteousness but as robed in His righteousness."[55] Consequently, "The sacrifice and the obedience of Christ are corollaries which can never truly be separated."[56] He adds that this "righteousness of God" is a gift given "unto all those who believe" (Rom 3:22; cf. Gal 3:22; Phil 3:9). "And so Paul says in Romans 10:4 that 'Christ is the end of the law

---

53. Osiander was a close associate of Luther's who took some of Luther's earlier emphases on Christ's indwelling in a more radical direction, while Luther as well as Melanchthon were refining the doctrine along the lines of the doctrine of imputation found in *The Book of Concord*. Lutherans rejected Osiander's view in Solid Declaration III. Calvin joined the argument by adding a lengthy section to the final 1559 edition of the *Institutes* (1.3.5–6).

54. Richard N. Longenecker, *Paul, Apostle of Liberty*, 2nd ed. (Grand Rapids: Eerdmans, 2015), 138.

55. Longenecker, *Paul, Apostle of Liberty*, 138.

56. Longenecker, *Paul, Apostle of Liberty*, 139.

in its connection with righteousness to all who believe.'"[57] All of the pieces are here, just as they are in Paul, for justification as the imputation of Christ's righteousness in his active and passive obedience as well as his resurrection from the dead. All of Christ's saving benefits are communicated to us by our being united to him, but each gift is communicated differently: Life is *given*, guilt is *cancelled*, righteousness is *imputed*, holiness is *imparted*, and final glorification is *awarded* to the just in their resurrection.

Yet Wright does not seem entirely consistent. On the one hand, he is insistent that it is *not* "Christ's own righteousness that is reckoned to God's redeemed people."[58] On the other hand, he acknowledges that we are granted Christ's covenantal status and even that (as noted above) "the Reformers' proper sense of something being accomplished in Christ Jesus which is then reckoned to us."[59]

If the first contention is intended, then the believer is declared a "covenant member" or "justified sinner" without any relation to *what Christ did*. One could cite many other statements from Wright to show that he does not draw this conclusion, but this particular formulation detaches the *ordo salutis* from the *historia salutis* entirely. This is ironic since Wright is worried that the former has marginalized the latter in Reformed theology. However, the Reformed view makes the believer's justification dependent directly on Christ's fulfillment of his vocation as the Last Adam and the true and faithful Israel.

If the second view is intended, then the question is: What exactly is reckoned? If it is "something in Christ Jesus," then what? And how? It seems that the obstacle here is the reduction of God's righteousness to "God's *own* righteousness," which is assumed to be God's covenant faithfulness. In other words, once more, the missing party is Jesus Christ and his obedience as our covenant head. So Wright is stuck between the Scylla of "imputing God's own righteousness" (which can't be right) and the Charybdis of an infused righteousness (which also doesn't work).

The alternative to both is that God imputes the covenantal status (merits, obedience, whatever one wants to call it) of Jesus Christ to all who are united to him by faith. Obviously, God's covenant faithfulness

---

57. Longenecker, *Paul, Apostle of Liberty*, 139.

58. Wright, "New Perspectives on Paul," 253.

59. N. T. Wright, "Paul in Different Perspectives: Lecture 1: Starting Points and Opening Reflections," lecture, Auburn Avenue Presbyterian Church, Monroe, LA, January 3, 2005, http://www.ntwrightpage.com/Wright_Auburn_Paul.htm.

cannot be reckoned to us. *We* must be reckoned as faithful covenant partners. Justification is not God's reckoning of his faithfulness to the covenant of grace, but of Christ's faithfulness to the covenant of law, culminating in his obedience unto death. This is why God became human and, as the Last Adam, became our vicarious covenant head in both his active and passive obedience as well as his resurrection. According to Romans 5:13, sin is not counted or imputed where there is no law. The sin of Adam was imputed to humanity as a covenantal entity in solidarity because it was imputed to each member (Rom 5:12).

As David Shaw points out, Wright also seems to offer contradictory perspectives on Abraham and merit. In *Paul and the Faithfulness of God*, Wright is convinced that μισθός (reward) in Genesis 15:1 "re-orients our reading of Rom 4:4–5" away from the traditional emphasis on Abraham's unworthiness.[60] However, Paul interprets the whole event of Genesis 15 in precisely this manner, *contrasting* wages and gift. Wright's interpretation here not only contradicts Paul's argument; it fails to recognize that in Genesis 15:1 God was *promising* Abraham a reward without stipulations or conditions. However, Shaw observes, in his Romans commentary, Wright delivers his more customary verdict that Romans 4:4–5 is not very important. After all, he says, "This is the only time he uses this metaphorical field in all his discussions of justification, and we should not allow this unique and brief sidelight to become the dominant note, as it has in much post-Reformation discussion."[61] In spite of such careful exegesis elsewhere, Wright does not do justice to a passage that is of great importance for anyone who wants to understand Paul's doctrine of justification.

Wright wholeheartedly affirms that our guilt is imputed to Christ.[62] But if sin can be imputed, why not righteousness? Isaiah 53:11, in fact, refers to both imputations:

> Out of the anguish of his soul he shall see and be satisfied;
> by his knowledge shall the righteous one, my servant,
> *make many to be accounted righteous* [יַצְדִּיק],
> and he shall *bear their iniquities.*

---

60. David Shaw, "Romans 4 and the Justification of Abraham in Light of Perspectives New and Newer," *Themelios* 40, no. 1 (2015): 55, quoting N. T. Wright, "Paul and the Patriarch," 215.

61. N. T. Wright, *Romans*, in *The New Interpreter's Bible*, vol. 10, *Acts, Romans, 1 Corinthians* (Nashville: Abingdon, 2002), 491.

62. N. T. Wright, *Jesus and the Victory of God* (Minneapolis: Fortress Press, 1998), 604–10

In fact, is that not precisely what Paul is arguing in Romans 5: The bad news of Adam's imputation and the good news of Christ's? There is no place for a transfer of Christ's covenantal obedience to the believer in Wright's interpretation. For Paul, however, "the righteousness of God through faith in Jesus Christ" is a "justification" that is "a gift" given to "all who believe" (Rom 3:22–25).

Union, Not Imputation

Whereas the ancient fathers and the Reformers saw union with Christ as an umbrella-term for all the saving gifts, including justification, there is a growing emphasis among biblical scholars and theologians to pit union against justification. The shadow of Schweitzer looms large. If we share in Christ and all that he is, then why is a distinct move such as imputation even necessary?

Representing a brief but significant trend in the 1990s known as "Federal Vision," Rich Lusk argued that "in-Christ-ness makes imputation redundant." "I do not need the moral content of his life of righteousness transferred to me; what I need is a share in the forensic verdict passed over him at the resurrection. Union with Christ is therefore the key."[63] John Barclay suggests, "We do not have to imagine here a 'transfer' of 'the righteousness of Christ,' effected through a believer's union with Christ. It is enough to say that God recognizes as 'righteous' those who indicate, by faith in Christ, that the Christ-event has become the ground of their being."[64] But if Christ's righteousness is not actually given or transferred to us, then is not justification in truth a legal fiction? And if the relevant passages indicate that the verdict "righteous" is a gift that is actually *given to believers*, then does this not constitute some sort of "transfer"? Believers draw their life and ground of being not from "works of Torah" but from "faith in Christ," says Barclay.[65] This is true, of course, but the formulation appears too imprecise in comparison with Paul's straightforward and distinguishing terms. Union with Christ (or Christ as ground of our being) is the umbrella-term for the gifts (election, redemption, calling, justification,

---

63. Rich Lusk, "A Response to 'The Biblical Plan of Salvation,'" in *The Auburn Avenue Theology: Pros and Cons; Debating the Federal Vision*, ed. E. Calvin Beisner, The Knox Theological Seminary Colloquium on the Federal Vision (Fort Lauderdale, FL: Knox Theological Seminary, 2004), 142. This brief movement within conservative Presbyterian and Reformed circles in North America was decisively rejected by their general assemblies and synods.

64. John M. G. Barclay, *Paul and The Gift* (Grand Rapids: Eerdmans, 2015), 379.

65. Barclay, *Paul and the Gift*, 379.

adoption, sanctification, glorification), not a substitute for any one of them, including justification. With respect to *justification*, the issue is a δικαίωμα (declaration of righteousness) that answers to the κατάκριμα (condemnation). The question is whether one is reckoned as having kept the righteous requirements of the law. This cedar of Lebanon seems to get lost in the forest of "the ground of their being." Apart from the "great exchange"—our sins imputed to Christ and his righteousness imputed to us—I cannot see how this avoids the charge of a legal fiction, a matter on which I focus below.

In addition, Barclay reduces justification to nonimputation, suggesting that Paul "says that 'to credit righteousness' (Rom 4:6) is equivalent to 'not crediting sin' (4:8)."[66] But it is one thing for a friend to forgive a debt and quite another to credit my account with his inheritance. More importantly, does Paul in fact say that justification is merely nonimputation of sin (i.e., forgiveness)? It is interesting that although Paul's quotation of Psalm 32:1 speaks of the nonimputation of sin to David, Paul adds a positive imputation of righteousness just before his quotation: "And to the one who does not work but believes in him who justifies the ungodly, his faith is *counted as righteousness, just as David also speaks* of the blessing of the one to whom God *counts righteousness* apart from works" (v. 5). Crediting righteousness is different from merely forgiving transgressions, and Paul affirms both here.

Michael Bird suggests that Romans 5:19 (like 2 Cor 5:21) refers to a transformative "becoming."[67] Bird is willing to focus on the *ordo salutis* and even to bring sixteenth-century debates into Pauline exegesis when "becoming righteous" is affirmed. However, there are several problems with this view—two that are especially worth mentioning: lexical and exegetical.

First, it is precarious to hang too much on the phrase "will be *made* righteous" [δίκαιοι κατασταθήσονται] in 19b, since καθίστημι means to appoint, declare, make, or constitute.[68] Second, why should "become the righteousness of God" refer to a progressive sanctification any more than Christ being "made sin" refers to a process of degeneration? If Jesus was "made sin" by imputation, then we are made righteous by the same.

---

66. Barclay, *Paul and the Gift*, 486.

67. Michael Bird, "Progressive Reformed Perspective," *Justification: Five Views*, ed. James K. Beilby and Paul Rhodes Eddy (Downers Grove, IL: InterVarsity, 2011), 148–49.

68. BDAG, 492.

In any case, I think that Bird here (like Wright) is too *ordo*-centered when Paul's point belongs more to the *historia salutis*. In Romans 5 Paul has told us how it is *in history* that all people "were made sinners" (v. 19a)—namely, that "one trespass led to condemnation for all people" (v. 18a). This is not a process within individuals but a universal and continual imputation since the fall. Recall my point made in chapter 5 from 1 Corinthians 15. "Thus it is written, 'The first man [ὁ πρῶτος ἄνθρωπος] Adam became a *living being*' [ψυχὴν ζῶσαν]; the last Adam [ὁ ἔσχατος Ἀδὰμ] became a *life-giving spirit*" [πνεῦμα ζωοποιοῦν] (v. 45). Ἐγένετο ("became") becomes the head verb shared by the two Adams, with the contrast of the first Adam becoming alive at creation and the Last Adam becoming life-giving at his resurrection. "So as in Adam all die, so in Christ are all made alive" (v. 22). "Became" here refers to a new condition or state that appeared (a) when the first Adam sinned and (b) when the last Adam was raised. We should assume a similar redemptive-historical meaning in Romans 5:12–19.

Further, as we have seen, the opposite of judicial condemnation is justification, not renewal. Although the *transformative impact* of union with Christ is highlighted in Romans 6, in chapter 5 we are told *how* believers "will be made righteous" (Rom 5:19) *in history*—namely, through "one act of righteousness" (v. 18). It is there, in Christ's death and resurrection, where the gift of justification was accomplished objectively and then applied in time to believers.

Although 1 Corinthians 1:30 does not mention imputation, how else is Christ "our righteousness" in a forensic or legal sense, as Bird agrees it is? Bird grants that in Philippians 3 "there is clearly a righteousness from God that is given to believers."[69] Then why not imputed or credited, particularly since Paul actually uses the term? And if one agrees that believers receive Christ's status, then how?

Yet just at this point, Bird challenges Wright's suggestion that "union with Christ" accomplishes everything intended by "imputation."

I accept Wright's sketch, but I do think we are still left with the question, what does union actually do that makes us "righteous" before God? This is where a concept like imputation is a necessary implicate of the biblical materials. If we take all the bits and bobs

---

69. Bird, "Progressive Reformed Perspective," 149.

together, including this language of "counting" from Romans 4, the gift of righteousness in Romans 5:17 and Philippians 3:9, the representative natures of Adam and Christ as federal heads, the forensic nature of *dikaioō* and *dikaiosyne* in several passages (e.g., Rom 3:21–26; 10:10; Gal 2:15–21; 5:4–5), and the indebtedness of salvation to Jesus' faithfulness and obedience in his task as Son, then, something like "imputation" sounds like a logical necessity of describing the application of salvation for those who are "in Christ."[70]

This is a terrific summary of the Reformation position. However, just at this point, Bird registers disagreement with the imputation of Christ's active obedience. It was the Lutheran and Reformed scholastics who emphasized "the accounting metaphor of 'credit,' . . . glossing over Paul's 'in Christ' language of justification for a model that looks like an abstract transaction of righteousness and myopically focusing on the sequence of events in personal salvation (*ordo salutis*) without integrating it into the overarching story of salvation history where God brings Jews and Gentiles into the family of the Messiah (*historia salutis*)."[71]

Although he fleshes out this complex of charges a bit, they remain rather sweeping and unsupported. I cannot take the space to address each of them here. Surely Bird knows that union with Christ was as major a motif in Reformed theology after Calvin as it was for the Reformer. Neither the doctrine of the merit of the fathers in rabbinical teaching, nor "the accounting metaphor of 'credit'" in Second Temple Judaism, nor the exchange of sin and righteousness in Isaiah 53 and several New Testament passages are distinctly medieval or early modern ideas. If we can agree that "Jesus was obedient where Adam and Israel failed to be,"[72] then a question arises: "To what purpose?" What is he obeying and how does his fulfillment of covenantal righteousness in the place of Adam and Israel differ in substance from saying that Christ—the Last Adam—fulfilled the covenant of works, bore its sanctions, and rose again triumphantly as the firstfruits of the whole harvest, all so that in him we could inherit his estate with his wealth credited or imputed to us?[73] For Paul, a creature's righteousness is covenant faithfulness

---

70. Bird, "Progressive Reformed Perspective," 152.
71. Bird, "Progressive Reformed Perspective," 152.
72. Bird, "Progressive Reformed Perspective," 145.
73. In a footnote, Bird asserts that the Westminster Confession (11.1) "deliberately omits reference to the 'active' obedience of Christ." However, the Confession affirms the covenant of

as (rather than in opposition to) conformity to the law. Christ is the Second Adam in whom we are justified. Paul's dots are not difficult to connect: in Adam (under the law's curse), Jews and gentiles alike are judged guilty and therefore liable to death; in Christ, Jews and gentiles alike are declared righteous because of the obedience of Christ.

Like Wright, Bird keeps moving the pieces of the puzzle around: yes to a new status in Christ, and yes even to imputation (as long as it is not transferring "frequent flyer points").[74] Then he says no to the only thing that could be imputed: namely Christ's righteousness—i.e., his covenant faithfulness to the law. Finally, he obfuscates the whole issue by pressing the false choice between union with Christ and the imputation of Christ's obedience; at least according to the Reformers and their scholastic heirs, the latter is the gift of the former.

It becomes quite evident that for many critics the "Reformation perspective" or "justification theory" has more to do with Billy Graham and/or Rudolf Bultmann than with Luther and Calvin.[75] I have also

---

works in 7.2 and adds references to his active as well as passive obedience securing redemption in 8.5 and 9.3. In fact, by the time of the Westminster Confession, the denial of Christ's active obedience was associated with the Amyraldian and Arminian schools as a defection from the Reformed system.

74. Bird, "Progressive Reformed Perspective," 145. This comparison is only a slightly greater caricature than Wright's analogy of a gas being passed from one person to another.

75. Some of Karl Barth's revisions seem driven in part by his revulsion at the psychological gymnastics of pietistic revivalism. Eberhard Busch, *Karl Barth and the Pietists*, trans. Daniel W. Bloesch (Eugene, OR: Wipf and Stock, 2016), 38. James Dunn identifies Bultmann and Billy Graham as primary examples of the individualistic soteriology he opposes. James D. G. Dunn, "New Perspective View," *Justification: Five Views*, ed. James K. Beilby and Paul Rhodes Eddy (Downers Grove, IL: InterVarsity, 2011), 185n38. Similarly, the foil for N. T. Wright's treatments of the atonement and justification is the crudest evangelistic presentations that I too have encountered, but they are hardly representative of Reformation theology, whose standard works he repeatedly admits he has not read. After hundreds of pages of trying to discern the target of Douglas Campbell's "justification theory," one finally discovers it: Billy Graham and the Four Spiritual Laws (*The Deliverance of God*, 291, 337, 1029). One would be hard-pressed, I think, to find references to justification in Billy Graham's books and sermons, and there is nothing about justification in the Four Spiritual Laws. (Likewise, not a single primary source is cited from the classic Reformed theologians he criticizes ad nauseam.) In any case, the undergirding theology (Arminian synergism) is not even remotely related to the magisterial Reformation. Consequently, much of the contemporary criticism of the traditional evangelical doctrine of justification comes from those who hail from broadly evangelical-revivalist traditions (Sanders and Dunn, Methodist, and Wright, evangelical Anglican). Michael Bird, Peter Leithart, and Matthew Bates are evangelicals. There is a tendency to claim the label "Reformed" on the part of those who have no ecclesial commitment to the Reformed confessions. I say all of this merely to suggest that the bulk of contemporary criticism of the Reformation comes from scholars with some background in evangelical-revivalist traditions whose biblical scholarship considerably outweighs their familiarity with the actual texts of confessional Lutheran and Reformed traditions. Consequently, the impressive guns of biblical scholarship are often aimed at straw opponents. Frustrations with an evangelical subculture in which one was reared are often directed at the Reformation more broadly when in fact there is a very real difference.

heard popular presentations of imputation that sound a lot like the frequent-flier-points analogy, with little grounding in the Christ-event and union with Christ. But these are not credible formulations of Reformation and confessional Lutheran or Reformed teaching. Besides the fact that all the elements for active obedience and imputation are present in Bird's helpful and compact summary above, Reformed theology emphasizes union with Christ, and covenantal participation in his active obedience as well as his death and resurrection can hardly be said to detract from "in Christ" language.

Mark Seifrid also argues that if justification grants forgiveness of sins, then an imputation of righteousness on the basis of Christ's active obedience is "unnecessary and misleading."[76] "In reducing 'justification' to a present possession of 'Christ's imputed righteousness,'" he says, "Protestant divines inadvertently bruised the nerve which runs between justification and obedience. It is not so much *wrong* to use the expression 'the imputed righteousness of Christ' as it is *deficient*."[77]

However, the first question is whether Scripture teaches imputation, not whether one considers it unnecessary or as endangering sanctification. Furthermore, the Reformation interpretation cannot be reductive or deficient if it actually says *more* than Seifrid allows: namely, that justification includes forgiveness *and* the imputation of righteousness.[78] But more to the point, forgiveness by itself does not establish rectitude. It is not *forgiveness* (negation of guilt) that withstands the last judgment, but *righteousness* (positive standing). Without the latter, the goal of the covenant as well as its conditions are left unfulfilled. The familiar shibboleths drawn from Cremer, Schweitzer, Stendahl, and others present themselves in Seifrid's assertion: "justification" cannot be "reduced to an event which takes place for the individual at the beginning of the Christian life" within "an 'order of salvation' (*ordo salutis*)."[79] Yet does

---

76. Mark A. Seifrid, *Christ, Our Righteousness: Paul's Theology of Justification* (Downers Grove, IL: IVP Academic, 2001), 175

77. Seifrid, *Christ, Our Righteousness*, 175.

78. In an intriguing remark, Herman Bavinck judges, "The rationalistic school is rooted basically in Piscator's teaching, according to which the righteousness we need is accomplished not by the active but solely by the passive obedience of Christ!" (Bavinck, *Reformed Dogmatics*, ed. John Bold, trans. John Vriend [Grand Rapids: Baker Academic, 2006], 3:531). I am in no way placing Seifrid in the "rationalistic school" but noting that all of these alternative moves have been made before, as we see again below in relation to Gundry's objection to imputation that repeats the Arminian and Neonomian argument. That doesn't make it wrong, but it does challenge the common assumption that "it's just exegesis."

79. Seifrid, *Christ, Our Righteousness*, 176

not Paul place it in an *ordo salutis* in Romans 8:30? There seems to be enough of a logical progression in his thought from predestination to calling to justification to glorification that one might be warranted in calling an *ordo*. Where, if anywhere, does Seifrid think that justification belongs in it?

Legal Fiction?

When Paul says, "So you also must consider [λογίζεσθε] yourselves dead to sin and alive to God in Christ Jesus" (Rom 6:11), he is not saying, "Pretend that you are dead to sin and alive to God in Christ." Instead, he is calling hearers to recognize what is in fact the case. Analogously, for God to reckon, impute, consider, or count us as righteous for Christ's sake is not to pretend that we are righteous but for him to acknowledge what is true about us when Christ is our righteousness. Because Christ's righteousness is imputed or credited in the declaration itself, justification cannot be considered a legal fiction. It is therefore unwise to jettison imputation in an effort to save justification from this charge when in fact imputation saves the doctrine from it.

It is not a legal fiction to have an inheritance credited to one's account—any more than it is to have one's debts canceled or credited to another. As Paul looks over his ledger in Philippians 3, he places his righteousness in the liabilities column and Christ's righteousness in the assets column. In the alternative accounts, the inheritance does not seem to allow for giving anything to anyone in particular. Justification may be forensic (that is, judicial), but there can be no transfer of assets, if you will, from a faithful representative to the ungodly. Yet Paul says that instead of possessing a righteousness of his own, he possesses the righteousness of Christ. How can we understand that other than a *transfer* of liabilities and assets—a great exchange? This stock of legal and commercial imagery is not the stuff of Sunday school legend but belonged to the world of ancient Judaism that Paul knew well.

A major plank of the Roman Catholic critique of the Reformation doctrine is that it is a legal fiction: God merely declaring something to be the case contrary to fact. Many Protestant scholars today concur, as we have seen, including Douglas Campbell, Hans Boersma, Wolfhart Pannenberg, and Peter Leithart. As in the Roman Catholic view, baptism transforms one's state and condition such that the only relevance of a forensic declaration is to recognize that deliverance has taken place.

As we have seen, N. T. Wright also treats justification merely as analytic, as declaring what is already the case apart from justification itself. In neither view does justification itself accomplish anything (either infusion or imputation), but where Campbell and Leithart view justification as a declaration that transformation has occurred, Wright sees it as a declaration that one is a covenant member.

According to Wright, "Paul's doctrine of justification is focused on the divine law-court," *over against* "the supposed moral achievement of Jesus in gaining, through his perfect obedience, a righteousness which can then be passed on to his faithful people."[80] But I cannot see how this false dichotomy does not raise the specter of justification as a legal fiction. First, it rests, once again, on the unfounded claim that the righteousness of God is a relational-concept and not a norm-concept. Bultmann's "relational not ethical" dichotomy is Wright's "covenantal not moral achievement," but the distinction goes back to Diestel and Cremer. However, what sort of court, especially God's, makes judgments that have nothing to do with whether laws have been broken or fulfilled (i.e., "moral achievement")? Second, it is difficult to see how the crediting of the believer with Christ's covenantal standing *undermines* a legal justification. On the contrary, it renders justification something other than a mere decree and without foundation in reality.

Yet Wright does seem to think that *somehow* what is true of Jesus is now true of us who believe in him. According to Romans, he says, "The long entail of Adam's sin and death can be undone (5.12–21) through his obedience."[81] In spite of Israel's unfaithfulness, "God must stick to the plan." "But that means that sooner or later he will require a representative Israelite who *will* be faithful, who will be obedient to God's purpose not only for Israel but through Israel for the world."[82] He even affirms that, again *somehow*, this righteous status is communicated to them: "The Messiah represents his people so that what is true of him is true of them."[83] Happily, this is the opposite of Wright's strong claims elsewhere: namely, that justification is not about how people are saved, nor about a status that God somehow grants to us in the Messiah, but about God's own faithfulness. Here at least, justification is a legal,

80. Wright, *Justification*, 12.
81. Wright, *Paul: In Fresh Perspective*, 47.
82. Wright, *Paul: In Fresh Perspective*, 47.
83. Wright, *Paul: In Fresh Perspective*, 113.

courtroom verdict that somehow grants the Messiah's representative status to his people "so that what is true of him is true of them." All the ingredients of a chocolate chip cookie are present except the chocolate chips: what is still missing even from this formulation is the mechanism for this sharing of covenantal status—imputation.

We have seen that Wright affirms that the *guilt* of believers is imputed to Christ, so *forgiveness* is not a legal fiction in his view. As with all attempts to affirm a forensic account of justification while rejecting imputation, justification is left suspended in midair. It is indeed a legal fiction.

Adding another false dichotomy, he says, "It is not the 'righteousness' of Jesus Christ which is 'reckoned' to the believer. *It is his death and resurrection.*"[84] This seems to differ from his formulation above, where he says that it is *not* "Christ's own righteousness that is reckoned to God's redeemed people but, rather, *the fresh status of 'covenant member.'*"[85] In the former statement, Wright does see Christ's death and resurrection as "'reckoned' to the believer." But then why not his obedient life as well?

The alternative views are reductive. When Christ's active obedience is left out of the equation, one may legitimately question whether there is in fact any basis in fact for the divine verdict.

But the difference runs deeper. By presupposing Cremer's thesis, Wright denies himself the option of treating justification as a declaration that one is righteous because one shares Christ's covenantal status of "righteous" before the law. The relevant phrases have been so completely redefined that even the formulas that approach the Reformation construction lack any semantic or exegetical foundation. This comes in contrast with the Reformation view, in which Christ's curse-bearing and fulfillment of the law constitute the basis for forgiveness and righteousness, respectively; the *ordo salutis* is firmly grounded in the *historia salutis*. Wright discounts the idea of justification involving moral achievement, yet this is precisely how Paul says that God justifies and condemns—hence our need for "the gift of righteousness" achieved by Jesus in his incarnation, life, death, and resurrection.

Seeking to overcome false choices (especially forensic versus participationist and soteriology versus ecclesiology), Michael Bird recognizes that the problem that Paul addresses is deeper and wider than ethnic

---

84. Wright, *Justification*, 232, emphasis added.
85. Wright, "New Perspectives on Paul," 253, emphasis added.

exclusion (viz., "the curse of the law"; Gal 3:10). He properly observes that the solution yields an ecclesiological result: "so that in Christ Jesus the blessing of Abraham might come to the Gentiles" (Gal 3:14). "So when you think gospel, think Abrahamic promises," Bird rightly counsels.[86]

However, in spite of his own judgment, Bird finds the Reformation's interpretation of imputation untenable. It is "still trapped in medieval categories of merit; and it doesn't adequately grasp the implications of union with Christ."

> So Jesus' obedience does become ours—but not through artificially dividing Jesus' obedience into active and passive varieties, not through a medieval concept of "merit" that is imputed instead of imparted, not because Jesus is the exemplary pelagian who earns salvation when we cannot, not by fulfilling a covenant of works that did not contain grace, not by way of righteousness molecules floating through the air to us—rather, we become "righteous" in Christ when by faith we participate in the vicarious death and resurrection of Jesus Christ.[87]

It is difficult to take such a lampoon seriously. However, against this imaginary position, Bird suggests that "righteousness here is not a property to be transferred, but a status to be conferred."[88]

Yet again, there is no transfer of *property* in the Reformation view of justification; on the contrary, this was the doctrine they rejected. What is transferred or conferred—it is the same idea—is Christ's meritorious status before God. There is no transfer of God's essential righteousness—whether gas, steam, solid, or liquid—across the courtroom or righteousness molecules floating through the air to us; just "the free gift of righteousness . . . through the one man Jesus Christ" (Rom 5:17). Bird affirms, "There is indeed a gift of a righteous status from God (see Rom 5:17; Phil 3:9)."[89] So I am not quite sure why he is so reticent to identify this with the imputation of Christ's righteousness to believers. Indeed, Paul *says* that Christ is our righteousness (1 Cor 1:30; 2 Cor 5:21; Phil 3:9, perhaps glossing Jer 23:6; Isa 53:11; 61:10).

---

86. Bird, "Progressive Reformed Perspective," 138.
87. Bird, "Progressive Reformed Perspective," 150.
88. Bird, "Progressive Reformed Perspective," 147.
89. Bird, "Progressive Reformed Perspective," 141.

There are indeed other metaphors for justification than "crediting," but they all point to the same reality: clothed with Christ, cancelled debts, full inheritance, and so forth. Paul seems to connect more dots than Bird suggests. When Wright and Bird concede that righteousness is a *status conferred*, they are recognizing at least implicitly the point that the Protestant Reformers intended by Paul's λογίζομαι. However, both scholars resist the idea of imputation largely because of the standard assumption (via Cremer) that righteousness cannot be conformity to a norm and because of the canard that the idea of merit is medieval. But, as we have seen, the idea of merit is also Jewish, and the new perspective is eager to display the continuities between Paul and Judaism. Although Bird's final answer seems unclear to me, his refusal of imputation leaves him also open to the charge of a doctrine of justification that is a legal fiction. If Christ's righteousness is not made *my* righteousness by some glorious exchange, then any declaration is either going to be based on inner transformation or on an arbitrary decree contrary to fact.

According to Robert Gundry, it is not union with Christ but faith that takes the place of Christ's alien righteousness. This view indeed obviates the charge of a legal fiction, but it does so at the cost of making the inherent righteousness of the believer (the virtue of faith itself) the basis of justification.

First, Gundry agrees that there are explicit imputation passages. "But none of these texts says that Christ's righteousness was counted," writes Gundry, "so that righteousness comes into view not as what is counted but as what God counts faith to be."[90] What God counts or imputes is faith, not Christ's righteousness, Gundry argues.[91] Gundry clearly states that "the righteousness that comes 'from' (*ek*) faith (Rom 9:30; 10:6) and from God 'through' (*dia*) faith and 'on the basis of' (*epi*) faith (Phil 3:9) is the faith that God counts as righteousness. Paul's language is supple: faith is the *origin*, the means, and the *basis* of righteousness in that God counts it as righteousness" (emphasis added).[92]

However, *epi* has a broader lexical range than Gundry allows.[93] While in technical theological jargon the basis (or formal cause) of something

---

90. Robert Gundry, "The Nonimputation of Christ's Righteousness" in *Justification: What's at Stake in the Current Debates*, ed. Mark Husbands and Daniel J. Treier (Downers Grove, IL: IVP Academic, 2004), 18.

91. Gundry, "The Nonimputation of Christ's Righteousness," 22.

92. Gundry, "The Nonimputation of Christ's Righteousness," 25.

93. There are no fewer than eighteen possible renderings, according to BDAG, 363–67.

is distinguished from the means (or instrumental cause), *epi* and *dia* both are used with greater range and flexibility in scripture, as their English equivalents are in common use. In fact, *epi* appears as a basis ("on account of" or "because of"), a marker of basis for a state of being, an action, or a result in numerous places.[94] In other words, *epi* ("on account of") is interchangeable with *dia* ("through").

Even Luther can say, in his exegesis of Galatians, that we are justified "for the sake of our faith in Christ or for the sake of Christ," as if the two phrases are interchangeable.[95] He can do so, first, because he believes that Christ himself is present in faith (based on Rom 10:8, etc.). Faith is not like a transaction between the sinner and Christ; it is Christ's act of uniting the sinner to himself. It all depends on what one is contrasting: faith and works or faith as an inherently worthy basis versus passive instrument. For Luther, instead of being anthropocentric, faith negates the self as the source of righteous action altogether to cling to Christ.[96]

However, in dogmatics the choice of preposition is more precise, especially through the influence of Aristotle's *Categories*, with distinctions between various causes (formal, material, efficient, instrumental, final). With greater refinement during the heat of polemical battle, the magisterial Reformers favored the formula *iustificatio propter Christum per fidei* (justification on the basis of Christ through faith) precisely to avoid the error of thinking that the faith now constitutes the virtuous act that God graciously treats as if it were the fulfilling of the whole law. If Gundry is saying that faith is the *basis* in this technical sense, then it is the *material cause* of justification, which would be quite a radical position. In the Roman Catholic view, faith (and works) has a merely *instrumental* role in justification. Roman Catholic and Protestant systems agree that Christ is the *basis* (or material cause) of justification (although not the exclusive basis, in the former system). Gundry does say that "Paul rejects the Jewish tradition that God counted Abraham's faith as righteousness because it was a work (a good one, of course)."[97]

---

94. BDAG, 366.

95. Luther, *Lectures on Galatians Chapters 1–4* (1535), in *LW* 26:233.

96. See Jonathan A. Linebaugh, "The Christo-Centrism of Faith in Christ: Martin Luther's Reading of Gal 2.16, 19–20," *New Testament Studies* 59, no. 4 (2013): 535–44.

97. Gundry, "The Nonimputation of Christ's Righteousness," 25. Gundry notes the following survey of the Jewish literature: J. A. Ziesler, *The Meaning of Righteousness in Paul: A Linguistic and Theological Inquiry* (Cambridge: Cambridge University Press, 1972), 43, 103–4, 109, 123, 125–26, 175, 182–83.

Yet if faith is the ground of justification rather than the instrument, one wonders how that Jewish interpretation could be faulted.

On the basis of Paul's statement that the people's sinning before the law was "not after the likeness of Adam's transgression," Gundry denies the imputation of Adam's sin and therefore of Christ's righteousness.[98] Yet this verse (Rom 5:14) makes the opposite point—namely, that even though they did not commit the *same* sin, they were still the *same* sinner in, with, and through Adam. Further, Gundry speaks of "the failure of Paul, despite his extensive discussion of law and writing that Christ was 'born under the law' (Gal 4:4), ever to make a point of Christ's keeping the law perfectly on our behalf (not even his sinlessness in 2 Cor 5:21 being put in relation to law-keeping)."[99]

Yet what other import might the phrase "born under the law" have served? And how else would a Jewish contemporary have understood sinlessness other than "in relation to law-keeping"? And why does Paul contrast Adam's one act of disobedience and Christ's one act of obedience? Does this not suggest that Christ's obedience, rather than our faith, is imputed? Further, besides rejecting original sin, Gundry fails to consider the passages that refer to Christ's needing "to fulfill all righteousness" (Matt 3:15), "to fulfill the law" (Mt 5:17), and to sanctify himself "that they may be truly sanctified" (John 17:19), as well as Hebrews 10:5–7, which interprets Psalm 40:7–8 as referring to Christ's active obedience for us. Gundry argues, "To be sure, *dikaiōma*, translated 'act of righteousness' in Romans 5:18 and 'righteous requirement' in Romans 8:4 (also in Romans 1:32), may be collective in Romans 8:4 for all the requirements of the law. But that collective meaning is unsure, even unlikely, for Paul writes in Galatians 5:14 that 'the whole law is fulfilled in one command, 'You shall love your neighbor as yourself.'"[100]

Yet even such an interpretation of Galatians 5:14 seems strained. Paul was merely summarizing "the whole law" (i.e., all the requirements of the law collectively comprehended). Surely loving one's neighbor does not consist in one act. And in the context of the apostle's running polemic in Galatians, would it not be legitimate to assume here that he is simply repeating the claim in 3:10 that to offend at one point

---

98. Gundry, "The Nonimputation of Christ's Righteousness," 28.
99. Gundry, "The Nonimputation of Christ's Righteousness," 32.
100. Gundry, "The Nonimputation of Christ's Righteousness," 34.

(failing to love God and neighbor perfectly) is to be "under the curse" of the law?

Although he has argued that faith is not a work, Gundry says, "The righteousness of faith is *the moral accomplishment* that God counts faith to be even though it is not *intrinsically* such an accomplishment" (emphasis added).[101] Christ's "obediently righteous act of propitiation made it right for God to count faith as righteousness."[102] Thus our imperfect obedience ("moral accomplishment") is rewarded with final justification over and beyond its inherent value.

Gundry's critique of imputation is not new; it was advanced by Arminius, Hugo Grotius, and other Remonstrant (Arminian) theologians as well as by the English Puritan Richard Baxter.[103] It was for this reason that the Westminster Confession adds that believers are justified "not by anything wrought in them or done by them, *nor by imputing faith itself, the act of believing, or any other evangelical obedience to them, as their righteousness*; but by imputing the obedience and satisfaction of Christ unto them, they *receiving and resting on Him* and His righteousness by faith; which faith they have not of themselves, it is the gift of God."[104]

However, aside from historical parallels, is Gundry's position exegetically plausible? Responding to Gundry's argument, D. A. Carson points out that Paul was well aware of Jewish exegesis of Genesis 15:6 "to prove that Abraham was justified by faith and not by works" but rather as meritorious obedience.[105] "What this means, for our purposes, is that Paul, who certainly knew of these traditions, was explicitly interpreting Genesis 15:6 in a way quite different from that found in his own

---

101. Gundry, "The Nonimputation of Christ's Righteousness," 36, emphasis added.

102. Gundry, "The Nonimputation of Christ's Righteousness," 39.

103. See Arminius, The Works of Arminius, trans. James Nichols and W. R. Bagnall, 3 vols. (1825–28; repr., Grand Rapids: Baker, 1956), 2:42–50. The Puritan Richard Baxter made a similar argument, treating faith and evangelical obedience as the "new law" that replaces the "old law" as the basis for justification. Faith is "paying but a Pepper Corn" as a tenant to a landlord. In this way, "Faith shall be imputed to us for a sufficient personal Payment, as if we had paid the full rent." Richard Baxter, *An Extract of Mr. Richard Baxter's Aphorisms of Justification, Publish'd by John Wesley* (London: W. Strahan, 1745; Gale ECCO Print Editions, 2010), 19–20. Chapter 13 of the Westminster Confession targets this error when it states that believers are justified "not by imputing faith itself, the act of believing, or any other evangelical obedience to them as their righteousness; but by imputing the obedience and satisfaction of Christ unto them, they receiving and resting on him and his righteousness by faith; which faith they have not of themselves, it is the gift of God." In fact, it is possible to recognize parallels with the covenant (or better, contractual) theology of late medieval nominalism, according to which justification is granted on the basis of one's imperfect obedience. No one merits final justification according to strict merit (*de condigno*), but only according to God's gracious decision to accept it as if it were meritorious (*de congruo*).

104. Westminster Confession of Faith 11.1 (Glasgow: Free Church Publications, 1997), 56–57.

105. Examples include Rabbi Shemaiah, 50 BC; *Mekhilta* on Exod 14:15 [35b], 40b.

tradition, and he was convinced that this new way was the correct way to understand the text."[106]

More specifically, Carson draws our attention to the parallelism in Romans 4:5–6:

4:5—God *justifies* the ungodly.
4:6—God *credits righteousness* apart from works.

"In other words, 'justifies' is parallel to 'credits righteousness'; or, to put the matter in nominal terms, justification is parallel to the imputation of righteousness."[107] And it has to be an "alien" righteousness, since "God justifies *the ungodly* (Rom 4:5); he credits righteousness *apart from works* (Rom 4:6)."[108]

Carson reasons, "If God has counted or imputed our faith to us as righteousness, then, once he has so counted or imputed it, does he then count or impute the righteousness to us, a kind of second imputation?"[109] In Philippians 3, it is clearly not an inherent righteousness.[110] "In 2 Corinthians 5:19–21, we are told that God made Christ who had no sin to be sin for us, so that *in him* we might become the *righteousness* of God. It is because of God that we are in Christ Jesus, who has become for us *righteousness* (and other things: 1 Cor 1:30). Passage after passage in Paul runs down the same track."[111] Faith—even faith in Christ—is not the same as having a righteousness that is "not of my own." Faith, not Christ, becomes the basis for the transfer from unrighteous to righteous.[112]

It becomes clear that the case for justification rests on the case for imputation, for without the latter the former is indeed an arbitrary decree, a legal fiction, and, even more, an impossibility since God cannot justify without being just. Yahweh "will by no means clear the guilty" (Nah 1:3). Justification cannot therefore be a mere exoneration or pardon over against the law but must be accomplished with the concurrence

---

106. D. A. Carson, "The Vindication of Imputation: On Fields of Discourse and Semantic Fields," *Justification: What's at Stake in the Current Debates*, ed. Mark Husbands and Daniel J. Treier (Downers Grove, IL: InterVarsity, 2004), 56.
107. Carson, "The Vindication of Imputation," 61, emphasis added.
108. Carson, "The Vindication of Imputation," 61.
109. Carson, "The Vindication of Imputation," 64.
110. Carson, "The Vindication of Imputation," 69.
111. Carson, "The Vindication of Imputation," 72.
112. Carson, "The Vindication of Imputation," 72.

of the law. God's righteous law—the *norm* by which we are judged covenantally faithful—must declare whether one is righteous. But only with imputation is this law upheld rather than circumvented.

Furthermore, if the ground of justification is faith itself, then faith is no longer the passive instrument of receiving God's declaration but the one small work ("faithfulness") that saves, or in other words, as Gundry defines above, "*the moral accomplishment* that God counts faith to be."[113] We will consider the role of faith in justification in chapter 11.

One final note is worth mentioning in connection with the charge of a legal fiction. Reformation theology, both Lutheran and Reformed, has emphasized that all of God's works wear a covenantal aspect. God speaks creation into existence out of nothing, and Paul draws on this to highlight the *ex nihilo*, unconditional, and effective speech by which Yahweh fulfills his promise apart from anything in human beings (Rom 4:17). Justification itself is the forensic source, not the effect, of this speech. As the Reformers often said, when God declares a sinner to be just, apart from anything already existing in or done by the believer, he or she *is* just. This is true in both senses: legally just in God's courtroom and definitively just, holy, and righteous. Again, the latter is the result of justification, not justification itself. However, God's word cannot return to him without accomplishing *every* purpose for which he sent it (Isa 55:11).

Along these lines, Simon Gathercole argues, "We should more properly consider that God's 'speech-acts' are what *determine* reality; they do not merely create an alternative, Platonic reality," notes Gathercole. In a footnote, he says, "What I have in mind here is the view sometimes articulated, that although we are *really* sinners, yet, when God looks at us, God sees Jesus."[114]

> If God declares a sinner to be righteous, then he or she really *is* righteous. . . . This is not simply the imposition of a foreign philosophical or linguistic understanding of God's words—it comes from Romans 4. . . . The righteousness here should not be understood either as an infused moral power or as covenant membership. . . .

---

113. Gundry, "The Nonimputation of Christ's Righteousness," 36.

114. Simon Gathercole, "The Doctrine of Justification in Paul and Beyond," in *Justification in Perspective: Historical Developments and Contemporary Challenges*, ed. Bruce L. McCormack (Grand Rapids: Baker Academic, 2006), 226n10.

> By God's creative word, then, we stand as embodying everything that God requires. In our identity and being we have been determined righteous by God.[115]

"The category of 'alien' righteousness is vital in capturing the truth that our righteousness comes only from God and not from ourselves," Gathercole concludes. "But it should not be misinterpreted to mean that we are thereby not really righteous."[116] Not only because God's word is powerful and definitive but also because, via imputation, our "alien righteousness" is really ours, the charge of a legal fiction cannot be sustained.

COMPARISON WITH OTHER FACETS OF THE GREAT EXCHANGE

Like most doctrines, the debate over imputation will not be decided simply by the number of times *logizomai* appears. It is the task of biblical scholars and dogmaticians alike to gather the pieces of the puzzle together and see how they fit according to their intrinsic place in an overall pattern. The Westminster Confession offers one of the best summaries of the Scripture principle: "The whole counsel of God . . . is either expressly set down in Scripture, or by good and necessary consequence may be deduced from Scripture."[117]

This formula requires dogmas to be grounded in Scripture while avoiding a biblicism that has fueled many heresies in church history. For example, the doctrine of the Trinity is clearly taught in Scripture if one puts together the various pieces of its teachings (viz., God is one, but the Father is God, the Son is God, and the Holy Spirit is God). From the paucity of explicit formulations, some biblical scholars and theologians have also judged the doctrine of *ex nihilo* creation to be an early patristic development rather than a scriptural teaching. Nevertheless, Scripture does teach clearly and explicitly that God alone is eternal (Ps 90:2; Isa 44:6; 48:12; John 1:1–3; Rev 1:8), that creation came into being at a certain moment by his will and command (Gen 1:1; Pss 33:6; 104:24; Isa 45:18; 1 Cor 8:6; Heb 11:3; Rev 4:11), that nothing existed before God did so decree it (Isa 44:24; Rom 4:17), and that all things exist by

---

115. Gathercole, "The Doctrine of Justification in Paul and Beyond," 226–27.
116. Gathercole, "The Doctrine of Justification in Paul and Beyond," 229.
117. Westminster Confession of Faith, ch. 1 (p. 22).

him, through him, and for him (Isa 42:5–6; Rom 11:36; Col 1:16). On this basis, one not only may but must conclude that Scripture teaches that creation is a temporal and contingent effect of God's free speech, that is, the doctrine of *ex nihilo* creation.

Similarly, the exegetical support for the doctrine of justification through faith alone, on the basis of Christ's righteousness imputed to the sinner, should be determined not only by explicit proof texts but by drawing conclusions from good and necessary deductions from a variety of passages. It is not a question therefore of exegesis versus systematic theology. It should be evident by now that all the parties in this discussion are doing theology, interpreting particular passages in the light of other passages that form what each scholar takes to be the overall thrust of "Paul's theology."

In the light of this prolegomenon, only a crude biblicism would make the doctrine of imputation to depend on the prominence of the term itself. The New Testament offers a broad range of images, such as clothing, transferring debts and assets, a last will and testament, a gift of righteousness, and other metaphors for imputation.

I opened our historical exploration in volume 1 by focusing on the "great exchange" motif in the ancient church. This umbrella-term, which is synonymous with union with Christ, helps us to discern the broader semantic range of terms related to justification than the δίκ-group itself. Great-exchange language carries the same freight as the technical term *imputation*: "the righteous one, my servant, shall make many to be accounted righteous" (Isa 53:11); "the righteous for the unrighteous" (1 Pet 3:18); "[Christ] became to us wisdom from God, righteousness and sanctification and redemption" (1 Cor 1:30). We do not need the technical word "imputation." The concept is there.

It is not surprising that the ancient church found justification like a gleaming gem nestled in martial, clothing, commercial, legal, familial, and a host of other analogies. These are, after all, the ways justification appears in Scripture itself.

Clothing Metaphors

To "put on Christ" is to derive all of one's righteousness from him, both for justification and sanctification. That is not only because he is the eternal Son but because he is the justified covenant head of his people "and was declared to be Son of God with power according to the

Spirit of holiness by resurrection from the dead" (Rom 1:4). In Christ, our rags are exchanged for robes of regal splendor and we are seated at the same table with Abraham, Isaac, and Jacob.

The clothing analogy is not original to Pauline theology. It occurs first with God's clothing of Adam and Eve after the fall. At first, Job considered his integrity his clothing: "I put on righteousness, and it clothed me; my justice was like a robe and a turban" (Job 29:14), but he also recognizes, "Though I am in the right, my own mouth would condemn me; though I am blameless, he would prove me perverse" (Job 9:20). "I shall be condemned [lit., "am accounted wicked"]; why then do I labor in vain?" (v. 29). He realizes that God's justice penetrates into the depths of his heart. Who can win a case in court with God? (vv. 31–32). "There is no arbiter between us, who might lay his hand on us both. Let him take his rod away from me, and let not dread of him terrify me. Then I would speak without fear of him, for I am not so in myself" (vv. 33–35). Only at the end of the story does Job realize that his only hope is to have a mediator and to cast himself on God's mercy in sackcloth and ashes. "Even now, behold my witness is in heaven, and he who testifies for me is on high" (16:19). For I know that my Redeemer lives, and at the last he will stand upon the earth" (19:25).

The analogy reappears in the vision of Joshua the high priest in Zechariah 3, a courtroom scene with Yahweh the judge, the Angel of the LORD (who is also identified as God), Satan as the prosecutor, and of course Joshua himself. Satan accuses, and the Angel of the LORD commands his attendant to remove the high priest's filthy clothes (remission) *and* to exchange these for garments of righteousness (justification).

Similarly, Isaiah exults, "I will greatly rejoice in the LORD, my whole being shall exult in my God; for he has clothed me with the garments of salvation, he has covered me with the robe of righteousness, as a bridegroom decks himself with a garland, and as a bride adorns herself with her jewels" (Isa 61:10–11; cf. Rev 21:2, which paraphrases this verse, interpreting it as the clothing of the elect in robes of righteousness).

The guests at the wedding feast in Jesus's parable are adorned in festive garments (Matt 22:1–14), and the prodigal son is decked out by the father in the best clothes upon his return (Luke 15:11–32). So when Paul says that Christ is "our righteousness, holiness, and redemption" (1 Cor 1:30) and refers repeatedly to our being "clothed with Christ," "having put on Jesus Christ," and calls us on that basis to "put on

Christ" in our daily conduct, this same connection between justification and sanctification is being drawn.

Therefore, when N. T. Wright says, "But Paul does not say that God sees us clothed with the earned merits of Christ,"[118] I wonder what else he could possibly mean when he speaks of "the gift of righteousness" that is nothing less than "Jesus Christ" (Rom 5:17) or when he says that "all of you who were baptized into Christ have clothed yourselves with Christ" (Gal 3:27). Again, there is more to this great exchange than imputation, but there is nothing without the latter. We wear Christ's righteousness like a robe. And what is this righteousness if not his "earned merits"—that is, his fulfillment of the law? Justification is no more a legal fiction than it is an emperor with no clothes.

Adoption

We could refer to other gifts of our union with Christ that depend on justification. In adoption, the Father's reward given to Christ for his meritorious obedience is shared with his brothers and sisters. Everyone who is in Christ is a "firstborn son," coheir of the entire estate, a child of Abraham (Gal 3:28–29). Far from the false dichotomies that we have encountered, the judicial basis of justification provides the objective security for a genuine relationship.

In the economy of the Sinai covenant, Moses is a servant in God's house, while Jesus Christ is the firstborn son (Heb 3:1–6). So even Moses's justification and adoption are dependent not on the condition of his personal fulfillment of the law-covenant made at Sinai but on Christ's personal fulfillment of that covenant by which he has won our reward.

> For he who sanctifies and those who are sanctified all have one source. That is why he is not ashamed to call them brothers, saying, "I will tell of your name to my brothers; in the midst of the congregation I will sing your praise." And again, "I will put my trust in him." And again, "Behold, I and the children God has given me." (Heb 2:11–12)

Like justification, this adoption is not a legal fiction. The law is fulfilled: the first-born Son has won the entire estate by his victorious

---

118. Wright, "New Perspectives on Paul," 261.

service to the crown, but, as established in the mutuality of the covenant of redemption (i.e., election), every adopted child has an equal share.

If union with Christ in the covenant of grace is the matrix for Paul's *ordo*, justification remains its source, even for adoption. We do not move from the topic of justification to other (more interesting) ones but are always relating the riches of our inheritance to this decisive gift. In William Ames's words, "Adoption of its own nature requires and presupposes the reconciliation found in justification. . . . The first fruit of adoption is that Christian liberty by which all believers are freed from the bondage of the law, sin, and the world."[119] The children need not worry about their future or jockey for their Father's favor. After all, "He who did not withhold his own Son, but gave him up for all of us, will he not with him also give us everything else?" (Rom 8:32).

---

119. William Ames, *The Marrow of Theology*, ed. John Dykstra Eusden (Grand Rapids: Baker Academic, 1997), 165.

CHAPTER 9

JUSTIFICATION AND JUDGMENT

The Role of Works in the Day of Christ Jesus

One of the (if not *the*) key loci for revealing one's view of justification is the final judgment. The final salvation of the elect is already secured. It is based on the eternal covenant of redemption and the immutability of God's promise. The God who promised Abraham a redeemer-seed and passed alone between the pieces in a self-maledictory oath *cannot* fail to fulfill his purpose. "And those whom he predestined he also called, and those whom he called he also justified, and those whom he justified he also glorified" (Rom 8:30).

Can any link in this golden chain be broken? If not, then what do we make of the passages that clearly teach a final judgment according to works? Will there be some who are predestined, called, and justified (in the present) who will not be glorified (justified in the future)? The focus of this chapter is on justification and the final judgment. However, we begin with a brief analysis of the harmony between James and Paul to set the stage for that discussion.

JAMES AND PAUL

If, of the New Testament, we had only James's epistle without Paul's corpus, we still would have the teaching of Jesus in the synoptic gospels with clear reference to his coming for the ungodly rather than those who think that they are righteous, the justification of the wicked who call on God's mercy, the impossibility of entering his kingdom through the law rather than his gracious forgiveness, and the role of faith alone in receiving Christ with his benefits. The fourth gospel would confirm that all who trust in Christ have passed from condemnation to justification, from death to life, and we would still know from the sermons in Acts and the epistles of Peter and John that we are chosen, redeemed, called, and justified by grace alone in Christ alone. But we would have no knowledge of the background to James's polemic against those who imagine that they could be justified by a faith that does not produce the fruit of love and good works.

Paul did not teach what James excoriated, nor does the Jerusalem apostle claim that he did. However, Paul knew what some people were saying: "And why not do evil that good may come?—as some people slanderously charge us with saying. Their condemnation is just" (Rom 3:8). "What then shall we say? Shall we continue in sin so that grace may increase? By no means!" (Rom 6:1–2). "It is not surprising, then, if [Satan's] servants masquerade as servants of righteousness. Their end will correspond to their actions" (2 Cor 11:15). "What then shall we say? That the law is sin? By no means!" (Rom 7:7). "What shall we say then? Is there injustice on God's part? By no means!" (Rom 9:14). Yet if our interpretation of Paul does not lead to these accusations, then it is probably not what the apostle is saying.

All churches of the Reformation affirm the teaching of James (and the other apostles, including Paul) that genuine faith cannot fail to produce good works. In Solid Declaration IV ("On Good Works"), Lutherans confess that although the good works even of believers are so corrupt that they cannot merit God's justification (8),[1] deeds proceeding from faith are nevertheless rewarded by God, since it is impossible for genuine faith not to produce good works that are commanded by God (9). "It is impossible to separate works from faith, yea, just as impossible as it is for heat and light to be separated from fire" (12). It is therefore an "Epicurean delusion" by which some

> fabricate for themselves a dead faith or delusion which is without repentance and without good works, as though there could be in

---

1. Formula of Concord (1577), Solid Declaration 4, "Of Good Works," in *Book of Concord*, ed. Theodore G. Tappert (Philadelphia: Fortress, 1989), 51–58. Paragraph numbers indicated parenthetically.

a heart true faith and at the same time the wicked intention to persevere and continue in sins, which is impossible; or, as though one could, indeed, have and retain true faith, righteousness, and salvation even though he be and remain a corrupt and unfruitful tree, whence no good fruits whatever come, yea, even though he persist in sins against conscience, or purposely engages again in these sins, all of which is incorrect and false (15).

It must always be remembered that "St. Paul has entirely excluded our works and merits from the article of justification and salvation, and ascribed everything to the grace of God and the merit of Christ alone" (22). At the same time, invoking Paul's warnings (Rom 8:13; 1 Cor 6:9; Gal 5:21; Eph 5:5; Col 3:6), the confessors admonish against the "delusion" of thinking that one could give themselves over to their lusts and yet enter Christ's kingdom (32).

Attempts to reconcile James and Paul regarding Abraham did not begin with the Reformation. The eternal Sabbath "is obtained only by faith," says Augustine.[2] Since Abraham had no grounds for boasting before God, "it follows that he was not justified on the basis of works. So if Abraham was not justified by works, how was he justified?" Paul explains that it is by believing God, "and it was reckoned to him as righteousness," Augustine explains. "Abraham, then, was justified by faith. Paul and James do not contradict each other: good works follow justification." He explains further, "You see that Abraham was justified *not by what he did*, but *by his faith*," but woe to the person who reasons, "all right then, so I can do whatever I like, because even though I have no good works to show, but simply believe in God, that is reckoned to me as righteousness?" James was correcting misunderstandings of Paul, Augustine continues, reminding them "of the good works of this same Abraham whose faith was commended by Paul."

> James dwells on an action performed by Abraham that we all know about: he offered his son to God as a sacrifice. That is a great work, but it *proceeded from faith. I have nothing but praise for the superstructure of action, but I see the foundation of faith; I admire the good work as a fruit, but I recognize that it springs from the root of faith.* If Abraham had done

---

2. Augustine, *The Letters of St. Augustin* 36.25 (*NPNF*[1] 1:268).

it without right faith it would have profited him nothing, however noble the work was. On the other hand, if Abraham had been so complacent in his faith that, on hearing God's command to offer his son as a sacrificial victim, he had said to himself, "No, I won't. But I believe that God will set me free, even if I ignore his orders," his faith would have been a dead faith because it did not issue in right action, and it would have remained a barren, dried-up root that never produced fruit.[3]

Commenting on James and Paul in the late sixth century, Oecumenius in Asia Minor argued similarly that Abraham was justified by faith alone, but his faith was also revealed and approved in offering Isaac. Abraham's works are certainly worthy of celebrating, but because they are rooted in faith and they have no role in justification itself.[4]

According to the seventh-century writer Andreas, Paul is speaking of faith as it operates in justification, while James is speaking of the fruit of faith—namely, good works.[5] Similarly, Bede interprets James as speaking to the issue of how good works necessarily spring from justifying faith.

Although the apostle Paul preached that we are justified by faith without works, those who understand by this that it does not matter whether they live evil lives or do wicked and terrible things, as long as they believe in Christ, because salvation is through faith, have made a great mistake. James here expounds how Paul's words ought to be understood. This is why he uses the example of Abraham, whom Paul also used as an example of faith, to show that the patriarch also performed good works in the light of his faith. It is therefore wrong to interpret Paul in such a way as to suggest that it did not matter whether Abraham put his faith into practice or not. What Paul meant was that no one obtains the gift of justification on the basis of merits derived from works performed beforehand, because the gift of justification comes only from faith.[6]

3. Augustine, *The Works of Saint Augustine*, ed. John E. Rotelle, OSA, pt. 3, vol. 15, *Expositions of the Psalms 1–32*, trans. Maria Boulding, OSB (Hyde Park: New City Press, 2000), 364–65 (exp. 2 of Ps 31:2–4).
4. Oecumenius, in *Ancient Christian Commentary on Scripture*, New Testament 11, *James, 1–2 Peter, 1–3 John, Jude*, ed. Gerald Bray (Downers Grove, IL: InterVarsity, 2000), 33.
5. Andreas, in *Ancient Christian Commentary on Scripture*, NT 11:16 (on Jas 2:21).
6. Bede in Gerald Bray, ed., *Ancient Christian Commentary on Scripture, New Testament XI: James, 1–2 Peter, 1–3 John, Jude* (Downers Grove: InterVarsity Press, 2000), 31.

In short, James and Paul are approaching Abraham from different vantage points and with different interests. Since justifying faith produces love and good works, professing believers cannot say that they have the root without the fruit.

JUSTIFICATION AND FINAL JUDGMENT

Jesus warns,

> Not everyone who says to me, "Lord, Lord," will enter the kingdom of heaven, but the one who does the will of my Father who is in heaven. On that day many will say to me, "Lord, Lord, did we not prophesy in your name, and cast out demons in your name, and do many mighty works in your name?" And then will I declare to them, "I never knew you; depart from me, you workers of lawlessness." (Matt 7:21–23)

Later in Matthew's Gospel Jesus explains that at the last judgment he will separate the sheep from the goats, with a clear reference to the former's loving care and works of mercy toward their brothers and sisters in prison (Matt 25:31–46).

What stands out in these passages is the response of both groups. In Matthew 7, the condemned protest their judgment on the basis of their great works, including miracles, even in Christ's name. They do not appeal to God's mercy in Christ but assume that what they have done should qualify them for justification. In Matthew 25, the goats respond with astonishment that they are not found worthy, while the sheep are surprised that they are. Clearly, the elect did not pursue these works in order to merit final bliss; they were simply loving and serving their fellow believers under severe persecution. Furthermore, the sheep are welcomed into the kingdom "prepared for you from the foundation of the world"—grounding their right to enter not in their own works but in God's electing grace. Nevertheless, their good works evidenced the work of grace in their hearts.

In Revelation, John hears a multitude praising God and crying out,

> "Let us rejoice and exult
> and give him the glory,

> for the marriage of the Lamb has come,
>> and his Bride has made herself ready;
> it was granted her to clothe herself
>> with fine linen, bright and pure"—

> *for the fine linen is the righteous deeds of the saints.* (Rev 19:6–8, emphasis added)

What stands out here, as in Matthew 25, is the fact God "*granted* [the church] to clothe herself with fine linen." In Revelation 7:14 we are told that the ones dressed in white robes "are the ones coming out of the great tribulation." "They have washed their robes and made them white *in the blood of the Lamb*." Of further significance is the fact that at the great white throne of judgment in Revelation 20:8–15, there are two books: the book of life and the book of deeds. While the book of deeds is read out and is consistent with the lives of the saints versus the ungodly, the decisive issue is whether one's name is written in the Lamb's book of life from the foundation of the world. Thus, the judgment in which the sheep are separated from the goats is dependent on election and faith in "the blood of the Lamb," while there is also an awards ceremony in which suffering believers will be honored for their patience, endurance, and martyrdom for the sake of Christ.

Written to encourage persecuted Christians to keep the faith, the book of Revelation is not addressing the question, "How can I be accepted by a holy God?" but "How can I hope for justice in the face of manifest injustice?" The "great tribulation," I believe, refers in the immediate context to the widespread suffering of the saints in John's day, but it continues wherever the church is persecuted. Early on the martyred souls cry out "with a loud voice, 'O Sovereign Lord, holy and true, how long before you will judge and avenge our blood on those who dwell on the earth?'" (Rev 6:10). Though despised and disgraced by the world, the martyrs' testimony to Christ to the end is a glorious garment worn by the whole church.

The martyrs' cry echoes Asaph's prayer in Psalm 79. He first complains that

> the nations . . . have defiled your holy temple;
>> they have laid Jerusalem in ruins.

> They have given the bodies of your servants
>> to the birds of the heavens for food,
>> the flesh of your faithful to the beasts of the earth. (v. 1–2)

Complaint turns to an appeal for mercy:

> How long, O Lord? Will you be angry forever? . . .
> Do not remember against us our former iniquities;
>> let your compassion come speedily to meet us,
>> for we are brought very low.
> Help us, O God of our salvation,
>> for the glory of your name;
> deliver us, and atone for our sins,
>> for your name's sake! (vv. 5, 8–9)

Finally, the prayer turns to imprecation:

> Why should the nations say,
>> "Where is their God?"
> Let the avenging of the outpoured blood of your servants
>> be known among the nations before our eyes!
> Let the groans of the prisoners come before you;
>> according to your great power, preserve those doomed to die!
> Return sevenfold into the lap of our neighbors
>> the taunts with which they have taunted you, O Lord!
> But we your people, the sheep of your pasture,
>> will give thanks to you forever;
>> from generation to generation we will recount your praise.
>> (vv. 10–13)

As God's merciful atonement for their sins is the basis for Asaph's cry for deliverance on behalf of Israel, the blood of the Lamb has been mentioned repeatedly throughout John's vision. Nowhere do the saints appeal to their works as the ground of their deliverance. On the contrary, the hymn is sung to the Lamb:

> Worthy are you to take the scroll
>> and to open its seals,

> for you were slain, and by your blood you ransomed
>> people for God
>>> from every tribe and language and people and nation,
>> and you have made them a kingdom and priests to our God
>> and they shall reign on the earth. (Rev 5:9–10)

Clearly, the last judgment is a twofold event: final deliverance for the elect and judgment for those who have rejected the testimony of the saints.

We have already encountered the clothing metaphor. One must appear at the wedding feast with the appointed garment (Matt 22:11–14; cf. Isa 61:10–11; Zech 3).

In fulfillment of Jeremiah 23:5–6, David's righteous branch is Jesus, who in fact is no less than "Yahweh our righteousness." As Paul glosses in 1 Corinthians 1:30, "Because of him you are in Christ Jesus, who became to us wisdom from God, righteousness and sanctification and redemption."

Another passage appealed to in favor of a future justification by works is 1 Corinthians 3:12–15, where Paul warns against building on the foundation of Christ and the apostles with inferior materials. "If the work that anyone has built on the material survives, he will receive a reward. If anyone's work is burned up, he will suffer loss, though he himself will be saved, but only as through fire" (vv. 14–15). This has been used also for the doctrine of purgatory. However, it refers neither to purgatory nor to final salvation. On the contrary, Paul says that the minister "himself will be saved," but his "work is burned up." Especially in context, Paul is warning against teachers who, though building on the proper foundation (they are not the false teachers of Matthew 7:21–23), build shabbily. They suffer loss because they see their entire ministry go up in smoke, as it were, as it is tested by God's searching judgment. Since the passage says explicitly that these unsuitable builders themselves are saved, it can hardly be used as a proof text for final justification according to works.

Covenant Faithfulness or Conformity to a Norm?

In Wright's view, as we have seen, the righteousness of God (δικαιοσύνη Θεοῦ) means God's faithfulness, not a gift of right-standing before God.[7] We have examined the migration of the phrase from seeing

---

7. N. T. Wright, *What Saint Paul Really Said: Was Paul of Tarsus the Real Founder of Christianity?* (Grand Rapids: Eerdmans, 1997), 95–111; Wright, *Paul and the Faithfulness of God* (Minneapolis: Fortress, 2013), 2:925–66.

it as an attribute of God by which he judges according to a norm (the law) to seeing it as God's activity of being faithful to his covenant—a relational concept. It is this trajectory that Wright joins when he argues, "The best argument for taking *dikaiosynē theou* in Romans 1:17, 3:21, and 10:3 as 'God's faithfulness to the covenant with Abraham, to the single-plan-through-Israel-for-the-world,' is the massive sense it makes of passage after passage."[8] However, the real question first is what the phrase means semantically and what it is capable of referring to lexically. Wright's translation makes sense of so many passages only if one presupposes Cremer's thesis.

A great deal turns on how we understand the phrase *dikaiosyne theou* already at the beginning of Romans. In the ESV, it reads:

> For I am not ashamed of the gospel, for it is the power of God for salvation to everyone who believes, to the Jew first and also to the Greek. For in it the righteousness of God is revealed from faith for faith, as it is written, "The righteous shall live by faith." For the wrath of God is revealed from heaven against all ungodliness and unrighteousness of men, who by their unrighteousness suppress the truth. (Rom 1:16–18)

The best translation of the quote (Hab 2:4 in Rom 1:17) is "The righteous by faith shall live"—in other words, it is by the covenantal principle of grace alone, in Christ alone, through faith alone. In this sense, "The law is not based on faith" (Gal 3:12). Its covenantal principle is act-consequence: "Do this, and you will live." Habakkuk contrasts pride with faith, just as Paul does here. In Ezekiel 20:11–13 the phrase is repeated, "I gave them my statutes and made known to them my rules, *by which, if a person does them, he shall live.*" Paul is contrasting this principle at the heart of the Sinai covenant with the promise that is embraced by faith "from beginning to end," as I understand Romans 1:17. "*For* [γὰρ], the wrath of God is being revealed from heaven" (Rom 1:18).

In the light of this coming judgment, which will be just and inexorably based on God's righteous standard (the law), the gospel is the only hope. One will either attain everlasting life by the principle of *doing* what the law requires, which is impossible (Rom 3:19–20) or by

---

8. Wright, *Justification: God's Plan and Paul's Vision*, 179.

receiving "the righteousness of God through faith in Jesus Christ for all who believe" (vv. 21–22).

Goal or Origin?

Rewards retain an important place in Paul's letters as in the gospels, just as in Judaism. The difference is that according to Paul justification is accomplished once and for all in Christ. Whatever rewards believers receive in addition to justification, they are, as Augustine said, God's crowning of his own gifts. They are not merited but rewarded.

One way of stating the fundamental difference between Rome and the Reformation on this point is that whereas the former sees final justification as the *terminus ad quem* (goal), the latter sees it as the *terminus a quo* (origin). "There is therefore now no condemnation for those who are in Christ Jesus" (Rom 8:1). Hence, according to the Reformers and their heirs, justification is nothing less than the verdict of the last judgment pronounced in the present. Vos observes,

> It is sometimes alleged that Paul was the first to frame the concept of a comprehensive adjustment of all sins in the accounting of God. In this form the thought is not correct, because Judaism had already worked out the doctrine of a daily balance struck by God taking into account the works performed up to the point of reckoning, both as to merit and demerit, and not omitting to introduce the element of imputed righteousness from the fathers, who had a surplus of merit.[9]

But in the Judaic stream, "the balance struck is unstable," with the scales going up and down each day. Here is where the future meets the present in Paul's eschatology. In justification we have "a last judgment anticipated." There is no basis for the notion that Paul was thinking merely of past sins and a future justification based on works.[10]

One cannot read the Second Temple discussions of the coming judgment and the question of how many works (and of what quality) are required for justification and conclude that this personal anxiety

---

9. Geerhardus Vos, *The Pauline Eschatology* (repr., Philipsburg, NJ: P&R, 1994), 56.

10. Vos, *The Pauline Eschatology*, 56, *pace* Wernle's thesis in *Der Christ und die Sünde bei Paulus* (1897).

is merely the product of the introspective conscience of modernity. "The Apostle not seldom does speak of the consciousness of justification as needful for those who, within the Christian sphere, are subject to a daily sense of sin," Vos observes.[11] In sharp contrast is the confidence that comes from knowing that justification is a settled affair: "Through him we have also obtained access by faith into this grace in which we stand, and we rejoice in hope of the glory of God" (Rom 5:2; cf. 8:33–34; Phil 3:7–9; Eph 1:7, Col. 1:14).

> The language of Romans 8.33, 34: "Who shall lay anything to the charge of God's elect? It is God that justifies; who is he that condemns" could not be more absolute than the sentence rendered in the last judgment; in fact it is so absolute as to be indifferent to the categories of past, present or future. In this respect the fact of justification is only the reverse side of the facts of prognosis and predestination and it would be out of place in the *catena salutis* of vs. 29, if its scope were less unlimited and unconditional than that of the other conceptions enumerated.[12]

Though buffeted on every side by temptation, sin, doubt, despair, and anxieties of various kinds, the believer is secure in the objective certainty that Christ's life, death, resurrection, and ascension are completed events and that his ongoing intercession cannot fail. It is from this confidence that believers begin to love instead of dread or seek to appease, manipulate, or use God and their neighbors. For a more fulsome treatment of this point, see chapter 12 in the previous volume.

In none of these instances of final judgment to which Jesus refers above is justification attributed to the deeds of the saints. In Matthew 25, the sheep are not said to merit the kingdom but to inherit it: "Come, you who are blessed by my Father, inherit the kingdom prepared for you from the foundation of the world" (v. 34). Service to their brothers and sisters is not the condition for receiving but the characteristic of those who have been granted it already by grace. The righteous deeds of the saints do not qualify them for heaven but adorn the church—and themselves—with honors. Their final salvation is attributed to election:

---

11. Vos, *The Pauline Eschatology*, 56.
12. Vos, *The Pauline Eschatology*, 57.

whether their names were written in the Lamb's book of life from the foundation of the world (Rev 20:8–15). Yet those who have suffered much will be rewarded much. Because grace always produces the fruit of good works, these rewards are real tributes that we will share in celebrating.

Whereas Moses proclaimed the terms of attaining temporal beatitude through obedience, Jesus's mountain sermon proclaims beatitude first in Matthew 5. On the basis of their blessing, his followers are the meek who will *inherit the earth*, the mourners who are *comforted*, the merciful who make peace because they have been *given peace* with God. Similarly, the rewards given to believers at the last judgment do not constitute their salvation but their compensation for loss on behalf of Christ's name. One may even say that they are in a sense worthy of these rewards—due to God's grace at work within them. After all, they suffered and even lost their life for the sake of the Lamb. However, they do not merit these awards, either condignly or congruently. These rewards are granted by a Father in a way that far surpasses the legal verdict of a judge. And they have nothing to do with salvation in general or justification in particular but belong to the superabundance of God's gracious liberality.

Basis or Evidence? Romans 2

In addition to the question of whether justification is the goal or the origin of the Christian life, it is important to determine whether the relevant passages make works the basis or the evidence of justification. The weightiest passage adduced in favor of a final justification based on works is Romans 2:6–11, 13:

> He will render to each one according to his works: to those who by patience in well-doing seek for glory and honor and immortality, he will give eternal life; but for those who are self-seeking and do not obey the truth, but obey unrighteousness, there will be wrath and fury. There will be tribulation and distress for every human being who does evil, the Jew first and also the Greek, but glory and honor and peace for everyone who does good, the Jew first and also the Greek. For God shows no partiality. . . . For it is not the hearers of the law who are righteous before God, but the doers of the law who will be justified.

According to Wright, "Paul has spoken in Romans 2 about the final justification of God's people on the basis of their whole life."[13] In fact, Romans 2:13 is his *sedes doctrinae* for final justification by works.

> Paul, in company with mainstream Second Temple Judaism, affirms that God's final judgment will be in accordance with the entirety of a life led—in accordance, in other words, with works. He says this clearly and unambiguously in Romans 14:10–12 and 2 Corinthians 5:10. He affirms it in that terrifying passage about church builders in 1 Corinthians 3. But the main passage in question is Romans 2:1–16.[14]

"Present justification declares, on the basis of faith, what future justification will affirm publicly (according to 2:14–16 and 8:9–11) on the basis of the entire life."[15] Thus, "Justification, of course, therefore has two poles—present and future."[16] In sum, "Romans 3.21–4.25 is about *present* justification; but what Paul had set up in 2.1–16 was the question of *future* justification."[17] Interestingly, he concedes that the first half of Romans *is* about present justification and apparently about "how we are saved," since Wright describes *future* justification in clearly soteriological terms.

It seems that in Wright's account, present justification is less decisive than future justification. The former is merely a badge of membership; it does not accomplish anything salvific but testifies to what is already the case (viz., belonging to the people of God). The future justification, however, is decisive for salvation, determining one's everlasting destiny "on the basis of the entire life a person has led in the power of the Spirit—that is, it occurs on the basis of 'works' in Paul's redefined sense."[18] This is the justification that *saves*, and it is by works. "The Spirit is the path by which Paul traces the route from justification by faith in the present to justification, by the complete life lived, in the future."[19]

---

13. N. T. Wright, *Paul: In Fresh Perspective* (Minneapolis: Fortress, 2009), 121. John Piper also points out that Wright seems to use "according to" and "on the basis of" (works) as interchangeable (Piper, *The Future of Justification: A Response to N. T. Wright* [Wheaton, IL: Crossway, 2007]).

14. N. T. Wright, "New Perspectives on Paul," in *Justification in Perspective: Historical Developments and Contemporary Challenges*, ed. Bruce L. McCormack (Grand Rapids: Baker Academic, 2006), 253.

15. Wright, *What Saint Paul Really Said*, 129.

16. Wright, *Paul: In Fresh Perspective*, 58.

17. Wright, *Paul and His Recent Interpreters*, 208.

18. Wright, "New Perspectives on Paul," 260.

19. Wright, *Paul: In Fresh Perspective*, 148.

A few things may be said in response. First, with respect to justification, much of contemporary (especially new perspective) scholarship frequently critiques the traditional Reformation perspective on justification as too bound to an *ordo salutis*, while merely shifting the soteriological freight from justification to another aspect of the *ordo*. In other words, justification cannot pertain to how people are saved *unless* it refers to election (Barth), calling (Wright), sanctification (Bird), or glorification (Wright again). We have seen that Douglas Campbell insists that being "saved" in the present is nothing more than realizing one's election, redemption, and justification; Michael Bird suggests that Romans 5:19 (like 2 Corinthians 5:21) refers to a transformative "becoming." In various places, N. T. Wright identifies the moment of justification with calling,[20] being restored once again to our covenant vocation (i.e., sanctification), and a final justification based on works (i.e., glorification). In other words, revisionists do not actually reject an *ordo* approach; on the contrary, they select one event in the *ordo* as the central dogma or "Pauline center" from which they deduce the others. This is a far more *ordo*-centered approach than one finds in the traditional view. According to the latter, justification is sharing now (already) in Christ's own justification accomplished in the past (*historia salutis*)

The Reformed *ordo* is based on Romans 8:30: election, calling, justification, and glorification. Calling is indeed the moment when the Spirit unites us to Christ by faith through the preaching of the gospel, sealed by the sacraments (e.g., Heidelberg Catechism, Q. 65). Effectually called, we are united to Christ to receive all of his benefits. We are declared righteous in justification, are being sanctified, and will be glorified. Since everyone seems to finally adopt one *ordo* or another, there is no reason for singling out the Reformed view in this respect. In the end, Wright's doctrine of justification is just as much about "how to be saved" at least with respect to final justification, but it makes salvation finally to depend on Spirit-empowered works, which is exactly the Roman Catholic position.

---

20. Wright, *Paul: In Fresh Perspective*, 121–22. He says, "The word 'justification' does not itself denote the process whereby, or the event in which, a person is brought by grace from unbelief, idolatry and sin into faith, true worship and renewal of life. Paul, clearly and unambiguously, uses a different word for that, the word 'call'. The word 'justification' despite centuries of Christian misuse, is used by Paul to denote that which happens immediately after the 'call': 'those God called, he also justified.' In other words, those who hear the gospel and respond to it in faith are then declared by God to be his people, his elect, the 'circumcision,' 'the Jews,' 'the Israel of God.' They are given the status *dikaios*, 'righteous,' 'within the covenant.'"

Second, everything turns on how one reads Paul's larger argument in Romans 1–3. Has Paul been arguing that gentiles or Jews have in fact been doers of the law? Or is it rather his thesis that no one has, does, or will keep it? If the latter, then 2:13 is intended as an indictment, not an exhortation.[21]

Third, in the immediate context in Romans, Paul is not encouraging people to seek final justification by works—even if we bracket the rest of the epistle from our purview. The preceding verses read:

> Therefore you have no excuse, O man, every one of you who judges. For in passing judgment on another you condemn yourself, because you, the judge, practice the very same things. We know that the judgment of God rightly falls on those who practice such things. Do you suppose, O man—you who judge those who practice such things and yet do them yourself—that you will escape the judgment of God? Or do you presume on the riches of his kindness and forbearance and patience, not knowing that God's kindness is meant to lead you to repentance? But because of your hard and impenitent heart, you are storing up wrath for yourself on the day of wrath when God's righteous judgment will be revealed. (Rom 2:1–5)

Reformation exegesis is often criticized for always turning such warnings into a revelation of people's helplessness so that they will flee to Christ. Yet that is exactly what Paul does in this argument, leading up to 3:19–20, which then prepares his readers for the good news of a gift of righteousness through faith.

Wright's interpretation of Romans 2:13 simply does not fit the logic of Paul's argument, which is to challenge Jewish "boasting in the law," showing them that they too are "in Adam," so that "the whole world might become guilty before God." "None is righteous, no, not one" (3:10). "So by the works of the law no human being will be justified in his sight, since through the law comes knowledge of sin" (3:20). Therefore, "We hold that one is justified by faith apart from works of the law" (3:21).

Paul's massive transition in 3:21 only makes sense in the light of the universal condemnation of the world by the law: "But now the righteousness of God has been manifested apart from the law," which Jews

---

21. As John Piper observes, racial boasting and self-help moralism are not radically different, as Wright maintains, but are expressions of self-righteousness (Piper, *The Future of Justification*, 170).

and gentiles have only through faith in Christ. Having focused on the guilt of the gentiles and then the Jews, he offers a summation: Paul is *excluding* every possibility that *anyone* will be justified according to works, now or in the future. Paul's jeremiad is not a vilification of Jews as such; on the contrary, he is saying: *if this is how it has turned out with the special people God chose and called out from the world, then who can be saved?* If Jews, who are dedicated zealously to God's specially revealed Torah, are as corrupt as the gentiles, then who can hope to merit final vindication? The person whom Paul has in mind here is condemned not for trying to obey the law (*pace* Bultmann and Bornkamm) but for boasting in the law while having *failed to keep it.* "But because of your hard and impenitent heart you are storing up wrath for yourself on the day of wrath when God's righteous judgment will be revealed" (v. 5).

Paul sees no contradiction between justification by grace alone in Christ alone, received through faith alone, and the fact that those who are justified are also being sanctified—hence, his sobering warning that those who are unrepentant will not enter the kingdom of heaven (1 Cor 6:9–11; Gal 5:21). But his warning serves his larger argument that no one is righteous (Rom 3:10), and therefore no one will be justified by works. If Paul *says explicitly* that *no one will be justified by works*, then how can one say that *future justification* is in fact *by works*? It makes no difference to say that they are Spirit-empowered works versus circumcision; Paul does not include such nuance here. In short, Romans 2:13 is, as Chrysostom, Augustine, Melanchthon, Calvin, and a host of careful expositors have recognized, an empty set—a hypothetical argument. "The sense of this verse, therefore, is that if righteousness is to be sought by the law," says Calvin, "the law must be fulfilled, for the righteousness of the law consists in the perfection of works."[22]

The arguments of Wright and Gathercole in favor of seeing the "doers of the law" in Romans 2:13 as Christian gentiles are strong. If they are unbelievers, then why say, "So, if a man who is uncircumcised keeps the precepts of the law, will not his uncircumcision be regarded as circumcision?" (v. 26). Perhaps Paul is simply saying that if one takes pride in circumcision as a badge of law-keeping, then virtuous pagans are more "circumcised" in their noble behavior than Jews who fail to keep it. I confess to wavering on this question but am inclined to

---

22. Calvin, *New Testament Commentaries*, 12 vols., trans. Ross Mackenzie (Grand Rapids: Eerdmans, 1995), 8:46.

conclude against the view that Paul refers to believers here. It is uncharacteristic of Paul to say that Christians "do not have the law" yet "*by nature* [rather than by the Spirit or in Christ] do what the law requires." Paul's "gentiles, who do not have the law" are the same who "in their unrighteousness suppress the truth" (1:18), and it is these who know the law above Torah itself, "while their conscience also bears witness, and their conflicting thoughts accuse or even excuse them" (2:15).

In the argument so far, *natural* (φυσικὴν) is associated with gentile morality, both in their contempt for natural law and in the fact that sometimes they do what the law commands (e.g., not stealing, murdering, etc.). Following Paul and Augustine, the Reformers distinguished between a civil righteousness (*coram hominibus*, before fellow humans) and righteousness before God (*coram Deo*). Paul is not saying that pagans are devoid of the former, only the latter. Recall the irony of Abimelech, a pagan king, chastising Abraham for doing "things that ought not to be done" by passing off Sarah as his sister (Gen 20:9). And yet, Abraham is justified by faith. Apart from faith, good works are virtuous before humans but of no account before God (Rom 14:23). Paul also maintains that this civil righteousness is sufficient to curb unrighteous acts, to the point of shaming possessors of the written Torah for their hypocrisy (2:17–29). Douglas Campbell's extreme view of the total depravity of unbelievers echoes the Anabaptist tradition, against whom Calvin held up the example of the civil righteousness of the ancient jurists and moralists.[23] But even if they are Christians, it seems clear enough that Paul is saying that only doers of the law will be justified and that no one has fulfilled it. If he is saying that some are justified by their works on the last day, then Paul is contradicting his major thesis.

Fourth, the idea of a future justification based on works contradicts the major thrust of teaching where the term *justification* is mentioned explicitly. Paul is not alone in his contrast between works and faith in justification. The Gospels represent Jesus as teaching the same doctrine. In contrast with the boasting Pharisee and others "who trusted in themselves that they were righteous," the tax-collector cried out, "Lord, be merciful to me, the sinner." And the tax-collector "went home justified," not expecting a future justification based on a whole life lived (Luke 18:14). "Whoever believes in him is not condemned, but whoever

---

23. *Inst.* 2.2.15.

does not believe is condemned already, because he has not believed in the name of the only Son of God" (John 3:18). Condemnation and justification are present-tense objective facts if one trusts in Christ. Jesus promises, "Truly, truly, I say to you, whoever hears my word and believes him who sent me has eternal life. He does not come into judgment, but has passed from death to life" (John 5:24).

Paul moves from cause to consequence in many places, including Romans 5:1: "Therefore, since we *have been* justified by faith, we *have* peace with God through our Lord Jesus Christ." And again in chapter 8:

> There is therefore *now* no condemnation for those who are in Christ Jesus. . . . What then shall we say to these things? If God is for us, who can be against us? He who did not spare his own Son but gave him up for us all, how will he not also with him graciously give us all things? Who shall bring *any charge* against God's elect? It is God who justifies. *Who is to condemn?* Christ Jesus is the one who died—more than that, who was raised—who is at the Father's right hand, interceding for us. (vv. 1, 31–34, emphasis added)

Paul adds, "For with the heart one believes and is justified, and with the mouth one confesses and is saved. For the Scripture says, 'Everyone who believes in him will not be put to shame'" (10:10–11). There is no possibility that one of God's chosen, redeemed, called, and justified people will be condemned on the last day. What point is there then in talking about a future justification by works? "He *has delivered* us from the domain of darkness and *transferred* us to the kingdom of his beloved Son, in whom we *have redemption*, the forgiveness of sins" (Col 1:13–14). Since the list of our transgressions has been cancelled, nailed to the cross, there is no judgment to fear (Col 2:14).

Fifth, Wright's definition of "the works of the law" in some sense contradicts his insistence that the phrase refers exclusively to ethnic boundary markers (i.e., ceremonies).[24] It is striking that when it comes to *future* justification, the term "justification" is loosened from its new

---

24. John Piper provides this incisive comment by Simon Gathercole: "It is crucial to recognize that the New Perspective interpretation of [Rom] 4:1–8 falls to the ground on this point: that David, although circumcised, sabbatarian, and kosher, is described as without works because of his disobedience." Yet God counts righteousness to David (Rom 4:5, 8). Simon Gathercole, *Where Is Boasting? Early Jewish Soteriology and Paul's Response in Romans 1–5* (Grand Rapids: Eerdmans, 2002), 247.

perspective soil: there is no mention of the faithfulness of Christ (versus faith in Christ), nor ecclesiology rather than soteriology, nor justification meaning "table fellowship" and inclusion in the people of God as having nothing to do with how we are saved. Now it means a forensic declaration "on the basis of the entire life a person has led in the power of the Spirit—that is, it occurs on the basis of 'works' in Paul's redefined sense."[25] In other words, it is not by circumcision but by fulfilling the moral commands of Torah that one is finally justified. Taking the Origenist line of interpretation, Wright concludes that the works that justify are not the ceremonies but the Spirit-enabled works of the believer. In fact, he writes, "When, by clear implication, I am charged with encouraging believers to put their trust in someone or something 'other than the crucified and resurrected Savior,' I want to plead guilty." After all, we also trust in the Spirit's transforming work, he says.[26]

But to put one's *trust* in the transforming work of the Spirit within us is hardly grounds for the security that Paul establishes in these passages. In contrast to Christ's righteousness, our sanctification is always incomplete and imperfect. We indeed place our trust in the triune God, including of course the Holy Spirit, but the object of justifying faith is not the Spirit's transforming work within us. John Piper recognizes that Wright tends to merge "the imputation of a new position with the impartation of a new nature."[27] The view that Wright defends here is one of the reasons why the Westminster divines insisted that we are justified "not by anything done by us *or wrought within us*"—even by the Holy Spirit. This is sanctification, not justification.

Not only are faith and obedience necessarily connected, as the Reformation traditions maintain, but, according to Wright, "Indeed, very often the word 'faith' itself could properly be translated as 'faithfulness,' which makes the point just as well."[28] Similarly, Paul A. Rainbow suggests that justification "unfolds for an individual in two phases, marked by conversion and the last judgment. While faith alone is required to inaugurate it, evangelical obedience becomes a subordinate part of the basis for its culmination."[29] If I am not mistaken,

25. Wright, "New Perspectives on Paul," 260.
26. N. T. Wright, *Justification: God's Plan and Paul's Vision* (Downers Grove, IL: IVP Academic, 2009), 163–64.
27. Piper, *The Future of Justification*, 126.
28. Wright, *What Saint Paul Really Said*, 160.
29. This is the thesis of Paul A. Rainbow, *The Way of Salvation: The Role of Obedience in Justification* (Waynesboro, GA: Paternoster, 2005).

this interpretation is close to the one that Paul excoriated in Galatians 3:3, but in any case it is identical to the Roman Catholic position.

So while generally eschewing talk of the *ordo salutis* (how individuals "get saved"), Wright nevertheless offers an alternative *ordo*. However, rather than make sanctification ("a whole life lived") the consequence of justification, he renders it the *basis*, going beyond the Roman Catholic view, which treats the believer's works merely as the *instrument*. For both perspectives, however, the final verdict is analytic: God is declaring righteous those who actually are righteous. As in Roman Catholic teaching, the believer's transformed life grounds the verdict that one is at present a member of this community that will be justified on the last day.

Evangelical theologian Matthew W. Bates argues,

> Regarding the role of works in salvation, although many systematic treatments attempt to skate around this issue in a variety of ingenious ways, Paul himself states that we will be judged on the basis of our deeds: "But because of your hard and impenitent heart, you are storing up wrath for yourself on the day of wrath when God's righteous judgment will be revealed. *God will render to each one according to his works*: to those who by steadfastness in well-*doing* seek for glory and honor and incorruptibility—*eternal life,* but for those who are self-seeking and do not *obey* the truth, but obey unrighteousness—wrath and fury" (Rom. 2:5–8).[30]

In Bates's view, then, Paul is not addressing this specific warning to those who boast in Torah but fail to keep it; rather, he is teaching that the final judgment will in fact be based on works. The "systematic treatments [that] attempt to skate around this issue in a variety of ingenious ways" are in fact a trail of interpreters from Irenaeus, Chrysostom, and Augustine to the Reformers. Bates points up the major exegetical divergence at this point: Is Paul saying that the basis of the final judgment (and therefore justification) is works, or he is driving those who trust in their works (despite utter failure) to flee from trusting in their obedience to Christ?

But the crucial question exegetically is this: How does the final-justification-by-works interpretation find its climax in 3:20? As I have

---

30. Matthew W. Bates, *Salvation by Allegiance Alone* (Grand Rapids: Baker Academic, 2017), 107–8, emphasis original.

argued frequently, the climax of Paul's argument comes in Romans 3:20: "For by works of the law no human being will be justified in his sight, since through the law comes knowledge of sin." The "for" indicates the conclusion of the argument. No one is righteous: the law has exposed this. Therefore, the only expectation for those who trust in their own righteousness is a just verdict of condemnation.

The traditional interpretation therefore is not an evasion but an attempt to follow the logic of Paul's argument. Bates continues,

> Moreover, after the passage I just cited, Paul goes on to say that it is not the hearers of the law but the "*doers of the law*" who will be justified (Rom. 2:13), and that what is rendered on this day of judgment will extend even to sins committed in secret (Rom. 2:16). Paul is firm even if some modern commentators are not: we will be judged, at least in part, for eternal life *on the basis of* our works.[31]

But again, is Paul upbraiding his opponents for boasting in a law that they have not kept or exhorting them to work harder at keeping the law (at least the moral precepts) so that they can be justified by works at the end?

JUDGMENT ACCORDING TO WORKS

The other scriptural passages cited above do however teach a final judgment in which the works of believers are acknowledged and rewarded. The question turns largely on how one interprets κατά. Is it *according to* or *by* works? This question determines especially how we interpret Paul's reference in Romans 2:12–15 to a judgment "*in accordance with their works* [κατὰ τὰ ἔργα αὐτῶν]" (2:6).

Κατὰ: "According To" or "On the Basis Of"?

First, it is worthwhile to state the traditional Protestant position that many contemporary interpreters are rejecting. The magisterial Reformation wholeheartedly affirmed a final judgment in which all deeds will be made known and the faithfulness of believers will finally be rewarded. Yet, as Lutherans confess, it is "not on account of

---

31. Bates, *Salvation by Allegiance Alone*, 108.

works that follow, but of grace, through Christ," that we are "retained by faith."[32] Good works proceed from "God's will and express command, . . . which the Holy Ghost works in believers, and with which God is pleased for Christ's sake, and to which He promises a glorious reward in this life and the life to come."[33] A typical summary is found in the Belgic Confession (1561). Written by Guido de Bres, who was burned at the stake, Article 37 views the last judgment from a perspective that is closer than ours to first-century context. The souls of the dead will be "joined and united with their own bodies in which they lived," while those who are still alive "will be changed 'in the twinkling of an eye' from 'corruptible to incorruptible' [1 Cor 15:51–53]."

> Then "the books" (that is, the consciences) will be opened, and the dead will be judged according to the things they did in the world (Rev 20:12), whether good or evil. Indeed, all people will give account of all the idle words they have spoken (Matt 12:36), which the world regards as only playing games. And then the secrets and hypocrisies of men will be publicly uncovered in the sight of all.[34]

Notice, especially from the perspective of a mixed body within the context of persecution even by those who name Christ, the Belgic Confession treats this judgment as separating hypocrites from genuine believers.

> Therefore, with good reason the thought of this judgment is horrible and dreadful to wicked and evil people. But it is very pleasant and a great comfort to the righteous and elect, since their total redemption will then be accomplished. They will then receive the fruits of their labor and of the trouble they have suffered; their innocence will be openly recognized by all; and they will see the terrible vengeance that God will bring on the evil ones who tyrannized, oppressed, and tormented them in this world.

---

32. Formula of Concord (1577), Book of Concord, trans. and ed. Theodore G. Tappert (Philadelphia: Fortress, 1959), Solid Declaration 4.33 (p. 556).

33. Formula of Concord (1577), Solid Declaration 4.38 (p. 557).

34. This and the two subsequent block quotes from the Belgic Confession, art. 37, in *Psalter Hymnal* (Grand Rapids: Board of Publication of the CRC, 1976), 90.

No one but outright hypocrites—those who refuse to repent and believe the gospel yet are in some sense associated with the visible community—are meant to feel anxious about this final judgment. They will be convicted by their own deeds of never having been united to Christ in true faith.

> The evil ones will be convicted by the witness of their own consciences, and shall be made immortal—but only to be tormented in the everlasting fire prepared for the devil and his angels (Matt 25:14). In contrast, the faithful and elect will be crowned with glory and honor. The Son of God will "confess their names" (Matt 10:32) before God his Father and the holy and elect angels; all tears will be "wiped from their eyes" (Rev 7:17); and their cause—at present condemned as heretical and evil by many judges and civil officers— will be acknowledged as the "cause of the Son of God." And as a gracious reward the Lord will make them possess a glory such as the heart of man could never imagine. So we look forward to that great day with longing in order to enjoy fully the promises of God in Christ Jesus, our Lord.

Once more we see that the context—namely, of believers suffering now in view of a final vindication on the last day—provides the proper perspective for interpreting these seminal passages.

Second, we recognize that for interpreting Romans 2:12–15 much turns on whether the tradition has been justified in rendering κατά "according to" rather than "on the basis of." The question is not whether believers will be included in God's final assize but whether their *justification* depends upon it. If the Reformation interpretation is accurate, then justification is the rendering of that future verdict (concerning salvation) in the present. There is then no future verdict that could be different than the present declaration.

Διότι, ἐπεί, and ὅτι ordinarily mean "because / on account of," while κατά has a variety of denotations: "according to" (Matt 2:13), "down" (Matt 8:32; 9:29), or "in" (as "in" a dream, Matt 2:19, 22). Those accustomed to Aristotle's causal distinctions over centuries of use in theology may be inclined to impose a stricter reference range than these conjunctions and prepositions have in New Testament Greek. Nevertheless, we may reasonably assume that if Paul had wanted to say that the works of believers will be the *basis* for their final justification, he had at hand clearer words to make that point. Κατὰ means "down from," whether from a ladder or in an argument from greater to lesser, not "on the basis of" or "because of." For example, it is "in" or "according to" a dream that the Lord warns Joseph to flee Herod's wrath with Mary and Jesus (Matt 2:13). It is therefore unclear why Matthew Bates concludes that rendering κατά "according to" "is true neither in English nor in Greek." Rather, he says, "*Kata* gives the norm or the standard for judgment in a way that moves beyond mere congruency to basis."[35] Bates overstates his lexical case considerably. While acknowledging Thomas Schreiner's solid argument for rendering κατά "according to,"[36] Bates fails to engage his argument seriously, concluding that a simpler solution is that "we really are eternally judged, just as Paul indicates, in part on the basis of our works, but these works are part of *pistis* as embodied allegiance or enacted loyalty."[37]

Bates also appeals to Ephesians 5:5 and Galatians 5:19–21: the exclusion lists.[38] But whereas the Lutheran and Reformed confessions invoke these texts to warn against the delusion of a "faith" without repentance, Bates suggests that Paul's polemic is not directed at *all* works but "something more specific: 'works *of law*.'" "That is, Paul opposed the idea that anyone can perform the works of the law (as given by God to Moses)—and by extension any other rule-based system—in order to establish or confirm righteousness before God."[39] So is it obedience to "a legal code" or "allegiance (*pistis*) to the Christ as the Holy Spirit works in the community to actualize the power of God for salvation?"[40] This interpretation too is identical to Origen's: in contrast with the old

---

35. Bates, *Salvation by Allegiance Alone*, 108. He cites BDAG and Ps 61:13; Prov 24:12; Matt 16:27; John 7:24; 8:15; 2 Tim 4:14; 1 Pet 1:17; Rev 2:23. But in the John passages, Jesus upbraids the Pharisees for judging by appearances instead of reality. And 2 Tim 4:14 relates Paul's statement, "Alexander the coppersmith did me great harm; the Lord will repay him according to his deeds." Only Matt 16:27, 1 Pet 1:17, and Rev 2:23 refer specifically to God's payment according to deeds and the Reformation interpretation does not deny this. It is in fact the baseline of judgment from which justification obtains its significance. Only in Christ do we escape the penalty that our deeds deserve.

36. Thomas Schreiner, "Justification Apart From and By Works: At the Final Judgment Works Will *Confirm* Justification," in *Four Views on the Role of Works at the Final Judgment*, ed. Alan P. Stanley (Grand Rapids: Zondervan, 2013), 78, 97. See also Piper, *The Future of Justification*, 103–11, esp. 109–10.

37. Bates, *Salvation by Allegiance Alone*, 109.

38. Bates, *Salvation by Allegiance Alone*, 111.

39. Bates, *Salvation by Allegiance Alone*, 112.

40. Bates, *Salvation by Allegiance Alone*, 114.

covenant, the new covenant prescribes spiritual obedience (i.e., works done in the power of the Spirit) as necessary for final justification.

Are we saved by works? Bates asks. Yes, but not "on the basis of whether we ate meat with the blood still inside it," for example.[41]

> So while the answer is no because it is the allegiance to the king himself that counts rather than performance of the Mosaic law, it is also yes since allegiance (*pistis*) to Jesus as king demands obedience to the deepest intentions of the law of Moses (see Matt. 5:17–48) even though this law has now reached its climactic goal (Rom. 10:4). At the final judgment, we will not be evaluated on the basis of whether we kept a list of rules such as the Ten Commandments, except inasmuch as genuine fidelity to Jesus the king demanded it.[42]

"We are saved when our confessed and imperfectly maintained allegiance unites us to Jesus the king, for he has already been declared righteous, and we share that righteous standing."[43] But Jesus himself summarized the law as loving God and neighbor.

In Bates's account, the law indeed is set aside (contrary to Paul's conclusion that "we uphold the law," Rom 3:31); instead, we are saved by works that apparently have no foundation in God's law. Not even the moral law—the Ten Commandments—is valid: a legalism without the law. This view is not Pelagian or even Semi-Pelagian, since grace precedes all that we do. But it contradicts the heart of Paul's gospel. Interpretations such as those offered by Wright and Bates read Paul's later statements about the Spirit-led life of the justified into the basis of justification itself. Appealing to Spirit-wrought works does not eliminate the basic conclusion that justification is merited; the reward of everlasting life is not a unilateral gift but is *based upon* one's fulfillment of the oath, "All this we will do." Again, this is the rationale for the crucial clause in the Westminster Confession that the elect are not justified "not for any thing *wrought in them* [even by the Holy Spirit], or done by them, but for Christ's sake alone" (11.1). In any case, one cannot say that works are the ground of final justification *and* salvation is apart from human merits. Therefore, ironically, this position does hold implicitly

---

41. Bates, *Salvation by Allegiance Alone*, 118.
42. Bates, *Salvation by Allegiance Alone*, 118.
43. Bates, *Salvation by Allegiance Alone*, 123.

to a "covenant of works" but concludes that the believer rather than Christ must fulfill it in order to attain final justification.

Wright also takes Romans 2:12–15 as a straightforward account of final justification according to works. "Paul means what he says."[44] It is not "the unaided works of the self-help moralist" but "the obedient submission to the leading of the Spirit." He adds,

> I am fascinated by the way in which some of those most conscious of their Reformation heritage shy away from Paul's clear statements about future judgment according to works. It is not often enough remarked upon, for instance, that in the Thessalonian letters and in Philippians, he looks ahead to the coming day of judgment and sees God's favorable verdict not on the basis of the merits and death of Christ, but on the basis of his apostolic work [1 Thes 2:19–20; cf. Phil 2:16–17].[45]

It is of great importance to understand these texts to which he appeals, since his conclusion is so straightforward in claiming that "God's favorable verdict" on Paul is "*not* on the basis of the merits and death of Christ, but on the basis of his apostolic work." It is not only that Paul's obedience merits the reward but that Christ's does not even play a role. This view of course goes beyond the Roman Catholic teaching. More importantly, it is not what Paul says.

In the first passage that Wright cites (1 Thess 2:19–20), the apostle exults, "For what is our hope or joy or crown of boasting before our Lord Jesus at his coming? Is it not *you*? For *you* are our glory and joy." Paul seeks no more reward than the Thessalonians themselves. In the Philippians verses, he similarly commends them for "holding fast to the word of life, so that in the day of Christ I may be proud that I did not run in vain or labor in vain. Even if I am to be poured out as a drink offering upon the sacrificial offering of your faith, I am glad and rejoice with you all. Likewise you also should be glad and rejoice with me" (Phil 2:16–18). This rejoicing is nothing more than a faithful missionary looking forward to "the day of Christ" when he sees the fruit of his suffering labors. When it comes to his own status, however, Paul declares, "But far be it from me to boast except in the cross of our

44. Wright, "New Perspectives on Paul," 253.
45. Wright, "New Perspectives on Paul," 254.

Lord Jesus Christ, by which the world has been crucified to me, and I to the world" (Gal 6:14). Before God, he recognizes "that Christ Jesus came into the world to save sinners, of whom I am the foremost. But I received mercy for this reason, that in me, as the foremost, Jesus Christ might display his perfect patience as an example to those who were to believe in him for eternal life" (1 Tim 1:15–16).

Adherents of the Reformation interpretation hardly "shy away from Paul's clear statements about future judgment according to works," as Wright suggests. It is clearly affirmed in the Lutheran and Reformed confessions (see, e.g., Westminster Confession, ch. 33). This is because Paul has no difficulty acknowledging a final judgment that includes believers. "For we must all appear before the judgment seat of Christ, so that each one may receive what is due for what he has done in the body, whether good or evil" (2 Cor 5:10). In Romans 14:12 Paul says that "everyone will give an account of himself to God." Those who follow the Reformation interpretation hardly shy away from such clear statements; they simply interpret them differently: judgment according to (κατά) works rather than through or on account of (διά or ἐκ) works is well-attested in classic Reformed treatments. We may call them justifying in the sense that James meant: not justifying us before God but justifying our profession in this life. The final judgment will not render a verdict that is different from the one that believers enjoy now; rather, it will confirm the elect as those who have been not only justified but sanctified by grace.

God not only justifies the believer's person but also his or her works. No longer a judge but now a father, God does not treat us as our works (even good works) deserve but graciously regards them as the imperfect obedience of children. Even though they are imperfect before the bar of justice, the sin clinging to their works is forgiven. Because God cherishes the person, he also delights as a father in the incomplete and imperfect works of his people in whom his Spirit is at work. The whole church will stand before God vindicated only on the basis of an imputed righteousness, but they will not do so without an imparted righteousness as well.

These good works will be rewarded *but not with respect to justification.* As Calvin comments, "After he has received us into his favor, he receives our works also by a gracious acceptance. It is on this that the reward hinges. There is, therefore, no inconsistency in saying that he rewards good works, provided we understand that mankind, nevertheless, obtain eternal life gratuitously."[46] He adds that "the expression ['God will render to every one according to his works'] indicates an order of sequence rather than the cause." Believers "prove themselves access to the glory of the Heavenly Kingdom, but by which those chosen by their God are led to its disclosure."[47] In short, good works are necessary not *unto justification* but *as a consequence*. Those who are justified are being sanctified. Union with Christ delivers both gifts inseparably but distinctly to each believer. Since those who are declared righteous are also definitively holy in Christ and are being conformed to his image, the fruit of the Spirit will attest to the identity of the elect on the last day. They have not only been chosen, redeemed, and justified, but also sanctified and glorified. Their works will reveal that they are God's elect, but those works are not the basis of their election. While N. T. Wright sees present justification as nothing more than an identification of who belongs to the covenant people and future justification as salvific, it is just the opposite in Paul.

At this point I find helpful the distinction often drawn by the older Reformed theologians between justification apart from works, which is *declarative*, and the judgment according to works, which is *demonstrative*.[48] This distinction is useful for distinguishing between the different senses of justification in Paul and James. Nothing can be clearer in Paul than that Christ alone is the basis (i.e., meritorious cause) of salvation and that faith is the instrument, with love and good works as the fruit. To say that the believer's works are the *basis* of justification in any sense is to go even beyond the traditional Roman Catholic view. While, in the Reformation perspective, faith alone unites us to Christ—for justification, sanctification, and glorification—the fruit of new obedience begins immediately to blossom. Therefore, those who are justified now will also be able to show themselves in truth to be children of their heavenly Father, even though, unlike the "goats," they seem unaware of their good works. But this is not justification—first, middle, or final. In addition to justification, God will adorn his work of grace within the godly with rewards.

---

46. Calvin, *Calvin's Commentaries*, vol. 22, *Commentary on the Epistles of Paul the Apostle to the Corinthians*, trans. William Pringle (Grand Rapids: Baker, 1981), on 2 Cor 5:10.

47. *Inst.* 3.18.1.

48. See, e.g., John Owen, *The Works of John Owen*, ed. William H. Goold (Edinburgh: Banner of Truth Trust, 1965), 7:181–85.

PART 4

RECEIVING JUSTIFICATION

CHAPTER 10

FAITH

Looking to Christ

Having discussed what justification is and its mechanism (imputation), I turn now to the means. As the "apocalyptic" school emphasizes, faith is treated in Scripture as an event or epoch that arrives with Christ (Gal 3:22–26). However, this is merely shorthand for the new covenant in which the types and shadows have given way to the reality and believers were justified through faith in the Old Testament just as we are (e.g., Gen 15:6; Heb 11:4–40; Rom 4:11–16; Gal 3:7). Therefore, the identification of faith with an epoch hardly cancels the many passages that treat faith chiefly as the way one is justified. It is possible also to find exegetical support for the idea that faith is evidence of regeneration. However, nowhere is faith described as the badge of covenant membership, as the new perspective maintains. In other words, in terms of exegesis, the definition of faith as a badge of membership is a category mistake. No more than baptism in the New Testament is circumcision contrasted with *faith* in the Old Testament. On the contrary, Abraham's circumcision was "a seal of the righteousness that he had by faith while he was still uncircumcised" (Rom 4:11). In the Old Testament as in the New, justification is the reality, the sacraments are the sign and seal of God's promise, and faith is the means of actually possessing the reality that is pledged to all visible covenant members. Thus, it is baptism, not faith, that has replaced circumcision (Matt 28:19; Acts 2:38; Rom 4:11; 6:2–6; Gal 3:27; Col 2:11–12; Titus 3:5; 1 Pet 3:21). In both Testaments, it is possible to be a visible member of the covenant without actually embracing the reality promised in word and sacrament.

Both theses—faith as apocalyptic event or as ecclesial badge—are proposed as alternatives to the traditional view that faith is the means of receiving Christ's saving benefits. However, the preponderance of relevant passages in the New Testament treat faith as the instrument of receiving Christ with his benefits, which include the forgiveness of sins, justification, entrance into the kingdom, sanctification, and glorification.

One may cite only a few representative verses: "But to all who did receive him, who believed in his name, he gave the right to become children of God" (John 1:12). "Whoever believes in him is not condemned, but whoever does not believe is condemned already, because he has not believed in the name of the only Son of God" (John 3:18). Jesus said, "Truly, truly, I say to you, whoever hears my word and believes him who sent me has eternal life. He does not come into judgment, but has passed from death to life" (John 5:24). He also said, "Truly, truly, I say to you, whoever believes has eternal life" (John 6:47), and "everyone who lives and believes in me shall never die" (John 11:26). When the crowds asked what to do to be saved, "Peter said to them, 'Repent and be baptized every one of you in the name of Jesus Christ for the forgiveness of your sins, and you will receive the gift of the Holy Spirit'" (Acts 2:38). Proclaiming the gospel to Jews, Paul announced that "by him everyone who believes is freed from everything from which you could not be freed by the law of Moses" (Acts 13:39). "For we hold that one is justified by faith apart from works of the law" (Rom 3:28). "Therefore, since we have been justified by faith, we have peace with God through our Lord Jesus Christ" (Rom 5:1). The object of faith is Christ as he is revealed in the gospel. Receiving him as our righteousness, we are justified (Rom 1:17; 3:22; 4:23–25; 9:30; 1 Cor 1:30; Phil 3:9). The "if" of faith alone rings out in various passages, including Romans 10:

> If you confess with your mouth that Jesus is Lord and believe in your heart that God raised him from the dead, you will be saved. For with the heart one believes and is justified, and with the mouth one confesses and is saved. For the Scripture says, "Everyone who believes in him will not be put to shame." For there is no distinction between Jew and Greek; for the same Lord is Lord of all, bestowing his riches on all who call on him. For "everyone who calls on the name of the Lord will be saved." (Rom 10:9–13)

Therefore, Lutherans confess "that faith alone is the means and instrument whereby we lay hold of Christ, and thus in Christ of that righteousness which avails before God, for whose sake this faith is imputed to us for righteousness (Rom 4:5)." Further, "This faith is not a bare knowledge of the history of Christ, but such a gift of God by which we come to the right knowledge of Christ as our Redeemer in the Word of the Gospel, and trust in Him that for the sake of His obedience alone we have, by grace, the forgiveness of sins, are regarded as holy and righteous before God the Father, and eternally saved."[1]

Calvin defines faith in the Geneva Catechism as "a sure and steadfast knowledge of the fatherly goodwill of God toward us, as he declares in the gospel that for the sake of Christ he will be our Father and Savior."[2] The Heidelberg Catechism teaches (Q. 60–61),

> Q. How are you righteous before God?
> A. Only by true faith in Jesus Christ. Although my conscience accuses me that I have grievously sinned against all God's commandments, have never kept any of them, and am still inclined to all evil, yet God, without any merit of my own, out of mere grace, imputes to me the perfect satisfaction, righteousness, and holiness of Christ. He grants these to me as if I had never had nor committed any sin, and as if I myself had accomplished all the obedience which Christ has rendered for me, if only I accept this gift with a believing heart.
>
> Q. Why do you say that you are righteous only by faith?
> A. Not that I am acceptable to God on account of the worthiness of my faith, for only the satisfaction, righteousness, and holiness of Christ is my righteousness before God. I can receive this righteousness and make it my own by faith only.

So, once again, *sola fide* is merely shorthand for *solo Christo*. It is not because of faith itself—its quality, intensity, or virtue—that one is justified, but because of Christ, who becomes ours through faith alone.

---

1. Formula of Concord, Epitome to the Solid Declaration 3.5–6, in *The Book of Concord*, ed. Theodore G. Tappert (Philadelphia: Fortress, 1989), 473.
2. Geneva Catechism (1536), in *Selected Works of John Calvin: Tracts and Letters*, ed. Henry Beveridge and Jules Bonnet, 7 vols. (Grand Rapids: Baker, 1983), 2:132.

As the Westminster confession teaches, faith does many things: believes all that God teaches in his word, obeys God's commands, and so forth. "But the principal acts of saving faith are accepting, receiving, and resting upon Christ alone for justification, sanctification, and eternal life, by virtue of the covenant of grace."[3] The same views are found in the Thirty-Nine Articles (Anglican), the London/Philadelphia Confession (Baptist), and in other Protestant symbols. This chapter explores the scriptural doctrine of faith in conversation with Roman Catholic and Protestant challenges to the classic evangelical teaching.

OBJECT AND ACT OF JUSTIFYING FAITH

More than an object "at a distance," as it were, Christ himself is present in his word proclaimed and sealed in the sacraments and therefore also in the faith that he gives through the gospel. Christ absolves and justifies by speaking to us in person (Rom 10:8–9). In what then does the act of faith consist?

The Faith That Is Believed

Theologians have traditionally distinguished between the faith that is believed (*fides quae creditur*) and the faith that believes (*fides qua creditur*). Jude exhorts believers "to contend for *the faith* that was once for all delivered to the saints" (Jude 3). Faith is knowledge of and assent to particular truths. What the Reformers objected to was (a) reducing faith to assent to propositions and (b) a blind assent at that—submitting to all that the church teaches (*fides implicita*), which marks one of several points at which the Council of Trent was at odds with the tradition (especially Aquinas). Calvin judged, "It would be the height of absurdity to label ignorance tempered by humility 'faith'!"[4] Essentially, this makes the church rather than Christ the object of faith.

We are not justified by knowledge but by Christ. Nevertheless, in order to trust in Christ, there must be some knowledge of the triune God, revealed in Christ, who himself is known according to his gospel. "Now faith is the assurance of things hoped for, the conviction of things not seen" (Heb 11:1–2). A child need not know how the Santa Claus legend emerged or all the details surrounding it in order to anticipate

---

3. Westminster Confession of Faith 14.2, (Glasgow: Free Church Publications, 1997), 63–64.
4. *Inst.* 3.2.3.

with bated breath the arrival of the jolly saint. Yet there must be some content to the expectation. How much more so with the coming seed of the woman, offspring of Abraham and Sarah, of David, and of Mary the mother of the incarnate God. But knowledge and assent are directed to the principal element of faith: assurance or confidence. "Faith then is not a naked knowledge either of God or of his truth," says Calvin; "nor is it a simple persuasion that God is, that his word is the truth; but a sure knowledge of God's mercy, which is received from the gospel."[5]

Especially since Vatican II, the idea of implicit faith has been expanded to incorporate those who know nothing of Christ or who, "through no fault of their own," have not embraced the church formally—for example, members of other religions or of no affiliation.[6] Michael Schmaus argues,

> According to Hebrews [1:6], then, faith in God's existence and his justice is all that is necessary. It must be added, however, that such faith is sufficient only in the case of one who has not yet been reached by the revelation of Christ. Thus we should not exclude the possibility of a justifying faith on the part of the members of the great (perhaps atheistic) moral systems of Asia. For in acknowledging the authority of a conscience which is not subject to men's control they acknowledge implicitly, even though they are not clearly aware of it, God revealing himself to them in their conscience.[7]

This argument illustrates a deep tendency in Roman Catholic thought to identify faith with mere assent—and the fewer the propositions, the better.[8] Paul argues that the voice of God in his law resounds

---

5. Calvin, *Calvin's Commentaries*, vol. 19, *Commentaries upon the Epistle of Paul to the Romans*, trans. John Owen (Grand Rapids: Baker, 1996), 171.

6. See *CCC*, 847, quoting the Vatican II document, *Lumen Gentium*, 16; cf. *Gaudium et Spes*, 22.

7. Michael Schmaus, *Dogma*, vol. 6, *Justification and Last Things* (London: Sheed and Ward, 1977), 29.

8. Even appeals to the thesis of the development of dogma (formulated especially by Cardinal Newman) cannot save this interpretation of *fides implicita*, declared at the Second Vatican Council, from its contradiction of centuries of official church dogma. Defenders of the contemporary Roman Catholic view (including Protestants, even some evangelicals) often appeal to Cornelius in Acts 10, as an example of a gentile who was justified by an implicit faith even before Peter explained the gospel (Clark Pinnock, *A Wilderness in God's Mercy* [Grand Rapids: Zondervan, 1992], 84–85). However, this was far from Thomas's view. "With regard, however, to Cornelius," he says, "it is to be observed that he was not an unbeliever, else his works would not have been acceptable to God, whom none can please without faith. Now he had implicit faith, as the truth of

in the conscience to disclose universal guilt (Rom 1:17–2:16) but that another word—the gospel—is needed for salvation (3:21ff.), but Rome sees the gospel merely as a clearer revelation of the law. The Reformation position rejects the reduction of faith to assent (much less assent merely to the God of natural revelation) but recognizes that it involves knowledge, assent, and trust in God's promises in Jesus Christ.

The Faith That Believes

If Christ is the object, then what is the act of faith in the act of God's justifying? When used with a genitive case, the preposition διά in the New Testament always denotes instrumental efficacy. For example, in Romans 11:36 we read, "For from him and through him and to him are all things [ἐξ αὐτοῦ καὶ δι᾽ αὐτοῦ καὶ εἰς αὐτὸν]." In Galatians 3:2, the negation of ἐξ ἔργων νόμου ("from/by the works of the law") excludes every human cause from justification other than "receiv[ing] the Spirit by the hearing [of the gospel] with faith" [τὸ Πνεῦμα ἐλάβετε ἢ ἐξ ἀκοῆς πίστεως]. Wherever this language of ἐκ πίστεως or διὰ πίστεως occurs, we should assume, on purely lexical grounds, that faith is the *instrumental* cause and, on exegetical grounds, especially when opposed to all human works, that it is faith *alone*.

RECEIVING INSTRUMENT OR VIRTUOUS GROUND—GIFT OR WORK?

When Christ finds us, we are "dead in trespasses and sins" (Eph 2:1), but "even when we were dead in our trespasses, [God] made us alive together with Christ" (v. 5). It is remarkable that while in Deuteronomy 10:16 God commands Israelites to circumcise their own hearts, in 30:6 he promises, after their failure, to perform the operation himself. Thus, just as Paul announced (Rom 3:21), the gospel (as "good news") is already announced in the law (that is, the canon of the Mosaic covenant). God himself replaces the stony heart with a fleshly one and forgives their sins.

Faith is not the one work on the basis of which God justifies. It is the *instrument*, not *basis* of justification. Further, while faith is a condition in the sense that only those who believe in Christ are justified, even this faith is a gift of the covenant of grace, which is grounded in the

---

the Gospel was not yet made manifest: hence Peter was sent to him to give him fuller instruction in the faith" (II-II, Q. 10, A.4, Reply to the third).

eternal and unconditional pact between the persons of the Godhead in which we were not a party but solely beneficiaries. God not only makes it possible to believe but actually grants faith to whomever he will (Luke 10:22; John 1:18–19; 6:35–40, 63–65; 10:27–29; Acts 13:48; 16:14; Rom 8:30; 9:10–24; Eph 2:5; Jas 1:18). Paul's opposition of faith and works on the point of justification does not allow the former to be assimilated to the latter (e.g., by means of defining faith as obedience, works, faithfulness, etc.). This gift of faith is the result of God's effectual calling of sinners by the gospel.[9]

The notion that faith is a gracious gift of God is replete also in the patristic literature. Clement of Rome argued in his late first-century letter to the Corinthians that the great heroes of the old covenant "were highly honored, and made great, not for their own sake, or for their own works, or for the righteousness which they wrought, but through the operation of His will." "And we, too, being called by His will in Christ Jesus," he adds, "are *not justified by ourselves*, nor by our own wisdom, or understanding, or godliness, or works which we have wrought in holiness of heart; *but by that faith* through which, from the beginning, Almighty God has justified all men; to whom be glory for ever and ever. Amen" (32:1–4).[10] Even the faith that justifies is a gift, Ambrose contends.[11]

Chrysostom says that Paul "makes a wide distinction" between "faith and precept," believing in the word of Christ rather than ascending to the heavens. Notice the bishop's sweeping contrast between *doing* and *receiving*: "Instead of a certain manner of life, He brought in faith."[12] As we have seen, Chrysostom repeatedly affirms that even the faith by which we are justified is a gift.[13]

To be sure, Rome teaches that faith is a gift. However, faith does not *justify* until it becomes active in love—that is, works. For Chrysostom, however, the distinction is between doing and receiving. Faith cannot therefore be a virtue that qualifies one for justification. He adds,

---

9. Richard B. Gaffin Jr. expresses the view taught by the prophets, Jesus, and the apostles and summarized in the Reformed confessions and catechisms. "The origin of the believer's faith does not lie in himself," he says, "but in the calling of God, which in its irrevocable efficacy and power is life-giving and creative (Rom. 4:17; 11:29; Eph. 1:18–20; II Tim. 1:9)." Gaffin, *Resurrection and Redemption: A Study in Paul's Soteriology* (Phillipsburg, NJ: P&R, 1987), 142.

10. Clement of Rome, *Epistle to the Corinthians* 32 (*ANF* 1:13). Emphases in these quotations are added.

11. See George Finch, *A Sketch of the Romish Controversy* (London: G. Norman, 1831), 220.

12. Chrysostom, *Homilies on Ephesians* 2:11, 12, hom. 5 (*NPNF*[1] 13:72).

13. For my previous examination of Chrysostom on Romans, see vol. 1, ch. 2.

Now in what case, tell me, does faith save without itself doing anything at all? Faith's workings themselves are a gift of God, lest anyone should boast. What then is Paul saying? Not that God has forbidden works but that he has forbidden us to be justified by works. No one, Paul says, is justified by works, precisely in order that the grace and benevolence of God may become apparent.[14]

"It was not by your own pains that you found out God," he preached, "but while you continued in error, He drew you to Himself."[15]

Augustine also teaches, "And lest men should arrogate to themselves the merit of their own faith at least, not understanding that this too is the gift of God, this same apostle, who says in another place that he had 'obtained mercy of the Lord to be faithful,' here also adds: 'and that not of yourselves; it is the gift of God: not of works, lest any man should boast.'"[16] God's sovereign grace does not efface but frees the will from bondage to sin. "It goes before the unwilling to make him willing; it follows the willing to make his will effectual."[17]

The former immortality man lost through the exercise of his free will; the latter he shall obtain through grace, whereas, if he had not sinned, he should have obtained it by desert. . . . And the will owes its freedom in no degree to itself, but solely to the grace of God which comes by faith in Jesus Christ; so that the very will, through which we accept all the other gifts of God which lead us on to His eternal gift, is itself prepared by the Lord, as the Scripture says [Prov. 16.1].[18]

Boniface, bishop of Rome and friend of Augustine, is also representative of this point of view. "It appears obvious," he says, "that our faith in Christ, like all good things, comes to individuals from the gift of divine grace and not from the power of human nature."

---

14. Chrysostom, *Homily on Ephesians* 4.2.9, in *Ancient Christian Commentary on Scripture, New Testament VI: Galatians, Ephesians, Philippians*, ed. Mark J. Edwards (Downers Grove, IL: InterVarsity, 1998), 134.

15. Chrysostom, *Commentary on Galatians* 4:9 (*NPNF*[1] 12:31). Such comments, frequent especially throughout his homilies on Romans and commentaries on the Pauline epistles, serve at least to qualify the usual description of his soteriology as "synergistic."

16. Augustine, *The Enchiridion* 31 (*NPNF*[1] 3:247–48).

17. Augustine, *The Enchiridion* 32 (*NPNF*[1] 3:248).

18. Augustine, *The Enchiridion* 106 (*NPNF*[1] 3:271).

We rejoice that your brotherhood perceived this truth in accordance with catholic faith, when a council of some bishops of Gaul was held. As you have indicated, they decided unanimously that our faith in Christ is conferred on men by the intervention of divine grace. They added that there is absolutely nothing good in God's eyes that anyone can wish, begin, do, or complete without the grace of God, for as our Savior said, "Without me you can do nothing." For it is both a certainty and an article of catholic faith that in all good things, the greatest of which is faith, divine mercy intervenes for us when we are not yet willing [to believe], so that we might become willing; it remains in us when we are willing [to believe]; and it follows us so that we remain in faith.[19]

Augustine and Aquinas affirmed that faith is a gift that God gives to his elect and introduced the crucial distinction between the outward calling of all by the gospel and the effectual calling of the elect.[20] Libertarian accounts of free will as well as hyper-Calvinist views of divine sovereignty assume that to the extent that God's effectual grace is responsible for faith, the individual is less responsible and less free. However, with Augustine and Aquinas, the Reformers taught that the *more* that God works in our lives, the more active—the freer—we are.

In short, according to the leading interpreters of Paul throughout church history, faith is—like the cross itself—a humble (even according to the world), powerless thing. It is not the quality of the subjective act but the treasure it grasps that is "the power of God unto salvation for everyone who believes, to the Jew first and also to the Greek" (Rom 1:16).

Precisely because of its object, faith brings assurance. "Therefore, since we have been justified by faith, we have peace with God through our Lord Jesus Christ" (Rom 5:1). Warning against seeking assurance of election in the "hidden God," Luther emphasized throughout the *Bondage of the Will* that it is to be found in Christ as he is revealed in the gospel. Similarly, Calvin writes,

---

19. Quoted in William E. Klingshirn, trans., *Caesarius of Arles: Life, Testament, Letters*, Letter 20—Pope Boniface to Caesarius; 2 (Liverpool: University Press, 1994), p. 125.

20. Augustine, *On the Predestination of the Saints*, in *NPNF*[1] 5:513; Saint Thomas Aquinas, *Commentary on the Letter of Saint Paul to the Romans*, ed. J. Mortensen and E. Alarcón, trans. F. R. Larcher, OP (Lander, WY: Aquinas Institute, 2012), 1.4, 25.

> First, if we seek God's fatherly mercy and kindly heart, we should turn our eyes to Christ, on whom alone God's Spirit rests. . . . But if we have been chosen in him, we shall not find assurance of our election in ourselves; and not even in God the Father, if we conceive him as severed from his Son. Christ, then, is the mirror wherein we must, and without self-deception may, contemplate our own election.[21]

Christ alone is the "mirror of our election."[22] The only proper place to look is to the promise in God's word, Calvin concludes: "Let us hear what is said in the Gospel."[23]

Speaking for many of his Puritan associates, Robert Traill argued that "faith in Jesus Christ, in the office of justification, is neither a condition nor a qualification but in its very act a renouncing of all such pretenses."[24] In one sense, faith is not a condition but a gift of the covenant of grace, but in another it is a condition as the necessary instrument of justification, which the repeated biblical formula "through faith in God/Christ" underscores.

DOES FAITH JUSTIFY BECAUSE IT IS LOVE?

With Peter Lombard's *Sentences*, medieval theology adopted the view that faith is one of the cardinal virtues alongside hope and love. Thomas Aquinas understood faith to be assent to the truth of God's

---

21. *Inst.* 3.13.5.

22. As John Leith observes, for Calvin election is never to be sought apart from Christ. "The God who elects is the same God who was in Christ. The Christ who performs the deeds of salvation is the eternal Christ who is the register of election. He is the mirror in which election can be understood." John Leith, *John Calvin's Doctrine of the Christian Life* (Louisville: Westminster John Knox, 1989), 131.

23. John Calvin, *Calvin's Calvinism: God's Eternal Predestination and Secret Providence Together with "A Brief Reply" and "Reply to the Slanderous Reports"*, trans. Henry Cole; ed. Russell J. Dykstra (Jenison, MI: Reformed Free Publishing Association, 2009), 172. Although the contrast between Calvin and the Puritans has been exaggerated, it is worth noting that the continental Reformed tradition regarded assurance and faith as synonymous. To believe in Christ, in other words, *is* to be assured (besides Calvin, see Q. 21 of the Heidelberg Catechism: "What is true faith?" "True faith is not only a certain knowledge, whereby I hold for truth all that God has revealed to us in his Word, but also an assured confidence, created by the Holy Spirit in my heart, that not only to others but to me also, God has freely given remission of sins, everlasting righteousness, and salvation, merely of grace, only for the sake of Christ's merits." In contrast, the Westminster Confession teaches, "This infallible assurance does not so belong to the essence of faith, but that a true believer may wait long, and conflict with many difficulties, before he be partaker of it." (18.3). The Confession does emphasize that it is the subjective experience of assurance that waxes and wanes (with which the continental tradition would agree), but the Puritan view did open up a distinction that could be and indeed was by some taken in the direction of an unhealthy anxiety in the search for assurance based on inner experience and outward actions.

24. Robert Traill, *A Vindication of the Protestant Doctrine of Justification*, in *The Works of Robert Traill* (1810; repr., Edinburgh: Banner of Truth, 1975), 1:252–96.

word and the teachings of the church, which is why he believed that faith was inadequate to justify apart from being perfected by love. The first grace of justification (conversion) is not merited even by faith, says Aquinas, "but because the believing itself is the first act of the justice God works in him."[25] However, in order to bring complete justification (i.e., inward renewal or sanctification), faith must become love, and in order to attain final justification, meritorious works. Notice already that faith brings the first (unmerited) grace "because the believing itself is the first act of *the justice God works in him*," not because it clings to Christ. Everything turns on the movement of the soul from injustice to justice.

John Henry Newman correctly recognized the difference at this point. In the "Lutheran view," he says,

> Faith, it appears, is to be defined, not by its *nature*, but by its *office*; not by what *it is*, but by what it *does*. It is trust *in Christ*, and it differs from all other kinds of faith in That towards which it reaches forward and on which it rests. Thus it differs from historical faith, or intellectual knowledge, in that it is a taking Christ for our portion and (to use a familiar phrase) closing with His offers of mercy.[26]

Trust cannot exist without putting forth obedience, but it is not thereby justifying.[27] "It justifies then, not as being lively or fruitful, though this is an inseparable property of it, but as *apprehending* Christ, which is its essence."[28] Calvin, too, rejects the belief that faith must be formed by love in order to justify.[29] Newman even concedes in this work (written just prior to joining the Roman Catholic Church) that the "Roman school" differs from the patristic consensus in its reduction of justification to spiritual renewal. Even at Trent, "Spiritual renewal is said to be the '*unica formalis causa*,' the *one and only* true description of justification." The ancients did not speak like this, Newman observes.[30]

---

25. Quoted in Markus Bockmuehl, "Aquinas on Abraham's Faith in Romans 4" in *Reading Romans with St. Thomas Aquinas*, ed. Matthew Levering and Michael Dauphinais (Washington, DC: Catholic University of America Press, 2012), 44, from Aquinas, *Commentary on Romans*, para. 331.

26. John Henry Newman, *Lectures on the Doctrine of Justification*, 3rd ed. (London: Rivington's, 1874; repr., Nashotah House, 2012), 12.

27. Newman, *Lectures on the Doctrine of Justification*, 14.

28. Newman, *Lectures on the Doctrine of Justification*, 16.

29. Newman, *Lectures on the Doctrine of Justification*, 21, citing *Inst.* 3.11.20.

30. Newman, *Lectures on the Doctrine of Justification*, 31.

However, Newman himself takes the familiar Origenist path of concluding that the works that do not justify are "works of the Law" interpreted as the old covenant boundary markers as opposed to "works or fruits of the Spirit."[31] "St. Paul, then, by speaking of faith as justifying without works, means without corrupt and counterfeit works, not without good works. And he does not deny what St. James affirms, that we are justified in good works."[32]

It is important to remind ourselves that in the traditional Roman Catholic interpretation, the reason that faith must be perfected by love in order to be justifying is grounded not in human initiative but in God's grace. It is because the first grace is the infusion of love.[33] Michael Schmaus points out that the idea is grounded especially in Origen's notion of agape as "a process of purification, and so as a gateway to the vision of God."[34] How then can one be assured of being in a state of grace? According to the Council of Trent, "Without a special revelation it is neither possible nor necessary for anyone to have the certainty of faith about the state of justification."[35] The place of love in medieval scholasticism, however, Luther gave to Christ. It is Christ who gives form, color, and life to faith itself.[36]

There are two key verses for the view that justifying faith is completed by love. The first is Galatians 5:6: "For in Christ Jesus neither circumcision nor uncircumcision counts for anything, but only faith working through love." However, Paul has just spent the first four chapters of Galatians explaining, often in polemical detail, how justification before God is a gift through faith alone. It is not by their works but by embracing what they heard—namely, the gospel—that they were justified, if indeed they believed this gospel at all (Gal 3:2). Now (in Gal 5) he is not talking about the operation of faith in relation to justification but the way this same faith bears fruit in love and good works. Ironically, those who sought life by the law have not found righteousness, while those who seek life in Christ alone receive not only justification but sanctification (see also Rom 11:7).

31. Newman, *Lectures on the Doctrine of Justification*, 289–90.
32. Newman, *Lectures on the Doctrine of Justification*, 291.
33. Schmaus, *Dogma*, 6:91–92. Schmaus explains, "In ecclesiastical terminology this process whereby man is transformed is described as an infusion of heavenly love (DS 1530f.)."
34. Schmaus, *Dogma*, 6:96–97.
35. Council of Trent, Session 6, ch. 9, DS 1533f.
36. Luther, *Lectures on Galatians Chapters 5–6* (1535), in *LW* 27:129–30.

Thus the justified immediately begin to bear the fruit of the Spirit (Gal 5). Paul thinks that their backbiting and jealousy spring from their legalism. Yet, again ironically, it is those who have abandoned the law as their means of justification who actually begin to fulfill the law not as a covenant of works but as the inevitable fruit of the faith that justifies. The burden of justification has been lifted from our shoulders, so we are exhorted, "Bear one another's burdens, and so fulfill the law of Christ" (Gal 6:2). The law could command love but could not create it. Calvin paraphrases Paul's statement: it is "as if he said, 'If you desire to keep a law, Christ enjoins on you a law which you can only prefer to all others; and that is, to cherish kindness towards each other. He who lacks this has nothing.'" Thus, "Everything that is foreign to love is unnecessary." Yet even "he who is nearest to it in comparison with others, is yet far distant in respect of God."[37] Paul is not undoing his previous argument; rather, he is building on it. But they are different topics. Once again, we need to allow Paul to talk about justification *and* sanctification, faith *and* love, without reducing the former to the latter. Only those who are freed of the law's severe requirement ("do this, and you will live") are liberated to love and therefore to begin to obey the heart of the law.

The second major verse appealed to for the Roman Catholic view is Romans 5:5. The ESV renders it, "Hope does not put us to shame, because God's love [love of God] has been poured into our hearts through the Holy Spirit who has been given to us." Should "love of God" (ἀγάπη τοῦ Θεοῦ) be interpreted as God's love for us or our love for God? As even Roman Catholic biblical scholar Joseph Fitzmyer argues, the genitive here is subjective: God's love for us, not (as in the Vulgate translation) our love for God. Given the fact that the second part reads, "the Holy Spirit who has been *given to us*," it seems highly doubtful that the first part of the sentence would refer to our love for God.[38]

The Reformers saw faith as the instrument in justification not because of what it is in itself—its inherent strength or virtue—but simply because it embraces *Christ*. Faith is not to be conflated with love, repentance, or any other effect of regeneration. Calvin explains,

---

37. Calvin, *The Epistles of Paul the Apostle to the Galatians, Ephesians, Philippians and Colossians*, ed. David W. Torrance and Thomas F. Torrance, trans. T. H. L. Parker (Grand Rapids: Eerdmans, 1965), 110 (on Gal 6:2).

38. Joseph A. Fitzmyer, *Romans: A New Translation with Introduction and Commentary* (New York: Doubleday, 1993), 398.

Repentance can rightly and fittingly be called the beginning of the way that leads to salvation, but more as an accompaniment than a cause. These are not subtle evasions but a simple explanation of the difficulty, for while Scripture teaches that we never obtain the forgiveness of our sins without repentance, at the same time it teaches in many places that the only ground of our forgiveness is the mercy of God.[39]

Therefore, "It is false to say that any part of righteousness (justification) consists in *quality* or in the habit which resides in us, and that we are righteous (justified) only by gratuitous acceptance."[40] His critics turn accompaniments into instruments. "It is just as if they were to say that forgiveness of sins cannot be severed from repentance, and therefore repentance is part of it."[41] They confuse "an inseparable accident" with the "cause" of justification.[42] (To use my own illustration, it does not follow that because police officers carry a weapon, the weapon makes them a police officer.)

Yet, Calvin adds, one "can no more separate faith from charity than Christ from his Spirit."[43] "There would be no truth in the words of John, that faith is the victory by which we overcome the world (1 John v. 4) did it not engraft us into Christ (John xvi. 33), who is the only conqueror of the world." When the Council of Trent cites "faith that works by love" (Gal 5:6), it fails to see that "love is the fruit and effect of faith." After all, "Paul is not there considering in what respect faith or charity avails to justify a man, but what is Christian perfection; as when he elsewhere says, 'If a man be in Christ he is a new creature' (2 Cor. v. 17)."[44] However, love is not the completion of faith but the fruit. Word-faith-love-good works: this is the proper order according to the Reformers. John Milbank claims that the Reformers' emphasis on centrality of faith rather than love "is the *gravest imaginable heresy*."[45]

39. Calvin, *The Second Epistle of Paul to the Corinthians, and the Epistles to Timothy, Titus, and Philemon*, ed. David W. Torrance and Thomas F. Torrance, trans. T. A. Smail (Grand Rapids: Eerdmans, 1964), 100 (on 2 Cor 7:10).

40. Calvin, *Acts and Antidote*, vol. 3, *Selected Works of John Calvin: Tracts and Letters*, 7 vols., ed. Henry Beveridge and Jules Bonnet, trans. Henry Beveridge (Grand Rapids: Baker, 1983), 117.

41. Calvin, *Acts and Antidote*, 118.

42. Calvin, *Acts and Antidote*, 118.

43. Calvin, *Acts and Antidote*, 118.

44. Calvin, *Acts and Antidote*, 119.

45. John Milbank, "Alternative Protestantism," in *Radical Orthodoxy and the Reformed Tradition: Creation, Covenant, and Participation*, ed. James K. A. Smith and James H. Olthuis (Grand Rapids: Baker Academic, 2005), 33.

However, he draws the illegitimate inference that by identifying faith alone as the instrument of justification, the Reformers were ranking faith above love in general. But, again, how is love denied if it is said to be the inseparable and inevitable fruit of faith? "How shall the mind rise up to taste the divine goodness," asks Calvin, "and not at once be wholly set on fire with answering love for God?"[46]

DOES FAITH JUSTIFY BECAUSE IT IS OBEDIENCE?

In Protestant circles as well, faith and obedience are often conflated. Bultmann describes faith as "venture."[47] "Faith is a 'leap in the dark.' . . . For man is not asked whether he will accept a theory about God that may possibly be false, but whether he is willing to obey God's will." The meaning of Christ's cross, he says, is found in our "crucifying the affections and lusts . . . , overcoming our natural dread of suffering, . . . and the perfection of our detachment from the world." This constitutes "the judgment . . . and deliverance of man."[48] But here Bultmann not only confuses justification with sanctification but with a view of sanctification that can only be reckoned as gnostic. As Julius Schniewind points out, "The 'crucifixion of our passions' is then no more than a striking euphemism for self-mastery, which is the quest of all the higher religions and philosophies."[49] Faith as "making Jesus Lord and Master" (as Machen did nearly a century ago) is simply another way of saying the same thing.[50] If this is what one has in mind when using the term "faith," then it is indeed an anthropocentric conception.

There is some danger in using the shorthand, "justification by faith," since in technical terms "by" means "on the basis/account of." The Reformation formula is *propter Christum per fidem*—on the basis/account of Christ through faith. But the idea of faith itself as the one small work that God counts as sufficient for bestowing justification has appeared in Arminian, pietist, and revivalist Protestantism for a long time. When Richard Baxter and other seventeenth-century divines taught

---

46. *Inst.* 3.2.41.
47. Rudolf Bultmann, "Faith as Venture," in *Existence and Faith: Shorter Writings of Rudolf Bultmann* (London: Hodder and Stoughton, 1960), 57.
48. Rudolf Bultmann, "New Testament and Mythology," in *Kerygma und Myth: A Theological Debate*, rev. ed., ed. Hans Werner Bartsch, trans. Reginald H. Fuller (New York: Harper & Row, 1961), 64–65.
49. Julius Schiewind, "A Reply to Bultmann" in *Kerygma und Myth: A Theological Debate*, rev. ed., ed. Hans Werner Bartsch, trans. Reginald H. Fuller (New York: Harper & Row, 1961), 65–66.
50. J. Gresham Machen, *What Is Faith?* (Edinburgh: Banner of Truth, 1996), 192–93.

this view, it was dubbed "Neonomianism" by their Puritan colleagues. Neonomians taught that faith is a lesser work that counts as having fulfilled the whole law. In Baxter's *Aphorisms on Justification*, republished by John Wesley, Baxter in fact spoke of faith as "a Contract." "And all Contracts of such nature, do impose a necessity of performing what we consent to and promise, in order to the benefit." Similar to E. P. Sanders's formula for covenantal nomism, Baxter says, "Covenant-making may admit you, but it's the Covenant-keeping that must continue you in your privileges."[51]

The new perspective on Paul has also transformed faith into faithfulness. James Dunn thinks that it would make little sense in Paul's argument in Romans 4 to attack the widespread Jewish view of Abraham as "the archetype of *faithfulness*."[52] But I have already established the fact that this is precisely what Paul does (challenging the "merit of Abraham"), and it makes perfect sense. Abraham is held up not as an example of faithfulness (this would be to reverse his entire argument that the patriarch had nothing to boast of before God) but as an example of faith in Christ even against all odds and empirical evidence at hand (Rom 4:16–22). In fact, the Genesis narrative itself (Gen 12–25) includes Abraham's gross moral failures as well as faithfulness, which highlights God's faithfulness in spite of the patriarch's weaknesses.

More recently, evangelical theologian Matthew W. Bates, following N. T. Wright, argues that justifying faith is "allegiance."[53] He emphasizes Paul's reference to the "obedience of faith" in Romans 1:5. "If, as has traditionally been held since the Protestant Reformation, the gospel is all about faith alone, not faith plus works, then why doesn't Paul just say that the gospel is purposed toward *pistis*?"[54] Faith is allegiance, he says, transferring ultimate loyalty from Caesar to Christ, as in the case of the jailer in Philippi (Acts 16:31). "Obedient loyalty to the king is required as a condition as acceptance."[55] "Allegiance includes obedient

51. Richard Baxter, *An Extract of Mr. Richard Baxter's Aphorisms of Justification, Publish'd by John Wesley* (London: W. Strahan, 1745; Gale ECCO Print Editions, 2010), 19–20. See David C. Lachman, *The Marrow Controversy: An Historical and Theological Analysis* (Edinburgh: Rutherford House, 1988); Hans Boersma, *A Hot Pepper Corn: Richard Baxter's Doctrine of Justification in Its Seventeenth-Century Context of Controversy* (Vancouver: Regent College Publishing, 2003).

52. James D. G. Dunn, "Once More, ΠΙΣΤΙΣ ΧΡΙΣΤΟΥ," in *Pauline Theology*, vol. 4, *Looking Back, Pressing On*, ed. Elizabeth E. Johnson and David M. Hay (Atlanta: Scholars' Press, 1997), 61–81; Dunn, *The Theology of the Apostle* (Grand Rapids: Eerdmans, 1998), 379–85.

53. Matthew W. Bates, *Salvation by Allegiance Alone* (Grand Rapids: Baker Academic, 2017).

54. Bates, *Salvation by Allegiance Alone*, 34.

55. Bates, *Salvation by Allegiance Alone*, 104.

action," he says, drawing on Matthew 7:21–23.[56] "In short, we cannot say in an unqualified fashion that final salvation is by grace and by faith apart from embodied obedience, for this misunderstands the nature of both *charis* ('grace') and *pistis* ('faith') in antiquity and in Paul's Letters."[57]

Does Bates mean that allegiance is necessary for being welcomed finally into the everlasting kingdom? It is certainly true that "if we deny him, he also will deny us" (2 Tim 2:12). Faith definitely takes the form of allegiance, and we grow in allegiance daily. However, *in the act of justification*, faith is not allegiance but trust. From this root of trust, the fruit of love and allegiance blossom. Bates is saying more than that faith must become allegiance in sanctification in order to be genuine faith. Rather, he argues that faith must be allegiance in justification. So once again, as in the Roman Catholic version, the attempt among Protestants to define justifying faith *as obedience* (i.e., works) rests on a basic failure to distinguish faith's activity in *justification* from its activity in *sanctification*.

As one in a long line of criticism, Bates misunderstands the "Lutheran" view as teaching that a faith that does not work can nevertheless justify.[58] On the contrary, confessional Lutheran and Reformed churches see such faith as the dead faith that James and Paul reject. Faith can no more exist without works than a fire can exist without heat. "Oh, it is a living, busy, active, mighty thing, this faith. And so it is impossible for it not to do good works incessantly," Luther exults.

> It does not ask whether there are good works to do, but before the question rises, it has already done them, and is always at the doing of them. He who does not these works is a faithless man. He gropes and looks about after faith and good works and knows neither what faith is nor what good works are, though he talks and talks, with many words about faith and good works.[59]

As the Puritan divine Thomas Goodwin put it, the acts of faith are many. Faith is active in love, to be sure, active in suffering, in hope,

---

56. Bates, *Salvation by Allegiance Alone*, 99.

57. Bates, *Salvation by Allegiance Alone*, 105.

58. In the work cited above, John Henry Newman caricatured the "Lutheran" view as teaching that "trust then is not necessarily lively faith" (Newman, *Lectures on the Doctrine of Justification*, 8).

59. Luther, *Commentary on Romans*, trans. J. Theodore Mueller (Grand Rapids: Zondervan, 1954), xvii.

in serving neighbors, and so forth. However, *in the act of justification*, faith is merely a receiving and resting in Christ.[60] The Puritans often used the vivid term "recumbency": faith is reclining upon Christ. Even our faith is incomplete and imperfect, subject to wavering, doubt, fear, and stubborn sin. Only by the virtue of its object is faith the means of justification.

I have already dealt with "the obedience of faith" in Romans 1:5 in connection with N. T. Wright's interpretation, so I will be brief here in responding to Bates's appeal to it. Everything turns on the object of obedience. To obey the gospel is to believe it; to obey the law is to do it. If Romans 1:5 is saying that we are justified by works, then Paul has overlooked the glaring contradiction of everything else that he says on the subject. In context, Paul is issuing a declaration in his office as an ambassador of the Sovereign King, much like the one in 2 Corinthians 5:20: "Therefore, we are ambassadors for Christ, God making his appeal through us. We implore you on behalf of Christ, be reconciled to God." In Paul's thinking, to cling to one's own striving is the highest form of disobedience. Contrasting the righteousness that is by works and the righteousness that is by faith, he laments that his fellow Jews, "being ignorant of the righteousness of God, and seeking to establish their own, they did not *submit to God's righteousness*" (Rom 10:3). So he is surely not saying that they would be justified if only they had more fully obeyed or submitted to God's moral commands. The Gospels confirm this interpretation. For example, when Jesus is asked in John 6, "'What must we do, to be doing the works of God?' Jesus answered them, 'This is the work of God, that you believe in him whom he has sent'" (vv. 28–29). They are justified not by working but by believing.

FAITH IS THE MEANS OF INHERITING GOD'S ESTATE

Christ fulfilled the covenant of law (both the overarching covenant with humanity in Adam and the covenant at Sinai) so that he could dispense his reward to his coheirs. This is the heart of justification. Faith is the only human act capable of being exclusively a receiving instrument since faith is confidence in what *someone else* has accomplished. Faith does not attain the reward (in which case it

---

60. Thomas Goodwin, *The Object and Acts of Justifying Faith*, in *The Works of Thomas Goodwin*, vol. 8 (Edinburgh: Banner of Truth, 1985).

would be the meritorious basis) but claims it in Christ. When it comes to acquittal before God, Paul does not believe in grace and works, faith and works, or Christ and works. It is an either-or. Works are commands to be *done*, and the gospel is a report to be *heard* and *believed* (Rom 10:1–17; cf. Gal 3:2).

Like other new perspective scholars, Bates takes the Origenist line of exegesis that treats the new covenant as superior because it demands spiritual works (the law of Christ) for justification rather than external observances (the law of Moses). However, the "law of Christ" is in substance the Decalogue delivered through Moses: "Bear one another's burdens [the second table of the Decalogue] and so fulfill the law of Christ" (Gal 6:2). This moral law cannot justify, but freed from the law as a covenant of works ("Do this and you shall live"), believers are free for the first time to love without fear of punishment and without relating in envious competition (Gal 5:1–26).

There is also an essential apocalyptic-eschatological feature to this new covenant obedience. Since Christ has come, and the age to come has dawned in his resurrection, love is now possible in a new way. I have noted this point in reference to Galatians 5, but it is made also by John. John claims that even though the content of the law is the same (viz., love), in a sense it has changed completely now that Christ has come and inaugurated the new creation. So this new society of love is "true in him" and therefore "true in us" through union with him (1 John 2:7–8). Throughout 1 John the point is made that good works are the necessary evidence of genuine faith (2:3, 9, 15–16, 23, 29; 3:6, 9–10, 14; 4:2–3; 5:10–12). There is no indication in these passages or anywhere else that the keeping of commandments is instrumental to justification. On the contrary, as for Paul, obedience is a sine qua non of final salvation (glorification) because God finishes what he begins (Phil 1:6). But justification is not sanctification or glorification.

Faith is the gift of the Holy Spirit through the gospel that acknowledges and rests in God's covenant faithfulness—specifically, in the person and work of Christ for sinners. "For all the promises of God find their Yes in him. That is why it is through him that we utter our Amen to God for his glory" (2 Cor 1:20). The proclaimed gospel creates faith, faith bears the fruit of love, and love is active in good works.

FAITH *IN* OR THE FAITHFULNESS *OF* CHRIST: THE ΠΙΣΤΙΣ ΧΡΙΣΤΟΥ DEBATE

In 1983, New Testament scholar Richard B. Hays published an extensive argument in favor of reading the Pauline phrase πίστις Χριστοῦ as a subjective genitive: the faith *of* Christ instead of faith *in* Christ.[61] Ever since Hays's provocative essay, the subjective reading has taken Paul scholarship by storm.[62] The key verses in dispute are Galatians 2:16, 20; Romans 3:22, 26; and Philippians 3:9. According to this new point of view, the phrase "faith in Christ" should be translated "the faithfulness of Christ" in each case.

The Rationale for the Subjective Interpretation

The subjective reading is not altogether foreign to Protestant translations. The King James Version (1611) rendered the phrase "faith *of* Christ" in two of the controverted passages: Galatians 2:16, 20 and Romans 3:22. Further, as Hays documented, his conclusions were argued by several scholars in the twentieth century.[63]

In fact, the subjective view is part of the broader trend that we have explored. First, it involves the shift from seeing the "righteousness of God" as a divine attribute and norm (revealed in his law) by which he exercises judgment toward the idea of God's faithfulness to his covenant promise (i.e., saving deliverance). As we have seen, the new perspective generally presupposes this revised understanding of God's righteousness along with the redefinition of "works of the law" as referring to the boundary markers that separate gentiles from Jews (viz., circumcision and dietary laws). In fact, Hays argues that the premises of the new perspective require a subjective interpretation, although James D. G. Dunn

61. Richard B. Hays, *The Faith of Jesus Christ: An Investigation of the Narrative Substructure of Galatians 3:1–4:11*, 2nd ed. (Grand Rapids: Eerdmans, 2002).
62. Those who favor the subjective genitive include Karl Barth, *The Epistle to the Romans*, trans. Edwin C. Hoskyns (New York: Oxford University Press, 1968), 41, 96; Richard Longenecker, *Galatians*, WBC 41 (Dallas: Word, 1990), 87–88; F. J. Matera, *Galatians*, Sacra Pagina 9 (Collegeville, MN: Liturgical, 1983), 93–94; L. T. Johnson, *Reading Romans: A Literary and Theological Commentary* (New York: Crossroad, 1997), 58–61; J. Louis Martyn, *Galatians: A New Translation and Commentary*, AB 33A (New York: Doubleday, 1997), 251, 263–75. Barth, however, read the phrase as "the faithfulness of God" rather than, more specifically, "faithfulness of Christ." See Michael F. Bird and Preston M. Sprinkle, eds., *The Faith of Jesus Christ: Exegetical, Biblical, and Theological Studies* (Grand Rapids: Baker Academic, 2010), especially the surveys of the debate by Bird (1–14) and Debbie Hunn (15–32). Other good overviews may be found in George Howard, "On the 'Faith of Christ,'" *Harvard Theological Review* 60 (1967): 459–65; Paul Pollard, "The 'Faith of Christ' in Current Discussions," *Concordia Theological Journal* (1997): 213–28.
63. Hays, *The Faith of Jesus Christ*, 121–24, 142–47.

has been among the proposal's staunchest critics.[64] Second, it involves a shift from reading πίστις and its cognates as "faith" to "faithfulness."[65] Introduced by Johannes Haußleiter in 1891,[66] the subjective-genitive view was defended by Gerhard Kittel, and Gabriel Hebert mediated the view to T. F. Torrance.

Karl Barth also took a subjective-genitive view of key verses in Romans, but as the "faithfulness of God."[67] Benjamin Myers notes that Barth renders Romans 3:28 as "For we reckon that a person is justified by the faithfulness of God [*Treue Gottes*] apart from works of the Law" (as in 10:6, 8).[68] Barth came to defend the subjective genitive view on the other passages (e.g., Gal 2:20; Phil 3:9), Myers relates.[69] For Barth, Paul's opposition is not between "two different psychological conditions (active striving and passive reception)," but "a much more radical antithesis" between "*human religion* versus *divine action*," just as J. Louis Martyn proposes.[70] "Thus faith takes place not where one passively receives God's gift, but only where one's entire self is dissolved and done away with in the event of Jesus' death."[71]

Shaped by John Macleod Campbell's view of the atonement (by Christ's vicarious repentance) as well as Barth's doctrine of election, Torrance argued that Christ repented and believed in our place. Justified by Christ's faith, we must not only flee our unrighteousness and self-trust but "flee from even our own acts of faith, confession, trust and response, and take refuge in the obedience and faithfulness of Christ."[72] Since the faithfulness of Christ is alone necessary, and the faithfulness of

---

64. Dunn, "Once More, ΠΙΣΤΙΣ ΧΡΙΣΤΟΥ," 61–81; Dunn, *The Theology of the Apostle*, 379–85.

65. Charles Lee Irons, *The Righteousness of God: A Lexical Examination of the Covenant-Faithfulness Interpretation*, WUNT 2/386 (Tübingen: Mohr Siebeck, 2015), 329–33.

66. Johannes Haußleiter, "Der Glaube Jesu Christi und der christliche Glaube: Ein Beitrag zur Erklärung des Römerbriefes," *Neue kirchliche Zeitschrift* 2 (1891): 132–34.

67. Barth, *The Epistle to the Romans*, 41, 96.

68. Benjamin Myers, "From Faithfulness to Faith in the Theology of Karl Barth," in *The Faith of Jesus Christ: Exegetical, Biblical, and Theological Studies*, ed. Michael F. Bird and Preston M. Sprinkle (Milton Keynes: Paternoster, 2009), 293, from Barth, *Der Römerbrief 1922* (Zurich: EVZ, 1940), 72; ET, *Romans*, 107, 361, 377.

69. Myers, "From Faithfulness to Faith in the Theology of Karl Barth," 293. See Karl Barth, *The Epistle to the Philippians*, trans. James W. Leitch (Louisville: Westminster John Knox, 2002), 99–103. On Gal 2:20, see *CD* II/2, 559.

70. Myers, "From Faithfulness to Faith in the Theology of Karl Barth," 295.

71. Myers, "From Faithfulness to Faith in the Theology of Karl Barth," 295. Once more I have to observe the similarity of this view with the seventeenth-century antinomians, not to mention the *Gellasenheit* of German mysticism that influenced Anabaptist treatments of union with God. In more radical forms of mysticism generally, the self is lost in its union with God. Despite Barth's displayed contempt for mysticism and pietism, it is difficult to overlook the basic similarity at this point, although his interpretation is of course unyieldingly christocentric.

72. T. F. Torrance, *Theology in Reconstruction* (repr., Grand Rapids: Eerdmans, 1996), 159–60.

believers is a response to salvation which they already possess apart from it, faith *in* Christ becomes quite secondary. During these years, C. F. D. Moule and James Barr led the opposition to the subjective reading, as did C. E. B. Cranfield.[73]

Hays explains that his doctoral studies at Yale Divinity School in the 1970s were shaped by the narrative theology of Hans Frei as well as by Barth's *Church Dogmatics.* "In short, Barth's theology was already lurking in the background when Hays was writing his great dissertation on the faith of Jesus Christ," Myers observes.[74] Douglas Campbell's dependence on Barth is obvious throughout his *Deliverance of God.* Hays, Martyn, and especially Campbell are up front about the theological agenda, even conceding that their view cannot be established on merely semantic and exegetical grounds.

This dependence on Barth says nothing about how to translate πίστις Χριστοῦ, but it does help to explain the urgency, emphasis, and stark antitheses that advocates press. Something quite large is at stake for a subjective reading: nothing less than a "christocentric" versus "anthropocentric" gospel. Marcus Barth argued that if we are justified through faith *in* Christ, then people are "totally delivered to the sincerity, depth, certainty of their own faith."[75] Richard Hays goes further, judging that the traditional reading "verges on blasphemous self-absorption in our own religious subjectivity."[76]

Hays and, more radically, Campbell suggest that the new perspective is still too mired in Reformation debates. Paul is not contrasting works of the law (whatever they are) with faith. Rather, he is contrasting anything and everything that human beings do (including believing) with God's action. J. Louis Martyn says that for Paul πίστις Χριστοῦ *means* "an act of God carried out in Christ."[77] So faith is faithfulness, but it is always God's or Christ's, not ours. God's righteousness is manifested by

---

73. C. E. B. Cranfield, *A Critical Textual Commentary on the Epistle to the Romans* (Edinburgh: T&T Clark, 1975), 203.

74. Myers, "From Faithfulness to Faith in the Theology of Karl Barth," 292, from Hays, *The Faith of Jesus Christ,* xxiii–xxiv.

75. Debbie Hunn, "ΠΙΣΤΙΣ ΧΡΙΣΤΟΥ in Galatians 2:16," *Tyndale Bulletin* 57, no. 1 (2006): 23–33, quote from 24, quoting Markus Barth, "The Faith of the Messiah," *Heythrop Journal* 10 (1969): 363–70, esp. 368.

76. Richard B. Hays, "ΠΙΣΤΙΣ and Pauline Christology: What Is at Stake?," in *Pauline Theology,* vol. 4, *Looking Back, Pressing On,* ed. David M. Hay and E. Elizabeth Johnson (Atlanta: Scholars' Press, 1997), 46.

77. Martyn, *Galatians,* 270.

the faith of Christ and not by the faith of human beings, Hays insists.[78] The covenant-faithfulness interpretation and the subjective genitive stand or fall together.[79]

Like Barth and Käsemann, proponents contrast their view with the traditional view in terms of a theocentric versus anthropocentric emphasis. With the new perspective generally, Hays maintains that justification does not confer a new legal status ("declared righteous"), but includes those who were once excluded among the people of God.[80] Once again, Romans is not answering the question, "How can I be saved?"[81] It is about Jew-gentile relations in the church. The righteousness of God refers to God's covenant faithfulness. Hays (along with Martyn, Campbell, and others) see themselves as going beyond the new perspective in terms of a more theocentric/christocentric and apocalyptic perspective.

Thus, those who are in broad agreement with the Reformation's reading of Paul on justification find themselves fighting, as it were, on two fronts: against a neonomian tendency that makes justification depend finally on the believer's obedience and an antinomian tendency that makes even faith unnecessary for justification.[82] Since the active obedience of Christ lies at the heart of justification in both Lutheran and Reformed confessions, the addition of a few new passages on Christ's faithfulness to the arsenal in its favor would seem hardly to be cause for alarm. Yet the subjective rendering—hardly provoked by a fresh discovery of a purely lexical, grammatical, or even exegetical nature—is part of a broader theological agenda launched by Karl Barth.[83] Debbie Hunn observes, "Twelve years after Hebert reintroduced the πίστις Χριστοῦ debate, Markus Barth predicted a change in theological outlook that

---

78. Hays, "ΠΙΣΤΙΣ and Pauline Christology," 35–60.

79. Hays, *The Faith of Jesus Christ*, 283, 294.

80. Richard B. Hays, "Justification," in *The Anchor Bible Dictionary* (New York: Doubleday, 1992), 3:1131.

81. Richard B. Hays, "Psalm 143 and the Logic of Romans 3," *JBL* 99 (1980): 112.

82. This was the debate that roiled seventeenth-century English Puritanism. Antinomians like Tobias Crisp and John Saltmarsh taught a doctrine of eternal justification and Christ's vicarious faith and repentance that has a general similarity to Karl Barth and T. F. Torrance. On the antinomian controversy see Michael A. G. Haykin and Mark Jones, eds., *Drawn into Controversies: Reformed Theological Diversity and Debates within Seventeenth-Century British Puritanism* (Göttingen: Vandenhoek & Ruprecht, 2011).

83. Barth's novelty is the election of *all* in Christ; otherwise, much of his teaching on the subject (including justification and faith) is identical to that of the English antinomians, especially Saltmarsh and Crisp.

would break the traditional mould on Paul."[84] That change has come, to be sure, but it is important not to see the sweeping popularity of the subjective view as a sudden lexical and grammatical discovery that has eluded the whole church from its earliest days.

Hays, Martyn, and Campbell do not brook any half-measures. Campbell says, "Paul's theological description today resembles an Arctic ice-shelf—melting and rotting underneath, riven with fissures, and about to collapse into the sea. Either we do something about it, or we face real and terrible consequences for our inaction." It is nothing less than a contest between Athanasius and Arius, he says.[85] Peter Leithart adds his own alarm: this is "ultimately a question of what Paul is talking about in general, the fundamental thrust of the gospel he proclaims, what is in the foreground and what is in the background. Is Paul's presentation of the gospel in Romans and Galatians mainly an answer to the question, how can sinners be saved? (Answer: Trust in Christ!) Or is it mainly an answer to the question, how did God reveal and manifest his justice in the world? (Answer: Through the faithful work of Christ.)"[86] In other words, one must choose between the *ordo salutis* and the *historia salutis*. According to the traditional translation, Leithart recognizes, "To say one is justified by 'faith in Christ' is to say that one is justified (whatever *that* means) by trusting in Jesus."[87] But according to these scholars, this rendering, assumed by all branches of Christianity since the early patristic era, is wrong. In short, the gospel is either that the righteousness of God is a gift in Christ received through faith, not by any works of ours, or that God's faithfulness is proved in Jesus's faithfulness in defeating the powers, not the Jewish ceremonies or the power of Torah. But is this yet another false dilemma?

Lexical Analysis

At the outset, it is important to say that there are indeed many passages that attest the faithfulness of Christ—without which, by the way,

---

84. Debbie Hunn, "Debating the Faithfulness of Jesus Christ in Twentieth-Century Scholarship," in *The Faith of Jesus Christ: Exegetical, Biblical and Theological Studies*, ed. Michael F. Bird and Preston M. Sprinkle (Peabody, MA: Hendrickson, 2010), 29.

85. Douglas. A. Campbell, "The Current Crisis: The Capture of Paul's Gospel by Methodological Arianism," in *Beyond Old and New Perspectives on Paul: Reflections on the Work of Douglas Campbell*, ed. Chris Tilling (Eugene, OR: Cascade, 2014), 48.

86. Peter J. Leithart, *Delivered from the Elements of the World: Atonement, Justification, Mission* (Downers Grove, IL: IVP Academic, 2016), 155. Leithart provides a superb bibliography in the notes on pages 154–55.

87. Leithart, *Delivered from the Elements of the World*, 154–55.

there could be no traditional doctrine of justification (since it is based on Christ's faithfulness). Furthermore, we cannot assume that Paul must always intend the same meaning in every πίστις Χριστοῦ (or similar) phrase. It could well be that it is sometimes subjective, other times objective, and, as suggested below, something different altogether (e.g., genitive of origin/source). In Romans 3:3, πίστιν τοῦ Θεοῦ obviously means the "faithfulness of God." Paul of course was not working with such syntactical distinctions, so we have to allow the context to determine the meaning.

However, there are some important concerns with the subjective view of the relevant passages on entirely semantic grounds. The first move, already made by the new perspective, is to broaden "faith" in these passages to include "faithfulness." However, this conclusion remains highly contested. Barr accused Hebert and Torrance of importing heavily freighted theological interpretations of Hebrew words like אֱמֶת ('emeth) and אֱמוּנָה ('emunah), meaning "faithful" and "faithfulness" (rendered ἀλήθεια in the New Testament), into πίστις, disregarding what words actually mean as semantic markers distinguished from other words.[88]

Other words have been imported into πίστις from the New Testament itself, as Debbie Hunn observes. "Many have followed Kittel in his attempt to bring faith to encompass obedience in the phrase, 'obedience of faith' in Romans 1:5."[89] To the contrary, focusing on the determinative role of context, "Moule argues that the use of the verb πιστεύω determines the meaning of the noun πίστις in Galatians 2:16 where both words appear."[90] However, Douglas Campbell argues that it is "a fallacy to derive the meaning of πίστις from its cognate verb πιστεύω," while Barry Matlock points out that "Paul himself substitutes the noun πίστις for the verb πιστεύω when he quotes Genesis 15:6 in Romans 4:9." Thus, "πιστεύω has a narrower semantic range, one which does not include 'be faithful.'"[91]

---

88. James Barr, "Faith and Truth: An Examination of Some Linguistic Arguments," in *Semantics of Biblical Language* (London: Oxford University Press, 1961), 188. This recalls Irons's evaluation of the Cremer thesis that I drew upon in ch. 3.

89. Hunn, "Debating the Faithfulness of Jesus Christ in Twentieth-Century Scholarship," 18.

90. Hunn, "Debating the Faithfulness of Jesus Christ in Twentieth-Century Scholarship," 19, quoting C. F. D. Moule, "The Biblical Conception of 'Faith,'" *Expository Times* 68 (1957): 222.

91. Hunn, "Debating the Faithfulness of Jesus Christ in Twentieth-Century Scholarship," 19, referring to Douglas A. Campbell, "False Presuppositions in the ΠΙΣΤΙΣ ΧΡΙΣΤΟΥ Debate: A Response to Brian Dodd," *JBL* 116 (1997): 715–16, and R. Barry Matlock, "Detheologizing the ΠΙΣΤΙΣ ΧΡΙΣΤΟΥ Debate: Cautionary Remarks from a Lexical Semantic Perspective," *Novum Testamentum* 42 (2000): 4.

An objective genitive makes Abraham's faith the instrument of clinging to God's promise. However, "If we translate the genitive subjectively," says Leithart, "we come to this: 'the promise [which springs] out of the faith exercised by Jesus was given to all those who believe.'"[92] But this makes neither grammatical nor theological sense. The promise does not spring from Jesus's faith; rather, it anticipates and announces his person and work. Nowhere are we told that the patriarchs or prophets were justified by Jesus's faith; rather, they were justified through faith in the promise of his advent, as Hebrews 11 especially underscores.

Following Kittel, Hays argues that if Paul speaks of the faith of Abraham in Romans 4:16, he must be referring in to the faith of Christ in 3:26.[93] However, appealing to Philippians 1:27, Hans Leitzmann argues, τῇ πίστει τοῦ εὐαγγελίου is obviously "the faith *in*" rather than "*of* the gospel," so why would we not conclude that Paul intends an objective genitive in Romans 3:22 as well? Similarly, Thomas Schreiner "uses the objective genitive τῆς γνώσεως Χριστοῦ Ἰησοῦ in Philippians 3:8 to conclude that πίστις Χριστοῦ in 3:9 is objective."[94]

Kittel and others have argued for the subjective view also on the basis of a parallel in Galatians 2:16 between πίστις Χριστοῦ and ἔργα νόμου. If the latter is subjective (works *of* law), then surely the former is as well. However, Hunn notes, "In Acts 9:31, for example, Luke sets 'the fear of the Lord' beside 'the comfort of the Holy Spirit,' an objective beside a subjective genitive, which readers clearly understand. [Roy] Harrisville, in fact, found the early church fathers to understand Romans 4:16 as subjective and Romans 3:26 as objective without confusion or question."[95]

Even Richard Hays "thinks that the arguments from grammar are 'finally inconclusive.'"[96] Stanley E. Porter and Andrew W. Pitts observe

---

92. Leithart, *Delivered from the Elements of the World*, 156n20.

93. Hays, "ΠΙΣΤΙΣ and Pauline Christology," 47.

94. Hunn, "Debating the Faithfulness of Jesus Christ in Twentieth-Century Scholarship," 19–20, quoting Hans Leitzmann, *An die Römer* (Tübingen: Mohr Siebeck, 1933), 48; and referencing Thomas R. Schreiner, *Paul, Apostle of God's Glory in Christ: A Pauline Theology* (Downers Grove, IL: InterVarsity, 2001), 213.

95. Hunn, "Debating the Faithfulness of Jesus Christ in Twentieth-Century Scholarship," 24, referring to Roy A. Harrisville, "ΠΙΣΤΙΣ ΧΡΙΣΤΟΥ: Witness of the Fathers," *Novum Testamentum* 36 (1994): 233–41. Hunn also notes, "Most πίστις Χριστοῦ phrases include the proper name Ἰησοῦς, but proponents of the adjectival genitive have yet to address whether or not the Greek of Paul's time allowed a proper noun to modify πίστις as an adjectival genitive. And if it did, what did it mean? The definitions cited here are more theological than lexical and could hardly be inherent in the simple phrase" (26).

96. Stanley E. Porter and Andrew W. Pitts, "Πίστις with a Preposition and Genitive Modifier: Lexical, Semantic, and Syntactical Considerations in the πίστις Χριστοῦ Discussion," in *The Faith of Jesus Christ: Exegetical, Biblical, and Theological Studies*, ed. Michael F. Bird and

that many "despair of solving the issue linguistically and consign it to a matter of exegesis or even theology." However, "Lexical, grammatical, and syntactical factors are probably more important to the discussion than is usually assumed."[97] The semantic issue turns on disambiguating the meaning of the head term πίστις, they argue.[98] In other words, does πίστις mean "faith in the sense of 'faithfulness' or in the sense of 'belief'"?[99]

Porter and Pitts maintain that contemporary categories of Greek grammar are read back anachronistically into Paul, when it is "highly unlikely that he was working with notions of subjective or objective genitive, or corresponding categories, as he made linguistic choices."[100] The authors focus on the seven or eight πίστις Χριστοῦ uses (Gal 2:16, 20; 3:22; Rom 3:22, 26; Phil 3:9). After breaking down the three major collocational patterns of πίστις in the New Testament, they conclude that both the interpretation of πίστις as faithfulness and as a subjective genitive (faithfulness of Christ) are highly unlikely in the disputed verses.

In brief, they conclude, "The use of πίστις as a head term with a prepositional specifier, without an intervening article and followed by an element in the genitive, provides further evidence that, at least from a linguistic standpoint, when Paul used the phrase πίστις Χριστοῦ he was indicating that Christ was the proper object of faith."[101] Further, when Paul uses the subjective genitive to refer to a person's faith/faithfulness, it is with a definite article, but the definite article never appears with the πίστις Χριστοῦ phrase.[102] They note also that at Romans 3:22 the Codex Alexandrinus copied διὰ πίστεως Ἰησοῦ Χριστοῦ as διὰ πίστεως ἐν Χριστῷ Ἰησοῦ, assuming that an objective genitive.[103]

While I agree with the authors that the scribe was simply trying to clarify, it seems plausible that he was doing so by using the language of verse 24, which is exactly the same clause that he inserted here, including the reversal of "Jesus" and "Christ." This actually strengthens the authors' case that Paul was repeating the basic point of verse 22 ("the righteousness of God through faith in Jesus Christ") in verse 24

Preston M. Sprinkle (Milton Keynes: Paternoster, 2009), 35, from Hays, "Πίστις and Pauline Christology," 716.

97. Porter and Pitts, "Πίστις with a Preposition and Genitive Modifier," 36.
98. Porter and Pitts, "Πίστις with a Preposition and Genitive Modifier," 36.
99. Porter and Pitts, "Πίστις with a Preposition and Genitive Modifier," 37.
100. Porter and Pitts, "Πίστις with a Preposition and Genitive Modifier," 39.
101. Porter and Pitts, "Πίστις with a Preposition and Genitive Modifier," 53.
102. Porter and Pitts, "Πίστις with a Preposition and Genitive Modifier," 50–51.
103. Porter and Pitts, "Πίστις with a Preposition and Genitive Modifier," 52.

("and are justified by his grace as a gift, through the redemption that is in Christ Jesus").

Moisés Silva also reminds us that "Paul's many unambiguous statements" should govern our interpretation of the more ambiguous ones.

> If by *pistis Christou* (which in isolation can indeed signify any number of things) the apostle had meant either "Christ's faith" or "Christ's faithfulness," it would have been ridiculously easy for him to make that point clear beyond dispute. Among various possibilities, he could have, for example, indicated—in the same contexts—one or two ways in which Jesus believed and how those acts of faith were relevant to the matter at hand. Or he could have told us—again, in the same contexts—that his message of *dikaiosynē* ("righteousness, justification") is true because *Christos pistos estin* ("Christ is faithful"). What could have been simpler? And considering the theological importance of this issue, one would think that he might have made a special effort to clarify matters. Instead, if some scholars are to be believed, Paul did not have enough sense to realize that the phrase *pistis Christou* is ambiguous. And to make matters worse, he unwittingly misled his readers by using the verb *pisteuō* with *Christos* as direct object again and again in the very same passages that have the ambiguous phrase! His bungling proved spectacularly successful, for in the course of nearly two millennia, virtually every reader—including ancient scholars for whom Greek was their native language—understood the phrase to mean "faith in Christ" and gave no hint that it might mean something else.[104]

The controversy not only underappreciates the priority of disambiguating the head term πίστις but also, as we will see in considering particular passages, obscures the wider range of potential genitive variations. In particular, a number of verses arguably intend "the faith" (i.e., the content that is believed or *fides quae creditur*) as well as genitive of source (*genitivus auctoris*). It is entirely possible, in other words, to read some of the verses best in fact as neither objective nor subjective, but as referring to the faith that *comes from*, has *reference to*, is *due to*, or *originates in* Jesus and his faithful work on our behalf.

---

104. Moisés Silva, review of *The Faith of Jesus Christ: Exegetical, Biblical, and Theological Studies*, ed. Michael F. Bird and Preston M. Sprinkle, *Themelios* 35, no. 2 (2010): 305–11.

The first move, shared by new perspective scholars generally, that faith equals faithfulness, should not be taken for granted. "It is not clear," notes Mark A. Seifrid, "that the 'subjectivists' sufficiently have taken into account the radical shift in usage of the term πίστις from 'faithfulness' to 'faith' that appears in the New Testament writings, the Apostolic Fathers, and beyond."

> The use of the term πίστις to signify "faith" is not unique to the New Testament and early Christianity. What is new is the way in which faith—*fides specialis*—becomes decisive and determinative in the human relation to God. . . . Secondly, both "subjectivists" and "objectivists," by virtue of the categories they defend, assume that we should read the noun πίστις in a verbal sense. Whether it signifies Christ's faithfulness or our believing, πίστις is thought to function as a *nomen actionis*. It is not at all clear that this assumption is valid.[105]

Seifrid suggests, "In the first place, in the New Testament the noun πίστις does not serve as an appellative, but as an absolute."[106] But in some cases at least, the intended meaning is neither objective nor subjective, but the intention is *the* faith (*fides quae creditur*)—that is, the content of what is believed. Even Roy Harrisville overlooked this class of instances in the fathers.[107] The genitive is subjective (as in Ignatius's letter to the Magnesians, "in the faith of Jesus Christ," and in Polycarp's "concerning the faith of the Lord"), but it pertains to the content of what is believed.[108] "In all probability," Seifrid suggests, "we find here again a *genitive auctoris*."[109] It is clear also that *the* faith (*fides quae creditur*) is intended in Romans 1:16 ("I am not ashamed of the gospel . . ."), so "unless one is ready to sever Romans 1:17 from Romans 1:16, it is clear that the three occurrences of the term πίστις in verse 17 in one way or another reflect the content of the gospel." Seifrid goes so far as to say that "it is not clear that πίστις appears in *any* instance in Paul's letters as a merely verbal noun." In fact, "A nominal sense of πίστις

---

105. Mark A. Seifrid, "The Faith of Christ," in *The Faith of Jesus Christ: Exegetical, Biblical, and Theological Studies*, ed. Michael F. Bird and Preston M. Sprinkle (Milton Keynes: Paternoster, 2009), 130–31.

106. Seifrid, "The Faith of Christ," 130–31.

107. Seifrid, "The Faith of Christ," 136.

108. Seifrid, "The Faith of Christ," 136.

109. Seifrid, "The Faith of Christ," 136.

likewise is present where Paul speaks of faith as a gift and work of God in Christ." Paul does of course speak also of faith as an action, even in the immediate context (Rom 1:12), attaching the personal pronouns: "your faith" and "my faith."[110] In short, Seifrid wisely reminds us that, finally, the context must determine what Paul means, and we should not reduce the possibilities to objective and subjective options.[111]

Finally, a subjective reading of the disputed verses is unlikely given the fact that the earliest Christian readers and interpreters of Paul, for whom Greek was the mother tongue, simply took for granted the objective meaning. Scouring the *Thesaurus Linguae Graecae*, Roy Harrisville discovered that in the patristic sources πίστις Χριστοῦ was regarded in every case as an objective genitive.[112] It is difficult to imagine that the objective genitive construction of πίστις Χριστοῦ, which was assumed by every Christian writer since the apostolic fathers, "verges on blasphemous self-absorption in our own religious subjectivity."[113]

Exegetical Analysis

The decision over the objective or subjective rendering of Paul's πίστις Χριστοῦ verses cannot be made on semantic grounds alone. Before examining the key passages more closely, I should touch on three of the most central exegetical criticisms of the objective view.

---

110. Seifrid, "The Faith of Christ," 131.
111. Seifrid, "The Faith of Christ," 134.
112. Harrisville, "ΠΙΣΤΙΣ ΧΡΙΣΤΟΥ," 233–41.
113. Hays, "What Is at Stake?," 46. Proponents of the subjective view appeal to their own brief, produced by Ian Wallis, but Wallis' method and conclusions have been challenged. See esp. Mark W. Elliott: "Πίστις Χριστοῦ in the Church Fathers and Beyond," in *The Faith of Jesus Christ: Exegetical, Biblical, and Theological Studies*, ed. Michael F. Bird and Preston M. Sprinkle (Milton Keynes: Paternoster, 2009), 281. Barry Matlock observes, "Wallis does not attend specifically to early readings of Paul's πίστις Χριστοῦ phrases but searches more generally for texts that associate the language (or concept) of 'faith' with Christ. The two investigations thus overlap very little but nevertheless share an important result: neither finds an example of the subjective genitive reading of πίστις Χριστοῦ on the part of any early Greek reader, *nor indeed any discussion of the matter.* Nevertheless, Richard Hays pronounces Harrisville's evidence 'surprisingly slight' and prefers instead Wallis's account of the evidence, from which Hays infers that the subjective genitive would have been the normal reading of πίστις Χριστοῦ until fourth-century Christological controversies made it appear unorthodox to speak of Christ having 'faith'—Athanasius is the key witness here for Wallis and Hays is found and, more important methodologically, no debate on the πίστις Χριστοῦ phrases is found. It is not that the subjective genitive reading is explicitly rejected among early Greek readers (on theological grounds that Wallis and Hays might find suspect), but rather that no awareness is shown of this option nor indeed of any problem, and so the objective genitive is read without polemic or apology" (Matlock, "Saving Faith: The Rhetoric and Semantics of πίστις in Paul," in *The Faith of Jesus Christ: Exegetical, Biblical, and Theological Studies*, ed. Michael F. Bird and Preston M. Sprinkle (Milton Keynes: Paternoster, 2009), 87, quoting Hays, *The Faith of Jesus Christ*, xlvii–lii; Ian G. Wallis, *The Faith of Jesus Christ in Early Christian Traditions* (New York: Cambridge University Press, 1995), 200–212.

Redundancy

Advocates of the subjective view place considerable weight on the issue of redundancy, but this turns out to be a very weak argument. First, Paul refers to "the righteousness of God through faith in Jesus Christ for all who believe" (Rom 3:22). He is simply emphasizing that it is because justification is *through faith alone* that it is given to *all*. Reading the verse aloud even in English (recall that these were primarily *read* epistles), if one stresses *all* in the verse, there is no redundancy at all. On the contrary, Paul is making the same point that he has been making all along: namely, *because* justification is through faith alone, it is available to all, not just to Jews. (This also explains why he singles out Abraham, since he lived centuries before Torah and the Sinai covenant and was thereby justified through faith alone.)

In Galatians 2:16, Paul says that "we have believed in Christ Jesus so that we might be justified through faith in Christ and not by works of the law." The logic makes perfect sense and poses no concern about redundancy; we have believed in Christ in order to find our justification in him rather than in our own works. As John M. G. Barclay notes, "[Galatians] 2:16 is full of repeated or redundant expressions. The relevant genitival phrases in Galatians are all accompanied by verbs that unambiguously speak of human 'believing' (2:16; 3:6, 22), while nowhere in this letter is the verb πιστεύειν or the adjective πιστός used of Christ."[114] In fact, as Francis Watson points out, Paul's antithesis loses its precision on the subjective reading of Galatians 2:16. "The symmetry of 'justified by Law' and 'righteous by faith' has been lost."[115]

And, as Barry Matlock observes, even if Galatians 2:16 is a subjective genitive, "the passage affirms the necessity of believing." A subjective reading exhibits the same repetition, although it is more cumbersome: "Knowing that a man is not justified by the works of the law but by the faith that Jesus exercises, even *we have believed in Christ Jesus*, that we may be justified by the faith that Jesus exercises."[116] Since no one can dispute that the italicized clause is objective, it makes more sense to conclude that he was repeating the same point for emphasis than to

114. John M. G. Barclay, *Paul and The Gift* (Grand Rapids: Eerdmans, 2015), 381.

115. Francis Watson, "By Faith (of Christ): An Exegetical Dilemma and its Scriptural Solution," in *The Faith of Jesus Christ: Exegetical, Biblical, and Theological Studies*, ed. Michael F. Bird and Preston M. Sprinkle (Milton Keynes: Paternoster, 2009), 162.

116. Leithart, *Delivered from the Elements of the World*, 155.

say that the objective clause was preceded and followed by a subjective genitive. Either way, there is repetition, but it makes more sense to see "we have believed in Christ Jesus" as emphasizing the same idea as "a man is justified by faith" (not by works of the law) and "that we may be justified through faith."

Then there is Galatians 3:22: "But the Scripture imprisoned everything under sin, so that the promise by faith in Jesus Christ might be given to those who believe." This verse comes closest to redundancy, but Leithart rests too much on this fact.[117] Once again, even if the first clause were subjective, the second clause confirms faith in Christ as the action of believers. A subjective reading of the first clause gains nothing of substance for his argument. Further, on the subjective reading, the promise comes from (ἐκ) the faithfulness of Christ, but surely this is not right. While God *fulfills* his promise through Christ's faithfulness, it can hardly be said that the promise itself comes *from* Christ's faithfulness. After all, it was made to Abraham and Sarah—indeed, to Adam and Eve. The point is that God, by his law, arraigned everyone as guilty so that there was no way out except by relying on his promise, which is embraced through faith in Christ, who is the object of the promise. Hence, Christ is given to all who believe in him/the promise (δοθῇ τοῖς πιστεύουσιν).

Finally, Philippians 3:9 refers to being "found in [Christ], not having a righteousness of my own that comes from the law, but that which comes through faith in Christ, the righteousness from God that depends on faith." There is certainly repetition in this verse, but the repetition is obvious in the preceding verses as well, where there is no question of objective or subjective genitives:

> But whatever gain I had, I *counted as loss* for the sake of Christ. Indeed, I *count everything as loss* because of the surpassing worth of knowing Christ Jesus my Lord. For his sake I have suffered the loss of all things and *count them as rubbish*, in order that I may gain Christ and be found in him, not having a righteousness of my own that comes from the law, but that which comes through faith in Christ, the righteousness from God that depends on faith. (Phil 3:7–9, emphasis added)

---

117. Leithart, *Delivered from the Elements of the World*, 155n20.

If anything, there is more "redundancy" in verses 7–8 than in verse 9, but it emphasizes Paul's point: he counts his own righteousness as loss, even as rubbish, in order to have Christ's righteousness through faith. Further, as James Dunn notes,

> Paul's Greek in Philippians 3:9 "would scarcely be intelligible" if he meant the first occurrence of πίστις to refer to Christ's faith and the second to human faith. And because the second reference to faith modifies the first, there is a redundancy whether the genitive is subjective or objective. In fact, the twofold occurrence of δικαιόω and ἐξ ἔργων νόμου in the same verse show well enough that Paul did not share our aversion to repetition.[118]

Anyone familiar with Paul's teaching style knows that the rabbinical technique of resumptive repetition (*Wiederaufnahme*), or epanalepsis, is part of his stock-in-trade. One obvious example is Romans 5:9–10: "Since, therefore, we have now been justified by his blood, much more shall we be saved by him from the wrath of God. For if while we were enemies we were reconciled to God by the death of his Son, much more, now that we are reconciled, shall we be saved by his life." In fact, Romans 5 is a series of such phrases, repeating the same idea in slightly altered variations, akin to parallelism in Hebrew poetry. Rather than treating such instances as a problem to be solved, we should recognize them as Paul's flags indicating that he wants to drive this point home especially—and, in these instances, a point that defenders of the subjective view wish that he had not made.

ANTHROPOCENTRIC OR CHRISTOCENTRIC

As noted above, the heart of the argument in favor of the subjective genitive is that "faith *in* Christ" (objective genitive) is anthropocentric rather than christocentric. Richard Hays says that "we are saved by Jesus' faithfulness, not by our own cognitive dispositions or confessional orthodoxy."[119] If beneath the caricature Hays is saying that everyone is saved regardless of whether they believe in Christ, then a Barthian dogma is driving recklessly over exegesis. That simply is not true to what Paul says explicitly. For example, in Romans 10 he clearly states

---

118. Dunn, "Once More, ΠΙΣΤΙΣ ΧΡΙΣΤΟΥ," 75, 79.
119. Hays, "What Is at Stake," 55.

that there are certain articles of faith—doctrines, if you will—that are included in the act of faith and that it is the believer who confesses this faith unto salvation. "For with the heart one believes and is justified, and with the mouth one confesses and is saved" (Rom 10:10). *Something* is believed, and *someone* confesses and thereby "is saved." This is why there must be preachers, so that people may hear the gospel and believe and be saved (Rom 10:13–15).

Besides lacking exegetical warrant, Barth's interpretation of the relation of justification to faith seems incoherent. For Barth, according to Bruce McCormack, "Faith may not be the cause of our justification, but there is no justification of the individual without it."[120] McCormack does not identify what kind of cause he has in mind, but in traditional Protestant theology faith is identified as the *instrumental cause* of justification. But if "there is no justification of the individual without it," then how can it be anything other than a condition? Furthermore, Barth clearly teaches that everyone is justified; faith is merely the recognition of what is already the case.[121] So it is not clear how faith can be said to be necessary for justification. All the more problematic it is, then, to say with Barth that faith is "the human work that corresponds to [God's] work."[122]

Perhaps Hays and Campbell are seeking greater consistency at this point by simply eliminating any talk of faith as a condition. But it comes at the price of ignoring a host of passages. T. F. Torrance insists that we must not only flee our unrighteousness and self-trust but "flee from even our own acts of faith, confession, trust and response and take refuge in the obedience and faithfulness of Christ."[123] But what is it to "take refuge in the obedience and faithfulness of Christ" but "confession, trust and response"? The former is precisely what we mean by "faith in Christ." If faith itself were the object (viz., the quality of the act itself), then "faith in Christ" would indeed be anthropocentric—and that this is a real problem in many Protestant (especially pietist-revivalist traditions) I do not doubt. But this view is excluded explicitly in Reformation confessions.

---

120. Bruce L. McCormack, "*Justitia aliena*: Karl Barth in Conversation with the Evangelical Doctrine of Imputed Righteousness" in *Justification in Perspective: Historical Developments and Contemporary Challenges*, ed. Bruce L. McCormack (Grand Rapids: Baker Academic, 2006), 195.

121. *CD* IV/1, 742.

122. *CD* IV/1, 615.

123. T. F. Torrance, *Theology in Reconstruction* (repr., Grand Rapids: Eerdmans, 1996), 159–60.

Faith is an act of confession in Christ as Lord, as raised from the dead, and as the basis and source of justification. "That is why it depends on faith," Paul says, "*in order that the promise may rest on grace* and be guaranteed to all his offspring—not only to the adherent of the law but also to the one who shares the faith of Abraham, who is the father of us all" (Rom 4:16).[124] Therefore, *sola fide* cannot be set over against *sola gratia* and *solo Christo*; on the contrary, it secures them. In Philippians 3:8, faith is "knowledge *of Christ*." Faith is "*looking to Jesus*, the founder and perfecter of our faith," who was crucified, raised and intercedes for us (Heb 12:2). Similarly, Ephesians 4:13 exhorts us "to come to the unity of *the* faith *and of the knowledge of the Son of God* (καὶ τῆς ἐπιγνώσεως τοῦ Υἱοῦ τοῦ Θεοῦ)."[125] It is inconceivable how knowledge of and faith in the Son of God—*rather than ourselves*—could be considered anthropocentric.

As noted above, pietism introduced a new emphasis on the subjective act of faith—its quality, its various components, psychological stages, and experiences in the soul—that could turn faith into a work after all. Joining Kant's anthropocentric turn, Schleiermacher and other liberal pietists treated faith as a generic and universal attitude or feeling. We see the same tendency in Bultmann in the quotations above and in the attempts to render faith a virtue (love, obedience, allegiance), which of course would turn the focus back on the act rather than the object. However, this is not the Reformation position. John Barclay is right when he judges that "Campbell's claim that the objective genitive leaves faith 'anthropocentric' and Keck's assertion that the objective genitive 'separates Christ from justification, which now depends solely on human believing' both misrepresent what they oppose."[126] Richard Hays says that the objective view tends "to reduce the gospel to an account of individual religious experience, or even to turn faith into a bizarre sort of work, in which Christians jump through the entranceway of salvation by cultivating the right sort of spiritual disposition."[127]

---

124. Emphasis added to Scripture references in this paragraph.
125. Richard H. Bell, "Faith in Christ: Some Exegetical and Theological Reflections on Philippians 3:9 and Ephesians 3:12," in *The Faith of Jesus Christ: Exegetical, Biblical, and Theological Studies*, ed. Michael F. Bird and Preston M. Sprinkle (Milton Keynes: Paternoster, 2009), 121.
126. Barclay, *Paul and the Gift*, 382n88, quoting Douglas A. Campbell, "Romans 1.17—A Crux Interpretum for the *Pistis Christou* Debate?," *JBL* 113 (1994): 265–85, quote at 273, and L. E. Keck, "'Jesus' in Romans," *JBL* 108 (1989): 443–60, quote at 454. Barclay adds, and I can only concur heartily, "For a reminder of the original Lutheran reading, see Jonathan A. Linebaugh, 'The Christo-Centrism of Faith in Christ: Martin Luther's Reading of Galatians 2.16, 19–20,' *NTS* 59 (2013): 535–44."
127. Hays, "What Is at Stake?," 56.

Like Campbell, Hays must have sat through one too many student evangelistic meetings, with which I am familiar. But this type of piety belongs to a different universe than the churches of the Reformation.

In contrast with these anthropocentric conceptions of faith, Luther says that "faith clasps Christ as a ring clasps its jewel"—Christ, not faith, is not the gem itself. All the major Lutheran confessional statements on justification tie the "chief article" to the incarnation, cross, and resurrection of Christ. In fact, nothing could be further from an existentialist gospel than Luther's definition, which basically summarizes Romans 1:4: "The Word is the Gospel of God concerning his Son who was made flesh, suffered, rose from the dead, and was glorified through the Spirit of holiness."[128]

The Reformers were insistent upon the phrase *propter Christum per fidem*: by Christ through faith, not by faith through Christ. In fact, Luther accused Erasmus of being anthropocentric, and one can hardly find a more theocentric and christocentric theologian in the history of the church than Calvin. One key difference between Reformation teaching and pietism is that the former regards Christ not only as the object of faith but as the one who is present personally by his word and Spirit to *create* trust in him. Christ not only reconciled us objectively to God in his death and resurrection; he does so subjectively through his word and Spirit. The preaching of the gospel is not merely an occasion of information and exhortation for an autonomous act of signing a contract with God. On the contrary, it is through this event that Christ delivers himself to sinners in such a way that they find themselves trusting in him (Luke 8:11–21; Mark 4:24; John 1:13; Rom 1:16; 10:17; Gal 3:2, 5; 1 Thess 2:13; 2 Thess 2:13; Heb 4:2, 12–13; 1 Pet 1:23, 25; Jas 1:18). Christ does not descend to save us only to depart and expect us to claim the gift by our striving. "But what does [the righteousness that is by faith] say? 'The word is near you, in your mouth and in your heart' (that is, the word of faith that we proclaim)" (Rom 10:8). The Heidelberg Catechism summarizes this well in question 65:

> **Q.** It is through faith alone that we share in Christ and all his benefits: where then does that faith come from?
> **A.** The Holy Spirit produces it in our hearts by the preaching of the holy gospel, and confirms it by the use of the holy sacraments.

---

128. Luther, "The Freedom of a Christian," in *LW* 31:346.

Commenting on Galatians 2:16, Luther says that faith "takes hold of Christ in such a way that Christ is the object of faith, or rather not the object but, so to speak, the One who is present in the faith itself."

> Therefore faith justifies because it takes hold of and possesses this treasure, the present Christ. . . . Here there is no work of the Law, no love; but there is an entirely different kind of righteousness, a new world above and beyond the Law. . . . For the present let it be enough for us to have shown that Paul is speaking here not only about the Ceremonial Law but about the entire Law.[129]

Similarly, Calvin says that faith is not only justifying because of its object (Christ in the gospel) but because it "involves a relation to the Word of God that enables people to rest and trust in God." Faith comes through means: God's speech through human language. Consequently, he says,

> We are therefore said to be justified by faith, not because faith infuses into us some habit or quality but because we are accepted by God. Faith is only the instrumental cause of our justification. Properly speaking, our righteousness is nothing but God's free acceptance of us, on which our salvation is founded. . . . [Righteousness] is not even a reward for our faith, because faith is only the means by which we receive what God freely gives. We are justified by the grace of God. Christ is our righteousness, the mercy of God is the cause of our righteousness, righteousness has been obtained for us by the death and resurrection of Christ, righteousness is bestowed on us through the gospel, we obtain righteousness by faith.[130]

Faith is so associated with Christ that Paul is happy to use it as shorthand for "redemption by Christ," or "the gospel." The "word of faith" is equivalent to the "word of Christ" in Romans 10:8, for instance. In Galatians 3 he even uses faith and Christ interchangeably: *faith* came (v. 23) and *Christ* came (v. 24).

---

129. Luther, *Lectures on Galatians Chapters 1–4*, in *LW* 26:129–30. Jonathan A. Linebaugh makes a good case for seeing Luther's approach as a "third way" beyond objective and subjective-genitive interpretations. See his "The Christo-Centrism of Faith in Christ: Martin Luther's Reading of Galatians 2.16, 19–20, *New Testament Studies* 59, no. 4 (2013): 535–44.

130. John Calvin, *Commentary on Galatians*, in *Reformation Commentary on Scripture*, New Testament 10, *Galatians, Ephesians*, ed. Gerald Bray (Downers Grove, IL: InterVarsity, 2011), 95.

Along these lines Seifrid draws an intriguing conclusion from Romans 6:17, in which Paul "inverts the expected locution." "Rather than speaking of conversion in terms of 'a pattern of teaching which was handed over' to the Roman Christians, he speaks of their 'being handed over to a pattern of teaching.' The unexpected inversion serves to underscore the change of lordship worked by the gospel in which the human being is made new."

> The act of obedience that is faith is by no means excluded. It is encompassed within the work of the gospel, which creates the human being afresh. Paul's personification of "the righteousness of faith" in Romans 10:6 bears similar significance. . . . Yet Paul alters the expected wording in verse 6 so that it is not he who speaks, but "the righteousness of faith" (or, as in the following context, "word of faith," and the "word of Christ") that speaks in him (Rom 10:8, 17). Another voice, that of God, speaks in and through the Apostle. Here again, faith implies the presence of a new person. Likewise, in Galatians 1:23, Paul indicates that the churches of Judea reported his proclaiming (εὐαγγελίζεται) the faith *which he once persecuted*. He identifies the churches and their faith (Gal. 1:13, 23). . . . Of course, he also speaks of persons *having faith* (Rom. 14:22; 1 Cor. 13:2; Phlm. 5) and of persons *believing* and thus acting. . . . According to the Apostle, Christ in his saving work *communicates himself* to the fallen human being in the gospel by the means of faith.[131]

It is inconceivable that an act of human beings that not only has Christ for its object but Christ as the mediator of the act itself can be anthropocentric.

At the end of the day, I fear, Hays, Martyn, and Campbell are driven by an erroneous conception of divine and human agency that they have inherited from Barth. Assuming a univocal rather than analogical view of the Creator-creature relation, this perspective regards divine and human agency in competitive terms—to the extent that God is the actor in an event, human beings are not, and vice versa. Barth's tendency to see God and human beings in fundamental opposition is apparent in the apocalyptic school's criticisms of even the act of trusting in Christ

---

131. Seifrid, "The Faith of Christ," 132.

as "anthropocentric." However, Paul assumes what we may call an analogical perspective according to which human beings "live and move and have their being" in God (Acts 17:28). Grace does not cancel human activity but works effectually in people, raising to eschatological life those who are spiritually dead, freeing their will, giving them faith, and completing the good work that he has begun (Phil 2:12–13; Eph 2:1–10). Paul cannot even conceive of a πίστις Χριστοῦ that is an autonomous act of "human will or exertion" rather than the gift of "God, who has mercy" (Rom 9:16). For Paul, it is precisely to the degree that God is active in salvation that human beings are active in faith, love, and good works. He is not opposed to *human* acts, whether faith or even works, but rather to the idea that humans can elicit or merit God's favor by their free will and obedience or even believe apart from his effectual grace.

ROMANS 1:17 AND ΠΙΣΤΙΣ ΧΡΙΣΤΟΥ

Although it is not one of the πίστις Χριστοῦ verses, those who defend the subjective genitive also appeal to Romans 1:17, where Paul quotes Habakkuk 2:4: "Now that no man is justified by the law in the sight of God, is evident: for, 'The righteous shall live by faith'" (Rom 1:17; cf. Gal 3:11). Hays and Campbell think that Paul has in mind a messianic interpretation of Habakkuk 2:4, in which Yahweh declares, "Behold, his soul is puffed up; it is not upright within him, but the righteous shall live by his faith." Thus, according to these scholars, the verse (and Romans 1:17) should read, "'The righteous one (i.e., Jesus) by means of his faithfulness (i.e., to the point of death) will live (i.e., be resurrected).' And God's δικαιοσύνη is therefore disclosed by Jesus's faithfulness (so 1:17 and 3:21–22)."[132]

Although I agree with the emphasis on Christ's obedience and vindication before God by his resurrection, I am not convinced that this is what Paul is saying here. Even if Habakkuk 2:4 should be given a messianic reading (which I doubt), it is unlikely that this is the intention in Paul's citation in Romans 1:17, or Galatians 3:11 for that matter.

First, Paul has just said that he is "not ashamed of the gospel because it is the power of God unto/for salvation [εἰς σωτηρίαν] for all who

---

132. Hays, *The Faith of Jesus Christ*, 134–37; Douglas A. Campbell, "The Faithfulness of Jesus Christ in Romans 3:22," 66. Francis Watson reminds us, "According to the Masoretic text, 'the righteous one by *his* faith/faithfulness will live.' According to most Septuagint manuscripts, 'the righteous one by *my* faith/faithfulness will live.' The divergence probably arises from a confusion between Hebrew *waw* and *yod*" (Watson, "By Faith [of Christ]," 154).

believe [παντὶ τῷ πιστεύοντι], the Jew first and also to the Greek" (Rom 1:16). It seems to me that the same thought ("for all who believe") is present in his very next statement. It is true that it is the faithfulness of Jesus Christ that is saving (indeed imputed), but it is just as true that we receive this faithfulness of Jesus Christ through the faith that he gives us to be united to him. It helps to interpret verse 17 in light of verse 32: "God's righteous decree" is that all who practice perversions "deserve to die." Only the righteous deserve to live, but "there is no one righteous, no not one" (3:10). So the only way to be justified—declared righteous—is through faith in Christ (3:21ff.). It makes sense at the headwaters of this argument that Paul would draw on Habakkuk to make the point that life is found not in the law ("do this, and you will live") but through faith in Christ. Regardless of one's judgment on the passages in question, in these verses Paul says that justification comes only to those who believe.

Second, everywhere else in Paul the antithesis of "justified by the law" (v. 17) is "justified by faith"—that is, the faith of believers (and not the faithfulness of Christ). Thus, the most natural reading of Habakkuk is "The righteous by faith will live," in contrast with "The righteous by works will live." This fits well with the fact that the prophet contrasts this faith in God with pride, as Paul does frequently.

This reading becomes even clearer when Paul quotes the Old Testament in a similar context in Galatians 3:11–12. Galatians 3:11 and Romans 1:17 are identical: "Now it is evident that no one is justified before God by the law, for 'The righteous shall live by faith.'" But in Galatians an illuminating (if shocking) statement follows it: "But the law is not of faith, rather 'The one who does them shall live by them'" (Gal 3:12, quoting Lev 18:5). There should now be no question that in quoting Habakkuk Paul means "The righteous will live—that is, receive life—on the principle of faith rather than on the principle of works." This is Paul's typical contrast between law and gospel, the principle of inheritance: "do this, and you will live" versus "I will give you a new heart, justify, sanctify, and glorify you."

The law-covenant (Lev 18:5) formula appears also in the indictment in Ezekiel 20: "I gave them my statutes and made known to them my rules, by which, if a person does them, he shall live" (Ezek 20:11, 13). Paul is contrasting the two instrumental causes: "The one who does these things will live by them"—that is, have life from doing them—is juxtaposed with having life from faith, which is shorthand for "from Christ through faith." When it comes to the right of inheriting ever-lasting life, "law is not of faith." In justification, the two principles are totally opposed.

Third, as Watson observes, the meaning of Romans 1:17 ("from faith") should be consistent with Romans 10:6 ("the righteousness that comes from faith"), where it is clear that *believers* (not Christ) are the subjects of this believing. "The reference to Christ is absolutely fundamental in *both* cases, and it is disingenuous to play off a (virtuous) 'christocentric' reading against a (bad, protestant) 'anthropocentric' one. It is simply a matter of exegesis."[133] It is not exegesis but "claims of theological superiority" that subjectivists use to exhort readers to adopt their position. According to Watson,

> There is no reason to suppose that a focus on "our" faith rather than Christ's will inevitably issue in theological disaster. This is a faith that has its origin and content in God's reconciling work in the incarnate, crucified, and risen Jesus—an act whose scope is extended to us through the agency of the Holy Spirit in the proclaimed word and the communal and individual acknowledgement it evokes. Pauline faith is not self-generated or self-sufficient; it is not a "condition" of salvation; it is not a mere mental disposition; it is not a sanctuary for the solitary individual. It has to do with the human participation intended in the divine reconciling act, which does not reduce its objects to passivity but reconstitutes them as agents and subjects within the overarching, all-embracing sphere of grace.[134]

Furthermore, "The possibility of a subtle semantic distinction between ἐκ and διὰ is already excluded in 2:16, where the two forms are used interchangeably."[135] Basically, the longer forms are inextricable from the shorter ones.

> While Paul's usage is flexible, so that each occurrence will possess its own contextual nuance, it is unlikely that "by faith of Christ" will mean something quite different from "by hearing of faith" or simply

---

133. Watson, "By Faith (of Christ)," 159.
134. Watson, "By Faith (of Christ)," 163.
135. Watson, "By Faith (of Christ)," 152.

"by faith." The longer formulations *elaborate* the shorter one, but the shared structure means that they are unlikely to *deviate* from it. If "faith" is in the first instance "the faith of Christ" (that is, Christ's own faith or faithfulness), then this will be the case throughout.[136]

Fourth, while the meaning of "from faith to faith [ἐκ πίστεως εἰς πίστιν]" (Rom 1:17) is secondary to the decisions thus far, the most likely meaning is "of faith from beginning to end," in terms of both the *historia salutis* and the *ordo salutis*. With respect to the former, people have always been justified through faith: all who trust in Christ are Abraham's children, Paul argues in Romans and Galatians. This translation fits well with Paul's broader concern with God's faithfulness in light of the widespread apostasy from the Abrahamic covenant. "Has God's word failed?" No, it has always been from faith in the promise, rooted in God's electing grace (Rom 9–11). Indeed, even now "there is a remnant chosen by grace" (Rom 11:5). With respect to the latter, the gospel is "the power of God unto salvation for everyone who believes," not only in the beginning but to the day of judgment. There is no getting in by grace and staying in by obedience (Gal 3:3). It is by grace through faith from first to last (Eph 2:8–10).

Campbell makes a strong argument that a conventional reading of Romans 1:17 cannot explain how *faith* reveals God's righteousness.

> "Faith" simply does not function as the means by which something moves from a position of invisibility to one of visibility, from the unknown to the known, and to affirm that it does is to make a basic semantic error—to assert something meaningless or ungrammatical. "Faith" tends to affirm something already known as true, which is of course the way that it functions in justification, in response to Christian preaching and the gospel. *The gospel,* when preached, makes God's saving act in Christ known or "visible." And "faith" then *responds to* that prior disclosure as an act of affirmation, *and not the act of disclosure itself.*[137]

But my interpretation does not fall afoul of this critique. Paul says that the *gospel* reveals God's righteousness, which leads to justification for all who

---

136. Watson, "By Faith (of Christ)," 153–54.
137. Campbell, "The Faithfulness of Jesus Christ in Romans 3:22," 67–68.

believe, just as God's righteous wrath is being revealed in his law (v. 18). Faith is not the instrumental cause of the revelation; rather, the gospel that reveals justification is announced in the old covenant (from faith) as well as the new (to faith), as Paul argues specifically in relation to Abraham.

According to Campbell, Paul does not say in Romans 3:22 that faith is the means of appropriating justification, but that it is "the 'means by which' God's righteousness is disclosed, which is a rather different thing."[138] Thus, the apostle must mean not (our) faith but (Christ's) faithfulness. It is true that our faith does not reveal God's righteousness. But Paul does not say that our faith *or* Christ's faithfulness reveals God's righteousness. He says that "the righteousness of God through faith in Jesus Christ for all who believe" (v. 22)—*the gospel* of justification apart from the law (v. 21)—reveals God's *gift of righteousness.*

Watson is convinced that "Paul's 'by faith of Christ' formulations all derive from Habakkuk 2:4." It is a strong argument:

> Paul never speaks of "*the* faith of Christ," as he speaks of "the faith of our father Abraham" (Rom 4:12). If we are to understand Paul's language, we must not neglect his prepositions. Since διὰ [τῆς] πίστεως is simply a variant of ἐκ πίστεως, and since the latter phrase is clearly and explicitly derived from Habakkuk 2:4, the argument will further support the claim that Paul speaks of "justification by faith" in the context of his interpretation of Scripture, and not as a free-standing "doctrine" developed by himself or revealed on the Damascus Road.[139]

Watson says, "My argument is indebted to Douglas Campbell's observation that Paul uses the phrase ἐκ πίστεως only in the two letters where he cites Hab. 2:4."[140] However, Campbell "draws the opposite conclusion to mine from this observation because he does not see that Paul draws from Habakkuk not only ἐκ πίστεως but also δίκαιος ἐκ πίστεως."[141] Consequently, Watson judges, the subjective view is "*demonstrably* mistaken."[142]

---

138. Campbell, "The Faithfulness of Jesus Christ in Romans 3:22," 68.

139. Watson, "By Faith (of Christ)," 148–49.

140. Watson, "By Faith (of Christ)," 149n6, referring to Campbell, "Romans 1:17—*Crux Interpretum*," 268.

141. Watson, "By Faith (of Christ)," 149n6

142. Watson, "By Faith (of Christ)," 150n8. Cf. See Joseph A. Fitzmyer, "Paul's Jewish Background and the Deeds of the Law," in *According to Paul: Studies in the Theology of the Apostle* (New York: Paulist, 1993), 19–35.

In contrast with "faith *in* Christ," it does not make sense to juxtapose "faith *of* Christ" and "works of the Law," says Watson. What Paul is setting in antithesis is *doing* (works) and *believing* (in Christ). In both cases, the subject is man (doer/believer) and the object is God's word (Law/promise). "The children of Abraham are twice described as οἱ ἐκ πίστεως ([Gal] 3:7, 9). . . . The Law however is not ἐκ πίστεως (3:24)."[143] Thomas Schreiner similarly observes, "In Rom 10:3, 'their own righteousness' is explained as 'the righteousness of the law,' and 'the righteousness of God' is explained as 'that which is of the law,' and 'the righteousness from God' is explained as 'that which is by faith.' Therefore, 'the righteousness of God' (*theou*) in Rom 10:3 is equivalent to 'the righteousness from God' (*ek thou*) in Phil 3:9."[144]

We should recall that the larger question is whether God's word (promise) has failed. It has not because "[the gospel] is the power of God for salvation to everyone who believes, to the Jew first and also to the Greek" (Rom 1:16). In short, as Seifrid expresses it, "God's gift and work of justification in Jesus Christ creates its own reception within the fallen human being."[145] For Paul, the gospel "*imparts life*, as a speech-act that takes place in the proclamation of the gospel."[146]

> By implication, it is the faithfulness of Yahweh that is at stake in Habakkuk 2:4. . . . Just as the prophet formerly was commissioned to write the vision and make it plain for a messenger to read, run, and announce it, so the Apostle now announces the word of Christ that he has received. The faith of the Apostle as well as that of the prophet before him is created and sustained by the concrete promises of salvation given to them. Both of them live and speak out of the message they received. Faith has its source in the faithfulness of the God who promises and fulfils. In citing Habakkuk 2:4, Paul recalls this setting and draws out its theological significance. The context of the citation thus explains why the prior double phrase ἐκ πίστεως εἰς πίστιν in verse 17a is folded into a single phrase ἐκ πίστεως in verse 17b. There is no distinction between the Lord's messengers and

---

143. Watson, "By Faith (of Christ)," 151.
144. Thomas Schreiner, *New Testament Theology: Magnifying God in Christ* (Grand Rapids: Baker Academic, 2009), 335. Schreiner's argument has three steps (335–36) and a great summary on p. 336.
145. Seifrid, "The Faith of Christ," 143.
146. Seifrid, "The Faith of Christ," 139.

those who receive their message. Prophet and Apostle themselves are called to faith in the promise they are commissioned to bear.[147]

Seifrid rightly observes, "There is a significant connection between Rom. 1:16–17 and 10:14–17."[148] The gospel is a "report" and "message" that is "heard" from "the word of faith" and "then announced to others." A promise is meant to be *believed*. Indeed, it is through the gospel itself that the Spirit creates this faith. The law was in the heart and mouth in the old covenant, but now it is the gospel. To miss this is to go astray in the interpretation of Romans entirely.

NON-PAULINE EVIDENCE

In the synoptics, "faith *in* God/Christ" is consistent and recurring (Matt 8:10; 9:2, 22, 29; 15:28; 17:20; 21:21; 23:23; Mark 2:5; 4:40; 5:34; 10:52; 11:22; Luke 5:20; 7:9, 50; 8:25, 48; 17:5, 6, 19; 18:8, 42; 22:32). From the beginning of Mark, the command is to "repent and believe the gospel" (Mark 1:15). In fact, reference is made to "*their* faith" (πίστιν αὐτῶν; see Matt 9:2; Mark 2:5; Luke 5:20) and "*your* faith" (for πίστις σου; see Matt 9:22; 15:28; Mark 5:34; 10:52; Luke 7:50; 8:48; 17:19; 18:42; 22:32; and πίστιν ὑμῶν; see Matt 9:29; Luke 8:25). Further, Jesus was "saying to them, 'Have faith in God'" (Ἔχετε πίστιν θεοῦ; Mark 11:22). On one occasion the disciples asked Jesus, "Increase our faith!" (Πρόσθες ἡμῖν πίστιν; Luke 17:5). In many of these passages, as also in Acts 3:16, it is "through faith in [Christ's] name" (ἐπὶ τῇ πίστει τοῦ ὀνόματος) that people receive healings of various sorts. Jesus told Jairus, "Do not be afraid, only believe" (Mark 5:36), implying that through his faith his daughter would be healed. For "all things are possible to the one who believes" (9:23).

According to the author's testimony, the fourth gospel is "written so that you may believe that Jesus is the Christ, the Son of God, and that by believing you may have life in his name" (John 20:31). We should not be surprised, then, at the Gospel of John's emphasis on believing in Christ. The gospel's most famous verse relates that God "gave his only Son, that whoever believes in him should not perish but have eternal life" (3:16). Faith here is the condition or means through which one enters into the benefits of Christ's life, passion, and resurrection. "Whoever

---

147. Seifrid, "The Faith of Christ," 140.
148. Seifrid, "The Faith of Christ," 140n39.

believes in him is not condemned, but whoever does not believe is condemned already, because he has not believed in the name of the only Son of God" (3:18). Willis H. Sailer notes, "John will certainly refer to the importance of belief through his use of the verb and associated forms, but Jesus is almost always the object of these forms and never their subject (cf. 2:24)."[149]

Despite a lack of explicit references, it is clear implicitly from a host of passages that Jesus had faith in his Father, even to the point where he accedes to the Father's will in the crucifixion (Luke 22:42) and commits his soul to the Father (Luke 23:46). Jesus is not only the God in whom all are to look for salvation but the human servant who looks to his Father for everything that he needs and heeds his words above all else (Matt 4:4). Although Hebrews does not include Jesus on the "hall of faith" list in chapter 11, it does place an Old Testament reference on the lips of Jesus: "And again, 'I will put my trust in him'" (Heb 2:13). If works are only considered good by proceeding from faith (Rom 14:23), then Jesus must have had faith in God. Indeed, it is through his act of faith that he represents his new human family and persevered in his vicarious obedience for us. There is therefore no theological objection to *including* Jesus among those who trusted in God; there is, however, an objection to *excluding* everyone else.

Michael Bird helpfully brings to our attention other instances of grammatical ambiguity with respect to faith in/of Christ besides the several Pauline instances:

> (1) In Acts 3:16 we find reference to "the faith that is through him [i.e., Jesus] (ἡ πίστις ἡ δι' αὐτοῦ) has given him this complete health"; (2) Revelation 14:12 states: "Here is a call for the endurance of the saints, those keeping the commandments of God and holding fast to the faith of Jesus (τὴν πίστιν Ἰησοῦ)"; (3) James 2:1 says: "My brothers, do you with your acts of favoritism really have the faith of our glorious Lord Jesus Christ? (τὴν πίστιν τοῦ Κυρίου ἡμῶν Ἰησοῦ Χριστοῦ τῆς δόξης)."[150]

---

149. Willis H. Salier, "The Obedient Son: The 'Faithfulness' of Christ in the Fourth Gospel," in *The Faith of Jesus Christ: Exegetical, Biblical, and Theological Studies*, ed. Michael F. Bird and Preston M. Sprinkle (Milton Keynes: Paternoster, 2009), 223.

150. Michael F. Bird, "Introduction: Problems and Prospects for a New Testament Debate," in *The Faith of Jesus Christ: Exegetical, Biblical, and Theological Studies*, ed. Michael F. Bird and Preston M. Sprinkle (Milton Keynes: Paternoster, 2009), 3.

However, all three examples favor the objective (and/or source) construction. First, if Acts 3:16 is ambiguous, then it is clear enough in other passages I have cited above that *in every case* healing is attributed instrumentally (a) to *faith*, not to faithfulness (which in any case is impossible to attribute to people who are healed immediately without any prior acts of obedience) and (b) to the faith of the one being healed, never to the faith/faithfulness of God/Christ.

Second, with respect to Revelation 14:12, it may be said that believers do hold fast to Jesus's faithfulness, but even if the object is "Jesus's faithfulness," the saints are the ones who are *holding fast* to it, so his faithfulness cannot be a substitute for their faith. Revelation 14:12 is another instance, I suggest, of a genitive of source that is supported by the definite article: *the faith* (i.e., *fides quae creditur*). James 2:1 seems best translated as it appears above: as a genitive of source but as the act of faith in Christ—that is, the genuine faith that only Jesus gives. Yet it difficult to imagine that James is saying that their favoritism betrays a lack of *Jesus's* faithfulness.

CONCLUSION

The πίστις Χριστοῦ debate turns out to be a tempest in a teapot. Even if all of the four or five verses in question intend a subjective genitive, we are still left with a massive number of verses (including clauses within some of those disputed verses!) that teach what, according to Hays, "verges on blasphemous self-absorption in our own religious subjectivity."[151] In contrast, the traditional Protestant interpretation warmly embraces every passage, affirming both Christ's faithfulness as the basis and the believer's act of faith as the instrument of receiving the former. Jesus's faithfulness even unto death on a cross is precisely why he is the *object* of faith. The act of faith is directed outside of ourselves, to Christ Jesus as the one who has saved us by his faithfulness.

As with other false choices that we have encountered, I suggest that the subjective view is to be faulted not in what it affirms but in what it rejects. Reformed theologian Michael Allen explores in detail the many passages in Scripture that highlight the saving import of Christ's faithfulness, and he does so without embracing the subjective-genitive

---

151. Hays, "What Is at Stake?," 46.

interpretation of the passages we considered.[152] As James Dunn points out, "The Pauline emphasis on the gracious self-sacrifice of the cross is more clearly and more powerfully drawn in passages like Romans 5:6–11, 2 Corinthians 5:16–21 and Philippians 2:6–11, where again I find myself wondering why Paul did not include reference to Christ's faithfulness in such passages if it was indeed such an important motif in Paul."[153] In fact, Dunn adds,

> And the Reformation re-emphasis that God's grace comes to its most effective effect through faith alone, through trustful dependence on God alone (Rom. 4), quite apart from and without any added condition of "works of the law" (Gal. 2:16; 3:2, 5), needs to be clearly reaffirmed in a day when different church traditions increasingly take the place of the "works of the Law" against which Paul warned so fiercely.[154]

In most cases, the subjective-genitive interpretation goes hand-in-hand with a rejection of the traditional Protestant view of justification. The debate is really, as R. Barry Matlock suggests, "a proxy war" for "a corporate, participationist reading" versus "an individual, forensic one . . . and this, more than anything, accounts for its persistence."[155] Adding to the calls to arms noted above, Sigve Tonstad commends the subjective view for cutting "a wide swath in the theological landscape and rearranges the perspective around a new center." It is a view that "on the surface may seem like a minor revision" but "lays the groundwork for an entirely different paradigm in the theology of the NT."[156] Similarly, Mark Reasoner explains that it will change "how we present the gospel," moving us away from a focus on conversion and justification.[157] In addition to replacing justification with participation in Christ, Reasoner adds, "Proponents of the subjective genitive, who hold that Christ's faith is what saves, will not call for a distinct,

---

152. Michael Allen, *The Christ's Faith* (Edinburgh: T&T Clark, 2009).
153. James D. G. Dunn, foreword to *The Faith of Jesus Christ: Exegetical, Biblical, and Theological Studies*, ed. Michael F. Bird and Preston M. Sprinkle (Milton Keynes: Paternoster, 2009), xviii.
154. Dunn, foreword to *The Faith of Jesus Christ*, xviii.
155. Matlock, "Saving Faith," 74.
156. Sigve Tonstad, "Πίστις Χριστοῦ: Reading Paul in a New Paradigm," *Andrews University Seminary Studies* 40, no. 1 (Spring 2002): 56–57, quoted in Bird, "Introduction," 2.
157. Mark Reasoner, *Romans in Full Circle: A History of Interpretation* (Louisville: Westminster John Knox, 2005), 39–40, quoted in Bird, "Introduction," 3.

conversion-constituting act of *placing one's faith in Jesus*. They will rather call people *to join the church that lives out in a concentric pattern the faith that Jesus displayed*."[158] Thus, ironically, justification through faith in Christ is judged anthropocentric while the works of believers take its place. This only underscores the worry expressed by Mark Seifrid that the subjective interpretation ends up marginalizing the life, death, and resurrection of Christ (which is ironic, given Campbell's caricature of the Reformation position on this point) and giving prominence instead to the believer's imitation of Christ's faithfulness.

In contrast, Seifrid notes, "The recognition that in the expression 'faith of Christ' Paul speaks of Christ as the source and author of faith brings to light a fundamental theological dimension of his theology."

> For the Apostle, to believe in Jesus Christ is not first to act, but rather to be acted upon by God in his work in Jesus Christ. It is to know that our faith is the work of another. Here lies the connection between doctrine and doing that the "subjectivists" have sought but failed to find. Here our "doing" is not our own doing, but the doing and work of another, given to us in the apostolic proclamation of the gospel.[159]

The point at which the paths diverge sharply is over the distinctive doctrines introduced by Karl Barth, most centrally the election (and justification) of all people in Christ. Arguably, apart from the novel doctrines of election and justification developed by Barth, the πίστις Χριστοῦ controversy would never have emerged. However, as we have noted, Barth (as well as Campbell) ultimately back away from absolute universalism. At the end of the day, Barth and his followers also are inconsistent in their conclusions about the role of faith. On the one hand, in defense of the subjective view, Chris Tilling notes, "The key issue for Campbell is that faith *not* be understood . . . as the *condition* for salvation."[160] On the other hand, he says that faith is "necessary if final life or salvation is to be reached."[161] This is Barth's view too,

---

158. Reasoner, *Romans in Full Circle*, 39–40, emphasis added.

159. Seifrid, "The Faith of Christ," 146.

160. Chris Tilling, "Campbell's Faith: Advancing the *Pistis Christou* Debate," in *Beyond Old and New Perspectives on Paul; Reflections on the Work of Douglas Campbell*, ed. Chris Tilling (Eugene: Cascade, 2014), 237.

161. Douglas A. Campbell, *The Deliverance of God: An Apocalyptic Rereading of Justification in Paul* (Grand Rapids: Eerdmans, 2013), 68.

as McCormack notes above. But surely both propositions cannot be right. If one cannot reach final salvation without it, then it must be a condition. Then, if faith means faithfulness, we return to the traditional Roman Catholic teaching that final justification is conditioned upon one's lifelong obedience. How can this be construed as more christocentric, unconditionally gracious, "no strings attached," and objective than the Reformation position?

CHAPTER 11

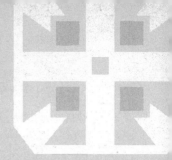

UNION WITH CHRIST

Justification and the Great Exchange

I close this second volume as I began the first, with the "great exchange." As I argued, the great exchange between Christ and sinners—debts for wealth, death for immortality, unrighteousness for righteousness, condemnation for justification, slavery for freedom—is the core of biblical soteriology. We often find justification nestled in the great exchange in patristic treatments. Justification is neither the sum nor a footnote of the great exchange but occupies a prominent place within it. Like propitiation in the doctrine of the atonement, justification is not the whole story, but apart from it there is no happy ending. Indeed, all the other gifts that we have in union with Christ—adoption, sanctification, glorification—are secured by justification.

I also argued at the outset that the great exchange—or union with Christ—is the most ecumenically significant starting point, where the greatest consensus is to be found in the past as well as in the present, among Orthodox, Roman Catholic, and Protestant theologies. At the same time, I demonstrated in the opening chapters of volume 1 that this motif achieves its clearest and most consistent articulation in forensic justification. Consequently, far from being an alternative paradigm to justification, union with Christ or the great exchange is the proper habitat for justification. In this concluding chapter I locate justification within the broader framework of union with Christ.

UNION *VERSUS* JUSTIFICATION?

Having already challenged the false choice between union with Christ and imputation, I will only briefly touch on the dichotomy between union and justification. For many, union with Christ has become the new *Christus Victor*: the way of avoiding Pelagian moralism on the one hand and "justification" on the other, simply by avoiding *legal* categories in favor of *ontological-eschatological* ones.[1] It also displays the enduring effects of Albert Schweitzer's remarkable study of Paul.[2] E. P. Sanders saw Paul's real difference with Judaism lying in his "participationist" soteriology (being in Christ) rather than in a putative difference over justification or faith and works per se. Interest in this theme is shared by classic Reformation theology, the new perspective, and the apocalyptic school.

Long before the new perspective, Reformed biblical theologians were interested in displaying the broader cosmic and eschatological canvas. Without discounting the *ordo salutis*, they nevertheless recognized that the *historia salutis* is that broader canvas. Anyone sympathetic to the seventeenth-century federal theologians and, more recently, Geerhardus Vos and Herman Ridderbos, will agree with the view that N. T. Wright attributes to the new perspective:

> What the new perspective has said . . . is that the triple reality of conversion, salvation, and "the gospel" is conveyed by Paul not primarily through the language of justification, though that is indeed closely aligned with this reality, but through the language about Jesus Christ; more exactly, about Jesus as the crucified and risen Messiah, and about what is true of humans who come to be "in him."[3]

---

1. See, e.g., Don Garlington, "Imputation or Union with Christ? A Response to John Piper," *Reformation and Revival Journal* 12 (2003): 45–113; cf. John Piper, *Counted Righteous in Christ: Should We Abandon the Imputation of Christ's Righteousness?* (Wheaton, IL: Crossway, 2002); Michael F. Bird, "Incorporated Righteousness: A Response to Recent Evangelical Discussion Concerning the Imputation of Christ's Righteousness in Justification," *Journal of the Evangelical Theological Society* 47 (2004): 253–75.

2. Where the history of religions school sought to interpret the New Testament in comparison with Hellenism (especially Mediterranean mystery religions), Schweitzer pointed to Jewish apocalyptic as the more likely source. See Albert Schweitzer, *The Mysticism of the Apostle Paul*, trans. W. Montgomery (Baltimore: Johns Hopkins University Press, 1998), 26–40.

3. N. T. Wright, *Paul and His Recent Interpreters: Some Contemporary Debates* (Minneapolis: Fortress, 2015), 118.

Elsewhere he adds, "The irony is that at this point Sanders and others, including the present writer, are standing firmly in line (via Albert Schweitzer) with Calvin himself, though it is from would-be Calvinists that some of the sharpest criticism has come."[4] However, one will not find in Calvin an ally for any false choice between union with Christ and forensic justification.

The choice that is pressed between union and justification involves a category mistake. Union with Christ is not actually an element of the *ordo salutis* but the umbrella-term (equivalent to the "great exchange") for the *ordo* as a whole. It makes as little sense to treat union as an alternative to justification as it does to see it as an alternative to election, redemption, effectual calling, sanctification, or glorification. This is the weakness of all "central dogma" approaches, as they deduce an entire system from a single idea. Regardless of one's interpretation of its meaning, anyone who thinks that the doctrine of justification is a "subsidiary crater" in Paul's thinking must push deliberately to the background what the apostle clearly places in the foreground, at least in Romans and Galatians.

Matthew W. Bates represents a growing number of evangelical theologians and biblical scholars when he says that union with Christ makes debates over imputed and infused beside the point.[5] Thus in the Roman Catholic view (defended here by Bates, *mutatis mutandis*) emphasizing union with Christ *over against* justification ensures that "infused righteousness does front union" and therefore any divine verdict.[6] Bates judges that the Council of Trent "helpfully" and "straightforwardly affirms that Scripture does not make a clean conceptual division between initial righteousness (traditionally 'justification' proper for Protestants) and subsequently enjoyed righteousness (traditionally part of 'sanctification' for Protestants)."[7] Justification must be legal and transformative. Trent is also correct to insist that "the final judgment will be (at least in part) on the basis of works."[8]

Ironically, while some Protestants are attracted to Trent, the great Jesuit New Testament scholar Joseph Fitzmyer defends the view articulated by

---

4. Wright, *Paul and His Recent Interpreters*, 119.
5. Matthew W. Bates, *Salvation by Allegiance Alone* (Grand Rapids: Baker Academic, 2017), 166. He adds, "Although subsequently in the *Institutes* John Calvin is perhaps not as clear on the precise relationship between justification and union as one might wish, he nevertheless does clearly affirm the primacy of union in salvation" (167).
6. Bates, *Salvation by Allegiance Alone*, 189.
7. Bates, *Salvation by Allegiance Alone*, 185.
8. Bates, *Salvation by Allegiance Alone*, 186.

the Reformers. Justification is strictly forensic in Scripture, he argues, but "salvation" is broader than justification. "When Paul looked back at the Christ-event, he saw it as a complex unit, something like a ten-sided solid figure. When he gazed at a panel of it from one direction, he said that Christ 'justified' us; when he gazed at it from another, he said that Christ 'saved' us; or from another, Christ 'transformed' us, and so on."[9] And union with Christ, I suggest, is the wider rubric of "salvation" in its application. Along the same lines Richard Gaffin observes,

> Paul's notion of Christ as a corporate person does *not* eliminate the necessity of reflecting on the place of an *ordo salutis* in Paul, on how he relates the benefits possessed (existentially and individually) by believers to the past historical accomplishment of Christ. In the language of classical theology, so far as the property of the believer in Christ is concerned, justice must be done both to the *alienum* and the *proprium*, and neither aspect may be stressed to the exclusion of the others.[10]

UNION *AND* JUSTIFICATION

The triune God is not a being among beings but *is* life and "has life in himself" (John 5:26). He grants creatures participation in his life—never univocally, as if we possessed a portion of deity, but analogically, as those spoken into and sustained in existence by his powerful word—from the Father, in the Son, and by the Spirit. Furthermore, the God who grants us analogical participation in his life is the Trinity; hence, each person is participated in distinctly. For example, we participate in the Father as the source of our adoption, in the Son as the mediator and elder brother who makes us coheirs of his estate, and in the Holy Spirit as the one who unites us to Christ and thereby justifies, sanctifies, and glorifies us. The Spirit by whom the Son assumed our humanity also sustained the incarnate Word in his trial as the Last Adam and raised him from the dead as the beginning of the new creation. And now the same Spirit grants us faith to be united to Christ, the now-exalted God-human.

---

9. Joseph A. Fitzmyer, *According to Paul: Studies in the Theology of the Apostle* (New York: Paulist, 1993), 11.

10. Richard B. Gaffin Jr., *Resurrection and Redemption: A Study in Paul's Soteriology* (Phillipsburg, NJ: P&R, 1987), 58.

Union is not a goal but the source of our life. Chosen in him, redeemed by him, and crucified, buried, and raised with him, we share in Christ's pioneering journey in an "already" and "not-yet" manner. Justification is the fundamental turning-point in the sinner's status before God, while sanctification is the turning-point in the sinner's condition, and glorification will be the turning-point in the whole existence of the saints. Although we will be all that he is in his glorified humanity, we are not yet raised bodily. Yet we have been raised from spiritual death, justified and definitively renewed. We are being conformed to the image of Christ daily, suffering in the joy of the prize that has already been won for us. "There is therefore now no condemnation for those who are in Christ Jesus" (Rom 8:1). Although we still struggle mightily against Satan, sin, and the realities of a fallen world, Christ has already subdued Satan. "The God of peace will soon crush Satan under your feet" (Rom 16:20).

Union with Christ (or the "great exchange") is the broader intersection where rival perspectives demand a fork in the road—the false choices that we have met frequently along the way—but where, in a more integrated account, they meet without any contradiction. Covenantal and apocalyptic, personal and corporate, soteriology and ecclesiology, the *historia salutis* and the *ordo salutis*, forensic justification and transforming renewal, faith and works all find unity without conflating one with the other.

Paul, John, and Union

If it is an exaggeration, it is only slight when Richard Longenecker says that there is really nothing surprising in Paul after reading John's Gospel.[11] Jesus is the Bread of Life (John 6:48–58), and followers must eat his flesh and drink his blood to abide in him. Jesus teaches, "In that day you shall know that I am in my Father and you in me and I in you" (John 14:20), which is followed by the analogy of vine and branches in 15:1–11. His followers are simultaneously "in the world" and "in me." He says "In me you may have peace. In the world you have tribulation" (John 16:33). Finally, in his prayer in chapter 17, Jesus speaks of his intimate bond with his own: "that they also may be one in us" (v. 21)

---

11. Richard N. Longenecker, *Paul, Apostle of Liberty*, 2nd ed. (Grand Rapids: Eerdmans, 2015), 149–50.

and "I in them" (vv. 23, 26). Throughout this farewell discourse, Jesus refers to the Spirit as the one who accomplishes this union.

In the Synoptic Gospels as well, Jesus presents himself as the true temple. Separating Israel from the world, Torah binds God's bride to Yahweh. But Jesus is the eternal Word even above Torah who binds believers to himself. He is the place of union between Lord and servant in his incarnation and, for us, in the communion of saints. The stock of images is drawn from ancient Near Eastern *politics*, not Greco-Roman mystery religion. This is a significant point especially in light of the way the history of religions school attributed the Pauline motif of mystical union to a supposed Hellenizing process. Ridderbos explains this perspective as it centered around F. C. Baur:

> While Reformation theology viewed justification by faith as the center of Paul's doctrine and associated sanctification, the struggle between flesh and Spirit, and the like very closely with it, in this period [after Bauer] scholars proceeded to distinguish beside the judicial-forensic "line," which they explained from Judaism, an ethical (or mystical-ethical) "line," which was said to find its expression in the contrast of flesh and spirit and to be oriented, not to Judaism, but to Greek-Hellenistic thinking. . . . This communion is thought of as an ethically-oriented mysticism, not as an objective inclusion of believers in Christ, but as a spiritual and mystical connection, out of which then, understood in a general religious sense, a life of love and spiritual freedom would flourish.[12]

However, the theory was speculative and failed to comprehend the roots of Paul's concept of union in the Old Testament, especially the Prophets, as well as its radical differences from Greek mystery religion. Schweitzer was among the first to challenge the history of religions interpretation on this score. For Paul, he perceived, union with Christ is not Greek-symbolic, but realistic. "This union with Christ, sharing in his new corporeality, comes about by baptism. Together with Christ the elect form a 'joint personality of which the *pneuma* is the vital force."[13]

---

12. Herman Ridderbos, *Paul: An Outline of His Theology*, trans. John R. de Witt (Grand Rapids: Eerdmans, 1975), 18.

13. Albert Schweitzer, *The Mysticism of Paul the Apostle* (Baltimore: Johns Hopkins University Press, 1998), 117–18, 227–30; cf. Ridderbos, *Paul*, 18.

Longenecker observes that in the mystery religions and in Philo, *mysterion* is a secret. "With Paul, however, the term takes the Palestinian sense of Amos 3:7, Psalm 25:14, Proverbs 3:32, and Sirach 3:20; i.e., of a hitherto unknown aspect of God or His dealing which has now become known, either to all or to those who will accept such revelation."[14] Paul's thinking is far from the dualism of Greek religion and philosophy. In fact, it is far removed even from the Hellenistic Judaism of Philo. Paul's comparison of the two Adams in 1 Corinthians 15 is the reverse of Philo's, in which the *first 'adam* was the "man from heaven" (an ideal form) and the *second 'adam* was the "man of dust."[15] For Paul, the first and last Adam have an eschatological meaning: Adam, the living being by whom death entered the world, and Christ, the life-giving Lord. There really is no comparison between Paul and Philo.[16] Whereas the goal of Paul's argument is the resurrection, "Philo has no objection to the body of Moses being 'stripped off him like a shell that has grown about the soul' and his soul as stripped naked set free to ascend to heaven."[17] Qumran was more purification of the body, not getting rid of it.[18] For Philo, the body is defiling, for Qumran, defiled, for Paul, captive along with the soul to sin.[19] Paul does not view salvation as absorption into the divine, and it is not individualistic.[20] This last point was emphasized by W. D. Davies: "There is a social aspect to the Pauline concept of the being 'in Christ'; union with Christ however personal had meant incorporation into a community that could be described as one body. As far as we know, however, the mysteries were individualistic."[21] In mystery religions, the goal was freedom from fate, but in Paul it is freedom from sin.[22]

Longenecker concludes, "The Mystery interpretation of Paul's use of 'in Christ' seems to have lost its case."[23] Paul's thought is also far from Adolf Deißmann's notion of the resurrected Christ as a "semiphysical and ethereal reality . . . permeating the Christian and the Christian living in

---

14. Longenecker, *Paul, Apostle of Liberty*, 41.
15. Longenecker, *Paul, Apostle of Liberty*, 43.
16. Longenecker, *Paul, Apostle of Liberty*, 44–45.
17. Longenecker, *Paul, Apostle of Liberty*, 48.
18. Longenecker, *Paul, Apostle of Liberty*, 48.
19. Longenecker, *Paul, Apostle of Liberty*, 49.
20. Longenecker, *Paul, Apostle of Liberty*, 148.
21. W. D. Davies, *Paul and Rabbinic Judaism: Some Rabbinic Elements in Pauline Theology* (London: SPCK, 1970), 90.
22. Longenecker, *Paul, Apostle of Liberty*, 148.
23. Longenecker, *Paul, Apostle of Liberty*, 149.

Christ."[24] Here Christ's humanity not only vanishes into thin air, but this docetic Christ becomes indistinguishable from the Holy Spirit, much as in Origen's conception.[25]

Others more recently have recovered Deißmann's emphasis, Longencker observes, but interpret it as "not primarily denoting individual and personal communion with Christ but as being a locution for corporate communion in the Church."

> Of course, the Roman Church has always taken this position, asserting that to be in the living Christ was to be in "the Church with its centre in Rome." But in the reaction to philosophic individualism and the rediscovery of the thought of corporate personality in the Scriptures, many non-Romanists have also viewed the phrase as speaking primarily of corporate life in the Body of Christ—i.e., the organic Church. Albert Schweitzer argued that "'being-in-Christ' is the prime enigma of Pauline teaching" if we view it as "an individual and subjective experience" rather than "a collective and objective event."[26]

"Similarly, Rudolf Bultmann states that '"in Christ," far from being a formula for mystic union, is primarily an ecclesiological formula'; and thus 'to belong to the Christian Church is to be "in Christ" or "in the Lord."'"[27] J. A. T. Robinson and L. S. Thornton, among others, promoted this idea in Britain "as a corollary to the insistence that 'the Church is literally now the resurrection "body" of Christ' was dominant in the thought of Paul."[28]

But after reviewing the many "in Christ" passages in Paul, Longenecker concludes,

> Thus, while not assenting to all of Deissmann's positions, nor insisting that there be a unitary exegesis of the phrase, it seems one must

---

24. Longenecker, *Paul, Apostle of Liberty*, 150, quoting A. Deißmann, *Di neutestamentliche Formel "in Christo Jesu"* (Marburg: Elwert, 1892).

25. Origen, *Spirit and Fire*, ed. Hans Urs von Balthasar, trans. Robert J. Daly, SJ (Washington, DC: Catholic University of America Press, 1984), 183.

26. Longenecker, *Paul, Apostle of Liberty*, 151–52, quoting Schweitzer, *Mysticism of Paul*, 3, 123. On this history of the *totus Christus* concept, especially as assimilated to German idealism's idea of a "corporate personality," see Michael Horton, *People and Place: A Covenant Ecclesiology* (Louisville: Westminster John Knox, 2008), 155–89.

27. Longenecker, *Paul, Apostle of Liberty*, 152, from *Theology of the NT*, 1:311.

28. Longenecker, *Paul, Apostle of Liberty*, 152, quoting Robinson, *The Body* (London: SCM, 1957), 51; and Thornton, *The Common Life in the Body of Christ* (London: Dacre, 1941).

assert that Paul's "in Christ" carries a quite definitely local flavor. It is not just a bit of "verbal ingenuity" or one of many metaphors subservient to the controlling concept of "the Body of Christ", but it is the dominant expression of the Apostle's thought for the relationship of the believer to Christ.[29]

This union is personal and individual as well as corporate: Vine and branches, head and members, firstfruits and harvest, King and kingdom. Made visible in the confession of sin and confession of faith, in hearing the Word of law and gospel, and in receiving Christ together in baptism and Eucharist, the body is one with Christ. There is no union with Christ that is not simultaneously union with his visible church, but it is not merely—or even primarily—an institutional unity but a mysterious, true, and intimate binding of many into one in their inmost being. The Father is in the Son without losing his own personality: "You, Father, are in me, and I in you" (John 17:21). In the surrounding verses, Jesus prays that "those who will believe in me" will also "be in us" and "be one even as we are one" (vv. 20–22). Incorporation does not entail the loss of individual personhood or personality, but rather the communion of persons as they are united together in one head. Longenecker also points out along these lines,

So Paul, with his high Christology, can speak of being "in Christ" without that concept of person "in" person softening or dissolving the fixed outlines of personality for either Christ or the Christian. To have been forced to give a definite psychological analysis of this relationship would have left Paul speechless. But he was convinced that he had experienced just such intimacy with Christ. . . . It is not the pagan mysticism of absorption, for the "I" and the "Thou" of the relation retain their identities. But it is the "I and Thou" communion at its highest.[30]

Further, "Baptism signifies and seals a *transition* in the experience of the recipient, a transition from being (existentially) apart from Christ to being (existentially) joined to him. Galatians 3:27 is even more graphic:

---

29. Longenecker, *Paul, Apostle of Liberty*, 154, quoting Schweitzer, *Mysticism of Paul*, 117; and Robinson, *The Body*, 58–67, respectively.
30. Longenecker, *Paul, Apostle of Liberty*, 155.

'Those who have been baptized into Christ have put on Christ' (cf. I Cor. 12:13)."[31] This is not a metaphor; it is the real history:

> If then you have been raised with Christ, seek the things that are above, where Christ is, seated at the right hand of God. Set your minds on things that are above, not on things that are on earth. For you have died, and your life is hidden with Christ in God. When Christ who is your life appears, then you also will appear with him in glory. (Col 3:1–4)

To be "in Christ," Vos notes, is not just a change in subjective conditions, but "the old things are passed away, new things have come into being."

> There has been created a totally new environment, or, more accurately speaking, a totally new world, in which the person spoken of is an inhabitant and participator. It is not in the first place the interiority of the subject that has undergone the change, although that, of course, is not to be excluded. The whole surrounding world has assumed a new aspect and complexion. . . . Christ nowhere with the Apostle figures merely as a productive center of new individuals: He is everywhere, where the formula in question occurs, the central dominating factor of a new order of affairs, in fact nothing less than the originator and representative of a new world-order. . . . Nor does the context permit any restriction to the renovated inner nature of the Christian subjectively considered. . . . It belongs to the chapter on "Justification" equally much as to that on inward renewal.[32]

The prophet Isaiah had already announced that "the righteous one, my servant, shall make many to be accounted righteous" (Isa 53:11). This great exchange also appears in 1 Peter 3:18: "For Christ also suffered once for sins, the righteous for the unrighteous, that he might bring us to God, being put to death in the flesh but made alive in the spirit." The same point is emphasized by Paul: the "righteous for the unrighteous" (see 1 Cor 1:30; 1 Tim 3:16, etc.).

We do not need the technical word "imputation" for this; the concept is there in any case. Where some see imputation as superfluous in

---

31. Gaffin, *Resurrection and Redemption*, 50–51.
32. Geerhardus Vos, *The Pauline Eschatology* (repr., Philipsburg, NJ: P&R, 1994), 47.

the Johannine and Pauline treatments of union, others (like myself) see it as ubiquitous. Vine and branches, head and members, firstfruits and harvest, bridegroom and bride—these are all *sedes doctrinae* for the "great exchange" in which all that Jesus Christ is and possesses as the "firstborn from the dead" is granted freely to all who identify with him.

Union and the Overcoming of False Choices: Bernard, Luther, and Calvin

On all sides in recent decades, there is a recognition that union with Christ is a crucial—even central—element in patristic soteriology. It was also a prominent motif in Byzantine and medieval spirituality, and Bernard of Clairvaux (1090–1153) serves as an especially important example. In *Against the Antinomians*, Luther declared, "This doctrine is not mine, but St. Bernard's. What am I saying? St. Bernard's? It is the message of all Christendom, of all the prophets and apostles."[33] In *The Freedom of a Christian*, Luther wrote,

> We conclude, therefore, that a Christian lives not in himself, but in Christ and his neighbor. Otherwise he is not a Christian. He lives in Christ through faith, in his neighbor through love. By faith he is caught up beyond himself into God. By love he descends beneath himself into his neighbor. Yet he always remains in God and in his love.[34]

Faith not only justifies; it also "unites the soul with Christ as a bride is united with her bridegroom," he says. "At this point a contest of happy exchanges takes place. . . . Is that not a happy household, when Christ, the rich, noble, and good bridegroom, takes the poor, despised, wicked little harlot in marriage, sets her free from all evil, and decks her with all good things?"[35] We must be united to Christ because "all our good is outside us, and that good is Christ."[36]

Calvin was a first-rate patristics scholar in his own right, but Luther, the monk, had been deeply schooled in Bernard's spirituality. The early editions of the *Institutes* are based largely on Luther's work, while the

---

33. Luther, "Against the Antinomians," in *LW* 47:10.
34. Luther, "The Freedom of a Christian," in *LW* 31:351.
35. Luther, "Two Kinds of Righteousness," in *LW* 31:298.
36. Luther, *Lectures on Romans*, in *LW* 25:267.

later versions culminating in the final 1559 edition display Calvin's independence as a thinker. Nevertheless, Calvin quotes Bernard more than twenty-nine times in the section devoted to the subject in the 1559 *Institutes*.[37] He fleshes out Paul's teaching in a way that displays richly how union with Christ is the intersection between aspects that we have seen throughout our study to be often subjected to false dichotomies.

First, union with Christ is the intersection between legal and organic aspects of salvation. In Calvin's exegesis, there is a wonderful interaction between organic and legal metaphors in their discussions of the mystical union of branches to the vine, bodily members to their head, adopted coheirs to their firstborn brother, bride to her bridegroom, and so forth. By itself, the imitation of Christ does not appreciate the intimate union of believers with Christ. Paul "has something higher in mind"—namely, "that the death of Christ is efficacious to destroy and overthrow the depravity of our flesh, and His resurrection to renew a better nature within us. It also states that by baptism we are admitted into participation in this grace." "Having laid this fundamental proposition" of *union*, he says, "Paul may very properly exhort Christians to strive to live in a manner that corresponds to their calling."[38]

Second, the lines of soteriology and ecclesiology intersect in the union-motif. In fact, the covenant of grace integrates soteriology and ecclesiology. Election pertains to individuals: "God chose *us*" in Christ (Eph 1:4). "Those whom he predestined, these he also called, and those he called, these he also justified" (Rom 8:30). Yet these individuals are chosen to be part of Christ's *bride*, members of his *body*. Ephesians 2:15 refers to Jew and gentile in Christ as "one new person" (see also Gal 3:28). Paul labors the point that the church is one body with many members and Christ as the head (Rom 12:5; 1 Cor 12:12–27; Eph 1:22; 5:23). The visible church, the covenant community, is the historical institution within history where the promise becomes a reality.

Although the *totus Christus* motif—the union of Christ and his members as "one new person"—is often attributed to Augustine, it can be found as early as Clement of Alexandria: "The complete man—if one

---

37. *Inst.* 3.20.1. On the number of references to Bernard, see François Wendel, *Calvin: Origins and Development of His Religious Thought*, trans. Philip Mairet (New York: Harper & Row, 1963), 127n43.

38. Calvin, *Calvin's New Testament Commentaries*, vol. 8, *The Epistles of Paul the Apostle to the Romans and to the Thessalonians*, ed. David W. and Thomas F. Torrance, trans. Ross Mackenzie (Grand Rapids: Eerdmans, 1973), 123 (on Rom 6:4).

may use the phrase, the total Christ—is not divided. He is neither barbarian, nor Jew, nor Greek, neither male nor female, but the New Man, completely transformed in the Spirit."[39] Everything that has happened to Jesus Christ according to his humanity *must* happen eventually to his whole body. Emphasizing this point, Calvin goes so far as to say,

> This is the highest honor of the Church, that until he is united to us, the Son of God reckons himself in some measure imperfect. What consolation is it for us to learn that not until we are along with him does he possess all his parts or wish to be regarded as complete. Hence, the First Epistle to the Corinthians, when the apostle discusses largely the metaphor of a human body, he includes under the single name of Christ the whole Church.[40]

We have seen that many of the criticisms of the "Lutheran" or "Reformation" perspective by contemporary biblical scholars are actually targeting pietistic revivalism. Whatever one might conclude from contemporary representatives, confessional Lutheran and Reformed churches define their faith and practice consensually, in the ecumenical creeds and their respective confessions. In those sources, there is no contrast drawn between cosmic and individual, between ecclesiological and soteriological. Indeed, the usual criticism by evangelicals, from conservative to progressive, has often been that Reformed theology is too ecclesial and sacramental.[41] The faith that unites us to Christ is indeed the act of the church, but the church defined not as the magisterium nor even as the ministerium but as the "Amen" of all of God's people together as hearers of the faith-engendering word, baptized together into Christ and nourished in common by his body and blood (1 Cor 10:14–17).

39. Clement of Alexandria, *Protrepticus*, 11, quoted in Michael Schmaus, *Dogma*, vol. 6, *Justification and Last Things* (London: Sheed and Ward, 1977), 49.

40. Calvin, *Calvin's New Testament Commentaries*, vol. 11, *The Epistles of Paul the Apostle to the Galatians, Ephesians, Philippians and Colossians*, eds. David W. and Thomas F. Torrance, trans. T. H. L. Parker (Grand Rapids: Eerdmans, 1965), 138 (on Eph 1:23).

41. Wayne Grudem, *Systematic Theology* (Grand Rapids: Zondervan, 1994), 950–51, 976–77; Charles Ryrie, *Basic Theology: A Popular Systematic Guide to Understanding Biblical Truth* (1986; repr., Chicago: Moody Press, 1999), 467, 487; Millard Erickson, *Christian Theology* (Grand Rapids Baker, 1985), 3:1093–94, 1096, 1101, 1120, 1122, 1126. From a more progressive evangelical direction, see Stanley Grenz, *Revisioning Evangelical Theology: A Fresh Agenda for the 21st Century* (Downers Grove, IL: InterVarsity, 1993), 17, 30–34, 38, 41–42, 44–46, 51–52, 55, 62, 77, 80, 88, 122; Grenz, *Theology for the Community of God* (Nashville: B&H, 1994), 644, 670.

Third, union with Christ is the intersection of the historia salutis *and the* ordo salutis, *redemption accomplished and applied.* No one is clearer than Calvin in arguing that Christ has fully merited our salvation, outside of us in history. Yet, he adds, all of this is all for nothing unless the Spirit unites us to Christ now, and one cannot be united to Christ for justification without also receiving in him sanctification and glorification.[42] "Not only does he cleave to us by an invisible bond of fellowship, but with a wonderful communion day by day, he grows more and more into one body with us, until he becomes completely one with us."[43] Through the word and sacraments the Spirit works "to lead us little by little to a firm union with God."[44] In Calvin's view, "Paul not only exhorts us to follow Christ, but also takes hold of something far higher, namely, that through baptism Christ makes us sharers in his death, that we may be engrafted in it."[45] To be sure, we are called to follow Christ's example, but the root of sanctification is union with Christ, not imitation, he says.[46]

Much of late medieval piety (especially in the widely popular *devotio moderna*) turned on the imitation of Christ with a view toward final union with God. A more radical mysticism, with roots in Meister Eckhart via the *Theologia Germanica*, pursued direct union with God's essence by fleeing everything temporal and material. Even Scripture, preaching, and sacraments were on the former side of the letter-spirit divide and had to be transcended by the divine spirit within oneself. Early Anabaptism was steeped in this tradition. It is fascinating to find Anabaptist scholar Curtis W. Freeman pointing out Douglas Campbell's

---

42. *Inst.* 3.1.1–2.

43. *Inst.* 3.2.24. Mosser notes that in the 1545 edition Calvin says "daily he more and more unites himself to us in one, same substance" (p. 48), but this disappears in the 1559 edition—which not incidentally includes the polemic against Osiander.

44. *Inst.* 2.15.5. Elsewhere: "It is because he consecrated himself to the Father that his holiness might come to us; for as the blessing on the first fruits is spread over the whole harvest, so the Spirit of God cleanses us by the holiness of Christ, and makes us partakers of it. Nor is this done by imputation only, for in that respect he is said to have been made our righteousness; but he is likewise said to have been made to us sanctification (1 Cor 1:30), because he has, so to speak, presented us to his Father in his own person, that we may be renewed to true holiness by his Spirit" (Calvin, *Calvin's Commentaries*, vol. 17, *Commentary on the Gospel according to John*, trans. William Pringle [Grand Rapids: Baker, 1996], on 17:19).

45. *Inst.* 4.15.5.

46. *Inst.* 3.3.9. Origen bequeathed a spirituality of ascent through various stages: purgation, contemplation, and union. Calvin reversed this order: beginning with union, the believer fixes his or her eyes on Christ, and grows in sanctification as a branch bears fruit from its vine. Late medieval piety, especially as influenced by the Brethren of the Common Life, placed its stress on the imitation of Christ. Here too, Calvin differs. While affirming the imitation of Christ, he suggests that union with Christ is more fundamental to the believer's identity.

proximity to this view, a connection to which Campbell himself nods. Campbell's alternative to justification is "in fact repeating an argument that is quite old," says Freeman, explaining,

> Luther's Wittenberg colleague, Andreas Karlstadt, diverged from the teaching of the justification of sinners by grace through faith. He believed that God's grace would remake sinners and lead to a life of discipleship and obedience in which sin would be overcome. For Karlstadt sin was conquered through the "yieldedness" (*Gelassenheit*) of the Christian's will to God's will. This notion of *Gelassenheit* became central in Anabaptist theology and spirituality.[47]

This is an interesting point, especially since Luther, in the introduction to his lectures on Galatians, explains that Anabaptists and Rome join in their rejection of justification.

According to Calvin, John and Paul do not teach either imitation or *Gelassenheit* as the nature of this union.[48] There is certainly a mysticism in Luther and Calvin, the same type that Schweitzer identified in Paul. But there could never be any of the Creator-creature confusion or spirit-matter dualism that fed radical mysticism. The critique of Osiander's position (itself indebted directly to the *Theologia Germanica*) clearly articulates Calvin's difference with this type of piety, as does Solid Declaration 3 of the Formula of Concord. Indeed, as articulated by Torrance, Hays, Martyn, and Campbell, the subjective interpretation reflects something close to late medieval German mysticism that features passivity, or even self-annihilation, as the primary means of union with God.

In addition to the aforementioned differences, the focus of the magisterial Reformers is not on the believer's activity—or even passivity—but on the redemptive-historical fact that every believer participates in *Christ's* activity (his historical life, death, resurrection, and ascension) by which (in the power of the Spirit) the believer who passively receives

---

47. Curtis W. Freeman, "The Faith of Jesus Christ: An Evangelical Conundrum," in *Beyond Old and New Perspectives: Reflections on the Work of Douglas Campbell*, ed. Chris Tilling (Eugene, OR: Cascade, 2014), 258.

48. Thomas N. Finger observes that the early Anabaptists assumed a strong Neoplatonic opposition between spirit and matter, with everything natural being "smashed" and obliterated so that the soul could be united with God. They staunchly rejected the magisterial Reformation's teaching on justification (Finger, *A Contemporary Anabaptist Theology: Biblical, Historical, Constructive* [Downers Grove, IL: InterVarsity, 2004], 109).

all righteousness from God in Christ is active in love and good works toward his or her neighbor (see again Luther's *Freedom of a Christian*). The self is not annihilated or absorbed into God and his will. On the contrary, the self, dead and condemned, is justified and enlivened as an agent who freely loves and serves others.

As in the older version, the contemporary approach of Hays, Campbell, and others makes much of imitating Christ's faithfulness while denying that Christ's faithfulness is actually credited to believers. While various lay movements (such as the Brethren of the Common Life) emphasized following Christ's example, Calvin says union with Christ is far deeper:

> Let us know that the Apostle does not simply exhort us to imitate Christ, as though he had said that his death is a pattern which all Christians are to follow; for no doubt he ascends higher, as he announces a doctrine with which he connects an exhortation; and his doctrine is this: that the death of Christ is efficacious to destroy and demolish the depravity of our flesh, and his resurrection, to effect the renovation of a better nature, and that by baptism we are admitted into a participation of this grace. This foundation being laid, Christians may very suitably be exhorted to strive to respond to their calling.[49]

This "engrafting is not only a conformity of example, but a secret union."[50]

In Christian (including evangelical) piety generally, there seems often to be a disconnect between what happened to Christ and what happens to us. Or to put it more technical terms, the *historia salutis* (Christ's incarnation, life, death, resurrection, ascension, and second advent) and the *ordo salutis* (our election, redemption, justification, sanctification, and glorification). Jesus-history is seen as an essential prerequisite for one's personal salvation here and now, but it is our activity (conversion, repentance, faith, new obedience) that is seen often as salvific. Instead, Reformed soteriology emphasizes our insertion here and now through faith into Jesus-history, so that we are baptized into his death and resurrection, and so that we participate in the new creation that has dawned

---

49. Calvin, *Calvin's Commentaries*, vol. 19, *Commentaries upon the Epistle of Paul to the Romans*, trans. John Owen (Grand Rapids: Baker, 1996), 221.

50. Calvin, *Calvin's Commentaries*, 19:222.

in him. Paul can no longer even think of himself existing apart from being "in Christ." And, as noted from Calvin above, even Christ can no longer think of himself apart from us. (In Acts 9:4, being addressed by Christ with the query, "Saul, Saul, why do you persecute *me*?" must have launched Paul's consciousness of this intimate connection.)

I know what Tom Wright is talking about when he says, "My anxiety about what has now been seen as *the traditional Reformed view*, . . . is that it focuses all attention on 'me and my salvation' rather than on 'God and God's purposes', which—as we see in the Gospels, and in e.g. Romans 8—are much wider than just my salvation."[51] Traditional Reformed theology, exegesis, and practice are marked by an emphasis on "God and God's purposes," as well as an ecclesial consciousness and an eschatology of cosmic redemption. However, pietism (and revivalism) have made considerable inroads into Reformed churches too. Influencing both liberal and conservative Protestants, pietism reverses this relation: not our union with Christ in his death, burial, and resurrection as much as his union with us, living in our heart.

The "Christ within" bears the seed of truth: Christ has given us his Holy Spirit who indwells us (Rom 8:10; Gal 2:20; Eph 3:17–19; Col 1:27; 1 John 3:24). However, *Christ* remains outside of us, living, dying, being raised, ascending, and returning. Yet our lives now are mapped onto his by the same Spirit who raised Jesus from the dead. However, many biblical scholars and theologians reared in this implicit Gnosticism (or at least Platonism), whether more liberal or conservative, have overreacted by marginalizing or rejecting Paul's equally important emphasis on the application of redemption. To suggest that Paul is not interested in the question, "How are we saved?" is quite simply to miss much of what he says.

"The justification by faith perspective on Christ's work," Campbell alleges, "while placing a satisfactory emphasis on the cross, evacuates his incarnation, much of his life, his resurrection, and his ascension, of all soteriological value."[52] Such statements will strike anyone familiar

---

51. Trevin Wax, "Interview with N. T. Wright—Responding to Piper on Justification," January 13, 2009, http://trevinwax.com/2009/01/13/interview-with-nt-wright-responding-to-piper-on-justification/, emphasis added.

52. Douglas A. Campbell, *The Quest for Paul's Gospel* (London: T&T Clark, 2005), 168. Cf. Douglas A. Campbell, *The Deliverance of God: An Apocalyptic Rereading of Justification in Paul* (Grand Rapids: Eerdmans, 2013), 708–9. Especially given the emphasis of confessional Lutheran and Reformed traditions on the priority of the *historia salutis*—namely, Christ's history—and the weight that they place on the salvific importance of the incarnation, active obedience,

with Lutheran and Reformed confessional theologies as ill-informed. In addition, it is ironic, since the more likely target of this criticism is Karl Barth, who insisted that the resurrection and ascension contributed nothing of saving significance beyond Christ's death.[53]

The *historia salutis* must always remain at the forefront. Christ's incarnation, life, death, and resurrection—indeed also his ascension and return—must be what we mean by "the gospel." Yet he "was delivered up *for our trespasses* and raised *for our justification*" (Rom 4:25). Rather than being sidelined, the *ordo salutis* needs to be connected to the *historia salutis*. And that connector is union with Christ, as Calvin observed. God bestowed blessings on the Son, "not for private use, but to enrich the poor and needy."

> And the first thing to be attended to is, that so long as we are without Christ and separated from him, nothing which he suffered and did for the salvation of the human race is of the least benefit to us. To communicate to us the blessings which he received from the Father, he must become ours and dwell in us. Accordingly, he is called our Head, and the first-born among many brethren, while, on the other hand, we are said to be ingrafted into him and clothed with him (Eph 4:15; Rom 6:5; 11:17; 8:29; Gal 3:27).[54]

---

resurrection, and ascension of Christ, this statement is quite ill-informed. Robert Preus underscored the point that in Lutheran theology *sola gratia* and *sola fide* are simply appendages to (or, better, entailments of) *solo Christo*. The Reformers would say that not even the most monergistic doctrine of grace is adequate unless it affirms that all benefits of salvation are both achieved by Christ and found in Christ alone. This is seen for example in Melanchthon's Apology to the Augsburg Confession, says Preus. "One cannot fail to note that Article IV . . . addresses the propitiatory and mediatory work of Christ as directly as the article on justification by faith" (Robert Preus, *Justification and Rome* [St. Louis: Concordia Academic Press, 1997], 16). Luther follows the same route in the Smalcald Articles (2.2.1–5, 15–16). "It is because of this article that all other articles touch us" (18, from *Second Disputation Against the Antinomians*, in *WA* 28:271). Actually, it is Rome that treated justification in relation to the subjective work of the Spirit within us (*ordo salutis*) rather than to the objective work of Christ for us (*historia salutis*). "These teachers regarded the aphorism [*articulus stantis et cadentis ecclesiae*] not as a mere cliché, useful for polemics against Roman Catholic theology, but a fundamental, integrative principle in their theology, worship and practice, and in their ministry in the Church" (18–19). Thus, in the Augsburg Confession, justification is tied directly to Christ's atoning work on the cross. Justification is not an abstract or arbitrary decree of a *potentia Dei absoluta*. It is only on the basis of Christ's cross that God is gracious to sinners (46–49). It is his incarnation, life, death, resurrection, and ascension rather than our "appropriation" that actually saves—a point that Calvin movingly expressed, as we saw above.

53. *CD* IV/2, 291. Peter Leithart makes the same charge by selectively quoting from the Lutheran and Reformed confessions. The very articles that he quotes include the resurrection as an essential part of justification. See Peter J. Leithart, *Delivered from the Elements of the World: Atonement, Justification, Mission* (Downers Grove, IL: IVP Academic, 2016), 331n33.

54. *Inst.* 3.1.1. Beveridge translation.

Fourth, union with Christ is the intersection of the "already" and "not-yet." As I have argued, not every aspect of the *ordo salutis* has a "not-yet." There is no future election or future effectual calling. Jesus spoke of the "regeneration of all things," when he assumes his throne (Matt 19:28). The spiritual regeneration of the inner self (the new birth) is the "already" of that cosmic renewal that will be realized fully in the resurrection of the body (2 Cor 4:13–18). Sanctification will be realized in glorification (1 Cor 13:11–12; 2 Cor 3:18). However, justification *is* the verdict of the last day rendered in the present—a fully realized treasure. At the same time, we grow more and more into our union with Christ, as in any marriage. We need not turn *justification* into an intersection of the already and not-yet in order to affirm *union* as the site where this age and the age to come overlap in a fruitful, if often frustrating, tension.

Luther and Calvin both affirmed the maxim *simul iustus et peccator*: before God we are always justified in Christ although we remain inherently sinful. The believer never outgrows their dependence at every moment on the righteousness of Christ, as if he or she now had at least something to offer God. Before God, we are in ourselves still ungodly enough to be condemned. Our best works are stained by sin. Nevertheless, because Christ's righteousness is imputed to us, we are not regarded as ungodly but as cherished and spotless members of the bride of Christ. Because of this, we are now recipients of those other graces, of adoption and sanctification, that lead us by degrees to greater conformity to our elder brother.[55]

Yet to this traditional theologoumenon of "simultaneously righteous and sinful" must be added the maxim of "simultaneously regenerated and sinful." While it is true that a believer remains just in Christ and inherently sinful, it is also important to recognize that the believer is not unregenerate, under the dominion of sin, any more than he or she is under sin's condemnation. Since sanctification always accompanies justification, the elect are being conformed to the image of Christ even at the moment that they first trust in him. Thus, they are no longer "dead in trespasses and sins" (Eph 2:1), incapable of understanding and embracing the truth (1 Cor 2:14)—even in their lowest moments of disobedience and doubt. Thus, while the *simul* says something important,

---

55. Michael Allen develops the relationship between justification and sanctification well in his volume in the New Studies in Dogmatics series: *Sanctification* (Grand Rapids: Zondervan Academic, 2017).

it does not say everything that needs to be said about the paradox of "saint and sinner."

Fifth, closely associated with the previous point, union with Christ is the intersection of Christology and pneumatology. All that he is, has done, and possesses are "nothing to us until we become one with him," Calvin writes. This is accomplished by "the secret efficacy of the Spirit." "The whole comes to this, that the Holy Spirit is the bond by which Christ effectually binds us to himself," and it is by this same Spirit that we share in Christ's anointing.[56] It is because of a robust pneumatology that he is able to stress participation. To speak of Christ being present apart from the Spirit's distinctive operation necessarily encourages a tendency to transform Jesus—the still-incarnate Lord who has ascended—into a cosmic Christ who is virtually indistinguishable from the Holy Spirit, as in Deißmann's view above.

The distinction of persons and their operations must be preserved in order to ensure that the one to whom we are united remains the one whose nature we share. Otherwise we cannot be glorified with him. What would the resurrection of the dead mean if our head is merely a cosmic spirit? This pneumatological emphasis, in my view, is the distinctive insight of Vermigli and Calvin over against Luther and Zwingli.

The "mystical" aspect of union owes nothing to Greek mystery religions or the mysticism of "surrender" but to the Holy Spirit's act of uniting us here and now to Christ's historical existence, which he now carries with him into the age to come. The impulse is Irenaean through-and-through.[57] As Philip Walker Butin notes, Calvin affirms as strongly as Luther the descent of the eternal Son in our flesh but "complements and completes the 'downward' emphasis on incarnation with an equal and 'upward' emphasis on resurrection and ascension" by the Holy Spirit.[58] As Douglas Farrow, Julie Canlis, and others have argued, Calvin's emphasis is deeply Irenaean rather than Origenist.[59]

---

56. *Inst.* 3.1.1.

57. See my essay, "Atonement and Ascension," in *Locating Atonement: Explorations in Constructive Dogmatics*, ed. Fred Sanders and Oliver Crisp (Grand Rapids: Zondervan Academic, 2015), 226–50.

58. Philip Walker Butin, *Revelation, Redemption, and Response: Calvin's Trinitarian Understanding of the Divine-Human Relationship* (New York: Oxford University Press, 1995), 118.

59. Douglas Farrow, *Ascension and Ecclesia* (New York: Bloomsbury T&T Clark, 2004). Throughout this work, Farrow compares Calvin to Irenaeus (over against Origen). Similarly, see Julie Canlis, *Calvin's Ladder: A Spiritual Theology of Ascent and Ascension* (Grand Rapids: Eerdmans, 2010).

Paradoxically, it is precisely by departing in the flesh that Jesus is able to send the Holy Spirit to bind his people to himself more intimately than the disciples had experienced even walking at his side. Not merely alongside Jesus, following his teaching and example, they were now inserted into his eschatological existence, becoming beneficiaries of his justification and glorification. By his ascension Christ has opened a space within our history for the descent of the Spirit, who brings the powers of the age to come into the present age. Just as Calvin added to Luther's emphasis on Christ's descent the equally Pauline emphasis on ascent with Christ through the Spirit, he added to Luther's "once-and-for-all" emphasis the "more-and-more" aspect of our union.[60] This is *sanctification*, however, since justification is an already completed verdict at the headwaters of the believer's new existence.

It is the Spirit who united Jesus to our flesh and raised him from the dead as the head of his new humanity and who now unites us to Jesus so that all that he has and is becomes ours. A de-eschatologized and individualized soteriology will inevitably cause the *ordo salutis* ("getting saved") to drift apart from the *historia salutis* (redemption accomplished). But a weak pneumatology (or one in which the Spirit arrives too late on the scene) will inevitably cause the *historia salutis* to drift apart from the *ordo salutis*. Either way, the bond between our life and Christ's would be severed.

Our personal salvation is to be found in Christ, not the "Christ in my heart"—an experience in my own existence—but in Christ *as he was incarnate—fulfilled the law, bore its curse, rose again, and ascended on high*. In Calvin's thinking, as in Paul's, Christ's history is not merely analogous to ours. Nor is it even merely the basis for our redemption. Rather, he means literally that every benefit of salvation (the *ordo salutis*) is nothing but a sharing in each event of Christ's historical existence. Christ's death did not make our justification possible; "we are justified *by* his blood" (Rom 5:9). We really are crucified and raised with Christ; this is not mere rhetorical flourish. For Calvin, the resurrection is more than proof of a proposition; it is an event that has turned the tide of history decisively away from death to life, condemnation to justification,

---

60. Although somewhat overstated, there is some truth to George Hunsinger's suggestion that while Calvin embraces Luther's "once and for all," he goes beyond Luther by stressing also the "more and more" aspect of salvation. See George Hunsinger, *Disrupting Grace: Studies in the Theology of Karl Barth* (Grand Rapids: Eerdmans, 2004), 14.

flesh to Spirit, for all who are united to Christ. Christ's history neither becomes assimilated to mine ("Christ in my heart") nor does mine become assimilated to his—the abolition of the self. Rather, through faith I am united to Christ so that his history and future become mine.

Calvin expresses this most poignantly in a lyrical summation:

> We see that our whole salvation and all its parts are compre-hended in Christ (Acts 4:12). We should therefore take care not to derive the least portion of it from anywhere else. If we seek salvation we are taught by the very name of Jesus that it is "of him" (1 Cor 1.13). If we seek any other gifts of the Spirit, they will be found in his anointing. If we seek strength, it lies in his dominion; if purity, in his conception; if gentleness, it appears in his birth. For by his birth he was made like us in all respects (Heb 2:17) that he might learn to feel our pain (Heb 5:2).
>
> If we seek redemption, it lies in his passion; if acquittal, in his condemnation; if remission of the curse, in his cross (Gal 3:13); if satisfaction, in his sacrifice; if purification, in his blood; if recon-ciliation, in his descent into hell; if mortification of the flesh, in his tomb; if newness of life, in his resurrection; if immortality, in the same; if inheritance of the Heavenly Kingdom, in his entrance into heaven; if protection, if security, if abundant supply of all blessings, in his Kingdom; if untroubled expectation of judgment, in the power given to him to judge. In short, since rich store of every kind of good abounds in him, let us drink our fill from this fountain and from no other.[61]

Sixth, union with Christ is the intersection between justification and sanctifi-cation. Justification is strictly forensic: the imputation of Christ's merits. However, "You cannot grasp this," he says, "without at the same time grasping sanctification also."[62] After all, one is not grasping a gift but *Christ himself.*

> As long as Christ remains outside of us, and we are separated from him, all that he has suffered and done for the salvation of the human race remains useless and of no value for us. Therefore, to share with

---

61. *Inst.* 2.16.19.
62. *Inst.* 3.16.1.

us what he has received from the Father, he had to become ours and dwell within us. For this reason, he is called "our Head" [Eph. 4:15] and "the first-born among many brethren" [Rom. 8:29].[63]

When we begin to discuss sanctification, we are not moving from *what God* does to *what we do* but from *one work of God* (viz., to declare us righteous) to *another work of God* (viz., to make us righteous).

Like Luther, Melanchthon, Bucer, and Vermigli, Calvin spoke of a *duplex beneficium*—twofold benefit—of this union: justification and renewal. Precisely in their distinction from each other, both gifts are equally precious. Matthew Bates laments Calvin's treatment of sanctification as "merely the inevitable outworking of a prior justification."[64]

It is true that Calvin saw sanctification as dependent on justification. This has become a matter of trifling debate in Reformed circles in recent years. Some have argued that justification has no relation to sanctification; rather, both are gifts of union.[65] To say that sanctification depends logically on justification is a Lutheran approach rather than Reformed, they insist.[66]

I call this a trifling debate because it introduces yet another false choice, this time between union with Christ and the *ordo salutis*. Reformed theologians have never felt any sense of self-contradiction in saying that justification and sanctification are twin benefits of union with Christ and that within the *ordo* sanctification depends on justification.[67] The very notion of an *ordo* requires logical dependence.

---

63. *Inst.* 3.1.1.

64. Bates, *Salvation by Allegiance Alone*, 185. See *Inst.* 3.11.6.

65. See for example William Evans, *Imputation and Impartation: Union with Christ in American Reformed Theology* (Eugene, OR: Wipf and Stock, 2008); Mark A. Garcia, *Life in Christ: Union with Christ and Twofold Grace in Calvin's Theology* (Milton Keynes, UK: Paternoster, 2008); Lane G. Tipton, "Union with Christ and Justification," in *Justified in Christ: God's Plan for Us in Justification*, ed., K. Scott Oliphint (Fearn, Ross-shire, UK: Mentor, 2007), 23–50. The *ordo* of the Westminster Confession, however, is clear: effectual calling-justification-sanctification-glorification—with union with Christ being an umbrella-term rather than one of the elements of the *ordo* itself.

66. For example, Robert Letham makes the extraordinary claim that by stressing union with Christ, Reformed theologians "differ from a purely external justification as is seen in Lutheranism." Letham, *Union with Christ in Scripture, History, and Theology* (Phillipsburg, NJ: P&R, 2011), 82. For the Reformed justification is no less a purely external/extrinsic verdict, and Lutherans affirm union with Christ as clearly as the Reformed.

67. See for example the Belgic Confession (art. 24). The Westminster Larger Catechism says that "sanctification is inseparably joined with justification" (Q. 77). J. Todd Billings, *Calvin, Participation, and the Gift: The Activity of Believers in Union with Christ* (New York: Oxford University Press, 2009); cf. Michael Horton, "Calvin's Theology of Union with Christ and the Double Grace: Modern Reception and Contemporary Possibilities," in *Calvin's Theology and Its Reception: Disputes, Developments, and New Possibilities*, ed. I. John Hesselink and J. Todd Billings (Louisville: Westminster John Knox, 2012), 72–96.

Each of the benefits depends on the others that are prior to it. Just as glorification depends on election, redemption, calling, justification, and sanctification, sanctification depends on everything leading up to justification.

For his part at least, Calvin sees no difficulty in affirming both points: sanctification depends on justification, and both are inseparable gifts of union with Christ.[68] He says, for example, "For *since* we are clothed with the righteousness of the Son, we are reconciled to God, and renewed by the power of the Spirit to holiness."[69] "Sanctification, for Calvin, grows out of justification," Herman Selderhuis explains, "and the glory of Christ's perfect righteousness may never be obscured, not even for a moment." "Therefore, justification is the cause and sanctification is the effect."[70] Both justification and sanctification are dependent on effectual calling, for example, even though they are equally gifts of union.

As Louis Berkhof summarizes, "The mystical union in the sense in which we are now speaking of it is not the judicial ground, on the basis of which we become partakers of the riches that are in Christ," but rather "the righteousness of Christ is freely imputed to us." The demands of the law are met "in view of the fact that the righteousness of Christ is imputed" to the believer.[71] Similarly, Geehardus Vos argues,

In our opinion, Paul consciously and consistently subordinated the mystical aspect of the relation to Christ to the forensic one. . . . Paul's mind was to such an extent forensically oriented that he regarded the entire complex of subjective spiritual changes that take place in the believer and of subjective spiritual blessings enjoyed by the believer as the direct outcome of the forensic work of Christ applied in justification.[72]

I would only add two important caveats. First, this forensic basis even for the union itself is the judgment and justification of Jesus Christ

---

68. *Inst.* 3.11.6.

69. *Inst.* 3.11.17, emphasis added.

70. Herman Selderhuis, *Calvin's Theology of the Psalms* (Grand Rapids: Baker Academic, 2007), 195–98.

71. Louis Berkhof, *Systematic Theology* (Grand Rapids: Eerdmans, 1996), 452, 517.

72. Geerhardus Vos, "The Alleged Legalism in Paul's Doctrine of Justification," in *Redemptive History and Biblical Interpretation: The Shorter Writings of Geerhardus Vos*, ed. Richard B. Gaffin Jr. (Phillipsburg, NJ: P&R, 1980), 384.

himself. Second, in logical order the gift of new birth does indeed precede faith and justification. Nevertheless, as Berkhof and Vos properly observe, logical priority does not determine basis. We are not justified by virtue of the fact that we are regenerated, but we are justified only because Christ's righteousness is imputed. This forensic justification remains the firm basis for the believer's free and secure pursuit of conformity to Christ's image by his Word and Spirit. Consequently, we yield freely to his Spirit not only because we are united to Christ and receive our sanctification and justification in him but also because we have the confidence that only justification can bring.

Yet it is surely correct and important to point out that Calvin (like Luther) saw justification and sanctification as twin benefits of union with Christ, over against the one-sided interpretation of Matthew Bates's characterization. In short, whereas Luther and Calvin see *union with Christ* (the great exchange) involving both legal (justification) and transformative (sanctification) elements, Bates and numerous others see *justification* itself as legal and transformative.

The gift of salvation is Christ himself. To receive Christ is to receive election, redemption, the Holy Spirit, justification, sanctification, and glorification. According to the Westminster Confession,

> They, who are once effectually called, and regenerated, having a new heart, and a new spirit created in them, are further sanctified, really and personally, through the virtue of Christ's death and resurrection, by His Word and Spirit dwelling in them: the dominion of the whole body of sin is destroyed, and the several lusts thereof are more and more weakened and mortified; and they more and more quickened and strengthened in all saving graces, to the practice of true holiness, without which no man shall see the Lord.[73]

Though "inseparably bound," these gifts remain distinct, as the Westminster Larger Catechism observes:

> Although sanctification be inseparably joined with justification, yet they differ, in that God in justification imputeth the righteousness of Christ; in sanctification of his Spirit infuseth grace, and enableth

---

73. Westminster Confession of Faith, ch. 8, in *The Trinity Hymnal* (Atlanta: Great Commission Publications, 1990), 853–54.

to the exercise thereof; in the former, sin is pardoned; in the other, it is subdued: the one doth equally free all believers from the revenging wrath of God, and that perfectly in this life, that they never fall into condemnation the other is neither equal in all, nor in this life perfect in any, but growing up to perfection.[74]

We merit nothing before God (Luke 17:10; Rom 11:35), the Belgic Confession teaches.

Yet we do not wish to deny that God rewards good works—but it is by his grace that he crowns his gifts. Moreover, although we do good works we do not base our salvation on them; for we cannot do any work that is not defiled by our flesh and also worthy of punishment. And even if we could point to one, memory of a single sin is enough for God to reject that work. So we would always be in doubt, tossed back and forth without any certainty, and our poor consciences would be tormented constantly if they did not rest on the merit of the suffering and death of our Savior.[75]

On the basis of justification, the verdict of the last judgment has been rendered in the present: "There is therefore now no condemnation for those who are in Christ Jesus" (Rom 8:1). "This alone is of importance: having admitted that faith and good works must cleave together," Calvin says, "we still lodge justification in faith, not in works. We have a ready explanation for doing this, provided we turn to Christ to whom our faith is directed and from whom it receives its full strength."[76]

The most egregious mistake that critics of the Reformation interpretation (especially but not exclusively biblical scholars) make is to read the Reformers' polemics against good works *in relation to justification* as a more general polemic against good works; these critics interpret the Reformers' dogmatic rejection of identifying human actions as an instrumental (much less efficient or meritorious) cause of *justification* as a general wariness of human agency in the pilgrimage of salvation. This gospel, says Luther, "will cause the heart to rejoice and find delight in

---

74. Westminster Larger Catechism, Q. 77 (Glasgow: Free Church Publications, 1997), 169.
75. Belgic Confession, art. 24, in *Psalter Hymnal* (Grand Rapids: Board of Publication of the CRC, 1976).
76. *Inst.* 3.16.1.

God and will enable the believer to keep the law cheerfully, without expecting reward, without fear of punishment, without seeking compensation, as the heart is perfectly satisfied with God's grace, by which the law has been fulfilled. . . . Behold, thus the Law is delightful now and easy which before was disagreeable, difficult, and impossible; for it lives in the heart by the Spirit."[77] Following Paul's logic in Ephesians 2:8–10, the Reformers were united in teaching that we are saved by grace alone, through faith alone, precisely in order to be freed for the first time to the good works that God preordained for us.

For Jesus, the covenant of creation even trumped Sinai (Mark 10:2–12; Matt 5:31–32; 19:3–12; 1 Cor 7:10–11). When he says he has not come to abolish the law but to fulfill it, he means not only the ceremonies but especially the moral law, which remains the Great Commandment from creation to consummation. As the creator God himself, the Word of the Father, Jesus will not—cannot—ignore the command to love; he fulfills it. Justification is taken care of, so "if anyone does sin, we have an advocate with the Father, Jesus Christ the righteous. He is the propitiation for our sins, and not for ours only but also for the sins of the whole world" (1 John 2:1–2). On this secure basis, the call to love is no longer a fearful command (rendering our brothers and sisters and neighbors a threat rather than a gift) but our reasonable service. Far from unleashing a reign of antinomian terror, the advent of Christ and the reign of the Spirit ushers in a new eschatological reality—the new creation—that makes possible for the first time a genuine family of love.

The promise of the new covenant was anticipated in the text of the Sinai covenant itself. "For this commandment that I command you today is not too hard ['wonderful'] for you, neither is it far off" (Deut 30:11). Although the Sinai covenant commands the people to circumcise their hearts (Deut 10:16), Yahweh promises that after Israel fails "the LORD your God will circumcise your heart and the heart of your offspring, so that you will love the LORD your God with all your heart and with all your soul, that you may live" (30:6). This is why Paul said in Romans 10:6–8 that the *gospel* ("the word of faith that we are proclaiming") is not too far away that we should have to seek it out. Bryan Estelle offers a persuasive interpretation of Deuteronomy 30:1–14:

---

77. Luther, "Sermon for the Second Sunday after Epiphany," in *The Complete Sermons of Martin Luther*, 7 vols., ed. John Nicholas Lenker (repr., Grand Rapids: Baker, 2007), 1.2:68.

It will not be "too wonderful" in the sense of not too baffling for them to understand. Moshe Weinfeld eloquently explains this "intellectual accessibility" view from the standpoint of wisdom, biblical and otherwise, in its ancient Near Eastern context. If Deuteronomy 30:1–14 is a prophecy of the new covenant, then it would be teaching that at that time obedience would not be beyond Israel's capacity or ability. Once God circumcises a believer's heart, meeting the demands of his law will no longer be beyond one's ability, albeit still performed imperfectly. The Spirit's presence in sanctification enables the person's will to be God's will. . . . Since Christ will have descended in the new covenant age to usher in the promises, the people will have no need to say, "who will go up for us heavenwards?"[78]

It would be a serious error, then, for a Christian to live on the basis of confidence in Christ for justification while succumbing to the dominion of sin and death. I have in mind something like the following assumption: "I am sinless in Christ because of justification, but I cannot expect much in the way of freedom from the power of sin and for genuine growth in conformity to Christ and love for my neighbors." This attitude comes perilously close to the type of "faith" that James said cannot save since it is not genuine faith at all. But we do not need to add love and works to faith or transform faith into love and works to counter this heresy. We merely need to recognize that the same faith that passively receives Christ and his gifts bears the fruit of love and good works.

Since we have been justified, we now have neighbors to care for, justice and charity to be done. In fact, we are called to a higher standard of righteousness than the Pharisees with their external observances and oral traditions that neglected "the weightier matters of the law," which Jesus identified as belonging to neighbor-love (Matt 23:23–28). "For I tell you," Jesus says, "unless your righteousness exceeds that of the scribes and Pharisees, you will never enter the kingdom of heaven" (Matt 5:20).

In the Sermon on the Mount, Jesus contrasts the leniency of the old covenant, because of the weakness of sinful flesh, with the demands of love. Hateful insults are now murder, and the first religious obligation

---

78. Bryan Estelle, "Leviticus 18:5 and Deuteronomy 30:1–14 in Biblical-Theological Development," in *The Law Is Not of Faith: Essays on Works and Grace in the Mosaic Covenant*, ed. Bryan Estelle, J. V. Fesko, and David VanDrunen (Phillipsburg, NJ: P&R, 2009), 128.

is to reconcile with our brothers and sisters (Matt 5:21–26). Lust now counts as adultery (vv. 27–30). Divorce, except for adultery, is forbidden now (vv. 31–32). Believers are to be ruled by honest speech, without recourse to the courts (vv. 33–37; cf. 1 Cor 6:1–8). Selfish retaliation should be replaced with selfless gifts (vv. 38–42), and enemies are to be loved and prayed for rather than cursed (vv. 43–48). The new covenant is easier in the sense that it comes not only with the command but with the security of "no condemnation" and the eschatological power of Christ's new-creation life, but its demands are greater: nothing less than the deep longing of the Creator for that fellowship for which he created humanity. "Under the law" as a covenant ("do this, and you will live"), the command to love is not only difficult but impossible and, finally, condemning; under the covenant of grace, it becomes not only possible but real and, finally, a testimony to the faith that overcomes the world.

This gift is certainly free, without any basis in the deserts of the recipient, but it is not "without any strings attached." In fact, it is with *all the strings attached.* Joseph Fitzmyer makes the point well:

> It is not merely that "no living human being is righteous" before him (Ps 143:2), but that Yahweh gratuitously seeks out faithless Israel and will not let it go off of him. Listen to Hosea's prophecy, "I will heal their faithlessness; I will love them freely, for my anger has turned from them" (14:4); or earlier, "I will make for them/you a covenant on that day with the beasts of the field . . . , and I will betroth you to me forever; I will betroth you to me in righteousness and in justice, in steadfast love, and in mercy" (2:18–19).[79]

Because God is too gracious, merciful, and loving to purchase our redemption only to leave us in the grip of sin, it is impossible for those who are justified to be left unrenewed. The point of the gift is to bind us to the triune God and each other. Furthermore, those who are justified are also renewed and are being sanctified. If they do not forgive others, they are not forgiven; if they do not have works, then they do not have genuine faith. But their act of forgiving others does not make them

---

79. Joseph Fitzmyer, SJ, response to John Reumann, in *"Righteousness" in the New Testament: "Justification" in the United States Lutheran-Roman Catholic Dialogue, with Responses by Joseph A. Fitzmyer and Jerome D. Quinn,* by John Reumann (Philadelphia: Fortress; New York: Paulist, 1982), 199.

worthy of forgiveness, nor is their faith the one work on which salvation depends; rather, the nature of the gift itself makes them worthy. Romans 11 does not say that we cannot return anything to God. Rather, it says, "Who has given a gift to him that he might be repaid?" (Rom 11:35). Every good gift comes from God. But what is returned? Nothing of a compensatory nature. The return is in a completely different register, not in the category of quid pro quo but the kind of grateful worship in which God delights (Ps 40:6). And that grateful worship consists in praising God chiefly by loving others.

"By now it should be self-evident that from such faith deeds of gratitude proceed quite spontaneously," as Eberhard Jüngel argues.

> These are deeds freely performed. Yet they arise of necessity from the gratitude of faith; they cannot help coming out of persons who are grateful to God. In thankfulness, freedom starts to press the issue. Faith, which is nothing other than receiving, is a taut coil springing creatively into action for the common good. . . . For believers know that since God has done enough for our *salvation*, we can never do enough for the *good* of the world. . . . There is no more liberating basis for ethics than the doctrine of justification of sinners by faith alone.[80]

In making thankfulness the root of deeds, Jüngel follows the familiar biblical and Reformation path. The Heidelberg Catechism in fact is divided into the three parts of guilt, grace, and gratitude. The key is to ensure that the right doctrines come under the right headings, or the Decalogue may be misplaced under the second.

It is significant that Paul sees *ingratitude* as the root of idolatry and immorality in Romans 1:21. Relieved of the burden of the guilt, condemnation, and dominion of sin and the law, believers go on their way rejoicing. Since their works cannot serve God, their energy and service are freed for the neighbor who needs them. Returning to our house justified like the tax-collector in Jesus's parable (Luke 18:14), we find someone to cherish as a gift rather than to dread as a threat to our autonomy. "Because of justification," argued the Puritan William Ames, "the defilement of good works does not prevent their being

---

80. Eberhard Jüngel, *Justification: The Heart of the Christian Faith*, trans. Jeffrey E. Cayzer (London: T&T Clark, 2001), 259.

accepted and rewarded by God."[81] Justification is not the enemy of inner renewal, love, ethical activity, or rewards. On the contrary, justification is the only basis on which any of these other gifts is possible.

THE MEANS OF EFFECTING AND STRENGTHENING UNION

If faith is the instrument of our being united to Christ, where does this faith come from? In many of the proposals that we have encountered in this volume, it is unclear how union with Christ comes about. Evidently, there is no event of being united here and now to Christ, no temporal distinction between redemption accomplished and applied. For most of the Christian traditions, however, this union is accomplished by the Holy Spirit at a certain point in one's life. Most churches hold that the Word is a means (if not the primary means) of the Spirit's uniting sinners to Christ, while many also see baptism and the Eucharist as means of grace and Orthodox and Roman Catholic traditions add other sacraments as well. It is beyond our scope to offer a full treatment of this topic, but if we are faithful to the New Testament some inclusion is important for concluding this study of justification.

Word and Faith

We have seen the tendency either to confuse or to separate things that God has joined together without losing their own integrity: law and gospel, *historia* and *ordo*, individual and church, soteriology and ecclesiology, justification and sanctification, legal and transformative, norm and relationship, redemptive-historical and apocalyptic, Christology and pneumatology, already and not-yet, and so forth. To these may be added a tendency either to conflate or separate the means of grace and the gift of grace. We have seen repeatedly that the primary target for the backlash against Protestant interpretation of justification is an individualistic, voluntaristic, and contractual soteriology. This target does actually exist; indeed, it is widely pervasive, especially in a Protestantism that has been shaped by a pietistic-revivalist heritage. In this milieu, union with Christ and justification become not only a personal but often private affair, with little connection to the socializing

---

81. William Ames, *The Marrow of Theology*, ed. John Dykstra Eusden (Grand Rapids: Baker Academic, 1997), 171.

word and sacraments through which Christ by his Spirit creates and sustains faith.

In contrast, Paul teaches that faith comes by hearing the word of God, specifically the gospel (Rom 10:17). The first mark of the church is the preaching of the word. Through his word and Spirit (never separated), Christ is truly present in the world.[82] God created the world by the words of his mouth and by his speech also brings a new creation into being. Through the proclamation of his word, God is not just speaking about what might happen if we bring it about but is actually speaking it into being. As God proclaims his gospel, a church is created, sustained, expanded, and deepened. Hence, the repeated announcement in Acts, "the word of God spread," is equivalent to "the church grew." Thus, the church is the creation neither of a papal hierarchy nor of the decision of many people willing, but of the word (*creatura verbi*). Herman Ridderbos notes that Jesus was not just preaching a promise during his earthly ministry, yet his preaching inaugurated its reality: "His word is not only a sign, it is charged with power. . . . For the new and unprecedented thing here is not that forgiveness is being *announced*, but that it is being *accomplished on earth*."[83] His word brings the kingdom with it, and it is founded in his blood. Thus, only as prophet and priest is Jesus Christ also the king.

Even now the "age to come" is reconfiguring reality around its glorified head. The time that the church thus occupies because of the ascension is defined neither by full presence nor full absence but by a eucharistic tension between "this age" and "the age to come." Douglas Farrow succinctly expresses this point:

> The comfort of the *Christus praesens* is clearly grounded in the stubborn and troubling fact of the *Christus absens*. . . . Covenant history and world history have divided in this departure, for in and with Jesus the former has already reached its goal. In the resulting gap a place has opened up for the eucharistic community as a genuinely new entity within world history, albeit a peculiar one with its own peculiar view of the way things are.[84]

---

82. Selderhuis, *Calvin's Theology of the Psalms*, 134.
83. Herman Ridderbos, *The Coming of the Kingdom* (St. Catherines, Ontario: Paideia, 1979), 73–74.
84. Ridderbos, *The Coming of the Kingdom,* 37, 40.

Christ's repatriation in our exalted humanity marks a radical detour from the form of this present age, ensuring that it is passing away and therefore does not have the last word. Yet because it is *Christ's* repatriation, this detour is not away from this world as nature and history but toward its future consummation beyond sin and death. The preaching of the gospel is not merely instruction or exhortation; it is "the power of God for salvation" (Rom 1:16). This event does not merely provide the occasion and impetus for people to regenerate themselves by accepting the information for and exhortation to faith. Rather, it is through this proclaimed gospel that the Spirit creates faith.

Like Luther, Calvin called this proclamation of the gospel the "sacramental word" because it is not only instruction about Christ but is Christ's means of uniting us to himself.[85] Instead of driving us deeper into our individual selves, this preached word draws us out of ourselves to cling to Christ (Westminster Larger Catechism, Q. 155) and therefore to each other as members together of his body. We hear this word together and are thereby made one people, confessing sins, gathering in common faith and prayer. We are baptized into Christ and therefore into his visible church, always in a public gathering of his people, and are made more and more one with Christ, the members with their head, in the Lord's Supper. Faith is therefore personal but never private. Nor is it a transaction in which God merely promises to give something (e.g., salvation) if we promise to give something of our own (e.g., faith and obedience). Rather, Christ comes to deliver *himself* and all his gifts *to us* through this very human and frail ministry of preaching and sacrament. Even the faith to receive Christ with his gifts is created and sealed by Christ's own operation by his Spirit through these creaturely means. B. A. Gerrish explains, "It is crucial to Calvin's interpretation that the gospel is not a mere invitation to fellowship with Christ, but the effective means by which the communion with Christ comes about."[86] In proclaiming God's Word, the minister is not merely describing a new creation and exhorting us to enter into it; through this proclamation, Christ himself is speaking a new creation into being.[87]

---

85. B. A. Gerrish, *Grace and Gratitude: The Eucharistic Theology of John Calvin* (Minneapolis: Augsburg Fortress, 1993), 85, referring to *Inst.* 4.14.4.

86. Gerrish, *Grace and Gratitude*, 84. His references to Calvin are from *Inst.* 3.5.5.

87. See *Inst.* 3.2.6–7; 3.2.28–30; 4.14.4. See also Gerrish, *Grace and Gratitude*, 84–85.

In the words of the Second Helvetic Confession, "The preached Word is the Word of God."[88] The biblical canon is the completed foundation, and the preached word is the primary means of the Spirit's ongoing building project. Even in this present evil age we "taste of the goodness of the word of God and the powers of the age to come" (Heb 6:5). Without the work of the Spirit, the word would fall on deaf ears, but the Spirit opens deaf ears *through* the external word.[89] Following the logic of Romans 10, Calvin emphasizes that we must refuse any contrast between the outer and inner word.[90]

For Rome, faith is created by the church; for the Anabaptists, faith is created by the free will of the individual, but for the magisterial Reformers, faith is created by the Spirit through the word. Faith is not merely the believer's response to the word but is created through the word and sealed by the sacraments (Heidelberg Catechism, Q. 65). No medium is more suited to God's objective promise-making than preaching. John Leith observes, "For Calvin as for Luther, 'The ears alone are the organ of the Christian.'"[91]

Calvin also shares Luther's view that it is specifically the preaching of the *gospel* that is the primary means of salvation. Especially from Paul, and assisted by Augustine's *The Spirit and the Letter*, Luther came to distinguish the law and the gospel as the two ways God speaks to us.[92] This emphasis is just as clear in Calvin (as well as his Reformed colleagues and theological heirs).[93] Calvin points out that "faith through

---

88. The Second Helvetic Confession, in *The Constitution of the Presbyterian Church (U.S.A.): Part I, Book of Confessions* (Louisville: Office of the General Assembly, 1991), ch. 1.

89. Calvin, *Calvin's New Testament Commentaries*, vol. 4, *The Gospel According to St. John, 1–10*, ed. David W. Torrance and Thomas F. Torrance, trans. T. H. L. Parker (Grand Rapids: Eerdmans, 1959–72), on John 15:27.

90. *Inst.* 4.1.5–6.

91. John H. Leith, "Doctrine of the Proclamation of the Word," in *John Calvin and the Church: A Prism of Reform*, ed. Timothy George (Louisville: Westminster John Knox, 1990), 212.

92. W. H. T. Dau, *The Proper Distinction Between Law and Gospel: Thirty-Nine Evening Lectures* (St. Louis: Concordia, 1929): Luther wrote, "Hence, whoever knows well this art of distinguishing between the Law and the Gospel, him place at the head and call him a doctor of Holy Scripture." See the Apology to the Augsburg Confession (1531), Art. 4. Article 5 of the Formula of Concord adds, "We believe, teach, and confess that the distinction between the Law and the Gospel is to be maintained in the Church with great diligence" (F. Bente and W. H. T. Dau, eds. and trans., *Triglot Concordia: The Symbolical Books of the Evangelical Lutheran Church* [St. Louis: Concordia Publishing House, 1921]).

93. Wilhelm Niesel observes, "Reformed theology recognises the contrast between Law and Gospel, in a way similar to Lutheranism. We read in the Second Helvetic Confession: 'The Gospel is indeed opposed to the Law. For the Law works wrath and pronounces a curse, whereas the Gospel preaches grace and blessing'" (Niesel, *Reformed Symbolics: A Comparison of Catholicism, Orthodoxy and Protestantism*, trans. David Lewis [Edinburgh: Oliver and Boyd, 1962], 217). See Michael Horton, "Calvin and the Law-Gospel Hermeneutic," *Pro Ecclesia* 6 (1997): 27–42; Horton,

the word of the gospel" is the proper formula for Paul. When Paul specifically refers to "the word of faith that we preach" (Rom 10:8), he means the gospel.[94] "Faith is not produced by every part of the Word of God, for the warnings, admonitions and threatened judgments will not instill the confidence and peace requisite for true faith."[95] "This is the true knowledge of Christ: if we take him as he is offered by the Father, namely, *clothed with his gospel.* For as he himself has been designated the goal of our faith, so we shall not run straight to him unless the gospel leads the way."[96]

Without the clear and regular proclamation of the gospel, faith shrivels along with its fruit. Once this sacramental aspect of God's word is embraced, we are able also to affirm that it teaches us truths to be believed and exhorts us to obey its commands. It not only creates and sustains our faith but also regulates our doctrine and life.

Baptism and Faith

Paul does not see circumcision or baptism as an external sign of inward grace, nor as a symbol of something else, but as the seal of God's pledge. Baptism is the public, visible, and real participation in the apocalyptic in-breaking of the kingdom of God, the new creation with Christ as the inaugural prototype. Like many distinctions, the external-internal dichotomy is drawn from a Neoplatonist anthropology rather than from the eschatological division between "this age" (flesh) and "the age to come" (Spirit) as announced by the prophets, reflected in the less Hellenized (i.e., less Philonic) texts of early Judaism, and extrapolated in the New Testament.

Aquinas held that while the old covenant sacraments (especially circumcision) were valid through faith in the coming Christ, the sacraments of the "new law" are actually effectual in regenerating and remitting sin.[97] The great Franciscan theologian Bonaventure held that sacraments merely afford occasions for the Spirit to work rather than being means of grace in themselves. It was against Bonaventure's view that Aquinas defended an *ex opere operato* formulation of the sacraments.[98]

"Law and Gospel, with Response by Mark Garcia," in *The Confessional Presbyterian* 8 (2012): 154–76.

94. Calvin, *Calvin's Commentaries*, 19:389–91 (on Rom 10:8).
95. I. John Hesselink, *Calvin's Concept of the Law* (Allison Park, PA: Pickwick, 1992), 28.
96. Hesselink, *Calvin's Concept of the Law*, 3.2.6, emphasis added.
97. Cross, *Duns Scotus*, 136, from *ST* 3.62.4.
98. Cross, *Duns Scotus*, 136, referring to *ST* 3.62.1.

After Aquinas, Duns Scotus followed his Franciscan forebear, even radicalizing his teaching in the direction of what we might call from the sixteenth-century perspective a more "Zwinglian" view.[99]

Settling these differences within the medieval schools, the Council of Trent formulated an explicit *ex opere operato* interpretation. Cardinal Newman explains, "Or, in other words, Faith justifies, *because* Baptism has justified."[100] Faith is "the instrument of justification after Baptism."[101] More recently, Michael Schmaus argues that faith and baptism "form a unified whole (Mark 16:16), but faith is the more comprehensive and formative element."

> This arises from the fact that the word is the formative element of the sacrament. Just as the saving word of preaching takes concrete, visible form in the enactment of the saving sign (sacrament), so faith embodies itself in the reception of baptism. . . . Through the reception of the sacrament in which faith attains visible form the believer takes hold of the salvation present in the sacrament (cf. Basil, *On the Holy Spirit*, 12).[102]

According to Trent, nothing before faith merits justification; faith is the ground, root, and foundation of it all.[103] But not faith alone.[104] Faith is assent to the gospel's truth. "This is first a *fides generalis*. However, the council also stressed the *fides actualis et individualis*. According to the council, one who in the acknowledgement of his own sinfulness affirms Jesus Christ has undergone a stirring experience and thus is confident that God will remit his sins for Christ's sake."[105] It is not faith *and* works, but a working faith that justifies.[106]

As we have seen at various points along the way, a growing number of evangelical scholars, often reacting against a more traditional evangelical antisacramentalism, embrace an essentially Roman Catholic view (especially of baptism in relation to faith), insisting that the Reformation

---

99. Cross, *Duns Scotus*, 136, referring to *ST* 3.62.1.

100. John Henry Newman, *Lectures on the Doctrine of Justification*, 3rd ed. (London: Rivington's, 1874; repr., Nashotah, 2012), 232.

101. Newman, *Lectures on the Doctrine of Justification*, 251.

102. Schmaus, *Dogma*, 6:33.

103. Council of Trent, Session 6, ch. 8, DS 1532.

104. Schmaus, *Dogma*, 6:32–33. See Council of Trent, Session 6, Canon 9, DS 1559; Canon 12, DS 1562; and esp. ch. 9, DS 1533.

105. Schmaus, *Dogma*, 6:33.

106. Schmaus, *Dogma*, 6:34.

was an unfortunate product of late medieval nominalism (i.e., Duns Scotus and William of Ockham).[107] However, even Luther singled out Scotus's view (as well as Thomas's) for censure in the Smalcald Articles:

> Baptism is nothing else than the Word of God in the water, commanded by His institution, or, as Paul says, *a washing in the Word*; as also Augustine says: *Let the Word come to the element, and it becomes a Sacrament.* And for this reason we do not hold with Thomas and the monastic preachers [Dominicans] who forget the Word (God's institution) and say that God has imparted to the water a spiritual power, which through the water washes away sin. Nor [do we agree] with Scotus and the Barefooted monks [Minorites or Franciscan monks], who teach that, by the assistance of the divine will, Baptism washes away sins, and that this ablution occurs only through the will of God, and by no means through the Word or water.[108]

As I observed in volume 1, Reformers such as Bucer, Vermigli, and Zanchi were traditional Augustinian-Dominican Thomists in their metaphysical system. To the extent that Calvin was trained in philosophy as a master of arts student at the University of Paris, he leaned in a traditional direction and explicitly singed out the nominalists for reproach.

For Reformed theology, the word and the sacraments link the *historia salutis* (Christ's incarnation, life, death, resurrection, ascension) to the *ordo salutis* (the application of redemption to the believer). "For in his flesh was accomplished man's redemption," he argues.[109] Calvin employs the realistic language of the patristic era to affirm this bond created by the Spirit between *signum* and *res*. "Christ communicates his

---

107. A major source of this trend is a rediscovery of the *nouvelle théologie* associated with Henri de Lubac, Hans Urs von Balthasar, and the Radical Orthodoxy movement identified especially with John Milbank. Christian Reformed theologian Hans Boersma contends, "The Reformation teaching of justification by faith alone (*sola fide*), exemplified a great deal of continuity with the nominalist tradition. This continuity centered on the imputation of Christ's righteousness." Boersma, *Heavenly Participation: The Weaving of a Sacramental Tapestry* (Grand Rapids: Eerdmans, 2011), 92; cf. Boersma, *Nouvelle Theologie and Sacramental Ontology* (New York: Oxford University Press, 2013). Peter J. Leithart, a minister of the Communion of Reformed Evangelical Churches, argues similarly that the Reformation was an unfortunate product of late medieval nominalism. For him, baptism is not only the sign and seal but the instrumental cause of union with Christ (Leithart, *Delivered from the Elements of the World*, 182, 187–91, 222–23, 228).

108. The Smalcald Articles 3.5, "Of Baptism," in *Book of Concord: Confessions of the Evangelical Lutheran Church*, ed. and trans. Robert Kolb and Timothy Wengert (Minneapolis: Fortress, 2000).

109. Calvin, *Calvin's New Testament Commentaries*, vol. 4, *The Gospel According to John, 1–10*, ed. David W. Torrance and Thomas F. Torrance, trans. T. H. L. Parker (Grand Rapids: Eerdmans, 1959–72), 167.

riches and blessings to us by his word," writes Calvin, "so he distributes them to us by his sacraments."[110] The Spirit creates faith through the Word, says Calvin. "But the sacraments bring the clearest promises."[111] "For baptism attests to us that we have been cleansed and washed; the Eucharistic Supper, that we have been redeemed."[112]

On the heels of treating justification, the Heidelberg Catechism (1564) asks, "Then from where does this true faith come?" and answers, "The Holy Spirit creates it in our hearts by the preaching of the holy gospel and confirms it through the use of the holy sacraments."[113] At least according to the Reformed symbols, Scripture treats the sacraments as instruments of covenant ratification, as in Paul's language of "sign and seal" in Romans 4:11.

Calvin saw in both Roman Catholic and Anabaptist views a common tendency to treat sacraments as human works. However, Calvin argues, "In Sacraments God alone properly acts; men bring nothing of their own."[114] God is the promise-maker. "Baptism testifies to us our purgation and ablution; the Eucharistic supper testifies our redemption. Water is a figure of ablution [washing], and blood of satisfaction."[115] "Christ communicates his riches and blessings to us by his word," writes Calvin, "so he distributes them to us by his sacraments."[116] The Spirit creates faith through the Word, says Calvin. "But the sacraments bring the clearest promises."[117] "For baptism attests to us that we have been cleansed and washed; the Eucharistic Supper, that we have been redeemed."[118] While denying that they confer salvation apart from faith, he says that "they are not empty and naked signs of a distant grace."[119] According to Calvin, Rome binds God to earthly means, while the Anabaptists disallow that God can freely bind himself to them.[120]

---

110. Calvin, "Form for Administration of the Sacraments," in *Selected Works of John Calvin: Tracts and Letters*, ed. Henry Beveridge and Jules Bonnet, 7 vols. (Grand Rapids: Baker, 1983), 2:115.

111. *Inst.* 4.14.5.

112. *Inst.* 4.14.22.

113. Heidelberg Catechism, LD 24, Q. 64.

114. Calvin, "Antidote to Trent," in *Acts of the Council of Trent: With the Antidote*, in *Selected Works of John Calvin: Tracts and Letters*, 7 vols., ed. Henry Beveridge and Jules Bonnet, trans. Henry Beveridge (Grand Rapids: Baker, 1983), 3:176.

115. *Inst.* 4.14.22.

116. Calvin, "Form for Administration of the Sacraments," 2:115.

117. *Inst.* 4.14.5.

118. *Inst.* 4.14.22.

119. Calvin, *Selected Works of John Calvin: Tracts and Letters*, vol. 3, *Acts and Antidote*, ed. Henry Beveridge and Jules Bonnet, trans. Henry Beveridge (repr., Grand Rapids: Baker, 1983), 175, emphasis added.

120. *Inst.* 4.1.5.

For generations, especially through the influence of pietism and revivalism, Anglo-American Protestantism has leaned in a decidedly "Zwinglian" direction. Though he did not take it as far as the Anabaptists, Zwingli assumed a Platonic dualism between sign and reality, spirit and matter, God's work and the church's ministry. "For faith springs not from things accessible to sense nor are they objects of faith," he insisted.[121] However, Calvin had early on rejected the contrast between "flesh" and "Spirit" as equivalent to "matter" and "spirit."[122] In short, he saw the physical aspect as the means chosen by God for delivering and strengthening the spiritual communion with Christ.[123] As evidenced in the *Antidote to the Council of Trent*, it becomes clear that for Calvin the central issue is *solo Christo*: Christ alone "as he is clothed in the gospel."[124] Even Roman Catholic scholars who have studied Calvin's work closely point up his realistic view of the sacraments as means of grace, as opposed to Zwingli and the Anabaptists. Roman Catholic scholar Kilian McDonnell, OSB, observes, "Rather than denying the real presence" in the Eucharist "he presupposes it. None of the Reformers defended it more forcibly than Calvin."[125]

Some readers may be wondering what justification has to do with the sacraments. "Everything," the Reformers would reply. When anxious parishioners felt that the good news was for others and that they remained under God's judgment, the Reformers could point them to their union with Christ made visible and tangible in their baptism. The same apostle who proclaimed the justification of the ungodly through faith alone also taught that baptism is the sign and seal of God's gracious covenant and that the Holy Supper also assures us of our justification. Even when we are convinced of the truth of this amazing doctrine, it is easy to turn back into ourselves in practice apart from a robust sense of the Spirit's working through these means that Christ has appointed for our good.

---

121. Huldrych Zwingli, *Commentary on True and False Religion*, ed. Samuel Macauley Jackson and Clarence Nevin Heller, trans. Samuel Macauley Jackson (Durham, NC: Labyrinth, 1981), 214. Of course, if followed consistently (which, happily, he did not do), one wonders how faith could come by *hearing* (Rom 10:17).

122. Calvin, *Calvin's Commentaries*, 19:224–25 (on Rom 6:6).

123. Willem Balke, *Calvin and the Anabaptist Radicals*, trans. William J. Heynen (Grand Rapids: Eerdmans, 1981), 53.

124. *Inst.* 3.2.32.

125. Kilian McDonnell, OSB, *John Calvin, The Eucharist and the Church* (Princeton: Princeton University Press, 1967), 224. Yves Congar adds concerning Luther and Calvin, "Both Reformers kept to a middle road, or rather a synthesis, and each in his own way insisted on a close relationship between an external 'instrument' of grace . . . and the activity of the Spirit" (Yves Congar, *I Believe in the Holy Spirit*, trans. David Smith [New York: Crossroad, 1997], 138).

There has been a resurgence of "Calvinism" within evangelicalism recently in North America and beyond. However, it may surprise many to learn that, despite their differences, both Lutheran and Reformed confessions are no less opposed to the Anabaptist than the Roman Catholic views of the sacraments. Until this part of the Reformation heritage is rediscovered, otherwise admirable defenses of justification will lack a crucial dimension, and the fateful dichotomies that we have encountered will only continue to find fresh targets.

Union with Christ and the Communion of Saints

United to Christ, we are simultaneously united to his body. Because we truly feed on Christ in the Lord's Supper, we are drawn "both to purity and holiness of life, and also to charity, peace, and concord" with each other.[126] Although each of us receives Christ personally, no one receives him privately. Just as we are made part of his new creation together through the public preaching of the word, we feed on Christ's body and blood together as coheirs of a common estate. "Christ, presenting himself to us, not only invites us by his example to give and devote ourselves mutually to each other, but inasmuch as he makes himself common to all, [he] also makes us all to be one in him." From the fellowship with Christ in the Supper,

> We will take care that none of our brethren is hurt, despised, rejected, injured, or in any way offended, without our, at the same time, hurting, despising, and injuring Christ; that we cannot have dissension with our brethren, without at the same time dissenting from Christ; that we cannot love Christ without loving our brethren; that the same care we take of our own body we ought to take of that of our brethren, who are members of our body; that as no part of our body suffers pain without extending to the other parts, so every evil which our brother suffers ought to excite our compassion.[127]

Grace leads to gratitude—a thanksgiving toward God that turns us outward to our brothers and sisters and then also out to our neighbors, whoever they may be. Luther observed that God does not need our

---

126. *Inst.* 4.17.38. See also 1 Cor 10:15–16.
127. *Inst.* 4.17.38.

good works but our neighbors do.[128] Similarly, for Calvin, "The only way to serve God well is to serve our fellow believers. Since our good deeds cannot reach God anyway, he gives us instead other believers unto whom we can do good deeds. The one who wants to love God can do so by loving the believers."[129]

THE GOAL OF UNION

Because of the Spirit, who unites us to Christ, we can pass from the guilt offering to the peace offering—to the life of thanksgiving for which we were created. It is striking that when Paul relates our "sacrifice" to old covenant types, it is not to the atonement offering for guilt but to the "living sacrifice of praise" (Rom 12:1–2), the thank offering. Christ gave himself as the guilt offering and in his resurrection became the firstfruits as well. And now, "If the dough offered as firstfruits is holy, so is the whole lump, and if the root is holy, so are the branches" (Rom 11:16). We enter through the torn veil of his flesh to enter the Holy of Holies and join our fellow guests at the feast.

However, we have not yet located our identity on the christocentric map until we have recognized our participation in Christ's *ascension*. The ascension is not merely an exclamation mark for the resurrection; it is a new stage in Christ's life and ministry that guarantees a further event of salvation for us. Having laid the basis for this in the *historia salutis* in chapter 6, we now connect it to the final link in the *ordo salutis*: glorification.

Even to the very end, Jesus fulfills the eternal pledge to the Father and the Spirit as mediator of his elect. "There is no gift that has not been earned by Him," as Vos observes.[130] He adds,

> [Robert] Rollock already demonstrates how the work of the Mediator with respect to the covenant of grace was nothing but a carrying through in him of the covenant of works broken in Adam. "Christ, therefore, our Mediator, subjected himself unto the covenant of works, and unto the law for our sake, and did both fulfil the condition of the covenant of works in his holy and good life . . .

---

128. Luther, "The Freedom of a Christian," in *LW* 31:351.
129. Selderhuis, *Calvin's Theology of the Psalms*, 235.
130. Vos, *The Pauline Eschatology*, 248.

and also did undergo that curse with which man was threatened in that covenant of works, if that condition of good and holy works were not kept. . . . Wherefore we see Christ in two respects, to wit, in doing and suffering, subject to the covenant of works, and in both respects he has most perfectly fulfilled it, and that for our sake whose Mediator he is become" (Rollock, *Works*, I, 52f).[131]

We have so far referred to glorification in its relation to Christ's intercession and entrance into glory in our humanity. With these themes in mind, we come to the most controversial aspect of this doctrine and one that, in comparison with previous eras, has received too little attention in contemporary Reformed theology.

The doctrine known most familiarly in the West as glorification or the beatific vision is referred to in the Christian East as deification or *theōsis*.[132] It may surprise some, including Calvinists, that Calvin considered "deification"—the most perfect participation in God by grace possible for a creature—"the greatest thing" conceivable.[133] He writes, "Let us mark that the end of the gospel is to render us eventually conformable to God, and, if we may so speak, to deify us." Nevertheless, he immediately adds,

But the word nature [in 2 Pet 1:4] is not here *essence* but *quality*. The Manicheans formerly dreamt that we are a part of God, and

---

131. Vos, *The Pauline Eschatology*, 249.

132. For descriptions of deification from Orthodox theologians, see Vladimir Lossky, *The Mystical Theology of the Eastern Church* (Crestwood, NJ: St. Vladimir's Seminary Press, 1997), 29–33. I devote more than a chapter to deification in *Covenant and Salvation: Union with Christ* (Louisville: Westminster John Knox, 2007), first in dialogue with new Finnish proposals, 174–80, 209, 214–15, 306, and then in conversation with the Orthodox doctrine of theosis in chapter 14. On various approaches to deification, see in relation to Calvin, Carl Mosser, "The Greatest Possible Blessing: Calvin and Deification," *Scottish Journal of Theology* 55, no. 1 (2002): 34–50; A. J. Ollerton, "Quasi Deificari: Deification in the Theology of John Calvin," *Westminster Theological Journal* (2011): 251. In relation to Aquinas, see Daniel Keating, "Justification, Sanctification and Divinization in Thomas Aquinas," in *Aquinas on Doctrine*, ed. Thomas Weinandy et al. (T&T Clark, 2004), 139–58. Some evangelicals, like Pentecostal-Lutheran theologian Veli-Matti Kärkkäinen, are attracted to the new Finnish Perspective on Luther, which treats deification as an alternative to forensic justification ("Salvation as Justification and Deification: In Search of an Ecumenical Convergence"). Arguing that Luther himself favored the former while confessional Lutheranism (following Melanchthon) took the latter route, this view builds on Gustaf Aulén's highly contested work. The same is true on the Reformed side with those influenced by Thomas F. Torrance (including Douglas Campbell), for whom a poorly understood Melanchthon and federal theologians provides the foil of "justification theory." But the new view is closer to that of Andreas Osiander, rejected not only by fellow Lutherans but by Calvin (who added a new section of refutation to the final 1559 *Institutes*). On this point, see Carl Trueman, "Is the Finnish Line a New Beginning?" in the *Westminster Theological Journal* 65, no. 2 (2003): 231–44. See also Robert W. Jenson's response to Trueman in the same volume.

133. *Inst.* 3.25.10.

that after having run the race of life we shall at length return to our original. There are also at this day fanatics who imagine that we thus pass over into the nature of God, so that he swallows up our nature. . . . But such a delirium never entered the minds of the holy Apostles; they only intended to say that when divested of all the vices of the flesh, we shall be partakers of divine and blessed immortality and glory, so as to be as it were one with God *as far as our capacities will allow.*[134]

"Plato recognized man's highest nature as union with God," yet even he "could not even dimly sense its nature apart from Christ." Far from raising our minds away from the body to incorporeal universals, Calvin says that "they alone receive the fruit of Christ's benefits who raise their minds *to the resurrection.*"[135] As Philip Walker Butin points out, "Calvin's most complete definition of the *imago Dei* in the *Institutes* is based on the assumption that 'the true nature of the image of God is to be derived from what scripture says of its renewal through Christ.'"[136] The justified are assured that they will be raised bodily, free of the curse of sin and death, for the glorifying—indeed deifying—vision of God.

There are two ways to be "deified" in the history of the church's reflection. The first way is for the divine part of us to be swallowed up in the divine world (the One or God), that is, by being *freed of our humanity* with its bondage to the material world and history. The purest version of this thesis is ἕνωσις (*henōsis*), as found in Indian and Greek religions and refined by Plotinus.[137] Although Origen was a Christian presbyter and teacher, his views were controversial in his own time, and after his death the Christian East judged several of his teachings heretical (including universal salvation and the pantheistic implications of his thought).

---

134. Calvin, *Calvin's Commentaries*, 22:371, emphasis added.

135. *Inst.* 3.25.2, emphasis added.

136. Philip Walker Butin, *Revelation, Redemption, and Response: Calvin's Trinitarian Understanding of the Divine-Human Relationship* (New York: Oxford University Press, 1995), 68.

137. Influenced by Indian religious thought as he encountered it in Alexandria, Plotinus sought to mediate Plato's thought in a system that became known as Neoplatonism. He writes in his *Enneads*, "To this end [of *henōsis*], you must set free your soul from all outward things and turn wholly within yourself, with no more leaning to what lies outside, and lay your mind bare of ideal forms, as before of the objects of sense, and forget even yourself, and so come within sight of that One" (6.9.7). The goal of the ascent is that one "remembers who he became when he merged with the One," without even consciousness of his own personal existence (6.9.11). Plotinus, *The Enneads*, ed. Stephen MacKenna, LP Classic Reprint Series (New York: Larson, 1992).

Despite his orthodox intention, Origen's view of deification, at least in *On First Principles*, can be seen as a variation of *henōsis*. In any case, he conceived of deification in terms of the believer's ascent of mind corresponding to that of Jesus. At the cross, says Origen, "the dispensation of the flesh was ended."[138] We must no longer think of Christ as a human being circumscribed by space. "For it is not a man who is 'wherever two or three are gathered in' his 'name' (Mt 18:20); nor is a man 'with' us 'always, to the close of the age' (Mt 28:20); and when the faithful are gathered everywhere, what is present is not a man but the divine power that was in Jesus."[139] Similarly, Origen counsels, the soul that will "climb to the heights of heaven shall no longer be a man, but according to his word, will be 'like an angel of God'" or perhaps divine; but in either case, "he shall certainly no longer be a man."[140]

The second way to think about deification (or *theōsis*, as it is typically designated in the Orthodox tradition) is for our *human nature to be perfected by grace*, that is, brought to its fulfillment with the image of God not only restored but fully and immutably confirmed in righteousness.[141] This deification can only occur by the power of the Spirit. Our spirit cannot ascend and be absorbed into the Godhead. That would be fatal for us since "our God is a consuming fire" (Heb 12:29). Instead, the Holy Spirit—God himself—descends and unites us to Christ our head.

This was the path of Irenaeus, particularly as he battled the Gnostics, whose worldview shared important similarities with Neoplatonism.[142] For Irenaeus and his heirs, however, deification is our true humaniza-

---

138. Origen, *Spirit and Fire*, 135.

139. Origen, *Spirit and Fire*, 136–38.

140. Origen, *Spirit and Fire*, 358. In the soul's fall before the creation of this world, "because he abandoned life and chose death, man became a human being; and not just a human being, but also earth. . . . In the resurrection, however, the flesh will cleave to the soul and will become a soul which . . . will become 'one spirit with him' (1 Cor 6:17), and become a 'spiritual body' (1 Cor 15:44)."

141. This contrast between Irenaeus and Origen is admittedly a gross generalization. Origen displayed enormous reverence for Scripture and the rule of faith, even if he interpreted it in a Neoplatonist frame. Further, the Cappadocian fathers, who formulated the Orthodox doctrine, were sympathetic to Origen while still rejecting his most controversial ideas. Neoplatonism was the air that the early fathers breathed, but some were more successful in allowing the biblical narrative to challenge inherited assumptions. As Roman Catholic theologian Michael Schmaus notes, the concept of deification was developed especially in the fourth century by the great Cappadocian theologians. "In the translation of Platonic ideas to the realm of Christian teaching on salvation, the scriptural texts concerning the only-begotten Son of God (Jn 1:14), the firstborn among many brothers (Rom. 8:29; Col. 1:15), and the indwelling of the Spirit became the foundation of the deification theory" (Schmaus, *Dogma*, 6:46–47).

142. So much so, in fact, that Plotinus wrote a diatribe against the Gnostics (as he had the Christians), many of whom had been his former students.

tion in union with Christ. Athanasius insists that we will be deified only in the Son "without losing our own proper substance."[143] Irenaeus had made the same point: "Neither is the substance nor the essence of the creation annihilated."[144] The Son "became what we are, that He might bring us to be even what He is Himself," says Irenaeus.[145] A little later, he stipulates that this consummate union "will render us like unto [Christ]."[146] Deification is the full realization of the gifts of immortality, complete restoration of the image of God, adoption, and the vision of God in Christ.[147] Irenaeus's and Athanasius's accounts are united by a Trinitarian, christocentric, and pneumatological pattern that instead of transcending humanity and this world's history *saves* it by uniting humanity to the glorified humanity of Christ—not by a "casting away of the flesh," Irenaeus insists, "but by the imparting of the Spirit."[148] Glorification is our true humanization.[149] "The glory of God," he says marvelously, "is a human fully alive."[150]

Douglas Farrow suggests that Calvin, like Irenaeus, brought attention back to the economy and thus to the *problem* of Christ's absence. "'But why,' asked Calvin, 'do we repeat the word "ascension" so often?' To answer in our own words, it was because he found it necessary to reckon more bravely than the other Reformers with the absence of Christ as

---

143. Athanasius, *De Decretis* 3.14 (*NPNF*² 4:159); cf. Athanasius, *Against the Arians*, 1.39 (*NPNF*² 4:329).

144. *Haer.* 5.36.1 (*ANF* 1:566).

145. *Haer.*, preface to Book 5 (*ANF* 1:526).

146. *Haer.* 5.8.1 (*ANF* 1:533).

147. Carl Mosser notes that in the Orthodox tradition deification includes motifs such as adoption, participation in God, immortality, restoration of the *imago Dei*, glorification, and "consummation of the marriage between Christ and the Church." Carl Mosser, "The Greatest Possible Blessing: Calvin and Deification," *Scottish Journal of Theology* 55, no. 1 (2002): 36.

148. Canlis, *Calvin's Ladder*, 183–84, quoting *Haer.* 581.

149. Reflecting a proper wariness of the pantheism rife in neo-Protestantism as well as in some versions of Roman Catholic piety, Barth wrote, "God becomes man in order that man may—not become God, but come to God" (*CD* IV/2, 106). However, this also reflects Barth's own Zwinglian presuppositions. Especially in the Eucharistic debates, Calvin criticized Zwingli's overreaction against the domestication of God by underscoring with Paul the importance of our being united to Christ's humanity (and therefore to God in Christ) for our salvation. It was not merely his divinity that saved us, but Christ the God-man. (Interestingly, Zwingli did affirm deification without any apology [Stephens, *Theology of Huldrych Zwingli* (Oxford: Clarendon, 1988), 56–67], but he was not working with the sort of Christological assumptions that could warrant a sound conception of it.) Properly understood, the Athanasian formula in no way threatens the Creator-creature distinction. Deification is always qualified by "as far as it is possible for a creature to be," "not a mixture of essences," and so forth. The point is that when we are united to Christ, we become more and more like God—in other words, like the human images of God that we were created to be. It is the moral attributes, not the incommunicable attributes, that the patristic sources have in mind. Barth's substitute formula elides the mystical union of God and human beings in Jesus Christ through the power of the Spirit.

150. *Haer.* 4.20.7 (*ANF* 1:490, which reads, "The glory of God is a living man").

a genuine problem for the church." Apart from the ascension in the flesh, says Calvin, we are robbed of Christ's likeness to us; we lose the significance of the Spirit's role in uniting us to the ascended Christ, and the reality of Christ's bodily return is called into question. More like Irenaeus, then, Calvin returns our focus to the economy of redemption, that is, to the actual history of Jesus of Nazareth from descent (incarnation and his earthly ministry of redemption) to his ascension and heavenly ministry and to the Parousia at the end of the age.[151]

Like Calvin, the most formative Reformed theologians were happy to speak interchangeably of glorification and deification, identifying this event with the resurrection of the dead as one event that glorifies us in body as well as soul.[152] In his commentary on the Westminster Confession, Thomas Watson rhapsodizes concerning the soul's reunion with its flesh, concluding, "The dust of a believer is part of Christ's mystic body."[153]

For those conditioned by the false choices of current discussions (as well as classic Orthodox-Catholic-Protestant debates), this may seem strange. Indeed, Luther too considered deification to be the goal of justification without, as the new Finnish school argues, collapsing the latter into the former. In fact, to conflate justification with deification is to deprive the latter of its basis. While having criticized the reduction of δικαιοσύνη Θεοῦ to "God's covenant faithfulness," the narrative that I have offered fully incorporates this meaning, even as Wright defines it as "the creation thereby of a people who embody the creator's will

---

151. Farrow, *Ascension and Ecclesia*, 176–77.

152. Francis Turretin, *Institutes of Elenctic Theology* (Philadelphia: P&R, repr. 1992), 3:209, 609, 611–12. As the Belgic Confession concludes, "And for a gracious reward, the Lord will cause [his elect] to possess such a glory as never entered the heart of man to conceive" (Belgic Confession, art. 37). When Christ returns in the flesh, the Westminster Confession adds, "The bodies of the unjust shall, by the power of Christ, be raised to dishonor: the bodies of the just, by His Spirit, unto honor; and be made conformable to His own glorious body" (Westminster Confession of Faith, 32.3). Only Jonathan Edwards seems to represent a significant departure from this norm on key points, affirming deification in a more Origenist or at least Neo-Platonist direction. See Michael J. McClymond and Gerald. R. McDermott, *The Theology of Jonathan Edwards* (New York: Oxford University Press, 2012): "The whole body of Edwards' metaphysical and typological reflections rested on a notion of continuity between Creator and creation" (105). Cf. Edwards, *The Works of Jonathan Edwards*, ed. Thomas A. Schafer, vol. 13, *Miscellanies* (New Haven: Yale University Press, 1995), 295. According to 2 Cor 3:18, the divine light "changes the nature of the soul," and "it assimilates the nature [of the soul] to the divine nature" (Edwards, *A Divine and Supernatural Light* [Boston: S. Kneeland and T. Green, 1734], 16). McClymond compares Edwards's view of theosis to that of Gregory Palamas (McClymond, "Salvation as Divination: Jonathan Edwards, Gregory Palamas and the Theological Uses of Neoplatonism," in *Jonathan Edwards: Philosophical Theologian*, ed. Paul Helm and Oliver Crisp [Aldershot: Ashgate, 2003], 145).

153. Thomas Watson, *A Body of Divinity* (repr. Edinburgh: Banner of Truth Trust, 1986), 309.

for human community."[154] The idea is present even where the phrase is not used, just as this meaning is not always intended when the phrase is employed.

In light of the arguments offered here, while the distinctions remain, false choices fade away. Not only sanctification but deification is affirmed precisely because a purely forensic justification grounds these other gifts. After justification—and because of it—there is purification (sanctification) and communion ("eating and drinking with God" together with the brothers and sisters to whom he has joined us in Christ). Just as Christ is Victor because he cancelled the debt (Col 2:14), and conquered death because he removed its legal curse (1 Cor 15:55–56), so also he merited our deification by his incarnation, life, death, resurrection, and ascension. It is no slight to justification to say that it is but a means to an end, especially when it is this end in view:

> On this mountain the LORD of hosts will make for all
>   peoples
>   a feast of rich food, a feast of well-aged wine,
>   of rich food full of marrow, of aged wine well refined.
> And he will swallow up on this mountain
>   the covering that is cast over all peoples,
>   the veil that is spread over all nations.
>   He will swallow up death forever;
> and the Lord GOD will wipe away tears from all faces,
>   and the reproach of his people he will take away from
>   all the earth,
>   for the LORD has spoken.
> It will be said on that day,
>   "Behold, this is our God; we have waited for him,
>   that he might save us.
>   This is the LORD; we have waited for him;
>   let us be glad and rejoice in his salvation." (Isa 25:6–9)

---

154. N. T. Wright, *Paul and His Recent Interpreters* (Minneapolis: Fortress, 2015), 328.

SUBJECT INDEX

ablution, 483, 484
Abraham, 39, 59, 64, 71, 72, 73–74, 77,
    78, 81, 86, 87, 89, 94–95, 97, 106,
    111, 113–14, 117, 119, 120, 124, 126,
    128, 137–38, 139, 140, 189, 208, 209,
    216, 232, 255, 268, 287, 288, 296,
    300, 302, 305–13, 317–20, 322–24,
    327–28, 330, 331, 333, 345, 355, 357,
    359, 364, 365, 367, 369–71, 375, 383,
    397, 401, 412, 422, 427, 428, 431,
    438, 439–40
Abrahamic covenant. *See under* covenant
absolute will of God, 248
absolution, 249
Achan's theft, 330
act-consequence connection, 61, 62, 66,
    81–82, 84–85, 86, 117, 147–48, 232,
    333, 375
adoption, 124, 170, 183, 241, 279, 347,
    365–66, 447, 450, 465, 491
adultery, 90, 137, 173, 216, 475
Adam, Israel and, 66–76 (*see in general*
    chapter 1, "Adam and Israel," 57–75)
  the two Adams, 64, 71, 74, 206, 265,
    348, 453
Adamic covenant. *See under* covenant
advocate, our heavenly, 269, 270, 473
agape, 408
age to come, 33, 34, 49, 101, 126, 131,
    178, 194, 237, 242, 257, 265, 271,
    279, 415, 465, 466, 467, 478, 480,
    481
agnosticism, 177, 202
Agnus Dei, 40, 183, 197, 200–205, 213,
    239, 240, 249, 257
  recent criticism of 201–5
allegiance, 108, 245, 287, 338, 390–91,
    412–13, 431
Anabaptism, 204, 460–61

Anabaptists, 35–36, 201–2, 209, 461, 480,
    484–85
anti-Judaism of Christianity, 203
angels, 95, 199, 239, 266, 272, 389
anointing with oil, 269
antinomianism, 18
antinomians, 417, 419
Antiochus IV Epiphanes, 190
Apocalypse of Zephaniah, 238, 323–24
apocalyptic (interpretation), three essential
    elements of, 33
apocalyptic school, 176, 180, 297, 305,
    306, 397, 434, 448
  Romans 4 and the, 317–20
Apocrypha, 327
apologetics, 18–19
apostasy, 278, 438
appropriation, 28, 37, 464
Arianism, 19
Arminians, 197
Asaph (psalmist), 62, 82, 190, 194, 229,
    372, 373
ascension (Christ's), 31, 37, 38, 40, 187,
    207, 231, 260, 270, 272, 273–74, 276,
    278, 279–80, 377, 461, 462, 463,
    466–67, 478, 483, 487, 492, 493
assurance, 314, 400, 401, 405–6
Athanasianism, 47
atonement, 34, 40, 45, 58, 59, 66, 91,
    153, 154–56, 159, 160, 178, 180,
    193, 195–201, 203, 205, 208, 211,
    212, 213–14, 216–20, 222–224, 226,
    235–38, 242, 243, 246, 248, 249–50,
    252, 255, 260, 272, 273, 275, 284,
    309, 314, 323, 331, 350, 373, 417,
    447, 464, 487
Anselmian view of the (or, the theory of
    Anselm), 197–98, 199, 200, 249
Christus Victor theory of the, 40, 41,

495

Lutheran Book of Concord, 335
Lutheranism, 18, 49, 199, 469, 480, 488
"Lutheran" perspective (on justification), 19, 24, 108
Lutheran and Reformed confessions, 195, 273, 390, 393, 419, 464, 486. *See also* Westminster Confession of Faith
Lutherans, 18, 343, 368, 387–88, 399, 469, 488
"Lutheran" view, 178, 407, 413
LXX (*also*, Septuagint), 130, 132, 159, 169, 175, 185, 186, 218, 219, 290, 435
Maccabean revolt, 190, 312
Marcionite
  antinomianism, 18, 57, 155
  hermeneutics, 161, 201, 237, 242
Marxism, 49
Mary (mother of Jesus), 209, 321, 334, 390, 401
mediation, 140, 216, 232, 274, 331. *See next*
mediator, 47, 57, 64, 77, 78, 83, 84, 95, 136, 139, 158, 172, 208, 212, 216, 222, 232, 272, 273, 287, 288, 331, 335, 343, 364, 434, 450, 464, 487–88
Melanchthon, 19, 105, 299, 343, 382, 464, 469, 488
membership, 106, 114–15, 131, 137, 139, 140, 164, 295, 296, 297, 299, 302, 310, 311, 312, 340, 361, 379, 397
mercy, 40, 46, 61, 66, 73, 75, 83, 84, 91, 92, 94, 101, 103–4, 107, 110, 111, 114, 124, 126, 148, 152, 155, 169, 172–73, 175, 192, 227, 238, 242, 289, 292, 300, 323–24, 364, 368, 371, 373, 393, 401, 404, 405, 406, 407, 410, 433, 435, 475
mercy seat, 166, 219, 228, 272
merit(s), 58, 77, 103, 106, 110–14, 116, 118, 124, 138, 148, 152, 188, 207–8, 237, 283, 291, 303, 306, 309, 312, 314, 320, 321–25, 327–30, 332–37, 341–42, 343, 344–45, 349, 355–56, 359, 365, 368, 369, 370, 371, 376, 377, 378, 391–92, 399, 404, 406, 407, 412, 435, 468, 472
  the difference between condign and congruent, 113
  of the fathers, 111, 322

and imputation in ancient Judaism, 322–24
and imputation in Christianity, 332–37
Midrashim, 100
Mishnah, 116, 322, 324. *See also* oral Torah
modernism, 21. *See next*
modernity, 158, 199, 205, 254, 377
modern theology, 11, 50, 153, 177, 236–37, 273
moral example/influence, 157, 197, 199, 245, 254–55
moral government, 236, 247–53, 254
moral law, 23, 61, 64, 69, 75, 94, 134, 136, 137, 139, 141, 143–44, 155, 173, 303, 306, 391, 415, 473
Mosaic covenant. *See* Sinai covenant
Moses, 64, 70, 78, 79, 85, 88, 89, 90, 92, 95, 104, 114, 119, 120, 122, 127, 128, 140, 144, 147, 157, 209, 213, 216, 229, 232, 242, 268, 323, 331, 365, 378, 390, 391, 415, 453
  a new, 333, 334
murder, 90, 173, 211, 383, 474
mysticism, 22, 37, 105, 417, 452, 455, 460, 461, 466
natural law, 48, 62, 75, 84, 306, 383
Neonomianism, 411–12
Neoplatonism, 35, 259, 489, 490
neo-Protestantism, 37, 491
new birth, 197, 262, 465, 471
new covenant, 23, 57, 59, 72, 73, 74, 76, 78–80, 89, 91, 95, 101, 102, 107, 111, 129, 131, 136, 146, 171, 173, 176, 192, 215, 224, 231, 232, 288, 305, 309, 331, 333, 338, 391, 397, 415, 473–75
  basic difference between the old covenant and the, 107
new creation, 33, 37–38, 131, 144, 158, 204, 240, 255, 257–59, 262, 265, 268, 269, 339, 415, 450, 462, 473, 475, 478, 479, 481, 486
new Finnish school/interpretation of Luther, 34, 50, 199, 284, 301, 326, 488, 492
New Testament, 21, 26, 34, 38, 42, 65, 71, 79, 80, 105, 126, 143, 163, 172, 173, 184, 188, 202, 203, 208, 211, 212, 218, 219, 220, 223, 246, 250, 253, 257, 287, 289, 290, 298, 305–6, 321,

151, 152, 184, 196, 341, 432, 460–62, 491

Plato's "two worlds," 262

political and judicial practices in ancient Israel, 211–13

pollution of the sanctuary, the cosmic significance of the, 229–30

powers of darkness, 33, 243, 257. *See also* demons; evil powers

preaching, 18, 37, 46, 51–52, 185, 187, 196, 280, 380, 432, 438, 460, 478–80, 482, 484, 486

predestination, 177, 352, 377

present evil age, 33, 241, 243, 257, 267, 480

problem of evil, 71, 73

promises, 27, 59, 68, 72, 76, 78, 80, 81, 89, 111, 124, 131, 136, 165–69, 171, 172, 175, 232, 287, 288, 292, 295, 306, 307, 355, 384, 389, 402, 415, 440, 474, 484

prophecies, 187

prophecy, 97, 199, 474, 475

prophetism, 120, 121

prophets, 58, 65, 73, 78, 84, 86, 89, 90, 95, 98, 99, 111, 114, 120, 121, 127, 168, 170, 171, 181, 183, 187, 189, 191, 202, 268, 269, 292, 315, 324, 332, 403, 422, 457, 481

Prophets, the, 71, 76, 90, 98, 286, 305, 317, 331, 452

propitiation, 156, 158, 201, 203, 218–19, 220, 223, 227, 249, 250, 255, 286, 287, 315, 332, 359, 447, 473

Protestantism, 21, 28, 121, 197, 283, 284, 411, 477, 485. *See also* neo-Protestantism

Protestant liberalism, 205, 261

Protestant Reformation. *See* Reformation

Protestant Reformers. *See* Reformers

protoeuangelion, 57

Pseudepigrapha, 327

punishment, 70, 161, 167, 191, 198–99, 221, 224, 232, 236, 237, 247, 250, 251, 252, 333, 415, 472, 473

purgatory, 112, 152, 200, 325, 374

purification, 208, 213, 214, 216, 217, 218, 227–32, 235–36, 249, 250, 258, 260, 274, 408, 453, 468, 493

and peace offerings, 227–33

Puritans, 406, 414

Quakers, 36

Qumran, 65–66, 99–100, 102, 103, 110, 121, 122, 132, 174, 187, 190–92, 218, 289–90, 307, 329, 453

Radical Orthodoxy, 34, 35, 50, 51, 284, 483

"radical Protestants," 35, 38

ransom, 91, 211–12, 217, 235, 236, 240, 243–44, 246, 252

"rationalistic school," 351

reaping what you sow, 62. *See* act-consequence connection

reason, 18, 154, 241, 283

recapitulation, 203, 205–10, 235–36, 243, 273

reconciliation, 28, 43, 161, 197, 198, 201, 213, 235, 243, 250, 335, 339–40, 343, 366, 468

redemption, 28–29, 31, 34, 37–40, 42, 43, 47, 48, 51, 52, 57, 67, 71, 74, 75, 76, 86, 97, 108, 148, 151, 153, 155, 156, 158–59, 177, 193, 195, 197, 198, 201, 204, 208, 211, 213, 214, 219, 224, 230, 231, 240, 242, 243, 244, 248, 250, 251, 259, 260, 265, 272, 274, 276, 286, 300, 301, 303, 309, 315, 317, 318, 324, 328, 331–32, 338, 339, 346, 350, 363, 364, 366, 367, 374, 380, 384, 388, 424, 433, 449, 460, 462, 463, 467, 468, 470, 471, 475, 477, 483, 484, 492

the means of, 201

Reformation, 17–22, 24, 26, 31, 34–38, 41–43, 45, 47, 50, 79, 112, 160, 162, 177, 182, 196, 198, 200, 260, 283, 284, 285, 288, 299, 300, 303, 315, 317, 321, 324–26, 332, 337, 342, 343, 349–52, 354, 355, 361, 368, 369, 376, 380, 381, 385, 387, 389, 390, 392, 393, 394, 402, 411, 412, 418, 419, 430–32, 444–46, 448, 452, 459, 461, 472, 476, 482–83, 486

Reformation exegesis, 315, 381

Reformed *and* Reformed orthodox confessions, 200, 350, 403, 430. *See also* Lutheran and Reformed confessions; *individual confessions by name*

Reformed tradition, 31, 57, 79, 206, 303, 350–51, 406, 463

SCRIPTURE INDEX

AUTHOR INDEX

Abegg, Martin, Jr., 102
Adam, Karl, 283
Adams, Rebecca, 202
Alarcón, E., 405
Alexander, Philip S., 100, 115, 313–14, 323, 329
Allen, Michael, 25, 152, 286, 302, 443–44, 465
Ames, William, 274–75, 366, 476–77
Andersen, F. I., 101
Anderson, Clifford B., 28, 174
Anderson, Gary A., 217
Anderson, James, 335
Andreas, 370
Anselm, St., 198, 199, 249–52
Aquinas, Thomas. *See* Thomas Aquinas, Saint
Arminius, 247, 248, 359
Asselt, Willem J. van, 31, 60
Athanasius, 44, 45, 47, 48, 236, 243, 420, 426, 491
Augustine, 23, 45, 47, 57, 105, 156, 226–27, 236, 243, 334, 335, 369–70, 376, 382, 383, 386, 404, 405, 458, 480, 483
Aulén, Gustaf, 198–201, 207, 209, 237, 240, 248, 488
Avemarie, Friedrich, 319
Backus, Irena, 31, 60, 206
Bagnall, W. R., 359
Bailey, Daniel P., 85, 212, 223, 226
Balke, Willem, 485
Balthasar, Hans Urs von, 454, 483
Baker, Mark D., 200, 219
Barclay, John M. G., 26, 60, 68, 109, 110, 112, 113, 123–26, 133, 138, 145, 161, 179, 187, 346–47, 427, 431
Barr, James, 163, 165, 285, 294, 418, 421
Bartsch, Hans Werner, 411

Barth, Karl, 25, 27–32, 34, 38, 40, 44–45, 47, 48, 50, 60, 64, 67, 104, 106, 151, 174, 176–79, 221, 260, 263, 284, 301, 350, 380, 416–19, 430, 434, 445, 464, 491
Barth, Markus, 419–20
Bartlett, Anthony, 203–4
Bassler, J. M., 317
Bates, Matthew W., 350, 386–87, 390–91, 412–13, 414, 415, 449, 469, 471
Bauckham, Richard, 101, 238, 324
Bavinck, Herman, 272–73, 277, 351
Baxter, Richard, 359, 411–12
Beale, G. K., 63, 68
Beilby, J. (James K.), 252, 347, 350
Beisner, E. Calvin, 346
Beker, J. Christiaan, 32, 33, 39, 42–43, 192, 204, 261
Bell, Richard H., 431
Bente, F., 480
Berkhof, Louis, 249, 470, 471
Berkouwer, G. C., 11, 28
Bethune-Baker, J. F., 199
Bettenson, Henry, 57
Beveridge, Henry, 335, 399, 410, 464, 484
Billerbeck, Paul, 105, 118, 323 (*see* Strack-Billerbeck), 324
Billings, J. Todd, 41, 469
Bird, Michael F., 32, 41, 44, 347–51, 354–56, 380, 416, 417, 420, 422, 424, 425, 426, 427, 431, 442, 444, 448
Bird, Phyllis, 61
Blackwell, Ben C., 64, 99, 100, 101, 113, 148, 185, 193, 313
Bloesch, Daniel W., 350
Blumenfeld, Bruno, 326
Bockmuehl, Markus, 106, 307–8, 319, 320, 407
Boer, H. R., 28

521